D0153410

*Major Problems in the
History of American Medicine
and Public Health*

MAJOR PROBLEMS IN AMERICAN HISTORY SERIES

GENERAL EDITOR

THOMAS G. PATERSON

Major Problems in the History of American Medicine and Public Health

DOCUMENTS AND ESSAYS

EDITED BY

JOHN HARLEY WARNER
YALE UNIVERSITY

JANET A. TIGHE
UNIVERSITY OF PENNSYLVANIA

HOUGHTON MIFFLIN COMPANY
Boston   New York

Editor-in-Chief: Jean L. Woy
Senior Associate Editor: Frances Gay
Associate Project Editor: Jane Lee
Editorial Assistant: Martha Rogers
Associate Production/Design Coordinator: Lisa Jelly
Senior Manufacturing Coordinator: Sally Culler
Senior Marketing Manager: Sandra McGuire

Cover image: *The Field Hospital,* 1867, Jonathan Eastman Johnson, Gift of Maxim Karolik
for the M. and M. Karolik Collection of American Paintings, 1815–1865, 1948. Courtesy,
Museum of Fine Arts, Boston.

Printed in the U.S.A.

Library of Congress Catalog Card Number: 00-133849

ISBN: 0-395-95435-5

123456789-CRS-04 03 02 01 00

For
Rudolph E. Tighe, Jr.
and
Dorothy Nies Warner

Contents

C H A P T E R   7
Reconfiguring "Scientific Medicine," 1865–1900
Page 196

CHAPTER 8
The Gospel of Germs: Microbes, Strangers, and Habits of the Home, 1880–1925
Page 234

CHAPTER 9
Strategies for Improving Medical Care: Institutions, Science, and Standardization, 1870–1940
Page 275

CHAPTER 10
Expert Advice, Social Authority, and the Medicalization of Everyday Life, 1890–1930
Page 317

CHAPTER 11
The Technological Imperative? Hospitals, Professions, and Patient Expectations, 1890–1950
Page 349

CHAPTER 12
The Culture of Biomedical Research: Human Subjects, Power, and the Scientific Method, 1920–1965
Page 388

C H A P T E R   1 3
Public Health and the State During an Age of Biomedical Miracles, 1925–1960
Page 424

C H A P T E R   1 4
Rights, Access, and the Bottom Line: Health Politics and Health Policies, 1960–2000
Page 459

CHAPTER 15

The Persisting Search for Health and Healing at the End of the Twentieth Century

Page 499

Preface

Health and health care loom unmistakably large in the national consciousness of Americans at the start of the twenty-first century. It is difficult to pick up a newspaper, to watch the nightly news, or to surf the Internet without encountering debates over health care financing, new health risks, new medical technologies that promise a fuller or longer life, or the implications of mapping the human genome. The exploits of physicians in emergency rooms and courtrooms persistently win audiences for films and television programs that dramatize the ethical dilemmas raised by organ transplantation, gene therapy, access to abortion, physician-assisted suicide, and balancing the individual's rights to privacy against the public's health— dilemmas faced by health care providers, politicians, and patients alike. At the same time, medical advisers with diverse claims to expertise tell us how we should conduct our daily lives: what we eat, whether we smoke or drink, how we have sex, and what we must do to stay fit. The urgency of decisions about our health as individuals and as a nation, at a time when 14 percent of our Gross Domestic Product is consumed by health care and when the medical world is changing at a dizzying pace, is an unavoidable part of our experience as Americans. For all their immediacy, many of today's medical preoccupations have deep roots in the past, and learning about the history of our health culture helps us understand its present configuration, its failings, and its potential.

This book explores the diverse ways in which Americans have experienced sickness and sought to maintain or restore health. It examines why and how the experiences of illness and healing have been shaped by racial, ethnic, class, gender, religious, and regional differences. It asks who has been held responsible for health and culpable for illness, and how changes in biomedical science, moral values, and political agendas have transformed widely shared assumptions about accountability. It investigates the changing role of institutions—such as the hospital, the diagnostic laboratory, the medical school, the state, and the home—in structuring America's health culture. It traces the checkered education and status of the physician in American society while at the same time exploring the variety of healers who competed with one another in what always has been a competitive medical marketplace. And it shows the shifting, often contested role of medical authority as a force in directing the conduct of daily life. The documents and essays in *Major Problems in the History of American Medicine and Public Health* reveal the extent to which the characteristics of a good healer, the meanings of disease, and the nature of a healthy society have been vigorously debated from the colonial period through the present.

Medical history had long been cultivated as a professional history, written chiefly by physicians for other physicians. Starting in the 1960s, however, this approach began to change profoundly, as scholars interested in social history started to ask new historical questions not only about medical practitioners and practices but also about disease, the body, interactions between healers and sufferers, public health, medical institutions, and health policy. Indeed, by the 1970s some historians asked whether the newly vitalized field might better be characterized as the history of *health care* rather than as the history of *medicine,* a category that taken literally would exclude, to cite only one crucial example, the history of nursing. By and large, historians, like the professional associations and journals of the field, have retained the label "history of medicine," while insisting—as we do in this volume—on a very expansive and inclusive interpretation of its scope. At the same time, though, as we planned our volume on the history of *medicine,* we became increasingly aware of how many of the issues we regarded as integral to understanding the culture of health and system of care that have come to exist in the United States conventionally fall under the heading of *public health,* and our convictions about what an introduction to this field should encompass are reflected in our expanded title: medicine *and* public health.

Individuals interested in learning more about the history of American medicine and public health are invited to join the American Association for the History of Medicine (AAHM). This organization publishes one of the leading journals in the field, the *Bulletin of the History of Medicine;* and an informative newsletter; offers book and article prizes; and holds an annual conference. For contact information, see the AAHM's web site at *http://www.histmed.org/* where you will also find links to other sites related to the history of medicine and public health. The History of Health Sciences web site at *http://www2.duke.edu/misc/MLA/HHSS/histlink.htm* contains more valuable references. For online discussion of topics in the field and more related research information, consult H-SCI-MED-TECH at *http://www.h-net. msu.edu/~smt/index.html.*

Like other volumes in this series, *Major Problems in the History of Medicine and Public Health* approaches its subject in two ways: first, through primary sources; and second, through the interpretations of scholars. We invite readers to examine critical issues through diverse viewpoints and approaches. Each chapter begins with an introduction that identifies problems or themes, places them in a larger context, and poses questions to think about in reading the documents and essays. The headnotes also suggest key questions. The documents reflect the temper of the times and allow students to immerse themselves in the historical moment, develop their own perspectives, and evaluate the explanations of others. The essays demonstrate that scholars can read documents in multiple ways or choose to examine different aspects of the same problem; like the documents, the essays are intended to provoke discussion. Each chapter ends with a brief bibliography to guide further investigation, and teachers will recognize that an abundance of websites and films, which we draw upon in our own classrooms, are available to supplement these printed sources. The format of the books in this series enables students to appreciate the complexity of not only history itself but the *writing* of history.

We have accumulated many debts in the course of preparing this volume. We are grateful to the series editor, Thomas G. Paterson, for recognizing that the history of medicine and public health belongs in larger discussions of American history, and to the Houghton Mifflin staff—Jean Woy, Frances Gay, and Jane Lee for their fine editorial advice and overseeing the book's production, and Katie Huha and Marcy Lunetta for their work in clearing permissions. We are grateful as well to Toby Appel, Jack Eckert, Sam Fore, Henry Fulmer, Martha Smart, and Christopher Stanwood for their assistance in acquiring documents; to Pat Johnson and Joyce Roselle of the University of Pennsylvania and to Patricia Johnson and Ramona Moore of Yale University for their administrative support; to Janet Tighe's graduate assistants, Erin McLeary and Audra Wolfe, for both their scholarly and technological assistance; and to the students in her undergraduate survey and graduate seminar who, during the past two years, tested much of the material in this collection. We also wish to acknowledge the detailed and helpful written comments on the draft table of contents provided by the reviewers: Allan M. Brandt, Harvard University; Lisa Herschbach, Rutgers University–Newark; Susan D. Jones, University of Colorado; Michael E. Samuels, University of South Carolina; and Carolyn G. Shapiro-Shapin, Grand Valley State University. For their suggestions, support, and enormously helpful advice, we would like to thank our colleagues Caroline J. Acker, Rima D. Apple, Robert Aronowitz, Anne-Emanuelle Birn, Monique Borque, Charlotte G. Borst, Allan M. Brandt, Gert H. Brieger, JoAnne Brown, Theodore M. Brown, Karen Buhler-Wilkerson, John C. Burnham, Colin G. Calloway, Ann Carmichael, Adele E. Clarke, David T. Courtwright, Jacalyn M. Duffin, Julie Fairman, Norman J. Gevitz, Janet Golden, Gerald Grob, Jennifer Gunn, Beth Haiken, Evelynn M. Hammonds, Bert Hansen, Victoria A. Harden, William H. Helfand, Joel D. Howell, Kathleen W. Jones, Susan D. Jones, Suzanne White Junod, Gwen E. Kay, Alan Kraut, Maneesha Lal, Susan E. Lederer, Barron H. Lerner, Susan Lindee, Kenneth Ludmerer, Elizabeth Lunbeck, Howard Markel, Harry M. Marks, Jacquelyn Miller, Ellen S. More, Edward Morman, Ronald L. Numbers, John Parascandola, Martin Pernick, Heather M. Prescott, Leslie J. Reagan, Guenter B. Risse, Charles E. Rosenberg, Barbara Gutmann Rosenkrantz, John W. Servos, Carolyn G. Shapiro-Shapin, Merritt Roe Smith, Rosemary Stevens, Molly P. Sutphen, Janet Theophano, Nancy J. Tomes, Elizabeth Toon, Sarah W. Tracy, Clifford E. Trafzer, Keith Wailoo, and Daniel J. Wilson. For assistance in the final stages of book preparation, we would also like to thank Toby Appel, John Brembeck, Eve Buckley, Carita Constable, Andrew Rizzo, Anthony Rizzo, Chris Versen, and Theresa Walls. We are especially indebted to Naomi Rogers, who has been our most ruthless and caring critic, and to Albert A. Rizzo, whose clinical insight and culinary skill proved invaluable.

J.H.W.
J.A.T.

CHAPTER
1

What Is the History of Medicine
and Public Health?

The history of medicine and public health explores fundamental realities of human existence that, at first glance, might seem to be universal, such as birth, death, aging, trauma, suffering, diet, bodily functions, and exposure to physical and social environments that can promote or undercut health. What health, illness, and the life cycle mean, however, and how they are managed, are highly changeable and culturally contingent, both time- and place-specific. Accordingly, a central task of historians is to explore and explain change and choice to understand how Americans thought about their bodies; how they interpreted the meaning of sickness; what conceptual and technical tools lay healers and medical professionals brought to their efforts to palliate or cure; and how private and state institutions sought to prevent the spread of disease and maintain a healthy society.

The study of history engages us in a dialogue between past and present: historians inevitably view the past from our standpoint in the present. And even if the particular problems and dilemmas of contemporary health culture are strikingly different from those confronted by earlier generations, historians of medicine and public health often find themselves asking how Americans in the past—both professionals and lay men and women—answered questions about health and illness that concern us today: What is health? What is disease? Who is responsible for maintaining health? Who is culpable for illness? To what extent should the physical and mental well-being of American citizens be left up to each individual, and to what extent should prevention and care be the province of the state? Are domestic violence, drug abuse, and poverty best seen as social ills or as public health problems? And who should decide? What constitutes a healthy society? Historians have revealed how profoundly the answers to these questions have changed over time. Exploring the history of medicine and public health—investigating how questions such as these were understood and debated in the past—helps us to view contextually the particular health culture we live with today.

Questions such as these are persistent themes running through this volume, as are other fundamental questions about the production of medical knowledge and provision of health care: How and why did medical knowledge and practice change? What were the social and political processes that determined who tested

*new therapies and regulated their use? How have health and access to health care
been shaped by such factors as gender, ethnicity, race, region, and class? Who
decided what constituted acceptable training for a health care provider, and what
determined who had access to education as a physician, nurse, midwife, chiropractor,
or naturopath? How have Americans selected their health care providers in a pluralistic marketplace? Here again, the answers can be powerfully salient for understanding the present and even envisioning the future.*

*The study of medical history is not itself a recent development: in earlier cen-
turies doctors looked to the past to chart the advancement of medical ideas and to
establish their professional lineage by celebrating the accomplishments of famous
forebears. As a part of the larger discipline of* history*, however, rather than as a
branch of* medicine*, history of medicine is a relatively new field of inquiry. Especially since the 1960s, the study of American medicine and public health has
emerged as a vibrant field of social and, more recently, cultural and policy history.
The ideas and practices of physicians and the changing course of biomedical knowledge remain central, important topics for historical investigation. Yet the scope of
the field has expanded, and scholars challenging earlier interpretations and exploring new territory have increasingly asked new questions, often drawing on
sociology, anthropology, linguistics, demography, and historical epidemiology. The
layperson's experience of his or her own body in illness and wellness; the use and
abuse of medical authority in governing everyday life; the social and economic determinants of physical and mental illness; the cultural construction of what disease
means; and the variety of healers competing with one another in what often has
been a remarkably open American medical marketplace—themes such as these
have moved to the forefront. The history of medicine and public health can help us
understand how and why health care has come to be such a central preoccupation
in American society, evident in the seemingly paradoxical celebration of biomedical
marvels and lament over an inequitable health care delivery system in crisis. One
thing we share with all Americans, past and present, is the experience of living in a
human body, and history offers a source of insight into the choices we have as we
manage that experience in sickness and in health.*

 ## E S S A Y S

When it first appeared in 1979, under the title "Beyond 'the Great Doctors,'" the first
essay was a controversial rallying call for the "new social history" in American medicine and public health. Susan Reverby of Wellesley College and David Rosner of
Columbia University—both now senior scholars but at the time fresh from graduate
school—first sketch the early history of the field in the United Stated, characterizing a
history of medicine chiefly cultivated by doctors and rooted in medical culture. They
then turn to the activist concerns of historians of health, illness, and health care that
grew from a wider social, political, and intellectual upheaval represented by the civil
rights, antiwar, and feminist movements of the 1960s and 1970s. How much is the analytical program they called for reflected in essays by other historians that appear in later
chapters of this anthology? How has work by other historians moved in different directions that Reverby and Rosner, when they wrote two decades ago, did not envision?

The second essay is by Charles E. Rosenberg of the University of Pennsylvania,
the historian who has most visibly led the program for the social history of American
medicine and public health and whose pioneering work powerfully influenced historians like Reverby and Rosner. Rosenberg's essay exemplifies the focus on institutions

that is a central preoccupation of the history of medicine and public health. In his hands, exploring the history of a single health care institution—the hospital—is an occasion for displaying complex interactions among the various elements that have shaped America's shifting health culture: the intellectual aspirations and career options of doctors and nurses; health care financing and issues of welfare; the cognitive and social roles of science and technology; the experiences of illness and patienthood; and the relationship of class to health and health care. Written for an interdisciplinary symposium convened at the end of the 1980s on the future of the American hospital, Rosenberg's essay displays the double aim that animates much of the work in American medical history—namely, to understand the past in its own terms while at the same time using historical insight to inform discussions of current health care policy.

In the final essay, Brown University historian James T. Patterson explores the history of disease, one of the most vibrant areas in the history of medicine and public health. His essay points to the whole host of themes in the history of medicine and public health that studying disease can open up. Indeed, as the work of such historians as Allan M. Brandt, Judith Walzer Leavitt, and Charles E. Rosenberg has amply shown, disease is not merely an important topic but an analytical tool for historically investigating the values, expectations, and cultural assumptions (about gender, race, and class, for example) of American society, which are brought into sharp relief in the representation and management of disease.

Medical Culture and Historical Practice

SUSAN REVERBY AND DAVID ROSNER

"The history of medicine is infinitely more than the history of the great doctors and their books," wrote Henry E. Sigerist, a prominent medical historian, nearly a half century ago. In light of our recognition of the complexity of health care delivery and the post–World War II growth of the health industry, this dictum is now even more relevant.

A history that both illuminates health policy concerns and explores the subtleties of medicine's past is being built with the questions and tools of what is called the "new social history." This history explicitly examines the growth and transformation of society's structures, institutions, and culture. Its current formulation has been shaped in part by contemporary political struggles. The Civil Rights, Anti-War, and Women's movements all focused the historian's attentions on class and familial relations and the different historical experiences of minorities, women, and the working class. In the absence of an abundance of the usual written sources to explore this history, social historians have turned to social science methodology, computer technology, and new sources of data such as manuscript censuses, city directories, and tax lists.

The social history perspective raises important questions when applied to medical and health care issues. Some of these questions concern the social and political responses to disease, the social epidemiology of health and illness, the changing definition and importance of professionalism, the ideological and social control aspects of medicine, and the social role of health care institutions.

Until recently these social concerns were not central to the history of medicine because the field focused primarily on the unfolding of medical science and "the ideas that have animated physicians." This dominant medical history tradition reflects both a pervasive societal faith in the potential and efficacy of medical science and the fact that much of this history was written by physicians. As Owsei Temkin has noted, "the history of medicine . . . [was] conceived as a march of progress culminating in the present state of superior medical and scientific knowledge." With the growing understanding of both the social causation of health and disease and the way in which science is embedded in a society's social relations, however, historians have begun to reanalyze medical history.

. . . [Historians are addressing in particular] three themes of central concern to the health field:

1. the shifting boundaries between professional and lay control over the definition of health and disease;
2. the social and economic consequences of the changing locus of health care delivery; and
3. the complex relationship between workers, professionals, and health care institutions.

The linking of contemporary medical issues with the writing of history has a long tradition. At certain historical moments, medical history was valued as a way to keep physicians in touch with humanistic concerns in the face of an increasingly technological and specialized medical practice. At other times, medical history has been marshalled in support of different positions in the battles over medical and health care reforms. In the following pages we will briefly trace the close relationship between the history of medicine and medicine, emphasizing the political nature of this alliance. We do this to ground the new social history of health care in its past.

Until the end of the nineteenth century, many of the theoretical and practical formulations of medical practitioners were derived from history. An understanding of the Ancients, their therapeutic regimens and theoretical justifications, lent credence to various medical practices. Hippocrates, Aristotle, and Galen dot the pages of pre-twentieth-century medical writings just as references to current research appear in this year's publications. Medical history was written by practitioners for practitioners.

With the development of science as the dominant ideology and material base of medicine, history lost its function as medicine's source of authority. In medicine, as in other aspects of American life, innovation, progress, and scientific advance, rather than recourse to ancient authorities, became highly valued. In centers where this scientific medicine was most advanced, the history of medicine took on a new function.

Nowhere was this clearer than at the medical and nursing schools organized at Johns Hopkins University in Baltimore in the 1880s. The men and women of the new scientific generation at Hopkins were aware that medicine and nursing entailed more than scientific knowledge and technical skills. With the growing importance of science, they were deeply concerned that the art of medical and nursing practice might be lost. For them, the art entailed clinical decision-making, "bedside manner," the development of the physician's and nurse's "character," and a sensitivity to the patient's humanity. They saw the training of their students in this "humanism" as an essential counterweight to the possible dehumanizing effects of the new science. For them, the study of history was the linchpin that could hold together both the science and the art of medicine and nursing. Harvey Cushing, the famed surgeon, later eloquently voiced this motive for his generation's abiding concern with history:

> In the modern development of the physician into a scientist have we not lost something precious that may without risk of pedantry be brought back to Medicine? Not only has the art of healing, *die Heilkunst,* come more and more to be lost sight of as the doctor arrives at his diagnosis in the laboratory rather than at the bedside, but less and less does he care to be reminded that poetry, history, rhetoric and the humanities once had close kinship with natural philosophy when *Doctores Medicinae* took the leadership among the *Artisti.*

The history of medicine functioned as an excursion into moral philosophy and ethics and as a unifying theme for an increasingly specialized profession. This history was to be, as George Sarton would later argue for the history of science, a new humanism that did not reject but rather embraced science and practical knowledge.

Thus, as soon as the nursing and medical schools opened at Hopkins, history lectures were given. In addition, William Osler, who headed the Hopkins medical department, merged medical history with his daily medical teaching on rounds. As he described it:

> A case of exopthalmic goitre comes in—the question at once is put, Who was Graves? Who was Parry? Who was Basedow? Of course the student does not know; he is told to bring, on another day, the original article, and he is given five or ten minutes in which to read a brief historical note.

"In this way," Harvey Cushing wrote, "many students who unquestionably would have sidestepped a formal course of lectures became unconsciously impregnated" with history. For those more consciously interested in history, a Johns Hopkins Hospital Historical Club was organized at which formal papers, later published in the hospital's *Bulletin,* were presented.

This generation's approach to history places medical ideas in a cultural context, although to the modern reader its erudite style appears inaccessible and flowery. In addition, the students acquired a peculiar vision of medical history—rooted deep in historical time but focused narrowly on specific individuals and discoveries. The Oslerian method of teaching the history of medicine was also predicated upon medical schools' having a faculty steeped in history.

Ironically, as this history strove to bind the student to his past, it severed these tenuous ties. As an intellectual history, dependent upon a knowledge of Greek and Latin and the skills imparted by a classical education, its lessons for the practically oriented medical student became less and less clear. Even when this history examined medicine in its American context, it appeared to have little to teach the new science-trained medical student, who was more concerned with breaks than continuities with the past. Similarly, it was assumed that only a physician, with the technical knowledge of medicine and an understanding of the subtleties of medical culture, could be a medical historian. Medical students were therefore isolated from general currents in history.

Medical history was becoming extraneous to medical education despite its proponents' attempts to make apparent its usefulness. Survey after survey in the 1900s through the 1920s drew dismal pictures of haphazard courses and occasional lectures in most medical schools. Yet a small coterie of physicians and medical educators banded together to give medical history an institutional form. In the 1920s medical history journals appeared sporadically and the American Association for the History of Medicine was organized. In 1926 the interest in medical history on the part of Johns Hopkins faculty culminated in the appointment of the then retiring William Henry Welch to a chair in the history of medicine and the beginning of plans for an institute in the history of medicine. Thus, the lack of widespread interest in the history of medicine pushed its proponents to establish an institutional base.

The relationship between history and medicine took on a new meaning with the appointment of Henry E. Sigerist as Welch's replacement as the head of the Johns Hopkins Institute of the History of Medicine in 1932. A physician-philologist, trained as a medical historian under Karl Sudhoff at the University of Leipzig's Institute of the History of Medicine, Sigerist professionalized the history of medicine in America. He combined the academic classical tradition with a new definition of the art of medicine. While previously the art had been seen as medical humanism, centered on the doctor-patient relationship, Sigerist expanded its boundaries to include social and political phenomena. He shared with the earlier medical generation a belief that:

> Modern medicine had become so specialized and so technical that some place had to be established in medical schools where medicine would be studied, not from the specialist's point of view, but as a whole, as an entity—and in its relationship to the other sciences, and to society as a whole.

His history of medicine had an additional element that Sigerist defined as "sociological," the study of the development of socioeconomic structures of various civilizations and their relationship to health care. Sigerist sought, in his voluminous historical writings, to place medicine in "a matrix that was at once cultural, social and economic."

Although his historical work was not always overtly political, he saw much of it as part of a larger political and educational effort to transform the health care system. His history was to serve two functions: "It should give us a more complete picture of the development of civilization and . . . should make us aware [of] where we come from in medicine, at what point we are standing today, and in what direction we are marching." Sigerist was very clear about that direction: "I do hope I will live long enough to see the triumph of socialism in the world, the beginning of a new era, the promise of civilization at last." Hence, during the Depression and war years, Sigerist, along with other physicians and public health workers, expanded the concern of medical humanism into the political arena.

Controversy was endemic to the medical politics of that period. In the context of the Depression, the issues centered on the access to and organization of medical care. The political left in medicine was struggling for the introduction of national health insurance, government-run clinics, salaried physicians, and pre-paid group practice. What now appear as basic political reforms was seen, in the highly charged atmosphere of the 1930s, as exceedingly radical. Advocates of these positions were often labeled "bolsheviks" and kept from academic appointments.

Sigerist's important role in these efforts was recognized nationally and symbolized by his appearance on the cover of *Time* magazine in 1939, under the lead "His philosophy; history spirals toward socialization." His advocacy of socialized medicine and the Soviet model of health care delivery further identified him as a national spokesman for these causes. Thus Sigerist infused history with a new immediacy. Not surprisingly then, his influence was greatest among an entire generation of physicians enmeshed in medical and health care reforms. . . .

Sigerist also influenced professional medical historians. . . . But the history of medicine in the 1930s and the 1940s still had a relatively limited institutional base. Chairs and academic appointments were few in number. Even Sigerist's most well-known and prolific intellectual heir, George Rosen, never held an appointment in the history of medicine until he joined the Yale faculty in 1969. Before that, he wrote history while he practiced medicine, worked for the New York City Health Department and the Health Insurance Plan of New York, and taught public health at Columbia.

While Sigerist and his students produced some of the most important work in the history of medicine, they did not represent the dominant approach. The history of medicine remained primarily intellectual history. In addition, both the prevailing political conservatism and the lack of institutional support served to isolate those who were writing left social history. With the rise of McCarthyism in the post–World War II years, the left political import of the social history approach was stifled. Sigerist himself, suffering from ill health, overcommitment, enormous administrative demands, and a growing political uneasiness, left the United States in 1947 to begin writing a synthetic work. He wrote in his diary in 1947:

> *I did not leave America in order to escape.* I left in order to be able to write my books and made the decision before the situation had become so acute. When it did become critical I actually thought of reconsidering my plan, of staying on, waiting for the challenge to come and of becoming the spokesman for the persecuted left-wing professors. The alternative was to write my books and to write articles, to carry on the fight with the pen, to continue my teachings through my books.

The "sociological approach" to medical history was also developed within the discipline of sociology and met with a parallel fate. Bernhard J. Stern, a friend and contemporary of Sigerist's, has been called "the father of medical sociology." His belief that history provided a framework for understanding contemporary medical problems is reflected in his pioneering dissertation on *Social Factors in Medical Progress,* in his books written for the New York Academy of Medicine, and in his activities within professional sociology associations. His clearly articulated Marxist interpretations set medicine within the contradictions of class conflict without being insensitive to its peculiarities and its special nature. As an open Marxist, Stern's academic career at Columbia University, despite his achievements and skill as a teacher, was precarious. Although his writing greatly influenced a generation of progressive physicians, his ideas come down to us mainly through his books. Unlike Sigerist, he had few graduate students and no institute behind him.

Sigerist, Stern, and their followers, despite their own political differences, had clearly established that the sociological approach had much to offer medicine. Although their political views were at odds with those of the majority of physicians, Sigerist and Stern were able to make medical history accessible and relevant to the profession at large. As in the pre-bacteriological era, they sought to make the history and sociology of medicine an integral part of medical concerns.

The task of integrating social history into the *mainstream* of medical history was pursued not by a physician but by a historian, Richard H. Shryock, Sigerist's successor in 1949 at the Hopkins Institute. Shryock brought to medical history a respect for the social sciences, a commitment to a comparative history perspective, a sense of the importance of external social forces, and, above all, the sensitivity of a social-cultural historian. His main contribution was to remove medial history from its parochialism and give it a more catholic airing. Shryock questioned the notion that medicine was always progressing toward truth. He clearly demonstrated that a professional historian, even though not a physician, could write insightfully about medicine's technical aspects. As with others trained in Progressive history, Shryock focused on broad social and cultural currents. Thus for today's social historian his work seems too general, lacking clear explanations of the mechanisms of change.

For intellectual and political reasons, Shryock, unlike Sigerist, was able to start a continuing social history tradition. Sigerist's work was often positivistic and iatrocentric, rooted in an older classical tradition. In contrast, Shryock was able to link medical history to the main currents in the historical profession and "to place medical history in a society-centered cosmos." Their approaches also differed politically. Owsei Temkin summed this up when he noted that there was little hostility toward Shryock because "shorn of political overtones medical sociology was very welcome at Johns Hopkins." Of course Shryock's work did have political overtones, but the tones were not as discordant as Sigerist's in the political and intellectual atmosphere of the 1950s.

Following Shryock, and in conjunction with the post–World War II growth in the field of social history, this approach has slowly become more prominent within the history of medicine. Charles Rosenberg's work is perhaps the clearest example of this. His landmark book, *The Cholera Years,* makes clear that medical history can inform us as much about general social and political change as about science and medicine. Rosenberg symbolizes the conjuncture of medical and general history since he was trained by both types of historians, Erwin H. Ackerknecht and Richard Hofstadter. . . .

Often those writing the social history of medicine today see themselves at the beginning of a new historical tradition. This is in part due to the influx of non-physician historians and to the minority status of the social history impulse within the history of medicine. Many social historians of medicine trace their ancestry to the great English working-class historian, E. P. Thompson, rather than through the intellectual tradition in medical history. The loss of this medical history lineage has import for the future development of the new social history of health care. First, social historians run the risk, as Gerald Grob has noted, of failing to understand the basis for the internal logic of medicine. Second, the sense of urgency and commitment which has fueled much of the important research in medical history may be lost. Social historians of health care are thus in danger of becoming sophisticated antiquarians.

To avoid these pitfalls, social history of health care has to be reinfused with the immediacy which characterized the endeavors of some of its past advocates. We are not trying to suggest that there will be what Paul Sanazaro has called "preventive history—drawing on the past to highlight for us potentially undesirable and avoidable consequences of future decisions." Nor do we intend to wrench historical events and forces from their context. Rather, social history can provide an essential tool for analyzing current health care problems by providing a sense both of their origins and the possibilities to affect change. Without this kind of history, the future appears full of chance, inevitability, or irony.

Medicine's Institutional History and Its Policy Implications

CHARLES E. ROSENBERG

American hospitals have always disappointed. Each generation during the past century has deplored some aspect of this seemingly necessary institution. In the late nineteenth century, critics were indignant at the use—and apparent abuse—of free hospital services by men and women able to pay private physicians for care. They were concerned as well about the difficulty of imposing cleanliness, economy, and order on an intractable institution. At the beginning of the present century, a concerned minority of progressive reformers assailed the hospital's forbidding impersonality and bureaucratic rigidity, while other critics (and sometimes the same ones) decried its failure to attain the standards of efficiency and productivity that prevailed in the business world. In the 1920s and 1930s, planners urged that hospitals be made accessible to all Americans regardless of class or place of residence.

After World War II, an expanding economy brought a solution to the problem of inadequate facilities; more seemed inevitably better and a suddenly generous federal government began to support the hospital enterprise in a variety of ways. By the 1960s, a new generation of critics had begun to bewail this very expansion of hospital beds and services; it had created, they charged, an institution dominated by bureaucracy and capital-intensive technology and controlled by career-driven physicians and socially insensitive administrators.

Since the mid-1970s, economic problems have seemed most pressing. Third-party payers, both private and public, have sought to cap runaway costs, while profit-making hospital corporations have sought to take advantage of a seemingly risk-free niche in the American economy. Hospital planners, administrators, and a good many physicians have fallen victim to an outbreak of acute "Chicken Little" syndrome, wringing their hands as they wait for some actuarial sky to fall. Probably no generation has undertaken a broader and more stressful examination of hospital services.

An institution that has never been more necessary has never seemed more problematic. Today, voluntary hospitals discuss their market share and place in what is now called "the health care industry." Their administrators negotiate with

Charles E. Rosenberg, "Looking Backward, Thinking Forward: The Roots of Hospital Crisis," *Transactions and Studies of the College of Physicians of Philadelphia* 12 (1990): 127–129, 134–145, 147–150. Reprinted with permission from Charles E. Rosenberg. Copyright © 1990.

health maintenance organizations and other wholesale customers, while casting about for "profit centers" in the form of outpatient surgery units, sports medicine, and eating disorder clinics. Hospital managers measure earnings against the cost of capital and, in many regions, look over their shoulders at competition from profit-making rivals—as both nonprofits and for-profits begin to look more and more alike. The situation seems unprecedented; to many in the health care professions, it is as offensive as it is uncomfortable.

All of this is very much in the here and now; conditions so novel and unsettling minimize concern for the past. "What are the hospital's *real* problems," a questioner asked me at a seminar some months ago, "aside from emotions and history?" But both history and emotions are fused reality; attitudes and historically determined interests are as "real," and can be as constraining, as any other marketplace variable. What individuals assume, value, and anticipate are structuring—and, in fact, structural—elements in defining the boundaries within which economic and professional motives operate.

And although many of the key elements in today's medical care system seem to have come into being during the past quarter-century, they have been built upon well-established foundations. As early as the 1920s, indeed, the fundamental aspects of our contemporary hospital system were already in place. Even then, most Americans expected a great deal of these impressive institutions and such enthusiastic anticipations were already tied to a vision of the hospital as scientific and therapeutically efficacious. No longer was it merely a refuge for the poor alone, as it had been since its origins in the eighteenth century and throughout the nineteenth. By the same time, an intense and intimate relationship between the hospital and medical profession had also come into being. The ambiguous and contradictory image of the hospital as social service institution, on the one hand, and, on the other, as purveyor of technically defined and legitimated services was already well-established. This confusion was paralleled and exacerbated by the voluntary hospital's place in an ill-defined terrain between the public and private sectors.

There have certainly been major changes in health care and for hospitals since World War II, among them, the emerging role of the federal government, the expansion of third-party payment, and the enormous and capital-intensive growth of technical capacity. But all of these elements of change were assimilated into a system already rigid and precisely articulated, strengthening, rather than challenging, the fundamental aspects of that system. . . .

American voluntary hospitals have never been private except in the narrowest legal sense. Until the recent past, the great majority of America's important and influential hospitals were either explicitly municipal, or not-for-profit institutions operating for the common good. Such hospitals paid no taxes, were immune from civil suits, and received a variety of subsidies from state and local governments. Their governing boards assumed that they acted as stewards of society's resources, which were to be expended in pursuit of the general welfare. A for-profit sector has existed ever since nineteenth-century surgeons rented houses in which to treat private patients, but until recent years it has never played a significant role in the provision of medical care. Both the hospital's healing function and the presumably selfless and necessarily benevolent nature of that defining purpose have always guaranteed that hospitals would be clothed with the public interest. Their mission constituted a "sacred trust" that differentiated the hospital corporation's activities from those of an ordinary marketplace actor.

Consistently enough, cities and states have supported voluntary hospitals since the founding of the Pennsylvania Hospital in 1751. Even explicitly religious institutions have been the beneficiaries of public subsidies. In the realm of ideology, however, Americans have historically held fast to one consistent distinction among hospitals, but it was not the distinction between public and private that a lawyer might have understood and defended. It was a traditional differentiation between almshouse and hospital, between municipal—or county—and voluntary institution, between welfare and technical functions, and between the unworthy and worthy poor.

The eighteenth- and early nineteenth-century almshouse was an undifferentiated receptacle for the "dependent," as the conventional phraseology termed those unable or unwilling to work. Almshouse "inmates" included the mentally and physically handicapped, the aged, the infant, and the sick. In larger cities, medical care and medical personnel soon became important in local almshouses, for many of those inhabiting their beds were, in fact, the sick and the chronically ill aged—even if they had been admitted as "indigent." . . .

. . . [T]he tenacious belief in a fundamental distinction between the culpably dependent and the guiltless victim of random sickness was important to nineteenth-century Americans. It served not only to justify a frugal regimen at almshouse facilities, but also as a major argument to justify the founding of our pioneer nineteenth-century hospitals.

The contentions of hospital advocates in the nineteenth century seemed reasonable and equitable to their peers. It was unfair to subject the honest working man or woman to demeaning contacts within the almshouse's stigmatizing walls. A hospital open only to the remediable sick could be presented as a very different sort of institution, one in which no factor other than sickness itself determined eligibility for admission. It was consistent, then, that admission policies at most such voluntary hospitals categorically excluded the presumed victims of their own misdeeds, such as syphilitics, alcoholics, and unmarried mothers.

The provision of medical care outside an almshouse setting was a necessary path to reform. So long as acutely ill patients were treated in an almshouse setting, the dominance of chronic and geriatric ailments would make the institution unattractive to elite physicians concerned with the hospital's potential teaching role. So long as laymen were aware that admission to a municipal hospital was determined exclusively by dependence, they would regard the institution with fear and hostility. To be treated in New York's Bellevue, Chicago's Cook County, or in Philadelphia General Hospital was to admit a culpable lack of options. Moreover, the frugal tradition of "less eligibility" meant that the municipal hospital's internal standards of diet and amenities would routinely be maintained at a minimum level. No one, after all, was to be encouraged to prefer public alms to even the most meager wages earned by his or her own efforts.

No respectable group of Americans were more aware of grim municipal hospital conditions than the physicians who practiced in them. It is no accident that staff physicians at such institutions were leaders in calling for the severing of hospital from welfare services. They sought to make the municipal hospital exclusively a healing institution, subject to the claims and judgments of medical science and no longer hostage to political expediency and to the crushing and irremediable burden of poverty and incapacity. Key to the logic of such reform pleas was an often-expressed faith in medicine's healing capacity, and the egalitarian corollary that every individual had a right of access to such undeniably therapeutic resources. This technological entitlement implied an increasing gap between the hospital's welfare and curative functions. . . .

The pressure for increased access to hospital facilities implicit in a growing faith in medical capacities had a number of consequences in the 1920s and 1930s. One was a widely shared concern with the fact that the most technologically advanced medicine seemed available only to the very poor and very rich. The hospital ward and its subsidized beds were still marked by the stigmatizing aura of charity, while the private room with its capacity to protect individual sensibilities was limited to a small percentage of Americans. One solution, of course, was the construction of "semi-private" wings or buildings intended to serve the needs of middle-class men and women. The assumed prerogatives of class and the equally unquestionable public mission of the not-for-profit hospital made such solutions plausible. But beneath these experiments in hospital care for middle-income Americans lay a powerful conviction: if the hospital and its technical skills provided the best hope for cure, then every American should have access to these resources.

The Great Depression raised the stakes in the 1930s; new solutions had to be found, tactics that would preserve both the hospital's fiscal integrity and the middle-class patient's access to the institution. The creation of Blue Cross and Blue Shield was one outcome of this configuration of need, interest, and assumption. These prepaid insurance schemes also reflected the peculiar status of the hospital as clothed with the public interest and somehow above the marketplace. Faith in medicine's technical capacities—as centered in the hospital—guaranteed that these prepayment mechanisms would occupy the generally unquestioned place of quasi-public agencies, but would be little constrained by public supervision.

These assumptions, coupled with bureaucratic necessity, led the Blue Cross and Blue Shield to adopt administrative strategies that reified and exacerbated the reign of acute, reductionist models in health care. No disease was legitimate unless it could be coded in a nosological system. The schematic logic that divided medical care interactions into the specifically diagnosable and thus legitimately reimbursable, as opposed to the preventive or chronic, paralleled in another sphere the distinction between worthy and unworthy poor, between the voluntary and almshouse hospital. It reflected as well existing professional priorities that put acute individual care at center stage and placed preventive and chronic care on the periphery. . . .

. . . The emergence of Medicare and Medicaid in the mid-1960s did not challenge the ideological assumptions or interests embedded in earlier prepayment schemes; they simply added a deep new pocket to subsidize an existing system.

It is hardly surprising that powerful interests should have found this a comfortable environment: a controlled context in which cost-plus procurement replaced normal, and sometimes chastening, market transactions. Third-party payment has in general reflected the interest of providers but has never been perceived in this potentially critical and antagonistic way by most Americans; the convenient and deeply rooted blurring of distinctions between the public and private sectors, between the technical and the egalitarian, helped disarm such skepticism. It is paralleled by the way in which programs that largely benefit middle-class constituencies, such as Medicare and tax deductions for home mortgage interest, have been perceived as rights, while those designed to help the less fortunate, such as Medicaid and rent subsidies, are seen as welfare and thus demeaning. In a fundamental way, these examples parallel the attitudes expressed in an older set of polarities that distinguished between almshouse and hospital, public and private, and welfare maintenance and scientific healing.

The American hospital is an American institution. As such, it partakes of and reflects more general aspects of American cultural values. It has also been seen as particularly praiseworthy, the product of a local, and in more recent years national, commitment to community in the highly valued—and value-legitimating—form of advanced technology. Throughout their history, Americans have esteemed countries and communities able to mobilize advanced technology as a social resource; such societies have seemed more admirable, more moral, somehow higher on the scale of worthiness.

Thus boosterism provided one motivation for the rapid spread of hospitals during the years between the late 1880s and 1910. . . .

Communities wanted hospitals not only because they provided trained nurses and 24-hour care, but because they seemed to incorporate and represent the most scientific and technically advanced form of the healing art. These were decades during which most prosperous and educated Americans were fascinated both by the regalia and the rhetoric of science, even if the content remained open to debate. This was a period during which the art of warfare became military science, and when domestic science, library science, and political science all came into being. In retrospect, it seems obvious that the impact of the laboratory on medicine's therapeutic capacities still lay largely in the future; but Americans had been enormously impressed by a seeming transformation in medical knowledge during the years between 1880 and the 1920s. Newspapers and magazines were quick to report the discovery that many of mankind's greatest killers were caused by specific microorganisms. They were equally enthusiastic in reporting that some of these ills could be averted through preventive "inoculations" or, in other instances, cured by the injection of substances discovered and manufactured in the laboratory. The public health worker's ability to evaluate water quality, to diagnose ailments, and to disclose healthy carriers of disease through the use of serological tests or bacteriological screening seemed enormously encouraging. . . .

These attitudes about medicine were coupled with an older American faith in technology, with the ordinarily unstated but deeply felt conviction that if something could be done, it should be done. And the healing of sickness provided an emotionally resonant and seemingly disinterested goal to justify the mobilization of social resources. This complex of assumptions about science and its necessary application constituted a compelling argument for the proliferation of hospitals and progressive upgrading of the technology that had come to provide their fundamental rationale. . . .

Health and healing had [by the 1920s] come to play an important role in a secular society, a society that was at the same time increasingly ill-equipped to deal with acute illness and death outside an institutional context. Funds to implement these assumptions became increasingly available after World War II. At the same time, technology grew rapidly in complexity and cost, increasing budgetary pressures and adding substance to arguments for expanding and renovating hospital facilities. Thus occurred the intersection of material and attitudinal factors that provided the legitimacy and guaranteed the inevitability of escalating hospital expenditures; it was demeaning to place a price on a man or woman's life or on their freedom from pain and incapacity. So long as the calculation could be seen in terms of a procedure or practice that might or might not be performed, the decision-making gradient would clearly be inclined in the direction of making that procedure available. And more and more of such procedures became real options in the decades after 1950; renal dialysis and coronary bypass surgery are only two such examples among a host of others. Quibbling over mundane dollars seemed inappropriate in the face of transcendent goals. The bottom-line was that there was no bottom line—and costs climbed dramatically in a highly bureaucratic and capital intensive enterprise.

In this sense, it would not be inappropriate to compare hospital costs with defense expenditures. In both cases money is spent in pursuit of a transcendent goal, in the one case "security," in the other "health." In both cases, cost-cutting could be equated with penny-pinching, an unworthy aim, given the gravity of the social goals involved.

In both areas, material interests obviously play a role; hospitals, doctors, and medical suppliers, like defense contractors and the military, have interests expressed in and through the political process. But ideas are significant as well: it is impossible to understand our defense budget without factoring in the power of ideology; it is impossible to understand the nature and style of America's health care expenditures without an understanding of the ideological allure of scientific medicine and the promise of healing. Both the Massachusetts General Hospital and General Dynamics Corporation operate in the marketplace, but they are not bound by market discipline; and both also mock the presumed distinction between public and private that places them both in the category of private enterprise.

Like many other institutions, the hospital of the 1920s had become a self-consciously rational and efficient institution. It was no accident that the efficiency movement helped shape the rhetoric and, to a lesser extent, the practice of hospital administrators, just as it had factory and public school administrators. At the same time, the hospital still bore the marks of its humanitarian and paternalist origins. (Religious hospitals in particular still reflected community values in a variety of ways.) Hospital workers were paid less than their similarly skilled peers, and compensated with a presumed paternalist security. House officers and student nurses still bartered their time for credentials and experience.

Nevertheless, the great majority of hospitals sought to follow the much-admired pattern of other large enterprises: the army, the corporation, the factory. The most efficient use of limited funds implied the careful evaluation of expenditures; exhaustive record-keeping, it was contended, guaranteed more consistent and higher-quality medical care as well as the possibility of monitoring and controlling costs. Few contemporaries anticipated circumstances in which conflict might arise between bureaucratic efficiency and the quality of care ultimately experienced by individual patients.

In any case, it is clear that key aspects of the hospital's internal order had been transformed by the 1920s; the hospital was a very different institution from its mid-nineteenth-century predecessor. One such aspect was the professionalization of administration; another, and perhaps even more important, was the professionalization of nursing.

Nothing was—and is—more significant than nursing in shaping a hospital's internal life. And the day-to-day routine of patient care in large and medium-sized hospitals of the 1920s was controlled by a staff composed largely of student nurses, supervised by a cadre of more experienced training school graduates. (In small hospitals, a trained nurse might serve simultaneously as superintendent and chief nurse.) A decisive gap had been opened between the patient as object of care and the nurse as would-be professional, allied in some necessary, if ordinarily subservient, way with the staff physicians who oversaw and legitimated the provision of that care. In earlier periods, hospital nurses had been recruited from among recovered patients or from the community's servant class. They were not expected to identify with physicians or to see themselves as professional in their training or prerogatives. In the first decades of the twentieth century, nurse administrators were well aware of their less-than-secure professional identity and, lacking a prestigious and laboratory-oriented body of knowledge, dedicated themselves all the more tenaciously to the ideals of order and efficiency.

Hospital administrators, too, had come a long way from their nineteenth-century origins. Prudence, morality, and a bit of business experience described the qualities desired in a mid-nineteenth-century hospital superintendent. Trustees neither assumed nor expected any specific experience in the man entrusted with the day-to-day administration of their institution. By the 1920s, however, the situation was rather different. . . . There was some disagreement as to whether medical or lay superintendents might be more appropriate, but "professionalism" was assumed. A hospital superintendent's association was organized in 1899, and textbooks and specialized journals had already become available for the would-be hospital chief executive.

The place of the medical profession in the hospital of the 1920s was more prominent as well as more formal than it had been in previous generations. The hospital had become more explicitly and self-consciously a technical institution; medical knowledge appeared increasingly effective and decreasingly accessible to lay understanding. It seemed both natural and appropriate that medical practitioners and medical judgments should play a commanding role in hospital governance. Physicians determined admissions policies and, often, capital expenditures as well. . . .

Meanwhile, every stage of the physician's career was becoming embedded in the hospital—in the large teaching hospitals most prominently, but to a degree in every institution. The needs of certification and teaching helped define the role and duties of house officers, and wedded individual hospitals to a national network of certifying agencies. Accreditation made the individual hospital and its traditionally autonomous governing board subject to external bureaucratic control. Less concretely, but perhaps even more important, the individual hospital was subordinate to the dictates of an internationally-agreed-upon body of medical knowledge. Such knowledge had a variety of implications, from the way in which surgical and radiological facilities should be built and maintained, to appropriate doctor-patient ratios. The hospital was well along in its shift from a paternalistic institution controlled by local laymen and reflecting traditional ideas of stewardship, to a professionally-dominated and bureaucratically ordered institution responsive to national and even international standards and constraints. . . .

. . . [I]n the years immediately following World War II . . . the long pent-up economy provided resources for hospital expansion. The Hill-Burton Act (1946) granted funds for hospital construction, while the National Institutes of Health supported research and training (and, indirectly, hospital teaching and staffing). Employee-connected third-party payment expanded as well, providing a reliable, predictable, and expanding stream of revenue for previously hard-pressed institutional budgets. With the passage of Medicare and Medicaid in the 1960s, the system was complete. . . .

At first, the expanding health care system seemed to be one in which everyone benefited and no one paid excessively. . . . The sick received prepaid inpatient and some outpatient care; physicians, a generous income; hospital administrators, a secure and profitable salary; suppliers, enthusiastic and free-spending customers. Even nurses and workers could band together to demand salaries approaching those available in the private sector. By 1965, the system was ideally positioned for a generation of expansion.

And, for a time, it seemed that many of the older dilemmas of medical care had been bypassed. The poor could, it seemed, be treated in less stigmatizing circumstances, while the working man and woman and the middle-class family benefited from a medicine whose quality would not be constrained by cost. The technical resources of the system both structured and legitimated reimbursement. Briefly, at least, it seemed that private hospitals could and would take over the burden of poverty and dependency that traditionally had been the responsibility of municipal and (a minority of) large urban voluntary hospitals. The egalitarian implications of a shared faith in technology made traditional distinctions between welfare and private medicine seem less and less defensible; technological entitlement became a force in itself, legitimizing increasing hospital-based expenditures.

But in some fundamental ways the hospital system had changed less than the scale of its funding and the diagnostic and therapeutic tools at its disposal. The priorities and characteristics already built into American medicine a half-century earlier were in some ways only intensified by these newly abundant sources of support. . . .

Perhaps the crisis in hospital finance will stimulate some general reflections. Although that crisis seems, in the 1980s, to have turned on questions of financing, public dissatisfaction with hospitals implicates other aspects of health care as well. The shocked reaction to rapid private sector growth shared by many laypersons as well as physicians and health care administrators reflects in part the deeply felt assumption that the hospital was, and is, clothed with a social mission that transcends its place as marketplace actor. It seems somehow wrong to many Americans that managers and stockholders should benefit from healing the sick. . . .

For generations the hospital has seemed a necessary and inevitable, thus laudable and legitimate, institution. Perhaps the most important truth that has emerged in the past decade is the conviction that hospitals are not inevitable institutional reflections of available technical capacity. Technology provides options; it does not choose among them. The American hospital is historical and contingent; its boundaries are not necessary but negotiated. Our contemporary sense of crisis is one aspect of an increasingly self-conscious process through which hospitals are in fact renegotiating accustomed boundaries. But such negotiations are never easy. Boundaries reflect accustomed privileges and habits of thought. They are not redrawn without a struggle.

Disease in the History of Medicine and Public Health

JAMES T. PATTERSON

[M]ost historians of medicine proudly and explicitly describe themselves as supporters of the larger enterprise that has taken historical writing by storm in the past thirty years: the writing of contextualized social history. No one, indeed, has urged this agenda more frequently than Charles Rosenberg, who, as a professor of the history of science at the University of Pennsylvania, has directed many of the best-known scholars in the field. While he is uncomfortable with the term "social construction" of disease—which he thinks can lead to politically charged depictions of medical practitioners as legitimizers of an oppressive social order—he nonetheless insists that we understand the history of medicine in its social context. As he phrased his stance in co-editing an influential collection of essays, *Framing Disease,* disease is

> at once a biological event, a generation-specific repertoire of verbal constructs reflecting medicine's intellectual and institutional history, an occasion of potential legitimization for public policy, an aspect of social role and individual—intrapsychic—identity, a sanction for cultural values, and a structuring element in doctor and patient interactions.

Many of the essayists in this important collection elaborate Rosenberg's point of view. Social, economic, and cultural forces, they emphasize, "frame" the ways in which societies understand diseases. Three maladies discussed in the collection—silicosis, chronic fatigue syndrome, and anorexia—have in fact been named as well as framed by circumstances. Other common diagnoses—hysteria, alcoholism, homosexuality, "hyperactivity"—have been framed and labelled as "diseases" even though we cannot prove the existence of biopathological mechanisms.

Some of the scholars writing for *Framing Disease* proceed also to question what they consider to be the over-reliance of people on the "expertise" of medical personnel. They are attracted to the insights of Arthur Kleinman, whose book *The Illness Narratives* describes how patients and their families relate their symptoms of illness to practitioners, who then reconfigure these symptoms as narrow, technical issues, or "disease problems." . . .

. . . [A] logical corollary of this socio-cultural approach . . . [is] that we must avoid talking about specific "diseases" as if they were always the same through time—or as if they are perceived in the same ways by patients and practitioners. One historian who has made this point forcefully is Katherine Ott, in *Fevered Lives,* a cultural history of tuberculosis in the United States. She begins her book,

> the cultural products accompanying consumptions, also called phthisis, the white plague, and wasting disease, differ from those of tuberculosis. There is neither a core "tuberculosis," constant over time, nor a smooth conceptual trajectory leading from the lungs of ancient Greeks to the AIDS ward of a modern hospital. What we call "tuberculosis" was not the same disease in 1850 that it was in 1900 or even 1950.

She does not mean that understandings of the etiology of tuberculosis have changed dramatically since the 1890s—rather, that the disease is perceived in varied ways

James T. Patterson, "How Do We Write the History of Disease?" *Health and History* 1 (1998): 8–28. Reprinted by permission of the author.

by different people at different times, that the patient population has changed considerably over the past 150 years, and that the larger culture (defined by Ott as nowadays "post-AIDS, postindustrial, [and] postmodern") helps to structure the way the disease is managed.

In a very different way, Susan Sontag's *Illness as Metaphor* makes a similar point, though in this case about broad cultural perceptions rather than about historians or scientific researchers. Sontag, a cancer patient, wrote the book at white heat—"spurred by evangelical zeal," she wrote later—in order to demolish what she considered to be the "mystifications" erected by western cultures concerning the nature of cancer and tuberculosis. "Metaphors," she argued, came to distort popular understandings of these ailments, with tuberculosis often described romantically and sentimentally, and cancer, by contrast, associated with "irrational revulsion, a diminution of the self." Both sets of metaphors, she insisted, were grossly misleading; the metaphors surrounding cancer, indeed, literally helped to kill people, who all too often blamed themselves (or "stress") for their troubles and who therefore gave up. It was imperative, Sontag declared, that cancer patients do as she had done: ignore the metaphors, seek up-to-date medical help (in her case, chemotherapy), and fight the illness off.

We do not really know how many cancer patients have taken Sontag's no-nonsense advice. What we do know is that her speculations about the metaphorical representations of illness have intrigued (though not necessarily convinced) historians and others who insist on understanding disease in its socio-cultural context. A number of writers about AIDS, for instance, find it relevant and interesting to explore some of the metaphors used in talking about the syndrome.

A related theme of writing about the disease explores the complex, often contested relationships among scientists, as well as between "expert" and "popular" understandings of biological processes and medical therapies at given times in history. Essays concerning the "germ theory" of disease, collected in a recent issue of the *Journal of the History of Medicine and Allied Sciences,* emphasize that such a theory has no ontological life of its own. As [Nancy J. Tomes and] John Harley Warner [put] it, the theory is a "construction, the product of many communities engaged in vigorous debate." [They add], "there was no 'germ theory of disease' transcendent over time, but rather many different germ theories of specific diseases being debated in specific communities, times, and places." Historians of medicine, therefore, should avoid teleological assumptions resting on notions about widespread acceptance of "the germ theory": "a master narrative of the growth of medical practice is not only misleading but dangerous."

This perspective informs the arguments of Howard Markel's book on epidemics (cholera and typhus) in New York City in 1892 and Naomi Rogers's book on polio. Both studies observe that the arguments of many experts, who stressed the role of germs, were slow to be understood among various groups in the culture at large. They remind us that the transmission of ideas about health and sickness, like the spread of ideas in general, does not feature "progressive" "breakthroughs" that quickly transform the intellectual universe of a culture. Rather, the transmission is halting and layered. Mediated by considerations of class, gender, ethnicity, and residence, ideas often encounter stubborn resistance in the society at large.

Markel's account emphasizes the eruption in 1892 of a nasty tension between the then relatively new science of bacteriology and the politics of nativism. While some "experts" argued that germs explained cholera and typhus, others, including many leaders in the growing field of public health, insisted on improving sanitation. Neither of these approaches, however, commanded much attention from political leaders, some of whom encouraged popular prejudices about the disease-carrying propensities of recent immigrants, notably the "hordes" of supposedly dangerous and dirty East European Jews. One result of the panic that developed in 1892 was rigid restrictions on and inspections of such people. Another was the passage of federal legislation in 1893 that created a national system of quarantine regulations and that authorized the President to suspend immigration on a temporary basis. This law centralized responsibilities and led to creation of the United States Public Health Service in 1912.

Much of Rogers's excellent book examines reactions to the frightening epidemic of polio in 1916. These exposed a still uneasy and often volatile coexistence of germ theories (wrong theories, as it happened) and notions blaming disease on dirt and disorder that supposedly spread like miasma from poor, immigrant neighborhoods of large cities. The house fly soon became the *bête noire* of the epidemic. As she explains, "the germ theory and the new scientific medicine did not magically dissipate the influence of cultural prejudice in defining the relationship among disease, environment, and individual behavior." Moreover, "experts" were themselves divided. Some advocates of public health, like the widely respected Charles Chapin of Providence (Rhode Island), insisted on greater integration of bacteriology into public health work. Others, however, continued to stress the sanitarian precepts that had guided the late-nineteenth-century pioneers in the field. These leaders, like many frightened citizens, equated dirt and disease.

It is a small step from this theme to another that is common in recent writings about the history of medicine: the limits in the past (and present) of scientific understanding of diseases—even after the much-hailed triumphs of the bacteriological revolution. . . .

. . . During the First World War, the United States Navy did away with doorknobs on its battleships, in the belief that venereal disease could be spread by casual contacts. Hookworm disease, which played havoc with the physical well-being of millions of Americans, especially southerners, went virtually unrecognized until after 1900 in the United States. Influenza, which killed 20 to 40 million people in 1918–19, including some 500,000 in the United States, baffled experts, reducing them to recommending mass adoption of gauze masks (which were ineffective) and to inoculating thousands of people with vaccines that were no better than useless. Even now, scholars debate the reasons for the catastrophic declines in population of various Amerindians. . . .

In dealing with such ignorance about diseases, most historians of medicine, true to their commitment to contextualism, have struggled to avoid censorious statements or tone. To be sure, historians discount what they consider to be exaggerated claims for the happy therapeutic outcomes of scientific researches. They avoid such a "master narrative." Instead, they bow respectfully (usually with a reservation or two) to the arguments of Thomas McKeown and his colleagues, who argued twenty years ago that improved mortality rates since the early nineteenth century owe more to economic growth and consequent improvements in nutrition than to advances in scientific research or medical therapy. Many historians also stress another point: much doctoring in the past, and present, should not be seen only from the perspective (and records) of articulate (usually male) scientists and physicians. Rather, we should appreciate that medical care often reflects complex negotiations between doctors, nurses, midwives, patients, and their families. Such narratives, moreover, can mine heretofore ignored archival lodes, notably the diaries of patients and obscure care-givers. Laurel Thatcher Ulrich's book *A Midwife's Tale,* about the ministrations between 1785 and 1812 of Martha Ballard, a midwife in rural Maine, made compelling use of such a diary. The book won a Pulitzer prize. . . .

An especially self-conscious scholarly effort to appreciate [that "experts" in the past did not "know" what we claim to know] . . . is [Judith Walzer] Leavitt's book *Typhoid Mary,* about a famous—indeed notorious—carrier of typhoid fever early in this century. Mary Mallon was a poor, unmarried immigrant from Ireland who hired out as a cook in various households in the New York City area in the 1890s and 1900s. Although healthy herself, she was ultimately shown to have caused (by handling food) the deaths of three people and to have infected many more. Leavitt's narrative explores a host of issues, focusing on the question of civil liberties: when if ever may a society isolate a person (as Mary was isolated for the last twenty-three years of her life) who is thought to be dangerous to society? Leavitt is also deliberately concerned, however, with helping her readers look at the phenomenon of typhoid from different perspectives—those of doctors, public health personnel, patients, stigmatizers, and Mary herself. Is there a single "truth"—an uncontested entity that we may call "typhoid"—to be derived from Mary's story? . . . Leavitt for the most part avoids censuring Mary's contemporaries. Her goal, like that of many others in the field, is to place her protagonists in their appropriate settings and to elucidate the contingencies of history.

I cannot leave you with the impression, however, that historians of medicine are wholly nonjudgmental or "objective" about their subjects. On the contrary, for all their efforts at "social construction," "framing," and contextualism, many tend to take a critical stance toward American elites that reflects the wider thrust of historiography in the past thirty years.

The reasons for such a judgmental position need not detain us for long. They are rooted in the same seminal developments that shook the American social order in the 1960s and early 1970s, notably the civil rights movement, the Vietnam War, and the rise of feminism and environmentalism. These and other developments spurred critical reconsiderations by historians of the American past, which, they said, has featured widespread racism, militarism, governmental excess, sexism, and disregard for nature. Elites of all sorts—politicians, diplomats, bureaucrats, lawyers, big businessmen, Big Labor—have been exposed, accused of egregious sins of omission and commission. At the same time, Americans generally, having come to expect more and more from life during the economically prosperous 1950s and 1960s, came to embrace a fervent rights-consciousness, which has persisted and grown since that time. Expecting the best of all possible worlds, Americans have become quick to snap at people—and institutions—who have failed to practice the near-utopian goals that they sounded ever readier to preach.

In such a contentious, antiauthoritarian culture, it is hardly surprising that scientists and physicians, too, suffered from the lash of criticism. In these years, the exalted, near-priestly reputations of white-coated medical personnel dropped precipitously. . . . Doubts and anger mounted among African-Americans following disclosure in 1972 of the federal government's infamous, forty-year-long "Tuskegee experiment," in which physicians and public health officials complacently observed the effects of untreated syphilis among selected black males, doing nothing (even after the introduction of penicillin in the 1940s) to help them. Since then, surveys indicate, many African-Americans appear to believe the worst about the claims and therapies of white physicians and government bureaucrats. . . .

The rising fears and resentments of women surfaced with special clarity in a large-selling book that appeared in 1973—*Our Bodies, Ourselves,* by the Boston Women's Health Collective. It exposed a host of sexist practices in male-dominated medicine in the United States. Since then, concerns such as these have frequently merged with an environmental consciousness which has perhaps been stronger in the United States in the past thirty years than in any other nation. Indeed, an early "bible" of the movement, Rachel Carson's *Silent Spring,* focused on the links between pesticides and cancer, from which she was suffering while writing the book. (She died of the disease, aged fifty-six, in 1964.) . . . [W]omen have often led the fight for government action against what they say are harmful substances. Former congresswoman Bella Abzug, a cancer survivor, recently helped to organize the first World Conference on Breast Cancer in Canada, at which some delegates insisted that links between breast cancer and the environment need not be proved conclusively before governments move to ban allegedly carcinogenic substances.

Doubts about scientific-medical expertise, however, have reached well beyond minority groups and women. Reflecting rising educational levels, Americans in general have become shrewder, tougher consumers of medical services. With the rise of managed health care in the past decade, many of these consumers have seemed especially confrontational. While most people still have faith in America's medical institutions, millions have sought the blessings of "alternative medicine"; the National Institute of Health now has an Office of Alternative Medicine; the subject is taught in more than fifty American medical schools; consumer spend $14 billion per year on such medicines, or approximately $70 per adult. Dr. Andrew Weil's *Spontaneous Healing,* which recommends (among other things) educated use of mind-expanding drugs, has been a best-seller for nearly a year; his Web site attracts 83,000 hits a day. Still other Americans turn to the Internet (especially the Medline Web offered by the National Library of Medicine) for advice that they do not get from their physicians. . . .

Reflecting such popular feelings, many historians of medicine have approached their work in a critical spirit. While I cannot do justice to the wide scope of this eclectic and unorganized enterprise, I will mention a few themes of these efforts. One such theme highlights the persistence of class and racial discrimination in the history of American health care. This is such a central theme that it is hardly necessary to single out particular histories as examples. Still, two may suffice. One is Charles Rosenberg's *The Care of Strangers,* which, like other recent studies of hospitals, describes the many ways that American hospitals in the nineteenth and early twentieth centuries reflected the ongoing strength of class divisions in American society. Another is Georgina Feldberg's revealingly entitled book on tuberculosis, *Disease and Class,* which has much to say on the "social" dimensions of the long struggle against the disease. One of Feldberg's objectives is to spotlight the need for a more "socially informed medicine."

Feldberg and others go beyond making such obvious points about American health care practices, past and present. Indeed, her book features another long-standing continuity in such practices: the gulf between high-sounding proclamations of public support for better health care and the realities of low levels of federal-state spending. The United States, she maintains, resisted the establishment of a wide-spread vaccination program with BCG (the bacillus Calmette-Guerin, widely used against tuberculosis in Australia and other nations) in large part because such an effort would have required what Americans derided as expensive and excessive "regulation." Instead, she adds, the United States, a conservative culture that resists state intervention, depended on comparatively ineffective programs of public exhortation and education, which were thought to have the capacity to persuade *individuals* to adopt better habits. Faith in such educational programs, which have been financed primarily by private organizations (such as the National Tuberculosis Association, the American Social Hygiene Association against venereal disease, the March of Dimes against polio, and the American Cancer Society) represent a mainly priva-tized, distinctively American approach to the struggle for a more healthy society. (An oft-heard argument about such "exceptionalism" of the United States is that along with South Africa it is the only major nation that has not instituted a compre-hensive, state-supported health insurance system). . . .

The title of [Allan] Brandt's widely praised book *No Magic Bullet* [which ex-plores American responses to venereal disease since 1880] captures another theme that many critically oriented historians of American medicine have underscored: the United States since the great discoveries of Koch and Pasteur has been a culture that flirts foolishly with quests for "magic bullets," or "breakthroughs," as the front line in a "conquest" of disease. One such breakthrough did occur in the 1950s, when Americans deliriously celebrated news that a vaccine against polio would prove suc-cessful in preventing the disease. In general, however, as Brandt and many others have emphasized, "breakthroughs" and "magic bullets" "targeted" at specific diseases are relatively rare in the history of science. It would be better, they argue, to give gen-erous support to research in basic biological science and to finance long-term pro-grams of care-giving that take into account the considerable costs of coping with complicated chronic diseases (such as cancer, AIDS and tuberculosis). . . .

In the same vein, many critics add, Americans are often cool to expenditures for preventive approaches. Brandt makes this a theme of his account of public inac-tion concerning venereal diseases. So does Robert Proctor, in a hard-hitting book on contemporary "cancer wars" in the United States. Proctor begins by arguing that "the causes of cancer are largely known—and have been for some time." These include chemicals and other substances in the air, food and water, workplace expo-sures, "bad habits" (such as overexposure to the sun, reckless sex, fat-filled diets, and smoking), "bad government," and "bad luck—including the luck of your genetic draw and the culture into which you have been born." Despite our under-standing of such facts, Proctor maintains, Americans—ordinary people (who de-mand their pleasures) as well as leaders (who often shelter powerful economic interests)—do not take strong preventive steps against the Number Two killer in the country. Proctor highlights a point often made by scientists and historians of medicine: it is not necessary to understand the precise etiology of a disease to know that some things we do are bad for us—and to retaliate vigorously with pre-ventive measures. . . .

A final, heavily documented theme of this critical literature points to the readiness of Americans to scapegoat people for the existence of diseases, especially epidemics. To be sure, there have been exceptions: it is remarkable, for instance, how little scapegoating occurred in the United States during or after the greatest epidemic of all, influenza in 1918–19. Otherwise, Americans (like people in other nations) have frequently been quick to blame the victim: Jews, Typhoid Marys, east European immigrants, city people (and city dirt), Chinese (who were roughly handled during a San Francisco smallpox epidemic in 1900), prostitutes, "immoral" people, Amerindians (who were thought to have introduced venereal disease to "civilization" in 1492), African-Americans, the unwashed poor. . . .

The sudden and frightening arrival of AIDS in the 1980s has shown anew how quick people can be to scapegoat others. To be sure, reactions to AIDS have been less extreme than panics had been amid earlier epidemics—in part because AIDS in the United States is a more discriminating attacker than, for instance, smallpox or cholera. When it first appeared, it seemed mainly to afflict gay people and needle-using drug addicts, not the "general" population. Moreover, gays in the United States mobilized effectively to prevent, at least until now, widespread adoption of such measures as mandatory reporting and isolation of people with HIV and notification of partners. The result has been policies described as "AIDS exceptionalism"—different from those employed concerning other epidemic diseases, such as tuberculosis. . . . Still, AIDS (especially before 1986) has prompted some overreactions: arbitrary imprisonment, deportation, bashings, isolation, the burning of houses and other forms of discrimination. . . .

In these and other ways AIDS has recapitulated the social history of other sexually transmitted diseases: the pervasive dread of contagion, uninformed notions about casual transmission, the stigmatizing of victims, agitated debates about civil liberties and public health, and divisions within the government, both in the early years and later, when it became clear that AIDS is a chronic affliction requiring long-term care. The incursions of AIDS have also generated many familiar expectations (especially after the identification of HIV) about the manufacture of "magic bullets": some have called for a "Manhattan Project" to fight AIDS. We also see abundant manifestations, similar to those that attended the spread of venereal disease in the progressive era, of a societal quest for moral purification. . . .

This does not mean, however, that nothing has changed over time. Let me offer two observations about such change in the very recent past. The first emphasizes an argument that Charles Rosenberg (among others) has insisted on: the arrival of AIDS forces us to avoid purely social constructions of disease in history. AIDS, he says, is a "postrelativist" phenomenon. To be sure, it is socially framed—among other things, people once again blame the victims. But "at the same time it fits nicely into a one-dimensionally reductionist and biologically based model of disease. . . . It is no mere text, words arranged to mirror and legitimate particular social relationships and perceptions." For these reasons AIDS requires social historians of medicine to think carefully about their presuppositions.

More important, AIDS is a sobering reminder of the omnipresence of diseases among us, and of the futility of expecting the eradication of suffering. While this may seem an obvious point today, such a sober outlook reveals that many Americans today, scientists included, look at the world in a considerably less rosy way than they did in the "Can Do" years of the 1950s and 1960s. . . .

. . . While the sobering phenomenon of AIDS has contributed to this development, it is by no means the only source of rising doubts about the capacity of "science" and medicine to wipe out disease. Knowledgeable people insist on reminding us nowadays that many infectious microbes mutate rapidly: malaria, polio, and tuberculosis are cases in point. Diseases once thought to be declining in the western hemisphere, such as dengue fever and malaria, threaten to become epidemic in parts of South America and the Caribbean. A strain of bubonic plague is now known to be resistant to all antibiotics normally used to fight the disease. We now understand that different strains of the HIV virus have resulted in varied epidemic patterns of AIDS, each with its own route of transmission and level of infectiousness and aggression. Drugs that kill certain microbes provide other microbes with greater opportunities to proliferate. Mysterious "new" agents, such as the sources of "mad cow disease" and the Ebola virus (out of "darkest Africa"), excite feelings of dread and uncertainty. Other dimly understood "new" conditions, such as attention deficit disorder (ADD), are being diagnosed in record numbers.

It is also obvious that government officials lied to the American people about nuclear testing and about its medical dangers in the 1950s. Moreover, the "war" on cancer, America's most heavily armed assault on disease, has not only failed to slow age-adjusted mortality from the disease; it has also featured grant-hungry researchers overselling a seemingly endless arsenal of "magic bullets"—interferon, interleukin 2 and others. Well-informed observers of the fight against cancer now predict that mortality from this disease—the number two cause of death in the United States since the 1920s—will soon take over first place.

 ## F U R T H E R   R E A D I N G

Rima D. Apple, ed., *Women, Health, and Medicine in America* (1990).
Allan M. Brandt, "Emerging Themes in the History of Medicine," *Milbank Quarterly* 69 (1991): 199–214.
Gert H. Brieger, ed., *Medical America in the Nineteenth Century* (1972).
John C. Burnham, *How the Idea of Profession Changed the Writing of Medical History* (1998).
W. F. Bynum and Roy Porter, eds., *Companion Encyclopedia of the History of Medicine*, 2 vols. (1993).
James H. Cassedy, *Medicine in America* (1991).
John Duffy, *The Healers: A History of American Medicine* (1976).
John Duffy, *The Sanitarians: A History of American Public Health* (1990).
Elizabeth Fee and Theodore M. Brown, eds., *Making Medical History: The Life and Times of Henry E. Sigerist* (1997).
Daniel M. Fox and Christopher Lawrence, *Photographing Medicine: Images and Power in Britain and America Since 1840* (1988).
Norman Gevitz, ed., *Other Healers: Unorthodox Medicine in America* (1988).
Ludmilla Jordanova, "The Social Construction of Medical Knowledge," *Social History of Medicine* 8 (1995): 361–381.
Kenneth F. Kiple, ed., *The Cambridge World History of Human Disease* (1993).
Judith Walzer Leavitt, "Medicine in Context: A Review Essay of the History of Medicine," *American Historical Review* 95 (1990): 1471–1484.
Judith Walzer Leavitt, ed., *Women and Health in America*, 2nd ed. (1999).
Judith Walzer Leavitt and Ronald L. Numbers, eds., *Sickness and Health in America: Readings in the History of Medicine and Public Health*, 3rd ed. (1997).

George Rosen, *A History of Public Health* (1958).

Charles E. Rosenberg, *Explaining Epidemics and Other Studies in the History of Medicine* (1992).

Charles E. Rosenberg, *No Other Gods: On Science and American Social Thought* (1961, 1976).

Charles E. Rosenberg and Janet Golden, eds., *Framing Disease: Studies in Cultural History* (1992).

Todd L. Savitt and James Harvey Young, *Disease and Distinctiveness in the American South* (1988).

Richard H. Shryock, *Medicine and Society in America, 1660–1860* (1960).

Paul Starr, *The Social Transformation of American Medicine* (1982).

Morris J. Vogel and Charles E. Rosenberg, *The Therapeutic Revolution: Essays in the Social History of American Medicine* (1979).

John Harley Warner, "The History of Science and the Sciences of Medicine," *Osiris* 10 (1995): 164–193.

John Harley Warner, "Science in Medicine," in *Historical Writing on American Science*, ed. Sally Gregory Kohlstedt and Margaret Rossiter (1986), pp. 37–58.

James Harvey Young, *American Health Quackery* (1992).

Colonial Beginnings:
A New World of Peoples,
Disease, and Healing

With the European colonization of North America, Native Americans, Europeans, and Africans began not only a cultural exchange of medical knowledge and healing practices but also a biological exchange of diseases. British, Spanish, French, and Dutch settlers faced a new habitat with the expectation, firmly rooted in early modern European thought, that a new environment—with climate, topography, diet, and customs unlike those of their homelands—would alter both the temperament of its inhabitants and the character of their diseases. European immigrants brought with them their own healing traditions, which centered on a notion of sickness as imbalance of the body's humors, to be remedied by purging, vomiting, bleeding, and other means of restoring health. At the same time, however, they expected that plants native to American soil would provide particularly efficacious remedies for treating local American ailments. Explorers, missionaries, and settlers learned from Native Americans about the medicinal powers of indigenous plants, and such Native American knowledge was selectively appropriated by European American folk practice and mainstream learned medicine. As printing presses became more common in the colonies, this knowledge was disseminated in almanacs, newspapers, and domestic health guidebooks.

European explorers and colonists also brought with them infectious diseases new to the Americas, such as smallpox, measles, mumps, and influenza. The arrival of African slaves introduced diseases such as yellow fever and hookworm. For Native Americans in particular the consequences of this new intermixing of peoples and infections was devastating. Lacking immunity against these unfamiliar pathogens, Native American populations were decimated, with in some places nine-tenths of the population killed off. Although the health consequences of the European invasion often were unanticipated and poorly understood, the fact that Europeans sometimes intentionally resorted to what we now would regard as germ warfare testifies to their grasp of the contagious nature of a deadly disease such as smallpox.

Most Europeans and Africans in the colonies lived on farms, on plantations, or in small towns, and when ill relied chiefly on domestic medical self-help and

neighborly lay healing. In a society with few formally educated physicians, communities often looked to respected laypeople for their medical acumen, especially to
clergymen (all the more so because illness could be explained not only by natural
causes but also as a consequence of sin or providential design). The preacher-
physician was an established figure in many communities into the eighteenth
century, with Boston's Congregational minister Cotton Mather probably the best-
known example. Epidemics posed special problems for the entire community, not
just for sick individuals and their families. In the seventeenth century fear of
plague from ships crossing the Atlantic from Europe and of yellow fever from the
Caribbean led colonial governments to establish the first quarantines; and in
the eighteenth century smallpox epidemics prompted the building of pest houses,
where infected, dangerous people could be isolated from the rest of the population.
What warranted granting governments such powers to prevent the spread of disease? Who should assess the risks involved in such measures, and how should they
determine what would best serve the welfare of the community? How should a
proper balance be struck between individual civil liberties and the public's health?
And who should decide what constitutes appropriate authority over medical
knowledge and practice? These questions were vigorously debated in the American
colonies during the eighteenth century—as in the 1721–1722 smallpox inoculation
controversy in Boston, the most renowned medical debate of the colonial period in
the British colonies—and are questions that public health officials, lawmakers,
and the American public continue to grapple with today.

 ## D O C U M E N T S

Antoine Simon Le Page du Pratz recollects personal observations he made in the French
colony of Louisiana from 1718 through 1734 (which he published in France in 1758).
For eight of those years, starting in 1720, Le Page du Pratz, an adventurer and trader,
lived on a plantation he established north of New Orleans along the Mississippi River,
among the Indians of the Natchez Nation. He became a trusted friend, observed their
customs, and described their social structure, religion, and daily life. In Document 1,
Le Page du Pratz recounts how his own illness in 1723 was treated by a Natchez
shaman, explains why he judges Natchez therapies superior to those of French doctors,
and describes Indian herbal remedies for his European readers.

Documents 2, 3, and 5 are from the pamphlet war that was part of the Boston
smallpox inoculation controversy of 1721–1722 and give voice to both sides of this
bitter debate. In Document 2, the prominent Boston minister Cotton Mather recounts
how he initially heard about inoculation against smallpox from a slave, then interrogated other slaves about its use in Africa, and later heard about the introduction of the
practice from Constantinople to England. He tells about the first use of the practice in
New England by the Boston physician Zabdiel Boylston in 1721; the opposition it met
with in the community (not only from such physicians as William Douglass, who questioned the safety of the practice, but also from lay people who protested against a practice "learnt from the Heathens"). Mather explains his advocacy of inoculation, refutes
the objections brought against it, and affirms its success in preventing smallpox.

Douglass, at the time the only Boston physician with an M.D. degree, counters
Mather in Document 3. He decries what he regards as the intemperate promotion of
smallpox inoculation in Boston, comparing this "infatuation" with the movement in
Massachusetts three decades earlier that culminated in the hanging of people suspected of witchcraft. He particularly assails Mather for meddling in medical affairs
beyond his competence. In Document 5, Boylston, the physician-ally of Mather,

responds to Douglass. In his preface he recounts his first "experiment" with inoculation in 1721, performed on two of his slaves and his six-year-old son. He then presents case histories of his inoculations, which reveal some of the problems he encountered but emphasize the efficacy of the practice. The broadside reproduced as Document 4 laments fatalities in a Hartford epidemic in 1725. The poem intermingles religious themes with information about the people who died from the unspecified disease; the list of names points to clusters of deaths in certain households and underscores the racial mix in this early-eighteenth-century Connecticut town.

Document 6 is an excerpt from *Every Man His Own Doctor: Or, the Poor Planter's Physician* (1734), which was reissued in the colonies more than a dozen times before the Revolutionary War and was one of the earliest American popular guides to health care. The volume, widely ascribed to the Virginia-born physician John Tennent, emphasizes the singularity of illnesses arising from the American land and climate, and for their treatment recommends inexpensive remedies grown in American soil. Document 7 comes from a short history of the Ottawa Nation written in 1887 by Andrew Blackbird, son of an Ottawa chief and brought up in traditional ways in Michigan. Blackbird recounts a story from Indian oral tradition about the depopulation of a large Ottawa community along the upper shore of Lake Michigan, just below the Straits of Mackinac, when in the early 1760s the British sent a tin box containing smallpox scabs to kill the Indian allies of their rivals in the region, the French.

1. Le Page du Pratz, a French Observer in Louisiana, Reports on Natchez Nation Healing Practices, 1720–1728

For some days a *fistula lacrymalis* had come into my left eye, which discharged an humour, when pressed, that portended danger. I shewed it to M. *St. Hilaire,* an able surgeon, who had practised for about twelve years in the *Hôtel Dieu* at *Paris.*

He told me, it was necessary to use the fire for it; and that, notwithstanding this operation, my sight would remain as good as ever; only my eye would be blood-shot: And that if I did not speedily set about the operation, the bone of the nose would become carious.

These reasons gave me much uneasiness, as having both to fear and to suffer at the same time: However, after I had resolved to undergo the operation, the *Grand Sun* [a Natchez leader] and his brother came one morning very early, with a man loaded with game, as a present for me.

The *Great Sun* observed I had a swelling in my eye, and asked me what was the matter with it. I shewed it him, and told him, that in order to cure it, I must have fire put to it; but that I had some difficulty to comply, as I dreaded the consequences of such an operation. Without replying, or in the least apprizing me, he ordered the man, who brought the game, to go in quest of his physician, and tell him, he waited for him at my house. The messenger and physician made such dispatch, that this last came in an hour after. The *Great Sun* ordered him to look at my eye, and endeavour to cure me: After examining it, the physician said, he would undertake to cure me with simples and common water. I consented to this with so much the greater pleasure and readiness, as by this treatment I ran no manner of risque.

[Antoine Simon] Le Page du Pratz, *The History of Louisiana, or the Western Parts of Virginia and Carolina* (London: T. Becket and P. A. De Hondt, 1763; trans. from the first French ed., Paris, 1758), 2 vols.; vol. 1, pp. 77–81; vol. 2, pp. 38–40, 44, 133–134.

That very evening the physician came with his simples, all pounded together, and making but a single ball, which he put with the water in a deep basin, he made me bend my head into it, so as the eye affected stood dipt quite open in the water. I continued to do so for eight or ten days, morning and evening; after which, without any other operation, I was perfectly cured, and never after had any return of the disorder.

It is easy, from this relation, to understand what dextrous physicians the natives of *Louisiana* are. I have seen them perform surprizing cures on *Frenchmen;* on two especially, who had put themselves under the hands of a *French* surgeon settled at this Post. Both patients were about to undergo the grand cure: And after having been under the hands of the surgeon for some time, their heads swelled to such a degree, that one of them made his escape, with as much agility as a criminal would from the hands of justice, when a favourable opportunity offers. He applied to a *Natchez* physician, who cured him in eight days: His comrade continuing still under the *French* surgeon, died under his hands three days after the escape of his companion, whom I saw three years after in a state of perfect health.

In the war which I lately mentioned, the Grand Chief of the *Tonicas,* our allies, was wounded with a ball, which went through his cheek, came out under the jaw, again entered his body at the neck, and pierced through to the shoulder-blade, lodging at last between the flesh and the skin: The wound had its direction in this manner, because when he received it, he happened to be in a stooping posture, as were all his men, in order to fire. The *French* surgeon, under whose care he was, and who dressed him with great precaution, was an able man, and spared no pains in order to effect a cure. But the physicians of this Chief, who visited him every day, asked the *Frenchman* what time the cure would take? he answered, six weeks at least: They returned no answer, but went directly and made a litter; spoke to their Chief, and put him on it, carried him off, treated him in their own manner, and in eight days effected a complete cure.

These are facts well known in the Colony. The physicians of the country have performed many other cures, which, if they were to be all related, would require a whole volume apart; but I have confined myself to the three above mentioned, in order to shew, that disorders, frequently accounted almost incurable, are, without any painful operation, and in a short time, cured by physicians, natives of *Louisiana.* . . .

The *Bearded-creeper* is so called from having its whole stalk covered with a beard about an inch long, hooked at the end, and somewhat thicker than a horse's hair. There is no tree which it loves to cling to so much as to the *Sweet Gum.* . . . This is likewise the tree upon which it thrives best. It has the same virtue with its balm of being a febrifuge, and this I affirm after a great number of proofs. The physicians among the natives use this simple in the following manner. They take a piece of it, above the length of the finger, which they split into as many threads as possible; these they boil in a quart of water, till one third of the decoction evaporate, and the remainder is strained clear. They then purge the patient, and the next day, upon the approach of the fit, they give a third of the decoction to drink. If the patient be not cured with the first dose, he is again purged and drinks another third, which seldom fails of having the wished-for effect. This medicine is indeed very bitter, but it strengthens the stomach; a singular advantage it has over the *Jesuits bark,* which is accused of having a contrary effect.

There is another *Creeper* very like *Salsaparilla,* only that it bears its leaves by threes. It bears a fruit smooth on one side like a filbert, and on the other as rough as the little shells which serve for money on the *Guiney* coast. I shall not speak of its properties; they are but too well known by the women of *Louisiana,* especially the girls, who very often have recourse to it. . . .

Ground-ivy is said by the natives to possess many more virtues than are known to our botanists. It is said to ease women in labour when drank in a decoction; to cure ulcers, if bruised and laid upon the ulcered part; to be a sovereign remedy for the head-ach; a considerable quantity of its leaves bruised, and laid as a cataplasm upon the head, quickly removes the pain. As this is an inconvenient application to a person that wears his hair, I thought of taking the salts of the plant, and I gave some of them in vulnerary water to a friend of mine who was often attacked with the head-ach, advising him likewise to draw up some drops by the nose: he seldom practised this but he was relieved a few moments after. . . .

I mentioned that nature had contributed no less than war to the destruction of these people [the Native American peoples of Louisiana]. Two distempers, that are not very fatal in other parts of the world make dreadful ravages among them; I mean the small-pox and a cold, which baffle all the art of their physicians, who in other respects are very skillful. When a nation is attacked by the small-pox, it quickly makes great havock; for as a whole family is crowded into a small hut, which has no communication with the external air, but by a door about two feet wide and four feet high, the distemper, if it seizes one, is quickly communicated to all. The aged die in consequence of their advanced years and the bad quality of their food; and the young, if they are not strictly watched, destroy themselves, from an abhorrence of the blotches in their skin. If they can but escape from their hut, they run out and bathe themselves in the river, which is certain death in that distemper. The *Chatkas,* being naturally not very handsome, and not so apt to regret the loss of their beauty; consequently suffer less, and are much more numerous than the other nations.

2. Cotton Mather, a Boston Minister, Proselytizes for Smallpox Inoculation, 1772

A Gentleman [that is, Cotton Mather] well known in the City of *Boston,* had a *Garamantee* Servant, who first gave him an Account, of a Method frequently used in *Africa,* and which had been practis'd on himself, to procure an *easy Small-Pox,* and a perpetual [s]ecurity of neither *dying* by it, nor being again infected with it.

Afterwards he successively met with a Number of *Africans;* who all, in *their* plain Way, without any Combination, or Correspondence, agreed in *one Story, viz.* that in their Country (where they use to die like *Rotten Sheep,* when the *Small-Pox* gets among them) it is now become a *common Thing* to cut a Place or two in their Skin, sometimes one Place, and sometimes another, and put in a little of the Matter of the *Small-Pox;* after which, they, in a few Days, grow a *little Sick,* and a few *Small-Pox* break out, and by and by they dry away; and that no Body ever dy'd of doing this, nor ever had the *Small-Pox* after it: Which last Point is confirm'd by

[Cotton Mather], *An Account of the Method and Success of Inoculating the Small-Pox, in Boston in New-England* (London: J. Pells, 1722), pp. 1–2, 8–11, 14–18, 23–26.

their constant Attendance on the Sick in our Families, without receiving the Infection; and, so considerable is the Number of these in our Neighbourhood, that he had as evident Proof of the *Practice, Safety,* and *Success* of this Operation, as we have that there are *Lions* in *Africa.*

After this, he heard it affirm'd, That it is no unusual Thing for our Ships on the Coast of *Guinea,* when they ship their Slaves, to find out by Enquiry which of the Slaves have not yet had the *Small-Pox;* and so carry them a-shore, in this Way to give it to them, that the poor Creatures may sell for a better Price; where they are often (inhumanly enough) to be dispos'd of.

Some Years after he had receiv'd his first *African* Informations, he found published in our *Philosophical Transactions,* divers Communications from the *Levant,* which, to our Surprize, agreed with what he had from *Africa.* . . .

About three Months ago, the *Small Pox* broke in upon the City of *Boston,* where it very much appeard with the *Terrors of Death* to the Inhabitants. On this Occasion, there was address'd a Letter to the *Physicians* of the City, with an Account of the Communications from the illustrious *Timonius,* and *Pylarinus,* entreating them to meet for a *Consultation* upon it, *Whether the new Practice might be introduc'd and countenanc'd among us?* The Writer was persuaded, that herein he did but his Duty, and express'd no other than the *Charity of a Christian,* and a proper Concernment and Compassion for his poor Neighbours, whom he saw likely to die by Hundreds about him. His Address found (for what Reasons I know not, or am not willing to know) an *indecent Reception* with our Physitians; all the Return he had, was a Story which they spread about the Town and Country, that he had given an *unfaithful Account* of the Matter to them, tho' they had it in the printed *Philosophical Transactions* before their Eyes to justify it. . . . Nevertheless, one who had been a more *successful Practitioner* than most of them, and had, with a singular Dexterity in his Practice, perform'd Things not attempted by any of them, (namely, Mr. *Zabdiel Boylston*) was prompted, by his enterprizing Genius, to begin the Operation. He thought it most generous to make his first Beginning upon his *own Family;* and here, to make not only two *Slaves,* but a beloved *Son* of his own, (about five or six Years of Age) the Subjects of it: He made the *Transplantation* into them with two or three *Incisions* a-piece, taking the *Leg* as well as the *Arm* (and in one of them the *Neck*) for the Places of them: He did not use the *Precaution* of sending for the fermenting *Pus* by a third Person: He staid not for what some would have thought more *proper Seasons;* but he did it in the very *Heat of Midsummer,* which, with us, is hot enough: He did nothing at all to *prepare* their Bodies, and he chose to leave them to the *Liberties,* which Persons infected with the *Small-Pox* in the *common Way,* do generally take, before their *Decumbiture,* without any Detriment to them.

Under all these Disadvantages, did this Gentleman make his Experiments; but *they succeeded to Admiration.* About the seventh Day the Patients began to grow Feverish, and out of Order; on the third and fourth Day from their falling ill, his Child's Fever grew to an Height, beyond his Expectation, which (from the *Novelty* of the Business) did, for a few Hours, considerably terrify him: He had Recourse to the common Remedies of Blisters, and gave the Child a *Vomit,* and presently all the Fright was over: The *Eruption* began; and from the Time of its doing so with the *Child,* and with the two *Slaves,* there was no Occasion for any *other Medicine;* they were easy from this Time; their *Pustules* (which were, tho' not many, yet somewhat more for Number, than what is usual in the *Levant*) grew, and fell off, as they do in the *Levant;* and their *Sores,* which had an agreeable Discharge at them, seasonably dry'd up of themselves; and they all presently became as hail and strong as ever they were in their Lives.

It is incredible, what a *Storm* was rais'd, and very much of it principally owing to Some of our enrag'd *Physicians,* on this Occasion.

The Gentleman was threaten'd with an *Indictment* for *Felony;* . . . and Words were given out, which had a Tendency to raise the *Mob* upon him. . . .

But the Gentleman . . . took *little Notice* of the *Inhibition* that had been given him. Divers pious and worthy People consider'd how dreadfully the *Small-Pox* handled many of their Neighbours, and how much the *sixth Commandment* order'd them the Use of Means to preserve and prolong their Lives. . . . They therefore apply'd themselves to Dr. *Boylston,* with Desires to come under the Operation; and he charitably gratify'd them in the Thing desir'd; tho' the *Objects* were most of them, either so *Old,* or so *Weak,* that they would have been the *last* that one would have chosen for it; and one would have apprehended no little Hazard of the *Event:* But they all got *well* and *soon* through it, and so much beyond their Expectation, that they zealously gave Thanks to God, for leading them into it; and seriously pro-fess'd to their Neighbours, that they had rather suffer the Operation *twice* every Year, than *once* to undergo the *Small Pox,* as it is most *commonly suffer'd,* tho' they should be sure of surviving it.

. . . [But] truly, while these Things were doing, the Town was fill'd with Iniquity, to a Degree which good Men could not observe, without being more than a little *griev'd* at it.

I must say it, I never saw the Devil so *let loose* upon any Occasion. A *lying Spirit* was *gone forth* at such a Rate, that there was no believing any Thing one heard. If the *inoculated Patients* were a little *sickish,* or had a *Vomit* given them, it was immediately reported, That they were at the *point of Death, or actually dead.* While the Patients lay blessing and praising Almighty God, for shewing them this *easy Way to escape* a formidable Enemy, it was confidently reported, *That they bitterly repented of what had been done upon them, and would not, upon any Terms, be brought into it, if it were to do again.* . . .

That which much added to the Misery, was, that the People who made the *loudest Cry,* . . . had a very *Satanic Fury* acting them.

They were like the *possess'd People* in the Gospel, *exceeding fierce;* . . . they pretend *Religion* on their Side; and charg'd all that were not so, with denying and renouncing the *divine Providence,* and I know not how many more *Abominations;* yea, with *going to the Devil,* and the *God of Ekron.* And how strangely they treated the most meritorious Ministers of the Gospel, who did not come into their *Frenzies,* I leave unmention'd. *Father forgive them.*

. . . [Our opponents] plead, That the *Whole have no Need of a Physician;* and that it is not lawful for me to *make myself sick, when I am well;* and bring a *Sickness* on myself; no, tho' it be to *prevent a greater Sickness.* 'Tis to no Purpose to tell them, that they cavil against the Use of all *preventing Physick.* . . .

They plead, *That what is now done, is a Thing learnt from the* Heathens; *and it is not lawful for* Christians *to learn the Way of the* Heathen. *'Tis to no Purpose to tell them, that Hippocrates, and Galen were Heathen;* . . . And how many noble

Specificks have we *learnt* from our *Indians?* And from whom did they *learn* to smoak *Tobacco;* or drink *Tea* and *Coffee?*

. . . Their main Cavail against it . . . [is]: That God has *decreed when,* and *how* we shall *dye,* and for us to pretend a Remedy that won't fail to *save our Lives,* and secure us from *Death* by the *Small Pox,* is to take the *Work of God* out of his Hands. And how do we know, that God will send the *Small-Pox* upon us at all, since there will be some that will escape it, where-ever it comes? 'Tis to no Purpose to attempt their *Instruction;* for if one does, they will quickly, in express Terms, tell him, *You shall never convince me.* . . .

To quiet the Minds of People that would *think Soberly,* the Doctor stated *the Case of Conscience* in these Terms,

> Almighty God, in his great Mercy to Mankind, has taught us a *Remedy* to be used, when the Dangers of the *Small Pox* distress us; upon the Use of which *Medicine,* they shall, in an ordinary Way, be sure to have it not so severely as in the other Way, and consequently, not to be in such Danger of *dying* by this dreadful Distemper; as also to be deliver'd from the *terrible Circumstances* which many of them, who recover of this Distemper, do suffer from it. Whether a Christian may not employ this *Medicine* (let the *Matter* of it be what it will) and humbly give Thanks to God for his *good Providence,* in discovering it to a miserable World; and humbly look up to his *good Providence* (as we do in the Use of any other *Medicine*) for the Success of it?

And he thought it Answer enough to say upon it, *It may seem strange, that any Wise Christian cannot answer it.*

3. William Douglass, a Boston Physician, Decries the Dangerous "Infatuation" with Smallpox Inoculation, 1722

Six Men (commonly call'd the six INOCULATION MINISTERS) without any weight of Argument, by meer importunity, and reiterated Praying, Preaching, and Scribling . . . do indeavour that the infatuation of *Self-procuring the Small Pox,* may become universal. . . .

. . . The *Small Pox* being so universal for some time past, the Practitioners could not find Time to persue their Scribles and give them suitable Answers upon this the Parsons became uppisn, thinking they had gain'd the Field of Battle; but now, GOD be thanked the Small Pox is over and the Practitioners are like to find leisure Time to amuse the Town and themselves in driving them home within their own *Lines.* . . .

What has been said in favour of it by way of *Cant,* &c. does not deserve mentioning; as the calling of it a *discriminating Mark* of the Good from the Ungodly, the Saints from the Wicked; their throwing the Odium of *Party* on the *Anti-Inoculators:* They who continue in an even steedy Course, as before, are said to form a *Party;* not they who are active; and endeavour to introduce new and *dubious Practices* and Customs. *O BRASS!* If it be a *Party Business,* it is of their own making; for we may generally observe, the Inoculated are generally the *Devotees* of some *Inoculating*

[William Douglass], *Inoculation of the Small Pox as Practiced in Boston, Consider'd in a Letter to A—S—M.D. & F.R.S. in London* (Boston: J. Franklin, 1722), pp. [i], 2, 12–14, 16, 19–20.

Parson: At first it was *Congregational,* being almost confined to Mr. *W—b's* Heaters; then it spread among the *Devotees* of Dr. *M.* and Mr. *C.;* and lately many being buzz'd in the Ear with the great *Losses* sustain'd in the Natural Way, have as it were in *Despair* come into it. . . .

Poysoning and spreading infection, are by the penal Laws of England *Felony.* Inoculation falls in with the first without any Contradiction, and if a Person of so *weak a Constitution,* that any the least Illness may prove fatal to him; should be inoculated, and suffer but the tenth part of what several of the *Inoculated* have done, he must unavoidably perish, and his *Inoculator* deem'd guilty of wilful *Poysoning.* This is the Reason I suppose, why the Practitioners of *Boston* thought themselves not *safe* to venture on a Thing of such Consequence. Supposing only One in a Thousand should die of this Method, it cannot with Safety to the *Inoculator* be practis'd, without an Act of Parliament, exempting *Inoculation* by a sworn Practitioner from the Penaltys of *poysoning and spreading Infection.* . . .

Instead of contriving Methods to secure the *Inoculated* from taking the Infection the common Way, and their Neighbours from being infected by them, they inoculate indifferently in all Corners, and set the Town all in a Flame in one Moment as it were; *many perish* who had the Infection from the Inoculated, whose Deaths perhaps *in foro divino* they may be found guilty of. Their Authors *Timonius* and *Pylarinus* tell them, The Person who collects the Matter, ought not to apply it, least a *double Infection* ensue; and that the Advantage of this Practice is, that a *suitable Season* and a *well prepared Body* may be had to rencounter the Infection; but these things, as trivial, they neglect, and run headlong as if push'd on by Some *Fury.* . . .

If the Inoculators had designed a publick Good, why did they run headlong unto it, without observing the *Circumstances* and *Cautions* which might have made it useful; to begin in the Heart of the Town, where was no Infection; to inoculate all *Ages* and *Constitutions* from the very Beginning, without being first assur'd of it's Success on the *Young and Healthy.* Why did they not *petition the Government,* that none should be inoculated till his Name was recorded, that for the publick Good *in times to come,* it might be known who dy'd, and what *state of Health* they afterwards enjoy'd who surviv'd; say also have contriv'd some Method, that none might take the Infection from the *Inoculated:* This Neglect has occasioned the Death of many. . . .

We have learnt from our 5 or 6 Mo[nths] Experience of Inoculation, *1. That the* Small Pox *may sometimes be communicated by Inoculation.* I cannot say always, because some have been Inoculated more than once before it wrought; and many have from thence had only a sort of *eruptive Fever,* but no genuine Small Pox, so far as I am able to judge. *2. That the* Small Pox *so acquired, is frequently more favourable than in the common way of Infection, and not altogether so mortal:* What the dismal Consequences may be, I shall not pretend to determine; but Reason and the Testimonies of some Gentlemen from the *Levant,* give us ground to *suspect.* *3. That not one of the inoculated during the space of five or six Months has had the* Small Pox *in the natural way,* so far as we know; for the Inoculators in every thing that makes against them, by *LYES* and *EQUIVOCATIONS* endeavour to keep us in the dark. It is then a *palliative Prevention* of the Small Pox for some time, and not *very mortal;* and consequently may be of great Use to the *Guinea Traders,* when the Small Pox gets among their Slaves aboard to inoculate the whole Cargo, and patch them up for a *Market.*

4. A Broadside Laments the Death of Fifty-Four in a Hartford Epidemic, 1725

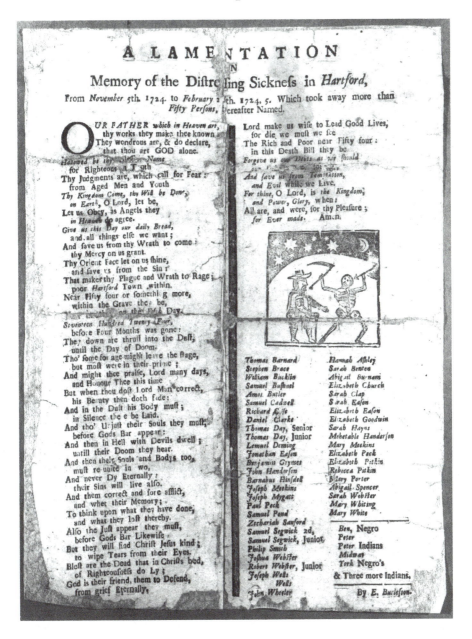

E. Burlesson, "A Lamentation in Memory of the Distressing Sickness in Hartford, from November 5th, 1724 to February 20th, 1724, 5" [New London, Conn.: Timothy Green, 1725], broadside in The Connecticut Historical Society, Hartford, Connecticut.

5. Zabdiel Boylston of Boston Recounts His Experiences as the First Physician to Inoculate Against Smallpox in the American Colonies, 1726

I began the Practice [of inoculation, concerned that] . . . *my children, whose Lives were very dear to me, were daily in Danger of taking the Infection, by my visiting the Sick in the natural Way; and altho' there arose such a Cloud of Opposers at the Beginning, yet finding my Account, in the Success, and easy Circumstances of my Patients (with the Encouragement of the good Ministers), I resolv'd to carry it on for the saving of Lives, not regarding any or all the Menances, and Opposition that were made against it. . . .*

I have not used this Practice only to the healthful and strong, but to the weak and diseased, the aged and the young: Not only to the rich, but have carried it into the Houses of the poor, and laid down whole Families; and tho' thro' my own Hurry in Business, and their living out of Town, I have been forced to leave them to the Management of unexperienced Nurses, yet they all did well.

And as to those six who died under Inoculation, I would observe that Mrs. Dix-well, *we have great Reason to believe, was infected before. Mr.* White, *thro' splenetic Delusions, died rather from Abstinence than the Small-Pox. Mrs.* Scarbrough *and the Indian* Girl *died of Accidents, by taking cold. Mrs.* Wells *and* Searle *were Persons worn out with Age and Diseases, and very likely these two were infected before. Neither can it be said, that there was one sound and healthful Person amongst them.*

. . . I do not recommend this Practice to be carry'd on and manag'd by old Women and Nurses; no, I would have it carry'd on and manag'd by good Physicians and Surgeons, where they are to be had; but rather than the People should be left a Prey to the Small-Pox in the natural Way, let it be manag'd by Nurses, for I cannot help thinking that even in their Hands, many less would die of the Small-Pox by Inoculation, than there does in the natural Way, tho' in the best of Hands, and under the best of Care.

And for those that have not yet come into this Practice, for their Assistance, until they have gain'd better Knowledge, I have given some short Directions how they may proceed with their Patients, when they begin this Practice of inoculating the Small-Pox. . . .

. . . [W]hen my Wife and many others were gone out of Town to avoid the Distemper, and all Hope given up of preventing the further spreading of it, and the Guards were first removed from the Doors of infected Houses, I began the Experiment; and not being able to make it upon myself (such was my Faith in the Safety and Success of this Method), I chose to make it (for Example sake) upon my own dear Child, and two of my Servants.

JUNE the 26th, 1721, I inoculated my Son *Thomas,* of about six, my Negro Man, *Jack,* thirty six, and *Jackey,* two and an half Years old. They all complain'd on the 6th Day; upon the 7th, the two Children were a little hot, dull, and sleepy, *Thomas* (only) had twitchings and started in his sleep. The 28th, the Children's Fevers continued, *Tommy's* twitchings and startings in sleep increased; and tho' the

Zabdiel Boylston, *An Historical Account of the Small-Pox Inoculated in New England, upon All Sorts of Persons,* Whites, Blacks, *and of All Ages and Constitutions* (London: S. Chandler, 1726), pp. ii–v, 2–3, 17, 21, 27, 39.

Fever was gentle and his Senses bright, yet as the Practice was new, and the Clamour, or rather Rage of the People against it so violent, that I was put into a very great Fright; and not having any Directions from D. *Timonius* and *Pyllarinus* concerning this Practice, I had nothing to have Recourse to but Patience, and therefore waited upon Nature for a Crisis (neither my Fears nor the Symptoms abating) until the 9th; when early in the Morning I gave him a Vomit, upon which the Symptoms went off, and the same Day, upon him and the black Child, a kind and favourable Small-Pox came out, of about an hundred a piece; after which their Circumstances became easy, our Trouble was over, and they soon were well. . . .

It was plain and easy to see, (even in these two) with Pleasure, the difference between having the Small-Pox this way, and that of having it in the natural way. . . .

[September] 20th, I inoculated Mrs. *Eliz. Valentine* about 18, Mr. *Warner* 21, and Mr. *Procter's Indian* Man 20 Years old; these all had the Small-Pox at the usual Time, of a good distinct Sort: The *Indian* had 3 or 4 uneasy Nights, after which his Rest return'd, and they were all soon well. Mrs. *Valentine* had but very few. . . .

[October 31st] I inoculated Mr. *Nathaniel Loring's* only Child, about 9 Years old, his Father being much concern'd for him, on Account of the Small Pox having been very fatal to their Family; he had the Small-Pox at the usual Time, very kindly, few in Number, and he soon was well. . . .

[November 26th] I inoculated Mr. *Tufts* of *Cambridge*, about 31, and his Negroe Boy 12 Years old. I was now so much employ'd in *Boston* and *Roxbury*, when their Sickness came on, that when Mr. *Tufts* sent for me, I could not go to them, and only sent Directions, with some few Medicines, and never saw either until they were well. They had the Small-Pox at the usual Time, and of the favourable Sort, as he gave me the Account some time after, when he came to pay his Bill. . . .

Now if there be any one that can give a faithful Account or History of any other Method of Practice that has carried such a Number, of all Ages, Sexes, Constitutions, and Colours, and in the worst Seasons of the Year, thro' the Small-Pox; or, indeed, thro' any other acute Distemper with better Success, then I will alter my Opinion of this; and until then, I shall value and esteem this Method of inoculating the Small-Pox, as the most beneficial and successful that ever was discover'd to, and practised by Mankind in this World.

6. A Virginia Domestic Guide to the Diseases of the American Colonies Makes "Every Man His Own Doctor," 1734

OUR Country is unhappily subject to several very sharp Distempers. The Multitude of Marshes, Swamps, and great Waters, send forth so many Fogs, and Exhalations, that the Air is continually damp with them. . . .

. . . [T]his is a cruel Check to the Growth of an Infant Colony, which otherwise, by the Fruitfulness of our Women, and the great Number of Recruits, sent from our Mother Country, would, in a few Years, grow populous, and consequently considerable. . . .

[John Tennent], *Every Man His Own* Doctor: *or, the* Poor Planter's *Physician,* 2nd ed. [Williamsburg, Va.]: William Parks, 1734, pp. 4–9, 29, 35, 38–39, 43–44, 55–56.

. . . [S]ome would be glad of Assistance, if they did not think the Remedy near as bad as the Disease: For our *Doctors* are commonly so exorbitant in their Fees, whether they kill or cure, that the poor Patient had rather trust to his Constitution, than run the Risque of beggaring his Family.

THESE Considerations made me account it a Work of great Charity and Publick Spirit, to communicate to the poor Inhabitants of this Colony, a safe Method of curing themselves, when they shall be so unhappy as to fall into any of our common Maladies. And for their greater Encouragement, the Remedies I shall prescribe, may be procured with little Trouble and Expence, being, for the most Part, such as grow at their own Doors, or may be easily propagated.

PROVIDENCE has been so good, as to furnish almost every Country with Medicines proper for the Distempers incident to the Climate; and such Domestick Remedies are always sufficient for the Poor, who live upon homely Fare, and for the Temperate, who make a right Use of God's Blessings. . . .

IN setting down the following Prescriptions, I have been cautious of talking like an *Apothecary;* that is, of using hard Words, that perhaps neither my Patient, nor my self understand. Nor have I taken them lightly upon Trust; but am able to recommend most of them upon more than Twenty Years Experience; and for the rest, I have credible Authority. . . .

BEFORE I mention the *Cure,* I shall endeavour to describe the *Symptoms* of each Distemper, in so plain a Manner, that any Person may be Master of his own Case, if he will but attend carefully to what he feels; otherwise he might mistake his Illness, and apply an improper Remedy. I shall also recommend the *Diet* fittest to be used in each Case; which often contributes more to the Patient's Recovery, than his *Physick:* At the same Time, he shall have my best Advice, to prevent every particular Ailment; which will be happier for him, than to know how to cure it.

I SHALL begin with the most fatal of all our Distempers, a PLEURISY; which discovers it self by a brisk Fever, and sharp Pain, pretty low in one of the Sides, shooting now and then into the Breast, and sometimes quite back into the Shoulder-Blades: It is uneasy every Time the Patient draws his Breath, and more so when he coughs; which is generally the Case in this Disease.

THE Moment any Person finds these Tokens upon him, he must, without Loss of Time, take away 10 Ounces of *Blood,* and repeat the same three or four Days successively, if the Pain go not away before. On the third Day, he may vomit with 80 Grains of *Indian Physick (Ipecacuania),* and every Night, drink 7 Spoonfuls of *Pennyroyal Water,* or the Decoction of it, moderately sweeten'd. In the mean Time, let him, every three Hours, take Half a Spoonful of *Honey* and *Linseed Oyl,* mixt together. He should also strew *Indian Pepper,* upon *Pennyroyal Plaister,* and apply it very hot to the Place where the Pain lies, and be sure to keep himself warm, and abstain from cold Water: Tho' if the Distemper should prove obstinate, you must apply a *Blister* to his Neck, and one to each Arm, on the fleshy Part above the Elbow. . . .

IN Case of a CONTINUAL FEVER, *bleed* immediately 10 Ounces. The Day following, *vomit* with *Indian Physick;* and the Morning after, *purge* with the same. And if you should be light headed, be convuls'd, or incline too much to Sleep, lay a large *Blister* to the Neck, and to the fleshy Parts of each Arm; and take a *Glister* every Night, of *Mallows,* and *Syrup* of *Peach Blossoms,* to abate the Heat of the Distemper. . . .

A DROPSY first shews it self, by the Swelling of the Legs about the Ancles, in such a Manner as to retain the Impression of your Finger. The Swelling appears most at Night, and is usually attended with a Shortness and Difficulty of Breath, ever most troublesome when the Patient lies down. . . .

IN Men, the excessive FLUX OF THE BLEEDING PILES sometimes ends in a *Dropsy,* if not stop'd in Time. In that Case, *purge* with *Indian Physick* 2 or 3 Times; and the Mornings you do'nt do that, drink the *Exprest Liquor* of *fresh Ass-dung,* sweetened with *Syrup* of *Quinces,* to be repeated 3 Times. In the mean while, take an Ounce of *Conserve* of *Roses,* twice or thrice a Day; and after every Stool, wash your Fundament clean with *Decoction* of *Comfry Leaves,* made very warm. . . .

IN Women, a *Dropsy* is often caus'd by FLOODING, OR THE IMMODERATE FLOW-ING OF THEIR COURSES. Let them for this, in the first Place, take away 8 Ounces of *Blood,* and then proceed as in the foregoing Case; only they must inject the *Decoction* of *Comfry Leaves,* and govern their Passions, if they can; nor must any Part of them, not so much as their Tongue, be allow'd to have too much Motion. . . .

NOW I am upon *Female Infirmities,* it will not be unseasonable to touch upon a common Complaint among unmarry'd Women, namely, THE SUPPRESSION OF THE COURSES. This don't only disparage their Complexions, but fills them, besides, with sundry Disorders. For this Misfortune, you must *purge* with *Highland Flagg* (commonly call'd *Belly-ach Root*) a Week before you expect to be out of Order; and repeat the same 2 Days after: The next Morning, drink a Quarter of a Pint of *Pennyroyal Water,* or *Decoction,* with 12 Drops of *Spirits* of *Harts-horn,* and as much again at Night, when you go to Bed. Continue this, 9 Days running; and after Resting 3 Days, go on with it for 9 more. Ride out every fair Day, stir nimbly about your Affairs, and breath as much as possible in the open Air. . . .

TO prevent this Complaint, young Women must shake off Sloath, and make Use of their Legs, as well as their Hands. They shou'd be cautious of taking *Opiats* too often, or *Jesuits-Bark,* except in Cases of great Necessity; nor must they long for *pretty fellows,* or any other *Trash,* whatsoever. . . .

THUS I have run through most of the common Complaints, to which the inhabitants of this Colony are subject; and prescrib'd such innocent Cures, as will generally succeed, if timely made Use of; yet am far from pretending, that any of them are infallible: We all know, that *Death* strikes so home in some Cases, that all *Physick* will be vain. . . .

IN the mean Time, it may seem strange, that, among the Remedies I have prescrib'd, no Mention is made of *Mercury, Opium,* or the *Peruvian Bark,* which have almost obtain'd the Reputation of *Specificks.* I acknowledge the powerful Effects of these Medicines; but am perswaded, they ought to be administered with the greatest Skill, and Discernment. And, as I write only for the Service of the Poor, who are wholly left to judge for themselves, I was fearful of putting such dangerous Weapons into their Hands.

IF those of better Circumstances find any Thing here, that may in any Manner deserve their Attention, I should be exceedingly glad: Tho' I own, these Directions were not designed for such as are in Condition to purchase more *learned Advice.* It was only to those whom Fortune has placed below the Regard of our *Doctors,* that I address this short Essay: And if one single Person shall be recovered thereby, or receive the least Relief, I shall account my Pains happily bestow'd.

7. Andrew Blackbird of the Ottawa Nation Records a Story from Indian Oral Tradition About the Decimation of His People by Smallpox in the Early 1760s, 1887

[T]he Ottawas were greatly reduced in numbers from what they were in former times, on account of the small-pox which they brought from Montreal during the French war with Great Britain. This small pox was sold to them shut up in a tin box, with the strict injunction not to open the box on their way homeward, but only when they should reach their country; and that this box contained something that would do them great good, and their people! The foolish people believed really there was something in the box supernatural, that would do them great good. Accordingly, after they reached home they opened the box; but behold there was another tin box inside, smaller. They took it out and opened the second box, and behold, still there was another box inside of the second box, smaller yet. So they kept on this way till they came to a very small box, which was not more than an inch long; and when they opened the last one they found nothing but mouldy particles in this last little box! They wondered very much what it was, and a great many closely inspected to try to find out what it meant. But alas, alas! pretty soon burst out a terrible sickness among them. The great Indian doctors themselves were taken sick and died. The tradition says it was indeed awful and terrible. Every one taken with it was sure to die. Lodge after lodge was totally vacated—nothing but the dead bodies lying here and there in their lodges—entire families being swept off with the ravages of this terrible disease. The whole coast of Arbor Croche, or Waw-gaw-naw-ke-zee, where the principal village was situated, on the west shore of the peninsula near the Straits, which is said to have been a continuous village some fifteen or sixteen miles long and extending from what is now called Cross Village to Seven-Mile Point (that is, seven miles from Little Traverse, now Harbor Springs), was entirely depopulated and laid waste. It is generally believed among the Indians of Arbor Croche that this wholesale murder of the Ottawas by this terrible disease sent by the British people, was actuated through hatred, and expressly to kill off the Ottawas and Chippewas because they were friends of the French Government or French King, whom they called "Their Great Father." The reason that today we see no full-grown trees standing along the coast of Arbor Croche, a mile or more in width along the shore, is because the trees were entirely cleared away for this famous long village, which existed before the small-pox raged among the Ottawas.

 *E S S A Y S*

In the first essay, Dartmouth College historian Colin G. Calloway draws on historical, ethnohistorical, and demographic scholarship to provide a vivid historical account of the decimation of the Native American population of what is now the United States between first contact with Europeans and the late eighteenth century. He explores not

Andrew J. Blackbird, *History of the Ottawa and Chippewa Indians of Michigan* (Ypsilanti, Mich.: The Ypsilantian Job Printing Office, 1887), pp. 9–10.

only the exchange of diseases, however, but also the interchange between Indian and European medical knowledge and healing practices. In the second essay, John B. Blake, long an historian at the National Library of Medicine, narrates the course of the controversy that erupted in Boston when, in 1721, the newly introduced technique of preventive inoculation against smallpox was first tried in the American colonies. Was inoculation a major medical advance in the 1720s, or was it a dangerous new practice? When and how should societal leaders impose public health initiatives? Bringing together issues of religion, medicine, and public health, and underscoring the place of both Europeans and African Americans in this story, Blake's essay, read in conjunction with the Mather, Douglass, and Boylston documents (Documents 2, 3, and 5), provides ample foundation for rethinking and even restaging the inoculation debate.

Indians, Europeans, and the New World of Disease and Healing

COLIN G. CALLOWAY

When Indians and Europeans met, they benefited from each other's medical knowledge and exchanged healing practices. Europeans also brought with them germs and viruses that erupted into epidemics of killer diseases among Indian populations. For Indian peoples, the new world often became a biological nightmare, in which impotent healers and distraught relatives watched helplessly as friends and loved ones succumbed to terrible plagues imported from Europe, as well as from Asia and Africa.

North American Indians did not inhabit a disease-free paradise prior to European invasion. The great epidemic diseases and crowd infections that ravaged Europe and Asia—smallpox, diphtheria, measles, bubonic and pneumonic plague, cholera, influenza, typhus, dysentery, yellow fever—were unknown in America. Indian peoples faced other, less devastating, problems. Bioarchaeological studies reveal evidence of malnutrition and anemia resulting from dietary stress, high levels of fetal and neonatal death and infant mortality, parasitic intestinal infections, dental problems, respiratory infections, spina bifida, osteomyelitis, nonpulmonary tuberculosis, and syphilis. Indian people also suffered their share of aches and pains, breaks and bruises, digestive upsets, arthritis, wounds, and snakebites. To deal with these things, Indian doctors employed a rich knowledge of the healing properties of plants and what today we would call therapeutic medicine. They combined knowledge of anatomy and medicinal botany with curative rituals and ceremonies.

. . . [I]n early America, European and Indian cures could work together. Contrary to the popular modern stereotype that all Indians were and are attuned to plant life, all Europeans totally out of touch with nature, many early explorers and colonists possessed an extensive knowledge of plants and their properties, knowledge that modern urban Americans have lost. Europeans in the seventeenth century generally believed that for every sickness there were natural plant remedies, if one only knew

Colin G. Calloway, "Healing and Disease," in *New Worlds for All: Indians, Europeans, and the Remaking of Early America* (Baltimore and London: Johns Hopkins University Press, 1997), pp. 25–28, 30–31, 33–41. Copyright © 1997 Johns Hopkins University Press.

where to find them. Indian healers, many of them women, knew where to find them, and Europeans were receptive to the cures they could provide.

Europeans who were dissatisfied with contemporary medical practices—purging, bleeding, and other drastic measures—often were inclined to see Indian healers as at least equal in ability to European physicians. Then as now, Western medicine offered a "disease cure" rather than a "health care" system. Many European observers spoke highly of Indian healers and regarded Indian life as "more healthful" than their own. . . . Englishman John Lawson, who traveled more than a thousand miles through Indian country in North and South Carolina in 1701, said the Indians displayed "extraordinary Skill and Success" in dealing with common ailments. He said they were "the best Physicians" for snakebites, and he saw them perform "admirable Cures . . . which would puzzle a great many graduate Practitioners." The cures he saw were "too many to repeat." Often, Indians went no more than a hundred yards from their homes to locate the remedy, and some of their chief physicians carried "their Compliment of Drugs continually about them, which are Roots, Barks, Berries, Nuts, &c. that are Strung upon a Thread." . . . Indian people obtained through trade plants that did not grow locally: Pueblo communities traded plants, and they also obtained certain herbs from Jicarilla Apaches on the plains.

Like other forms of life, plants possessed power. Shamans and healers handled them with care and performed special rituals such as smoking and offering prayers as they collected, prepared, and administered herbal cures. Heckewelder dismissed such rituals as "superstitious practices," but, then as now, Native healing had a vital spiritual dimension as well as a physical one. Medicine men and women were people who had been given a special gift of power, often through a dream or a vision, and they demonstrated their spirituality in the healing ceremonies they performed. Coocoochee, a Mohawk medicine woman living on the Maumee River in the 1780s and 1790s, was esteemed for her skill in preparing and administering medicines and "for the power of her incantations which gave her insights into the future." Among the Hurons, shamans often were members of curing societies: they diagnosed illnesses, treated injuries, set broken bones, rendered spells powerless, and organized rituals to bring comfort to the sick. Missionaries—the shamans' cultural equivalents and rivals—often were impressed by Indian knowledge and use of curative herbs, but they could not condone or tolerate medicine healers and their rituals. Jesuit Pierre Biard denounced Huron shamans as "sorcerers." They were "jugglers, liars, and cheats," he said. "All their science consists of a knowledge of a few simple laxatives, or astringents, hot or cold applications, . . . leaving the rest to luck, nothing more." Europeans often displayed equally cynical attitudes toward their own physicians, but such hostility toward the spiritual dimension of native healing no doubt reinforced the Indians' determination to keep their practices secret from prying Europeans, who might offend the spirits.

Nevertheless, settlers not only used Indian remedies but sometimes did so in accordance with Indian customs and rituals. "In the days of our sickness," said Crèvecoeur, "we shall have recourse to their medical knowledge." European botanists compiled an impressive list of plants and cures employed by Indian healers, and Indian doctors compiled an impressive record in ministering to Europeans. As Cabeza de Vaca and his companions wandered across the American Southwest in the 1530s, they earned a reputation as healers, and Indian people brought their sick to them to be cured. De Vaca also experimented with Indian curing practices "with good results." John Lawson noted that "an *Indian* hath been often found to heal an *English*-man of a Malady . . . which the ablest of our *English* Pretenders in *America,* after repeated Applications, have deserted the Patient as incurable." . . . Indians used sassafras as a medicine, applying the leaves directly to wounds. Sassafras proved so effective that Europeans came to think of it as a kind of wonder drug, and as early as 1602–3 English ships sailed to Virginia and Massachusetts to trade with the Indians for it. New England Indians, and then their colonial neighbors, used the plant known as white or green hellebore as an emetic. . . .

Indian healers helped cure Europeans as well. European medical care was virtually nonexistent in seventeenth-century New Mexico—Franciscan friars carried rudimentary surgical equipment but generally lacked formal medical training. Rather than travel to a mission and entrust their recovery to a friar's uncertain skills, Hispanic settlers frequently turned to Indian neighbors and relatives for remedies, as well as for love potions and aphrodisiacs. That often led to their participating in the Native rituals that accompanied curing—and that attracted the attention of the Inquisition. Some Europeans, however, balked at the idea of seeking cures from Indians. According to one chronicler, English colonists in the late seventeenth century recognized that Indians were "Incomparable Physicians," but would not use them. Ministers had convinced the colonists that the Indians' healing skills were the work of the Devil.

However willing they might be to provide healing, Indians generally endeavored to keep their knowledge hidden. This did not prevent Europeans from trying to learn their secrets. English physicians and apothecaries in colonial Virginia apparently sent their apprentices into the woods to search out Indian herbal medicines. . . . John Lawson advocated intermarriage between Indians and Europeans, not least because "we should then have a true knowledge of all the Indian's Skill in Medicine and Surgery." When Crèvecoeur visited the Indian town of Oquaga on the Susquehanna River just before the American Revolution, he met colonists from Pennsylvania who had gone there in search of cures from the Indian healers. Crèvecoeur tried to get one healer drunk to make her reveal her secrets. Henry Tufts, a rather disreputable character, lived for three years or so among the Abenakis in western Maine about the same time, having gone to "the Great Indian Doctress," Molly Ockett, to find a cure for a knife wound in his thigh. Molly Ockett cared for him and cured him "with a large variety of roots, herbs, barks and other materials." Tufts had a hard time swallowing some of the potions, but, "having much faith in the skill of my physician," he forced them down. Tufts served as an apprentice to his healer, hoping to learn her medicinal secrets. Convinced she was holding out on him, Tufts, like Crèvecoeur, resorted to rum. He then returned home and used the knowledge he had acquired to pass himself off as a physician in the colonies. Molly Ockett continued as an itinerant physician, catering to Abenakis and settlers alike and becoming part of the folklore of western Maine. According to one legend, she healed a sick infant named Hannibal Hamlin, thereby saving the life of Abraham Lincoln's future vice-president. . . .

Unfortunately, traditional Indian cures offered little protection against the new diseases that swept the land after Europeans arrived in North America. Separated from the Old World for thousands of years, the peoples of America escaped great epidemics like the Black Death, which killed perhaps a third of the population in fourteenth-century Europe. But they were living on borrowed time. Lack of exposure to bubonic plague, smallpox, and measles allowed Indian peoples no opportunity to build up immunological resistance to such diseases. From the moment Europeans set foot in America, hundreds of thousands of Indian people were doomed to die in one of the greatest biological catastrophes in human history. . . .

Established and well-traveled trade routes helped spread disease. Indians who came into contact with Europeans and their germs often contaminated peoples farther inland who had not yet seen a European; they in turn passed the disease on to more distant neighbors. It is likely that most Indian people who were struck down by European diseases like smallpox died without ever laying eyes on a European. In tracing the course of imported plagues among Indian populations in colonial America, many scholars describe them not as epidemics but as pandemics, meaning that the same disease occurred virtually everywhere.

As many as 350,000 people lived in Florida when the Spaniards first arrived, but the populations of the Calusa, Timucua, and other tribes plummeted after contact. Calusas who canoed to Cuba to trade may have brought smallpox back to the Florida mainland as early as the 1520s. When Hernando de Soto invaded the Southeast in 1539, the Spaniards found that disease had preceded them. In the Carolina upcountry, they found large towns abandoned and overgrown with grass where, said the Indians, "there had been a pest in the land two years before." In 1585, Sir Francis Drake's English crew, returning from plundering Spanish ships in the Cape Verde Islands, brought a disease that was probably typhus to the Caribbean and Florida. Indians around St. Augustine died in great numbers, "and said amongste themselves, it was the Inglisshe God that made them die so faste." The population collapse continued in the seventeenth century. Governor Diego de Rebolledo reported in 1657 that the Guale and Timucua Indians were few "because they have been wiped out with the sickness of the plague and smallpox which have overtaken them in past years." Two years later the new governor of Florida said 10,000 Indians had died in a measles epidemic. . . . The Apalachee Indians of northern Florida numbered 25,000–30,000 in the early seventeenth century; by the end of the century, less than 8,000 survived. Two and a half centuries after contact with the Spaniards, all of Florida's original Indian people were gone.

The pattern repeated itself elsewhere. In 1585, the English established a colony at Roanoke Island in Virginia. Almost immediately, local Indians began to fall ill and die. "The disease was so strange to them," wrote Thomas Hariot, "that they neither knew what it was, nor how to cure it." Across the continent, Pueblo Indians in New Mexico may have suffered from a huge smallpox epidemic that spread as far south as Chile and across much of North America in 1519–24. When they first encountered Europeans in 1539, the Pueblos numbered at least 130,000 and inhabited between 110 and 150 pueblos. By 1706, New Mexico's Pueblo population had dropped to 6,440 people in 18 pueblos. . . .

Deadly pestilence swept the coast of New England in 1616–17. Indians "died in heapes," and the Massachusett Indians around Plymouth Bay were virtually exterminated. As reported by Governor William Bradford, the Pilgrims found cleared fields and good soil, but few people, the Indians "being dead & abundantly wasted in the late great mortality which fell in all these parts about three years over before the coming of the English, wherin thousands of them dyed, they not being able to burie one another; their sculs and bones were found in many places lying still above ground, where their houses & dwellings had been; a very sad spectacle to behold."

Smallpox was a fact of life—or death—for most of human history. An airborne disease, normally communicated by droplets or dust particles, it enters through the respiratory tract. People can become infected simply by breathing. Not surprisingly, it spread like wildfire through Indian populations. However, because early chroniclers sometimes confused smallpox with other diseases and because the contagions came so quickly, it is difficult to discern which disease was doing the killing at any particular time. By the seventeenth century, smallpox in Europe was a childhood disease: most adults, having been infected as children, had acquired lifelong immunity and were not contagious. The long transatlantic crossings further reduced the chances that European crews could transmit the disease to America. Not until children crossed the Atlantic did smallpox, and the other lethal childhood diseases that plagued Europe, take hold on Native American populations. The Spanish brought children to the Caribbean early, but not until the beginning of the seventeenth century did Dutch and English colonists bring their families to New York and New England. The arrival of sick European children sentenced thousands of Indian people to death.

Smallpox struck New England in 1633, devastating Indian communities on the Merrimack and Connecticut Rivers. . . . The epidemic reduced the Pequots in southern Connecticut from perhaps as many as thirteen thousand people to only three thousand, setting the stage for their defeat by the English in 1637, and it may have reduced the Mohawks in eastern New York from almost eight thousand to less than three thousand. Such mortality rates were not unusual when virulent new diseases cut through previously unexposed populations. Indians from the Hudson River told Adriaen Van der Donck in 1656 "that before the smallpox broke out amongst them, they were ten times as numerous as they are now." John Lawson estimated that in 1701 there was "not the sixth Savage living within two hundred Miles of all our Settlements, as there were fifty Years ago." A recent smallpox epidemic in the Carolina upcountry had "destroy'd whole towns."

At the beginning of the seventeenth century, the Huron Indians numbered as many as 30,000–40,000 people, living in perhaps twenty-eight villages on the northern shores of the Great Lakes in southern Ontario. The French identified them as crucial to their plans for North American empire. The Hurons were the key to extensive trade networks reaching far beyond the Great Lakes, and their villages could also serve as "jumping-off points" for Jesuit missionary enterprises among more distant tribes. French traders and missionaries arrived in Huronia, and it was not long before the new diseases were reaping a grim harvest among the Hurons. Their longhouses were transformed into death traps. The smallpox epidemic that ravaged New England in 1633 reached Huronia in 1634. Smallpox or measles was thinning Huron numbers in 1635–36. A Huron elder, blaming the epidemic on the Jesuits, said, "The plague has entered every lodge in the village, and has so reduced my family that today there are but two of us left, and who can say whether we two will survive." Influenza struck in 1636–37. Smallpox returned in 1639. Huron population was scythed in half between 1634 and 1640. In

1648–49, famine and the attacks of the Iroquois completed the deadly work the diseases had begun. The Hurons scattered, most of the survivors being absorbed by other tribes.

Smallpox continued throughout the eighteenth century. It killed half the Cherokees in 1738 and returned in 1760; the Catawbas of South Carolina lost half their number to the epidemic of 1759. In 1763, the British doled out blankets from the smallpox hospital at Fort Pitt to visiting Indians; smallpox erupted among the tribes of the Ohio Valley soon thereafter. Outbreaks of smallpox were reported among Indian populations in New Mexico in 1719, 1733, 1738, 1747, and 1749; in Texas recurrently between 1674 and 1802; and in California, where Indian neo-phytes congregated in Spanish mission villages made easy targets for new crowd-killing diseases.

The massive smallpox epidemic that ravaged western North America between 1779 and 1783 illustrates the speed with which the disease could spread its tentacles throughout Indian country. The epidemic seems to have broken out in Mexico, and it afflicted Indian peoples in Peru and Guatemala. Spreading north to Spanish settle-ments like San Antonio and Santa Fe, it was picked up by Indians who visited the area to trade for horses. It was then quickly transmitted north and west, through the Rockies and across the plains, slaughtering as it went. It spread into the Canadian forests, killed as many as 90 percent of the Chipewyans in the central subarctic, and by 1783 was killing Cree Indians around Hudson Bay. . . .

Smallpox was probably the number-one killer of Indian people, but it was by no means the only fatal disease. Epidemics of measles, influenza, bubonic plague, diphtheria, typhus, scarlet fever, yellow fever, and other unidentified diseases also took their toll. Alcoholism added to the list of killer diseases imported from Eu-rope. "A person who resides among them may easily observe the frightful decrease of their numbers from one period of ten years to another," said John Heckewelder, lamenting the impact of alcohol. "Our vices have destroyed them more than our swords." . . .

Traditional healing practices proved powerless against the onslaught. Fasting, taking a sweat bath, and plunging into an icy river—a common Indian remedy for many ailments—aggravated rather than alleviated the effects of smallpox. Just as some Europeans looked to Indian skills and practices to deal with snakebites and ailments native to North America, so some Indian people looked to Europeans to provide relief from European sicknesses. Some believed that European witchcraft caused the new diseases; so it made sense to combat them with European power and medicine. Others, with their loved ones dying around them, were willing to try anything. Many Hurons accepted baptism from Jesuit priests, regarding it as a cura-tive ritual and hoping it could save their children.

Despite instances of genocide and germ warfare against Indian populations, Europeans frequently provided what help and comfort they could. Dead Indians were of no value to European missionaries seeking converts, European merchants seeking customers, or European ministers seeking allies. Hearing that Massasoit "their friend was sick and near unto death," Governor William Bradford and the Plymouth colonists "sente him such comfortable things as gave him great con-tente, and was a means of his recovery." French nuns ministered to sick Indians in seventeenth-century Quebec. Most Spanish missions in eighteenth-century California had dispensaries. . . . British Indian superintendent Sir William Johnson had the Mohawks inoculated against smallpox. . . .

Nevertheless, the protection was too little and too late to stop demographic disaster. Not all Indian populations suffered 75 percent or 90 percent mortality rates—indeed, in some areas of the country Indian populations were on the rise in the eighteenth century—but the result was a world newly emptied of Indian inhabitants. Europeans arriving in Indian country in the wake of one or more epidemics made inaccurate estimates of precontact Indian population size on the basis of head counts of survivors. Seeing remnant populations, they gained a distorted impression of the size and sophistication of the societies that had once existed—and that distorted impression entered the history books. America, many believed, was an "empty wilderness," a "virgin land." If the country was empty, that was a recent development; it was depopulated rather than unpopulated. The new world of opportunity, which "free lands" opened for Europeans in North America, was in itself a by-product of European invasion. . . .

Though scholars disagree widely in their estimates, it is likely that in what is today the United States, Indian population stood at somewhere between 5 million and 10 million in 1492. By 1800, the figure had fallen to around 600,000. By contrast, the European population of the English colonies in America doubled every twenty-five years in the late eighteenth century. The first U.S. census in 1790 counted a total population of 3.9 million people. By 1800, North America had just under 5 million whites and about 1 million blacks. As James Axtell points out, the Indian people who survived in the eastern United States were being engulfed in a sea of white and black faces. The demographic complexion of the new world created by the interaction of Europeans, Indians, and Africans was very different in 1800 from what it had been three centuries before.

Nevertheless, the American population of 1800 combined Indian and European healing practices. Indians and Europeans alike employed "folk remedies" as well as doctors to cure diseases and injuries. The British lagged behind the Spaniards in establishing hospitals in the New World: Cortez built the first hospital in Mexico City for Indian and Spanish poor in 1521, and by the end of the seventeenth century, there were more than one hundred fifty hospitals in New Spain. In contrast, the first general hospital to care for the sick poor in the British colonies was established in Philadelphia in 1752; Massachusetts General Hospital, not until 1811. The first medical school was established at the University of Pennsylvania in 1765; Harvard Medical School, not until 1783. For most of the eighteenth century, American physicians who wanted a medical education had to go to Europe. With few trained physicians and few medical facilities available, people in rural and small-town communities turned in times of sickness to family, neighbors, clergymen, skilled women, and local healers. In many areas of the country, itinerant Indian physicians remained common well into the twentieth century, providing health care for America's poor, whether Indian, white, or black. Many Indian people preserved their belief in the efficacy of traditional medicine—both herbal and spiritual—even as they benefited from European medicine as practiced by white doctors. False Face societies and curing rituals continued among the Iroquois long after many Iroquois had embraced Christianity. Medicine was power, and Indian people needed to draw on all the power available to them as they struggled to survive in the disease-ridden land that was their new world.

Smallpox Inoculation Foments Controversy in Boston

JOHN B. BLAKE

Of all the diseases affecting colonial America, none caused more consternation than smallpox. Highly contagious, once it gained a foothold, it spread rapidly and with fearful mortality. Recognizing these facts, the authorities of Massachusetts developed certain techniques designed to keep this scourge under control. They required incoming vessels with smallpox aboard to perform quarantine at Spectacle Island in Boston harbor, and when cases appeared in town, the Selectmen removed the patients to a pesthouse or placed guards about the infected dwellings. Although these precautions often proved successful, they were unable entirely to prevent periodic epidemics. During one of these outbreaks, in 1721, inoculation of the smallpox was first tried in the colonies. It enraged the town and called forth a bitter newspaper and pamphlet war, but it was the earliest important experiment in preventive medicine in America.

The practice was not new in 1721. People in certain parts of Africa, India, and China had been using inoculation for centuries. . . .

. . . [A]fter inoculation had become popular in Turkey, it was more fully studied, reported, and recommended in the western world. During a smallpox epidemic in 1713 it again came up for discussion in the Royal Society. In May, 1714, Dr. John Woodward, Professor of Physic at Greshman College, communicated to this scientific organization an enthusiastic endorsement from Dr. Emanuel Timonius of Constantinople. Other correspondents also reported on the practice, and two years later the Society published another favorable account by Jacobus Pylarinus. Not until April, 1721, however, did the first recorded inoculation take place in England, on the daughter of Lady Mary Wortley Montagu. Another child received the treatment in May. Princess Caroline became interested, and in August six felons offered themselves for experiment. After other trials the two royal daughters were successfully inoculated in April, 1722.

In Massachusetts, meanwhile, some of Cotton Mather's parishioners gave him a Negro slave in 1706. No doubt Mather asked him if he had had the smallpox, and received then his first confused intimation of the practice of inoculation as some of the African natives carried it out. Further questioning of several other Negroes and some Guinea slave traders confirmed the tale. Sometime before July, 1716, Mather also received a copy of Timonius's communication in the *Philosophical Transactions*. In a letter to Dr. Woodward of July 12, 1716, he corroborated this account with what he had heard and inquired why the practice was not tried in England. "For my own part," he wrote, "if I should live to see the *Small-Pox* again enter into

John B. Blake, "The Inoculation Controversy in Boston: 1721–1722," *New England Quarterly* 25 (1952): 489–506.

our City, I would immediately procure a Consult of our Physicians, to Introduce a Practice, which may be of so very happy a Tendency." At least five years in advance, therefore, Mather had seriously considered the policy he was later to follow.

On April 22, 1721, among several ships arriving from the West Indies was H.M.S. *Seahorse*, which brought the smallpox. Not until May 8, however, did the Selectmen learn that a Negro who came on the naval vessel was in town with the disease. When they heard of another case at Captain Wentworth Paxton's house, they ordered two men to stand guard there and let no one in or out without their permission. A few days later, at the request of the town, the Governor and Council ordered the *Seahorse* down to Bird Island to prevent further infection from this source, but not until after several other sick members of the company had come ashore. As late as May 20 the Selectmen could find no more cases, but two days later the town nevertheless instructed its representatives to seek further legislation to enable the Selectmen to prevent the spread of infectious sickness. On the twenty-fourth the Selectmen set twenty-six free Negroes to work cleaning the streets as a preventive measure, but without avail. On May 27 there were eight known cases, and by the middle of June the disease was in so many houses that the Selectmen abandoned the system of guards.

By this time Cotton Mather had decided to carry out his previous plan. Considering it his Christian duty—and worrying about his own children—on June 6 he circulated a letter about inoculation among the physicians of Boston, along with an abstract of the accounts by Timonius and Pylarinus. *"Gentlemen,"* he wrote, "My *request* is, that you would *meet for a Consultation* upon this Occasion, and to *deliberate* upon it, that whoever first begins this practise *(if you approve that it should be begun at all)* may have the concurrence of his *worthy Brethren* to fortify him in it." Whatever their reasons, they made no reply. On June 24, after the guards had been taken off the houses, he wrote another letter strongly recommending the technique to Dr. Zabdiel Boylston. This may have convinced the physician, for two days later he inoculated his six-year-old son Thomas and two of his Negroes. After several anxious days the experiment proved successful, and on July 12 he inoculated Joshua Cheever. Two days later John Helyer and another Negro underwent the operation. On the seventeenth Boylston treated his son John, and on the nineteenth three more people, bringing the total to ten.

The populace was quickly aroused. The idea had caused talk soon after Mather brought it up; within four days after Boylston's first experiment it "raised an horrid Clamour. . . ." In an advertisement in the *Boston Gazette* on July 17 the physician justified his action on the grounds of the reports of Timonius and Pylarinus and his own successful experiments, but when he indicated his intention to continue by the announcement that *"in a few Weeks more, I hope to give you some further proof of their just and reasonable Account,"* he no doubt increased the people's wrath. Cotton Mather, convinced of the value of the practice, thought the Devil had "taken a strange Possession of the People," and noted sadly in his diary that not only Boylston but he himself was also "an Object of their Fury; their furious Obloquies and Invectives."

Soon the Selectmen felt they must act. On July 21 they and some Justices of the Peace met with several members of the medical profession. Disregarding Boylston's invitation to see some of his patients, they accepted instead Dr. Lawrence Dalhonde's statement that inoculation in Italy, Spain, and Flanders had led to horrible *sequelae,* and pronounced that it "has proved the Death of many Persons," that it "Tends to spread and continue the Infection," and that its continuance "is likely to prove of most dangerous consequence." On this basis the Selectmen and Justices severely reprimanded Boylston and forbade him to continue the practice.

Three days later Dr. William Douglass, who led the professional opposition, tried a new attack in a communication to the *News-Letter.* He credited Mather with "a Pious & Charitable design of doing good," but attacked Boylston for "*His mischievous propagating the Infection* in the most Publick Trading Place of the Town. . . ." He called on the ministers to determine "how the trusting more the extra groundless *Machinations of Men* than to our Preserver in the ordinary course of Nature, may be consistent with that Devotion and Subjection we owe to the *all-wise Providence* of GOD Almighty." Of the lawyers he inquired "how it may be construed a *Propagating of Infection and Criminal.*" On the thirty-first the minister's reply appeared in the *Gazette,* signed by Increase and Cotton Mather, Benjamin Colman, Thomas Prince, John Webb, and William Cooper. After upholding Boylston's professional skill, they declared that if, as they believed, inoculation could save lives, they accepted it "with all thankfulness and joy as the gracious Discovery of a *Kind Providence* to Mankind. . . ." Use of this operation, they said, like that of any other medical treatment, depended on God's blessing and was fully consistent with "*a humble Trust . . . and a due Subjection*" to the Lord. When James Franklin's new paper, the *New-England Courant,* appeared on August 7, the anti-inoculators had their medium, and a furious newspaper and pamphlet war ensued.

Boylston, meanwhile, backed by the six ministers, disregarded the Selectmen's orders and on August 5 resumed inoculating. During that month he performed the operation on seventeen people, in September on thirty-one, and the next month on eighteen. Among the last were three men from Roxbury who, after their recovery, returned to recommend it there. November was his busiest month, with one hundred and four inoculations. Several ministers and other prominent men encouraged the practice by their example. On September 23 the Honorable Thomas Fitch, Esq., tried the new technique. Others included the Reverend Thomas Walter on October 31, and in November, the Reverend Ebenezer Pierpont, Anthony Stoddard, Esq., John White, Esq., the Honorable Judge Quincy's son Edmund, Edward Wigglesworth, and William Welsteed, professor and fellow respectively at Harvard, Justice Samuel Sewall's grandson Samuel Hirst, the Honorable Jonathan Belcher's son Andrew, and the Reverend Nehemiah Walter. On December 8, even a doctor, Elijah Danforth of Roxbury, submitted to the test.

Whatever the clergymen and esquires may have thought of inoculation, the people as a whole continued to oppose it violently. They were urged on by most of the local physicians, one of whom went so far as to assert that it would breed in Boston bubonic plague, which was then devastating southern France. One man vented his feelings about three in the morning of November 14 by throwing a lighted grenade into Cotton Mather's house. Ten days previously, shortly after Boylston began receiving patients from Roxbury and Charlestown, the town had expressed its official attitude by voting that anyone who came into Boston to be inoculated should be forthwith sent to the pesthouse unless he returned home. . . . The Selectmen thereupon requested the Justices for warrants to remove such persons. . . .

Meanwhile the epidemic also raged. Soon after it began, trade was disrupted, and many people fled. One person died in May, eight in June, eleven in July, and twenty-six in August. That month the General Court, which was sitting at the George Tavern on the Neck, appointed three men to stand guard at the door of the House of Representatives to prevent anyone from Boston entering without special license. In September, when the deaths jumped to one hundred and one, the Selectmen severely limited the length of time funeral bells could toll. . . .

By [mid-November] the epidemic was beginning to decline. October had been the worst month, with four hundred and eleven deaths. In November the total dropped to two hundred and forty-nine, and by mid-December, according to the Selectmen, the mortality was not much higher than in time of health. During January and February Boylston inoculated only twelve people, none in Boston. On February 26 the Selectmen issued an official statement that there were no more known cases in the town. Altogether, since April, 5,889 people, of whom 844 died, had had the smallpox. This one disease caused more than three-fourths of all the deaths in Boston during the year of the epidemic. During the same period Boylston inoculated 242 persons, with 6 deaths. Except for a few recurrences in April and May the epidemic was over in the capital.

Then, on May 11, 1722, Boylston inoculated Samuel Sewall, a Boston merchant and nephew of the diarist, his wife, three boys in his household, and Joanna Alford, the first he had done since February 24, and the first in Boston since December. The people were incensed. The Selectmen quickly removed these new cases to Spectacle Island to keep them from communicating the infection to anyone else, and called Boylston before the town meeting, where he "did solemnly promise to Inoculate no more without the knowledge & approbation of the Authority of the Town." Douglass gloated:

> Last January *Inoculation* made a Sort of *Exit,* like the Infatuation Thirty Years ago, after several had fallen Victims to the mistaken Notions of Dr. *M—r* and other learned Clerks concerning Witchcraft. But finding Inoculation in this Town, like the Serpents in Summer, beginning to crawl abroad again the last Week, it was in time, and effectually crushed in the Bud, by the *Justices, Select-Men,* and the *unanimous Vote* of a general Town-Meeting.

The voters also instructed their representatives to seek legislation regulating inoculation and prohibiting it in any town without the Selectmen's permission. Since some question had arisen over the interpretation of the act relating to contagious diseases, the people wanted their officials "Clothed with full power to obtain the great End & Designe of that Law, which is for the Preservation, Health, and Safty, of the Inhabitants." . . .

An analysis of the whole controversy shows that several factors were involved. One source of opposition to inoculation was the religious scruples of earnest and devout people. Some maintained that it was a sin for a healthy person to bring the sickness upon himself, especially since he might otherwise escape it altogether, and that he should in submission to God's will leave it to Him to determine whether or not he would suffer the disease. Another argument was that since the epidemic was sent by God, the only proper recourse was repentance and reformation; inoculation only increased the guilt because it was a rebellious attempt to take God's work out of His hands and showed distrust in His promises. . . .

Some of Boston's leading ministers, however, easily answered these arguments. It was not unlawful to make oneself sick in this manner, they declared; rather it was a duty because it was a protection against a worse sickness. In the same way, they pointed out, other preventive medicines such as purges and vomits were used, and no one considered that sinful. William Cooper provided the most complete rebuttal. It was not faith, he said, but presumption for anyone to think that God would preserve him when walking in an infected atmosphere. One must, of course, rely primarily on the Lord, he said, but this did not preclude the use of the best human help afforded by His providence. . . .

The religious question, though significant, should not be overemphasized. While much of the argument was couched in religious terms, the real dividing point was medical. The Sixth Commandment was frequently mentioned, but whether for or against depended on what the medical results of inoculation were alleged to be. None of the opponents was content to rest his case on the necessity of trusting in God's providence; however they phrased it, they all thought the practice harmful to the health and lives of their fellow-citizens.

In the passion of the fight both sides exaggerated either the ease and safety of the practice on the one hand, or its horrors and dangers on the other. The proponents' fundamental argument, however, was that it gave the patient a mild case of smallpox which protected him from the natural one. They cited the reports of Timonius and Pylarinus, and Boylston published Mather's abstracts. They pointed out that in Africa the Negroes had long carried on this practice to great advantage. They ridiculed the assertions that it would cause plague or debilitate the constitution. In particular they called to witness the results of Boylston's own trials. Old and young, weak and strong, had been inoculated, they said, with success beyond expectation. . . .

Although some objections were fantastic and some picayune, anti-inoculators also had sound arguments. They emphasized the known deaths among the inoculated—which the Mathers tried to explain away—and hinted of others. They said, rightly, that the technique endangered the individual who submitted to it. Their chief contention was that inoculation as performed by Boylston spread the epidemic. John Williams maintained that anyone who voluntarily took the smallpox violated the moral law of God—"Therefore all things whatsoever ye would that Men should do to you, do ye even so to them"—by bringing the disease to his neighbor. . . .

Religious and medical divisions were not the only causes of the heat of the controversy. In part they were due to the personalities involved, particularly those of Cotton Mather and William Douglass. The former, pedantic, tactless, egotistical, convinced that those who opposed him were possessed of the Devil, yet rejoicing in the prospect of martrydom at the hands of Satan's minions (the town), asserted that raving and railing against "*the* Ministers, *and other serious* Christians, *who favour this Practice, is a very crying Iniquity; and to call it a* Work of the Devil . . . *is a shocking* Blasphemy. . . ." He or one of his cohorts accused the anti-inoculation physicians of being another "Hell-Fire Club," a current, notorious group of blasphemers in England. Douglass, on the other hand, accused Mather of credulity, whim, and vanity, of omissions and errors in his abstracts of Timonius and Pylarinus, and of misrepresentation; and he called Boylston an illiterate quack. Douglass, apparently, thought he should be the leader of whatever was happening in local medical affairs and was prone to disparage any who were not his sycophants. Nine years later he declared that Mather had "surreptitiously" set Boylston to work, "that he might have the honour of a Newfangled notion." One suspects that some of his bitterness resulted from his own failure to take the lead. Eventually he came to favor the practice, but he never forgave his two opponents.

The clash between Mather and Douglass stemmed from more than their personalities, for they also stood for two different principles. The minister was in effect maintaining the right of his profession to interfere with and control the life of the community. . . .

Douglass, on the other hand, was defending the integrity of the medical profession against the interference of those whom he considered to be credulous laymen. He pointed out that no one should accept all the quaint things published in the *Philosophical Transactions,* that Mather's sources of information—accounts from the Levant and from untutored Negroes—were at best questionable. His principal complaint was that despite the opposition of the town, the Selectmen, and the medical profession, *"Six Gentlemen of Piety and Learning, profoundly ignorant of the Matter,"* rashly advocated a new and doubtful procedure in "a Disease one of the most intricate practical Cases in Physick. . . ." By January, 1721/1722, Douglass was willing to admit that inoculated smallpox was frequently more favorable than natural and that the practice was at least a temporary, palliative preventive. Though pessimistic, he thought that it might with improvement become a specific smallpox preventive. But, he declared, it must be allowed by an act of the legislature and carried out by "abler hands, than *Greek old Women, Madmen and Fools.*" He wanted a period of cautious experimentation. "For my own Part," he said, *"till after a few Years, I shall pass no positive Judgment of this bold Practice."*

Douglass' attitude toward the clergy brought him allies who opposed them chiefly for political reasons. . . . Claiming that inoculation was "a Delusion of the Devil," he compared it to "the Time of the Witchcraft at Salem, when so many innocent Persons lost their Lives. . . ." He blasted the ministers for going outside their calling by trying to control such public affairs as inoculation and paper money. . . .

. . . The most thorough rebuttal was a pamphlet inspired by Cotton Mather, the *Vindication of the Ministers of Boston.* The anonymous author lauded the clergy as worthy men seeking the best for their people and gave the pro-Mather version of the beginning of the whole controversy. He was chiefly concerned, however, with maintaining the ministers' leadership in all things:

> If this *impious* & Satanic Custom [of attacking the clergy] prevail, we shall involve our
> selves into a thousand pernicious *Evils.* . . . Our *Reprovers* and *Prophets* being Silenced,
> *Iniquity* and every *Abomination* will break in among us, and bear down like an irre
> sistible Torrent, all *Virtue,* and *Religion* before it. And what is mostly to be deprecated,
> all manner of *Spiritual Plagues* will follow this our degeneracy; and the *Town* grow
> ripe for a *Wrath unto the Uttermost.*

Inoculation had become a bitter party cause.

Reviewing the controversy, we must credit Cotton Mather and Boylston for their courage in experimenting with and continuing what seemed on fairly good evidence to be a means of saving life. But they cannot escape censure for their neglect of the rights of the community by their failure to take any steps to prevent those who were inoculated from transmitting the disease to others. Moreover, though Mather was not as credulous in this case as Douglass thought, it is difficult to escape the conclusion that he and Boylston were lucky that the experiment worked so well. On the other hand, Douglass' cautious approach toward an obviously dangerous medical innovation was a sane one. Unfortunately the vehemence of his opposition and his credulity in accepting Dalhonde's report becloud the positive values of his attitude. Furthermore, despite his expressed preference for cautious experiments, he himself would probably never have undertaken them.

 F U R T H E R   R E A D I N G

Whitfield J. Bell Jr., *The Colonial Physician and Other Essays* (1975).

Whitfield J. Bell Jr., *John Morgan: Continental Doctor* (1965).

John B. Blake, *Public Health in the Town of Boston, 1630–1822* (1959).

Philip Cash, Eric H. Christianson, and J. Worth Estes, eds., *Medicine in Colonial Massachusetts, 1620–1820* (1980).

James H. Cassedy, *Demography in Early America: Beginnings of the Statistical Mind* (1969).

Joyce E. Chaplin, *An Anxious Pursuit: Agricultural Innovation and Modernity in the Lower South, 1730–1815* (1993).

Alfred W. Crosby Jr., *The Columbian Exchange: Biological and Cultural Consequences of 1492* (1972).

Alfred W. Crosby Jr., *Ecological Imperialism: The Biological Expansion of Europe, 900–1900* (1986).

Henry F. Dobyns, *Their Number Became Thinned: Native American Population Dynamics in Eastern North America* (1983).

John Duffy, *Epidemics in Colonial America* (1953, 1971).

Norman Gevitz, "Samuel Fuller of Plymouth Plantation: A 'Skillful' Physician or 'Quacksalver'?" *Journal of the History of Medicine* 47 (1992): 29–48.

Gerald N. Grob, *The Mad Among Us: A History of the Care of America's Mentally Ill* (1994).

Robert H. Jackson, *Indian Population Decline: The Missions of Northwestern New Spain, 1687–1840* (1994).

Mary Ann Jimenz, *Changing Faces of Madness: Early American Attitudes and Treatment of the Insane* (1987).

Susan E. Klepp, "Lost, Hidden, Obstructed and Repressed: Contraceptive and Abortive Technology in the Early Delaware Valley," in *Early American Technology: Making and Doing Things from the Colonial Era to 1850,* ed. Judith A. McGaw (1994), pp. 68–113.

Karen Ordahl Kupperman, "Fear of Hot Climates in the Anglo-American Experience," *William and Mary Quarterly* 41 (1984): 213–240.

H. Roy Merrens and George D. Terry, "Dying in Paradise: Malaria, Mortality, and the Perceptual Environment in Colonial South Carolina," *Journal of Southern History* 50 (1984): 533–550.

Perry Miller, "The Judgment of the Smallpox," in *The New England Mind: From Colony to Province* (1953), pp. 345–366.

Ronald L. Numbers, ed., *Medicine in the New World: New Spain, New France, and New England* (1987).

Darrett B. Rutman and Anita H. Rutman, "Of Agues and Fevers: Malaria in the Early Chesapeake," *William and Mary Quarterly* 33 (1976): 31–60.

Rebecca J. Tannenbaum, "What Is Best to Be Done for These Fevers: Elizabeth Davenport's Medical Practice in New Haven," *New England Quarterly* 70 (1997): 265–284.

Russell Thornton, *American Indian Holocaust and Survival: A Population History Since 1492* (1987).

Virgil J. Vogel, *American Indian Medicine* (1970).

Patricia Ann Watson, *The Angelical Conjunction: The Preacher-Physicians of Colonial New England* (1991).

Patricia Ann Watson, "The Hidden Ones: Women and Healing in Colonial New England," in *Medicine and Healing,* ed. Peter Benes (1992), pp. 25–33.

Peter H. Wood, *Black Majority: Negroes in Colonial South Carolina* (1974).

The Medical Marketplace in the Early Republic, 1785–1825

In the early republic, physicians did not dominate medical practice even in the new nation's largest cities, and there was no consensus that they should. Indeed, male physicians played only a modest role in the medical care of Americans, who much more frequently turned to midwives and other women healers as well as to herbalists, bone setters, bleeders and cuppers, nostrum vendors, domestic healers, and home medical guidebooks. Although such healers did not offer identical services, and families often enlisted the aid of multiple providers of health care, these practitioners often competed with one another in a remarkably open medical marketplace.

At the same time, during the early decades of the republic, the expansion of medical institutions sustained a new, confident professionalism among those who identified themselves as "regularly bred physicians" or "regulars," as they were increasingly called. The establishment during the 1760s of medical schools (starting with the University of Pennsylvania in 1765 and King's College in New York in 1767), societies, and licensing laws had encouraged a sense of collective identity among physicians. In the new nation, regular physicians increasingly sought to set themselves apart from other healers, claiming both special learning (marked by allegiance to highly theoretical systems of pathology and therapeutics) and superior ability to explain and manage illness. The organization of local and state medical societies—which adopted formal ethical codes and fixed fee scales—helped regulars distinguish themselves as a group, a move state legislatures reinforced by placing licensing powers in the hands of the societies. Of about thirty-five hundred physicians in America at the time of the Revolutionary War, only one in ten held an M.D. degree, and apprenticeship remained the core of medical education. Some physicians, even if they did not seek an M.D. degree, supplemented apprenticeship by attending medical lectures—medical departments at Harvard (1782), Dartmouth (1798), and Transylvania University in Lexington, Kentucky (1799), joined existing schools—and a small elite studied abroad as they had before the Revolution, especially in Edinburgh and in London. Physicians founded medical journals, starting with New York's Medical Repository *in 1797, and even though the small number of hospitals in American cities were chiefly asylums for the sick poor, elite physicians sought charitable hospital appointments, partly for access to clinical experience, teaching, and investigation. Regular physicians also were distinguished by their practices, including the use of instruments (such as obstetrical forceps) in childbirth and by their reliance on so-called heroic medicine. Aggressive bleeding and purging that aimed at restoring the body's humors to a proper balance came to be one of the most readily recognized emblems of the regular medical profession.*

Who was qualified to practice as a healer? How should their qualifications be established and recognized by other practitioners and by the public? What were the claims of competing healers on the trust and business of the sick? These were questions debated with intensifying vigor in the late eighteenth and early nineteenth centuries. It was during this period that regular physicians sought to edge out competitors, including women practitioners and other rivals they lumped together as "irregulars" and discredited as "quacks." Yet, at a time when most patients relied on multiple sources of health care, the more regular physicians distanced themselves from competitors, the more they incurred hostility from other practitioners and from the public.

D O C U M E N T S

Document 1 is a newspaper article in which George Washington's physicians narrate his final illness in 1799. They recount how the former president had himself bled by "a bleeder in the neighbourhood" before giving in to his family's urging that he send for physicians and describe what treatments (including bleeding and purging) they administered after their arrival. In Document 2, Philadelphia Quaker Elizabeth Drinker, writing in the same year, reflects in her diary on the birth of her daughter Sally's sixth child. The birthing mother, like the dying former president, used more than one medical practitioner: Drinker reports on the services of both a male bleeder and the eminent physician William Shippen, whose use of drugs and obstetrical instruments left her apprehensive.

Document 3 is an 1803 address by Benjamin Rush—a 1768 medical graduate of the University of Edinburgh, a signer of the Declaration of Independence, a leading proselytizer for heroic medicine, and the most prominent medical teacher of the early republic—to his medical students at the University of Pennsylvania. He tells them about the frustrations and satisfactions they will encounter as practicing physicians, citing the ingratitude of the public in Philadelphia's savage 1793 yellow fever epidemic, an epidemic in which Rush gained notoriety for his advocacy of heroic bloodletting. The diary excerpts in Document 4, written in 1807 by a medical apprentice in Camden, South Carolina, provide a brief glimpse into the workaday routine through which most students acquired their knowledge of medicine. In Document 5, James Jackson, a leading Boston physician, and John Collins Warren, a prominent Boston surgeon, appeal in 1810 to affluent Bostonians for support of a hospital (what would become the Massachusetts General) to provide care for the worthy sick poor and to further the interests of medical education in New England (more particularly at Harvard) by giving students an opportunity to observe extensive practice without traveling to "the only medical school of eminence in this country"—the University of Pennsylvania in Philadelphia, the chief medical rival to Boston.

In Document 6, an anonymously authored pamphlet attributed to Harvard medical professor Walter Channing warns against the dangers of allowing women to practice medicine and celebrates the exclusion of women from the practice of obstetrics. Document 7, a letter from a young physician, Joseph Stanton (who apparently has neither attended lectures at a medical school nor served a formal apprenticeship), to his brother, reflects the difficulties many practitioners experienced figuring out medical licensing rules (which were highly variable and unevenly enforced) and finding a town where there are realistic prospects for establishing a medical practice. Stanton has decided to attend lectures at a new medical school in Cincinnati, and he notes the advantages of a new western school.

In Document 8, Samuel Thomson, founder of Thomsonianism, the first major antiorthodox medical movement in America, assails "learned doctors" for poisoning their patients with heroic mineral drugs and for keeping the simple truths of healing from the common man and woman, championing instead his system of domestic healing using natural botanic remedies. He derived his therapeutic approach around 1800 from folk practice in rural New Hampshire, where he was a farmer. Thomson's highly successful book *New Guide to Health; Or Botanic Family Physician,* first published in 1822 and excerpted here, was much more stridently antiprofessional than *Every Man His Own Doctor* (see Chapter 2, Document 6) of half a century earlier. It propelled Thomsonianism to enormous popularity as the first organized antiorthodox system of medical belief and practice.

1. George Washington's Physicians Narrate His Final Illness and Death, 1799

Messrs. J. & D. Westcott,

Presuming that some account of the late illness and death of General WASHINGTON will be generally interesting, and particularly so to the professors and practitioners of medicine throughout America, we request you to publish the following statement.

JAMES CRAIK,
ELISHA C. DICK.

Some time in the night of Friday the 13th instant, having been exposed to rain on the preceding day, General Washington was attacked with an inflammatory affection of the upper part of the wind-pipe, called in technical language, *cynanche trachealis.* The disease commenced with a violent ague, accompanied with some pain in the upper and fore part of the throat, a sense of stricture in the same part, a cough, and a difficult rather than a painful deglutition, which were soon succeeded by fever and a quick and laborious respiration. The necessity of blood-letting suggesting itself to the General, he procured a bleeder in the neighbourhood, who took from his arm, in the night, twelve or fourteen ounces of blood: he would not by any means be prevailed upon by the family to send for the attending physician till the following morning, who arrived at Mount Vernon at about eleven o'clock on Saturday. Discovering the case to be highly alarming, and foreseeing the fatal tendency of the disease, two consulting physicians were immediately sent for, who arrived,

[James Craik and Elisha C. Dick], "News. From 'The Times,' a Newspaper Printed in Alexandria (Virginia), dated in December, 1799," *Medical Repository* 3 (1800): 311–312.

one at half after three, the other at four o'clock in the afternoon. In the interim were employed two copious bleedings; a blister was applied to the part affected, two moderate doses of calomel were given, and an injection was administered, which operated on the lower intestines—but all without any perceptible advantage, the respiration becoming still more difficult and distressing. Upon the arrival of the first of the consulting physicians, it was agreed, as there were yet no signs of accumulation in the bronchial vessels of the lungs, to try the result of another bleeding, when about thirty-two ounces of blood were drawn, without the smallest apparent alleviation of the disease. Vapours of vinegar and water were frequently inhaled, ten grains of calomel were given, succeeded by repeated doses of emetic tartar, amounting, in all, to five or six grains, with no other effect than a copious discharge from the bowels. The powers of life seemed now manifestly yielding to the force of the disorder. Blisters were applied to the extremities, together with a cataplasm of bran and vinegar to throat. Speaking, which was painful from the beginning, now became almost impracticable; respiration grew more and more contracted and imperfect, till half after eleven o'clock on Saturday night, when, retaining the full possession of his intellect, he expired without a struggle.

He was fully impressed at the beginning of his complaint, as well as through every succeeding stage of it, that its conclusion would be mortal, submitting to the several exertions made for his recovery rather as a duty than from any expectation of their efficacy. He considered the operations of death upon his system as coeval with the disease; and several hours before his decease, after repeated efforts to be understood, succeeded in expressing a desire that he might be permitted to die without interruption.

During the short period of his illness he enconomized his time in the arrangement of such few concerns as required his attention, with the utmost serenity, and anticipated his approaching dissolution with every demonstration of that equanimity for which his whole life had been so uniformly and singularly conspicuous.

JAMES CRAIK,
Attending Physician.
ELISHA C. DICK,
Consulting Physician.

2. Elizabeth Drinker, a Philadelphia Quaker, Recounts in Her Diary the Physician-Attended Birth of Her Daughter's Sixth Child, 1799

[Oct.] 23 [1799].   My poor dear Sally was taken unwell last night, Dan came for us early this morning Sister is gone there—I stay to see Dr. Kuhn when he visits [my son] William who has not yet this morning had a return of the disorder—he is in bed and I hardly know how he is as yet—Sally has always been very lingering, how it will be this time, the Lord only knows, I am to be sent for if she should grow

Elizabeth Drinker, Diary, entries for October 23 and 24, 1799, in *The Diary of Elizabeth Drinker,* 3 vols., ed. Elaine Forman Crane (Boston: Northeastern University Press, 1991), vol. 2, pp. 1226–1229. Copyright © 1991 by Elaine Forman Crane. Used with the permission of Northeastern University Press.

worse—this is her birth-day. . . . Nancy Skyrin came in, she had been to see Sally. I believe she dont intend, if she can help it, to be with Sally at the extremity, she says that I need not leave William yet, that they will let me know when I ought to come, but having my cloak on and ready to go, and all things in order at home, I went—found Dr. Shippen half asleep in the back parlor by himself—I question'd him relative to Sallys situation, he said she was in the old way, and he thinks she dont require bleeding by her pulse—I went up stairs, . . . into Sallys Chamber she is in pain at times, forerunning pains of a lingering labour, a little low Spirited, poor dear Child—This day is 38 years since I was in agonies bringing her into this world of trouble; she told me with tears that this was her birth day, I endeavor'd to talk her into better Spirits, told her that, the time of her birth was over by some hours, she was now in her 39th. year, and that this might possiably be the last trial of this sort, if she could suckle her baby for 2 years to come, as she had several times done heretofore &c.—I came home to dinner, found WD. neither better or worse, brought little Henry home with me,—O dear! only to think that I have eat my dinner almost as heartily as usual, my Son pale and poorly up stairs, tho' on the recovery, and my Eldest daughter in actual labour, tho' not yet come to the extremity, could I have done so once? I think not; I believe that as we grow in years, we become more callous, or in some measure loose that quick sense of feeling, that attends us in our more youthful days. . . . I went again after-noon . . . found no change had taken place: Sally in almost continual pain, I came home again in the evening William better; . . . 'twas near 11 o'clock when I got there—Sally was all night in great distress, the pain never quite of, sometimes on the bed, but most of the night in the Easy chair; as it is called,—between two and 3 o'clock in the morning Dr. Shippen desired Jacob to call up a John Perry, who lives near them, to open a vain, 'tho it is a opperation she very much dreads, she gave up to it without saying a word: he perform'd with great care and dexterity as I thought, he took twelve or 14 ounces. Sally had two smart, or rather hard pains while the bleeder was there, he is a married man; she has taken 80 or 90 drops liquid ladanum during the day and night, but has not had many minuits sleep for 48 hours—the Doctor says the Child is wedg'd on or near the shear bone and he cannot get at it, to alter the position of its head, I came home between 7 and 8 in the morning of the—

24th.   after breakfast, and giving orders for dinner &c. WD. up stairs, I went again to Sally, the Doctor had giving her an Opium pill three grains he said, in order to ease her pain, or to bring it on more violently: neither appear'd to happen—in the Afternoon the Doctor said, the Child must be brought forward—he went out, which he had not done before, that he was going for instruments occur'd to me but I was afraid to ask him, least he should answer in the affermative—towards evening I came home as usual, and after seeing all things in order, was getting ready to depart, when little Dan enter'd, the sight of him flutter'd me, yet I had a secret hope that it was over, when Dan told us, that his mistress had a fine boy and was as well as could be expected— . . . this joyfull intelligence quite changed my feelings, I was apprehensive that the Child would not be born alive;—My husband went with me there, they were at supper, very Chearful, like Sailors after a storm—I went up to Sally, would not suffer her to talk.—I was thankful, that I happened to be absent at the time, tho' I intended otherwise, Dr. Shippen told me that he thought he should have had occasion for instruments, which said he I have in my pocket, claping his hand on his side, when I heard them rattle, but some time after you went away, I found matters were chang'd for the better, The Child, said he, is a very large one for Sally.—It is a very fine lusty fatt boy, the same countenence as little Sally: they talk of nameing him Sandwith, sister said it should be Jacob after his Father, what they have concluded on I dont yet know—The Doctor was very kind and attentive during the whole afflecting scene, was there two nights and 2 days, and sleep't very little—My husband, Nancy and self came home about 11 o'clock— as I had not had my cloaths off for two days and one night, going backwards and forwards, with my mind disturbed, I felt exceedingly weary when I went to bed.

3. Benjamin Rush Tells His Medical Students at the University of Pennsylvania of the Trials and Rewards of a Medical Career, 1803

GENTLEMEN,

You are convened this day for the purpose of hearing an introductory lecture to a course of lectures upon the institutes and practice of medicine. Previously to my entering upon those subjects, I shall deliver a few remarks upon the pains and pleasures of a medical life. The detail, of the former, will serve to show you the evils to which you will be exposed, in a greater or less degree, in your present pursuits; and thereby prepare you to meet them with dignity and resignation. The history, of the latter, will serve to animate you in your studies, and to lessen, if not destroy, the fears which may be excited by the previous detail of the pains which accompany the life of a physician. . . .

. . . The sources of VEXATION to a physician arise from the ignorance of mankind of the nature of medicine. This ignorance discovers itself in different degrees of credulity and superstition. It leads to a preference of quacks; also of artful, vulgar, and sometimes of brutal manners, to such as are candid, simple, and polite; and of pretensions to skill, though accompanied with levity, profanity, and even drunkenness, to a conduct uniformly grave, decent, and sober, in regularly bred physicians. . . .

. . . A physician is exposed to vexation, from the false judgment which the bulk of mankind often entertain of the nature of certain medicines which he employs in his practice. I well recollect the time when the prejudices against opium and bark were so great, that it was often necessary to disguise, in order to exhibit, them; and few persons are ignorant of the unfounded and illiberal clamours, which exist, at this day, in every part of the world, against the use of mercury and the lancet. . . .

. . . Public ingratitude is another source of vexation to a physician. In the month of December, 1793, the citizens of Philadelphia assembled at the statehouse, and voted their thanks to the committee who had superintended the city, during the prevalence of the fever of that year. A motion was afterwards made to thank the physicians of the city for their services. This motion was not seconded. The services and sacrifices of those physicians may easily be estimated, when I add, that their patients were

---

Benjamin Rush, "On the Pains and Pleasures of a Medical Life" (delivered 7 November 1803), in *Sixteen Introductory Lectures to Courses of Lectures upon the Institutes and Practice of Medicine* (Philadelphia: Bradford and Innskeep, 1811), pp. 210–212, 214, 217–221, 224, 226, 228–230.

chiefly poor people; and that out of thirty five physicians who remained in the city, eight died; and of the survivors, but three escaped an attack of the fever. . . .

I proceed in the order laid down, to take notice of the sources of DISTRESS to a physician. These arise, in the first place, from our intercourse with our fellow citizens being confined chiefly to those times in which they are unhappy from sickness and pain. Secondly, from our being frequently obliged to witness the inefficacy of our attempts to arrest the gradual progress of death in certain diseases. . . . [H]ow shall I describe his feelings, when compelled to share in the grief occasioned by his inability to save the life of a favourite or only child? . . .

Besides the distress which physicians feel from the causes that have been mentioned, they are exposed to share largely in that which is introduced into a city, by the prevalence of a general and mortal epidemic. Citizens, agitated and distracted by the contradictory reports and opinions of physicians; streets crowded and obstructed by carriages conveying whole families, with piles of household furniture, into the country; parents deserted by their children; children deserted by their parents; the sick neglected, or attended only by ignorant and mercenary nurses; our ears assailed in walking the streets, by the groans and shrieks of the dying; and our eyes met, in entering the doors of our patients, by a wife or a parent in tears from an apprehension of the fatal issue of the prevailing disease in a husband or a child; gloom and dejection sitting upon every countenance; an awful stillness pervading every street; and finally nothing seen in them but herses conveying the dead to their hasty graves. . . .

It remains only to mention SOLICITUDE, as a source of the pains of a medical life. It includes all those painful feelings which are excited by doubts of the nature of our patients' diseases; by the occurrence of new or alarming symptoms; by unexpected and disagreeable effects from our medicines; by the anxious inquiries of the relations and friends of the sick, with respect to the issue of their diseases; by our own apprehensions of censure; in case of their fatal termination; and lastly, by our constant fears, of doing too little or too much for their recovery. . . .

. . . The pleasures of a medical life are of an intellectual and moral nature. All the branches of medicine are calculated to afford pleasure to the understanding.

Anatomy and physiology unfold a microcosm of wonders to the inquisitive mind. The structure and offices of the heart, the liver, the spleen, the omentum, the blood vessels, the brain, the nerves, the muscles, the lymphatics, the stomach, and the skin, contain inexhaustible matters of pleasant inquiry and reflection. The separate and combined actions of the senses, the causes of animal life, and, above all, the faculties and operations of the human mind are capable of affording pleasure, when properly contemplated, through the longest life. . . .

. . . [Another] source of the pleasures of a medical life consists in the discovery of new truths, whether they relate to anatomy, physiology, natural history, chemistry, or the practice of physic. How delightful must have been the feelings of Dr. Harvey when he discovered the circulation of the blood! What may we not suppose were the transports of Linnæus, when his great and comprehensive genius conceived and established a system of botany founded upon the sexual relations and attractions of the plants! . . . But still higher has been the tide of pleasure in those physicians who have discovered, by reasoning, or by accident, new remedies for diseases. . . .

. . .Let us next attend to the pleasures of a medical life which are of a moral nature.

. . . The gratification of the humane and benevolent affections by relieving pain and sickness, and prolonging life, are great sources of this pleasure to a physician. It is enhanced by the violence and danger of the diseases which he has cured, and the importance of the relation which the subjects of them bear to the public or to their friends. To snatch the chief magistrate of a country, on whose life a whole nation depends for the continuance of its safety and repose, from an untimely grave; to arrest a malignant fever in its progress to death, in the father, and a consumption in the mother of a numerous family of children; to restore the deranged faculties of the mind in an only daughter; to resuscitate, from apparent death, by drowning, an only son; to behold the tears of joy in the relations of the persons who have been the subjects of these cures, and to receive from them their almost idolatrous expressions of gratitude and attachment! how exquisite the pleasure to a physician! . . .

. . . The gratitude of patients and communities manifested in various ways is another of the pleasures of a medical life. The hand of a physician has often been seized and kissed by a patient when emerging from the lowest stage of a disease, before he was able to speak. . . .

I have thus, gentlemen, delivered an epitome of the pains and pleasures which are connected with the profession of medicine. It remains now to determine which of them predominate in the scale of a physician's life.

If a physician should rely exclusively upon the stock of knowledge he acquired at the university in which he was educated, and neglect to study after he enters into practice—if he should pass a long life without adding a single discovery or improvement to any branch of our science—if he has flattered the rich, oppressed the middle ranks of life, and neglected the poor—if he has neither sympathized with the sorrows, nor partaken of the joys of his patients—if in his intercourse with them, and with his brother physicians, he has formed no social connexions, nor friendships—and, if in a word he has practised medicine as a trade, instead of profession—then his pains greatly predominate over his pleasures. Such a man it is true often derives pleasure from his wealth, but the wealth thus acquired is the product of the labour of the limbs, and not of the mind: and the pleasure derived from it is that of a mechanic, and not of a physician.

If, on the other hand, a physician consider himself a student of medicine as long as he lives—if he make it part of his business to read all the new publications upon the practical parts of his science—if he feel himself under an obligation to leave his profession in a better state than he found it, by adding to it some discovery or improvement—if he prefer the life of a patient, at all times, to his own interest and reputation—if he has made the joys and sorrows of his patients his own—if he can look around him and see thousands of his fellow citizens, whose lives have been prolonged by his skill and humanity—if he has so relieved the wants and distresses of the poor, from sickness and pain, as to derive a daily revenue from their blessings and prayers—if he has occasionally restored himself from fatigue and depression of body and mind, by spending an evening or an hour in pleasant society—if he has earned a friend by offices of disinterested kindness and benevolence—and, if he has acquired the esteem and affections of his patients, by his integrity and humanity, as well as their confidence by his skill—then his pleasures greatly predominate over all the pains of his medical life.

4. A Medical Apprentice in Rural South Carolina Records Daily Life in His Diary, 1807

6 [June 1807] . . . Showers this evening & night. No Business; I'm low spirits, nothing new that for me.

7   Still no business—Very warm for me, but the people say this is no thing—if this is nothing what will something be?

As the heat increases my spirits become depressed and I feel languid and home rushes on my mind with double the effect as usual.

Doct^r. Trent pays but little attention to his business—he was called on the other day to go 18 or 20 miles but would not go—no one knows why—here was lost Thirty or forty dollars—so much for slugishness—!!

June 8   Warm with showers in every direction—Had Potatoes for Dinner or with our dinner, for the first time this season—

Were the poor people not so intolerable Sluggish they could have made up for the deficiency of Corn by raising Potatoes; but so it is, they had rather starve than labour! . . .

11   This day our limbs are a load. The heat very opressive thro' the day and Night; showers at the North was but none near—Doct^r. T—not at the shop nor very attentive to our business at home. . . .

13th   Cool, and no showers—This day sold about 60 Dols. worth of Medicines! . . .

16   Very warm. At 2, °Clock started for Mr. West's first stage at Saunderss Creek 6 miles, Then to Gum Spring 4 miles, then to Lockards 4 miles then to Little Lenches Creek 9 miles then to Mr. Wests near hanging Rock, 1 mile in all 25 by computation—This was one of the most dreary rides that ever I undertook. When I arrived there the woman had been in Labour for no less than 5 day and was nearly exhausted—. I say in labour, for the waters has come a way 5 day before by some means or other; altho' her time had not come by same day, by her calculation, and had she been put to bed at *that* time and kept composed as possible, I have no doubt but that she might have done well; but not so; the old midwife took her in hand nor would she give her any time to recruit or rest—When I arrived the Midwife was using every exertion in her power and said to me that if she had strength she could deliver her without any doubt. I made an Examination and found the parts much inflamed by ruf usage, still the Child was almost out of reach and the Os Uteri appeared to have suffered very much by the old woman's fingers, and it was dilated to a large size—I put her to bed and gave her an anodine, and she got some rest that Night and at 3 °Clock her pains came on rapidly, nor would the old woman give her a moments rest off of the seat; at 10 °Clock I found by examining from time to time that the child did not advance in the least nor did the pains appear to bear down—; The Childs head presented right, for the sutures were plainly to be felt. The Scalp was much thickened—Several Times when she had very strong pains and when the midwife was setting by her—there was some thing came a way like the Excrement from a Child, but this never happened at when I was examining her—; from this

William Blanding, Diary, 4 vols.; vol. 1, entries for June 6, 7, 8, 11, 13, 16, 17 and July 24, 1807, Manuscripts Division, South Caroliniana Library, University of South Carolina, Columbia.

appearance One would have been lead to think that it was a Britch presentation, but it was not the case; the matter was dark coloured—I was convinsed that the woman would not be delivered without Instruments and that even if she were she could not live—still the old Midwife would give her no time to rest: at length we came to open war, for she often told me that if she had my strength she could deliver her, she was shure—I then proposed to come home, get some Instruments and return my self or send Doct^r. Trent—the Midwife beged for me to stay a little while, for she knew the Child was advancing and would soon be bourn[.] I examined and found that all was as it had been for 4 hours and started for Camden about ½ past Eleven, directing her to be kept as easy as possible; Doct^r. Trent arived a bout 9 °C1. And from what he could learn, the Midwife had after I left her made some powerful exertions to deliver her but to no purpose—When the Doct^r. went in the Midwife called to him to come and take her seat, and take the Child for it was just coming in to the world—he went to the patient and to his great surprise she had no sirculation in her arm, examined and found the Child to be dead, put the patient in bed and she died in a bout an hour. I must think that if the woman had been put to bed when the waters first came a way and given her an ano[dyne] that she might have kept along a number of days and done well.

17th   When I returned from Mr. West it was in the middle of the day and the mercury stood at 93—perhaps I never suffered more in riding 25 miles in my life—For 24 hours I had not Eaten but very little—and there was but one or two houses that I could get any drink at—When I arived a home or at Camden, I was almost dead—and as soon as night came I took some Tea and went to bed. . . .

24 [July]   This day assisted in opening a Negroe Girl of Mr. McRa's who died last evening—She was an African and has been in a lingering way for a long time, but could get no relief—

On opening her every part was sound except Mesentery which was much diseased, having lumps from the bigness of a Buck shot to that of a Quail's Egg—She was nothing but skin & bones—.

5. James Jackson and John C. Warren, Leading Boston Doctors, Solicit Support for Founding the Massachusetts General Hospital, 1810

BOSTON, August 20, 1810.

Sir,—It has appeared very desirable to a number of respectable gentlemen, that a hospital for the reception of lunatics and other sick persons should be established in this town. By the appointment of a number of these gentlemen, we are directed to adopt such methods as shall appear best calculated to promote such an establishment. We therefore beg leave to submit for your consideration proposals for the institution of a hospital, and to state to you some of the reasons in favour of such an establishment.

James Jackson and John C. Warren, "Circular Letter" (Boston, August 20, 1810), in N. I. Bowditch, *A History of the Massachusetts General Hospital* (Boston: John Wilson and Son, 1851), pp. 3–9.

It is unnecessary to urge the propriety and even obligation of succouring the poor in sickness. The wealthy inhabitants of the town of Boston have always evinced that they consider themselves as "treasurers of God's bounty;" and in Christian countries, in countries were Christianity is practised, it must always be considered the first of duties to visit and to heal the sick. When in distress, every man becomes our neighbour, not only if he be of the household of faith, but even though his misfortunes have been induced by transgressing the rules both of reason and religion. It is unnecessary to urge the truth and importance of these sentiments to those who are already in the habit of cherishing them,—to those who indulge in the true luxury of wealth, the pleasures of charity. The questions which first suggest themselves on this subject are, whether the relief afforded by hospitals is better than can be given in any other way; and whether there are, in fact, so many poor among us as to require an establishment of this sort.

The relief to be afforded to the poor, in a country so rich as ours, should perhaps be measured only by their necessities. We have, then, to inquire into the situation of the poor in sickness, and to learn what are their wants. In this inquiry, we shall be led to answer both the questions above stated.

There are some who are able to acquire a competence in health, and to provide so far against any ordinary sickness as that they shall not then be deprived of a comfortable habitation, nor of food for themselves and their families; while they are not able to defray the expenses of medicine and medical assistance. Persons of this description never suffer among us. The Dispensary gives relief to hundreds every year; and the individuals who practise medicine gratuitously attend many more of this description. But there are many others among the poor, who have, if we may so express it, the form of the necessaries of life, without the substance. A man may have a lodging; but it is deficient in all those advantages which are requisite to the sick. It is a garret or a cellar, without light and due ventilation, or open to the storms of an inclement winter. In this miserable habitation, he may obtain liberty to remain during an illness; but, if honest, he is harassed with the idea of his accumulating rent, which must be paid out of his future labours. In this wretched situation, the sick man is destitute of all those common conveniences, without which most of us would consider it impossible to live, even in health. Wholesome food and sufficient fuel are wanting; and his own sufferings are aggravated by the cries of hungry children. Above all, he suffers from the want of that first requisite in sickness, a kind and skilful nurse.

But it may be said, that instances are rare among us, where a man, who labours, with even moderate industry, when in health, endures such privations in sickness as are here described. They are not, however, rare among those who are not industrious; and who, nevertheless, when labouring under sickness, must be considered as having claims to assistance. In cases of long-protracted disease, instances of such a description do occur amongst those of the most industrious class. Such instances are still less rare among those women who are either widowed, or worse than widowed. It happens too frequently that modest and worthy women are united to men who are profligate and intemperate, by whom they are left to endure disease and poverty under the most aggravated forms. Among the children of such families also, instances are not rare of real suffering in sickness. To all such as have been described, a hospital would supply every thing which is needful, if not all they could wish. In a well-regulated hospital, they would find a comfortable lodging in a duly attempered atmosphere; would receive the food best suited to their various conditions; and would be attended by kind and discreet nurses, under the directions of a physician. In such a situation, the poor man's chance for relief would be equal perhaps to that of the most affluent, when affected by the same disease.

There are other persons, also, who are of great importance in society, to whom the relief afforded by a hospital is exceedingly appropriate. Such are generally those of good and industrious habits, who are affected with sickness, just as they are entering into active life, and who have not had time to provide for this calamity. Cases of this sort are frequently occurring. Disease is often produced by the very anxiety and exertions which belong to this period of life; and the best are the most liable to suffer. Of such a description, cases are often seen among journeymen mechanics and among servants. . . .

There is one class of sufferers who peculiarly claim all that benevolence can bestow, and for whom a hospital is most especially required. The virtuous and industrious are liable to become objects of public charity, in consequence of diseases of the mind. When those who are unfortunate in this respect are left without proper care, a calamity, which might have been transient, is prolonged through life. The number of such persons, who are rendered unable to provide for themselves, is probably greater than the public imagine; and, of these, a large proportion claim the assistance of the affluent. The expense which is attached to the care of the insane in private families is extremely great, and such as to ruin a whole family that is possessed of a competence under ordinary circumstances, when called upon to support one of its members in this situation. Even those who can pay the necessary expenses would perhaps find an institution, such as is proposed, the best situation in which they could place their unfortunate friends. It is worthy of the opulent men of this town, and consistent with their general character, to provide an asylum for the insane from every part of the Commonwealth. But if funds are raised for the purpose proposed, it is probable that the Legislature will grant some assistance, with a view to such an extension of its benefits.

Of another class, whose necessities would be removed by the establishment of a hospital, are women who are unable to provide for their own welfare and safety in one of nature's most trying hours. Houses for lying-in women have been found extremely useful in the large cities of Europe; and, although abuses may have arisen in consequence, these are such as are more easily prevented in a small than in a large town.

There are many others who would find great relief in a hospital, and many times have life preserved when otherwise it would be lost. Such especially are the subjects of accidental wounds and fractures among the poorer classes of our citizens; and the subjects of extraordinary diseases, in any part of the Commonwealth, who may require the long and careful attention of either the physician or surgeon. . . .

In addition to what has already been stated, there are a number of collateral advantages that would attend the establishment of a hospital in this place. These are the facilities for acquiring knowledge, which it would give to the students in the medical school established in this town. The means of medical education in New England are at present very limited, and totally inadequate to so important a purpose. Students of medicine cannot qualify themselves properly for their profession, without incurring heavy expenses, such as very few of them are able to defray. The only medical school of eminence in this country is that at Philadelphia, nearly four hundred miles distant from Boston; and the expense of attending that is so great, that students from this quarter rarely remain at it longer than one year. Even this advantage is enjoyed by very few, compared with the whole number. Those who are educated in New England have so few opportunities of attending to the practice of physic, that they find it impossible to learn some of the most important elements of the science of medicine, until after they have undertaken for themselves the care of the health and lives of their fellow-citizens. This care they undertake with very little knowledge, except that acquired from books;—a source whence it is highly useful and indispensable that they should obtain knowledge, but one from which alone they never can obtain all that is necessary to qualify them for their professional duties. With such deficiencies in medical education, it is needless to show to what evils the community is exposed.

To remedy evils so important and so extensive, it is necessary to have a medical school in New England. All the materials necessary to form this school exist among us. Wealth, abundantly sufficient, can be devoted to the purpose, without any individual's feeling the smallest privation of any, even of the luxuries of life. Every one is liable to suffer from the want of such a school; every one may derive, directly or indirectly, the greatest benefits from its establishment.

A hospital is an institution absolutely essential to a medical school, and one which would afford relief and comfort to thousands of the sick and miserable. On what other objects can the superfluities of the rich be so well bestowed?. . .

Hospitals and infirmaries are found in all the Christian cities of the Old World; and our large cities in the Middle States have institutions of this sort, which do great honor to the liberality and benevolence of their founders. We flatter ourselves that in this respect, as in all others, Boston may ere long assert her claim to equal praise.

We are, sir, very respectfully, your obedient servants,

JAMES JACKSON,
JOHN C. WARREN.

6. Walter Channing, a Harvard Medical Professor, Warns of the Dangers of Women Practicing Midwifery, 1820

The attention of the public having been lately turned to the subject of the employment of females as accoucheurs, has led to some discussion among the faculty and others with regard to the safety and expediency of introducing them into the practice of midwifery instead of physicians. There is, perhaps, no place of equal size, in which this branch of medical practice has been so entirely confined to male practitioners, as in this town. This circumstance having rendered it more difficult to come at the facts on this subject, it has been thought desirable that some statement should be made to enable the public to judge with fairness and impartiality. The circumstances, which would render females agreeable and most desirable as attendants

[Walter Channing], *Remarks on the Employment of Females as Practitioners in Midwifery. By a Physician* (Boston: Cummings and Hilliard, 1820), pp. 3–7, 18–21.

in these cases, are obvious to every one, but the objections to their employment are of a nature not so immediately perceived, except by physicians and those conversant in the practice of midwifery; and since one side of the case, from its very nature, is clearly before the public and can and does have its influence, it seems right that the opposite should be so stated and explained, as to have its fair counteracting operation, and give the public an opportunity to judge impartially of the merits of the case.

The question is, can the practice of midwifery be carried on with equal safety by female as by male practitioners? This is the only question which ought fairly to be considered, for no one can deny that safety is the principal consideration; so important indeed that we can conceive of none that can come in competition with it. If this be decided in the affirmative, the controversy is settled; for every other consideration would lead us to the preference of females. But it appears to me that the objections to this are of a most serious nature. Both the character and education of women disqualify them for the office.

I do not intend to imply any intellectual inferiority or incompetency in the sex. My objections are founded rather upon the nature of their moral qualities, than of the powers of their minds, and upon those very qualities, which render them, in their appropriate sphere, the pride, the ornament, and the blessing of mankind.

Women are distinguished for passive fortitude, firmness, &c. to a much greater degree than men; and this whether they are called to endure suffering themselves, or only witness it in others. They bear painful operations in surgery or witness them with a resolution at least equal to that of men. But this is all; their virtues of this kind are wholly passive. They have not that power of action, or that active power of mind, which is essential to the practice of the surgeon. They have less power of restraining and governing the natural tendency to sympathy, and are more disposed to yield to the expressions of acute sensibility. Where the responsibility in scenes of distress and danger does not fall upon them, when there is some one on whom they can lean, in whose skill and judgment they have entire confidence, they retain their collection and presence of mind; but where they become the principal agents, the feelings of sympathy are too powerful for the cool exercise of judgment. The profession of medicine does not afford a field for the display and indulgence of those finer feelings, which would be naturally called into operation by the circumstances in which a practitioner is placed. Not that a physician should be devoid of these feelings, or that he should attempt to extinguish them, or prevent their operation upon his mind, but they are to be so restrained, modified, and governed, as rather to form a principle of action, an element in the general character, than to be indulged on those particular occasions which have a peculiar tendency to call them into operation. . . .

The nature and progress of the mechanical part of a simple natural labour can be easily explained, and may be comprehended by the most limited understanding. Where then is the danger of trusting these cases, which form allowedly a very large proportion, to the hands of an intelligent and well educated woman? I answer, that it is wrong to look on labour as a mere mechanical process; it is a process in which every part of the system more or less partakes. This is by no means the only thing to be attended to. The local situation of the infant may be every way favourable, and yet the mother may be dying from an affection of some other part of the system. No one can thoroughly understand the nature and treatment of labour, who does not understand thoroughly *the profession of medicine as a whole.* . . .

No part of the profession can be practised without an acquaintance with every other part. The surgeon must be a physician, the oculist must be a physician, the accoucheur must be a physician; he must understand the general principles of medical practice, or he cannot be considered adequate to the treatment of the simplest case of labour; for circumstances occur, which not only require other assistance than that of nature, but which cannot be even ascertained to exist, except by a medical practitioner.

And this is perhaps the strongest objection to the employment of female accoucheurs, that we cannot expect them to be possessed of this essential part of their education. It is needless to go on to prove this; it is obvious that we cannot instruct women as we do men in the science of medicine; we cannot carry them into the dissecting room and the hospital; many of our more delicate feelings, much of our refined sensibility must be subdued, before we can submit to the sort of discipline required in the study of medicine; in females they must be destroyed; and I venture to say that a female could scarce pass through the course of education requisite to prepare her, as she ought to be prepared, for the practice of midwifery, without destroying those moral qualities of character, which are essential to the office. . . .

. . . [S]ickness, which is a heavy infliction, derives perhaps its greatest temporal alleviation from the kind and soothing attentions of a physician. It is not the duty of a medical practitioner merely to pass in cold and distant pomp into the bed chamber of the sick, to be satisfied with the dry formality of a prescription, and pass out again as indifferent as he entered. The profession has moral relations and moral duties. We should serve our patients with all our heart and soul; and they should know that we do it not merely because it is our business, or because we expect to be supported or to grow rich by the occupation, but because we feel for their welfare as friends, and as friends will strive for their advantage.

To the existence of these mutual feelings, nothing contributes more than the attendance of physicians in cases of midwifery. The interest excited in these cases is strong. Women seldom forget a practitioner who has conducted them tenderly and safely through parturition—they feel a familiarity with him, a confidence and reliance upon him, which are of the most essential mutual advantage in all their subsequent intercourse as physician and patient. On the other hand, the physician takes a deeper interest and feels a more intimate and personal connexion with those, whom he has attended in this scene of suffering and danger, than with patients of any other description.

It is principally on this account that the practice of midwifery becomes desirable to physicians. It is this which ensures to them the permanency and security of all their other business. . . .

As medical science has improved, it seemed at last to have been settled, that physicians regularly educated could alone be adequate to the exigencies of obstetric practice. This is the opinion held, taught, and defended, by the most eminent lecturers on midwifery in Europe. . . . Among ourselves, it is scarcely more than half a century since females were almost the only accoucheurs. It was one of the first and happiest fruits of improved medical education in America, that they were excluded from the practice; and it was only by the united and persevering exertions of some of the most distinguished individuals our profession has been able to boast, that this was effected.

7. A Young Physician Struggles to Get into Practice in Ohio, 1822

Cincinnati 1st mo 20—1822

Dear Brother

I received thy letter and must confess that my condition needs some appology but perhaps I may not be able to give one that will be deemed reasonable by any person who has never been in the same situation that I have since I saw thee last but I think those who have will think me excusable.

Finding that I was likely to be disappointed in geting money in the way I expected I went to Pittsburg to try to get into practice with some of the physicians there but was disappointed there[.] I then went to Beallsville to see if I could get my money of Dr Fowler where I was also unsuccessful and in my return I heard there was an opening at New Lancaster and resolved to go immediately there and to some other places with a prospect of entering into business but on arivin in the lower part of the state where the medical law had been attended to I found that I could not be admited as a candidate for license with out either having studied three years; learned the Greek and Latin language or attended a course of lectures at some medical college so that I have had a continued series of disappointments until I arived at Cincinnati, where I have succeeded in geting a sit of tickets on credit so that I am likely to spend the winter heare but what I am to do after that I do not know. I expect to sell my horse in the spring (which I have got a man to keep for his use) to pay my board; and perhaps part or all my books. I have determined upon no place to settle in the spring.

I am in hopes the Medical Colege will after a while [illegible] through its difficulties and asume a respectable standing. There are about thirty students this winter who are all well pleased with the professors and I think it probable our opportunities are not a great deal inferior to those in any college in the United States for what we miss in other things I think is amply made up in the intercourse we have with the professors which if there were a great number of students we could not have.

Daniel Drake M.D. teaches the theory and practice Jesse Smith M.D. Anatomy John D. Godman M.D. Surgery & demonstrative obstetrics Benjamin S. Bohrer M.D. Materia Medica & clinical practice, all of whom though young men are well qualified to fill their offices. Smith I think could scarcely be excelled, and though lectures on Materia Medica are generally deemed of little importance, yet in the way in which Bohrer delivers them they are a great source of information.

Elijah Slack A.M. is professor of Chimestry but is not much admired but Mr Best (with whom I board) delivers an excelent popular course so that our opportunities in that are also great. J. L. Wilson A.M. presented me with a ticket to attend a course on Moral Philosophy. I attend twenty seven lectures per week so that thee will guess I have little leisure.

Thee wished to know whither I still wanted the money from Carolina; I have never recieved a letter from Mt Pleasant since I left home and had debated writing

Joseph Stanton to Benjamin Stanton, Cincinnati, Ohio, January 20, 1822 (VFM 387), Archives, Ohio Historical Society, Columbus, Ohio.

to thee on that account but think it probable I shall if I can get it as it is not likely. I shall get into business so as to colect in time to pay for my tickets.

My respects to M.

adieu

Joseph Stanton

8. Samuel Thomson, a Botanic Healer, Decries the Regular Medical Profession as a Murderous Monopoly, 1822

There are three things which have in a greater or less degree, called the attention of men, viz: Religion, Government, and Medicine. In ages past, these things were thought by millions to belong to three classes of men, Priests, Lawyers and Physicians. The Priests held the things of religion in their own hands, and brought the people to their terms; kept the Scriptures in the dead languages, so that the common people could not read them. Those days of darkness are done away; the Scriptures are translated into our own language, and each one is taught to read for himself. Government was once considered as belonging to a few, who thought themselves "born only to rule." The common people have now become acquainted with the great secret of government; and know that "all men are born free and equal," and that Magistrates are put in authority, or out, by the voice of the people, who choose them for their public servants.

While these, and many other things are brought where "common people," can understand them; the knowledge and use of medicine, is in a great measure concealed in a dead language, and a sick man is often obliged to risk his life, where he would not risk a dollar; and should the apothecary or his apprentice make a mistake, the sick man cannot correct it, and thus is exposed to receive an instrument of death, instead of that which would restore him to health had he known good medicine. . . .

It is true that much of what is at this day called medicine, is deadly poison; and were people to know what is offered them of this kind, they would absolutely refuse ever to receive it as medicine. This I have long seen and known to be true; and have laboured hard for many years to convince them of the evils that attend such a mode of proceedure with the sick; and have turned my attention to those medicines that grow in our own country, which the God of nature has prepared for the benefit of mankind. Long has a general medicine been sought for, and I am confident I have found such as are universally applicable in all cases of disease, and which may be used with safety and success, in the hands of the people.

After thirty years study and repeated successful trials of the medicinal vegetables of our own country, in all the diseases incident to our climate; I can with well grounded assurance, recommend my system of practice and medicines to the public, as salutary and efficacious.

Great discoveries and improvements have been made in various arts and sciences since the first settlement of our country, while its medicines have been very

---

Samuel Thomson, *New Guide to Health; Or, Botanic Family Physician* (Boston: E. G. House, 1822), [mispaginated] pp. 183–186, 202–203.

much neglected. As these medicines, suited to every disease, grow spontaneously upon our own soil; as they are better adapted to our constitution; as the price of imported drugs is very high; it follows, whether we consult health which is of primary importance, or expence, a decided preference should be given to the former, as an object of such magnitude as no longer to be neglected. Yet in the introduction of those medicines I have been violently opposed, and my theory and practice condemned, notwithstanding the demonstrative proofs in their favor. But those who thus condemn, have taken no pains to throw off prejudice, and examine the subject with candor and impartiality.—Such as have, are thoroughly satisfied of their utility, and superior excellence. . . .

Being born in a new country, at that time almost an howling wilderness, my advantages for an education were very small; but possessing a natural gift for examining the things of Nature, my mind was left entirely free to follow that inclination, by enquiring into the meaning of the great variety of objects around me.

Possessing a body like other men, I was led to inquire into the nature of the component parts of what man is made. I found him composed of the four elements—Earth, Water, Air and Fire. The earth and water I found were the solids; the air and fire the fluids. The two first I found to be the component parts; the two last kept him in motion. Heat, I found, was life; and Cold, death. Each one who examines into it will find that all constitutions are alike. I shall now describe the fuel which continues the fire, or life of man. This is contained in two things—food and medicines; which are in harmony with each other; often grow in the same field, to be used by the same people. People who are capable of raising their food, and preparing the same, may as easily learn to collect and prepare all their medicines and administer the same, when it is needed. Our life depends on heat; food is the fuel that kindles and continues that heat. The digestive powers being correct, causes the food to consume; this continues the warmth of the body, by continually supporting the fire.

The stomach is the deposit from which the whole body is supported. The heat is maintained in the stomach by consuming the food; and all the body and limbs receive their proportion of nourishment and heat from that source; as the whole room is warmed by the fire which is consumed in the fire-place. The greater the quantity of wood consumed in the fire-place, the greater the heat in the room. So in the body; the more food, well digested, the more heat and support through the whole man. By constantly receiving food into the stomach, which is sometimes not suitable for the best nourishment, the stomach becomes foul, so that the food is not well digested. This causes the body to lose its heat—then the appetite fails; the bones ache, and the man is sick in every part of the whole frame.

This situation of the body shows the need of medicine, and the kind needed; which is such as will clear the stomach and bowels, and restore the digestive powers. When this is done, the food will raise the heat again, and nourish the whole man. All the art required to do this is, to know what medicine will do it, and how to administer it, as a person knows how to clean a stove and the pipe when clogged with soot, that the fire may burn free, and the whole room be warmed as before. . . .

The practice of giving poison as medicine, which is so common among the medical faculty at the present day, is of the utmost importance to the public; and is a subject that I wish to bring home to the serious consideration of the whole body of the people of this country, and enforce in the strongest manner on their minds the pernicious consequences that have happened, and are daily taking place by reason of giving mercury, arsenic, nitre, opium, and other deadly poisons to cure disease. It is admitted by those who make use of these things, that the introducing them into the system is very dangerous and that they often prove fatal. . . .

Those who make use of these things as medicine, seem to cloak the administring them under the specious pretence of great skill and art in preparing and using them; but this kind of covering will not blind the people, if they would examine it and think for themselves, instead of believing that every thing said or done by a learned man must be right; for poison given to the sick by a person of the greatest skill, will have exactly the same effect as it would if given by a fool.—The fact is the operation of it is diametrically opposed to nature, and every particle of it, that is taken into the system, will strengthen the power of the enemy to health.

 E S S A Y S

Looking at health care providers and their clients in two local contexts, these two essays display the diversity of healers available to sick Americans in the early republic. In the first essay, Harvard University historian Laurel Thatcher Ulrich focuses on the practice of Maine midwife Martha Ballard from 1785 to 1800, which Ulrich reconstructs using Ballard's diary. Examining the interaction between male physicians and female midwives, Ulrich reevaluates the shift from female to male obstetrics and reveals the social and professional issues at stake when elite physicians such as Walter Channing began to argue stridently that women were not suited to either midwifery or the wider practice of medicine.

Lisa Rosner of Stockton State College, in the second essay, explores the variety of healers practicing in the nation's largest city. Her essay investigates how medical practitioners in early-nineteenth-century Philadelphia were affected by the presence of the University of Pennsylvania medical school, which, from its founding in 1765, was selectively modeled on Edinburgh University. Rosner shows that University of Pennsylvania graduates and auditors, however prominent, did not succeed in dominating the city's practice, and that most medical care continued to come from practitioners other than male physicians. The two essays invite the questions: How could prospective patients distinguish among these assorted practitioners? In selecting a healer, how might a sick American's choice be influenced by their own residence, status, and gender? How and why was the standing of regular physicians in this medical marketplace changing?

The Medical Challenge to Midwifery

LAUREL THATCHER ULRICH

Some time in the afternoon or evening of October 9, 1794, David Sewall of Hallowell sent word to Martha Ballard that his wife was "unwell." There was nothing unusual in the call or in the casual entry in Mrs. Ballard's diary, "I was there all night." In her sixteen years as a midwife, Martha Ballard had lost many nights' sleep attending a woman in labor. This birth would be unusual, however. On October 10,

Laurel Thatcher Ulrich, "Martha Ballard and the Medical Challenge to Midwifery," in *Maine in the Early Republic: From Revolution to Statehood,* ed. Charles E. Clark (Hanover and London: University Press of New England, 1988), pp. 165–172, 174–176, 179–180. Copyright © 1988 by University Press of New England, reprinted by permission of University Press of New England.

in Mrs. Sewall's chamber, a minor drama in the history of American midwifery unfolded. "They were intimidated," wrote Mrs. Ballard, "& Calld Dr. Page who gave my patient 20 drops of Laudanum which put her into such a stupor her pains (which were regular & promising) in a manner stopt till near night when she pukt & they returned & shee was delivered at 7 hour Evening of a son her first Born."

The three elements in this story—the patient's "intimidation," the doctor's employment of laudanum, and the midwife's annoyance—fit perfectly into the larger history of childbearing in late eighteenth century America. Recent studies have concluded that the transition from traditional midwifery to medical obstetrics began in the northern United States between 1760 and 1820 and that it was a consequence both of new medical technology and of changes in the attitudes of women. Midwives had always been taught to call doctors in medical emergencies, but beginning in the 1760s in urban centers like Philadelphia, New York, and Boston, doctors trained in Edinburgh and London began officiating at normal births, employing forceps to hasten delivery and administering opiates to relieve pain. . . .

Although traditional midwifery would persist among immigrants and in isolated rural communities to the end of the nineteenth century, the physicians who founded America's first medical societies and colleges were successful in associating medical delivery with scientific progress. By 1820, an influential Boston physician could pronounce the exclusion of women from the practice of obstetrics one of "the first and happiest fruits of improved medical education in America." . . .

Women's historians have argued that male doctors promoted "science" at serious cost to women. Midwives were not only deprived of their occupation but were also shut out of the new medical education. Childbearing women were also hurt as birth became a medical event to be managed by interventionist attendants. Giving up the comforting circle of female support, mothers faced an increasing threat of infection and the possibility of overdoses of anesthesia or damage from forceps, as medical education failed to keep pace with the expansion of the profession. "Only after 1940," Judith Walzer Leavitt has argued, "did medicine begin to achieve a record of safety commensurate with the promises it had held out to women centuries earlier."

Martha Ballard's account of Hannah Sewall's delivery seems to summarize, then, the key themes in the transformation of childbirth in the late eighteenth century: A traditional midwife patiently waiting for the operations of nature was upstaged by an interventionist physician whose opiates promised a frightened young woman relief from pain. A closer look at the participants in this drama reinforces that impression. At 59, Martha Ballard came to Mrs. Sewall's chamber with the authority of her own motherhood as well as with the specialized skills she had acquired in her sixteen years as a midwife. Benjamin Page, on the other hand, was barely 24, still unmarried, fresh from his apprenticeship with Dr. Thomas Kittredge of Andover, Massachusetts. Yet he brought the promise of the new "scientific" obstetrics. In Dr. Kittredge's library he had probably read the works of Dr. William Smellie, the British physician who popularized the new medical obstetrics. Under Kittredge's supervision he may have used the improved forceps Smellie designed. . . .

All the elements characterizing the transition to medical obstetrics seem to have been in place by 1794 on the Maine frontier. Yet Hannah Sewall's delivery was only one among 48 that Martha Ballard performed in that year, and only one of the 797 deliveries she recorded in her diary between January 1785 and May 1812.

Seen in this context, Dr. Page's intrusion was a minor annoyance, a bungling effort set right by nature. There was no question in Martha Ballard's mind that she knew more about delivering babies than Ben Page, whom she once described as "that poor unfortunate man in the practice." Her practice was increasing, not decreasing, in 1794. Only after 1800, when age and frequent illness undermined her strength and when a move to a new farm took her farther away from the river and from major roads, did she sharply curtail her practice.

Martha Ballard's diary gives us a surer sense of the differences between "male" and "female" obstetrics than earlier studies based largely on prescriptive literature and on the lives of medical leaders. In late eighteenth century Hallowell, doctors were not as scientific or midwives as ignorant as older accounts would suggest, nor was there as much friction between the two specialties as more recent literature might lead us to believe. For the most part, medical obstetrics and midwifery co-existed peacefully. Yet there were important differences between men and women practitioners. That doctors were both better paid and less experienced than midwives created a troublesome discrepancy between the promise and the practice of the new medical obstetrics. Ironically, it was not "science" that undermined traditional midwifery but a new appreciation by doctors of the "ordinary" births that had long been managed by women.

Born in Oxford, Massachusetts, in 1735, Martha Moore Ballard emigrated to the Kennebec River country in 1777 with her husband, Ephraim, and five children. . . . Ephraim Ballard was a miller and surveyor. Although by no means a wealthy man, he was a respected citizen who served for a time as selectman of Hallowell. Martha Ballard was a dutiful and productive housewife, who raised pigs and poultry, cultivated a large garden, and produced both woolen and linen cloth in addition to practicing midwifery and physic. There is no indication that she had anything more than a primary education, though her younger brother, Jonathan, graduated from Harvard College in 1761 and eventually became the minister of the First Church of Rochester, Massachusetts. She later noted that she delivered her first baby in 1778, just after coming to Maine. Although she may have kept some sort of record of deliveries from that point on, her diary begins in 1785, the year she turned fifty. It closes in May 1812, a month before her death at the age of 77. . . .

The categories *doctor* and *midwife* inadequately describe the diversity of medical practice in this eighteenth century town. Hallowell's "doctors" ranged from the eminently visible Dr. Daniel Cony, Justice of the Peace, Representative to the General Court, and founding President of the Kennebec Medical Association, to the anonymous "negro woman doctor" who appears two or three times in the diary. Not until after 1796, when Benjamin Vaughan arrived in Hallowell with an M.D. from Edinburgh, did the area have a college-trained physician. Although most male physicians had served apprenticeships, it would be a serious mistake to read back into this period twentieth century notions of "medical science."

Doctor Cony, for example, had trained with Dr. Samuel Curtis of Marlborough, Massachusetts, a Harvard graduate, who later practiced in New Hampshire where he published "A Valuable Collection of Recipes" that included, in addition to homespun medical remedies, formulas for removing grease spots, bedbugs, and fleas, and for bleaching straw, mending china, and making red hair black. His work is a striking example of the practicality and disdain for theory that characterized

New England medicine, even of the "professional" variety, in the late eighteenth century. In his *American Medical Biography,* published in 1828, Thomas Thacher praised Benjamin Page for his treatment of spotted fever between 1810 and 1816 and acknowledged the "Moral rectitude and public virtue" of Daniel Cony, but he concluded that the District of Maine "possessed little claim to the merit of contributing to the improvement of medical science." Clearly, though there were the beginnings of medical organization in Hallowell before 1800 (Dr. Cony was a member of the Massachusetts Medical Society as early as 1787), there was very little "science," even by contemporary standards.

It is equally inappropriate to distinguish between midwives and doctors, as some writers do, by saying that one group has been concerned with a natural process (birth) and the other with a medical event (illness). Like most early American midwives, Martha Ballard not only delivered babies but also treated the sick. She seems to have specialized in diseases of women and children, though she also treated grown men, especially those suffering from burns, rashes, or frostbite. Mrs. Ballard's patients came to her house seeking salves, pills, syrups, ointments, or simply advice. Forty to seventy times a year she went to them, spending a few hours or several days administering "clisters" (enemas), dressing burns, or bathing inflamed throats. She did not pull teeth, set bones, or let blood (though once she drew blood from a cat and applied it to a man who was suffering from shingles). She cut infant tongues, lanced abscessed breasts, and composed remedies for intestinal worms and the itch. She also dressed and laid out the dead. Martha Ballard was both a midwife and a doctor; significantly, her most frequent term for labor was "illness."

The diary mentions six women—Mrs. Fletcher, Mrs. Hinkley, Mrs. Ingraham, Mrs. Clark, Mrs. Cox, and Mrs. Winslow—often enough or in such a context as to suggest that they also were midwives. Whether they practiced physic is difficult to say, although it is perfectly clear that several local physicians practiced obstetrics. Doctors Cony, Williams, and Hubbard, who were working in Hallowell or nearby towns by 1785, performed deliveries. In fact, Dr. Cony's only known literary contribution to the Massachusetts Medical Society, a one-page paper submitted in 1787, described "a circumstance which I had never before met with" in a delivery that he himself had performed in August of that year. Dr. Page, who arrived in Hallowell in 1791, and Dr. Parker of Pittston, who appears in the diary at about the same time, also delivered babies. Dr. Samuel Colman did not, nor did Dr. Steven Barton of Vassalboro, Martha Ballard's brother-in-law.

Yet Martha Ballard's diary demonstrates that relations between midwives and physicians were more cooperative than competitive. Mrs. Ballard delivered Dr. Colman's children and even attended the doctor himself during an illness; she borrowed medicines from Daniel Cony and he from her; and on various occasions she summoned Drs. Hubbard, Williams, and Cony to her own patients. For the most part, her remedies seem to have been compatible with theirs. When her daughter, Hannah, became delirious about ten days after delivering, Mrs. Ballard sent for Dr. Cony, who simply, as she said, "approved of what I had done—advised me to continue my medisin till it had opperation." In general, her records support the conclusion of Richard Brown that "learned" and "folk" medicine in Massachusetts "were part of the same medical spectrum and overlapped considerably." . . .

In addition to their joint commitment to what Martha Ballard would have called "pukes" and "purges," doctors and midwives had something else in common: the part-time nature of their work. As housewives, the midwives had heavy burdens at home including responsibilities for gardening, food processing, and animal care, but the doctors also divided their interests, none so strikingly as Dr. Steven Barton, who was a carpenter as well as a physician. In June 1774, for example, he charged Jonathan Ballard for "Visits & attendance" to his sick child and then for making a coffin. Daniel Cony, Hallowell's most distinguished physician, was a judge, politician, agriculturist, and land speculator. His varied interests were typical of gentlemen physicians of the period. In 1808 he apologized to the President of the Massachusetts Medical Society for failing to convene a group of doctors in the District of Maine, explaining that "The dispersed situation of your Committee joined with their various avocations has prevented a meeting."

Nor did Hallowell's practitioners claim a certain set of patients as their own. In troublesome cases, nearly everyone with any expertise—and some without—offered advice. When Martha Ballard's niece, Parthena Pitts, was suffering from a prolonged illness, she got up one morning about an hour after sunrise, as her aunt reported it, and "went out & milkt the last milk from the Cow into her mouth & swallowed it." This peculiar remedy had been "recommended as very Beneficial by Mr. Amos Page." An eighteenth century patient might summon more than one doctor or midwife at once and then employ whomever she chose. Mrs. Parker did not think it amiss to borrow Mrs. Ballard's horse "to go and see the negro woman doctor." Nor did a sense of loyalty to Dr. Colman, who had earlier treated him, prevent Calvin Edson from summoning Dr. Williams as well, or from applying to Martha Ballard for salve. Some of this overlapping may have originated with the healers themselves—one practitioner might understandably consult with another—but even allowing for that, the territorial boundaries seem to have been very loose.

Perhaps the best evidence of Martha Ballard's cooperative relationship with male doctors is her attendance at autopsies. She observed at least three "dissections" between 1794 and 1801, carefully recording the results in her diary. Although none of these cases was obstetrical, two of the subjects were women and the third a small child. At Nabby Andrews' autopsy in September of 1800, Mrs. Ballard reported that twelve doctors and three midwives were present, though she did not give names. That the women were there at all argues that medical practice in frontier Maine was still relatively open; neither professional exclusiveness nor womanly delicacy barred Hallowell's midwives from what was after all an important educational experience. That they were outnumbered four to one by male doctors testifies to the localized nature of their specialty as much as to their minority position in the medical world. The twelve doctors had no doubt gathered from miles around.

Thus Martha Ballard's diary modifies the picture of late eighteenth century midwifery presented in secondary accounts. In Hallowell, relations between doctors and midwives were less antagonistic and the two specialties less separate than we might have supposed. . . .

. . . [B]y any numerical measurement, midwifery prevailed over medical delivery in late eighteenth century Hallowell.

Yet the seemingly casual appearances of Drs. Cony, Williams, Parker, and Hubbard at the bedsides of Hallowell women, like the more dramatic incursion of Benjamin Page, undermined a traditional distribution of responsibility. Midwives had always been taught to summon a doctor in an emergency. Dismembering a dead fetus was a necessary skill for a surgeon; knowing when to let blood or to prescribe drugs was a proper role for a physician. In normal deliveries, the quite different talents of a midwife were enough. That even a few Hallowell families could summon *both* a doctor and a midwife to a *normal* delivery, employing whichever attendant arrived first, suggests a remarkable change.

We must consider here the different backgrounds of doctors and midwives. Although medical reformers lamented the haphazard training of New England physicians, most male doctors could make some small claim to "learning." At the least they had mastered prescribed texts and spent a year or two as an apprentice. Dr. Page had attended Phillips-Exeter Academy before apprenticing with Dr. Thomas Kittredge. A hundred years earlier, of course, a literary education would have been enough; many New England ministers doubled as physicians.

For midwives, giving birth themselves was an essential part of the training process; assisting at other women's deliveries was another. A traditional midwife was simply the most skilled member of an assemblage of female neighbors who assisted at each birth. After one delivery, for example, Mrs. Ballard wrote, "my comp[anions] were Old Lady Cox, Pitts, Sister Barton, Moody, Soal, & Witherel." At the Abial Herington house in June 1796, she noted, "there were 22 in number slept under that roof the night." A doctor might be twenty-four years old and unmarried, like Benjamin Page, but only in middle age, and usually only after her own childbearing years were over, could a woman acquire the full stature of a midwife.

Physicians can be located in town records and on tax lists (as well as in Martha Ballard's diary) by the title *Doctor*, which originally was simply a designation for a man of eminent learning. No woman, whether a midwife or a practitioner of physic, can be discovered by title. Hallowell's mysterious black healer might be referred to as a "doctor" or "doctoress," but she is never called *Doctor* Black. If midwives had any sort of distinguishing label in this period, it was probably the word *old*. Mrs. Ballard referred to "Old Mrs. Fletcher," "Old Mrs. Ingraham," and "Old Lady Cox," and when Mrs. Marsh came to visit, she wrote of her as "The Old Lady." In traditional society such terms connoted respect, a respect for expertise acquired by experience rather than through systematic study.

Martha Ballard respected the formal training of Hallowell's physicians. She had obviously been taught, like other midwives, to call a doctor in an emergency. On November 11, 1785, when she arrived at Henry Babcok's house too late for the delivery and found the patient "greatly ingered by some mishap," though Mrs. Smith, who had delivered the baby, did "not allow that shee was sencible of it," Mrs. Ballard summoned Dr. Williams who "prescribed remedies." The inexperienced midwife had undoubtedly caused the injury. Though Martha Ballard felt competent to "inquire into the Cause," she did not attempt to correct it without a physician.

Only once in 797 births, however, did she herself feel incapable of handling a delivery. She described the delivery of Mrs. Prescott on May 19, 1792 in the following manner:

> Her Case was Lingering till 7 pm I removd dificulties & waited for natures opperations till then, when she was more severely atackt with obstructions which alarmed me much I desired Doct Hubard might be sent for which request was complied with but by Divine assistance I performed the oppration, which was blisst with the preservation of the lives off mother and infant the life of the latter I dispard of for some time.

In the margin, she wrote: "the most perelous sien [scene] I Ever past thro in the Cours of my practice blessed be God for his goodness." Her ability to negotiate this "perelous sien" without Doctor Hubbard's assistance may have given Martha Ballard renewed faith in her own abilities, although characteristically she gave the credit to God. . . .

. . . Midwives had skills that doctors needed.

The Massachusetts physician who in 1820 wrote *Remarks on the Employment of Females as Practitioners in Midwifery* understood the problem perfectly. "A man must be a universal practitioner in midwifery, before he is qualified for a practitioner in difficult cases," he wrote. That is, a person unfamiliar with normal deliveries could not manage preternatural ones. If midwifery were reintroduced among the upper classes in Boston, he argued, there would be an inevitable decline in the quality of emergency obstetrics because physicians would be denied the day-to-day experience that good medicine required. That midwives might learn to manage difficult as well as normal deliveries was to him simply unthinkable. No woman could pass through the dissecting room and the hospital without losing "those moral qualities of character, which are essential to the office." We can only wonder what he would have thought of Martha Ballard and the other midwives who attended autopsies in late eighteenth century Hallowell.

Seen in this light, Benjamin Page's effort to administer laudanum at the delivery of Hannah Sewall is hardly the ominous foreshadowing of later medical triumphs that it seemed at first glance. Rather, it is yet another example . . . of the limited obstetrical experience of eighteenth century physicians. As long as Martha Ballard continued to dominate the practice of obstetrics in the region, it is difficult to imagine Benjamin Page or any other doctor acquiring the practical expertise that the new medical obstetrics demanded. That was exactly the point: It was not Dr. Page's competence but his incompetence that made it essential for him to practice midwifery.

The history of midwifery in nineteenth century Maine is yet to be written, but the general direction of change can be glimpsed in a document published at Norridgewock in March of 1823 by an association of Somerset County physicians. Following the example of Boston doctors of a generation earlier, these men established fees for various treatments, from "Extirpating tumors" to performing an "Operation for Hare-Lip," each man agreeing not to "under value his own services" nor to "undermine the practice of others" by charging less than the minimum prescribed. The doctors also pledged not to visit a patient previously treated by another physician "unless it shall be the frank and unbiased wish of the party calling him to dismiss the other from further attendance." Significantly, their rates included $4 for attendance "in ordinary Obstetric cases" and $8 "In cases where a Midwife has been first employed."

The Somerset County agreement neatly defines the structural changes that transformed the medical world of Martha Ballard into the medical world with which most of us are familiar. These doctors cared about territorial boundaries in a way that she would have found puzzling. They were also bent on destroying the old system that had allowed midwives to perform "in ordinary cases" while calling doctors in an emergency. By charging twice as much for backup calls as for deliveries, they put extraordinary pressure on midwives as well as on their clients. The expected outcome, we may be sure, was that parturient women would call a doctor first.

Whether the Somerset physicians were successful in their reforms we do not know, yet the long-term direction of change is clear. The expansion of medical obstetrics was part of a larger process through which medicine changed from a learned specialty to a full-time profession. For women the consequences of that shift cannot be overemphasized. Martha Ballard had sustained her practice while simultaneously running a household, supervising textile production, and rearing her youngest children. In her century such a pattern of part-time specialization was not unusual—for men or women. By the middle of the nineteenth century, this condition was no longer so. Doctors were doctors; midwives were also housewives. Ironically, then, the medical enlightenment of the eighteenth century, in teaching physicians to value ordinary midwifery, eventually guaranteed the exclusion of women from its practice. Still denied "learning," women no longer had the advantage of "experience."

None of this could have been foreseen, of course, on that October day in 1794 when Martha Ballard encountered Dr. Page at the delivery of Hannah Sewall. Having delivered forty babies already that year and having made dozens of medical calls, she had reason to feel superior to young Ben Page, "that poor unfortunate man in the practice."

The Philadelphia Medical Marketplace

LISA ROSNER

The impact of Edinburgh medical education on Philadelphia medicine has been well-known and well-attested since 1765, when John Morgan first drew an explicit comparison between Edinburgh and Philadelphia in his *Discourse upon the Institution of Medical Schools in America.* "[T]he reputation of [Edinburgh] is raised to such a height," Morgan wrote, "that . . . it already rivals, if not surpasses that of every other school of Physic in Europe." The "great resort of medical students" attending classes, "bring to the university and city considerable advantages, and, in return, carry the fame of their learning and their professors to every quarter of the globe." Surely if a similar "school of Physic" was founded in Philadelphia, Morgan thought, the same advantages would accrue to the city and University. . . .

Yet . . . Russell Maulitz and John Harley Warner have shown that physicians educated abroad were selective in what they chose to import; their assessment or even memory of their own training sometimes differed considerably from the original model. It is therefore reasonable to inquire what the consequences were of transplanting it to a new setting. . . .

The "Edinburgh model" was . . . a two-tiered model of medical education. Any student, whatever his previous background or studies, could attend classes. But only the privileged few, whose families could support them through three years of study, and whose Latin could sustain them through a thesis and examination, could graduate. The result was to provide access to medical lectures for the many, while

Lisa Rosner, "Thistle on the Delaware: Edinburgh Medical Education and Philadelphia Practice, 1800–1825," *Social History of Medicine* 5 (1992): 19–20, 22–40. Reprinted by permission of Oxford University Press. Copyright © 1992.

limiting the highest honour of MD to the select few. It was a model finely tuned to accommodate conditions of medical practice in Great Britain, where incomes of practitioners could vary enormously, from £10,000 for prominent London physicians to £400 for country general practitioners without MDs. The accessibility of Edinburgh lectures allowed each prospective practitioner to invest as much in his education as he could afford based on his expectation of practice; predictably, students planning on provincial practice generally attended only one year of lectures. . . .

Like Edinburgh University medical faculty, professors in the University of Pennsylvania medical school offered courses in medical subjects and also examined students for graduation. They, too, received no salaries, and had to rely on student fees for their income. Wherever possible they took Edinburgh professors and teachings as their models. Clinical lectures at the Pennsylvania Hospital, for example, were offered within a year of the medical school's inception. As at Edinburgh, incorporation of clinical experience into medical education produced some tension between student demand and patient welfare. Elizabeth Drinker wrote with disapproval of an operation performed on a young servant by Professors Philip Syng Physick and Benjamin Rush "with 6 of their students." "It is right that [medical students] should learn," she thought, "but 'twas making a great matter out of a little business, and enough to frighten the child."

The faculty did make some concessions to what they believed to be American conditions: they offered classes for only four months of the year, rather than six, and required two, rather than three years for graduation. Graduation examinations were also held in English, rather than Latin. The result of these concessions was that a larger proportion of University of Pennsylvania medical students—thirty-eight per cent—graduated. However, the basic two-tiered system of the Edinburgh model persisted, with the majority of non-graduates, eighty per cent, studying for only one year. . . .

As in Great Britain, this system was well-suited to accommodating disparities in the expected income of practitioners. And as in Edinburgh, the faculty acquired fame and fortune, as well as a stable student body. By 1844, the University of Pennsylvania medical school could "boast among its alumni, of thousands of the most respectable practitioners in the country." . . .

Yet the very success of the University of Pennsylvania medical school brought its own problems. The example of a successfully functioning medical school where faculty income was based on student fees inspired many new medical schools, including what came to be called "proprietary" medical schools, a persistent feature of American medical education through to the early twentieth century. In Great Britain a combination of Parliamentary supervision of universities, and traditional guilds acting to preserve their privileges, restricted the number of institutions that could award MDs. The mere threat of a Royal Commission to Investigate the Universities of Scotland was enough to force the Universities of St. Andrews and Aberdeen to stop awarding MDs without examination. The London hospital schools, however well-established, could never persuade the Royal College of Physicians of London to accept their diplomas as the equivalent of a university MD. The United States, in contrast, imported the system of accessible medical education without governmental or guild control of it; the result was a proliferation of institutions offering medical education and degrees.

Another Old World feature of medical life that had not been imported were separate Colleges of Physicians and Surgeons which regulated the practice of medicine within Philadelphia. In Edinburgh, only MDs could belong to the College of Physicians, which had a monopoly over the practice of internal medicine in the city. Fellows of the College of Surgeons had a monopoly over the practice of surgery and pharmacy. John Morgan, in 1765, had called for the separation of physicians and surgeons within Philadelphia, as they were separated in Britain. "[L]et each cultivate his separate branch apart," Morgan wrote, "the knowledge of medicine will then be daily improved, and it may be practised with greater accuracy and skill as well as a less expence." This aroused great anger among Philadelphia physicians, who generally practiced medicine, surgery, and pharmacy. . . .

By ignoring Morgan's call for separate Colleges, then, the other founders of the University of Pennsylvania had transplanted the Edinburgh model of medical education without the legal privileges that had encouraged its growth. This meant that Philadelphia provided a much sterner test of that education than Edinburgh itself. Graduates of the University of Pennsylvania had no legal monopoly over the practice of any kind of medicine in their University's home town; Philadelphia surgeons had no guild regulations to force them to attend classes. If university-educated practitioners nonetheless dominated medical practice in Philadelphia, that would certainly be a convincing testimonial to the value accorded their education. In order to investigate this, we must turn from medical education to medical practice. The Philadelphia city directories for 1800, 1811, 1819, and 1825 list 709 people who can be taken as medical practitioners, variously described as "physicians," "cuppers and bleeders," "dentists," "leeches," "midwives," and "nurses." If we exclude for a moment the nurses on the assumption that they were usually called as auxiliaries to other practitioners, that leaves 501, only thirty-three per cent of whom were University of Pennsylvania MDs. An additional six per cent attended classes without graduating. That percentage is not quite fair to the graduates, though, since the number went up considerably in the period. If we just examine the practitioners listed in the city directory for 1825, excluding nurses, we find that forty-nine per cent of them were University of Pennsylvania MDs, with an additional seven per cent who attended courses without graduating. Obviously graduates and auditors did not monopolize medical practice, nor supplant other kinds of practitioners. Equally obviously the number of graduates in the city increased substantially, attesting to the perceived value of university study in medicine.

We can use city directories to analyse what was happening more closely. People could be designated as practitioners in the main part of the directory after their names, or in the separate listings of "Physicians," "Cuppers and Bleeders," "Bleeders with Leeches," "Dentists," "Midwives" and "Nurses" at the beginning or end of the directory. I have used both designations wherever possible to find out as much as possible about types of practice. . . .

Descriptions which come from the directories will be indicated in quotation marks because they were probably self-designations. For example, it is not clear that all of the "Physicians" who made up an average of forty-four per cent of the practitioners listed in fact had an MD degree; indeed it is likely that they did not. Another twenty-four per cent of practitioners were variously listed as "cuppers," "bleeders," "leeches," surgeons," "dentists," and "toothdrawers." Sometimes these designations were coupled with "hairdresser" or "barber," but I have not included anyone who was listed only as a hairdresser or barber. I have grouped them together because the same practitioners were often listed with several descriptions, suggesting that they carried out the functions of the group called "surgeon-apothecaries," later "general practitioners," in Great Britain. "Midwives" averaged six per cent of the practitioners over the period, but it is likely that they were under-represented in the directories, since women's occupations were not systematically collected. The percentage of "nurses" is complicated by the fact that only eight were listed in the 1800 directory, making them eight per cent of practitioners listed. Thereafter, however, they average twenty-eight per cent of practitioners. Again, there may well have been more who were not listed.

These types of practitioners were not evenly distributed around the city. The most obvious division was based on gender. Male practitioners, whether listed as "Physician" or the variants of "Cupper and Bleeder," were generally found on the wider central streets of the city between Arch and Spruce and between 2nd and 6th. Female practitioners, whether listed as "Midwife" or "Nurse" or "Doctress" or "Bleeder with Leeches," were nearly always located either in alleys and narrow cross streets or beyond the central section of the city, where rents were cheaper. The geographical distribution thus provides one more example of the historical commonplace that women practitioners earned less than men. More forcefully put, it suggests that male and female practitioners were often part of different social groups and lived in very different material circumstances. Stuart Blumin has demonstrated that "gentlefolk," by and large, dominated the streets, while artisans were clustered in the alleys; these differences in occupation led to striking differences even between the amount of space per occupant in houses on streets and in alleys. The difference also provides a kind of metaphor for the invisibility of female practitioners in histories of medicine, for many of the alleys in which they lived have disappeared.

The "Physicians" who made up the largest group of Philadelphia practitioners included all of the luminaries of Philadelphia medical life, such as the Professors of the University of Pennsylvania and the Fellows of the College of Physicians. These were generally the preferred practitioners for the well-to-do. Elizabeth Drinker's diary has many references to "Dr Shippen," Professor of Anatomy, Surgery, and Midwifery, "Dr Rush," Professor of the Institutes of Medicine and Clinical Medicine, and "Dr Kuhn," Professor of the Theory and Practice of Medicine. Adam Kuhn was also one of Mrs. Margaret Coxe's favourite sources for her medicinal recipe book, contributing "receipts" for such domestic health staples as beef tea and tooth powder, as well as treatments for indigestion, wounds, and ringworm. Professor Philip Syng Physick contributed a "receipt for Ashes Tea—to cure Indigestion, and a bilious habit;" and Thomas Tickell Hewson, President of the College of Physicians of Philadelphia, one for "Eye Water for inflamed—or weak eyes." As we will see, neither the Drinkers nor Margaret Coxe looked exclusively to élite physicians for medical care. The familiarity of the references to Dr Shippen or Dr Kuhn, though, and the extent to which their advice was incorporated into home health care shows that these men had established precisely the kind of cordial physician-family relationship that was the goal of well-educated and ambitious medical men.

The listing of "Physician" included the other, less prominent practitioners who can be documented as having received an MD. It could also include practitioners who cannot be so documented. This may be because they received a medical degree elsewhere and we simply have no record of it. It might also be that they simply called themselves "Physician" without bothering to take a degree. It is not clear that Isaac Cathrall, for example, who studied in Edinburgh in 1791 and practiced in Philadelphia as a "Physician" at least from 1800 through 1819, ever obtained an MD. The twenty-six "Physicians" who studied at the University of Pennsylvania without graduating also would have had little incentive to go elsewhere for the MD, since they could set up a practice without it. It seems unlikely that Clark Anderson, who attend lectures at the University in 1811 and was also listed as practising at 148 South Street that year, ever took time from his practice to travel to another state to graduate, even though he was listed as "MD" in the 1819 directory, still at 148 South Street. W. P. Chandler studied for three years from 1810 to 1812, but did not graduate; he was listed variously as "Physician," "Man-Midwife" and "Dentist" in the city directories in 1811 and 1819. He, like Thomas Hall, who also attended classes for three years without graduating and was listed as MD in 1825, could have argued that having studied for more years than was required for graduation made it unnecessary to formally obtain the MD. Certainly there was no law requiring them to do so, and they may have felt, like Alexander Lesassier after his year of study at Edinburgh, that their education allowed them to "rank with the highest of them." Even in 1825, when the Philadelphia directory explicitly stated that its list included only "MD Practising Physicians in the City and Suburbs," there is no evidence that all the "Physicians" listed really did have MDs. The only practitioners affected adversely by increased consciousness of credentials were those who obviously could not have obtained an MD, the small number of women and "persons of color" listed in the main part of the directory as "doctress" or "doctor" respectively. In 1800 Martha Brand, with "doctress" after her name, was also listed separately with other "Physicians." But neither Hannah Myers ("doctress") nor Bael Burton ("doctor," "person of color") in 1819, nor Ann Roberts ("doctress") in 1825, were included in the separate listing.

By 1825 the number of MDs in the city had increased to the point that they made up the majority of "Physicians." In some streets there was an MD every few doors; on Arch Street at 103, 122, 128, 157, 247, and 266; on Chestnut at 176, 191, 192, 196, and 204; on South 4th at 98½, 123, 124, 144, and 148. Even on the outskirts and suburbs of the city the concentration of MDs increased, as competition with established practitioners led new graduates to seek practice further afield. The preponderance of MDs made Philadelphia highly unusual. In rural New Hampshire, where Samuel Thomson grew up, he later wrote, "there was no such thing as a Doctor known among us; there not being any within 10 miles." His family had recourse to an old woman skilled "with roots and herbs" who lived nearby, and one of the attractions of Thomson's own practice as well as his medical system was that it made medical care more available. In Philadelphia, though, it was the Doctor who might be the closest available practitioner, and the old woman skilled "in roots and herbs" who would be the rarity, at least according to the directories.

On the main streets as well as elsewhere in the city (often next door to an MD) flourished other practitioners, listed as cuppers, bleeders, dentists, surgeon-barbers, and apothecaries. As mentioned earlier, a single practitioner might have more than one designation, and the designations remained stable over successive directory listings. For ease of reference I will refer to them as "Cuppers and Bleeders," but it must be remembered that they were not a homogeneous group. . . . "Cuppers and Bleeders" were no more peripatetic than the "Physicians." Thirteen of them even had the same education: one or more years of study at the University of Pennsylvania medical school. None had an MD, though: educational differences were reflected in their descriptions to that extent.

The activities indicated by their descriptions—cupping, bleeding, leeching, tooth-pulling, surgery, dentistry—were the usual activities of the British surgeon-apothecary who flourished outside of major cities. Yet in no way did Philadelphia medical practice deviate more from British than in the continued existence of practitioners who combined these activities with barbering. No Edinburgh physician would have recommended a barber to perform medical services; indeed, the surgeons' guild had formally excluded barbers from practising medicine from the seventeenth century. In Philadelphia, however, the term "Surgeon-Barber" was in use at least until the 1820s, for the "Mutual Assistant Society of Hairdressers, Surgeon Barbers, &c" was founded in 1796, and was still in existence in 1823. American barbers may have continued to provide at least some medical treatment until the later nineteenth century: the *Barber's Recipe Book* published in 1884 contained a section on medical recipes.

It is clear that these practitioners did provide medical, not just tonsorial, services. One of the vice-presidents of the Mutual Assistant Society, John Pierie, practised at 4th and Walnut from 1811 through 1825. He was probably the "John Perry" whom William Shippen recommended be called "to open a vein" during Sally Downing's pregnancy. Other physicians also recommended this kind of practitioner. . . . If this pattern of physicians recommending particular bleeders was often repeated, it helps to explain why "Cuppers and Bleeders" were often found on the same streets as élite physicians.

"Cuppers and Bleeders" must also have worked independently of physicians. "Nancy Skyrin was so unwell this fornoon, with a giddy head &c., that she sent for the bleeder," Elizabeth Drinker noted on one occasion. . . . General Anthony Wayne's receipt "for the Pleurisy," a home remedy involving the use of pleurisy root, also included the direction that the patient "be *bled* plentifully," suggesting that a patient would call a bleeder himself without waiting for a physician. If the treatment worked, he would never need to call in a physician at all.

Patients also consulted non-physician practitioners for other treatment besides bleeding. Margaret Coxe's recipe book included a "cure for the fever & ague" from "Mr Jacob C. Wikoff," an apothecary listed in city directories at 35 Market Street in 1800 and 1811. Fever and ague were internal diseases; if Wikoff routinely treated such cases, he was acting as a general practitioner, not merely compounding medication. Sally Downing applied to a woman "who is noted for reducing dislocated bones by greasing and gentle pulling." The few examples of what appear to be husband-and-wife practitioners also suggests general practice not limited to acting under a physician's direction. Hannah Drummond, for example, was listed as a cupper and leecher at the same address as Josiah Drummond, who practised on North 8th Street from 1811 to 1825. He was variously listed as hairdresser, surgeon, dentist, and bleeder with leeches; since he attended medical lectures at the University of Pennsylvania in 1815 we can assume a desire for general medical practice. . . . We cannot tell from directory listings whether wives were performing a separate function from husbands—using leeches, for example, rather than a lancet—acting as their husbands' assistants, or treating women and children while their husbands treated men. What the presence of couples and the variety of their descriptions suggests, though, is the desire to build up as large a practice as possible. That was often the motive for partnerships in medical practice, but fees collected by a male partner or assistant would have to be split, while fees collected by a spouse stayed within the household. Similar motives inspired husband and wife medical practices later in the nineteenth century.

Though cuppers and bleeders could maintain stable practices until 1825 without a university education, there is some evidence that those who could afford it, like Josiah Drummond, began to look to the University of Pennsylvania medical lectures for upward mobility, for their children if not themselves. James Gardette, for instance, practised as a dentist from 1800 until 1825. Elizabeth Drinker mentioned his cleaning her son's teeth. "They were not foul," she wrote, "he extracted one, and scraped the others, then rub'd them with dentifrice." His fee was five dollars, but, she added, "if what he does will tend to preserve the teeth, 'tis a trifle well laid out." Enough of his patients must have agreed for him to stay in practice and pass it on to his children, for an E. B. Gardette, dentist, was listed at 246 Walnut in 1837. It seems likely that the Charles D. Gardette who received an MD from the University of Pennsylvania medical faculty in 1851 was his son. A clearer case of the role of medical education in inter-generational mobility comes from the Gilliams, who were dentists at 35 Arch Street. Lewis Gilliams was listed as a dentist from 1800 to 1819; by 1825 he had moved, and was listed as "gent." Jacob Gilliams, who studied for a year at the University of Pennsylvania without graduating, also practised as a dentist at 35 Arch from 1819. Perhaps from his home he could see the steady increase in the number of MDs and "Physicians" on Arch Street: by 1825 only 2 of the 21 male practitioners were not listed as one or the other. Jacob Gilliams stayed at 35 Arch through 1851, but by the 1830s he had taken Hudson Burr, a University of Pennsylvania MD, as a partner. And in 1836 a Lewis S. Gilliams graduated from the University of Pennsylvania medical school with a thesis on the *Natural History of the Teeth.*

The third group of practitioners were midwives, whose numbers fluctuated between eleven and nineteen over the period. Judith Walzer Leavitt and Laurel Ulrich have convincingly demonstrated that midwives were not supplanted by male physicians during the late eighteenth century; Philadelphia city directories confirm that midwifery practices remained stable through 1825; the diary of Mrs. Joseph Sarber, midwife at the Falls of Schuykill from 1814 until 1831, allow[s] us to push the existence of midwives into the 1830s. . . .

. . . [M]idwives did not make the same smooth transition into physicians as male "cuppers and bleeders." The increasing number of male midwives was one factor. According to the directories, there were forty-two male midwives in 1819 and twenty-nine in 1825; it is not clear why the numbers fluctuated, but it is clear that there were more male midwives listed than female. There may have been more physicians who oversaw births as part of general family practice and so did not list themselves as man-midwives in directories. City directories were unreliable in listing women's occupations, especially married women's; even those listed one year might be omitted the next. Though midwives often built their practices through word-of-mouth within their neighbourhoods and did not rely on directories for advertising, this still put them at a competitive disadvantage compared to male midwives, especially as neighbourhoods changed and the city expanded. Moreover, midwives' practices apparently were shorter than male practitioners': thirty-seven per cent of midwives listed in 1811 were also listed in 1819, but only twenty-seven per cent were still listed in 1825. Again, the difference may also reflect the directories' more erratic record-keeping for women's occupations.

Male practitioners had other advantages, including, as Leavitt has argued, "the status advantage of their gender and of the popular image of superior education." Midwives may also have had the status disadvantage of a lower social position. Midwives lived either in alleys or outside the central section of town. They were thus geographically and presumably economically marginal. If we take males living at the same address with the same last names to be either husbands or sons, midwives seem to have been part of artisan households. Jane Houston was the only midwife whose husband, P. W. Houston, was listed as "MD," "surgeon," "dentist," and "man-midwife." They were listed only in the city directory for 1819. In contrast Honora Hartnett, who practised at 51 South 5th in 1800, was listed at the same address as Daniel Hartnett, stage-coach keeper; Rebecca Carlley, who practised at 56 Shippen from 1811 to 1825, was listed at the same address as Joseph Carlley, carter; Elizabeth Mingle, who practised at 22 Appletree Alley from 1811 to 1825, was listed at the same address as John Mingle, bellows maker. Midwifery, then, may have flourished as one component of artisan household economy. . . .

The general economic decline of the artisan household, coupled with the increasing number of competing male physicians, may have made midwifery a less viable occupation. There was not much midwives could do about this. Hannah January, who practised at 39 Arch Street from 1819 to 1825, could, like Jacob Gilliams, have watched the ever-increasing numbers of MDs down the street. We may surmise that the strategy adopted by the Gilliams family would not have been available to any children she may have had: study at the University of Pennsylvania would have been too costly for her sons, and simply not open to her daughters. I have no evidence whether any great-great-granddaughters of Philadelphia midwives became physicians, as Martha Ballard's did. The only social mobility I have found for a midwife is personal, similar to Lewis Gilliams' shift from dentist to "gent." Ann Zigler, who practised as a midwife on 74 New Street from 1811 to 1819, was listed as "gentlewoman" in 1825.

The final category of practitioners listed by city directories was nurses. It was the largest after "Physicians," making up an average of twenty-eight per cent of all practitioners. It was also the least stable. Only twenty-two per cent of those listed as nurses in 1811 were still listed in 1819, while only five per cent were still listed in 1825. Since 79—thirty-eight per cent—were listed as "widow," some of the transience might have been due to natural attrition from old age. It might also have been due to nursing itself, which, since it involved prolonged and intimate contact with the sick, was probably the most dangerous of all health-care activities. Charles Wilson Peale was worried enough about contagion to copy several "cautions in visiting the sick" into his "memorandum book." An extract from Hufeland's *Art of Prolonging Life* advised him not to:

> swallow your saliva as long as you are near the sick; do not place yourself so as to be exposed to their breath. Do not visit them in woolen cloaths, or with furs about you, because these most powerfully retain infection. . . . It is very beneficial also, as long as you remain with the diseased, to hold a sponge dipped in Vinegar before your mouth and nostrils, or to smoke Tobacco.

Although nurses would seldom have worn furs when tending a patient, the rest of this advice would have been impossible for them to follow. Catching diseases from patients was an occupational hazard of nursing.

Susan Reverby has found that nurses in the early nineteenth century were most likely to be poor widows with no other means of support, and Philadelphia city directories provide evidence for this. As mentioned earlier, thirty-eight per cent were listed as "widow." In addition, it is harder to find information about the families of nurses than of midwives, or of female cuppers and bleeders, because nurses were almost never listed as living at the same address as men with the same last name. Nor was I able to find men of the same name ever having lived at that address, suggesting that nurses could not stay at the same residence after their husbands died. . . . It seems reasonable to assume from this that nurses did not generally practise as nurses while their husbands were alive, unlike Mary Busman or Rebecca Carlley. It also seems reasonable to assume that a nurse did not generally move into her son's household on her husband's death, though they might have moved into married daughter's household. One of the more interesting patterns, though, was that nurses frequently lived at the same address as midwives or other nurses. Mrs Rushel and H. Roney, nurses, both lived at the same address as Elizabeth Mingle on Appletree Alley in 1811, for example, and Rebecca Murl and Rebecca Naglee, both nurses, lived at the same address on Little Water Street in 1819. Perhaps they shared a room, or perhaps they merely rented rooms in the same house. Either way, the pattern supports the assumption that they were not living with their families, taking up nursing as an extension of their familial role, but rather were forced into it on the deaths of their husbands and in the absence of other economic resources. As Reverby put it, "Older women did not so much choose nursing as slip into it through life experiences and lack of other options." This did not keep them from being essential to good medical care; as Elizabeth Drinker wrote, "To have a good Nurse ready is a comfort."

The city directories listed other ephemeral practitioners, like I. Smith, "Indian Doctor," or Charles Felton, "person of color" and "Herb Doctor." Neither apparently merited inclusion in the separate lists of "Physicians" or "Cuppers and Bleeders," but each might have attracted patients. If they were like the "root doctors" mentioned by Samuel Thomson, they relied on native herbs for their treatment. Belief in the efficacy of native American plants was widespread: we have already encountered General Wayne's interest in pleurisy root. Philadelphians also seem to have shared in the general fascination with treatment by Blacks and Indians. Elizabeth Drinker reported that when a family member had cancer she was treated by "A Sam'l Wilson a black man . . . as he is a Cancer Doctor." His treatment consisted of applying some form of caustic plaster to the cancer. It did not work, but then neither had the painful operation previously performed by Professor Philip Syng Physic. Margaret Coxe copied into her recipe book a cure for "the Stone . . . communicated by a negro man at Berkely Springs, in Virginia to a Physician, who cured himself by it, & as a reward & for discovering the secret, he purchased the Negro's freedom." Since even—or especially—social outcasts might know "secrets," the main criterion for choosing a practitioner or form of treatment was whether someone who could be trusted had found it to be efficacious. Margaret Coxe also wrote, for example, that Goulard Cerate was "recommended by Miss N. Shippen for hurts of any kind—*a quack remedy,* but well tested by herself, as well as by many others to whom she spoke of it." Obviously she made a distinction between quack and orthodox medicine, but equally obviously that did not lead her to always choose the latter over the former. The main distinction was whether the remedy did, or did not, produce results.

This examination of Philadelphia medical practice shows clearly that University of Pennsylvania professors and graduates did not entirely supplant other practitioners. The thistle, we might say, did not crowd out pleurisy root. Of course, there was nothing built into the Edinburgh University model of medical education that said that it should. The Edinburgh system was predicated on the assumption that every would-be practitioner should be free to choose for himself the kind of education best suited to his future practice. That practice would be constrained or expanded by patients' perception of his efficacy and by their ability to pay. The concentration of MDs in the wealthier part of the city suggests for graduates, at least, that perception of their efficacy and ability to pay often went hand in hand. In less wealthy areas, though, MDs flourished in conjunction with other practitioners. On 3rd Street north of Arch in 1819, for example, there were two MDs, two other "Physicians," four "Cuppers and Bleeders," one of whom had studied for a year at the University of Pennsylvania, and eight nurses. We cannot know whether they tended to co-operate or compete in attracting patients. Historians have often assumed the latter, but we have enough examples of physicians recommending bleeders to suggest the former as well.

Yet if University of Pennsylvania graduates did not take over practice, they nonetheless had a great impact. Their number increased, and the examples of intergenerational mobility we have seen suggests that formal education was considered an asset. This placed women and Blacks at a disadvantage, since they could not even attend lectures, let alone graduate. . . .

. . . MDs, of course, . . . increasingly agitated for some kind of legislation restricting practice to properly licensed physicians. The story of their limited success is well known. It has been linked to American dislike for élite titles and monopolies, as well as to lack of conclusive proof that MDs cured more patients than other practitioners. Yet some of the blame—if we wish to call it that—for the failure of licensing can surely be traced to the transplant of an educational system that promoted the proliferation of practitioners, without the corporate regulations that kept that proliferation in check. The transplant was successful, measured by the increasing number of students, and measured, too, by the increase in knowledgeable practitioners. But the very accessibility of education blurred the distinction between MDs and other practitioners. Moreover, it set up a conflict between the interests of medical professors and those of the physicians they graduated, one that divided the profession for most of the nineteenth century. John Morgan had been right: the same factors which contributed to the fame and fortune of the Edinburgh professors worked in favour of the University of Pennsylvania as well. Its impact on Philadelphia medical practice, though, was not precisely what he had expected.

 F U R T H E R   R E A D I N G S

Whitfield J. Bell Jr., *The College of Physicians of Philadelphia: A Bicentennial History* (1987).

Philip Cash, Eric H. Christianson, and J. Worth Estes, eds., *Medicine in Colonial Massachusetts, 1620–1820* (1980).

Jane B. Donegan, *Women and Men Midwives: Medicine, Morality, and Misogyny in Early America* (1978).

J. Worth Estes, *Hall Jackson and the Purple Foxglove: Medical Practice and Research in Revolutionary America, 1760–1820* (1979).

J. Worth Estes and Billy G. Smith, eds., *A Melancholy Scene of Devastation: The Public Response to the 1793 Philadelphia Yellow Fever Epidemic* (1997).

Mary C. Gillett, *The Army Medical Department, 1775–1818* (1981).

Maurice B. Gordon, *Naval and Maritime Medicine During the American Revolution* (1978).

Amalie M. Kass, "The Obstetrical Casebook of Walter Channing, 1811–1822," *Bulletin of the History of Medicine* 67 (1993): 494–523.

Joseph F. Kett, *The Formation of the American Medical Profession: The Role of Institutions, 1780–1860* (1968).

Judith Walzer Leavitt, *Brought to Bed: Childbearing in America, 1750–1950* (1986).

Constance McGovern, *Masters of Madness: Social Origins of the American Psychiatric Profession* (1985).

Kay K. Moss, *Southern Folk Medicine, 1750–1820* (1999).

Ronald L. Numbers, "William Beaumont and the Ethics of Human Experimentation," *Journal of the History of Biology* 12 (1979): 113–135.

Martin S. Pernick, "Politics, Parties, and Pestilence: Epidemic Yellow Fever in Philadelphia and the Rise of the First Party System," *William and Mary Quarterly* 29 (1972): 559–586.

J. H. Powell, *Bring Out Your Dead: The Great Plague of Yellow Fever in Philadelphia in 1793* (1949, 1993).

Charles E. Rosenberg, *The Care of Strangers: The Rise of America's Hospital System* (1987).

David J. Rothman, *The Discovery of the Asylum: Social Order and Disorder in the New Republic* (1971).

William G. Rothstein, *American Physicians in the Nineteenth Century* (1972).

Catherine M. Scholten, "On the Importance of the Obstetrick Art: Changing Customs of Childbirth in America, 1769–1825," *William and Mary Quarterly* 34 (1977): 426–445.

Laurel Thatcher Ulrich, "Derangement in the Family: The Story of Mary Sewall, 1824–1825," in *Medicine and Healing,* ed. Peter Benes (1992), pp. 168–184.

Laurel Thatcher Ulrich, "'The Living Mother of a Living Child': Midwifery and Mortality in Post-Revolutionary New England," *William and Mary Quarterly* 46 (1989): 27–48.

Laurel Thatcher Ulrich, *A Midwife's Tale: The Life of Martha Ballard, Based on Her Diary, 1785–1812* (1990).

CHAPTER
4

Antebellum Medical Knowledge, Practice, and Patients, 1820–1860

Regular physicians in the early nineteenth century found reassurance in the conviction that most diseases were essentially overexcited conditions that would be remedied by aggressively depleting the body through bloodletting and mineral purgatives such as calomel. This notion was sustained not only by the theoretical systems of European and American medical authorities but also by a larger set of assumptions about health as balance and disease as imbalance, widely shared by doctors and patients alike. By the 1820s and 1830s, however, there were signs that confident faith in established medical knowledge and practice was being destabilized. The heroic approach to treatment that gave doctors such a clear, active role in managing disease was coming under skeptical scrutiny and sometimes attack. This assault came both from antiorthodox opponents and from elite regular critics who were influenced by newer French medical thinking and who suggested that much of the credit conventionally given to therapeutic interventions in the cure of disease was in fact owed to the healing power of nature.

Moreover, even figures like Benjamin Rush, who advocated the use of heroic treatments, insisted that medical therapy was to be gauged to such distinctive features of the patient as age, gender, race, ethnicity, class, and moral status, and to attributes of place like climate, topography, and population density. Starting in the second quarter of the nineteenth century, American physicians affirmed the individuality of patient and environment in determining practice with a fresh vigor fueled in part by a growing, French-inspired faith in empiricism and reaction against rationalistic systems. Even when, in 1846 at the Massachusetts General Hospital in Boston, surgical anesthesia was introduced for the very first time, offering the possibility of transforming surgery from the grizzly, brutal affair it had been when all operations had to be performed on fully sentient patients, anesthesia was applied only selectively. The benefits of pain avoidance were weighed against potential risks in a calculus that differentiated among candidates for anesthesia according to gender, race, ethnicity, and class. Although physicians insisted on keen attention to difference in their efforts to

*heal their patients' bodies and minds, however, the particularity of the individual
tended to be glossed over in obtaining subjects for teaching and investigation: the
cadavers laid out on the dissecting tables of American medical schools, for example,
were almost invariably the bodies of the poor, and often those of African Americans.*

*Throughout the antebellum period, medical practice—even surgery—was
conducted for the most part in patients' homes, and hospitals remained chiefly
charitable institutions for the sick poor. In one field, however, that of mental illness,
the institution itself came to be seen as a key instrument in therapy. Hospitals for the
mentally ill dated from the colonial era, but the emergence of moral treatment
(a plan that emphasized a humane and uplifting environment), the conviction that
the asylum was curative, and the campaign that Dorothea Dix launched in 1841
to reform the care of the insane poor fostered the creation of a host of state insane
asylums during the years before the Civil War.*

The certainty of medical knowledge *became a freighted issue in antebellum
medicine, not least of all because an awareness of the inbuilt uncertainties of* practice *had the potential to threaten both professional confidence and claims to social
esteem. How could the profession's medical knowledge serve as a unifying and
stabilizing force when physicians distrusted universally applicable rules for practice?
Especially at a time of growing regional divisiveness, the conviction shared by all
American physicians that practice had to be individuated according to patient and
locale—different, that is, for African American and European American, for east-
erner and westerner—took on increasingly politicized force. This is particularly
evident in arguments for medical regionalism and, during the late antebellum
period, in strident southern calls for intellectual and institutional separatism.*

 D O C U M E N T S

In Document 1, Asa Fitch, a young student attending his first course of medical lectures
at Rutgers Medical College in New York City during the winter of 1828–1829, records
in a diary his emotional response to witnessing surgical operations in the era before
anesthesia. As his experience grows, his diary entries display an emotional hardening
and detachment. Document 2 is an excerpt from a widely influential and controversial
address by Harvard medical professor Jacob Bigelow to the members of the Massachusetts Medical Society. Speaking in 1835, Bigelow urges his audience to recognize
that most diseases are "self-limited"—that is, that they end either in recovery or death
regardless of the physician's therapeutic interventions. What are the implications for
heroic medicine of his assessment of the healing power of nature? How might his
listeners react to his remarks?

Studying medicine in the spring of 1841 as an apprentice in the Rochester, New
York, office of Frank H. Hamilton (who during the winter months lectured as professor
of surgery at the nearby Geneva Medical College), Ruel Smith writes smugly in a private letter (Document 3) to a friend about the commotion that the discovery of a partly
dissected body of an elderly African American man has caused in the community.
What do his remarks suggest about the place of anatomical dissection in antebellum
society, and about the relationship between dissectors and dissected?

In Document 4, Andrew Stone, who has moved to the West after studying medicine
in the East, writes in 1845 from Indiana to the *Boston Medical and Surgical Journal*
explaining how eastern medical teachings must be modified for practice in a western
climate, treating western diseases and western patients. In a petition to the legislature of

the state of Tennessee (Document 5), the well-known lay reformer Dorothea Dix boldly makes the case for the curative promise of the insane asylum and the need for improvements in hospital care for the mentally ill. Like petitions Dix submitted to other state legislatures during the 1840s, this tract from 1847 urges the responsibility and interests of the state in supporting such a project. Document 6 is an excerpt from an M.D. dissertation, a short manuscript essay required for graduation, written in 1848 by Yale medical student Lebbeus Eaton Marsh. He selects as his topic the sensation created in the medical community by the first application of surgical anesthesia two years earlier, and although he celebrates the new possibility of painless surgery and asserts that ether no longer can be regarded as "a scientific toy," he cautions against its indiscriminate use.

Documents 7 and 8 display the political potential of stressing local knowledge in medicine, and of the conviction that physicians needed to pay close attention to differences among places and peoples. Regular physician and racial theorist Samuel A. Cartwright presents in Document 7 the 1851 conclusions of a committee of four physicians appointed by the Medical Association of Louisiana to investigate "the diseases and peculiarities of our negro population." He calls on southern physicians to study the distinctive medical conditions and therapeutic needs of African Americans, and illustrates his point by including an account of "drapetomania"—his term for a mental disease that causes slaves to run away. To what extent is Cartwright's thinking sustained by beliefs about disease and therapy that physicians in all parts of antebellum America shared? Is it possible to separate politics and medicine in this article from the *New Orleans Medical and Surgical Journal,* one of the country's leading professional periodicals? In Document 8, excerpted from a Nashville medical journal, S. P. Crawford, a Greenville, Tennessee physician, attributes the shortcomings of medical practice in the South to a misleading, dangerous reliance on European and northern medical authorities. Writing in 1860 on the eve of the Civil War, he underscores the medical distinctiveness of the southern habitat and southern peoples, insisting that if there are to be reliable guides to practice in the South, then southern physicians will have to produce their own, separate medical literature.

1. A New York Medical Student Recounts in His Diary His Emotional Responses to Surgery, 1828

Sat 29th [Nov. 1828]   At 12 o'clock went to the Hospital as usual. The hardness of my heart was here unexpectedly brought to the test, & I found it wanting. An amputation was performed by Dr. Stevens, of the left leg, about half way between the knee & ankle. The mans affection was caries of the os. Calcis. But oh, how my feelings recoiled at the sight! To behold the keen shining knife drawn round the leg severing the integuments—to see these dissected up & folded over, while the unhappy subject of the operation uttered the most heart rending screams in his agony & torment—to see another stroke of the knife cut through the muscular calf of the leg to the bone—& to hear the saw working its way through the bone, produced an impression I never can forget. I could not look upon the operation, but covered my eyes to keep myself from fainting. A momentary glance was all I could bestow, & with my eyes averted, I would wait till I had collected strength enough for another

Asa Fitch, entries for New York, November 29 and December 9, 27, and 30, 1828, in Diary G, July 24–December 31, 1828, Fitch Family Papers, Manuscripts and Archives, Yale University Library, New Haven, Connecticut.

look, equally brief, & I was rejoiced when it was through. At 4 o'clock Dr. Stevens met us at the Hospital again & gave us a description of the more important cases that have fallen under his care the present month, with his manner of treating them. . . .

Tues 9th [Dec. 1828]   In the hospital today saw the operation of couching performed, for cataract. Were all the operations of Surgery like this, there would be some sense to it. This afternoon attended the lectures of Drs. Francis & Griscom. . . .

Sat. 27   . . . In the Hospital we saw a most tedious & painful operation—taking a necrosed os humerus from a small child. But I had none of the tenderness which I have always before felt on such occasions. After this was through, a case of fistula in ano was also operated on. In the evening we went to hear Dr. Bushes lecture. . . .

Tues 30   . . . Today in the Hospital, saw the operation of Couching repeated on a black woman, on whom it was performed some time ago, & a cancer of the under lip, & scirrhus submaxillary glands were removed from another person. The latter was a cruel operation—the lower lip was nearly all cut away—the integument down under the skin was dissected up, & brought round to form a new lip. But when through the appearance of the mans face was much better than before.

2. Jacob Bigelow, a Harvard Medical Professor, Challenges the Physician's Power to Cure, 1835

The structure and functions of the human body, the laws which govern the progress of its diseases, and more especially the diagnosis of its morbid conditions, are better understood now, than they were at the beginning of the present century. But the science of therapeutics, or the branch knowledge by the application of which physicians are expected to remove diseases, has not, seemingly, attained to a much more elevated standing than it formerly possessed. The records of mortality attest its frequent failures, and the inability to control the event of diseases, which at times is felt by the most gifted and experienced practitioners, give evidence that, in many cases, disease is more easily understood, than cured.

This deficiency of the healing art is not justly attributable to any want of sagacity or diligence on the part of the medical profession. It belongs rather to the inherent difficulties of the case, and is, after abating the effect of errors and accidents, to be ascribed to the apparent fact, that certain morbid processes in the human body have a definite and necessary career, from which they are not to be diverted by any known agents, with which it is in our power to oppose them. To these morbid affections, the duration of which, and frequently the event also, are beyond the control of our present remedial means, I have, on the present occasion, applied the name of *Self-limited diseases.* . . .

By a self-limited disease, I would be understood to express one which receives limits from its own nature, and not from foreign influences; one which, after it has obtained foothold in the system, cannot, in the present state of our knowledge, be eradicated, or abridged, by art,—but to which there is due a certain succession of processes, to be completed in a certain time; which time and processes may vary

Jacob Bigelow, *A Discourse on Self-Limited Diseases. Delivered before the Massachusetts Medical Society, at Their Annual Meeting, May 27, 1835* (Boston: Nathan Hale, 1835), pp. 7–9, 13–16, 29, 31–35.

with the constitution and condition of the patient, and may tend to death, or to recovery, but are not known to be shortened, or greatly changed, by medical treatment. . . .

. . . I am aware that the works of medical writers, and especially of medical compilers, teem with remedies and modes of treatment for all diseases; and that in the morbid affections of which we speak, remedies are often urged with zeal and confidence, even though sometimes of an opposite character. Moreover, in many places, at the present day, a charm is popularly attached to what is called an active, bold, or heroic practice; and a corresponding reproach awaits the opposite course, which is cautious, palliative, and expectant. In regard to the diseases which have been called self-limited, I would not be understood to deny that remedies capable of removing them may exist; I would only assert, that they have not yet been proved to exist.

Under the simple self-limited diseases, we may class *hooping cough.* This disease has its regular increase, height, and decline, occupying ordinarily from one to six months. During this period, medical treatment is for the most part of no avail. . . .

Most of the class of diseases usually denominated eruptive fevers, are self-limited. *Measles,* for example, is never known to be cut short by art, or abridged of its natural career. *Scarlet fever,* a disease of which we have had much and fatal experience during the last three years, is eminently of this character. . . .

Small Pox is another example of the class of affections under consideration. It may, at first view, appear, that inoculation has placed artificial limits on this disease. But it must be recollected, that inoculated Small Pox is itself only a milder variety of the same disease, having its own customary limits of extent and duration, which are fixed, quite as much as those of the distinct and confluent forms of the natural disease. . . .

It is a question of great interest to the medical profession, to determine whether *typhus* is a disease susceptible of control from medical means. On this subject no one now doubts, that if the disease is once fairly established in the system, it cannot be eradicated by art, but must complete a certain natural course, before convalescence can take place. But a question still exists, whether this disease is capable of being jugulated, or broken up, at its outset, by the early application of remedies. . . .

An inherent difficulty, which every medical man finds to stand in the way of an unbiased and satisfactory judgment, is the heavy responsibility which rests upon the issue of his cases. When a friend, or valuable patient, is committed to our charge, we cannot stand by, as curious spectators, to study the natural history of his disease. We feel that we are called on to attempt his rescue by vigorous means, so that at least the fault of omission shall not be upon our charge. We proceed to put in practice those measures, which on the whole have appeared to us to do most good; and if these fail us, we resort to other measures, which we have read of, or heard of. And at the end of our attendance we may be left in uncertainty, whether the duration of sickness has been shortened, or lengthened, by our practice, and whether the patient is really indebted to us for good or evil. . . .

It appears to me to be one of the most important desiderata in practical medicine, to ascertain, in regard to each doubtful disease, how far its cases are really self-limited, and how far they are controllable by any treatment. This question can be satisfactorily settled only by instituting, in a large number of cases, which are well identified and nearly similar, a fair experimental comparison of the different active and the expectant modes of practice, with their varieties in regard to time, order and degree. This experiment is vast, considering the number of combinations which it must involve; and even much more extensive than a corresponding series of pathological observations; yet every honest and intelligent observer may contribute to it his mite. Opportunities for such observations, and especially for monographs of diseases, are found in the practice of most physicians, yet hospitals and other public charities afford the most appropriate field for instituting them upon a large scale. The aggregate of results, successful and unsuccessful, circumstantially and impartially reported by competent observers, will give us a near approximation to truth, in regard to the diseases of the time and place, in which the experiments are instituted. The *numerical* method employed by Louis in his extensive pathological researches, and now adopted by his most distinguished contemporaries in France, affords the means of as near an approach to certainty on this head, as the subject itself admits. . . .

In regard to acknowledged self-limited diseases, the question will naturally arise, whether the practitioner is called on to do nothing for the benefit of his patient; whether he shall fold his hands, and look passively on the progress of a disease, which he cannot interrupt. To this I would answer,—by no means. . . . In the first place, we may save the patient from much harm, not only by forbearing ourselves to afflict him with unnecessary practice, but also by preventing the ill-judged activity of others. . . . In the second place, we may do much good by a palliative, and preventive course, by alleviating pain, procuring sleep, guarding the diet, [and] regulating the alimentary canal. . . . Lastly, by a just prognosis, founded on a correct view of the case, we may sustain the patient and his friends during the inevitable course of the disease; and may save them from the pangs of disappointed hope on the one side, or of unnecessary despondency on the other. . . .

. . . The longer and the more philosophically we contemplate this subject, the more obvious it will appear, that the physician is but the minister and servant of nature; that in cases like those which have been engaging our consideration, we can do little more than follow in the train of disease, and endeavor to aid nature in her salutary intentions, or to remove obstacles out of her path.

3. A Medical Apprentice Writes from Rochester About a Cadaver "Resurrected" for Dissection, 1841

Rochester May 21st—[18]41

Dear friend Robertson,

. . . I am well, & enjoy myself very much. I have been in this place since the middle of March, in the office of F. H. Hamilton, Professor of surgery in Geneva medical College. The more I become acquainted with medicine, the better I am pleased with the profession, & its prospects. I think it is one which presents as many facilities, & as fair prospects for distinction as any other.

We have had high times here this spring in the line of resurrectionising; which has kept the rabble, & the Police department in a compleat stew. A body partialy

---

Ruel Smith to Smith Robertson, Rochester, New York, May 21, 1841, Robertson Family Papers, Collection #243, Folder 1, Smith Robertson Papers, Division of Rare and Manuscript Collections, Cornell University Library, Cornell University, Ithaca, New York.

desected was found early in the spring, in the third story of a building on Main St. The Police justice has made great exertions to assertain the particulars of the case, but is now contented to let the matter drop, not knowing half so much about it as before the investigation. The subject, was supposed to be an old negro, who died in a fit of intoxication some six miles out of the city. He was buried in the clothing in which he died, & had not a friend on Earth; & probably not in Heaven, or any other place, whose feelings could [be] injured. The body could not be recognized, as it had shed its coat. Most of the witnesses swore that it was a female; but as some were disposed to question this point; they called upon a phisition to examine & testify, who swore that he had what he called good reasons for believing that it was a male, as it had two devilish fine testicles. By order of the Police justice, three students were commited to prison for contempt of court; in as much as they refused to answer certain questions, which they feared might criminate themselves. Judge Porters son of this Co was one of the three. The proceedings proved to be unlawful, & they were released. The justice is now under an arrest for false imprisonment: damages laid at $3000. Thus stands the matter. & (I think,) the justice is satisfied by this time, that medical students are hard colts to break as they have the favor of the legal profession, & all the inteligent part of [the] community. One of the students is a son of Ex Gov Pitcher. Thus you see, we have water sufficiently hot to wash off the scurf.

Never mind the fog but keep poking; as opposition is the life of business.

I have the pleasure of friend Green's company as he is also reading medicine in the same office. No doubt the world will be astonished one of these days, when we come upon the stage! ! ! . . .

In great haste,

I [am] Yours, &c &c

Ruel Smith

4. An Eastern-Educated Physician in Indiana Advises Other Emigrants About the Distinctive Character of Diseases of the West, 1845

It is now some seven years since, after having received the honors of my ALMA MATER, at the literary emporium of America, and seeing the profession was well crowded in that section of country, I, like many other youthful aspirants, sought the Far West as a place to commence my career in the healing art. And after a close and unremitted application to the duties of the profession for so long a time, I now attempt to delineate something of the diseases and medical practice in a new country.

Hundreds of our young and enterprising medical men are annually emigrating to the West, to commence practice in a new climate, and among new and strange diseases—diseases of the character of which they have no just conception, and

Andrew Stone, "Remarks on Diseases of the West.—No. I" (letter to the editors, Crown Point, Lake County, Indiana, December 12, 1845), *Boston Medical and Surgical Journal* 33 (1846): 476–478, 480.

consequently can form no proper and efficient plan of treatment. It is no unusual thing for such young men to come to this country, and commence practice under the most flattering auspices, having, they think, all the necessary education, for they have duly spent the required number of years in studying the rudiments of pathology, and all the conflicting theories of the schools, and have seen considerable of clinical practice at the East. But how soon is their most sanguine hopes and anticipations blasted; although they are here never at a loss for patients or practice, for go where they may, hardly a summer or autumn passes by, but what affords sufficient sickness to keep every one employed that gives himself the name of physician. And here lies the fault of young physicians, as well as some old ones, on coming into a new country; they do not discriminate between the diseases here and what they have been accustomed to; and so treating, at first, our diseases according to the letter of the books, they experience the sad mortification of losing a large number of their patients, and thereby obtain a bad reputation, and are compelled to move and re-locate, or else abandon their favorite object of pursuit. In this manner, I have known many young physicians, well qualified as far as theory and a good preparatory education were concerned, almost discouraged, because they happened to lose a large number of patients for the first season of their practice in this new country.

I do not know, Mr. Editor, in what way I can confer greater benefit on the profession, and through them, in all probability, on a large number of our fellow beings, than by devoting a few numbers in your Journal to the character and treatment of the diseases of the West. Having had an extensive practice for six years in a large scope of country, on the borders of Spoon River in Illinois, and one season (the present) in a section of country nearly approaching the head of Lake Michigan, . . . where the number of patients for the season whom I have visited and prescribed for, has exceeded four hundred, . . . I shall be able to communicate some facts and incidents, which will be interesting to the student and medical man in the East.

The diseases of the West, for the most part, come and recede according to the variations of the seasons, and the changes of the elements; and to a close and scrutinizing observer, can be easily accounted for, and their approach pretty accurately foretold. Our rivers are almost annually overflowed, either by the great thaw and breaking up of winter, or the vernal rains, or frequently both combined, which cause a dense body of alluvial matter to be added to the already abundant mass of virgin soil. As the waters recede, exposure to the penetrating power of the summer's sun causes an exhalation of *miasm* which fills the air with a stench, on the borders of the streams, at least, hardly supportable. . . . When the sickly season commences, it is sudden and rapid, and, as a general thing, confined to the settlers on the river borders. Here, then, is conclusive evidence of malaria contaminating the whole atmosphere.

What, then, is the physician to treat, when called to the bed-side of a sick patient? He has to treat a case of poison. . . . As much as it may be the case, that the diseases of the pure climate of New England are generated in the body, here it seems, generally, diametrically the reverse. Nearly every case of fever is preceded by a chill, of longer or shorter duration, according to the amount of poison inhaled, the contaminated state of the sanguiferous system, and the functional or organic derangement which has already taken place. . . . In the remitting form, if the physician see the patient during the chill or the cold paroxysm, he will find him, perhaps, with a pulse hardly perceptible, weak and thready, and apparently indicating great debility; his countenance is livid, features ghastly, extremities and often the whole surface of the body cold; a sighing disposition for breath, and great difficulty of breathing. He complains, if sensible, of feelings of oppression at the epigastric region and a sensation of heaviness. There are often retching, vomiting and yawning; and great restlessness and uneasiness are manifested, so that the patient can hardly lie quiet in bed. In the more aggravated cases, however, the patient may lie in a stupid manner, showing great oppression of the cerebral organ. Of all the diseases which are common to the West, the symptoms above described are more calculated to mislead the young and inexperienced physician than any other, and they serve to try his judgment and determine his future success. It is in such diseases, that quick discernment, close scrutiny and good judgment are required; and let me here advise the young physician to throw aside all theories, and depend solely upon his own judgment and ability. . . .

ANDREW STONE, M.D.

Crown Point, Lake Co., Ind., Dec. 12th, 1845.

5. Reformer Dorothea Dix Calls on Tennessee Legislators to Turn State Insane Asylum into a "Curative" Hospital, 1847

To the Honorable,
the General Assembly of the State of Tennessee.

GENTLEMEN:

I ask to lay before you, briefly and distinctly, the necessities and claims of a numerous, and unfortunately, an increasing class of your fellow-citizens—I refer to the Insane of this State; the various distresses of whose various condition can be fully appreciated only by those who have witnessed their miseries. Pining in cells and dungeons, pent in log-cabins, bound with ropes, restrained by leathern throngs, burthened with chains—now wandering at large, alone and neglected, endangering the security of property, often inimical to human life; and now thrust into cells, into pens, or wretched cabins, excluded from the fair light of heaven, from social and healing influences—cast out, cast off, like the Pariah of the Hindoos, from comfort, hope, and happiness, such is the present actual condition of a large number of your fellow-citizens—useless and helpless, life is at once grievous to themselves, and a source of immeasurable sorrow to all beside.

In some cases, indeed, pitying friends strive to procure comforts, and exercise consoling cares: how little, under the cloud of this malady, these avail, many can bear sorrowful testimony. The only remedy or alleviation is to be found in *rightly organized Hospitals,* adapted to the special care the peculiar malady of the Insane so urgently demands.

D. L. Dix, *Memorial Soliciting Enlarged and Improved Accommodations for the Insane of the State of Tennessee, by the Establishment of a New Hospital* (Nashville, Tenn.: B. R. M'Kennie, 1847), pp. 3–6, 21–22, 24, 28–29, 32.

Made conversant with the cruel sufferings and measureless distresses of which I speak, by patient investigations, reaching through long and weary years, over the length and breadth of our land, I represent the existence of troubles no imagination can exaggerate, and I have come now to Tennessee, as the advocate and friend of those who cannot plead their own cause, and for those who have no friend to protect and succor them, in this, the extremity of human dependence. . . .

There is less insanity in the southern, than in the northern States, proportioned to the inhabitants of each; for this disparity several causes may be assigned: there is, in the former, comparatively but a small influx of foreigners, while they throng every district of the latter. . . . But a more obvious cause is found in the fact of the much more numerous colored population here than there. The negro and the Indian rarely become subject to the malady of insanity, as neither do the uncivilized tribes and clans of European Russia and Asia. Insanity is the malady of civilized and cultivated life, and of sections and communities whose nervous energies are most roused and nourished.

Upon careful inquiry, it will be discovered that great suf[fer]ing is experienced in every county of this State, from the want of a suitable Hospital for the Insane poor, as well as for those who are in moderate or affluent circumstances. This proposition admitted, it is clearly a duty to adopt such measures as shall effectually remedy the evil. . . .

Skilful Physicians, of enlarged minds and liberal attainments in our country, spend the best strength of their best years, in conscientious and diligent exertions for the relief of patients entrusted to their care. . . .

It is knowledge of this fact which inspires me with confidence in the treatment of the Insane, in every correctly governed, rightly organized Hospital. Insanity requires a peculiar and appropriate treatment, which cannot be rendered while the patients remain at their own homes, or by even skilful Physicians in general practice. I confide in Hospital care for remedial treatment, and in no other care. One might quote volumes to show, that, however able the patient or his friends may be, to provide in private families every luxury and accommodation, it is hazarding final recovery to make even the experiment of domestic treatment.

Dr. Brighan, in one of his early reports of the New York State Hospital, remarks, that "when sufficient time has elapsed to show clearly that the case is Insanity, unaccompanied by acute disease, then *no time should be lost,* in adopting the most approved remedial measures, among which, as has often been stated, is *removal from home,* to a place where the exciting causes of disease are no longer operative." "Let the friends *fully satisfy themselves that the patient will receive kind treatment,* then, forbear all untimely interference with the remedial measures adopted in the Hospitals of their choice." An individual being Insane, *all ordinary considerations* should give place to the aim of recovery; and this should be steadily adhered to, however discouraging the circumstances, till it is entirely established that the case is beyond the reach of all available means of cure. . . .

. . . *It is not safe, nor is it humane,* to leave the Insane, *whether curable or incurable,* to roam at large, or abide in families, unguarded, unguided, and uncontrolled. For their own sake, for that of their friends, for that of the community, they should be rendered to the *kind, skilful, intelligent, judicious watch* of Hospital protection.

Beside the *propriety* and *general obligation* which I assert of placing patients in good Hospitals, there is the great probability of ultimate recovery of the healthy functional action of the brain.

Dr. Bell, of the McLean Hospital at Somerville—whose name commands a respectful confidence rarely exceeded, the skilful Physician, wise friend, judicious superintendent, the good man, he whose cares have restored so many sufferers to their homes, and the blessed affections centering there—has stated, in an early report, and repeated the proposition in succeeding documents, that, "*in* an Institution *fully provided with attendants,* there may be afforded to all except a few highly excited patients, any comfort to which they have been accustomed at home, *and all cases certainly recent,* whose origin does not date directly or obscurely back more than one year, *recover under a fair trial.* This being the general law, the cases to the contrary counting as the exceptions." . . .

Were I to recount but briefly, a hundredth part of the shocking scenes of sorrow, suffering, abuse, and degradation, to which I have been witness—searched out *in jails, in poor-houses, in pens, and block-houses, in dens and caves, in cages and cells, in dungeons and cellars;* men and women in chains, frantic, bruised, lascerated, and debased—your souls would grow sick at the horrid recital. Yet have all these been witnessed, and for successive years shocking facts have been patiently investigated; and why?—in order to solicit and *procure a remedy* for such heart-rending troubles: the only remedy—*the establishment of well-constructed curative Hospitals.* I desire not to nourish morbid sensibilities, nor to awaken transient emotions. The ills for which I ask relief, in the name of all who are suffering, are too real, too profound for transient emotions to work a remedy, or for sudden sensibilities to heal. I ask you, gentlemen of the Legislature, men of Tennessee, to think, to ponder well, to discuss fairly this subject; then you will not need that I urge other arguments to secure effective action. Fathers, husbands, brothers, friends, citizens—you will require no more earnest solicitations to incite to the accomplishment of this noble work of *benevolence,* of *humanity,* and of *justice.* . . .

Respectfully submitted,

D. L. DIX.

NASHVILLE, NOVEMBER, 1847.

6. A Yale Medical Student Decries the Use of Anesthesia in Childbirth, 1848

Let us now . . . see what is said . . . with regard to the *justifiability of the use* of the *Vapor of Ether.*

Pain may be considered a premonitory condition, . . . and therefore we *should* feel averse to prevent it. *Pain* is *preventive, preservative,* and *curative.*

Lebbeus Eaton Marsh, "On the Inhalation of the Vapor of Ether" (M.D. dissertation, Medical Institution of Yale College, 1848), Historical Library, Cushing/Whitney Medical Library, Yale University, New Haven, Connecticut.

The *sensation* of pain, rouses us suddenly from our sleep, and impels us to flee from impending danger; the *dread* of pain *preserves* us from that, which would prove prejudicial to moral, as well as physical health, it restrains us from rushing madly into the vortex of vice, merely for the sake of the transient pleasure it affords; and *actual* pain, under disease, induces us to resort to those means best calculated to remove its cause. Pain, may, in fact be considered as a sentinel, wisely stationed on the walls of the citadel of life, to guard it against danger, or to give warning of its approach.

A humane physician, or surgeon, then, should weigh well the consequences of driving this sentinel from his post; or of lulling him to sleep while there—

Numerous cases are reported, in which, not only was suffering removed or alleviated, during parturition, but even the process itself, conducted to a safe and speedy issue under the administration of the vapor of Ether.

Still, however, we cannot but deprecate the introduction of this adjuvant into obstetric practice. A quick and easy labor, is not, consequently, a safe one, for we must look at its remote results, and there is no pain which suffering humanity is called upon to endure, attend with so little danger, and so quickly forgotten, as that which attends upon parturient effort.

In ninety-nine cases out of a hundred, there is no danger in this process *without the use of ether,* (we would not venture to say the same *with its use*) and—notwithstanding the extreme suffering which is consequent, and, naturally, ought to be consequent on the act of parturition—in an equal proportion of cases, the woman forgets her sufferings the moment her child is born; unless it be those after-pains which the *vis-medicatrix naturæ* brings into play, to remove the congestion, and diminish the volume of the puerperal womb.

Were it possible to restrict the administration of the vapor of Ether, to the most skillful and judicious physicians, as has recently been done by the Grand Duke of Hesse-Darmstadt—who has prohibited the lower grades of medical practitioners, (Officiers de sante) dentists, and midwives, in his domain, from using it in their operations,—our apprehensions would be less serious. But, in our *blessed* land of liberty, where big bugs and little bugs, and humbugs, equally operate with impunity, such exclusiveness is repudiated and, therefore, they who have a name to gain, as well as those who have no fame to lose, will in all probability, be most eager to use it, even on hazardous, as well as unnecessary occasions.

Hence, many respectable physicians, though dubious as to its propriety, may be driven to administer it in self defence. For we are well aware, how strong is the desire of freedom from suffering, where pain is dreaded, and how natural it is to the afflicted to have recourse to those, who promise them such immunity, and to give them the preference over the more prudent and skillful physician; and we also well know what a high reputation, for the time being, clings to that accoucher, and what a halo of glory encircles him, who is notorious for expediting labor, and rendering it easy, be the consequences what they may. . . .

There *may* be cases, in which this article will prove serviceable, but it should not be administered merely to allay the fears and remove the sufferings of a female destitute of common fortitude.

7. Samuel Cartwright, a Medical Professor and Racial Theorist, Reports to the Medical Association of Louisiana on the "Diseases and Physical Peculiarities of the Negro Race," 1851

Gentlemen:—On the part of the Committee, consisting of Doctors Copes, Williamson, Browning and myself, to investigate the diseases and physical peculiarities of our negro population, we beg leave TO REPORT—

That, although the African race constitutes nearly a moiety of our southern population, it has not been made the subject of much scientific investigation, and is almost entirely unnoticed in medical books and schools. . . . The little knowledge that Southern physicians have acquired concerning them, has not been derived from books or medical lectures, but from facts learned from their own observation in the field of experience, or picked up here and there from others.

Before going into the peculiarities of their diseases, it is necessary to glance at the anatomical and physiological differences between the negro and the white man; otherwise their diseases cannot be understood. . . .

The excess of organic nervous matter, and the deficiency of cerebral—the predominance of the humors over the red blood, from defective atmospherization of the blood in the lungs, impart to the negro a nature not unlike that of a new-born infant of the white race. In children, the nervous system predominates, and the temperament is lymphatic. The liver, and the rest of the glandular system, is out of proportion to the sanguineous and respiratory systems, the white fluids predominating over the red; the lungs consume less oxygen, and the liver separates more carbon, than in the adult age. This constitution, so well marked in infancy, is the type of the Ethiopian constitution, of all ages and sexes. . . .

Negroes, moreover, resemble children in the activity of the liver and in their strong assimilating powers, and in the predominance of the other systems over the sanguineous; hence they are difficult to bleed, owing to the smallness of their veins. On cording the arm of the stoutest negro, the veins will be found scarcely as large as a white boy's of ten years of age. They are liable to all the convulsive diseases, cramps, spasms, colics, etc., that children are so subject to. . . .

. . . Anatomy and physiology have been interrogated, and the response is, that the Ethiopian, or Canaanite, is unfitted, from his organization and the physiological laws predicated on that organization, for the responsible duties of a free man, but, like the child, is only fitted for a state of dependence and subordination. . . .

A knowledge of the great primary truth, that the negro is a slave by nature, and can never be happy, industrious, moral or religious, in any other condition than the one he was intended to fill, is of great importance to the theologian, the statesman, and to all those who are at heart seeking to promote his temporal and future welfare. . . . [T]he science of Medicine has nothing to do, further than to uncover its light, to show truth from error. . . .

Samuel A. Cartwright, "Report on the Diseases and Physical Peculiarities of the Negro Race," *New Orleans Medical and Surgical Journal* 7 (1850–1851): 691–692, 694–696, 698–700, 703–704, 707–710, 712, 715.

One of the most formidable complaints among negroes, and which is more fatal than any other, is congestion of the lungs. . . . It is more common among those who sleep in open houses, without sufficient fires to keep them warm and comfortable. It is seldom observed among negroes who inhabit log cabins, with cemented or clay floors, or warm houses made of brick, or any material to exclude the cold wind and air. The frame houses, with open weather-boarding and loose floors, admitting air both at the sides and from below, are buildings formed in ignorance of the peculiar physiological laws of the negro's organization, and are the fruitful sources of many of his most dangerous diseases.

Want of sufficient fires and warm blankets, is also another cause of thoracic complaints. The negro's lungs, except when the body is warmed by exercise, are very sensitive to the impressions of cold air. When not working or taking exercise, they always crowd around a fire, even in comparatively warm weather, and seem to take a positive pleasure in breathing heated air and warm smoke. In cold weather, instead of sleeping with their feet to the fire, as all other kinds of people do, whether civilized or savage, they turn their head to the fire—evidently for the satisfaction of inhaling warm air, as congenial to their lungs, in repose, as it is to infants. In bed, when disposing themselves for sleep, the young and old, male and female, instinctively cover their heads and faces, as if to insure the inhalation of warm, impure air, loaded with carbonic acid and aqueous vapor. The natural effect of this practice is imperfect atmospherization of the blood—one of the heaviest chains that binds the negro to slavery. In treating, therefore, their pulmonary affections, the important fact should be taken into consideration, that cold air is inimical to the lungs of healthy negroes, when the body is in repose, and not heated by exercise, and consequently more prejudicial in the diseases of those organs. A small, steady fire, a close room, and plenty of thick blanket covering, aided with hot stimulating teas, are very essential means in the treatment of the pulmonary congestions to which their lungs are so prone. . . . [T]hey will not bear repeated blood-letting, as the white race do. . . .

. . . [I]t is most strange that our institutions for medical learning, South, should be doing nothing, with such ample materials around them, to overturn an hypothesis [that is, abolitionism], founded in gross ignorance of the anatomy and physiology of the African race—an hypothesis threatening to cause a disruption of our federal government, and that could be disproved and put down forever at the dissecting table; as it also could be by contrasting the phenomena, drawn from daily observations taken among three millions of negroes, in health and disease, with the phenomena already drawn from observations of the white race; and thereby proving the difference of organization in mind and body between the two races. Stranger still, that our Southern schools in Medicine should be content to linger behind those of the North, without even hope of rivaling them in the numbers of their students, when a provision for including, in their course of instruction, the three millions of people in our midst, not cared for by any school, would, in time, put them far a-head, by attracting the current of students South, who have heretofore been attracted to the North. Some provision in our schools especially devoted to the anatomy and physiology of our negroes,—to the treatment of their diseases,—to the best means to prevent sickness among them,—to improve their condition, and at the same time to make them more valuable to their owners, and governed with more ease and safety,—would be sending Science into a new and wide field of usefulness, to reap immense benefits for the millions of both races inhabiting the South. . . .

Drapetomania is from [the Greek words meaning] . . . a runaway slave, and . . . *mad or crazy.* It is unknown to our medical authorities, although its diagnostic symptom, the absconding from service, is well known to our planters and overseers, as it was to the ancient Greeks. . . . I have added to the word meaning runaway slave, another Greek term, to express the disease of the mind causing him to abscond. In noticing a disease not heretofore classed among the long list of maladies that man is subject to, it was necessary to have a new term to express it. The cause, in the most of cases, that induces the negro to run away from service, is as much a disease of the mind as any other species of mental alienation, and much more curable, as a general rule. With the advantages of proper medical advice, strictly followed, this trouble-some practice that many negroes have of running away, can be almost entirely pre-vented, although the slaves be located on the borders of a free State, within a stone's throw of the abolitionists. . . .

. . . Before negroes run away, unless they are frightened or panic-struck, they become sulky and dissatisfied. The cause of this sulkiness and dissatisfaction should be inquired into and removed, or they are apt to run away or fall into the negro consumption. When sulky and dissatisfied without cause, the experience of those on the line and elsewhere was decidedly in favor of whipping them out of it, as a preventive measure against absconding or other bad conduct. It was called whip-ping the devil out of them.

If treated kindly, well fed and clothed, with fuel enough to keep a small fire burning all night, separated into families, each family having its own house—not permitted to run about at night, or to visit their neighbors, or to receive visits, or to use intoxicating liquors, and not overworked or exposed too much to the weather, they are very easily governed—more so than any other people in the world. . . . They have only to be kept in that state, and treated like children, with care, kind-ness, attention and humanity, to prevent and cure them from running away. . . .

Dysæsthesia Æthiopis is a disease peculiar to negroes, affecting both mind and body, in a manner as well expressed by dysæsthesia. . . . It is much more prevalent among free negroes living in clusters by themselves, than among slaves on our plantations, and attacks only such slaves as live like free negroes in regard to diet, drinks, exercise, etc. . . .

From the careless movements of the individuals affected with the complaint, they are apt to do much mischief, which appears as if intentional, but is mostly owing to the stupidness of mind and insensibility of the nerves induced by the dis-ease. Thus, they break, waste and destroy everything they handle—abuse horses and cattle,—tear, burn or rend their own clothing, and paying no attention to the rights of property, they steal other's to replace what they have destroyed. They wander about at night, and keep in a half-nodding sleep during the day. They slight their work,—cut up corn, cane, cotton or tobacco when hoeing it, as if for pure mischief. They raise disturbances with their overseers and fellow servants without cause or motive, and seem to be insensible to pain when subjected to punishment. The fact of the existence of such a complaint, making man like an automaton or senseless machine, having the above or similar symptoms, can be clearly estab-lished by the most direct and positive testimony. That it should have escaped the attention of the medical profession, can only be accounted for because its attention has not been sufficiently directed to the maladies of the negro race. . . .

The complaint is easily curable, if treated on sound physiological principles. The skin is dry, thick and harsh to the touch, and the liver inactive. The liver, skin and kidneys should be stimulated to activity, and be made assist in decarbonising the blood. The best means to stimulate the skin is, first, to have the patient well washed with warm water and soap; then, to anoint it all over with oil, and to slap the oil in with a broad leather strap; then to put the patient to some hard kind of work in the open air and sunshine, that will compel him to expand his lungs, as chopping wood, splitting rails or sawing with the cross-cut or whip saw. Any kind of labor will do that will cause full and free respiration in its performance, as lifting or carrying heavy weights, or brisk walking; the object being to expand the lungs by full and deep inspirations and expirations, thereby to vitalize the impure circulating blood by introducing oxygen and expelling carbon. . . .

. . . The dysæsthesia æthiopis adds another to the many ten thousand evidences of the fallacy of the dogma that abolitionism is built on; for here, in a country where two races of men dwell together, both born on the same soil, breathing the same air, and surrounded by the same external agents—liberty, which is elevating the one race of people above all other nations, sinks the other into beastly sloth and torpidity; and the slavery, which the one would prefer death rather than endure, improves the other in body, mind and morals; thus proving the dogma false, and establishing the truth that there is a radical, internal, or physical difference between the two races, so great in kind, as to make what is wholesome and beneficial for the white man, as liberty, republican or free institutions, etc., not only unsuitable to the negro race, but actually poisonous to its happiness.

8. A Tennessee Physician Calls for the Cultivation of a Distinctive Southern Medical Literature, 1860

The earth is divided into many natural botanical and zoölogical provinces, each possessing their own pecular fauna and flora, differing materially from each other. The difference is not the result of mere parallels or meridians, but isothermal lines, elevations, soil, moisture, etc., which tend to form the habits of each special province. . . . Diseases have their origin in the force and combination of elements without, modified by many causes peculiar to the locality of their origin; being virulent or mild, either in combination of elements or capacity of resistance in the individual. Diseases differ in different individuals, and no one but the quack ever thought of curing the same disease in every individual with the same remedy. It is true the same remedy may be given to a large number of cases, but not without many preparatory steps in the case, and changes and new combinations of the remedy to meet individual peculiarities.

This every physician knows to be the case in diseases of the same localities, in the same neighborhood and in the same families. How widely different then

S. P. Crawford, "Southern Medical Literature," *Nashville Journal of Medicine and Surgery* 18 (1860): 195–198.

are diseases of the same type in different localities, even within the same iso-thermal lines, and the difference must be still greater as you go above or below the lines. The idea of a man writing a book upon diseases from his observation of disease in a northern climate, which is designed to be a faithful and reliable exponent of the diagnosis and treatment of even the same disease within the tropics, is absolutely ridiculous. The man who relies upon such a book in the treatment of tropical diseases, no matter how high the "authority," will have a fearful mortality to tell the tale of his faithful reliance. . . . We have often heard it remarked by the physician, after having struggled with disease for some time according to the "authorities," "that books will not do to rely upon." The reason is obvious in the foregoing facts. Southern physicians . . . have groped in darkness for the want of competent guides, relying upon light from a distant quarter, for-getting that a southern latitude requires a southern sun, a light more practical and powerful than the aurora borealis. We must work for ourselves by the light that is shed around our own special habitations. . . . The great error of the southern physician, I think, has been his tenaciously adhering to principles drawn from observations in widely different localities. . . . The principles to which he adhered were not incorrect in the locality in which they were demonstrated, but wholly in-applicable when attempted to be applied in a different locality and among a differ-ent people. . . .

Northern books are not adapted to southern disease upon principles here deduced. The same is true of northern colleges. The general principles of medicine may be taught there as well as anywhere, and anywhere as well as there. But the practise of medicine can never be taught there to meet the demands of the student, I care not how many clinics or hospital demonstrations may come before him in a day. One single well developed case of fever, for instance, demonstrated before a class in a locality its own, or similar to it, will be of more practical benefit than a hundred cases of the same disease in a high northern latitude. . . . Medicine, like disease, must spring from the very elements, soil, sunshine, moisture, etc., that produce disease. The very circumstances that develop the one, contains, and sug-gest also, the antidote. The study and cure of disease in one locality does not neces-sarily give the information requisite to success in another locality. . . . Again we have a population here that book-makers at the north know absolutely nothing about—a people widely different from the race with which they are familiar, and of whose diseases they are no more competent to write than to give a history of the inhabitants of the moon. A southern medical literature is the desideratum—a litera-ture that can be relied upon—a literature drawn from demonstrations in a southern field, whose fauna and flora are different, having different botanical and zoölogical provinces—whose geology is different—whose heat and moisture are different in degrees, and whose genus homo is different in dynamical force, and whose diseases are modified or rendered virulent by these many differences, all of which have to be studied in their natural relations.

. . . Drake has collected a vast heap of valuable material, Cartwright has added no little, and a host of others have thrown in their items. The question is, who will systematize and arrange the facts into a work, that can be a reliable standard in the treatment of southern diseases? Who, we ask, will undertake to put southern medi-cine upon her legs? Once there, a mighty host will cry amen!

ESSAYS

Charles E. Rosenberg of the University of Pennsylvania explains in the first essay the notion of the body and its functioning in sickness and in health that was shared by antebellum doctors and patients alike. Earlier historians had tended to dismiss early-nineteenth-century therapy as risible or tragic, but Rosenberg, enlisting anthropological perspective for historical understanding, characterizes a system of cognitive structures and social rituals that was compelling, just as in this medical cosmology he identifies fault lines that promoted challenges and change. What precisely does Rosenberg mean when he asserts that, in the early nineteenth century, a therapy such as bloodletting "worked"? In the next essay, University of Michigan historian Martin S. Pernick elucidates the framework sketched by Rosenberg, using the 1846 introduction of anesthesia into surgery as his focus, and traces not only the transformation of antebellum therapeutics but also how changing attitudes toward patients' suffering went hand in hand with shifting notions of medical professionalism. In the final essay, Todd L. Savitt, a historian at the Medical College of East Carolina University, investigates how race and class made the bodies of African American men and women—especially (though by no means exclusively) in the South—singularly vulnerable to medical experimentation and involuntary dissection by European American medical students, physicians, and anatomists. How might a racial theorist like Cartwright have reconciled his conviction that blacks differ from whites in mind and body with the reliance in medical schools on the bodies of slaves for teaching anatomy by dissection?

Belief and Ritual in Antebellum Medical Therapeutics

CHARLES E. ROSENBERG

Medical historians have always found therapeutics an awkward piece of business. On the whole, they have responded by ignoring it. Most historians who have addressed traditional therapeutics have approached it as a source of anecdote, or as a murky bog of routinism from which a comforting path led upward to an ultimately enlightened and scientifically based therapeutics. Isolated incidents such as the introduction of quinine or digitalis seemed only to emphasize the darkness of traditional practice in which they appeared. Among twentieth-century students of medical history, the generally unquestioned criterion for understanding pre-nineteenth-century therapeutics has been physiological, not historical: did a particular practice act in a way that twentieth-century understanding would regard as efficacious? Did it work?

Yet therapeutics is after all a good deal more than a series of pharmacological or surgical experiments. It involves emotions and personal relationships and incorporates all of those cultural factors which determine belief, identity, and status. The meaning of traditional therapeutics must be sought within a particular cultural context; this is a task more closely akin to that of the cultural anthropologist than the physiologist. Individuals become sick, demand care and reassurance, are treated by designated healers. Both physician and patient must share a compatible—though not necessarily identical—framework of explanation. To understand therapeutics in the opening decades of the nineteenth-century, its would-be historian must see

---

Charles E. Rosenberg, "The Therapeutic Revolution: Medicine, Meaning, and Social Change in Nineteenth-Century America," *Perspectives in Biology and Medicine* 20 (1977): 485–506. Copyright © The John Hopkins University Press.

that it relates on the one hand to a cognitive system of explanation and on the other to a patterned interaction between doctor and patient, one which evolved over centuries into a conventionalized social ritual. . . .

The key to understanding therapeutics at the beginning of the nineteenth century lies in seeing it as part of a system of belief and behavior participated in by physician and layman alike. Central to the logic of this social subsystem was a deeply assumed metaphor—a particular way of looking at the body and of explaining both health and disease. The body was seen metaphorically as a system of dynamic interactions with its environment. Health or disease resulted from a cumulative interaction between constitutional endowment and environmental circumstance. One could not well live without food and air and water; one had to live in a particular climate, subject one's body to a particular style of life and work. Each of these factors implied a necessary and continuing physiological adjustment. The body was always in a state of becoming—and thus always in jeopardy.

Two subsidiary assumptions organized the shape of this lifelong interaction. First, every part of the body was related inevitably and inextricably with every other. A distracted mind could curdle the stomach, a dyspeptic stomach could agitate the mind. Local lesions might reflect imbalances of nutrients in the blood; systemic ills might be caused by fulminating local lesions. . . . Second, the body was seen as a system of intake and outgo—a system which had necessarily to remain in balance if the individual were to remain healthy. Thus the conventional emphasis on diet and excretion, perspiration and ventilation. Equilibrium was synonymous with health, disequilibrium with illness.

In addition to the exigencies of everyday life which might destabilize that equilibrium which constituted health, the body had also to pass through several developmental crises inherent in the design of the human organism. Menstruation and menopause in women and teething and puberty in both sexes all represented points of potential danger, moments of structured instability as the body established a new internal equilibrium. Seasonal changes in climate constituted another kind of recurring cyclical change which might imply danger to health and require possible medical intervention; thus the ancient practice of administering cathartics in spring and fall so as to help the body adjust to the changed seasons. . . .

The idea of specific disease entities played a relatively small role in such a system. Where empirical observation pointed unavoidably toward the existence of a particular disease state, physicians still sought to preserve their accustomed therapeutic role. And the physician's most potent weapon was his ability to "regulate the secretions"—to extract blood, to promote the perspiration, urination, or defecation which attested to his having helped the body regain its customary equilibrium. Even when a disease seemed not only to have a characteristic course but, as in the case of smallpox, a specific causative "virus," the hypothetical pathology and indicated therapeutics were seen within the same explanatory framework. The success of inoculation and later vaccination in preventing smallpox could not challenge this deeply internalized system of explanation. When mid-eighteenth- and early nineteenth-century physicians inoculated or vaccinated they always accompanied the procedure with an elaborate regimen of cathartics, diet, and rest. . . .

The American physician in 1800 had no diagnostic tools beyond his senses and it is hardly surprising that he would find congenial a framework of explanation which emphasized the importance of intake and outgo, of the significance of perspiration, of pulse, of urination and menstruation, of defecation, of the surface eruptions which might accompany fevers or other internal ills. These were phenomena which he as physician, the patient, and patient's family could see, evaluate, scrutinize for clues to the sick individual's fate. . . .

The effectiveness of the system hinged to a significant extent on the fact that all the weapons in the physician's normal armamentarium worked, worked that is by providing visible and predictable physiological effects; purges purged, emetics vomited, opium soothed pain and moderated diarrhea. Bleeding too seemed obviously to alter the body's internal balance—as evidenced both by a changed pulse and the very quantity of the blood drawn. Blisters and other purposefully induced local irritations certainly produced visible effects—and presumably internal consequences proportional to their pain, location, and to the nature and extent of the matter discharged. Not only did a drug's activity indicate to both physician and patient the nature of its efficacy (and the physician's competence) but it provided a prognostic tool as well; for the patient's response to a drug could indicate much about his condition, while the product elicited—urine, feces, blood, perspiration—could be examined so as to shed light on the body's internal state. . . .

This same explanatory framework illuminates as well the extraordinary vogue of mercury in early nineteenth-century therapeutics. If employed for a sufficient length of time and in sufficient quantity, mercury induced a series of progressively severe and ultimately full-blown symptoms of mercury poisoning. The copious involuntary salivation characteristic of this toxic state was seen as proof that the drug was exerting an "alterative" effect—that is, altering the fundamental balance of forces and substances which constituted the body's ultimate reality. . . .

. . . Drugs reassured insofar as they acted and their efficacy was inevitably underwritten by the natural tendency toward recovery which characterized most ills. Therapeutics thus played a central role within the system of doctor-patient interaction; on the cognitive level, therapeutics confirmed the physician's ability to understand and intervene in the ongoing physiological processes which defined health and disease; on the emotional level, the very severity of drug action assured the patient and his family that something was indeed being done.

In the medical idiom of 1800, "exhibiting" a drug was synonymous with administering it (and the administration of drugs so routine that "prescribing for" was synonymous with seeing a patient). This term was hardly accidental. For the therapeutic interaction we have sought to describe was a fundamental cultural ritual—in a literal sense—a ritual in which the legitimating element rested at least in part upon a shared commitment to a rationalistic model of pathology and therapeutic action. . . .

. . . And indeed, the efficacy and tenacity of this system must be understood in relation to its social setting. Most such therapeutic tableaux took place in the patient's home and thus the healing ritual could mobilize all those community and emotional forces which anthropologists have seen as fundamental in their observations of medical practice in traditional non-Western societies. . . .

The physician's art in the opening decades of the nineteenth century centered on this ability to employ an appropriate drug or combination of drugs and bleeding to produce a particular physiological end. Thus the apparent anomaly of physicians employing different drugs to treat the same condition; each drug, the argument followed, was equally legitimate so long as it produced the desired physiological effect. And this was no mean skill, authorities explained, for each patient possessed a unique physiological identity and the experienced physician had to evaluate a bewildering variety of factors ranging from climatic conditions to age and sex in the compounding of any particular prescription. A physician who knew a family's constitutional idiosyncracies was necessarily a better practitioner for that family than one who enjoyed no such insight, or even one who hailed from a different climate. For it was assumed that both the action of drugs and reaction of patients varied with season and geography. The physician had to be aware as well that the same drug in different dosages might produce different effects. Fifteen grams of ipecac, a young Southern medical student cautioned himself, acted as an emetic, five induced sweating, while smaller doses could serve as a useful tonic. . . .

Early nineteenth-century American physicians unquestionably believed in the therapeutics they practiced. Physicians routinely prescribed severe cathartics and bleeding for themselves, for their wives and children. . . .

Individuals from almost every level in society accepted—in forms reflecting individual and class differences—the basic outlines of the cognitive system we have described. Evidence of such belief among the less articulate is not abundant, but it does exist. Patients, for example, understood that a sudden interruption of perspiration might cause a cold or even pneumonia, that such critical periods as teething, puberty, or menopause were particularly dangerous. The metabolic gyroscope which controlled the balance of forces within the body was delicate indeed and might easily be thrown off course. Thus it was natural for servants and laborers reporting the symptoms of their fevers to an alms-house physician to ascribe them to a sudden stoppage of the perspiration. It was equally natural for young ladies complaining of amenorrhea to ascribe it to a sudden chill. The sudden interruption of any natural evacuation would presumably jeopardize the end implicit in that function; if the body did not need to perspire in certain circumstances or discharge menstrual blood at intervals it would not be doing so. These were mechanisms through which the body maintained its health-defining equilibrium, and thus they could be interrupted only at great peril. Almanacs, patent medicine circulars, and the letters and diaries of undistinguished Americans all indicate the widespread acceptance of these beliefs. . . .

The widespread faith in emetics, in cathartics, in diuretics, and in bleeding is evidenced as well by their prominent place in folk medicine. Domestic and irregular practice, that is, like regular medicine, was shaped about the eliciting of predictable physiological responses. Home remedies mirrored the heroic therapeutics practiced by regular physicians. In the fall of 1826, for example, when a Philadelphia tallow chandler fell ill he complained of chills, pains in the head and back, weakness in the joints, and nausea. Then, before seeing a regular physician, he "Was bled till symptoms of fainting came on. Took an emetic, which operated well. For several days after, kept his bowels moved with Sulph. Soda, Senna tea &c. He then employed a Physician who prescribed another Emetic, which operated violently and whose action was kept up by drinking bitter tea. . . ." Only after 2 more days did he appear at the Alms-House Hospital. Physicians skeptical of traditional therapeutics complained repeatedly of lay expectations which worked against change; medical men might well be subject to criticism if they should, for example, fail to bleed in the early stages of pneumonia. Parents often demanded that physicians incise the inflamed gums of their teething infants so as to provoke a "resolution" of this devel-opmental crisis. Laymen could, indeed, be even more importunate in their demands for an aggressive therapy than the physicians attending them thought appropriate. . . .

Botanic alternatives to regular medicine in the first third of the century were also predicated upon the routine use of severe cathartics and emetics—if of vegetable origin. (In the practice of Thomsonian physicians, the most prominent organized botanic sect, such drugs were supplemented by sweat baths designed in theory to adjust the body's internal heat through the eliciting of copious perspiration.) Botanic physicians shared many of the social problems faced by their regular competitors; they dealt with the same emotional realities implicit in the doctor-patient relationship and in doing so appealed to a similar framework of physiological assumption.

Nevertheless, there were differences of approach—among physicians and in the minds of a good many laymen who questioned both the routinism and the frequent severity of traditional therapeutics. (The criticisms which greeted the atypically severe bleeding and purging advocated by Benjamin Rush are familiar to any student of the period.) America in 1800 was in many ways already a modern society, diverse in religion, in class, and in ethnic background. It would be naive to contend that the unity of vision which—presumably—united most traditional non-Western cultures in their orientation toward a particular medical system could apply to this diverse and labile culture. Yet, as we have argued, there are surprisingly large areas of agreement. Even those Americans skeptical of therapeutic excess and inconsistency (and in some cases more generally of the physician's authority) did not question the funda-mental structure of the body metaphor we have described, disagree though they may have with regard to the possible efficacy of medical intervention in sickness. . . .

In describing American medical therapeutics in the first quarter of the nineteenth century we have been examining a system already marked by signs of instability. . . .

By the 1830s, criticism of traditional therapeutics had become a cliché in so-phisticated medical circles; physicians of any pretension spoke of self-limited dis-eases, of scepticism in regard to the physician's ability to intervene and change the course of most diseases, of respect for the healing powers of nature. This point of view emphasized the self-limited nature of most ailments, and the physician's duty simply to aid the process of natural recovery through appropriate—and minimally heroic—means. "It would be better," as Oliver Wendell Holmes put it in his usual acerbic fashion, "if the patient were allowed a certain discount from his bill for every dose he took, just as children are compensated by their parents for swallowing hideous medicinal mixtures." Rest, a strengthening diet, and a mild cathartic were all the aid nature required in most ills. In those ailments whose natural tendency was toward death, the physician had to acknowledge his powerlessness and simply try to minimize pain and anxiety. This noninterventionist position was accompanied by increasing acceptance of the parallel view that most diseases could be seen as dis-tinct clinical entities with a characteristic cause, course, and symptomatology. . . .

American physicians were tied to the everyday requirements of the doctor-patient relationship and thus, even among the teaching elite, no mid-century Ameri-can practitioner rejected conventional therapeutics with a ruthless consistency. The self-confident empiricism which denied the utility of any therapeutic measure not proven efficacious in clinical trials seemed an ideological excess suited to a handful of European academics, not to the realities of practice. It is no accident that the radically skeptical position was christened therapeutic nihilism by its critics. Nihilism with its echoes of disbelief and destructive change—of "total rejection of current religious beliefs and morals," to borrow a defining phrase from the *Oxford English Dictionary*—was not chosen as a term of casual abuse, but represented precisely the gravity of the challenge to a traditional world view implied by a relentless empiricism and the materialism which seemed so often to accompany it.

There were enduring virtues in the old ways. "There is," as one leader in the profession explained, "a vantage ground between the two extremes, neither verging towards meddlesome interference on the one hand, nor imbecile neglect on the other." The physician had to contend, moreover, with patient expectations: "The public," as another prominent clinician put it, "expect something more of physicians than the power of distinguishing diseases and of predicting their issue. They look to them for the relief of their sufferings, and the cure or removal of their complaints." . . .

. . . Despite the growing plausibility of views emphasizing disease specificity, for example, most physicians still maintained an emphasis on their traditional ability to modify symptoms. The older assumption that drugs acted in a way consistent with the body's innate pattern of recovery was easily shifted toward new emphases. The physician's responsibility now centered on recognizing the natural course of his patient's ailment and supporting the body in its path to renewed health with an appropriate combination of drugs and regimen; even the course of a self-limited disease might be shortened, its painful symptoms mitigated. The secretions had still to be regulated, diet specified and modified, perhaps a plethora of blood lessened by cupping or leeching. Even in ills whose natural course was to death, the physician might still avail himself of therapeutic means to ease the grim road. Finally, no one doubted there were ailments in which the physician's intervention could make the difference between life and death; scurvy, for example, was often cited as a disease "that taints the whole system, [yet] yields to a mere change in diet." The surgeon still had to set bones, remove foreign bodies, drain abscesses. . . .

The decades between 1850 and 1870 did see an increased emphasis on diet and regimen among regular physicians, most strikingly a vogue for the use of alcoholic beverages as stimulants. It is hardly surprising that one reaction to the varied criticisms of traditional therapeutics was a consequent acceptance of a "strengthening and stimulating" emphasis in practice: it responded not only to criticisms by sectarian physicians of "depleting" measures such as bleeding and purging, but preserved an active role for the physician within the same framework of attitudes toward the body which had always helped order the doctor-patient relationship. . . .

. . . [O]lder modes of therapeutics did not die, but, as we have suggested, were employed less routinely and in generally smaller doses. Dosage levels decreased markedly in the second third of the century and bleeding especially sank into disuse. The resident physician at the Philadelphia Dispensary could, for example, report in 1862 that of a total of 9,502 treated that year, "general blood-letting has been resorted to in one instance only, . . . cupping twelve times and leeching thrice." Residents at Bellevue in New York and in Boston's Massachusetts General Hospital had reported the previous year that bloodletting was "almost obsolete." Mercury, on the other hand, still figured in the practice of most physicians: even infants and small children endured the discomfort of mercury poisoning until well after the Civil War. Purges were still administered routinely in spring and fall to facilitate the body's adjustment to the changing seasons. The blisters and excoriated running sores so familiar to physicians and patients at the beginning of the century were gradually replaced by mustard plasters or turpentine applications, but the ancient concept of counterirritation still rationalized their use. Even bleeding still lingered, though increasingly in the practice of older men and in less cosmopolitan areas. . . .

Indeed, it was not until the very end of the nineteenth century that an outspoken and thoroughgoing therapeutic skepticism came actually to be pronounced from some of America's most prestigious medical chairs. "In some future day," as one authority put it [in 1898]:

> it is certain that drugs and chemicals will form no part of a scientific therapy. This is sure to be the case, for truth is finally certain to prevail. . . . The principal influence or relation of materia medica to the cure of bodily disease lies in the fact that drugs supply material upon which to rest the mind while other agencies are at work in eliminating disease from the system, and to the drug is frequently given the credit. . . . Sugar of milk tablets of various colors and different flavors constitute a materia medica in practice that needs for temporary use only, morphin, codein, cocain, aconite and a laxative to make it complete.

A dozen drugs, a Hopkins clinician argued [by 1900], "suffice for the pharmacotherapeutic armamentarium of some of the most eminent physicians on this continent." . . .

Clearly, the physician and the great majority of his patients no longer share a similar view of the body and the mechanisms which determine health and disease. Differing views of the body and the physician's ability to intervene in its mysterious opacity divide groups and individuals, not unify, as the widely disseminated metaphorical view of body function had still done in 1800. Physician and patient are no longer bound together by the very physiological activity of the drugs administered. In a sense, almost *all* drugs now act as placebos, for with the exception of certain classes of drugs such as diuretics, the patient experiences no perceptible physiological effect. He does ordinarily have faith in the efficacy of a particular therapy, but it is a faith based not on a shared nexus of belief and participation in the kind of experience we have described, but rather on the physician and his imputed status—indirectly, on that of science itself. Obviously, one can draw facile parallels to many other areas in which an older community of world view and personal relationship has been replaced by a more fragmented and status-oriented reality. Such observations have become commonplace as we try to ascertain the shape of a gradually emerging modernity in the nineteenth-century West.

Pain, the Calculus of Suffering, and Antebellum Surgery

MARTIN S. PERNICK

It is hard for us today to recreate the surgeon's feelings before anesthesia became available. The emotional ability to inflict vast suffering was perhaps the most basic of all professional prerequisites. A nineteenth-century anesthesia promoter recalled the procedure to repair a dislocated hip.

Martin S. Pernick, "The Calculus of Suffering in Nineteenth-Century Surgery," *Hastings Center Report* 13, no. 2 (1983): 26–34. Reproduced by permission. Copyright © The Hastings Center.

Big drops of perspiration, started by the excess of agony, bestrew the patient's forehead, sharp screams burst from him in peal after peal—all his struggles to free himself and escape the horrid torture, are valueless, for he is in the powerful hands of men then as inexorable as death. . . . At last the agony becomes too great for human endurance, and with a wild, despairing yell, the sufferer relapses into unconsciousness. . . .

Under such conditions, the professional values adopted by surgeons for most of Western history emphasized that saving life held absolute priority over avoiding suffering. . . .

. . . Benjamin Rush's student Philip Syng Physick, the first American to gain prominence as a full-time surgeon, became so sick at his initial amputation that he had to be carried from the room in mid-operation. Those who could not learn to accept the value of the suffering had to leave the profession. Samuel Cooper's early-nineteenth-century textbook cautioned prospective young surgeons to heed the example of the Swiss physiologist Haller, who had studied diligently to become a surgeon but had failed in practice, due to his "fear of giving too much pain." Cooper told aspiring young surgeons to learn [that] . . . ["]undisturbed coolness, which is still more rare than skill, is the most valuable quality in the practice of surgery." . . .

Not surprisingly, those who managed to overcome their revulsion and master the professional ability to inflict suffering took a certain pride in their accomplishment. British surgeon John Hunter claimed that there was a certain "*éclat* generally attending painful operations, often only because they are so." And, also not surprisingly, the practice of surgery did sometimes produce callousness. . . .

While their traditions and training thus sanctioned the infliction of agonizing remedies whenever "necessary" to save life, practitioners varied widely in their concept of necessity. For most surgeons operations generally remained the last resort. Such surgical reticence derived mainly from the appalling mortality rates, the product of uncontrollable infections, hemorrhage, and shock. In major limb amputations, death rates of 30 to 50 percent were not uncommon. As a result, both surgeons and patients avoided operations as long as possible (thus perhaps further inflating the surgical mortality rates). But, at least some surgeons cited suffering, not simply mortality, as their reason for avoiding the knife. . . .

Within this general tradition, early-nineteenth-century American physicians and surgeons gained a reputation for the particularly unrestrained infliction of excruciating remedies. Central to the notoriety of American practice as uniquely harsh and cruel was the medical system of Dr. Benjamin Rush. Rush's remedies, such as bloodletting and emetics, were based on treatments for fever that had been common to many medical systems for centuries. But he employed these procedures in an extremely heroic, unrestrained fashion. For Rush, the more dangerous the disease, the more painful the remedy must be. Rush favored "that bold humanity which dictates the use of powerful but painful remedies in violent diseases."

A skilled propagandist, Rush promoted his therapies in part by convincing practitioners and patients alike that they were heroic, bold, courageous, manly, and patriotic. Americans were tougher than Europeans; American diseases were correspondingly tougher than mild European diseases; to cure Americans would require uniquely powerful doses administered by heroic American physicians.

Whether or not American physicians really inflicted more pain than Europeans, Rush's rhetoric led observers on both sides of the Atlantic to assume they did. In the West especially, "mildness of medical treatment is real cruelty," wrote a popular medical author from Cincinnati. What was needed, he declared, was a "vigorous mode of practice; the diseases of our own country especially require it."

The heroic reliance on massive doses and extreme measures, regardless of pain, was by no means limited to orthodox physicians. Many rival healing sects flourished in nineteenth-century America; some were as painful and heroic in their practices as their professional rivals. The "botanical physicians," followers of self-cure promoter Samuel Thomson, advocated many of the same therapeutic procedures as did Rush. Thomson purged, puked, and blistered excruciatingly; he differed mainly in using only natural herbal substances to produce his pharmaceuticals.

In surgery as in medicine, Americans portrayed their practice as uniquely painful. "Frontier" surgeons like Ephraim McDowell, Nathan Smith, and J. Marion Sims developed new operations which, they bragged, Europeans had been too sensitive and timid to perform. Smith's biographer boasted that "the surgeon . . . often feels it to be his duty . . . to perform a painful and hazardous operation. . . . The timid man shrinks from such high responsibility, and suffers his patient to be destroyed by disease. Such was not Dr. Smith." Nationalistic Americans pointed with vast pride to the agonizing accomplishments of their surgeons as examples of the virile new culture of the young Republic. . . .

Thus, in the half-century prior to the discovery of anesthesia, American physicians and surgeons generally defined professional duty as demanding the unhesitating infliction of extreme suffering in order to save lives. They were not cruel or indifferent; rather, they were totally dedicated to doing whatever seemed necessary to prevent death. Reared in this tradition, many midcentury practitioners found it understandably difficult to turn around and sanction the use of drugs that had the power to relieve suffering at the risk of life. This response can be seen most starkly in the reaction of some leading American practitioners to the discovery of anesthesia. . . .

On October 16, 1846, a Boston dentist named William T. G. Morton first demonstrated that the vapor of diethyl ether could prevent the pain of surgery. Within three months of this initial public experiment, the leading hospitals of New York, London, and Paris began employing ether anesthesia. By 1848, nitrous oxide (laughing gas), chloroform, and other compounds had been added to the list of known anesthetics. The use of anesthesia spread far more rapidly than such earlier innovations as smallpox vaccination, or such later discoveries as antisepsis. Vaccination remained bitterly controversial over a century after Jenner's initial experiments; antisepsis aroused strong opposition for decades after Lister's early work. Anesthetics won acceptance at most major world medical institutions within a few years of Morton's first demonstrations.

But despite the unprecedented speed with which anesthesia entered practice, few surgeons then or since have regarded anesthetics as completely safe. In today's aseptic and technically sophisticated operating rooms, general anesthesia is often regarded as more risky than the surgery itself. In the mid-nineteenth century, when anesthesia was an untested, poorly understood novelty, concerns about its safety filled the medical journals. . . .

Midcentury surgeons thus had to decide whether the benefits of painless operations were worth the risks. Not surprisingly, more than a few insisted that the duty to preserve life absolutely outweighed the duty to relieve what one doctor revealingly termed "mere anguish." . . . The *New York Journal of Medicine* ruled that "immunity of pain merely, should never be purchased at the risk to life."

For these practitioners, the duty to preserve life was absolute; the duty to prevent suffering was recognized, but only when there was virtually no degree of physical danger involved. Thus, one young doctor admitted, "The mission of the physician is undoubtedly two-fold—to relieve human pain as well as to preserve human life. . . ." Yet one had clear priority over the other. "Endangering the life of our patient, merely for the purpose of relieving . . . from pain," he found totally "unjustifiable." . . .

However, a growing number of other physicians angrily disagreed. They urged the use of anesthesia, based on what they claimed was a professional duty to prevent suffering, even when that meant taking some risks with life. "Pain is only evil. . . . We are not required to possess an innocuous agent" to fight it, declared New York surgeon Valentine Mott. . . .

. . . [M]id-nineteenth century American attempts to strike a balance between the duty to cure and the duty to relieve drew most directly upon a new, therapeutically moderate approach to medicine. Calling their practice "conservative" or "rational" medicine, physicians like Austin Flint, Worthington Hooker, Oliver Wendell Holmes, and surgeons like Frank H. Hamilton promulgated a professional philosophy that carefully avoided all extremes. These self-professed "conservatives" excluded the radical excesses of Rush's heroism; they likewise rejected the therapeutic nihilism of his most extreme critics. Conservatives still retained the use of painful orthodox remedies, from bleeding to cautery, but in a limited and cautious fashion.

What distinguished conservative medical decision making was its search for a moderate intermediate solution to therapeutic conflicts such as that between the duty to relieve pain and the duty to preserve life. Thus, these practitioners were willing to incur danger in order to prevent suffering, but only up to a moderate limit. . . .

The conservative search for a "middle course" between conflicting ethical imperatives was closely tied to nineteenth-century advances in medical statistics, particularly the revolutionary applications of mathematics to assessments of drug safety and efficacy developed in Paris by Pierre Louis. These techniques, combining recent advances in calculus and probability theory with Bentham's utilitarian ethics, allowed physicians to measure the risks and benefits of a drug, without invoking such ethical absolutes as the traditional injunction to "do no harm." Louis and his followers taught that neither the inflicted harm done by therapeutic side effects nor the natural damage of untreated pathology was inherently preferable to the other. Rather, the physician's task was to compare directly the objective statistical magnitude of each harm regardless of its source, and act so as to maximize the overall benefit to the patient. . . .

A medical student of 1853 put it this way: "Men of science have differed in opinion" concerning how to weigh "that most terrible of obstacles, *pain*, . . ." against "the injurious effects following the use of these valuable agents [anesthetics]. . . . Statistics can afford the only unfailing criterion and are indispensable to the formation of a judgment—they should be allowed to speak for themselves." The problem thus became entirely technical. The risks and benefits of pain relievers could be measured, and the decision made according to a "rational" calculus. The physician's duty was to minimize total harm—not to make value distinctions between one type of harm and another.

By the 1850s, this mathematical approach to medical ethics enjoyed considerable professional acceptance in the United States. Thus, in the decade following Morton's ether demonstration, medical journals carried a series of statistical reports attempting to quantify the relative value of anesthetics. Many of these studies suffered from a very primitive understanding of statistics. But they clearly reflected the importance of mathematics in the conservatives' attempt to choose between conflicting versions of professional duty. . . .

The new willingness of conservative physicians to inflict some harm for the relief of suffering derived not only from medical ideas, but grew in part from mid-century social criticisms of professional callousness. Nineteenth-century American lay writers produced a torrent of demands for sentiment, emotion, and the expression of feelings in the practice of the professions. Yet this sentimentalist support for what later came to be called "empathy" did not always lead directly to the active relief of suffering; the connection was far more subtle and complex.

Public pressure for physicians to feel more emotional involvement with their patients grew increasingly insistent over the ante-bellum years. According to a typical expression of such sentiments in the *Philadelphia Bulletin,*

> Assuredly it is not a pulseless, tideless being that is desired to officiate at the couch of sickness. Rather is the man most acceptable as a physician who most approximates the feminine type; who is kind, and gentle, and cautious, and sympathetic, and truthful, and delicately modest.

One of the most caustic attacks on unfeeling surgery was Herman Melville's 1850 portrait of Dr. Cadwallader Cuticle in *White-Jacket.* Cuticle is hard, callous, and unfeeling.

> [N]othing could exceed his coolness when actually employed in his imminent vocation. Surrounded by moans and shrieks, by features distorted with anguish inflicted by himself, he yet maintained a countenance almost supernaturally calm. . . . Yet you could not say that Cuticle was essentially a cruel-hearted man. His apparent heartlessness must have been of a purely scientific origin. It is not to be imagined that even Cuticle would have harmed a fly, unless he could procure a microscope powerful enough to assist him in experimenting on the minute vitals of the creature.

But Cuticle's cold, machine-like, unemotional science is an external shell, designed to cover his real feelings—not the pangs of compassion, but his perverse and sadistic pleasure.

> Cuticle, on some occasions, would affect a certain disrelish of his profession, and declaim against the necessity that forced a man of his humanity to perform a surgical operation. Especially was it apt to be thus with him, when the case was one of more than ordinary interest. In discussing it, previous to setting about it, he would veil his eagerness under an aspect of great circumspection; curiously marred, however, by continual sallies of unsuppressable impatience.

Conservative physicians endorsed such criticisms of the unfeeling practice of medicine. In 1849, Henry J. Bigelow urged curriculum reform at the Harvard Medical School in order "to re-establish a facility in the manifestation of that kindly feeling which is generally upon the surface in early youth, but which sometimes in the process of education gets embedded beneath a stratum of indifference and insensibility." Conservative spokesmen like Worthington Hooker insisted that "humane sympathies" actually exceeded technical "skill" in medical importance. In 1848, the New York surgeon Alexander H. Stevens told the AMA, "Our profession, gentlemen, is the link that unites Science and Philanthropy."

As expressed by conservative physicians, the demand for sentiment and feeling contained more than a little elitist bias. The callousness of heroic medicine was blamed on the general decline of those genteel graces that supposedly had elevated the tone of the eighteenth-century professional. Elitist conservative physicians equated the lack of sensitivity in treatment with a lack of sensibility in manner. They dismissed the average nineteenth-century practitioner as "uncouth in his manners, vulgar and indelicate in his language, slovenly in his dress, and harsh and unfeeling in his treatment." While followers of Rush had expounded the need for harshness in democratic and especially Western medicine, conservatives scorned the resulting insensitivity as a form of rustic barbarism increasingly limited to "country physicians." . . .

To resolve the paradoxical nature of nineteenth-century social attitudes toward pain, *both* the romantic preoccupation with suffering and the antiromantic cults of hardness and insensitivity must be seen as interrelated aspects of the midcentury penchant for dichotomizing all facets of human life. Victorian social iconography divided the world into the separate and distinct spheres of: Head vs. Heart, Reason vs. Sentiment, World vs. Home, Art vs. Nature—all seen as reflections of the great division between Masculine and Feminine. Although these were two antithetical worlds, the existence of each depended upon the existence of its opposite. To regard either the sentimental benevolence of Dorothea Dix or the mechanical, ruthless efficiency of William Tecumseh Sherman as uniquely characteristic of midcentury America would be to overlook the process of polarization by which each helped produce and define the other. Between romanticism and antiromanticism existed a profound Victorian dialectic of pain. . . .

In summary, conservative professionalism sanctioned taking some risks for the relief of suffering, thus marking a break with earlier medical traditions. This new departure was strongly influenced by the growth of social sensitivity to human suffering in mid-nineteenth-century life. But the conservative approach to pain involved more than emotional sensitivity. It was a self-consciously moderate attempt to synthesize the powerful, painful remedies of heroic medicine with the milder therapies of its critics, to restore unity and consensus within a divided profession. Those physicians who followed the new doctrines of professional duty thus found themselves faced with what Hooker called a "nice balance of probabilities." For them, choices like that between the duty to relieve suffering and the duty to preserve life came to depend not on absolute deontological imperatives, but upon a moderate utilitarian measurement of the pros and cons, a calculus of suffering.

Race, Human Experimentation, and Dissection in the Antebellum South

TODD L. SAVITT

[I]n the Old South[,] . . . white medical educators and researchers relied greatly on the availability of Negro patients for various purposes. Black bodies often found their way to dissecting tables, operating amphitheaters, classroom or bedside demonstrations, and experimental facilitates. This is not to deny that white bodies were similarly used. In northern cities and in southern port towns such as New Orleans, Louisville, Memphis, Charleston, and Mobile, where poor, transient whites were abundant, seamen, European immigrants, and white indigents undoubtedly joined blacks in fulfilling the "clinical material" needs of the medical profession. But blacks were particularly easy targets, given their positions as voiceless slaves or "free persons of color" in a society sensitive to and separated by race. . . .

Interestingly, people generally assumed that information gained from observation of Negro bodies was applicable to Caucasians. Despite the political rhetoric then current in the Old South about a separate medicine for blacks and for whites, the research and teaching reflected, in fact, the opposite. Negroes did not seem to differ enough from Caucasians to exclude them from extensive use in southern medical schools and in research activities.

Use of blacks for medical experimentation and demonstration was not the result of a conscious organized plan on the part of white southerners to learn more about the differences between the races or even how better to care for their black charges. The examples related in this article reflect the actions of individual researchers and medical institutions. Taken together, however, a pattern emerges. Blacks were considered more available and more accessible in this white-dominated society: they were rendered physically visible by their skin color but were legally invisible because of their slave status.

Throughout history medicine has required bodies for teaching purposes. Students had to learn anatomy, recognize and diagnose diseases, and treat conditions requiring surgery; researchers had to try out their ideas and new techniques; and practitioners had to perform autopsies to confirm their diagnoses and to understand the effects of diseases on the human body. The need for human specimens became more recognized and more emphasized in America during the first half of the nineteenth century as the ideas of the French school of hospital medicine reached this country. Bedside experience, clinical-pathological correlations, and statistical studies became increasingly important. And medical schools throughout the United States, including those in the South, attempted to meet the new demands of students for a modern education. Clinics, infirmaries, and hospitals were opened in conjunction with those colleges; patients, however, were not always willing to enter. To fill beds it became essential to use the poor and the enslaved. Medicine thus capitalized on the need of the indigent and the helpless for medical care. In the South white

Todd L. Savitt, "The Use of Blacks for Medical Experimentation and Demonstration in the Old South," *Journal of Southern History* 28 (1982): 331–333, 335, 337–340, 344–348. Copyright © 1982 by the Southern Historical Association. Reprinted by permission of the Managing Editor.

attitudes toward blacks ensured the selection of patients of this group as specimens, though some whites were also used. . . .

By 1841 the Medical College of the State of South Carolina had established a permanent year-round hospital with large wards for black and white patients. College officials claimed that they had little trouble filling beds at this new infirmary, because "the slave population of the city, and neighboring plantations, is capable of furnishing ample materials for clinical instruction." Students at the school saw not only "all the common diseases of the climate" but also a variety of operative procedures, owing to the presence of a slave population "peculiarly liable to surgical diseases requiring operations for their relief." The medical college continued to use black patients for surgical demonstrations throughout the antebellum years. During the late 1850s, for instance, surgical cases occurring among blacks while school was in session were admitted to the "Coloured Wards" of a newly constructed public hospital and were reserved for the exclusive use of student doctors. . . .

The attitudes of white southerners both toward the use of human bodies in medical education and toward blacks were silently but clearly revealed in the medical profession's heavy reliance on Negro cadavers. Human anatomical dissection was illegal in many states during the antebellum period, although medical schools continued to teach anatomy. Unless approached by angry relatives or friends of deceased persons city authorities rarely questioned medical educators as to the sources of their anatomical specimens. Southern blacks, because of their helpless legal and inconsequential social positions, thus became prime candidates for medical-school dissections. Physicians usually found it much more convenient to obtain black specimens than white. "In Baltimore," commented Harriet Martineau after an 1834 visit, "the bodies of coloured people exclusively are taken for dissection, 'because the whites do not like it, and the coloured people cannot resist.'" Dr. Henry M. Dowling of Leesburg, Virginia, had little difficulty receiving permission for an autopsy on a twelve-year-old slave girl with a suspected case of worms because the victim's owner was "a gentleman of intelligence, and unaffected by the vulgar prejudices entertained on this subject . . ." by others. . . .

Occasionally, the prevailing attitude of whites—that dissection was acceptable when confined to the black population–was expressed in print. A correspondent to the Milledgeville, Georgia, *Statesman and Patriot* in 1828 agreed that it was necessary to dissect corpses to learn anatomy but opposed the use of whites for such a procedure. He endorsed a proposal then before the state legislature that permitted local authorities to release bodies of executed black felons to medical societies for the purpose of dissection, assuring the safety of white corpses. "The *bodies of colored* persons, whose execution is necessary to public security, may, we think, be with equity appropriated for the benefit of a science on which so many lives depend, while the measure would in a great degree secure the sepulchral repose of those who go down into the grave amidst the lamentations of friends and the reverence of society."

The Kentucky House of Representatives seriously considered a similar proposal. It rejected by the narrow margin of seven votes a bill "to authorize and require the Judges of the different Circuit Courts of this state to adjudge and award the corpses of negroes, executed by sentences of said judges, to the Faculties of the different chartered Colleges in this state, for dissection and experiment." In Virginia the vast majority of cadavers obtained for dissection at the five antebellum medical schools were those of Negroes. The faculty of the Medical College of Georgia in Augusta hired, between 1834 and 1852, several slaves to act as intermediaries in the purchase of bodies from masters in the surrounding plantation country. In 1852 it purchased Grandison Harris in Charleston to obtain cadavers and to perform janitorial duties. He robbed graves and also bought black bodies for the next fifty years or so. And the Medical College of South Carolina openly acknowledged in its circular of 1831 that it obtained "Subjects . . . for every purpose" from the black rather than the white population of Charleston so as to carry on "proper dissections . . . without offending any individuals. . . ." This undisguised use of Negroes for dissection in Charleston continued into the postwar era.

. . . Black fear of medical schools and dissection inevitably carried over into the postbellum period, when whites, as a means of maintaining control over freedmen, reinforced the idea of "night-doctors" who stole, killed, and then dissected blacks. The accuracy of the belief that whites actually killed blacks for use in dissection is hard to verify. But the fear blacks harbored was well known. . . .

. . . [In most instances] experiments did little to advance medical knowledge. The same cannot be said for Dr. James Marion Sims's use of slave women to develop a cure for vesico-vaginal fistula. Vesico-vaginal fistula is a break in the wall separating the bladder from the vagina, which allows urine to pass involuntarily to the outside from the vagina rather than from the urethra. Women suffering from this defect, usually the result of trauma during childbirth, are incontinent of urine and continually uncomfortable. The constant flow of urine produces fetid odors, irritated skin, and frequent infections of the reproductive organs. Sims, a South Carolinian practicing in Montgomery, Alabama, during the 1840s and early 1850s, became interested in this condition when three cases among black servants came to his attention within a few months, and a chance occurrence gave him the idea of how to cure it. While treating a white patient for a traumatically malpositioned uterus by placing the woman on her knees and elbows, he suddenly realized that by putting vesico-vaginal fistula patients in that same position he would be able to visualize the fistula and perhaps even repair it. No physician prior to this had developed a consistently successful surgical treatment for the condition owing to difficulties in visualizing the defect, repairing the passage through the bladder wall, and preventing infection during the procedure.

Once Sims had conceived of a way to operate on patients with vesico-vaginal fistula he set about putting his ideas into practice with the cooperation of his slave subjects. He never disguised the fact that what he was doing was entirely experimental. The three black women who served as the first patients, Anarcha, Lucy, and Betsey, desperately wished relief from their sufferings. So, too, did several other patients, all slaves, who submitted to Sims's attempts at a cure over the next four years, 1845 to 1849. Each woman underwent up to thirty operations in quest of relief. When local physicians lost interest and ceased assisting Sims with the procedure, the persistent doctor trained the slave patients to assist him. Finally, in May 1849, Sims succeeded in overcoming all the complications that had been plaguing his procedure for four years. One by one, the black women were cured and sent home.

It is significant that all the subjects in Sims's experiments were black. When he decided to pursue his idea of curing vesico-vaginal fistula he "ransacked the country for [Negro] cases" and found enough to warrant enlarging his eight-bed slave infirmary. Sims agreed with each slaveowner to pay all costs of maintenance except taxes and clothing and "to perform no experiment or operation . . . to endanger their [slaves'] lives. . . ." It was not until after his success with the slave women became known that white women ventured to submit to the operations. Interestingly, Sims discovered that Caucasian patients often failed to persevere as well as Negroes during the painful and uncomfortable procedure. Typical of the problem was the patient about whom Sims remarked in his medical notes: "The pain was so terrific that Mrs. H. could not stand it and I was foiled completely." Perhaps it was Sims's recognition of this difference between slave and white patients that prompted him, in a speech several years after his successes, to praise so highly the black women upon whom he experimented.

> To the indomitable courage of these long-suffering women, more than to any one other single circumstance is the world indebted for the results of these persevering efforts. Had they faltered, then would woman have continued to suffer from the dreadful injuries produced by protracted parturition, and then should the broad domain of surgery not have known one of the most useful improvements that shall forever hereafter grace its annals. . . .

It is to be expected in a slave society that the subjugated will be exploited. Such was the case in the American South where blacks acted not only as servants and laborers but also as medical specimens. Some medical scientists living in that society took advantage of the slaves' helplessness to utilize them in demonstrations, autopsies, dissections, and experiments, situations distasteful to whites and rejected by them. Some whites, usually the poor and the friendless, found themselves in the same position as blacks. But given the racial attitudes of that time and place, blacks were particularly vulnerable to abuse or mishandling at the hands of researchers, medical teachers, or students.

 F U R T H E R   R E A D I N G

Robert L. Blakeley and Judith M. Harrington, eds., *Bones in the Basement: Postmortem Racism in 19th-Century Medical Training* (1997).
Thomas J. Brown, *Dorothea Dix: New England Reformer* (1998).
James H. Cassedy, *American Medicine and Statistical Thinking, 1800–1860* (1984).
James H. Cassedy, *Medicine and American Growth, 1800–1860* (1986).
Norman Dain, *Concepts of Insanity in the U.S., 1789–1865* (1964).
Ellen Dwyer, *Homes for the Mad: Life Inside Two Nineteenth-Century Asylums* (1987).
David Gollaher, *Voice for the Mad: The Life of Dorothea Dix* (1995).
Gerald N. Grob, *Mental Institutions in America: Social Policy to 1875* (1973).
Reginald Horsman, *Josiah Nott of Mobile: Southerner, Physician, and Racial Theorist* (1987).
Kenneth F. Kiple and Virginia Himmelsteib King, *Another Dimension of the Black Diaspora: Diet, Disease, and Racism* (1981).
Nancy Krieger, "Shades of Difference: Theoretical Underpinnings of the Medical Controversy on Black/White Differences in the United States, 1830–1870," *International Journal of Health Services* 17 (1987): 259–278.
Judith Walzer Leavitt, "'A Worrying Profession': The Domestic Environment of Medical Practice in Mid-Nineteenth-Century America," *Bulletin of the History of Medicine* 69 (1995): 1–29.

Peter McCandless, *Moonlight, Magnolias, and Madness: Insanity in South Carolina from the Colonial Period to the Progressive Era* (1996).

Sally G. McMillen, *Motherhood in the Old South: Pregnancy, Childbirth, and Infant Rearing* (1990).

Ronald L. Numbers, ed., *The Education of American Physicians* (1980).

Ronald L. Numbers and Todd L. Savitt, eds., *Science and Medicine in the Old South* (1986).

Martin S. Pernick, *A Calculus of Suffering: Pain, Professionalism, and Anesthesia in Nineteenth-Century America* (1985).

Charles E. Rosenberg, *The Care of Strangers: The Rise of America's Hospital System* (1987).

David J. Rothman, *The Discovery of the Asylum: Social Order and Disorder in the New Republic* (1971).

Sheila M. Rothman, *Living in the Shadow of Death: Tuberculosis and the Social Experience of Illness in American History* (1994).

Todd L. Savitt, *Medicine and Slavery: The Diseases and Health Care of Blacks in Antebellum Virginia* (1978).

William Stanton, *The Leopard's Spots: Scientific Attitudes Toward Race in America, 1815–1859* (1960).

Steven M. Stowe, "Seeing Themselves at Work: Physicians and the Case Narrative in the Mid-Nineteenth-Century American South," *American Historical Review* 101 (1996): 41–79.

Nancy Tomes, *A Generous Confidence: Thomas Story Kirkbride and the Art of Asylum-Keeping, 1840–1883* (1984).

John Harley Warner, *Against the Spirit of System: The French Impulse in Nineteenth-Century American Medicine* (1998).

John Harley Warner, *The Therapeutic Perspective: Medical Practice, Knowledge, and Identity in America, 1820–1885*, (1986; with new preface, 1997).

CHAPTER
5

The Healer's Identity in the Mid-Nineteenth Century: Character, Care, and Competition, 1830–1875

By the middle of the nineteenth century, the American medical marketplace was the freest, least regulated in the western world. Criticism of the professions, including medicine, had been infused with a new political urgency. Beginning in the 1830s, the Thomsonians and their Jacksonian allies, tapping into the era's democratic ethos and egalitarian distrust of claims to privilege based on special learning, led a drive against licensing statutes, and during the next two decades state legislatures revoked virtually all medical licensing laws. Even though such laws had played a largely honorific function, their formal repeal underscored the fact that any man or woman who wished could set up practice as a physician.

Newly prominent in this open medical marketplace were adherents of anti-orthodox medical movements that possessed both formal structures and shared creeds, often called "sects" by contemporary critics. During the 1820s and 1830s the number of professional Thomsonians (practicing medicine for fees rather than treating only their own families) grew markedly. Eclecticism—a parallel botanic healing system in which professional physicians supplanted self-help—and hydropathy, or water cure, flourished in the 1840s and 1850s and established their own M.D. degree–granting medical schools. During the same decades, homeopathy, introduced to America in 1825, became the most powerful challenge to the regular profession, boasting institutions such as the Homeopathic Medical College of Pennsylvania (1848) and the first national medical association, the American Institute of Homeopathy (1844). These groups of nonregular practitioners often had sturdy links to the wider American health reform movement, professed liberal social and political views, and were far more receptive than the regular profession to the education of women as physicians and their acceptance as professional colleagues.

The number of regular physicians also rapidly multiplied during these decades, making earning a living in this highly competitive occupation all the more difficult. Medical schools, mostly proprietary ventures run by the faculty for profit, proliferated: twenty-six new schools were founded between 1810 and 1840, and another forty-seven by 1877. Medical schools vied with one another for paying pupils, which kept requirements and standards low. It was in this context of over-crowding and attack by alternative physicians that a movement toward orthodoxy arose. In 1847 the American Medical Association (AMA) was founded, partly to promote educational reforms but chiefly to establish a unified front and demarcate the orthodox faithful. The association exerted little political influence before the late nineteenth century, but its code of ethics was a culturally powerful device to enforce orthodoxy by forbidding members to associate with any physicians the AMA regarded as "sectarians." The ideology of orthodoxy also fostered intolerance of even elite regular physicians who seemed to threaten the established order of medical practice and the physician's primary allegiance to healing.

Professional identity in antebellum medicine was further contested and desta-bilized by the American women (and their supporters) who demanded entrance to regular medical schools and access to regular M.D. degrees. Many male regular physicians feared that their already besieged profession would be degraded by the admission of women as professional equals, despite the long-established role of women as healers. Beginning in the late 1840s, the debate over the fitness of women to train and practice as physicians brought to the foreground larger questions about the proper role and character of the American physician. The absence of state regula-tion facilitated women's access to M.D. degrees in the United States earlier than in any other nation, with Elizabeth Blackwell, in 1849, being the first woman to receive an M.D. degree. Yet male opposition kept most regular schools shut to all but a few women. In 1850, however, the Female Medical College of Pennsylvania opened as the world's first M.D.-granting medical school entirely for women. Over the next several decades a number of other women's medical colleges (orthodox and homeopathic) opened, as did women's hospitals.

What defines the proper physician? How and why do medical practitioners select certain intellectual, social, moral, and physical qualities as requisite to making a good physician, and how might patients make their choices among a variety of healers? These questions remain salient in the changing health culture of today. In the open and diverse medical marketplace of mid-nineteenth-century America, gender, divergent systems of healing, and concerns about the proper relationship between enthusiasm for science and a commitment to healing all informed a vigorous debate over the problem of professional identity.

 D O C U M E N T S

At a time when most state legislatures were repealing medical licensing laws, the local Monroe County Medical Society in New York set up a committee to investigate the status of state laws regulating medical practice. Their 1843 report (Document 1) con-cludes that within the assertively egalitarian climate of American society, any lobbying for the restoration of restrictive licensing laws would be fruitless and recommends encouraging a higher standard of education for their fellow regular physicians as the most promising means of combating nonorthodox practitioners.

In Document 2, dated 1849, pioneer hydropathic physician Mary Gove Nichols describes the experiences that led her to become a water-cure practitioner and activist, exemplifying the links binding together women's health reform, alternative medicine, and opposition to orthodox drugging. Gove Nichols, who never received an M.D. degree, recounts how she cobbled together her medical training in the 1830s. Her depiction of the role of "nature" in disease echoes that drawn by regular physician Jacob Bigelow (see Chapter 4, Document 2), but they reach very different conclusions. Speaking the following year to a local New York State association, regular physician N. Williams, in Document 3, enumerates the reasons why women are unsuited by nature to be educated or to practice as physicians. Addressing other members of the orthodox brotherhood precisely at the moment when women were beginning to gain access to regular M.D. degrees, Williams asserts that the medical profession lies outside of women's proper "sphere."

Harvard medical professor John Ware, speaking in the same year, concurs with Williams but devotes his address to entering medical students (Document 4) to outlining the ingredients of character that are necessary for *any* physician's success in medicine. Ware cautions his students that their education should transform them into good practitioners, not scientists, and warns against the dangers of excessive zeal for scientific knowledge for its own sake, of the brutalizing potential of human dissection, and of the risks of developing a hardened manner in interacting with patients.

In Document 5, a woman in Iowa and a man who has recently made the journey by wagon to the Oregon Territory testify to their success using hydropathy in self-help practice. In letters written in 1854 to the editor of the *Water-Cure Journal, and Herald of Reforms,* they both display their antipathy toward regular doctors and orthodox drugging. In Document 6, a lecture given in 1859 to potential patrons, sisters Elizabeth and Emily Blackwell, the first and third women to receive a regular M.D. degree and founders of the New York Infirmary for Women, rally support for their women's medical school and clinic. Underscoring the special qualities of character that women can bring to medical practice and to health reform, they posit a role for the woman physician as a "connecting link" between the science of the medical profession and the everyday lives of American women. Document 7 is an excerpt from the book *Sex in Education; or, a Fair Chance for Girls* (1873), written by Edward H. Clarke, a Boston physician and former medical professor at Harvard. In this controversial book, which became a rallying point for opponents to the education of women, Clarke insists that it is not so much intellectual capacity or social duty as the limitations of biology that advise against women entering the medical profession.

1. A County Medical Society Bemoans the Prevalence of Quackery and Public Opinion Opposed to Legal Regulation of Medical Practice, 1843

Medical Legislation.—A committee was raised some time last season by the Monroe County, N.Y. Medical Society, to whom was referred the subject of medical legislation. Circulars were addressed to medical gentlemen in different States, to ascertain points like these—"Is there any law in your State regulating the practice of physic and surgery—and if so, what is it?" "If any law in your State, imposing penalties or disabilities upon the quack, has ever existed, has it ever been repealed on abolished; and if so, what influence has such abolishment had upon the increase

"Medical Legislation," *Boston Medical and Surgical Journal* 28 (1843): 323–324.

or decrease of quackery?" Having received twenty letters in answer, besides eleven pamphlets, the committee sum up their doings thus:

"From the facts thus adduced, it appears, that EIGHT of the States have never had any laws regulating the Practice of Medicine; that TEN have abolished all law on the subject; that FOUR only have any existing law, so far as known to us (for from the four following we have received no replies to our circular—viz.: ARKANSAS, ILLINOIS, MICHIGAN, and DELAWARE.) So that EIGHTEEN at least out of the twenty-six States have, at this time, no laws regulating the Practice of Medicine, nor prohibiting that of Quackery.

"With regard to the benefits to be derived from Legislation, in the matter before us, the testimony here adduced is somewhat discrepant, both as it regards the facts, and the opinions of the witnesses. But one thing is clear, viz.: that Quackery and Patent Nostrums every where abound, despite all law and the severest penalties. It is also equally evident that public opinion will not tolerate penal enactments prohibiting Empiricism. The Committee have, therefore, unanimously come to the following conclusions:

"FIRST—That in the present state of the public mind, all penal or prohibitory enactments are inexpedient.

"SECOND—That it is most conformable to the spirit of our civil institutions, to leave perfect liberty to all to practise Medicine, being amenable only for injury done.

"THIRD—That all Legislation relative to the Practice of Medicine and Surgery, as in all other Arts and Sciences, should only aim to encourage by affording such facilities as may be necessary to its highest prosecution.

"FOURTH—That the important, if not the only remedy against Quackery, is Medical Reform, by which a higher standard of Medical Education shall be secured."

The Committee, Drs. Reid, Backus, and Moore, who appear to have faithfully performed the duty entrusted to them, make the following, among other additional remarks:

"The object of Legislation is the public good. Medical law may be said to have a twofold object: first, the protection of the community against imposition, where health and life are involved; second, the improvement of Medical Science: both aiming at and resulting in the public good. But law is the expression of the public will, without which it can neither be enacted, sustained, nor executed. The written statute is, therefore, a dead letter, whenever the public mind is arrayed against it. And this is pre-eminently the case with regard to the medical law of this State at this time. Empiricism is every where rife, and was never more arrogant, and 'the people love to have it so.' That restless, agitating, agrarian spirit, that would always be levelling down, has so long kept up a 'hue and cry against calomel and the lancet,' that the prejudice of the community is excited against, and their confidence in the Medical Profession greatly impaired—and no law could be enforced against the Empiric, or nostrum vender. Every attempt of the kind would only create a deeper sympathy in their favor, and raise a storm of higher indignation against the Profession. This spirit cannot be controlled by arbitrary legislation. It only makes it, like compressed steam, the more elastic and more certain to explode. It is by seeming to yield, and giving it space, that it becomes quiescent and harmless. A repeal of all penalties and disabilities would take away from the quack his strong ground for appeal to the sympathies of the people."

2. Mary Gove Nichols, a Women's Health Reformer, Explains Why She Became a Water-Cure Practitioner, 1849

I do not know that I shall make any apology for being one of the first to step out of the old and prescribed path for women, and become a physician. I took my place in the great field of labor which I now occupy, from a necessity of my being. I first received benefit from the practice of water-cure in my own case, and then I sought to benefit others. . . .

It is not my wish to speak of my own course any further than is needful, in order that others may be benefitted by my experience. It would be wrong for me to withhold facts that might be of use, from fear that I should incur the charge of egotism.

When a young girl, at school, an incident occurred, which, though slight in itself, and apparently worthy of no particular notice, probably determined my position in life. I was away from home. The gentleman where I boarded had some medical works in his library. I read them from curiosity, and was much interested; so much that I was constantly thinking how I could procure more books. I read what I found in my friend's library secretly, and after some months I returned home. I found my eldest brother engaged in the study of medicine. He had Bell's Anatomy at home with him occasionally, and sometimes left it for some days at a time. Without his knowledge, and unknown, indeed, to any of the family, I commenced studying these books. Time passed, and I became deeply interested in the subject. One day my brother was explaining the circulation of the blood, and fœtal circulation was incidentally mentioned. He was not master of his subject. He made some mistakes which I corrected, and finished his explanation for him. He stared at me with much astonishment, and asked me if I had been reading his books. I was obliged to confess the truth. My brother was much dissatisfied with my unwomanly conduct, and was determined that I should read no more. He ridiculed me, as the most effectual means of influencing a timid young girl. He told me mockingly, that he would bring me a book on obstetrics. I blushed scarlet and could not talk with him; but nothing broke my habit of reading his books till he hid them. . . .

Shortly after this period I married and went to live in New Hampshire. I now procured medical books from editors for whom I wrote; these I exchanged with a physician in the town where I resided. It happened that one of the books [the *Book of Health*] that I had the good fortune to procure, was devoted largely to the illustration of the sanative effects of cold water; its use was particularly recommended for children. . . . I read these books in 1832, fifteen years before this present writing. About this time I had a child, and began the use of water by having her bathed in cold water daily from birth. Soon after I commenced using water in hemorrhages and fevers. The physician who had loaned me the books also used water in fevers, I think in all cases giving little medicine. The patient was bathed during the accession of the fever in cold water—ice-cold, for it was drawn from very deep wells, and cloths wet in cold water were laid on the head. The patient drank plenty of cold water. This practice was wholly successful. . . .

Mary S. Gove Nichols, "Mrs. Gove's Experience in Water-Cure," *The Water-Cure Journal, and Hearld of Reforms* 7 (1849): 40–41, 68–70, 135.

From this time I was possessed with a passion for anatomical, physiological and pathological study. I could never explain the reason of this intense feeling to myself or others; all I know is, that it took possession of me, and mastered me wholly; it supported me through efforts that would otherwise have been to me inconceivable and insupportable. I am naturally timid and bashful; few would be likely to believe this who only see my doings without being acquainted with me. But timid as I was, I sought assistance from scientific and professional men. I went through museums of morbid specimens that but for my passion for knowledge would have filled me with horror. I looked on dissections till I could see a woman or child dissected with far more firmness than I could before this have seen a loin of veal or a lamb cut up. . . .

After my marriage I had resided for several years in New Hampshire, and then moved to Lynn, Mass., near Boston. Here I engaged in teaching, and had many more facilities for pursuing my studies than ever before.

In 1837 I commenced lecturing in my school on anatomy and physiology. I had before this given one or two lectures before a Female Lyceum formed by my pupils and some of their friends. At first I gave these health lectures, as they were termed, to the young ladies of my school, and their particular friends whom they were allowed to invite, once in two weeks; subsequently once a week. In the autumn of 1838 I was invited by a society of ladies in Boston, to give a course of lectures before them on anatomy and physiology. I gave this course of lectures to a large class of ladies, and repeated it afterward to a much larger number. I lectured pretty constantly for several years after this beginning in Boston. I lectured in Massachusetts, Maine, New Hampshire, Rhode Island, New York, New Jersey, Pennsylvania, Maryland and Ohio, and also on the island of Nantucket. . . .

In 1843 I obtained books from England on the Water-Cure, and much verbal and practical information from Henry C. Wright, who spent some time in this country during that year. He brought several works on Water-Cure, and being in bad health he applied the water in his own case successfully at my father's house, where he remained some months. The books that he brought, the accounts that he gave me of Priessnitz' practice, and Water-Cure practitioners in England, and his application of the water in his own case, added to my practical knowledge and conviction on the subject, removed the last remnant of my faith in drugs, and induced me to practice Water-Cure alone in every case that came under my care. I soon saw what qualifications were requisite to make a successful practitioner of Water-Cure. There are no rules of practice applicable to all cases, but the Water-Cure physician must have judgment to adapt the treatment to the vital or reactive power possessed by the patient. A practice that would be eminently successful in one case would surely destroy life in another. Care and ability in the diagnosis of disease, and skill in adapting the treatment to the strength and peculiar idiosyncracy of the patient, are indispensable to success in Water-Cure. . . .

. . . If people only knew the remarkable and almost marvellous way in which all violent and febrile diseases yield to a judicious application of this cure, drugs would be at a discount, and blisters and the lancet among the thousand horrors of the past. In my water-cure experience, I have had abundant evidence that depletion by bleeding or purgatives is never required, that counter-irritants are unnecessary tortures, and that all the indications of a rapid cure, without unnecessary weakness or poisoning can be attained by this mode of treatment.

3. A New York State Doctor Rails to His Professional Brethren Against the Education of Women as Physicians, 1850

GENTLEMEN,—The recent agitation, in this country, of the subject of "female physicians," the extent to which it has been carried, and the effect which it is calculated to produce on the profession and community, are considerations which seem to require more than a passing notice. . . . For one, I had always supposed that the male sex was the legitimate and exclusive heirs of the "healing art"; that its rights and obligations were emphatically and strictly our own, and that we, as a sex, are better adapted to it than our fair competitors. But if I am wrong in all this, if our title is not good, if we are mere squatters, or tenants at will, I shall, on the conviction of my mistake, use my utmost exertions to restore to the opposite sex the things that are hers. And after all, I am not aware that we shall be losers by the operation; for when the *crisis* comes, instead of educating *ourselves* and our *sons* for medical men, we will educate our *wives* and our *daughters* for medical women; and thus, what we may be denied on the one hand, may be restored on the other. And besides all this, when we as *men* have been "thrust out," and our places are occupied by the *fair sex,* may we not hope to fill the very stations which they now occupy? And if they are to turn doctors, lawyers, clergymen, &c., why may not we turn our attention to sewing, knitting, tending babies, and other household employment? Surely when they occupy our places, we must of necessity take possession of theirs; and when they become to all intents and purposes *men,* will we become, to the same extent, *women.* . . .

In saying, therefore, that I am unqualifiedly opposed to educating females for the medical profession, and that they are not constituted for an employment of this character, I utter a sentiment for which nature is responsible, and to whose testimony I shall appeal for the correctness of the position which I have taken. . . . [T]here is a vast difference, a wide "gulf" in the instinctive faculties, tastes and propensities of the two sexes, and which declare to each, with all the force of philosophic truth, "thus far and no farther shalt thou go." In this light of the subject let us inquire, do *females* possess *equal* talents and facilities, with *males,* for the medical profession? To the solution of this inquiry, I will submit the following propositions, viz.:—

1st. The practice of medicine is necessarily a *laborious* employment. It does not simply consist in riding about in an easy carriage, from patient to patient, whilst the weather is fair and pleasant. . . . To what conclusion, then, must we come with reference to an entire sex, who are naturally more *delicate* than ourselves? Most certainly, if corporeal hardship and privation are the necessary consequences of the medical profession, that the *male* sex is better qualified in this respect to discharge its duties than the *female.* . . .

2d. *Marriage* is a natural and divine institution, and its duties by females incompatible with the practice of medicine. Imagine, if you please, a female physician, who is the mother of a large family of children; or suppose she has no more than two or three. I submit, whether even the smaller number does not present cares and responsibilities, which a humane mother would not and should not transfer to

N. Williams, M.D., "A Dissertation on 'Female Physicians,'" *Boston Medical and Surgical Journal* 43 (1850): 69–75.

another? . . . [D]o not the circumstances of *gestation* and *childbirth* present difficulties, which could not be surmounted by a female under such embarrassments? But
I need not extend the argument, for the bare mention of the thought of married
females engaging in the medical profession is too palpably absurd to require any exposition. It carries along with it, a sense of shame, vulgarity and disgust. But it may
be argued, that those who are destined for the profession should avoid the marriage
covenant, and hence these objections will be obviated. Such, I believe, is the course
of Miss Blackwell, and some others, who have openly declared their own conse-
cration to a life of celibacy, that the world may be benefited by their labors in the
department of medicine. Wonderful beings, truly! . . . Marriage, [however,] it will be
acknowledged, is a *natural* state of the two sexes; consequently, the reverse of this is
an *unnatural* one. And if it be a divine institution, then must its avoidance, *cæteris
paribus,* be morally wrong. The conclusion of the whole argument, then, is, that the
marriage condition is not compatible with the duties of a physician so far as regards
females, and that its refusal is *naturally, religiously and socially wrong.* . . .

3d. Females cannot practise medicine with so much convenience to themselves
and others, as males. This arises not only from their constitutional peculiarities, rendering hardship and exposure hazardous at particular times; but also from their
habits and education. Imagine a call for one of these *model physicians* at the dead
hour of night, and perchance some miles out of town. Does she repair to the stable,
harness her horse, and hasten with all possible despatch to the residence of her
patient? By no means. Her groom must at least deliver her carriage at the door
under all circumstances, and must frequently attend her doctorship to the place of
destination, lest some insult or injury befal her upon the road. . . . If, however, she
is amply provided for in all these respects, and has only to seat herself in a carriage
and be driven from place to place, and from patient to patient, at whose expense is
her coachman employed? Here is an *extra* charge, which some one must defray. . . .

4th. The *temperament* of females is less favorable for the medical profession
than that of males. I shall not urge, that a special temperament pertains to each of
the sexes; but rather, that, as a whole, there is a material difference in this respect.
To the female sex, then, may be ascribed the *nervous* or *excitable* temperament. To
the male sex, the lymphatic, bilious and sanguine are more common. The designation, therefore, of *excitable* and *non-excitable,* is something more than an imaginary
line distinguishing the two sexes. I scarcely, then, need to add, that in a profession
where the *utmost nerve* and *self-possession* are often required, the male sex is the
most favorably constituted. Habit and education may do much to improve the temperament for this or any other department; but it cannot wholly supply the deficiency,
or render the *artificial* arrangement of things equal to the *natural.*

5th. The bearing of phrenology upon the question under consideration, is
adverse to the proposition of creating physicians out of the female sex. . . . Inhabi-
tiveness and Philoprogenitiveness are much larger, comparatively, in *females* than
in *males.* The love of home, and of offspring, are consequently more fully exhibited
in the one, than the other. Indeed, they seem to bear sway in the mental constitution
of females, and bring almost every other organ into uniform and harmonious sub-
serviency. And, say what we will, or think as we may, it is in the domestic circle
that woman's talents and virtues display themselves with the greatest brilliancy. In
this sphere we love, cherish and admire her. And the day is not distant when her

worth in her own peculiar province will be more fully appreciated, and a brighter halo will illumine the brow of woman in woman's sphere. . . . But she must be content to labor in her sphere, rather than assume responsibilities for which she has no natural taste or affinity. When she does this, when she aspires to be the *competitor* of man, she must abandon all claim to the love, sympathy and affection which are so freely bestowed upon her. . . .

Let us, then, in conclusion, cherish the "rights of woman," as reason, philosophy and science have pointed them out, having an ear to hear and a heart to feel, whenever her claims for our aid and sympathy are presented. And, on the other hand, let *woman* not assume the prerogatives of *man,* by entering the arena and noisy business of life, for which she has not faculties in common with *man;* but rather let her, in her own sphere, seek to co-operate with him in every effort to improve, happily and elevate the race.

4. John Ware, a Harvard Medical Professor, Advises What Makes a Good Medical Education, 1850

It is too often overlooked, that the final purpose of all medical study is practice. The whole circle of sciences connected with medicine has been called into existence for this purpose, and their value depends upon their connection with it. I do not mean to say that they are not worthy to be pursued for their own sakes. They are so, richly. . . . But it is not as philosophers, as lovers of science, or even as admirers of the wonderful works of God, that we are called to interest ourselves in these subjects. It is solely that we may learn to treat disease. The direction and arrangement of our studies are to be wholly governed by this as their final purpose. . . .

What, then, is that thorough knowledge of the profession which is necessary to success? A man may know a vast deal of the profession, and yet be a very poor practitioner. He may be an excellent anatomist, pathologist, chemist—nay, he may be minutely acquainted with the history and treatment of disease, and yet be totally unfit to take charge of a single patient. The thorough knowledge of the profession to which I refer in this connection, is that which will make the physician a good practitioner. . . .

Hence, though it may be an ungrateful task to check the interest of the young man in any study which he is pursuing with zeal, yet is he often in danger of expending a disproportionate share of his time and faculties on some favorite but limited subject. He may acquire so exclusive a relish for anatomy, for chemistry, for the microscope, or for pathology, as to vitiate his character as a practitioner. Not that these are useless kinds of knowledge, but that an excessive devotion to them may impair the practical tendency of his pursuits, and give them a wrong bias.

Of course it is desirable that he should be a perfect anatomist. But if he takes the time necessary to make him a perfect anatomist, he may neglect what is necessary to make him a good practitioner. . . .

Moreover, some members of our profession, both as students and as practitioners, become interested in the history of disease for itself alone. . . . But there is

John Ware, *Success in the Medical Profession* (Boston: David Clapp, 1851), pp. 5–7, 11, 23–25.

danger of failing to keep constantly in mind its relation to practice; of regarding it too much as a mere scientific pursuit. This is a fault into which men of the highest education are perhaps the most apt to fall. They acquire the habit of studying disease merely as an object of science. It may, indeed, be worth studying as an object of science merely. But he who would practise medicine, must study it with a view to the practice of medicine.

. . . [I]t often must have occurred to most practitioners to observe, that they can treat many cases perfectly well although they may not have been able to make out their scientific distinction; and, on the other hand, that they are quite at a loss sometimes where this distinction is perfectly clear. Hence, too, we find, that a very excellent pathologist sometimes, nay, I am afraid, quite often, may make but an indifferent practitioner; whilst some men, with a very moderate amount of pathological learning, but a large fund of sound common sense and a natural talent for nice observation, will make very excellent ones. They seize, with an intuitive quickness of perception, upon those conditions of disease on which its management depends; they learn, by an experience guided by their original sagacity, how far diseases are controllable by art, what conditions of them are so, and the agencies by which it can be done—and they apply this knowledge with a wisdom which is sometimes altogether beyond that which merely high attainments in science can confer. . . .

There is unfortunately something in the first influences of our training which tends to impair the delicacy of our minds with regard to certain subjects. . . . Certainly the tendency of the habit of dissection is to produce a difference between us and other men in the feelings with which we regard the remains of the dead. Naturally we entertain a sort of reverence for the inanimate body of a fellow being; a kind of awe comes over us in contemplating it; we provide in the most respectful and affectionate manner, and often at great expense, for its sepulture; we accompany it with holy rites; we are shocked if even the remains of a stranger, or a criminal, are committed to the grave without them. Thus all our associations are of a tender and almost sacred nature. But the habitual dissection of the dead body, necessary as it is, surely has a tendency to destroy these associations; we may forget that the object before us is anything but a mere subject of our art; it may become to us no more than the inorganic materials of the chemist's retort are to him. Thence may arise an indifference and even a levity of speech and manner, which are abhorrent to the sensibilities of the rest of mankind.

Now it is not necessary that this should be. The influence exerted is so gradual, the change in our habits and feelings is so insensibly brought about, that we are not aware that it has taken place, and are, perhaps, surprised and offended if it be pointed out to us. But the testimony of others to its reality should teach us carefully to look to the influences to which we are exposed, on this and other subjects, in our habitual pursuits. It should teach us to resist whatever may tend, in any degree, to diminish the tenderness, the delicacy, the purity of mind, which are so peculiarly required in the performance of our duties.

These considerations suggest, and they afford an occasion for, a few remarks upon the position which becomes us towards those of the other sex who are candidates for practice in our profession. . . .

. . . I cannot withhold my conviction that the general practice of medicine would be found unsuited to her physical, intellectual, and moral constitution—that she could not go thoroughly through with the preparation necessary for it without impairing many of those higher characteristics for which we honor and love her. There may be exceptions, but a profession cannot be filled by exceptions. I have spoken of some of the unfavorable influences of professional pursuits on our own minds; such influences would be doubly hurtful in their results upon the mind of woman. It is difficult to conceive that she should go through all that we have to encounter in the various departments of the study of medicine, without tarnishing that delicate surface of the female mind, which can hardly be imagined even to reflect what is gross without somewhat of defilement. . . .

The office of the physician and surgeon calls for those qualities which are characteristic of man. It is attended by many hardships of body and trials of mind, which, though not greater than those which women undergo, are yet different from them. He must be exposed by night and by day, to the wind and the storm, to cold and to heat; he needs bodily strength, endurance, and activity. So, too, he must be unmoved by suffering; he must be firm amidst dangers; he must have presence of mind in doubt and difficulty; he must not shrink from inflicting pain; he must forget that he is doing so; he must not be carried away by his strong sympathies, he must often act as though he had them not. Is the nature of woman competent to this? Should we love her as well if it were? Would she not be less a woman? We have each our office at the bedside of the sick—but it is a different one. We cannot perform hers, and she cannot perform ours.

5. Domestic Practitioners of Hydropathy in the West Testify to Their Faith in Water Cure, 1854

FROM F. A. M. S., Wapello, Iowa.—My husband is trying to quit the use of tobacco; and I think it will be a great benefit to his health, for he is quite nervous. I have had the third-day ague all the time for four months, but still my faith is unshaken. I believe water will cure it. I have had also the neuralgia, mostly facial, all the fall, arising from debility and decayed teeth; but I have no one to pack me, as my husband has been from home all the fall; but I have had one tooth out, took a pack last week, and had a light chill last night. I have treated my youngest son, a boy of five years, who was always diseased, and had been drugged three or four years, this fall; and, although he had taken no calomel for eighteen months, he was salivated three weeks. His complaint is affection of the liver, with hemorrhoids, causing prolapsus of the lower bowel, which has had to be replaced after every evacuation for three years; he had more than forty boils, besides being covered with skin blisters; it has been about six weeks since his body became well enough for me to rub him; he was a perfect skeleton, but could stand alone all the time. My faith was almost shaken when his strength failed day by day; but still he would answer always to the question, "Do you want a doctor?" with great emphasis, "No." But now he is around all day, and can walk a quarter of a mile; although his digestive organs are quite weak. I am a hard-working woman, and I think the Water-Cure adapted to the working-class; but, alas! how blindly they cling to their idols, and say the doctor knows. One lady said she would rather die with the consumption than look like a fright with a loose short dress. But time and patience will even work wonders. I

"Home Voices. Extracts of Letters," *The Water-Cure Journal, and Herald of Reforms* 17 (1854): 107.

have been sent for in two families to bathe, and they begin to *believe* when they see my boy walking around, and our doctors have both buried theirs.

FROM D. T., Albany, Oregon Territory.—The health of emigrants this season was good compared with what it was last year. The diseases that prevail are bowel complaint, and what they call mountain-fever. Tetter, erysipelas, scurvy, and scrofula, frequently make their appearance in subjects predisposed to them. This is probably owing to the absence of fresh vegetable diet, and the enormous quantities of swine's flesh consumed on the journey. Most emigrants provide themselves with cholera medicine, pain-killer, brandy, quinine, &c., to repel the attacks of disease. The result of the contest is various with different persons, and at different times; sometimes the disease is victorious, and sometimes the medicine, or rather the vital energies of the persons attacked. The most of the emigrants are from Missouri, Illinois, and Iowa; and exceedingly few of them appear to be acquainted with the blessings of Water-Cure. The writer brought with him nothing in the shape of medicine; believing that wherever good water could be found, there Providence furnished him with medicine; and accordingly, when diarrhœa threatened our health, the abdominal compress or long wet towel was employed, and the quantity of food greatly diminished; and this consisted in boiled rice for the most part. Should the complaint appear a little obstinate, the syringe with cold water was employed once or twice, and no further doctoring was required. Two of my drivers, who held Water-Cure in contempt, but who were ignorant of its principles or practice, took dysentery, and used cholera medicine, pain-killer, opium, &c. The medicine, however, was like to *kill* one of *them,* as well as his *pains;* he therefore sent back for a doctor who was travelling in a train fifteen miles behind ours; and behold, when he came, he told the patient that his *main reliance* for *a cure* was on the use of the syringe and wet towels applied to the abdomen. With the use of these Water-Cure appliances, and some medicine from the doctor, he got over the disease in five or six weeks; but had he applied to me, and used the Water-Cure, he might, under Providence, have had his complaint removed in that many hours from its commencement. Having him and his brother sick in my wagons for about a month on Bear and Snake river, helped to break down two teams for me and occasion the death of some fine oxen.—Yours, &c.

[We thank our correspondent for his hints to emigrants, and commend them to all whom it may concern. Don't take the doctor's pill-bags with you when you go West.]

6. Elizabeth and Emily Blackwell, Pioneer Women Physicians, Extoll the Woman Physician as the "Connecting Link" Between Women's Health Reform and the Medical Profession, 1859

In inviting consideration to the subject of medicine as an occupation for women, it is not a simple theory that we wish to present, but the results of practical experience. For fourteen years we have been students of medicine; for eight years we have been engaged in the practice of our profession in New York; and during

Elizabeth Blackwell and Emily Blackwell, *Medicine As a Profession for Women* (New York: W. H. Tinson, 1860), pp. 3–4, 8–10, 13, 15, 18–24.

the last five years have, in addition, been actively occupied in the support of a medical charity. . . .

When the idea of the practice of medicine by women is suggested, the grounds on which we usually find sympathy expressed for it are two. The first is, that there are certain departments of medicine in which the aid of *women* physicians would be especially valuable to women. The second argument is, that women are much in need of a wider field of occupation, and if they could successfully practice any branches of medicine it would be another opening added to the few they already possess. . . .

Now, we believe that both these reasons are valid, and that experience will fully confirm them; but we believe also that there is a much deeper view of the question than this; and that the thorough education of a class of women in medicine will exert an important influence upon the life and interests of women in general, an influence of a much more extended nature than is expressed in the above views. . . .

That progress is needed in sanitary matters is widely admitted; sanitary conventions are held; the medical profession and the press are constantly calling attention to defects of public and private hygiene, pointing out the high rate of mortality amongst children, etc.; but it is far from being as generally recognized how essential to progress it is that women, who have the domestic life of the nation in their hands, should realize their responsibility, and possess the knowledge necessary to meet it. . . .

If, then, it be true that health has its science as well as disease; that there are conditions essential for securing it, and that every day life should be based upon its laws; if, moreover, women, by their social position, are important agents in this practical work, the question naturally arises, how is this knowledge to be widely diffused among them? At present there exists no method of supplying this need. Physiology and all branches of science bearing upon the physical life of man are pursued almost exclusively by physicians, and from these branches of learning they deduce more or less clear ideas with regard to the conditions of health in every-day life. But it is only the most enlightened physicians who do this work for themselves; a very large proportion of the profession, who are well acquainted with the bearing of this learning upon disease, would find it a difficult matter to show its relation to the prevention of disease, and the securing of health, by its application to daily life. If this be the case with regard to physicians, it must evidently be impossible to give to the majority of women the wide scientific training that would enable them from their own knowledge to deduce practical rules of guidance. This must be done by those whose avocations require wide scientific knowledge—by physicians. Yet the medical profession is at present too far removed from the life of women; they regard these subjects from such a different stand-point that they can not supply the want. The application of scientific knowledge to women's necessities in actual life can only be done by women who possess at once the scientific learning of the physician, and as women a thorough acquaintance with women's requirements—that is, by women physicians.

That this connecting link between the science of the medical profession and the every-day life of women is needed, is proved by the fact that during the years that scientific knowledge has been accumulating in the hands of physicians, while it has revolutionized the science of medicine, it has had so little direct effect upon domestic life. . . . [P]hysicians are too far removed from women's life; they can criticize but not guide it. On the other hand, it is curious to observe that, as within the last few years the attention of a considerable number of women has been turned to medicine, the first use they have made of it has been to establish a class of lecturers on physiology and hygiene for women. They are scattered all over the country; the lectures are generally as crude and unsatisfactory as the medical education out of which they have sprung; but the impulse is worthy of note, as showing the instinctive perception of women, as soon as they acquire even a slight acquaintance with these subjects, how directly they bear upon the interests of women, and the inclination which exists to attempt, at least, to apply them to their needs. As teachers, then, to diffuse among women the physiological and sanitary knowledge which they need, we find the first work for women physicians. . . .

The next point of interest to be noticed is the connection of women with public charities and benevolent institutions. . . .

The only way to meet the difficulty, to give a centre to women who are interested in such efforts, and to connect intelligent women with these institutions, is to introduce women into them as physicians. If all public charities were open to *well* educated women physicians, they would exert upon them . . . [a] valuable influence . . . ; they would bring in a more respectable class of nurses and train them, which no men can do; they would supervise the domestic arrangements, and give the higher tone of womanly influence so greatly needed.

They would be at the same time a connecting link between these establishments and women in general life, enlisting their interest and active services in their behalf, far more effectually than could be done by any other means. A real and great want would thus be supplied, and one which no other plan yet proposed has proved at all adequate to meet.

We come now to the position of women in medicine itself. . . .

. . . The same reason which especially qualifies women to be the teachers of women, in sanitary and physiological knowledge, viz., that they can better apply it to the needs of women's life, holds good in regard to their action as physicians. So much of medical practice grows out of every-day conditions and interests, that women who are thoroughly conversant with women's lives will, if they have the character and knowledge requisite for the position, be as much better qualified in many cases to counsel women, as men would be in similar circumstances to counsel men. At present, when women need medical aid or advice, they have at once to go out of their own world, as it were; the whole atmosphere of professional life is so entirely foreign to that in which they live that there is a gap between them and the physician whom they consult, which can only be filled up by making the profession no longer an exclusively masculine one. Medicine is so broad a field, so closely interwoven with general interests, dealing as it does with all ages, sexes, and classes, and yet of so personal a character in its individual applications, that it must be regarded as one of those great departments of work in which the cooperation of men and women is needed to fulfill all its requirements. . . .

We have now briefly considered the most important grounds on which the opening of the profession of medicine to women is an object of value to society in general, and consequently having a claim upon the public for aid in its accomplishment. Let me now state briefly what are the means needed for this purpose.

The first requirement for a good medical education is, that it be practical, i.e., that the actual care of the sick and observation by the bedside should be its foundation. For this reason, it must be given in connection with a hospital. . . .

The chief difficulty in the way of women students at present is, as it always has been, the impossibility of obtaining practical instruction. There is not in America a single hospital or dispensary to which women can gain admittance, except the limited opportunities that have been obtained in connection with the New York Infirmary. This difficulty met us during our own studies, and we were obliged to spend several years in Europe to obtain the facilities we needed. . . .

This troublesome and expensive method is still the only way in which a woman can obtain any thing that deserves to be called a medical education, but it is evidently beyond the means of the majority of women. The instruction that they have hitherto been able to obtain in the few medical schools that have received them has been purely theoretical. It consists simply of courses of lectures, the students being rigorously excluded from the hospitals of the city, which are only open to men. Some three hundred women have attended lectures in these schools, the majority of them being intelligent young women, who would probably have been teachers had they not chosen this profession. They enter the schools with very little knowledge of the amount and kind of preparation necessary, supposing that by spending two or three winters in the prescribed studies they will be qualified to begin practice, and that by gaining experience in practice itself they will gradually work their way to success. It is not until they leave college, and attempt, alone and unaided, the work of practice that they realize how utterly insufficient their education is to enable them to acquire and support the standing of a physician. Most of them, discouraged, having spent all their money, abandon the profession; a few gain a little practical knowledge and struggle into a second-rate position. No judgment can be formed of women as physicians under such circumstances. It would be evidently an injustice to measure their capacity for such occupation by their actual success, when all avenues to the necessary instruction are resolutely closed to them.

Realizing the necessity of basing any system of instruction for women on actual practice, we resolved, seven years ago, to lay the foundation of such an institution as was needed. A number of well-known citizens expressed their approval of the undertaking, and kindly consented to act as trustees. We then took out a charter for a practical school of medicine for women. . . .

When we took out our charter we knew that, having few friends to aid in the effort, we must work gradually toward so large an end. We accordingly began the New York Infirmary, as a small dispensary, in a single room, in a poor quarter of the city, open but a few hours during the week, and supported by the contributions of a few friends. Three years ago we had grown sufficiently to take the house now occupied by the institution, No. 64 Bleecker street, and with the same board of trustees and consulting physicians we organized a small house department. This year the number of patients treated by the Infirmary is about three thousand seven hundred. Although the institution is much too small to enable us to organize any thing like a complete system of instruction for students or nurses, we have received into the house some of the elder students from the female medical schools, and a few women who have applied for instruction in nursing. We have thus become more familiar with their needs, and better able to shape the institution toward meeting them. . . .

. . . [I]t is already a valuable medical centre for women. The practice of a public institution, however small, establishes connexions between those who conduct it and others engaged in various public charities; and from the relations thus formed we have already been able to obtain facilities for students in the city dispensaries, and in private classes, that could not be obtained had we not such a centre to work from. . . .

We believe, therefore, that, quite independent of the broader work that may be ultimately accomplished, in its present shape as a charity to poor women, as a proof of women's ability to practice medicine, and as a medical centre for women, this institution is well worthy of support.

What we ask from those who are interested in the objects we have stated is to assist in raising a fund for endowment which shall place the institution on a secure foundation. . . .

Help us to build up a noble institution for women, such an institution as no country has ever yet been blessed with, a national college hospital in which all parts of the Union shall join. Let it not be a name merely, but a substantial fact, wisely planned and liberally endowed.

7. Edward H. Clarke, an Eminent Boston Physician, Asserts That Biology Blocks the Higher Education of Women, 1873

The problem of woman's sphere, to use the modern phrase, is not to be solved by applying to it abstract principles of right and wrong. Its solution must be obtained from physiology, not from ethics or metaphysics. The question must be submitted to Agassiz and Huxley, not to Kant or Calvin, to Church or Pope. Without denying the self-evident proposition, that whatever a woman can do, she has a right to do, the question at once arises, What can she do? And this includes the further question, What can she best do? . . . The *quæstio vexata* of woman's sphere will be decided by her organization. This limits her power, and reveals her divinely-appointed tasks, just as man's organization limits his power, and reveals his work. . . .

. . . If we would give our girls a fair chance, and see them become and do their best by reaching after and attaining an ideal beauty and power, which shall be a crown of glory and a tower of strength to the republic, we must look after their complete development as women. Wherein they are men, they should be educated as men; wherein they are women, they should be educated as women. The physiological motto is, Educate a man for manhood, a woman for womanhood, both for humanity. In this lies the hope of the race. . . .

. . . Woman, in the interest of the race, is dowered with a set of organs peculiar to herself, whose complexity, delicacy, sympathies, and force are among the marvels of creation. If properly nurtured and cared for, they are a source of strength and power to her. If neglected and mismanaged, they retaliate upon their possessor with weakness and disease, as well of the mind as of the body. . . .

CLINICAL observation confirms the teachings of physiology. The sick chamber, not the schoolroom; the physician's private consultation, not the committee's public

Edward H. Clarke, *Sex in Education; or, a Fair Chance for Girls* (Boston: James R. Osgood and Company, 1873), pp. 12–13, 19, 33, 61–62, 79–82, 85–87, 116–117.

examination; the hospital, not the college, the workshop, or the parlor,—disclose the sad results which modern social customs, modern education, and modern ways of labor, have entailed on women. Examples of them may be found in every walk of life. On the luxurious couches of Beacon Street; in the palaces of Fifth Avenue; among the classes of our private, common, and normal schools; among the female graduates of our colleges; behind the counters of Washington Street and Broadway; in our factories, workshops, and homes,—may be found numberless pale, weak, neuralgic, dyspeptic, hysterical, menorraghic, dysmenorrhœic girls and women, that are living illustrations of the truth of this brief monograph. . . .

Miss D—— entered Vassar College at the age of fourteen. Up to that age, she had been a healthy girl, judged by the standard of American girls. Her parents were apparently strong enough to yield her a fair dower of force. The catamenial function [that is, menstruation] first showed signs of activity in her Sophomore Year, when she was fifteen years old. Its appearance at this age is confirmatory evidence of the normal state of her health at that period of her college career. Its commencement was normal, without pain or excess. She performed all her college duties regularly and steadily. She studied, recited, stood at the blackboard, walked, and went through her gymnastic exercises, from the beginning to the end of the term, just as boys do. Her account of her regimen there was so nearly that of a boy's regimen, that it would puzzle a physiologist to determine, from the account alone, whether the subject of it was male or female. She was an average scholar, who maintained a fair position in her class, not one of the anxious sort, that are ambitious of leading all the rest. Her first warning was fainting away, while exercising in the gymnasium, at a time when she should have been comparatively quiet, both mentally and physically. This warning was repeated several times, under the same circumstances. Finally she was compelled to renounce gymnastic exercises altogether. In her Junior Year, the organism's periodical function began to be performed with pain, moderate at first, but more and more severe with each returning month. When between seventeen and eighteen years old, dysmenorrhœa was established as the order of that function. Coincident with the appearance of pain, there was a diminution of excretion; and, as the former increased, the latter became more marked. In other respects she was well; and, in all respects, she appeared to be well to her companions and to the faculty of the college. She graduated before nineteen, with fair honors and a poor physique. The year succeeding her graduation was one of steadily-advancing invalidism. She was tortured for two or three days out of every month; and, for two or three days after each season of torture, was weak and miserable, so that about one sixth or fifth of her time was consumed in this way. The excretion from the blood, which had been gradually lessening, after a time substantially stopped, though a periodical effort to keep it up was made. She now suffered from what is called amenorrhœa. At the same time she became pale, hysterical, nervous in the ordinary sense, and almost constantly complained of headache. Physicians were applied to for aid: drugs were administered; travelling, with consequent change of air and scene, was undertaken; and all with little apparent avail. After this experience, she was brought to Boston for advice, when the writer first saw her, and learned all these details. She presented no evidence of local uterine congestion, inflammation, ulceration, or displacement. The evidence was altogether in favor of an arrest of the development of the reproductive apparatus, at a stage when the development was nearly complete. Confirmatory proof of such an arrest was found in examining her breast, where the milliner had supplied the organs Nature should have grown. It is unnecessary for our present purpose to detail what treatment was advised. It is sufficient to say, that she probably never will become physically what she would have been had her education being physiologically guided. . . .

It may not be unprofitable to give the history of one more case of this sort. Miss E—— had an hereditary right to a good brain and to the best cultivation of it. Her father was one of our ripest and broadest American scholars, and her mother one of our most accomplished American women. They both enjoyed excellent health. Their daughter had a literary training,—an intellectual, moral, and æsthetic half of education, such as their supervision would be likely to give, and one that few young men of her age receive. Her health did not seem to suffer at first. She studied, recited, walked, worked, stood, and the like, in the steady and sustained way that is normal to the male organization. She *seemed* to evolve force enough to acquire a number of languages, to become familiar with the natural sciences, to take hold of philosophy and mathematics, and to keep in good physical case while doing all this. At the age of twenty-one she might have been presented to the public, on Commencement Day, by the president of Vassar College or of Antioch College or of Michigan University, as the wished-for result of American liberal female culture. Just at this time, however, the catamenial function began to show signs of failure of power. No severe or even moderate illness overtook her. She was subjected to no unusual strain. She was only following the regimen of continued and sustained work, regardless of Nature's periodical demands for a portion of her time and force, when, without any apparent cause, the failure of power was manifested by moderate dysmenorrhœa and diminished excretion. Soon after this the function ceased altogether; and up to this present writing, a period of six or eight years, it has shown no more signs of activity than an amputated arm. In the course of a year or so after the cessation of the function, her head began to trouble her. First there was headache, then a frequent congested condition, which she described as a "rush of blood" to her head; and, by and by, vagaries and forebodings and despondent feelings began to crop out. Coincident with this mental state, her skin became rough and coarse, and an inveterate acne covered her face. She retained her appetite, ability to exercise and sleep. A careful local examination of the pelvic organs, by an expert, disclosed no lesion or displacement there, no ovaritis or other inflammation. Appropriate treatment faithfully persevered in was unsuccessful in recovering the lost function. I was finally obliged to consign her to an asylum. . . .

In concluding this part of our subject, it is well to remember the statement made at the beginning of our discussion, to the following effect, viz., that it is not asserted here, that improper methods of study and a disregard of the reproductive apparatus and its functions, during the educational life of girls, are the *sole* causes of female diseases; neither is it asserted that *all* the female graduates of our schools and colleges are pathological specimens. But it is asserted that the number of these graduates who have been permanently disabled to a greater or less degree, or fatally injured, by these causes, is such as to excite the *gravest alarm,* and to demand the serious attention of the community.

E S S A Y S

Sorting out the place of gender, therapeutic orientation, and social function in defining a professional identity compelling to colleagues and potential patients was a key issue for physicians in the mid-nineteenth century, as it is today. In the first essay, Yale University historian John Harley Warner explores the social, political, and intellectual contexts that shaped the ways orthodox male physicians sought to define and defend their collective identity. He particularly emphasizes how appeals to character helped sustain professional identity during a period of sectarian warfare among medical practitioners and at a time when the important French impulse in American medicine prompted some leading physicians to reflect on the tension between their identity as scientists and identity as healers. In the second essay, historian Regina Morantz-Sanchez of the University of Michigan traces the emergence of the antebellum health reform movement and the public's growing dissatisfaction with orthodox medicine. She explains how the movement to teach women medicine developed from both the denigration of regular heroic practice and the associated health reform activism that grew especially prominent among middle-class, European American women. Morantz-Sanchez looks not only at the arguments for and against the education of women as physicians, but also at the deeper controversy over the proper role of women in medicine—that is, over the role of gender in defining the physician's professional and civic identity.

Science, Healing, and the Character of the Physician

JOHN HARLEY WARNER

In contrast to much of the twentieth century, when American doctors as a group enjoyed considerable security, affluence, and cultural authority, during the decades before the Civil War there was a widespread perception that the medical profession was degraded. From the 1820s onward, physicians believed with good reason that the power and prestige of their profession were declining. Medicine, like the other professions, was one target for popular animosity against all groups claiming special privilege. In the face of radical democratic protest against monopoly, state legislatures revoked medical licensing laws, legally opening up practice to everyone. Though an M.D. degree was not required for practice as a physician, one could easily be obtained by spending three months attending medical lectures, usually taken twice. The scientific content of such training was meagre, and instruction in a hospital or extensive experience at dissection were exceptions rather than the rule. The proliferation of for-profit medical schools, often characterized by low educational standards and ethics, greatly increased the production of poorly trained practitioners, leading to overcrowding and divisive competition. Many orthodox physicians found it difficult to earn a living from medical practice alone, and were compelled to supplement their income by trade or farming. "This country is overrun with half educated physicians," the Philadelphia medical professor

John Harley Warner, "Science, Healing, and the Physician's Identity: A Problem of Professional Character in Nineteenth-Century America," in *Essays in the History of Therapeutics,* ed. W. F. Bynum and V. Nutton, special issue of *Clio Medica* 22 (1991): 66–77. Reprinted with permission.

Alfred Stillé wrote in 1844 to a medical friend in Boston, echoing a commonplace complaint among the well-educated minority, "and the chances of earning one's meat & drink are just about in proportion to one's disregard of truth, honor, and modesty." But what even more disturbed regular (that is, orthodox) physicians was the rising power of alternative medicine, such as homoeopathy, hydropathy, and the botanic healing sect Thomsonianism. Sectarian practitioners attacked the pretensions and heroic therapies of orthodox physicians, and successfully competed with them for paying patients.

The link between scientific knowledge and the regular physician's professional identity was tenuous. To be sure, physicians such as Stillé who valued their own professional learning often looked down with disdain upon their ill-educated brethren, those "who," as another critic put it, "know as much about Anatomy, Physiology, Pathology, Materia medica and Pharmacy, as a pet cat does about the battle of Waterloo"; but they nonetheless recognized that scientific expertise was not a necessary criterion for membership in the regular medical profession. . . . The knowledge required to sustain professional identity was knowledge about practice, the sort that most practitioners initially gained by apprenticeship and developed by experience at the bedside.

The possession of extensive knowledge about medical science, conversely, was insufficient to make a person an acceptable physician. It neither established identity as a regular physician nor guaranteed success as a healer. Harvard medical professor John Ware made this point clearly in speaking to his students in 1850. "The main purpose of the study of medicine," he told them, "is to enable us to treat disease." Warning against the pursuit of scientific knowledge for its own sake, he cautioned that a zealous student of anatomy, chemistry, or pathology might be completely incompetent as a healer. Ware recognized that scientific knowledge might be admirable in the American physician, and noted, for example, that "of course it is desirable that he should be a perfect anatomist. But if he takes the time necessary to make him a perfect anatomist, he may neglect what is necessary to make him a good practitioner." . . . There was no place in American society for a career in medical research, and even medical school professors were private practitioners who taught as a sideline. A widespread belief even held that, as another physician put it, "there is a natural antagonism between profound scientific knowledge and great practical skill . . . that, in short, the study of the *science,* unfits a man for the *practice,* of medicine." . . .

What was critical to the physician's image and performance, however, was *character.* It was above all character—something antebellum Americans regarded as difficult to define but easy to recognize—that signified medical integrity and guaranteed correct behaviour. The American physician functioned in a remarkably open medical marketplace, one in which, as one medical student astutely noted in his thesis, "his position is rather felt than defined." . . . Character was the basis of reputation and respectability as well as guarantor of personal and professional morality, but more, it was an essential ingredient in the practitioner's success as a healer.

. . . In the wake of the [French] Revolution, . . . Paris became [the most vibrant center of western medicine and] a mecca for foreign medical students and practitioners, including at least 700 Americans between the 1820s and the 1850s. They went for a variety of reasons, but overwhelmingly were drawn by the opportunity to gain practical experience in the hospitals and dissecting rooms of the French capital, where access to bodies (living and dead) was so much freer than in their own country. . . . [As one physician] just returned from Paris concluded, "In no part of the world can the same practical experience be acquired by the attentive student as in the French capital." Bred up in a country with meagre opportunities for systematic study in the clinic or autopsy room, Americans were dazzled by the facilities of Paris. There they followed the medical lions on their clinical rounds, paid interns for private courses of bedside instruction on physical diagnosis, and practised surgical techniques on the dead body.

Yet even though access to practical experience—not novelty—was what chiefly drew Americans to France in the first place, once in Paris some among them increasingly became enticed by the scientific activity they found. The young physician Oliver Wendell Holmes wrote from Paris to his parents in Boston, "Merely to have breathed a concentrated scientific atmosphere like that of Paris must have an effect on any one who has lived where stupidity is tolerated, where mediocrity is applauded, and where excellence is defied." The French Revolution in politics had signalled a revolution in medicine as well, a time noted for such technical and conceptual innovations as the stethoscope and physical examination, tissue pathology, systematic clinical instruction and autopsy, clinical statistics, and the anatomo-clinical viewpoint. This was a medical science not of the laboratory bench but of the bedside and autopsy table, a medical science centred on close symptom-lesion correlation. For a physician from the New World newly arrived in Paris, being on the cutting edge of medical knowledge could be an exhilarating experience.

What some Americans in Paris found so seductive was the ideal of science as much as its content. They admired the allegiance to scientific investigation witnessed in their French mentors. But more than this, they were attracted by the particular attitude toward knowledge the Parisian ideal of medical science involved. In the eyes of Americans, the Paris Clinical School stood above all else for *empiricism*—a strident, sceptical clinical empiricism explicitly set against the rationalism that had dominated medicine through the early nineteenth century. . . . [O]rdinarily they expressed it in simple terms: what was most significant about French medical science was its allegiance to empirical fact, to truth, to knowledge attained and verified by direct observation and analysis of nature[,] . . . an assault on rationalistic, speculative systems of practice. . . . They saw French empiricism as the vehicle for a thoroughgoing reconstruction of medical knowledge, in which reliance on speculation would be supplanted by an allegiance to observation and empirically determined fact.

Yet underlying the reverence some Americans felt for their Parisian mentors was a profound ambivalence. As one American physician who in 1843 had recently arrived in Paris put it concisely in a letter to his father, "It is astonishing that the French who excel so much in the science of medicine should be so far behind in practice." Even those who most devoutly admired the French clinicians as the best medical scientists in the world at the same time judged them to be deplorable healers. . . . In the letters Americans wrote home, they regularly denounced the French physicians' therapeutic passivity, indifference to patient modesty, and brutality. Observing the French clinicians at work during his recent visit to Paris, one Kentucky medical professor told his students, he had found "their treatment of disease to be inert, lame and inefficient, to a degree surprisingly in contrast with the show of science and research which appears in their writings." All too often, in his appraisal, French therapeutics was "a meditation on death."

Many Americans shared the perception that the clinicians of the Paris School, in their enthusiasm for pathological science, did not particularly care about curing their patients. . . . And some Americans seriously worried that the clinical values of the Parisian clinicians reflected a deeper flaw in their character, one that made them more eager to gain new knowledge than to heal the sick. "As a matter of scientific research it might be interesting to understand disease, even if we did not attempt to cure it," a Philadelphia physician critical of the French preoccupation with investigating the natural history of disease told his students; "but as practising physicians and philanthropists, the alleviation and cure of disease must be the grand desideratum." He was left with the impression, however, that in Paris, "the physician did not prescribe treatment in many cases, under the apprehension, that if he did, he might thereby disturb the *post mortem* appearances!"

Some American chauvinism surely was at work in the judgment that whatever their claims to scientific excellence, the French clinicians ranked far below the Americans as practical healers. Yet many observers were seriously concerned that American physicians might be corrupted by the French model, seduced by its perverse inversion of the proper ranking of healing above science. What was threatened was not the physician's knowledge but his values, the integrity of his character. . . . The fear that devotion to science could corrupt the practitioner made many American physicians who studied in Paris wary of being tainted by it.

There was even a concern that the young American's character might be corrupted in more mundane ways by the very experience of living in Paris, a city not renowned for moral virtue. Taking notes on Charles Caldwell's lectures on the institutes of medicine in 1841 in Louisville, Kentucky, one medical student recorded in his class notebook that "the temptations and dangers that young men are exposed to in visiting the contaminated atmosphere of Paris is very great—There are more snares for virtue, and vice is clothed in more seductive charms & alluring colours than in any other city in the world." . . .

But while the concern that American physicians might be corrupted by the vices of Parisian life was serious, the concern that their values as healers might be undercut by excessive enthusiasm for science was much more disturbing. This was a danger more difficult to guard against, partly because it was less easy to recognize soon enough to forestall ruin. . . .

So long as Americans were still in Paris, they were to a large extent free to indulge their scientific inclinations while reassuring themselves that their integrity remained sound. . . .

Once these innocents abroad made the return voyage across the Atlantic, though, matters became more difficult. . . . They had to make choices about what . . . role they would assign [to French medical science] in American medicine and in their own identity as American physicians.

Some among them actively took up the task of proselytizing Parisian medical science to the profession in America. And collectively, they made up the group of American physicians best situated to do so. The fact that they could afford the time and expense of travelling to Paris in the first place meant they tended to come from a socioeconomic élite, while the experience they acquired in France enhanced their professional prestige. They were the physicians most likely to teach at medical schools, to serve as medical officers at hospitals, and to edit and write for medical journals, and they used all these forums to urge the ideals they had acquired in France.

Yet they found it difficult to pursue scientific investigations in the American context. Energy for investigations had to be stolen away from practice, and no one was paid for the time they put into research. . . . As Samuel Parkman, nostalgic for Paris after his return to Boston, wrote sardonically to a medical friend, "Science does not pay."

. . . "I am very far from feeling satisfied and contented with my present position," the Paris-returned Elisha Bartlett wrote from Lowell, Massachusetts, to a medical friend who shared his allegiance to French ways. "I have a practice, to be sure, pleasant and respectable enough, and by many of my brother doctors my situation would be regarded as an enviable and desirable one. But the opportunities here, for the study of medicine, as a great and progressive science, are almost nothing, and I feel, every day, with more and more earnestness, the want of these opportunities, and of kindred and co-operating associates in medical studies." The massive clinical institutions of Paris did not exist in the United States, and most practitioners had no association whatsoever with a hospital. John Young Bassett, who returned from Paris to Huntsville, Alabama, lacked access even to [a] tiny clinic, and so instead expressed the passion for empirical investigation he had acquired in France by keeping meticulous meteorological records and systematically correlating changes in climate with empirical observations of southern diseases.

Those who tried to engage in scientific work also lamented the lack of a community in America to encourage and appreciate their efforts. . . . Antebellum American society was highly distrustful of bids to authority based on the possession of specialized knowledge. Epitomized in the political and social ethos usually called Jacksonian Democracy, there was a prevalent faith that all authentic knowledge should be fully comprehensible to the common man and woman. . . . The abolition of virtually all medical licensing laws during precisely these decades starkly demonstrated the fact that the public did not recognize scientific training as a dependable sign of medical qualification.

Indeed, to the extent that science did become one emblem of the regular medical profession, it became a usable target for assaults upon orthodoxy and its putative evils. On the one hand, science was identified with heroic depletive therapies such as bloodletting and calomel, distinctive symbols of orthodox medicine that sectarians energetically pilloried. "Thousands of invalids are sickly by the poisons they have taken in the name of Science," one hydropathic practitioner snipped in a letter to his father. "Men are palsied, puralised, swollen, gouty, &c. by taking arsenic, quinine, strychnine and a host of other medicines under the garb of *Science*." At the same time, sectarian critics took "science" to stand for the mystification of the laws of healing, a device by which an aristocratic profession sought to maintain its monopoly by keeping simple medical truths "under lock and key," out of the hands of the public where they belonged. Science, according to this depiction of it, served the orthodox profession as a platform—a thoroughly corrupted one—for making claims to privileged status entirely at odds with the democratic spirit of the times.

As disturbing as this assault on scientific pretensions from outside the orthodox medical profession was the fact that the rank and file of regular American physicians were notoriously apathetic about scientific work. . . . [M]ost who studied in France were to be disappointed by their American professional brethren, and scorned their apathy. Thus Stillé bemoaned the "large number of young men who might have made good citizens as farmers, tradesmen, or mechanics," but who had trained as physicians instead, only to "plod along as stupid routinists." . . .

More than this, . . . [t]hose who committed themselves to cultivating science had to be on guard that their allegiance to science stay visibly subordinate to their obligations as healers. This concern was not just the anti-intellectual grumblings of the medical masses but an issue of professional integrity that even those who had studied in Paris took seriously.

This concern that too great a passion for science could become a threat to the American physician's character is lucidly illustrated by the scientific aspirations that the young James Jackson, Jr. developed while studying medicine in Paris, and by the anxieties that these aspirations roused in his physician-father, James Jackson, Sr., for his son's future. After studying medicine at Harvard, in the spring of 1831 the younger Jackson set off for Paris, where he spent the next two years studying in its clinics and dissecting rooms. He made it clear that gaining experience, not being on the cutting edge of science, was what had drawn him to the French capital, writing to his father not long after his arrival that "I have learned very little that is *new*— but it was not for novelty that I crossed the waters to visit foreign hospitals." At first he deplored the therapeutic impotence of the French clinicians, and, while he took full advantage of a "touching" class in which pregnant women were freely and fully examined by students, he wrote to his father that "I cannot but rejoice that the state of society is such in our own country that the same knowledge cannot be acquired there."

Over time, however, as he studied with the clinician Pierre Louis, Jackson became increasingly intrigued by the approach to investigating the natural history of disease that his French mentor exemplified. More and more he took up a new image of his future and his identity, as he sought to emulate the devotion to scientific investigation he witnessed in Louis. "In my idea of the end I shd. propose to my life, my mind has greatly changed since you rocked last my cradle," he wrote to his father in Boston early in 1833. "My view was then almost bounded to becoming a good physician—now my much more ardent desire is to do my part in clearing away some of the clouds wh. hide the truth in our difficult medical sciences. I am beginning to regard myself as one whose education has been such that it is in his power & whose disposition is such that it wld. be his delight to seek & find *truth,* pathological and therapeutic." The young Jackson eagerly announced to his father his plan to devote five years to pure investigation before starting practice, and Louis (whom James had come to describe as "my second father") wrote to Jackson, Sr. enthusiastically endorsing this plan.

Jackson, Sr., however, saw no choice but to reject the plan, and insisted that his son return home to begin medical practice. A medical professor at Harvard, founder of the Massachusetts General Hospital, and one of the most eminent physicians in the United States, the elder Jackson did not dismiss lightly his son's intellectual aspirations, and unmistakably was proud of James's professional commitment and industry. But he understood something that his son had yet to learn: too much scientific interest by an American physician could be seen as an outward flaw that pointed to an inward want of grace. Even the appearance of excessive devotion to science threatened to taint his character, and thereby to corrupt his integrity and identity as a healer. Jackson, Sr. later made precisely this point when he said that his son's plan had been impossible "because," as he explained,

> in this country his course would have been so singular, as in a measure to separate him from other men. We are a business doing people. We are new. We have, as it were, but just landed on these uncultivated shores; there is a vast deal to be done; and he who will not be doing, must be set down as a drone. If he is a drone in appearance only and not in fact, it will require a long time to prove it so, when his *character* has once been fixed in the public mind.
>
> This view of the subject is too vague, at least for those who belong to other and older countries. Let me then state the matter more definitely. Among us, where the hands are yet few in proportion to the work to be done, every young man engages as soon as he can in the business of life. The public estimation of his character is decided early in life; earlier than in Europe. . . . But, if an individual were to go very far in the other extreme, his reputation would be fixed, as one, who perhaps loved knowledge and knew how to acquire it; but who was not disposed to use it, and who perhaps did not know how to apply it. . . . Such at least were my fears.

The father's fears were not groundless, for he had a good grasp of the realities of his profession and of his nation. His son's scientific ardour, however genuine, was also naive. As it happened, Jackson, Jr. never really had to come to terms with all the difficulties that freighted his aspirations. Forced to return home to Boston in 1833, he began plans to start practice and announced the opening of his office in the newspaper. But, at the age of twenty four, just before his practice was to start, he grew ill and died. Aptly, his father kept a detailed case history of his son's final illness, and, reverently observing the French zeal for pathoanatomical correlation that James had so admired, invited a medical friend (whom James had taken to see Louis in Paris) to perform the autopsy.

Science, Health Reform, and the Woman Physician

REGINA MARKELL MORANTZ-SANCHEZ

By midcentury dissatisfaction with established medical practice had reached astonishing proportions; doctors had good reason to feel on the defensive. "The practice, or so-called *science* of medicine, has been little else than one of experiment," observed the health reformer Mrs. Marie Louise Shew in a scathing indictment. Standard medical therapeutics, she claimed, had hitherto been characterized by "uncertainty" and "chance." Little progress had been made in alleviating the sufferings of mankind. "Why," asked Shew's colleague Mary Gove Nichols, "are we sick?

Regina Markell Morantz-Sanchez, *Sympathy and Science: Women Physicians in American Medicine* (New York and Oxford: Oxford University Press, 1985), pp. 29–35, 37–38, 42–43, 45–59, 61. Copyright © 1985. Reprinted by permission of the author.

Why cannot the doctors cure us?" Men, women, and society had sought a cure so long in vain that they began to distrust their doctors. "We are tired of professions and promises." . . .

Jacksonian antielitism added to the profession's difficulties, as hostility to all professional distinctions became a featured aspect of American political rhetoric. Beginning around 1830, most states responded by abolishing restrictive licensing legislation, which already had proved difficult to enforce. Although the American Medical Association and the New York Academy of Medicine were founded in 1846 to counter such trends, there was only slow progress in medical education until the end of the century. . . .

Sectarians presented a . . . [special] challenge. Responding in part to the growing dissatisfaction with heroic medicine, the followers of several new medical systems began to compete with the regular profession for public patronage, legitimacy, and authority. Some of these sects opposed the physician's heroic methods and use of drugs and substituted for them the belief that only nature should do the healing. Hydropaths, for example, used only water internally, and externally in the form of baths and hot and cold compresses, shunning surgery and drugs altogether. Others, like the Botanics, later known as Eclectics, substituted so-called natural remedies for chemical and mineral ones. Homeopaths, although they used a variety of drugs, believed in such miniscule doses that their prescriptions had no deleterious effect— and possibly no effect at all. Like other sectarians, they too believed strongly in the healing powers of nature.

In time these sectarians formed their own professional institutions—schools, journals, and societies. Favoring the popular diffusion of professional knowledge, and respecting women's enhanced responsibilities in the family, their schools often welcomed women students, and consequently middle-class women initially gravitated to sectarian medicine. Many of the first generation of women doctors received their degrees from sectarian institutions. The challenge posed by sectarian medicine to older concepts of professionalism worked in favor of women. Paradoxically, in the mid-nineteenth century the abandonment of licensing legislation and the ease of access to a medical degree actually served to maintain a professional identity for all medical practitioners by conferring the title of doctor on a large proportion of them. This temporary fluidity allowed women who wished to achieve professional status to do so before definitions of professionalism crystallized once more.

The health-reform movement provided a different alternative to a dissatisfied public, and it grew and flourished in the atmosphere created by vociferous debate between sectarians and regulars over more humane methods of treatment. Beginning in the antebellum period, self-help in health matters, public hygiene, dietary reform, temperance, hydro-therapy, and physiological instruction merged as ingredients in a coherent and articulate campaign to save the nation by combating the ill-health of its citizenry. Although such attention to personal health and hygiene was not wholly original, never before had the regard for good health given rise to such widespread public activity. . . .

The concern with hygiene was an integral part of the antebellum reformist world view. The popularity of both sectarian medicine and health reform helped to shape the character of the midnineteenth-century reform consciousness. Indeed, the health crusade converged with several better-known radical concerns. Historians have been quick to point out this identity of ideas and personnel. Abolitionist speakers, for example, lodged at health-reform boarding houses, and a large number of women's-rights advocates followed some form of Sylvester Graham's vegetarian diet. Oberlin College, familiar as a breeding ground for abolitionism and women's rights, adopted strict vegetarianism in its dining-room in 1835. Asa Mahan, the college's president, put a "reformation in food, drink, and dress" high on the list of important causes. . . .

A shared theme of all health advocates was the inhibition of disease through the teaching of the laws of physiology and hygiene. Over and over again they argued that disease was *preventable;* that it was up to the individual to keep himself well. No longer were sickness and death to be tolerated with a stoicism and resignation that contrasted the limited moral choices of man with the all-powerful inscrutability of God. . . .

In a flurry of antielitist rhetoric, health reformers deplored the complicated language of most medical journals. "Reader," warned the editor of the *Water-Cure Journal,* "if you cannot understand what an author is writing about, you may reasonably presume he does not know himself." "I would have the *highest science,* clothed in words, that the people can understand," wrote Aurelia Raymond, in her graduate thesis at the Female Medical College of Pennsylvania. "I have studied medicine because I am one of the people . . . to enter my protest against the exclusiveness, which sets itself up as something superior to the people. . . ." . . .

Although the health-reform movement attracted both men and women, it was to the middle-class woman, by virtue of her new role in an increasingly complex society, that many of the health reformers addressed themselves. . . . Women took to the field as lecturers. Ladies' Physiological Societies appeared throughout the Northeast and West. The names of Mary Gove Nichols, Harriot Hunt, and Lydia Folger Fowler are only the most familiar of the dozens of women who taught enthusiastic female audiences the "laws of life." . . .

Good health became a prerequisite to woman's new place in the world. "Woman was neither made a toy nor a slave, but a help-meet to man," wrote "A Bloomer to Her Sisters," "and as such devolves upon her very many important duties and obligations which cannot be met so long as she is the puny, sickly, aching, weakly, dying creature that we find her to be; and woman must, to a very considerable extent, redeem herself—she must throw off the shackles that have hitherto bound both body and mind, and rise into the newness of life."

Women could achieve none of these goals until they learned to dress properly. Health reformers made dress reform a symbol of women's new aspirations. Impractical clothes immobilized women and kept them from their responsibilities. Some regular physicians had linked fashionable dress to female ill health, but health reformers succeeded in making dress reform a moral imperative. Good health was doomed, they argued, as long as women clung to the dictates of French fashion. They called upon women to liberate their souls by freeing their bodies from the harmful effects of tight lacing and long, heavy unhygienic skirts. . . .

By the end of the nineteenth century, reform ideas about personal cleanliness, public health, and family hygiene had become familiar axioms of middle-class American culture—a badge of distinction by which members could set themselves off from "illegitimate" immigrant groups, many of whom retained distinctly premodern daily habits and attitudes toward disease. Holding out to confused wives and mothers the prospect of improving the quality of life, not merely by changing the environment, but by gaining control of themselves, health reformers promised women that they could raise healthy children and keep husbands moral by cooking the right foods, and promoting exercise, cleanliness, and fresh air. The health-reform regimen established new standards by which middle-class women could measure their respectability and self-worth. Elevating the art of domesticity to a science, re-formers restored to their followers a sense of purpose and direction, while, unwit-tingly perhaps, preserving in a new form traditional assumptions about woman's role which were deeply imbedded in the culture. . . .

. . . [T]he entrance of women into the medical profession received powerful stimulus from the health-reform movement. "In sickness there is no hand like a woman's hand," the *Water-Cure Journal* reminded its readers. "The property of her nature," argued a contributor to *Godey's Lady's Book,* "which renders her the best of nurses, with proper instruction, equally qualifies her to be the best of physicians. Above all is this the case with her own sex and her children." . . .

. . . [T]he close relationship between feminists, health reformers, and pioneer women physicians clearly illustrates their common goals. In time these early women physicians, who were attracted to medicine out of an ardent desire to fulfill their des-tinies as superior moral beings with natural abilities to cure, would be transformed into full-fledged professionals by their contact with an increasingly scientific and empirical discipline. They, as well as their system of values, would be permanently altered in the process. . . .

When the young audience attending the fall session of Geneva Medical College in upstate New York listened to the dean of the faculty one morning in 1847, they probably only dimly comprehended the historical significance of the gentleman's words. In quavering tones, he spoke to them of a letter from a prominent physician in Philadelphia and sought their response to the writer's unconventional request.

For several months the physician had been preceptor to a lady student who had already attended a course of medical lectures in Cincinnati. He wished her to have the opportunity to graduate from an eastern medical college, but his efforts in secur-ing her acceptance had thus far ended in failure. A country college like Geneva, he hoped, would prove more open-minded. If not, the young woman's only other recourse would be to seek training in Europe. As the dean spoke, a silence fell upon the room. For several moments the students sat transfixed as he concluded his remarks with the comment that the faculty would accede to the request only if the students favored acceptance unanimously.

The students themselves did not realize that the faculty was emphatically opposed to the admission of a woman. Not wanting to assume the sole responsibil-ity for denying the request, they had thought the students would reject the pro-posal, and they planned to use the actions of a united student body to justify their own response.

Steven Smith, then a bright young member of the class and later a prominent New York physician and public-health advocate, witnessed the ensuing events. Over half a century later at a memorial service for his longtime friend and colleague, Elizabeth Blackwell, he recalled:

But the Faculty did not understand the tone and temper of the class. For a minute or two, after the departure of the Dean, there was a pause, then the ludicrousness of the situation seemed to seize the entire class, and a perfect Babel of talk, laughter, and cat-calls followed. Congratulations upon the new source of excitement were everywhere heard, and a demand was made for a class meeting to take action on the Faculty's communication. . . . At length the question was put to vote, and the whole class arose and voted "Aye" with waving of handkerchiefs, throwing up of hats, and all manner of vocal demonstrations. . . .

Blackwell studied medicine for two full terms at Geneva, but in an insulting footnote to the story, the school closed its doors to women soon after she received her degree. Such was the inauspicious start of the formal movement to train women as physicians.

Undaunted, women continued to seek medical training. Within two years three more graduated from the eclectic Central Medical College in Syracuse, the first co-educational medical school in the country. In Philadelphia a group of Quakers led by Dr. Joseph Longshore pledged themselves to teach women medicine and established the Woman's (originally Female) Medical College of Pennsylvania in 1850. The following year eight women were graduated in the first class. A Boston school, founded originally by Samuel Gregory in 1848 to train women as midwives, gained a Massachusetts charter in 1856 as the New England Female Medical College. Here Marie Zakrzewska, former medical associate of Elizabeth Blackwell, early female graduate of the Cleveland Medical College, and the influential founder of the New England Hospital for Women and Children, came to teach in 1859.

Meanwhile, in New York the Homeopathic New York Medical College for Women, established in 1863 by still another early graduate, Clemence Lozier, enjoyed such success that by the end of the decade it had matriculated approximately one hundred women. Five years later Elizabeth Blackwell, now joined in practice by her sister Emily, also a doctor, opened the Women's Medical College of the New York Infirmary.

Armed with the conviction that medical science needed a woman's influence, hundreds of women received medical training in the decades following Elizabeth Blackwell's graduation from Geneva Medical College. By 1880 a handful of medical schools accepted women on a regular basis. But female pioneers, still dissatisfied with what they believed to be the slow progress of medical coeducation, founded five "regular" and several sectarian women's medical colleges. They built dispensaries and hospitals to provide clinical training for female graduates. By the end of the nineteenth century, female physicians numbered between 4 and 5 percent of the profession, a figure that remained relatively stable until the 1960s. . . .

Women entered the profession as part of a broad effort toward self-determination in which all reformist women, from conservative social feminists to radical suffrage advocates, played varying parts. Like these, women doctors sought to redefine womanhood to fit better the demands of an industrializing society. Medicine, indeed, attracted more women votaries in the nineteenth century than any other profession except teaching, and female physicians took seriously their role in health education.

Although they remained a small minority of the profession, women doctors were conspicuous because they violated nineteenth-century norms for female behavior in a way that teachers did not. No wonder they became the focus of a debate over women's proper role in and relationship to public and private health. Whereas amateur instructors of physiology could be dismissed as objects of public ridicule, professionally trained women physicians were another matter entirely. By the end of the 1860s, protest against them mounted from within the profession, requiring them to refine and elaborate an ideological defense of their cause. . . .

The opponents of medical education for women, of course, were not interested in the socially transforming aspect of the new reverence for the female character. Placing women on a pedestal located firmly within the confines of the home, they justified an emotional preference for sequestered women by making them the moral guardians of society and the repositories of virtue. Fearing that women who sought professional training would avoid their child-rearing responsibilities, they reminded their colleagues in overworked metaphors that "the hand that rocks the cradle rules the world." Woman, argued a spokesman, held "to her bosom the embryo race, the pledge of mutual love." Her mission was not the pursuit of science, but "to rear the offspring and even fan the flame of piety, patriotism and love upon the sacred altar of her home." . . .

Conservatives also worried that teaching women the mysteries of the human body would affront female modesty. "Improper exposures" would destroy the delicacy and refinement that constituted women's primary charms. John Ware's conviction that medical education with its "ghastly" rituals and "blood and agony" in the dissecting room would harden women's hearts and leave them bereft of softness and empathy reappeared in elaborate guise.

Despite the popularity of this defense of female delicacy, conservatives compromised their case when they readily admitted that women's special sympathy made them excellent nurses. Praising Florence Nightingale's achievements in the Crimea, they credited her work primarily to her ignorance of scientific medicine. Medical education, they argued, would surely have hardened her heart, leaving her bereft of softness and empathy.

Supporters of female education quickly discovered that respect for feminine delicacy could work in their favor. Was the mother who nursed her family at the bedside ever shielded from the indelicacies of the human body? they asked. If the issue was female modesty, then why should men—even medical men—*ever* be allowed to treat women? As the use of pelvic examinations became part of ordinary practice, male physicians posed a greater threat to feminine delicacy than women practitioners. Indeed, the doctrine of "passionlessness" gave rise to such elaborate exaggerations of womanly delicacy that some social conservatives and some feminists alike viewed the training of women physicians as a necessary solution to the problems arising from female reluctance to disclose symptoms to male practitioners. Elizabeth Blackwell, for example, admitted in her autobiography that her first encounter with the idea of studying medicine arose from the agonized suggestion of a friend, dying of what was probably uterine cancer, that her sufferings would have been considerably alleviated had she been "treated by a lady doctor." . . .

But male physicians alleged other unsuitable character traits against women besides their innocence. Many agreed that Nature had limited the capacity of women's intellect. Women were impulsive and irrational, unable to do mathematics, and deficient in judgment and courage. Their passivity of mind and weakness of body left them powerless to practice surgery. And if these disadvantages were not enough, there remained the enigmatic side of the female temperament. Dependent, "nervous," and "excitable," women, "as all medical men know," were subject to uncontrollable hysteria. "Hysteria," regretted J. S. Weatherly, M.D., "is second Nature to them."

Even more subtle and insidious was the fear that the influx of women would alter the image of the profession by feminizing it in unacceptable ways. "The primary requisite of a good surgeon," insisted Edmund Andrews, "is *to be a man,—a man of courage.*" Few physicians were prepared to surrender their masculinity gracefully, especially when technical developments like the discovery of anesthesia actually were rendering harsher images of the doctor obsolete. One Boston doctor taunted women physicians with the remark, "If they cannot stride a mustang or mend bullet holes, so much the better for an enterprizing and skillful practitioner of the stern sex."

The editor of the *Boston Medical and Surgical Journal* continually grumbled about women becoming an economic threat in a profession already burdened with an oversupply of practitioners. When the graduates of the orthodox female medical colleges sought admission to local and national medical societies in the 1870s, they were rejected on the grounds that their training was either irregular or of poor quality. Opponents held women's allegedly inferior schooling against them, yet denied them access to the type of education that was acceptable and often refused to consult with them or ostracized those male practitioners who did. . . .

. . . [I]t was the group of physicians who managed to cloak their prejudices in the guise of science that proved the most injurious to women's free development. In the 1870s and 1880s these physicians transferred the grounds for the argument over "female nature" from the spiritual to the somatic.

Rallying around a book entitled *Sex in Education: A Fair Chance for Girls,* published in 1873 by the Harvard professor Dr. E. H. Clarke, they based their case against women almost entirely on biological factors. Menstruation was depicted as mysteriously debilitating and higher education in any subject, as sapping the energy needed for the normal development of the reproductive organs. The results, lamented Clarke with total seriousness, were "those grievous maladies which torture a woman's earthly existence: leuchorrhoea, amenorrhea, dysmenorrhea, chronic and acute ovaritis, prolapsus uteri, hysteria, neuralgia, and the like." He concluded that higher education for women produced "monstrous brains and puny bodies; abnormally active cerebration and abnormally weak digestion; flowing thought and constipated bowels."

When they chose to emphasize the devitalizing and still-ambiguous effects of menstruation, traditionalists were indeed effective. Physicians knew little about the influence of women's periodicity, and the culture treated menstruation as a disease. Reasoning that only rest could help women counteract the weakness resulting from the loss of blood, complete bedrest was commonly prescribed. Thus even if opponents appeared willing to concede women's intellectual equality—and many were prepared to do so—women's biological disabilities seemed insurmountable. Since menstruation incapacitated women for a week out of every month, could they ever be depended on in medical emergencies?

The biological argument proved particularly vexing to feminists. As M. Carey Thomas, the indomitable president of Bryn Mawr and a fierce supporter of women physicians, recalled years later, "We did not know when we began whether women's health could stand the strain of education. We were haunted in those days, by the clanging chains of that gloomy little specter, Dr. Edward H. Clarke's *Sex in Education.*"

Female physicians helped to dispel doubts about the effect of menstruation by functioning skillfully in their own professional lives. Many joined with the feminist community to launch a full-scale counterattack against the Clarke thesis. Outraged by the influence of Clarke's book, a group of women in Boston cast about for a woman doctor with the proper credentials to call its thesis into question. In 1874 they gained the opportunity for a public forum when Harvard Medical School announced that the topic for its celebrated Boylston Essay would be the effects of menstruation on women. Writing to Dr. Mary Putnam Jacobi in the fall of that year, C. Alice Baker urged her to take up the "good work," and "win credit for all women, while winning for yourself the Boylston Medical Prize for 1876." Jacobi met the challenge. Because the essays were submitted anonymously, the judges did not know that the author was female. Her essay "The Question of Rest for Women During Menstruation" won the prize, to the opposition's chagrin. The study challenged conservative medical opinion on the subject with sophisticated statistical analyses and case studies, concluding that there was "nothing in the nature of menstruation to imply the necessity, or even the desirability, of rest for women whose nutrition is really normal." . . .

Much like their opponents, female physicians took seriously the idea of their own moral superiority as women and their abilities as natural healers. They rarely quarreled directly with the concept of separate spheres, although their interpretation of this concept was quite different from that of the conservatives. Like other social feminists, women physicians defined "woman's sphere" as broadly as possible and connected it quite directly with the surveillance of and participation in public life. Examining the ethical implications of the scientific method for medicine and society, women physicians claimed for themselves the task of integrating Science and Morality. . . .

Like their opponents, supporters constantly connected womanhood with the guardianship of home and children. Women were morally superior to men, claimed Elizabeth Blackwell, because of the "spiritual power of maternity." The true physician, male or female, she argued, "must possess the essential qualities of maternity." . . .

Medical women also insisted that they had special contributions to make to the profession. Feminization could enhance the practice of medicine, whose goal was the eradication of suffering. Association with female colleagues would "exert a beneficial influence on the male," making men more gentle and sensitive in their practice. Combining the best of masculine and feminine attributes would raise medical practice to its highest level. Occasionally supporters carried the implications of this reasoning even further. Female physicians expected to challenge heroic therapeutics directly. As the "handmaids of nature," women would place greater value on the "natural system of curing diseases . . . in contradistinction to the pharmaceutical." They would promote a "generally milder and less energetic mode of practice." . . .

Nineteenth-century women doctors never drifted too far out of the ideological mainstream. As proponents of the expansion of women's role, they perceived gradual change to be the only kind the public would tolerate. Slowly they succeeded in creating a positive image for the female physician. A minority proved that wives and mothers could handle a professional career, and the inevitable interaction with male colleagues eventually convinced many critics that women could be competent doctors and still maintain their femininity.

Female physicians largely confined themselves to what became feminine specialties—obstetrics and gynecology in the nineteenth century, pediatrics, public health, teaching, and counseling later on. Such specialization was not due solely to resistance from male professionals, although women doctors occasionally blamed discrimination. Women practitioners also gravitated to these specialties because they were conscious of their "special" abilities. They concerned themselves with the health problems of women and children because they hoped to raise the moral tone of society through the improvement of family life.

But confining themselves to women's concerns also circumscribed women physicians' professional influence. A few even willingly advocated an informal curtailment of their medical role, hoping to gain support by taking themselves out of competition with men. Others disdained this approach. Such women were converted early to the modern and empirical world of professional medicine, and their first love was science. Uneasy in the moralistic world of their medical sisters, they exhibited a toughness and clarity of vision that set them apart from those women who used medicine primarily as a moral platform. Physicians like Mary Putnam Jacobi and Marie Zakrzewska insisted from the beginning that medical women needed to be of superior mettle. Fearing that specialization in diseases of women and children would mean a loss of grounding in general medicine, they warned that women would be justly relegated to the position of second-class professionals. Eventually their performance even within their specialty would become second-rate. If women would succeed in medicine, they asserted, they had to be thoroughly trained. Despite such predictions, specializing remained popular throughout the nineteenth century and into the next because it continued to provide advantages in blunting the resentment of male colleagues.

 F U R T H E R   R E A D I N G

Susan E. Cayleff, *Wash and Be Healed: The Water-Cure Movement and Women's Health* (1987).

Harris L. Coulter, *Divided Legacy: The Conflict Between Homoeopathy and the American Medical Association. Science and Ethics in American Medicine, 1800–1910* (1973, 1982).

Kenneth Allen De Ville, *Medical Malpractice in Nineteenth-Century America: Origins and Legacy* (1990).

Jane B. Donegan, *"Hydropathic Highway to Health": Women and Water-Cure in Antebellum America* (1986).

Robert C. Fuller, *Alternative Medicine and American Religious Life* (1989).

John S. Haller Jr., *Medical Protestants: The Eclectics in American Medicine, 1825–1939* (1994).

John S. Haller Jr., *A Profile in Alternative Medicine: The Eclectic Medical College of Cincinnati, 1845–1942* (1999).

Martin Kaufman, *Homeopathy in America* (1971).

Constance McGovern, *Masters of Madness: Social Origins of the American Psychiatric Profession* (1985).

James C. Mohr, *Doctors and the Law: Medical Jurisprudence in Nineteenth-Century America* (1993).

Regina Markell Morantz-Sanchez, *Sympathy and Science: Women Physicians in American Medicine* (1985; with new preface, 2000).

Stephen Nissenbaum, *Sex, Diet, and Debility in Jacksonian America: Sylvester Graham and Health Reform* (1980).

Ronald L. Numbers, *Prophetess of Health: Ellen G. White and the Origins of Seventh-Day Adventist Health Reform*, revised ed. (1992).

Steven J. Peitzman, *A New and Untried Course: Woman's Medical College and Medical College of Pennsylvania, 1850–1998* (2000).

Naomi Rogers, *An Alternative Path: The Making and Remaking of Hahnemann Medical College and Hospital of Philadelphia* (1998).

Naomi Rogers, "Women and Sectarian Medicine," in *Women, Health, and Medicine in America,* ed. Rima D. Apple (1990), pp. 273–302.

William G. Rothstein, *American Physicians in the Nineteenth Century* (1972).

Cynthia Eagle Russett, *Sexual Science: The Victorian Construction of Womanhood* (1989).

Martha H. Verbrugge, *Able-Bodied Womanhood: Personal Health and Social Change in Nineteenth-Century Boston* (1988).

John Harley Warner, *Against the Spirit of System: The French Impulse in Nineteenth-Century American Medicine* (1998).

John Harley Warner, "Orthodoxy and Otherness: Homeopathy and Regular Medicine in Nineteenth-Century America," in *Culture, Knowledge, and Healing,* ed. Robert Jütte, Guenter B. Risse, and John Woodward (1998), pp. 5–29.

John Harley Warner, *The Therapeutic Perspective: Medical Practice, Knowledge, and Identity in America, 1820–1885* (1986; with new preface, 1997).

James C. Whorton, *Crusaders for Fitness: The History of American Health Reformers* (1982).

James Harvey Young, *The Toadstool Millionaires: A Social History of Patent Medicines in America Before Federal Regulation* (1961).

CHAPTER
6

The Civil War, Efficiency, and the Sanitary Impulse, 1845–1870

In the first decades of its existence, many citizens of the United States congratulated themselves on the healthfulness of the new nation and the vast superiority of our climate and environment over those of disease-ridden Europe. By the 1830s, a small but increasingly vocal group of reformers began to cast doubt upon this health exceptionalism. These reformers fretted over a long list of sanitation and health problems, but it was the growth of urban centers that inspired their greatest concern as the nation's population density grew and the number of towns and cities increased. To early public health reformers, the voluntary measures and private funds used in these new cities and towns to combat such health hazards as improper sewers, epidemics of infectious diseases, and the crowded living conditions of immigrant-clogged slum areas seemed grossly inadequate. Building up a sizable body of descriptive data and a widening network of concerned citizens with volunteer experience, reform advocates began pushing for more assistance from state and local governments. By the 1850s a number of public health workers even advocated for the federal government to play a role in improving health conditions. Unfortunately for these reformers, the sectional tensions that would ultimately lead to the Civil War had already begun to absorb most of the nation's political attention.

What effect did the Civil War, the most devastating biological event of nineteenth-century American history, have on medicine and public health? Whose responsibility was it to provide care for the millions of men who would ultimately be caught up in this struggle? What kind of care should they receive? Where should it take place? Who should provide it? Were women to play a role in this care-giving endeavor? Should health care provisions for this conflict include a program of disease prevention, hygiene maintenance, and public sanitation? If so, who should establish and maintain this program—the army, the federal or Confederate government, private citizens? In the wake of the twentieth century, which witnessed such wartime medical miracles as the development and mass production of penicillin and the MASH (mobile army surgical hospital) unit, it is hard to imagine an era in

159

which such basic military health issues were unresolved. Yet that is precisely the situation in which Americans, northern and southern, found themselves during the early years of the Civil War.

At the start of the war, even in the Union army, hospital and ambulance facilities were almost nonexistent for a conflict that began with a call for 750,000 volunteers and would ultimately produce over 6 million sick and injured soldiers. Wounded and dying men often lay on a battlefield for days without care or transport. Health regulation and administration of basic health and hygiene rules were so lax that dysentery, typhoid, and other bacterial infections were endemic to camp life. Resolving these problems would require years of heated public debate, vicious political and military infighting, and a widespread popular reform effort. New private, voluntary soldiers' aid groups, such as the United States Sanitary Commission, were so much more effective than early medical efforts by the military that they received quasi-governmental status. Many of the key players in this struggle to improve the health of Civil War combatants were drawn from the same group of reformers that had been working on sanitary and hygiene issues since midcentury. What emerged from their efforts was a startling reorganization of medical practices and institutions that would have a profound effect on postwar-America's public health and medicine.

The legacy of the Civil War can be seen most clearly in the late-nineteenth-century transformation of the hospital from a charity institution for the destitute into a curative institution that appealed to all classes. It can also be seen in the rise of a formally trained, sought-after, and respected cadre of professional nurses, as well as in the development of a new government-sanctioned, bureaucratic structure for public health. A less visible but no less important Civil War legacy is the expansion of medical science to include such principles as sanitation, standardization, and organizational efficiency.

 # DOCUMENTS

In Document 1, dated 1845, New York physician and pietistic reformer John Griscom urges that city government should energetically use the law to transform the sanitary condition of New York City's poor. Arguing that an unsanitary and debilitating physical environment is a leading source of not only sickness but also poverty and immorality, he sees sanitary reform as the vehicle to economic and moral upliftment. Like English reformer Edwin Chadwick, whose *Report on the Labouring Population of Great Britain* (1842) was the cardinal document of the sanitary revolution, Griscom describes in vivid detail the conditions of the tenements that he regards as the source of sickness, poverty, and immorality. Document 2 is excerpted from one of a series of articles that English traveler and author Harriet Martineau wrote in 1861 for the popular journal *Atlantic Monthly*. Full of advice on how Americans can keep troops healthy and nurse those who fall in battle, Martineau's comments draw directly on the British experience in the Crimean War (1853–1856) and Florence Nightingale's nursing reforms. Written with a keen sense of how America is different from Europe, Martineau's practical suggestions provide an important glimpse into an international body of new ideas about hygiene and health care that powerfully influenced the United States.

Document 3 excerpts the 1862 diary of Kate Cumming, a twenty-seven-year-old unmarried woman from Mobile, Alabama. The journal entries of this nursing volunteer who left home despite family opposition are full of details of daily life in Confederate hospitals. Laced with Cumming's own painful confrontation with the belief that it was not "respectable" for a southern "lady" to serve as an army nurse, the diary provides an interesting contrast with Martineau's account of the heroic and vitally necessary role played by Nightingale and her nurses in the Crimea. Document 4 is an 1863 editorial by the prominent prewar sanitary reformer and physician Stephen Smith. Using his editorship of the *American Medical Times* to advance the cause of the U.S. Sanitary Commission and the reform of the army medical corps, Smith outlines the main principles of a new field he calls military hygiene. The reforms Smith advocates, particularly the work of the privately organized Sanitary Commission, have, as Smith recognizes, important implications for society even in peacetime. The author of Document 5, Louisa May Alcott, who would go on to write the novel *Little Women* (1868), ponders similar questions in an 1863 article for the Boston newspaper, the *Commonwealth*. Calling herself Tribulation Periwinkle, Alcott sent the newspaper a set of dispatches about her experience as a nurse for the Union army. These hospital sketches provide a window into the barrack's hospital, which she called Hurlyburly House, and give a poignant sense of the vital link between the home front and the battlefield during the Civil War.

Alcott's account and Cumming's journal entries offer a revealing contrast to Document 6, a set of letters written in 1864 by Maine physician James Moore while he was serving in the Union army in Virginia. Detailing the suffering in the camp hospital, which he likened to "a big slaughter house," Moore struggles to prepare himself for the army examination required of all surgeons. Although he appreciates the wonderful opportunity the war offers for him to improve his surgical technique, Moore is concerned about how much harder the examiners would be on him if they knew he favored homeopathy (a fact that he has kept secret), even though, as he observes, many of the men in the regiment prefer homeopathic treatment. Document 7 is quite different from these wartime accounts but grew directly out of the Civil War experiences of such reformers as Smith and Alcott. In 1865 the Council of Citizens' Association of New York, a civic organization that counted among its membership many former members of the U.S. Sanitary Commission (including commissioners Stephen Smith and Elisha Harris) submits a report they believe provides compelling evidence of the need for massive sanitary and hygiene reform. Engaging in the same kind of exposé as Griscom's *Report* of the 1840s, but following the more forceful lobbying strategy of the Civil War sanitary reformers, the Citizens' Association surveys New York City living conditions and presses their findings on public officials. This survey was the impetus for legislation that established the first major municipal health department of the modern era, An Act to Create a Metropolitan Sanitary District and Board of Health (1866). The survey and the subsequently established New York Board of Health became models for other communities striving in the late nineteenth century to improve their public health response.

1. John Griscom, a Physician and Reformer, Reports to the Municipal Government on the Sanitary Condition of the Laboring Population of New York, 1845

No duty can engage the attention of the magistracy of a city or state, more dignified in itself, more beneficial to the present generation, or more likely to prove useful to their descendants, than that of procuring and maintaining a sound state of the public health.

Of the three objects contemplated in the Declaration of Independence as necessary to be secured by government, the first named is "Life." Higher purposes cannot be conceived for which governments should be instituted.

John H. Griscom, *The Sanitary Condition of the Laboring Population of New York* (New York: Harper and Brothers, 1845), pp. 1–9, 46–47.

As upon the condition of health of an individual are based his physical and mental strength, his ability for self-maintenance, his personal happiness, and that of others dependent on him, and also his usefulness to his family, to the community and his country; and as the community depends for its prosperity upon the performances of its members, individually and collectively, in the measure of influence committed to them respectively, so does the health of the people affect the capacity and interests of the state.

As upon the individual, when sick, falls an increased pecuniary burden, with (in general) a suspension of income, so upon the state or city, must rest, not only the expenses of removing an unsound condition of public health, but also, from the attendant loss of character, a diminution of its resources.

When individuals of the pauper class are ill, their entire support, and perchance that of the whole family, falls upon the community. From a low state of general health, whether in an individual or in numbers, proceed diminished energy of body and of mind, and a vitiated moral perception, the frequent precursor of habits and deeds, which give employment to the officers of police, and the ministers of justice.

These, among other considerations, together with the recent expression by the chief magistrate of the city of his interest in the sanitary condition of his constituency, by the recommendation to the Common Council of a measure of no ordinary importance to their welfare and comfort, induce me to urge attention to a measure of improvement which has long impressed my mind, as one, above all others, demanding the action of the City Government. . . .

The objects of this communication, briefly stated, are these;—1st, to show that there is an immense amount of sickness, physical disability, and premature mortality, among the poorer classes;—2d, that these are, to a large extent, unnecessary, being in a great degree the results of causes which are removeable;—3d, that these physical evils are productive of moral evils of great magnitude and number, and which, if considered only in a pecuniary point of view, should arouse the government and individuals to a consideration of the best means for their relief and prevention; and 4th, to suggest the means of alleviating these evils and preventing their recurrence to so great an extent. . . .

Sanitary regulations affect the pauper class of the population more directly than any other, because they live in situations and circumstances which expose them more to attacks of disease. They are more crowded, they live more in cellars, their apartments are less ventilated, and more exposed to vapors and other emanations, &c., hence, ventilation, sewerage, and all other sanitary regulations, are more necessary for them, and would produce a greater comparative change in their condition. The influence of drainage upon the health and lives of the population, is too well known to require, at this day, any argument. Almost every one has heard of the effects of marshy soil, in country situations, producing Intermittent Fever, or Fever and Ague, and of the entire disappearance of the disease, simply by draining off the water, and permitting the ground to become dry. Its results in populous cities are equally well marked. . . .

The system of tenantage to which large numbers of the poor are subject, I think, must be regarded as one of the principal causes, of the helpless and noisome manner in which they live. The basis of these evils is the subjection of the tenantry, to the merciless inflictions and extortions of the *sub-landlord*. A house, or a row, or court of houses, is hired by some person of the owner, on a lease of several years, for a sum which will yield a fair interest on the cost. The *owner* is thus relieved of the great trouble incident to the changes of tenants, and the collection of rents. His income is sure from one individual, and obtained without annoyance or oppression on his part. It then becomes the object of the lessee, to make and save as much as possible, with his adventure, sufficient sometimes to enable him to purchase the property in a short time.

The tenements, in order to admit a greater number of families, are divided into small apartments, as numerous as decency will admit. Regard to comfort, convenience, and health, is the last motive; indeed, the great ignorance of this class of speculators (who are very frequently foreigners and keep a grog shop on the premises) would prevent a proper observance of these, had they the desire. These closets, for they deserve no other name, are then rented to the poor, from week to week, or month to month, the rent being almost invariably required in advance, at least for the first few terms. The families moving in first, after the house is built, find it clean, but the lessee has no supervision over their habits, and however filthy the tenement may become, he cares not, so that he receives his rent. He and his family are often found steeped as low in depravity and discomforts, as any of his tenants, being above them only in the possession of money, and doubtless often beneath them in moral worth and sensibility. . . .

In these places, the filth is allowed to accumulate to an extent almost incredible. Hiring their rooms for short periods only, it is very common to find the poor tenants moving from place to place, every few weeks. By this practice they avoid the trouble of cleansing their rooms, as they can leave behind them the dirt which they have made. The same room, being occupied in rapid succession, by tenant after tenant, it will easily be seen how the walls and windows will become broken, the doors and floors become injured, the chimneys filled with soot, the whole premises populated thickly with vermin, the stairways, the common passage of several families, the receptacle for all things noxious, and whatever of self-respect the family might have had, be crushed under the pressure of the degrading circumstances by which they are surrounded.

Another very important particular in the arrangements of these tenements must here be noticed. By the mode in which the rooms are planned, *ventilation is entirely prevented.* It would seem as if most of these places were built expressly for this purpose. They have one or two windows, and a door at one side of the room, but no opening anywhere else. A draught of air *through,* is therefore an utter impossibility. . . .

I have had recent occasion to visit several of these pestiferous places, and I pen these paragraphs in the month of August, with their sight and smell fresh upon my senses.

The almost entire absence of household conveniences, contributes much to the prostration of comfort and self-respect of these wretched people. The deficiency of water, and the want of a convenient place for washing, with no other place for drying clothes than the common sitting and bed room, are very serious impediments in the way of their improvement. Without any convenient or safe place to deposit wood, or coal, or food in large quantities, all their purchases are by "the small," from the neighboring grocer (who is perhaps the landlord), at prices from 10 to 50 per cent. above the rates at which they might be obtained, under better circumstances.

But the most offensive of all places for residence are the *cellars.* It is almost impossible, when contemplating the circumstances and condition of the poor beings who inhabit these holes, to maintain the proper degree of calmness requisite for a thorough inspection, and the exercise of a sound judgment, respecting them. You must descend to them; you must feel the blast of foul air as it meets your face on opening the door; you must grope in the dark, or hesitate until your eye becomes accustomed to the gloomy place, to enable you to find your way through the entry, over a broken floor, the boards of which are protected from your tread by a half inch of hard dirt; you must inhale the suffocating vapor of the sitting and sleeping rooms; and in the dark, damp recess, endeavor to find the inmates by the sound of their voices, or chance to see their figures moving between you and the flickering blaze of a shaving burning on the hearth, or the misty light of a window coated with dirt and festooned with cobwebs—or if in search of an invalid, take care that you do not fall full length upon the bed with her, by stumbling against the bundle of rags and straw, dignified by that name, lying on the floor, under the window, if window there is;—all this, and much more, beyond the reach of my pen, must be felt and seen, ere you can appreciate in its full force the mournful and disgusting condition, in which many thousands of the subjects of our government pass their lives.

> "There vapors, with malignant breath
> Rise thick, and scatter midnight death."

. . . From what has been related respecting the effects of the habitations of the poor, upon their health, lives, and morals, the evils are attributable to three things, viz., 1st, the living in damp, dark, underground, and other ill-ventilated apartments. 2d. The dirty and injured condition of the floors, walls, yards, and other parts of the premises. 3d. The crowding too many persons in single rooms of inadequate size and accommodations. To correct the first two of these evils, there appears but one way, and that is to place all the dwellings of the city under the inspection of competent officers, who shall have power *to enforce a law of domiciliary cleanliness.* For this purpose, those places known or suspected to be kept usually in improper condition, should be visited periodically, say once in one, two, or three months. The law should be so arranged as to make the cleansing bear upon the owner or lessee, and not upon the tenant directly, who is generally so poor, as to be unable to perform the necessary purgation and rectification of the premises. . . .

The effect of such a law upon the habits of the tenant would not be *direct,*—his personal condition can only be reached by the moral law,—but the landlord, under this compulsory process, urged by the fear of having his premises out-lawed would, in letting them, stipulate with his tenants to keep them clean, to whitewash the walls and ceilings, wash the floors, remove the collections of dirt and garbage, and keep the yards and cellars in good order. And knowing that the health officer will pay them frequent visits, armed with the power of the law, it is altogether reasonable to suppose that the tenants themselves would be stimulated to maintain a better appearance of persons and domicils—that many would feel a pride in a good and cleanly aspect—that the smothered feelings of self-respect, love of praise, and desire for the comforts of cleanliness, would, in hundreds of bosoms, be re-awakened into life and energy.

2. World Traveler Harriet Martineau Advises America on Keeping Troops Healthy During Wartime, 1861

What are the functions of General Hospitals, besides curing the sick and wounded? some readers may ask, who have never particularly attended to the subject.

The first business of such institutions is undoubtedly to restore as many as possible of the sufferers brought into them: and this includes the duty of bringing in the patients in the most favorable way, receiving them in an orderly and quiet manner, doctoring, nursing, feeding, clothing, and cleaning them, keeping their minds composed and cheerful, and their manners creditable, promoting their convalescence, and dismissing them in a state of comfort as to equipment. This is the first duty, in its many subdivisions. The next is to obviate, as far as possible, future disease in any army. The third grows out of this. It is to improve the science of the existing generation by a full use of the peculiar opportunities of observation afforded by the crop of sickness and wounds yielded by an army in action. . . .

The excellent and devoted managers of the hospitals of the Union army need no teaching as to the daily administration of the affairs of the wards. They will never have to do and dare the things that Miss Nightingale had to decide upon, because they have happily had the privilege of arranging their hospitals on their own principles. They will not know the exasperation of seeing sufferers crowded together on a wooden divan (with an under-stratum of dead rats and rotting rags) while there is an out-house full of bedsteads laid up in store under lock and key. Not being disposed to acquiesce in such a state of things, and failing in all attempts to get at the authority which had charge of the locked door, Miss Nightingale called to an orderly or two, and commanded them to break open the door. They stared; but she said she assumed the responsibility; and presently there were as many men in bed as there were bedsteads. Her doctrine and practice have always been,—instant and silent obedience to medical and disciplinary orders, without any qualification whatever; and by her example and teaching in this respect she at length overcame the jealousy and prejudices of authorities, medical and military: but in such a case as the actual presence of necessaries for the sick, sent out by Government or by private charity for their use, she claimed the benefit, and helped her patients to it, when there was no other obstruction in the way than forms and rules never meant to apply to the case. . . .

Of every hundred on board the transport, an average of ten had died since leaving the Crimea. . . . No one could wonder at this who had for a moment looked upon the scene. The poor fellows just arrived had perhaps not had their clothes off since they were wounded or were seized with cholera, and they were steeped in blood and filth, and swarming with vermin. . . . Before the miserable company could be fed, made clean, and treated by the surgeons, many were dead; and a too large proportion were never to leave the place more, though struggling for a time with death. It was amidst such a scene that Florence Nightingale refused to despair of five men so desperately wounded as to be set aside by the surgeons. The surgeons were right. As they said, their time was but too little for the cases which were not hopeless. And Florence Nightingale was right in finding time, if she could, to see

Harriet Martineau, "Health in the Hospital," *Atlantic Monthly* (December 1861): 724, 726–730.

whether there was really no chance. She ascertained that these five were absolutely given over; and she and her assistants managed to attend to them through the night. She cleaned and comforted them, and had spoonfuls of nourishment ready whenever they could be swallowed. By the morning round of the surgeons, these men were ready to be operated upon; and they were all saved.

It would have been easier work at a later period. Before many months were over, the place was ready for any number to be received in peace and quietness. Instead of being carried from one place to another, because too many had been sent to one hospital and too few to another, the poor fellows were borne in the shortest and easiest way from the boat to their beds. They were found eager for cleanliness; and presently they were clean accordingly, and lying on a good bed, between clean, soft sheets. . . . The cleaning of the wards was done in the mornings, punctually, quickly, quietly, and thoroughly. The doctors came round, attended by a nurse who received the orders, and was afterwards steady in the fulfilment of them. The tables of the medicines of the day were hung up in the ward; and the nurse went round to administer them with her own hand. Where she was, there was order and quietness all day, and the orderlies were worth twice as much as before the women came. Their manners were better; and they gave their minds more to their business. The nurse found time to suit each patient who wished it with a book or a newspaper, when gifts of that sort arrived from England. . . .

What were the changes in organization needed to produce such a regeneration as this?

They were such as must appear to Americans very simple and easy. The wonder will be rather that they were necessary at last than that they should have been effected with any difficulty. But Americans have never known what it is to have a standing army as a long-established and prominent national institution; and they can therefore hardly conceive of the strength of the class-spirit which grows up in the various departments of the military organization. . . . The old medical officers were incapable, pedantic, and jealous; and no proper relation had ever been established between them and the military authorities. The imbecility of the system cost the lives of others than the soldiers who died in hospital. . . . The citizens are accustomed to organize themselves for action of all sorts; and no stiff-necked classes stand in the way of good management. The difficulty in America must rather be to understand how anything so perverse as the management of British military hospitals ten years ago can have existed to so late a date.

. . . This is enough to say of the old methods.

In the place of them, a far simpler system was proposed at the end of the war. The eternal dispute as to whether the commandant should be military or medical, a soldier or a civilian, was set aside by the decision that he should be simply the ablest administrator that could be found, and be called the Governor, to avoid the military title. Why there should be any military management of men who are sick as men, and not as soldiers, it is difficult to see; and when the patients are about to leave the hospital, a stated supervision from the adjutant-general's department is all that can be required. Thus is all the jealousy between military and medical authority got rid of. The Governor's authority must be supreme, like that of the commandant of a fortress, or the commander of a ship. He will not want to meddle in the doctors' professional business; and in all else he is to be paramount. . . .

Of female nurses it is not necessary to say much in America, any more than in England or France. They are not admissible into Regimental Hospitals, in a general way; but in great military and civil hospitals they are a priceless treasure.

The questions in regard to them are two. Shall their office be confined to the care of the linen and stores, and the supplying of extra diets and comforts? If admitted to officiate in the wards, how far shall that function extend?

In England, there seems to be a strong persuasion that some time must elapse, and perhaps a generation of doctors must pass away, before the ministration of female nurses in military hospitals can become a custom, or even an unquestioned good. . . . Nobody doubts that many lives would be saved in every great hospital from the time that fevered frames and the flickerings of struggling vitality were put under the charge of the nurses whom Nature made. But the difficulties and risks are great. On the whole, it seems to be concluded by those who know best, that only a few female nurses should be admitted into military and naval hospitals: that they should be women of mature age and ascertained good sense, thoroughly trained to their business: that they should be the women who have been, or who would be, the head nurses in other hospitals, and that they should be paid on that scale: that they should have no responsibility,—being wholly subject to the surgeons in ward affairs, and to their own superintendent in all others: that no enthusiasts or religious devotees should be admitted,—because that very qualification shows that they do not understand the business of nursing: that everything that can be as well done by men should be done by trained orderlies: that convalescents should, generally speaking, be attended on by men,—and if not, that each female nurse of convalescents should have a hundred or so in her charge, whereas of the graver cases forty or fifty are as many as one nurse can manage, with any amount of help from orderlies. These proposals give some idea of what is contemplated with regard to the ordinary nurses in a General Military Hospital. The superintendent of the nurses in each institution must be a woman of high quality and large experience. And she will show her good sense, in the first place, by insisting on a precise definition of her province, that there may be no avoidable ill-will on the part of the medical officers, and no cause of contention with the captain of service, or whatever the administrator of the interior may be called. She must have a decisive voice in the choice of her nurses; and she will choose them for their qualifications as nurses only, after being satisfied as to their character, health, and temper.

. . . [T]he two sorts of women who really and permanently become nurses are those who desire to make a living by a useful and valued and well-paid occupation, and those who benevolently desire to save life and mitigate suffering, with such a temper of sobriety and moderation as causes them to endure hardship and ill-usage with firmness, and to dislike praise and celebrity at least as much as hostility and evil construction. The best nurses are foremost in perceiving the absurdity and disagreeableness of such heroines of romance as flourished in the press seven years ago,—young ladies disappointed in love, who went out to the East, found their lovers in hospital, and went off with them, to be happy ever after, without any anxiety or shame at deserting their patients in the wards without leave or notice. Not of this order was Florence Nightingale, whose practical hard work, personal reserve, and singular administrative power have placed her as high above impeachment for feminine weaknesses as above the ridicule which commonly attends the striking out of a new course by man or woman. Those who most honor her, and most desire to follow her example, are those who most steadily bring their understandings and their hearts to bear upon the work which she began. Her ill-health has withdrawn her from active nursing and administration; but she has probably done more towards the saving of life by working in connection with the War-Office in private than by her best-known deeds in her days of health. Through her, mainly, it is that every nation has already studied with some success the all-important subject of Health in the Camp and in the Hospital. It now lies in the way of American women to take up the office, and, we may trust, to "better the instruction."

3. Kate Cumming, an Alabama Nursing Volunteer, Writes in Her Journal About Conditions in the Confederate Army Hospital Service, 1862

April 22.   All the patients are being sent away on account of the prospects of a battle; at least, those who are able to be moved.

We have had a good deal of cold, wet weather lately. This is the cause of much sickness. Dr. Hereford, chief surgeon of Ruggles's brigade, has just informed me, that nearly our whole army is sick, and if it were not that the Federals are nearly as bad off as ourselves, they could annihilate us with ease. . . .

April 23.   A young man whom I have been attending is going to have his arm cut off. Poor fellow! I am doing all that I can to cheer him. He says that he knows that he will die, as all who have had limbs amputated in this hospital have died. It is but too true; such is the case. It is said that the reason is that none but the very worst cases are left here, and they are too far gone to survive the shock which the operation gives the frame. The doctors seem to think that the enemy poisoned their balls, as the wounds inflame terribly; but I scarcely think that they are capable of so great an outrage. Our men do not seem to stand half so much as the northerners. Many of the doctors are quite despondent about it, and think that our men will not be able to endure the hardships of camp-life, and that we may have to succumb on account of it; but I trust that they are mistaken. None of the prisoners have yet died; this is a fact that can not be denied; but we have had very few of them in comparison with the number of our own men.

April 24.   Mr. Isaac Fuquet, the young man who had his arm cut off, died to-day. He lived only a few hours after the amputation. The operation was performed by Surgeon Chaupin of New Orleans, whose professional abilities are very highly commended. Dr. Hereford was well acquainted with Mr. Fuquet and intends to inform his mother of his death. . . .

The amputating table for this ward is at the end of the hall, near the landing of the stairs. When an operation is to be performed, I keep as far away from it as possible. To-day, just as they had got through with Mr. Fuquet, I was compelled to pass the place, and the sight I there beheld made me shudder and sick at heart. A stream of blood ran from the table into a tub in which was the arm. It had been

Kate Cumming, *Kate: The Journal of a Confederate Nurse by Kate Cumming*, ed. Richard Harwell (Baton Rouge: Louisiana State University Press, 1959), pp. 24–25, 28, 33–39, 40, 65.

taken off at the socket, and the hand, which but a short time before grasped the musket and battled for the right, was hanging over the edge of the tub, a lifeless thing. I often wish I could become as callous as many seem to be, for there is no end to these horrors.

The passage to the kitchen leads directly past the amputating room below stairs, and many a time I have seen the blood running in streams from it.

There is a Mr. Pinkerton from Georgia shot through the head. A curtain is drawn across a corner where he is lying to hide the hideous spectacle, as his brains are oozing out. . . .

April 30. . . . The hospital is nicely fixed up; every thing is as neat and clean as can be in this place.

Mrs. Glassburn has received a great many wines and other delicacies from the good people of Natchez. I believe they have sent every thing—furniture as well as edibles. We have dishes in which to feed the men, which is a great improvement. The food is much better cooked. We have negroes for cooks, a good baker, a nice dining-room, and eat like civilized people. If we only had milk for the patients, we might do very well.

There is a young man here taking care of his brother, who is shot through the jaw. The brother procures milk from one of the farmhouses near, and had it not been for this I believe the sick man would have died of starvation. We have a few more such, and they have to be fed like children. One young man, to whom one of the ladies devotes her whole time, has had his jaw-bone taken out. We have a quantity of arrow-root, and I was told that it was useless to prepare it, as the men would not touch it. I thought that I would try them, and now use gallons of it daily. I make it quite thin, and sometimes beat up a few eggs and stir in while hot; then season with preserves of any kind—those that are a little acid are the best—and let stand until it becomes cold. This makes a very pleasant and nourishing drink; it is good in quite a number of diseases; will ease a cough; and is especially beneficial in cases of pneumonia. With good wine, instead of the preserves, it is also excellent; I have not had one man to refuse it, but I do not tell them of what it is made. . . .

May 7. . . . I had a slight quarrel with our ward-master. One of the men, lately wounded, was in a room where were some who had occupied it since the battle of Shiloh. One of them—a mere boy—was wasted to a skeleton; his back was covered with bed-sores. Poor child! he was very fretful. I observed that it annoyed the new patient, and requested Dr. Allen, who is very kind to the soldiers, to allow me to have him removed to a room by himself. He kindly gave his consent. While doing it, the ward-master objected; but as I had obtained leave, I had him removed, and he commenced to improve immediately.

I have been through the ward to see if the men are in want of anything; but all are sound asleep under the influence of morphine. Much of that is administered; more than for their good, and must injure them. I expressed this opinion to one of the doctors; he smiled, and said it was not as bad as to let them suffer. . . .

May 8. A number of men, wounded in a skirmish, have been brought in to-day. The surgeons dressed their wounds; there is always plenty for us to do without that. We wash their hands and faces which is a great treat to them, as they are covered with dust; we bathe their wounds, which are always inflamed, and give them something refreshing to drink. . . .

May 9.   A great many wounded men, both Federal and Confederate, were brought in to-day. About twenty-five of ours were shot through mistake. A fine-looking Federal captain is wounded in three or four places. His head and face are tied up, and he can not speak. He has a Bible, on the back of which is printed the Union flag. Some of us were looking at it; one of the ladies remarked that it was still sacred in her eyes. This astonished me, after the suffering which we had seen it the innocent cause of. I said that it was the most hateful thing which I could look at; as every stripe in it recalled to my mind the gashes that I had witnessed upon our men. I have conversed with a number of the prisoners; they all express the same opinion as the others, that they dislike Lincoln and the abolitionists as much as we do, but they are fighting for the Union. What a delusion!

I am no politician. I must own to ignorance in regard to federal or state rights; but I think I have a faint idea of the meaning of the word "union." According to Webster and other authorities, it is concord, agreement, and conjunction of mind. We all know how little of that and happiness exists in a forced union of man and wife, where there is neither love nor congeniality of feeling. Can these men really think it when they say it?. . .

May 10.   The hospital is again filled with the badly wounded. There is scarcely an hour during which they are not coming in from skirmishes. I sat up all night to see that the nurses performed their duties properly, and assisted in bathing the wounds of the men. They all rested quite well, excepting one, who was severely wounded in the hand. He suffered a great deal. One died suddenly this morning. I gave him his toddy; he was then quite cheerful; and I went to give him his breakfast, but his bunk was empty—he was dead and gone. He was wounded in the arm. The doctor desired him to have it amputated, which he would on no account permit. The result was hemorrhage ensued, and he bled to death before assistance could be rendered. I did not learn his name, nor any thing about him. . . .

Sunday, May 11.   A very hot, sultry day. I am very tired, as I have all to attend, the other ladies being sick; many of the nurses are sick also. It is more unhealthy now than ever, and unless some change takes place I fear that we will all die. . . .

May 12.   Two men died this morning, Mr. Adams and Mr. Brennan, from Coffee County, Alabama. Mr. Brennan was wounded. As a friend, Mr. Adams came to nurse him. Both were taken sick this morning, and died after a few hours' illness.

We have the same sad scenes to witness as ever—sick and wounded men lying on the platform at the depot, night and day, and we are not allowed to take them any thing to eat. Dr. Smith is obliged to prohibit it, as it is contrary to orders, and he has not the food to spare for them.

A terrible circumstance happened a few nights since. Our druggist, Dr. Size-more, went out about 9 o'clock to see some one. When within a short distance from the hospital he heard groans; went to the place from which they proceeded, and found a box-car, that had been switched off the track, filled with wounded men, some dead and others dying, and not a soul with them to do any thing for them. The conductor was censured, but I think whoever sent the men off are in fault for not sending proper persons to take care of them. If this kind of treatment of our brave men continues much longer, I fear that we will have none to fight for us, for such a total disregard of human life must have a demoralizing effect. If we had many more such kind-hearted officers as Dr. Smith, our men would suffer little through neglect.

None leave this hospital without he is certain they can go comfortably, and have plenty of nourishment to last them on their journey. I have seen him, many a time, go to the cars himself, to see that they were properly put in. I am informed that he spends every cent of his pay for their comfort. He will reap his reward. . . .

Sunday, May 18.   A very hot day. Our patients are nearly all gone. Captain Dearing left to-day. He is in a fair way to recover. He was one of the worst of the wounded. Three of the ladies are very sick. Miss Marks is not expected to live. She has made up her mind to that effect, and is perfectly resigned. She is a member of the Episcopal Church. . . .

May 23.   Have had two very nice men here, wounded—a doctor and a captain. They are friends of Mrs. Glassburn. Dr. Smith sent them to Rienzi, where the Mobile ladies are. Mrs. Glassburn visited them, and came back perfectly delighted with the hospital arrangements there. She says that Mrs. Ogden is an excellent manager. I am glad of this, as she has had a great deal of opposition from surgeons, as all of the ladies have who have desired to go into hospitals. I can not see what else we can do, as the war is certainly ours as well as that of the men. We can not fight, so must take care of those who do.

I think as soon as surgeons discover that ladies are really of service, that prejudice will cease to exist. The patients are delighted to have us, and say that we can cause them to think of the dearest of places to them now—home.

Miss Marks is a little better, and has been sent to Okolona. The other two ladies who were sick have returned to Mobile.

Every corner of the hospital is clean, and ready for patients. The last of my patients died this morning. He was a German, named Ernest; was wounded at Shiloh. He wandered a good deal in his mind; but just before he died he sent for Dr. Smith, and requested him to write to his wife, and send her all the money he had. She lived on Magazine Street, New Orleans.

One of the saddest sights witnessed are two Federals, who have been here since the battle of Shiloh. One has had his arm, the other his leg amputated. They are seventeen and eighteen years of age, respectively. They look very pitiful, dying among strangers, far away from their homes and relatives. They have been cared for the same as our own; but that is not all that is wanted. They need sympathy, and of that character which it is impossible for us to extend to them, as they came here with the full intention of taking all that is dear to us. They may have been conscientious, and thought that they were doing their duty, but we are of a different opinion, and it will be some time before we change. They will soon die; both are religious. I never look at them without thinking of the thousands of our poor men who are in the same condition in the North. I do sincerely trust that they are as well treated as these poor fellows have been. . . .

May 28.   Arrived at Okolona yesterday. I am staying at Judge Thornton's. The place is much changed since we were last here; it is filled with refugees, and sick and wounded soldiers. Mrs. Thornton has every corner of her house filled with the latter. I am informed that all private dwellings in the place are in the same condition. . . .

September 8.   . . . There is a good deal of trouble about the ladies in some of the hospitals of this department. Our friends here have advised us to go home, as they say it is not considered respectable to go into one. I must confess, from all I had heard and seen, for awhile I wavered about the propriety of it; but when I remembered the suffering I had witnessed, and the relief I had given, my mind was made up to go into one if allowed to do so. Mrs. Williamson and Mrs. May have come to the same conclusion on the subject as myself. God has said, "Who can harm you if you be followers of that which is good?" I thought of this, and believed it, and gained strength from it. Christians should not mind what the world says, so that they are conscious of striving to do their duty to their God.

It seems strange that the aristocratic women of Great Britain have done with honor what is a disgrace for their sisters on this side of the Atlantic to do. This is not the first time I have heard these remarks. Not respectable! And who has made it so? If the Christian, high-toned, and educated women of our land shirk their duty, why others have to do it for them. It is useless to say the surgeons will not allow us; we have our rights, and if asserted properly will get them. This is our right, and ours alone.

4. Medical Editor Stephen Smith Preaches the Gospel of Sanitary Reform During Wartime, 1863

Taken in a strictly economic point of view, the cash value of every soldier's life in the loyal army exceeds one thousand dollars, if that life can be preserved at full vigor during the war, or until lost in battle. Such is the simple arithmetic of war. The soldier's health and life become mathematical quantities, are made the basis of grand estimates in levying for recruits and conscripts, and in massing of forces in the field. Sound lungs, strong muscles, nerves well strung, senses perfect, and all functions in healthy action in the soldier, become and are essential elements in the military successes and prowess that crown the national arms. Thus Mars pays homage to Hygiene.

Life-saving, or its equivalent, health-saving, has become a most important branch in the art of war, and it has its full share in all grand strategic successes. A sickly army is a demoralized army, and must soon become a conquered force. And do we not see in the patriotic gratitude and munificent support that is given to the Sanitary Commission of our War Department, evidence of the enlightened confidence of the popular mind in reference to this principle? Fearfully is the truth on this subject brought home to the people as their choicest regiments return, after only two years' service, reduced ten *per cent.* by casualties of battles, thirty *per cent.* by deaths from disease, and twenty *per cent.* by invaliding or discharges on account of disability. Yet these are about the average ratios of losses; and few are the regiments that after two years' service in this bloody war can muster thirty-five *per cent.* of the men who first entered the field. . . . All this is a matter of momentous concern to the nation, and to the homes that furnished the volunteer soldiers. Thus is brought home the idea of the value and economy of health and lives—the fundamental idea, and the very animus of all true plans for promoting the science and works of Hygiene.

Stephen Smith, "War and Hygiene," *American Medical Times* (1863): 89–90.

. . . [T]he SURGEON GENERAL of our army has planted his standard, both as an instructor and chief executor in works and measures for promoting the hygienic welfare of the national forces. In seconding and officially sustaining the vast undertakings of the Sanitary Commission, he has but done justly; for that Commission commenced its work at the opening of the war . . . without mandatory power [and] it has laid the basis of the broadest system of scientific and practical inquiries and works that has ever been put into operation. To the patriot, longing for the reestablishment of the national power and the restoration of rightful peace, such labors and their results afford a positive source of reliance, while science and the interests of humanity are to reap richest fruits. It is honorable to the spirit and purposes of our profession, that chief officers of the army medical service cordially recognise and appreciate such sanitary works and labors. We believe the fact will yet be acknowledged, that the men who have thus earnestly studied and successfully labored to promote the national cause, and to save life in this war, have merited the eternal gratitude of their country. . . .

Another point worthy of attention in the progress of the war, is the wide extent to which the knowledge and principles of Hygiene have become popularized, and the lively interest of all intelligent men, in civil as well as military life, in the facts and purposes of sanitary science and hygienic improvements. We need not allude to the special causes that produced this result, for they are sufficiently obvious. But it is a result full of promise and significance, which must be followed up by comprehensive plans and earnest efforts of not only the few well known and skilled hygienists, but by the organized masses of the medical profession. The people have begun to appreciate the priceless value of human life; and the vocabulary of sanitary knowledge, and the elementary facts of hygiene, are becoming familiar in every household. Our medical schools have each a professor for instruction in military hygiene, and every practitioner of medicine finds himself invited to be a private teacher of sanitary science in the homes of the people.

5. Nursing Volunteer Louisa May Alcott Reports to Readers at Home About Her Experiences with the Union Army, 1863

The first thing I met was a regiment of the vilest odors that ever assaulted the human nose, and took it by storm. Cologne, with its seven and seventy evil savors, was a posybed to it; and the worst of this affliction was, every one had assured me that it was a chronic weakness of all hospitals, and I must bear it. I did, armed with lavender water, with which I so besprinkled myself and premises, that, like my friend, Sairy, I was soon known among my patients as "the nurse with the bottle." Having been run over by three excited surgeons, bumped against by migratory coal-hods, water-pails, and small boys; nearly scalded by an avalanche of newly-filled tea-pots, and hopelessly entangled in a knot of colored sisters coming to wash, I progressed by slow stages up stairs and down, till the main hall was reached, and I paused to take breath

---

Louisa May Alcott, *Hospital Sketches* (Boston: J. Redpath, 1863), pp. 33–35, 43–45.

and a survey. There they were! "our brave boys," as the papers justly call them, for cowards could hardly have been so riddled with shot and shell, so torn and shattered, nor have borne suffering for which we have no name, with an uncomplaining fortitude, which made one glad to cherish each as a brother. In they came, some on stretchers, some in men's arms, some feebly staggering along propped on rude crutches, and one lay stark and still with covered face, as a comrade gave his name to be recorded before they carried him away to the dead house. All was hurry and confusion; the hall was full of these wrecks of humanity, for the most exhausted could not reach a bed till duly ticketed and registered; the walls were lined with rows of such as could sit, the floor covered with the more disabled, the steps and doorways filled with helpers and lookers on; the sound of many feet and voices made that usually quiet hour as noisy as noon; and, in the midst of it all, the matron's motherly face brought more comfort to many a poor soul, than the cordial draughts she administered, or the cheery words that welcomed all, making of the hospital a home.

The sight of several stretchers, each with its legless, armless, or desperately wounded occupant, entering my ward, admonished me that I was there to work, not to wonder or weep; so I corked up my feelings, and returned to the path of duty, which was rather "a hard road to travel" just then. . . . Forty beds were prepared, many already tenanted by tired men who fell down anywhere, and drowsed till the smell of food roused them. Round the great stove was gathered the dreariest group I ever saw—ragged, gaunt and pale, mud to the knees, with bloody bandages untouched since put on days before; many bundled up in blankets, coats being lost or useless; and all wearing that disheartened look which proclaimed defeat, more plainly than any telegram of the Burnside blunder. I pitied them so much, I dared not speak to them, though, remembering all they had been through since the route [*sic*] at Fredericksburg, I yearned to serve the dreariest of them all. Presently, Miss Blank tore me from my refuge behind piles of one-sleeved shirts, odd socks, bandages and lint; put basin, sponge, towels, and a block of brown soap into my hands, with these appalling directions:

"Come, my dear, begin to wash as fast as you can. Tell them to take off socks, coats and shirts, scrub them well, put on clean shirts, and the attendants will finish them off, and lay them in bed."

If she had requested me to shave them all, or dance a hornpipe on the stove funnel, I should have been less staggered; but to scrub some dozen lords of creation at a moment's notice, was really—really——. However, there was no time for nonsense, and, having resolved when I came to do everything I was bid, I drowned my scruples in my washbowl, clutched my soap manfully, and, assuming a businesslike air, made a dab at the first dirty specimen I saw, bent on performing my task. . . .

The amputations were reserved till the morrow, and the merciful magic of ether was not thought necessary that day, so the poor souls had to bear their pains as best they might. It is all very well to talk of the patience of woman; and far be it from me to pluck that feather from her cap, for, heaven knows, she isn't allowed to wear many; but the patient endurance of these men, under trials of the flesh, was truly wonderful; their fortitude seemed contagious, and scarcely a cry escaped them, though I often longed to groan for them, when pride kept their white lips shut, while great drops stood upon their foreheads, and the bed shook with the irrepressible tremor of their tortured bodies. . . .

It was long past noon before these repairs were even partially made; and, having got the bodies of my boys into something like order, the next task was to minister to their minds, by writing letters to the anxious souls at home; answering questions, reading papers, taking possession of money and valuables; for the eighth commandment was reduced to a very fragmentary condition, both by the blacks and whites, who ornamented our hospital with their presence. Pocket books, purses, miniatures, and watches, were sealed up, labelled, and handed over to the matron, till such times as the owners thereof were ready to depart homeward or campward again. . . .

Then came the doctor's evening visit; the administration of medicines; washing feverish faces; smoothing tumbled beds; wetting wounds; singing lullabies; and preparations for the night. . . .

I witnessed several operations; for the height of my ambition was to go to the front after a battle, and feeling that the sooner I inured myself to trying sights, the more useful I should be. Several of my mates shrunk from such things; for though the spirit was wholly willing, the flesh was inconveniently weak. . . .

Dr. Z. suggested that I should witness a dissection; but I never accepted his invitations, thinking that my nerves belonged to the living, not to the dead, and I had better finish my education as a nurse before I began that of a surgeon. But I never met the little man skipping through the hall, with oddly shaped cases in his hand, and an absorbed expression of countenance, without being sure that a select party of surgeons were at work in the dead house, which idea was a rather trying one, when I knew the subject was some person whom I had nursed and cared for.

But this must not lead any one to suppose that the surgeons were willfully hard or cruel, though one of them remorsefully confided to me that he feared his profession blunted his sensibilities, and, perhaps, rendered him indifferent to the sight of pain.

I am inclined to think that in some cases it does; for, though a capital surgeon and a kindly man, Dr. P., through long acquaintance with many of the ills flesh is heir to, had acquired a somewhat trying habit of regarding a man and his wound as separate institutions, and seemed rather annoyed that the former should express any opinion upon the latter, or claim any right in it, while under his care. He had a way of twitching off a bandage, and giving a limb a comprehensive sort of clutch, which, though no doubt entirely scientific, was rather startling than soothing, and highly objectionable as a means of preparing nerves for any fresh trial. He also expected the patient to assist in small operations, as he considered them, and to restrain all demonstrations during the process.

"Here, my man, just hold it this way, while I look into it a bit," he said one day to Fitz G., putting a wounded arm into the keeping of a sound one, and proceeding to poke about among bits of bone and visible muscles, in a red and black chasm made by some infernal machine of the shot or shell description. Poor Fitz held on like grim Death, ashamed to show fear before a woman, till it grew more than he could bear in silence; and, after a few smothered groans, he looked at me imploringly, as if he said, "I wouldn't, ma'am, if I could help it," and fainted quietly away.

Dr. P. looked up, gave a compassionate sort of cluck, and poked away more busily than ever, with a nod at me and a brief—"Never mind; be so good as to hold this till I finish."

I obeyed, cherishing the while a strong desire to insinuate a few of his own disagreeable knives and scissors into him, and see how he liked it. A very disrespectful and ridiculous fancy, of course; for he was doing all that could be done, and the arm prospered finely in his hands. But the human mind is prone to prejudice; and, though a personable man, speaking French like a born "Parley voo," and whipping off legs like an animated guillotine, I must confess to a sense of relief when he was ordered elsewhere; and suspect that several of the men would have faced a rebel battery with less trepidation than they did Dr. P., when he came briskly in on his morning round.

As if to give us the pleasures of contrast, Dr. Z. succeeded him, who, I think, suffered more in giving pain than did his patients in enduring it; for he often paused to ask: "Do I hurt you?" and, seeing his solicitude, the boys invariably answered: "Not much; go ahead, Doctor," though the lips that uttered this amiable fib might be white with pain as they spoke. . . .

Speaking of the surgeons reminds me that, having found all manner of fault, it becomes me to celebrate the redeeming feature of Hurlyburly House. I had been prepared by the accounts of others, to expect much humiliation of spirit from the surgeons, and to be treated by them like a door-mat, a worm, or any other meek and lowly article, whose mission it is to be put down and walked upon; nurses being considered as mere servants, receiving the lowest pay, and, it's my private opinion, doing the hardest work of any part of the army, except the mules. Great, therefore, was my surprise, when I found myself treated with the utmost courtesy and kindness. Very soon my carefully prepared meekness was laid upon the shelf; and, going from one extreme to the other, I more than once expressed a difference of opinion regarding sundry messes it was my painful duty administer. . . .

The next hospital I enter will, I hope, be one for the colored regiments, as they seem to be proving their right to the admiration and kind offices of their white relations, who owe them so large a debt, a little part of which I shall be so proud to pay.

> Yours,
> With a firm faith
> In the good time coming,
> Tribulation Periwinkle.

6. A Maine Physician Writes to His Wife About His Experiences in the Union Army, 1864

> City Point Hospital
> June 18th 1864

My Dearest Lizzie

Since I last wrote you there has been a great change in Military affairs. Grant has moved his whole army around to this place. His head quarters are within a hundred yards of this place. We have also had a battle within four miles of here. 420 wounded men have been brought to this place. I can aprise you that we have had plenty to

James Otis Moore to "My Dear Lizzie," April 12, June 18, and July 2, 1864, James Otis Moore Papers, Rare Book, Manuscript, and Special Collections Library, Duke University, Durham, North Carolina.

do.—day before yesterday or rather night before last I did not sleep a wink worked hard all night. We [had] all kinds of wounds, any quantity of amputations. . . . Have been at it all day long. Have just got through 11 oclock P.M. It would make your heart sick to see the wounds some shot through the head—some with legs blown off, others with arms, off. I have seen any quantity with bullet holes through the chest. We put them under the influence of Chloroform and then amputate. Our Lieut. Colonel was wounded, one Lieut. with bullet hole through head—died of course. Another Lieut. lost an arm. We had in our Regt six officers wounded. Lost in killed & wounded about 200, poor fellows, they fought bravely. . . . We performed an amputation on a rebel prisoner to day. . . . He was wounded by a colored boy & succeeded in wounding him: tonight they lay side by side in the same hospital. There are in this place about six hundred sick & wounded & five of us have to attend them whole. Dont you believe we have something to do. After I got through the other day I rode out within a mile of where the battle was raging there was a field Hospital. Men were lying all around on the ground & it was heart renching to hear their groans & take on. Many a poor boy lost a leg or an arm, an old house was cleaned out, & the wounded lay all over the floor it looked j[us]t like a big Slaughter house. . . .

> . . . Division Hospital 18 Army Corp
> Camp near Petersburg June 2nd 1864

Dearest Lizzie

I improve the present opportunity to write you a few lines informing you of my continued good health. When I last wrote you I was with my Regt but since have been detailed to Hospital & I suppose you are not sorry at any rate I am not sorry. I have a good opportunity to see practice & surgery much better than I should if I had if I was with the Regt for I see all the sick & wounded there are in the Division and all operations that are performed in the Division are performed here so you see that I could not be better situated to see surgical practice than what I am here. It is a great school for me & I have learned already a good deal & hope I may learn more at any rate there is need enough of it. . . .

. . . It is a cruel war & my position leads me to see its effects. I have seen men wounded in all possible ways & shapes—Men with both legs shot off with one leg off, arms shot off, skulls blown open & their brains protruding & bullet wounds without number. But still my mind has not changed in the least in relation to the justice of the cause & I think it the imperative duty of the North to rise en masse & crush out the rebellion. Those who cannot go to war must pray. . . .

> Headquarters . . .
> Williamsburg April 12/64

My Dear Lizzie

. . . I am posting myself up on Anatomy & Surgery & have facilities for so doing which I could not possibly have at home. . . . [The examination board is] very strict here indeed. . . . I have a homoeopathic physician and if the board should know it they would probably examine me the closer for it. Dr Merrill was at Yorktown the other day & saw Lieut. Piper, [illegible] Piper's son of Biddeford. He is a Lieut in one of our colored Regts who told the Dr all about it. So he came home at night, &

came in & said "Doc," I have heard some news about you. Ah said I what is it. I hope it is nothing bad. I heard said he that you was a Homoeopathic Physician. Well said I, what of it. I suppose I am no worse for it am I. No said he but it is a good thing that board at Boston did not know it! Said he I care nothing about it of course, as long as you do your duty as well as you have done it I have nothing to say & so the matter dropped. I have found a number in the Regt who are homoeopathics. I mean of the officers. The Lieut Col. employs a homeopathic in his family at home. I tell you Lizzie the more I see of allopathic practice the more strong I am the faith once delivered to Homeopathists. . . . We have lost since we have been here eighteen men. The most of them have died of inflammatioins [*sic*] of the lungs. You know that is more than I ever lost since I have been in practice, I mean of the same disease. But there is one thing to be taken into consideration. The men cannot have that care bestowed upon them here that we have bestowed upon patients at home.

The peach trees are in blossom here, & beautifuly[;] look grass is springing into existence. I have been interupted in writing by attending a post mortem examination. . . .

Accept the renewed assurances of my love & esteem. Kiss the dear children for papa. You didn't say a word about them.

Good night good night. I hope angels are guarding your pillow. . . .

J. O. Moore

7. Sanitary Reformers Build upon Civil War Precedents to Clean Up Post-War Cities, 1865

Of the 714 buildings classed as tenant-houses, less than one-half were found to have a waste-pipe or drain connected directly with the sewer. Where this is wanting, liquid refuse is emptied on the sidewalk or into the street, or in some instances into sinks in the domiciles communicating with a common pipe which discharges its content into the open gutter to run perhaps hundreds of feet, giving forth the most noisome exhalations, and uniting its fetid streams with numerous others from similar sources, before reaching its subterranean destination.

Slops from rear buildings of such premises are usually emptied into a shallow gutter cut in the flagging and extending from the yard, or space between front and rear buildings, to the street. This is often clogged up by semi-fluid filth, so that the alley and those parts of the yard through which it runs are not unfrequently overflown and submerged to the depth of several inches.

There are more than four hundred families in this district whose homes can only be reached by wading through a disgusting deposit of filthy refuse. In some instances, a staging of plank, elevated a few inches above the surface, is constructed through the alleys. This affords to the residents the advantage of a dry walk, but in a sanitary point of view its influence is scarcely favorable, since it prevents the removal of the offensive matters beneath. . . .

Council of the Citizens' Association of New York, *Report of the Council of Hygiene and Public Health upon the Sanitary Condition of the City* (New York: D. Appleton and Company, 1865): 43–44, 49, 52, 64–65.

My district contains one tenant-house which has become rather notorious in consequence of having been the subject of several special reports, one of which I made about three years since. . . . [A]nd as the description of these premises and their population which I gave in that report is equally applicable now, I quote from it here:

"The building known as No.—— and No.—— Cherry Street forms a part of what has heretofore been known as 'Gotham Court.' As measured, it is 34 feet 4 inches wide in front and rear, is 234 feet long and 5 stories high. On the north it is contiguous to a large tenant-house fronting on Roosevelt Street. On the west an alley 9 feet wide separates it from a similar structure forming a part of the 'Court.' On the east another alley, 7 feet wide, divides it from the rear of a number of houses on Roosevelt Street. . . .

"At the time of visit 49 of the tenements were either vacant or the occupants absent. In the remaining 71 there were reported as residing 504 persons, averaging a little more than 7 persons to each occupied domicile. The entire amount of space in the rooms occupied is 138,840 cubic feet, which would be equal to a single room 118 feet square, and about 10 feet high, giving each individual an average of about 275 cubic feet, equal to a closet 5 feet square and 11 feet high. It must be recollected that the above total space contains not only its 504 inhabitants, but their furniture, bedding, and household utensils, besides no small portion of their excretions, as is painfully evident to every one who, in these regions, has the misfortune to possess an acute sense of smell. Of the entire number of tenements, four only were found in a condition approaching cleanliness. It need scarcely be said that the entire establishment swarms with vermin.

"In seven of the tenements tailoring was carried on. In five out of seven the articles manufactured were for the use of the army. In two of these rooms patients were found sick of contagious diseases. One was a case of typhus fever, the other of measles.

"It was admitted that 19 persons were unvaccinated. These were chiefly children, but it is probable that a much larger number are unprotected from variola, for in several instances those who asserted that the operation had been successfully performed, failed, on examination, to exhibit a vaccine scar.

"The average length of time that the residents have occupied the premises is reported to be about two years and eight months. There have been 138 births, including 12 still-born, in these families during their term of residence in the building. Of these only 77 are now living, showing an infant mortality of over 44 per cent. in two years and eight months; but as by far the greater number of these deaths occur during the first year, it may be safely assumed that 30 per cent. of those born here do not survive a twelvemonth. The total number of deaths reported as occurring in the families now occupying the premises during their term of residence there, is 98, or about 19½ per cent. of the population for that period.

"Of the 504 inmates, 146, or about 29 per cent., were found to be suffering from diseases of a more or less serious character, among which were four cases of small-pox (three of them unvaccinated), eight cases of typhus fever, seven cases of scarlatina, and four of measles in the eruptive stage, twenty-seven cases of infantile marasmus, twelve cases of phthisis pulmonalis, five cases of dysentery, three cases of chronic diarrhœa, [*sic*] and a large number of slight cases of diarrhœa and of cutaneous eruptions.

"It is difficult to form a satisfactory estimate of the comparative frequency of the different diseases heretofore prevailing, the inmates being, in a great proportion of cases, ignorant of their character. It is, of course, equally difficult to arrive at the causes of death, but it is pretty well ascertained that at least twenty cases of small-pox occurred during the past year, of which six were fatal. Scarlatina is assigned as the cause of sixteen deaths occurring during the above period. Typhus fever undoubtedly claimed numerous victims, as it has been quite prevalent. To the unaccustomed eye it is a sad and striking spectacle to witness the attenuated forms, the sunken eyes, the pinched and withered faces of the little patients, young in years but old in suffering, who are the prey of infantile marasmus. A glance is sufficient to designate *this* as one of the ghostly janitors, ever ready to open wide the gate which leads to early death.

"A description of these premises would be incomplete without, at least, a passing notice of two establishments occupying the front portion of the first story. One is termed a grocery, the other a liquor store. Both are apparently pretty well patronized. At the former are retailed a variety of articles of food, including partially-decayed vegetables, rather suspicious looking solids, bearing respectively the names of butter and cheese, and a decidedly suspicious fluid bearing the name of milk. Beer and alcoholic compounds are also dispensed. At the adjoining shop the staple commodities are those indescribable compounds of sundry known and unknown ingredients, which are sold as 'pure imported wines and liquors.' I believe from what I could ascertain that these liquors are used to a considerable extent by almost every family on the premises, a fact, indeed, which might be expected, for in such apartments as they occupy the poisonous air begets a deadly lassitude, and generates an inordinate desire for stimulants. To the effect of these unwholesome viands and poisonous beverages may probably be traced much of the diarrhœa which prevails here even at this season, and which is vastly increased in amount during the summer months.

"On the whole, perhaps, this section of Gotham Court presents about an average specimen of tenant-houses in the lower part of the city in respect to salubrity. There are some which are more roomy, have better means of ventilation, and are kept cleaner; but there are many which are in far worse condition, and exhibit a much higher rate of mortality than this." . . .

The evils attendant upon a residence in crowded localities are not always manifested in distinct forms of disease. There is a tenant-house cachexy [emaciations] well known to such medical men as have a practical acquaintance with these abodes; nor does it affect alone the physical condition of their inmates. It has its moral prototype in an ochlesis [crowd disease] of vice—a contagious depravity, to whose malign influence the youthful survivors of the terrible physical evils to which their infancy is exposed, are sure to succumb. . . .

The Tenant-House Rot.—The state of physical, mental, and moral decline to which I have adverted, is so well recognized and its causes so well understood, that it has received a name, less elegant than expressive; it is called the TENANT-HOUSE ROT.

Under such influences are reared to-day a large proportion of the future citizens of New York, who will control its social and political destinies. Under such influences have been reared a large class, already so numerous as at times to seriously disturb the public peace and to endanger the safety of our social and political fabric.

The terrible elements of society we saw brought to the surface during a great popular outbreak, are equally in existence at the present moment; nay, more, they are increasing year by year. The tocsin [*sic*] which next summons them from their dark and noisome haunts may be the prelude to a scene of universal pillage, slaughter, and destruction. We must reap that which we sow. Pestilence and crime are fungi of hideous growth, which spring up side by side from such pollution as we allow to rankle in our midst.

 E S S A Y S

Suellen Hoy, an independent scholar in South Bend, Indiana, gives a detailed account of the roles played by women in the U.S. Sanitary Commission and the various other organized responses to the medical needs of American soldiers during the Civil War. She explains the gospel of sanitation and personal hygiene that underlay the actions of many of these women. In connecting women's wartime activities to both their prewar domestic concerns and to postwar public health campaigns, Hoy shows the pivotal role the war played in redirecting American health culture. Chicago-based historian and teacher Bonnie E. Blustein's purpose in her provocative essay is to draw attention to the significance of science in the medical reforms that took place during the Civil War. A key part of this argument hinges on recognizing the multiple meanings given to the word *science* during this era: efficiency and accountability were central themes in the drive to make the U.S. Army Medical Department more scientific. Blustein is careful to place this intellectual debate in a well-developed social and political context, so that the links between middle-class interests and calls for greater efficiency are clear.

American Wives and Mothers Join the Civil War Struggle in a Battle Against Dirt and Disease

SUELLEN HOY

By the 1850s the largest eastern cities contained ever-widening extremes of wealth and poverty. New York City, Philadelphia, and Boston had slums as filthy and as deadly as those in Paris and London. The squalid conditions of these slums and the fears they fostered resulted in new concerns about public health. Until then, city dwellers tended to become anxious about health matters only when they felt threatened by periodic epidemics. But the large numbers of poor working-class families that had appeared during the 1840s seemed to forecast an impending disaster. Various welfare organizations and leading sanitarians, most notably John H. Griscom of New York and Lemuel Shattuck of Boston, attempted to ameliorate these conditions and to turn personal and local concerns into a national public health movement.

Griscom, a physician who served briefly as a health inspector for New York City during the early 1840s, underpinned his sanitary reform work with an avid interest in science and public welfare. He was also an influential member of the

Association for Improving the Condition of the Poor, whose missionaries visited working men and women in their homes. Considering them the best-informed citizens on the living conditions of the poor, Griscom used their testimony as well as his own experiences in preparing his report of 1845, *The Sanitary Condition of the Laboring Population of New York.* Perhaps for this reason he was able to understand what so many of his contemporaries did not.

In Griscom's view, poverty, not moral weakness or lack of self-control, generated the high incidence of disease and death among the urban masses. He knew that the rich, like the poor, were often "equally ignorant of the laws of life." Yet the rich had the means to obtain "greater comfort and more luxuries," which accounted "for their prolonged lives." Cleaner surroundings and better food, Griscom argued, could improve everyone's health and promote a more law-abiding community. He insisted that an educated child would be no better than his ignorant and unruly companions if he were "surrounded with dirt, foul air, and all manner of filthy associations." . . .

. . . Strong sanitary measures could cause the destruction of profitable tenements and create a demand for the construction of large and expensive drains and sewers. Physicians, who should have been willing and able to argue on behalf of such measures, were not well respected or well organized in the 1850s. Furthermore, public attention was distracted from health matters by the debate over slavery and its impact on the nation.

In May 1857, when Philadelphia hosted the first national quarantine convention, seventy-three zealous public officials and physicians attended. Not long after they convened, the group broadened the scope of its discussions to include issues of public hygiene as well as quarantine regulations and changed its name to "The Quarantine and Sanitary Convention." In April 1859, when the delegates met in New York City, they elected Griscom president and focused most of their attention on sanitary reform. Elisha Harris, later a founder with Henry W. Bellows of the United States Sanitary Commission, attended the 1859 and 1860 conventions. All of these early public health reformers agreed that disease could be prevented and controlled by cleaning up the environment. Although the mechanisms by which diseases were transmitted (such as microorganisms) were not understood until late in the century, the connection between filth and disease was a powerful one. This idea had served local communities well during epidemics. It would soon prove to have lasting effects during wartime. . . .

The Civil War provided public health reformers with a national laboratory in which to test their theories and apply their principles on hygiene. Unlike an epidemic, the war was neither local nor seasonal; but, like an epidemic, the Civil War created a full-blown crisis that captured everyone's attention. Far-sighted civilians mobilized a "sanitary" crusade in the North to guard the health of the fighting men by keeping their disease and death rates as low as possible. Women formed the shock troops who nursed Union soldiers amidst the filth and horror of hospital and battlefield during the bloody days of war and, with peace, headed south to minister to "contraband" former slaves. This shared purpose not only "brought home the idea of the value and economy of health and lives" but also contributed to "the wide extent to which the knowledge and principles of Hygiene" became "popularized . . . in civil as well as military life."

During the Civil War era, appreciation for cleanliness mushroomed. Stephen Smith, editor of the *American Medical Times* from 1860 to 1864 and later the first president of the American Public Health Association, recognized that by 1863 "the vocabulary of sanitary knowledge" and "the elementary facts of hygiene" had become "familiar in every household." By the end of the war, most Americans had gained some new ideas about the meaning of cleanliness, and about "women's place." . . .

Of the innumerable individuals who offered instruction in the principles and practice of sanitary science during this period, none would become as well known and venerated throughout the United States as [Florence] Nightingale, the Crimean War's "apostle of cleanliness." Although she never visited America, this "lady with a lamp" became famous for her much-publicized work in the Barrack Hospital of Scutari from 1854 to 1856. A year later her involvement in the investigation by the Royal Commission on the Sanitary Condition of the Army brought her more acclaim, as did her *Notes on Nursing* which, when published in London in December 1859, sold 15,000 copies within a month. . . .

A powerful force for sanitary reform[,] . . . Nightingale wasted little time in changing hospital policy within the British army. She assumed the duties of "Barrack Administrator" and devised various organizational plans so that the hospitals would run "upon a principle of centralization." Concerned about diet, supplies, and the patients' cleanliness (including their bedding, personal linen, and surgical appendages), she permitted few aspects of hospital routine to escape her notice. She usually described herself as "cook, house-keeper, scavenger . . . washerwoman, general dealer, store-keeper."

. . . Her disciplined attention to cleanliness brought order out of chaos and reduced the number of deaths from disease. Portions of the Nightingale legend, at least, are true and account in many ways for her extraordinary influence in the second half of the nineteenth century. Her defense of cleanliness and hygiene rested on an obsolescent but popular view that "miasmas," or a noxious atmosphere, caused disease—a view that emphasized the importance of being clean. Although Nightingale was incorrect about miasmas, her beliefs nevertheless gave force and even efficacy to her practical suggestions regarding sanitation. . . .

American women took pride in Nightingale's recognized accomplishments in Crimea, and they relished the prestige it gave their work. Their satisfaction must have been considerable when they read her responses to written questions posed by the British Sanitary Commission as reported in the *New York Times* on March 11, 1858. Without equivocation, Nightingale told the royal commissioners that "the woman is superior in skill to the man in all points of sanitary domestic economy, and more particularly in cleanliness and tidiness." For this reason, she insisted, "great sanitary reformers . . . look to the woman to carry out practically their hygienic reforms." Since women have "a superior aptitude in *nursing*," she concluded that "the Anglo-Saxon would be very sorry to turn women out of his own house, or out of civil hospitals, hotels, institutions of all kinds, and substitute men-housekeepers and men-matrons."

In 1860 Nightingale's *Notes on Nursing* appeared in the United States, where "its very extensive circulation" had important results. *Godey's* magazine, which reprinted portions of it, advised "every lady" to study and practice its precepts. Large numbers obviously did. For in 1862 *Harper's Weekly* acknowledged Nightingale's wide-ranging influence; in North *and* South her name had become synonymous with nursing. A teenager in Mississippi, for example, demonstrated her patriotism by going to battle "in the capacity of Florence Nightingale," while numerous other women simply "threw open sickroom windows and dedicated themselves to cleanliness." Military and civilian medical people also admired Nightingale's work, and a few met with her in London.

During 1861 thousands of resolute women in the North and South put aside their private household cares and offered their services, both as volunteers and as paid nurses. For the first time in the United States, women were to play a significant role in a major war. Working-class women, who had experience as laundresses and domestics, joined the ranks of middle-class women who had nursed family or friends but had never cared for strangers or worked for wages. They hoped that the skills they had acquired as mothers, housekeepers, and caretakers, along with the inspiration and instruction they had received from Nightingale, "could be put to useful and patriotic ends."

Women were accustomed to volunteering their services for the public good. The 1850s had been a decade rich in humanitarian reform activities. In all parts of the country, institutions for the deaf, blind, insane, and orphaned had been built or expanded; the decade's economic uncertainties as well as its growing immigrant population and public health concerns had given Americans many opportunities to become involved in social welfare efforts. Very often middle- and upper-class women in cities had taken the lead in these benevolent causes and established extensive networks of voluntary associations. . . .

In the Confederacy, women were "knitting socks, making shirts, and stitching underwear . . . turning out everything from caps to sandbags, and sometimes supplying entire regiments." Up and down the South's class structure, from plantation matrons to ordinary housewives, women organized hundreds of relief societies to sew, raise money, make flags, and send off blankets. They did much for their cause and would have done more, if the makeshift Confederate government had been better organized and funded. But it was unable to create a sanitary commission comparable to that of the North. Consequently these pages say much more about what happened in the Union than in the Confederacy, where the obstacles limiting the effectiveness of the South's women contributed to higher death rates from dysentery, malaria, pneumonia, and other diseases than from gunshots.

Only a month after the Civil War began, Mary Bache Walker in Hoboken, New Jersey, speculated that enough havelocks, drawers, shirts, and hospital dressing gowns had been made "for both armies." But organization and distribution problems prevented many of these goods from reaching those troops most in need. . . . Katharine P. Wormeley observed from Providence, Rhode Island, that "little circles and associations were multiplying, like rings in the water, over the face of the whole country; they were all in need of direction, information, guidance, and they felt it."

In response to this obvious need, fifty-five women and a few men assembled on April 25, 1861, at the New York Infirmary for Women and Children in New York City. Elizabeth Blackwell, physician and friend of Nightingale, chaired the meeting and discussion centered on how to consolidate and direct the activities of aid societies around the country. Those present ended their deliberations by drafting an appeal, emphasizing "the importance of systematizing and concentrating the spontaneous and earnest efforts" of New York women, and by setting April 29 as the date for a follow-up meeting. . . .

At the April 29 meeting, the Cooper Institute hall was "crowded with an earnest, enthusiastic, and patriotic assembly of women"—many of them from New York's most distinguished families. Numerous physicians well known to city residents also attended, as did the prominent Unitarian minister Henry W. Bellows. Together they organized the Woman's Central Association of Relief (WCAR) and elected surgeon Valentine Mott president and Bellows vice president. The group then discussed what it could do to supply goods and nurses to the army (which it did throughout the war, in cooperation with the Sanitary Commission). On the subject of nurses, the women pointed out that the Crimean War had proven "the total uselessness of any but picked and skilled women in this department of duty."

Indeed, the Crimean experience overshadowed the deliberations of this organization, as it would those of the United States Sanitary Commission throughout the Civil War. Blackwell, who chaired WCAR's Registration Committee on Nurses, considered Nightingale one of her "most valued acquaintances" and shared her anti-contagionist views (the belief that disease spread through filth and "miasmas" rather than by contact with infectious organisms). Blackwell had recently visited Nightingale in London and become convinced that "sanitation is the supreme goal of medicine, its foundation and its crown. She too believed in the unique capabilities women brought to nursing. Thus, even before creation of the Sanitary Commission, Blackwell's committee on nursing had joined with physicians at New York's Bellevue Hospital in providing one month's training to women before sending them to Dorothea Dix, recently appointed superintendent of women nurses in Washington, D.C. . . .

Such was not the case, however, in the federal capital in May 1861. When WCAR representatives—Bellows and Dr. Elisha Harris, together with physicians W. H. Van Buren and Jacob Harsen—arrived in Washington on May 16, 1861, they were aghast. Not only had "the country town" been "turned into a great, confused garrison," but even "quiet residential neighborhoods were in an uproar." Young soldiers, most of whom were away from home for the first time, crowded into the ill-prepared city and acted "as irresponsible as children." Having left mothers, sisters, and wives behind, they behaved as boys, whooping it up in the streets with their bugles and drums, getting drunk, firing weapons, relieving themselves in public, and neglecting to wash and "change their underwear for weeks at a time." Many of them had grown up on farms and had never been exposed to childhood diseases like measles; they promptly caught them. Almost a third of the troops got sick in 1861 before ever leaving their Washington staging areas, especially from gastrointestinal infections and the often lethal typhoid fever. . . .

Most disturbing was that the army had made so few preparations to receive these young soldiers. Arriving in cattle cars from different parts of the country, they had waited in line for hours to ascertain where they would be sheltered and fed, "while their ignorant and inexperienced Commissaries and Quartermasters" learned their duties. Once in camp, regiments spent the night as they had en route to Washington, sleeping on rotten straw covered with shoddy blankets. The water supply at inland depots was not adequate for washing, and government rations were generally unwholesome and poorly cooked. Bellows and Harris feared that if these conditions persisted there would be disastrous results.

On the thirteen-hour train trip from New York to Washington, Bellows and his companions had talked at length about how civilians could serve their country during war. . . . Harris suggested that they meet with the secretary of war and ask him to create a sanitary commission similar to the one that "had produced such happy results in the Crimea." By the time their train pulled into Union Station, they had unanimously agreed that they would urge the government "to establish a preventive hygienic and sanitary service for the benefit of the army."

After a month-long struggle, on June 9, 1861, Secretary of War Simon Cameron gave his approval to a commission, but one that would restrict its "meddling" to the volunteer army. Several days later President Lincoln signed an executive order authorizing what he suspiciously called "a fifth wheel" to the coach of state. This new agency, the United States Sanitary Commission, immediately took action and shape, selecting Bellows as president, scientist Alexander Dallas Bache vice-president, and lawyer George Templeton Strong treasurer. Then on June 20 the commission appointed Frederick Law Olmsted secretary and chief executive officer.

By wrapping cleanliness and order in the mantle of patriotism and victory, the commissioners defined a clear-cut mission: to teach the government, the medical bureau, the army, and the nation at home that "gunshots and cannon wounds, and death from battle, were not the enemies most to be feared in war." They had to learn that "the diseases of camp, arising from private ignorance, inexperienced officers, neglected or unknown sanitary police, the recklessness of raw soldiers, and the influences of exposure, unaccustomed food, and bad cookery" were the killers to guard against daily. For these reasons, Bellows and his colleagues had initially hoped they would be given "ample powers for visiting all camps and hospitals, advising, recommending, and if need be, enforcing, the best-known and most approved sanitary regulations in the army." But, in the end, the secretary of war made the commission simply advisory. Comparing it to its British model, Bellows complained that the United States Sanitary Commission had "been born paralytic" and was to be "endured" by government officials out of "deference towards a respectable body of supposed fanatics and philanthropists, backed by a large class of anxious and sympathetic women."

Despite its disabilities, this group of health "fanatics" and philanthropists, supported by thousands of concerned women, devised an energetic program of action "to *prevent* evils to the health of the army." The commission began its work by inspecting camps around Washington and giving advice on "the choice of camp sites, the importance of drainage and police, and the character and cooking of food." Although the commissioners showed an early interest in preparing women for work on the battlefield, they and Dix agreed that "attention to hygiene in the Army [was] far more important than any present *added* efforts to assure nursing." . . .

. . . Olmsted was a remarkable administrator. Fresh from his success as architect and superintendent of construction of Central Park—arguably the country's major municipal public work to that point—he had enhanced his reputation as a public administrator and broadened his interest in public health. He would go on to many more architectural and civic triumphs in his long career, but in 1861 he faced a huge challenge as inexperienced recruits poured into military camps (and before long, the hospitals). Olmsted accepted the Sanitary Commission's day-to-day leadership because he saw in it "an opportunity to educate the common soldiers, who in turn would propagate such ideas among the American people." . . .

In early July, when Olmsted and Harris examined the conditions of twenty camps around Washington, they were appalled and afraid. Every camp lacked "a system of drains," and "the sinks were unnecessarily and disgustingly offensive." They also saw that "cleanliness among the men was wholly unattended to," and their "clothing was of bad material and almost always filthy." . . .

These disgraceful living conditions help explain the Union army's defeat and rout at Bull Run in late July 1861. The extent of the panic and confusion provoked by the beating proved worrisome to all, but particularly to those who had expected a one-battle war. . . .

Olmsted prepared the Sanitary Commission's official report on the troops' defeat at Bull Run. He drew his conclusions on their performance from "about two thousand items of evidence" collected by inspectors for the commission and physicians and examiners of life insurance companies. In a "General summary," Olmsted pointed out that the volunteers had entered combat prepared "little better than a mob"; and those who fled to Washington, during or following the battle, looked like "wo-begone rabble." . . .

Before the commission succeeded in orchestrating a campaign to reorganize and expand the army's antiquated Medical Department, it began inspecting camps. It hoped to "inspire officers and men with a sense of the nature and importance of sanitary laws, and with the practical application of hygienic principles." If successful, they would certainly prevent the spread of contagious diseases. But Olmsted, who believed slovenliness to be the nation's "most characteristic" vice, wanted more. He wanted to show these young men from mostly rural areas how to live healthy lives. . . .

As preventive medicine, the Sanitary Commission's education and inspection program made significant gains. It developed manuals of procedure for field hospitals, proposed revampings to improve the Medical Department, and devised statistical forms to record levels of food supplies, camp drainage and sewerage, personal hygiene, and other sanitary matters. Its inspectors, the majority of whom had solid reputations as physicians or teachers, viewed their assignment as one of "suggesting, advising, and instructing the officers in camp" on ways to preserve the health of their troops. The inspectors tried not to cause unnecessary ill will when visiting camp sites, but they also knew that "the standard of the volunteers" regarding discipline should be "at least as high as that of the regulars." . . .

By 1862 it had become clear that a much more vigorous inspection system was necessary if the troops' hygienic condition were to show much improvement. For this reason, as well as to secure the appointment of a surgeon general who would acknowledge the serious deficiencies in the army's medical services, the Sanitary Commission undertook and successfully obtained passage of an act to reorganize the Medical Department. On April 16, 1862, President Lincoln signed legislation that included a provision for commissioning sanitary inspectors and for appointing the surgeon general and his assistants on the basis of merit rather than seniority. This law allowed the commission to reduce the number of its inspections in 1862 and completely discontinue them in 1864.

Since it had many other concerns, the Sanitary Commission was not left idle by the new law. It showed a real interest, for instance, in the needs of uncommissioned surgeons who worked under contract and also in the construction of military hospitals. Contract surgeons were frequently no more acquainted with the precepts of preventive medicine than were many of the regimental officers. In addition these surgeons were often required to treat wounds or diseases they had not seen in civilian practice. To assist them, the commission devised and disseminated a series of about twenty manuals or tracts, outlining the most up-to-date information on prevention and treatment of prevalent camp maladies and answering medical and surgical questions of a military nature. Influenced once again by Nightingale's successes in Crimea, the commission promoted the building of commodious pavilion hospitals. In them, they thought, heavy concentrations of "poison" or "effluvia" from the large number of patients gathered under one roof would be dissolved in plenty of fresh air. . . .

As a follow-up to its successful inspection program and the government's acceptance of its plans for model hospitals, the Sanitary Commission decided in September 1862 to take a look at the condition of general hospitals throughout the North. . . .

Despite the disheartening findings of many inspectors, the commissioners praised the medical staffs of half the hospitals they examined, rating 30 percent "Highly praised"; 20 percent, "Good"; 10 percent, "Adequate"; 40 percent, "Poor"; and none, "Terrible." One wonders whether 50 or 60 percent of the staffs were truly "adequate" to "highly praised," or whether the inspectors were being politic. For many in the army's Medical Department—and Secretary of War Edwin Stanton himself—had become irritated by the intrusion of civilian physicians posing as experts. At the end of 1864, Stanton banned commission inspectors from combat zones and closed patients' records to them; the "Sanitary" was "no longer completely indispensable." But Stanton's action was at least a tacit admission that the commission had got results. . . .

What then was the impact of the Sanitary Commission and the men and women who worked through it? They saved many lives and helped shape postwar behavior, despite Secretary Stanton's disapproval and the army's less than full cooperation. Olmsted, who always prized statistics, in 1861 employed the Boston actuary E. B. Elliott to analyze the Bull Run casualty figures and other data. In 1863, at the Fifth International Statistical Congress in Berlin, Elliott reported that in the first two years of the Civil War the Union army "had suffered distinctly lower rates of disease than had European armies in wars earlier in the century," as a result of the commission's preventive efforts. These, he acknowledged, were modeled after British initiatives during and after the Crimean War.

In 1862 the Union army's rates of sickness and death had soared in comparison with the prewar years, with diarrhea, measles, typhus, typhoid fever, malaria, various fevers, and scurvy the leading afflictions. This occurred before the Sanitary Commission's reforms took effect. As the war wore on, the diarrhea plague diminished.

The Sanitary Commission and its nurses did not eliminate disease in the Union army, any more than Nightingale had done in the British; more men continued to die of disease than from battle. But their work greatly reduced disease mortality. The ratio of disease deaths to battle deaths for the Union in the Civil War was about three to two. In the Mexican-American War of 1846–48, the ratio had been more than six disease deaths to one battle death. . . .

The Civil War experience unquestionably shaped the sanitary reform movement in the critical decades of the late nineteenth century. By 1865 the war's lessons were widely known; physicians along with the public had generally come to understand that disease could be prevented. This concept had been central to the public health recommendations offered by John H. Griscom and Lemuel Shattuck in the 1840s and 1850s. But professional apathy and public indifference had discouraged any action leading to a national movement. . . .

New York City was home to the founders of the Sanitary Commission and many of its most active members. During the closing months of the Civil War, it also became the focus of the first major confrontation for improved sanitary conditions and the birthplace of what was later described as "the fundamental movement for environmental sanitation in the United States." On February 13, 1865, Stephen Smith appeared before a joint committee of the New York state legislature and reported the findings of a metropolitan sanitary survey conducted in 1864 by the Council of Hygiene and Public Health of the Citizens' Association. Smith had been the principal organizer of the survey; Elisha Harris, his colleague and former secretary of the Sanitary Commission, had prepared the final report. The investigation, conducted by a staff of thirty-one physicians, adopted procedures similar to those used by the Sanitary Commission when it inspected military camps and hospitals. Inspector-physicians gave an account of their districts "mainly in terms of cleanliness and filth."

Smith's testimony and Harris's final report presented graphic descriptions of New York's miserably dirty neighborhoods and accused municipal authorities of gross negligence. Both men believed that the health and well-being of a locale could be "measured by its cleanliness." They were not surprised, therefore, that such outright neglect—which could have been "prevented by sanitary regulations"—resulted in "a fearfully HIGH DEATH RATE" and the social degradation of those living in them. Smith and Harris felt, in fact, that the city's draft riots in July 1863 would not have occurred had these conditions not existed. For these reformers and others, cleanliness provided a practical solution to many of the bewildering social problems facing urban America. Hence they confidently urged immediate and city-wide sanitary improvements.

. . . Even during the Civil War public-spirited citizens had introduced health bills into the state legislature each winter. Although none passed, daily newspapers, popular journals, and Smith's influential *American Medical Times* had steadfastly supported them. But during the war years, New York and other municipalities undertook almost no public improvements in sanitation, and most urban conditions grew worse because of the war's dislocations. In the end it was pressure from the press, sanitarians, and a certain enlightened public—urged along by another terrifying cholera threat—that resulted in passage of the Metropolitan Health Bill of February 1866.

Linking Science to the Pursuit of Efficiency in the Reformation of the Army Medical Corps During the Civil War

BONNIE E. BLUSTEIN

This study of medical science in the Union army explores the interconnections between the reorganization of the U.S. Army Medical Department and mid-century American medicine as a whole. . . . [T]he Civil War experience was critically important in setting not only the pace but the pattern of civilian medical science and practice in the last third of the century. . . .

The United States Sanitary Commission (USSC) played a leading role in organizing the provision of health care for Union troops, especially the tens of thousands in volunteer regiments, from almost the outset of the war. The leaders and most other commissioners came from the elite of New York City and other northern commercial and manufacturing centers. For them, medical reform was part and parcel of the general war aim: national unification in accordance with a "blueprint for modern America" conceived and dominated by representatives of the propertied classes of the North. In this context, there were two medical goals. The overt aim was the maintenance of troops capable of waging war: in a sense, improving and streamlining a key productive resource—labor power. A more subtle aim was the establishment of medical institutions that would mirror and reinforce the pattern of elite domination. . . .

The sharp controversies over key legislative measures to upgrade U.S. Army medical care, notably the Wilson bill (1862) "to increase the efficiency of the Medical Department," illustrate the very real medical/political struggle which accompanied Sanitary Commission efforts to implement its plans. The extensive correspondence of the surgeon general's office provides detailed confirmation that for many doctors, as well as for congressmen and others, these medical reforms did not appear to be progress at all. Three issues dominated this debate: the creation of a hospital system, the search for the "best men" to assume its leadership, and the attempt to establish and enforce professional standards for doctors in the service. . . .

The enforcement of reform measures by military discipline made it possible for the Medical Department to transcend many of the limitations of medical work in the civilian context and to create institutions, despite widespread dissent, which would later come to characterize American medicine as a whole. Yet these measures were enacted democratically, by legislation rather than by administrative fiat, in spite of the openly antidemocratic leanings of their most energetic advocates. This somewhat paradoxical result owed much to the persuasiveness of an outlook which has been described by Daniel Kevles (in the case of physics) as "best-science elitism." To many, the urgency of the wartime medical crisis required, in Kevles's words, "the construction of an institutional pyramid . . . open to the talents at the bottom, and commanded at the heights by a best-science elite" capable as no others

Bonnie E. Blustein, "To Increase the Efficiency of the Medical Department": A New Approach to U.S. Civil War Medicine," *Civil War History* 33 (1987): 22–32, 36–38, 40. Reprinted with permission of The Kent State University Press.

seemed to be of setting standards of excellence. The commissioners themselves drew this conclusion. By the end of the war, "science" had come to encompass, even to transcend, the values of efficiency, discipline, progress, national unification, and elite authority relationships so important to the commissioners' vision of America.

The reorganization of the Army Medical Department, carried out by Surgeon General William A. Hammond and his successor Joseph K. Barnes under the terms of the Wilson bill, represented a radical departure from previous medical practice both in and out of the army. This restructuring would have deep implications for health care in the United States as a whole. First, it would set an example for sanitation and public hygiene. In New York, agitation for sanitary reform had begun by 1842, but the effort which proved successful in securing the passage (in 1866) of key legislation began in December 1863. The New York law, first of its kind in the United States, was used as a model for bills in other states and localities. The movement behind it was consolidated with the formation of the American Public Health Association (APHA) a few years later. Both key leaders in New York sanitary reform acquired important experience in the war effort. Elisha Harris, secretary to the New York Sanitary Association and later to the APHA, was also secretary to the USSC. Stephen Smith, author of the New York sanitary bill and the first president of APHA, served as an acting assistant surgeon to U.S. military hospitals in Virginia and, in effect, as medical publicist for the USSC. Second, the Civil War promoted hospital organization. Rosemary Stevens has noted that the Civil War left Pennsylvania with "a legacy of hospitalized soldiers . . . and of a large number of influential citizens with experience in and outside the army [notably those who had worked with the USSC, which was active throughout Pennsylvania] with experience of hospital establishment, utility, and logistics." . . .

Additionally, Union army medical reorganization directly affected some twelve thousand physicians and surgeons out of fifty-five thousand listed, from North and South, in the 1860 census. These men, most of them accustomed only to the near-anarchy which prevailed in American medicine, were summarily subjected to examinations and regulations. These tests and rules, moreover, were administered and enforced by a small fraction of the profession that oriented itself more toward European medical science than toward its less distinguished counterpart at home. Finally, research sponsored by the Medical Department provided a basis for later development of medical science in the United States on a significant scale. Thousands of doctors were involved (sometimes reluctantly) in collective investigations of medical statistics and surgical pathology. More important, for the first time in the United States large numbers of patients were treated in hospitals where their histories were taken and written records kept, making possible the specialized study of injuries of the eye, the nerves, "soldier's heart," and the like. Not entirely by accident, this facilitated the rise of clinical specialism, which emerged immediately after the war as a scientific form of practice and research. The restructured Medical Department became an institution which would mediate intellectual changes deeply affecting the content of postwar medical science. While adopting the European context of scientific medicine, it directed American scientific research energies into physiological and surgical approaches rather than toward the pathological anatomy of the Parisian hospital and German laboratory traditions. The full significance of the resultant differences between American and European medical science would only surface with the large-scale importation of German science to the United States a generation later. . . .

The bill for reorganization of the Medical Department was introduced by Henry Wilson, a Free-Soil Republican from a New England farm family who would later serve as Vice-President of the United States under President Grant. Though considerably weaker than that proposed initially by the Sanitary Commission, both the bill's spirit and its specific provisions, providing a new structure for the centralized direction and inspection of medical work in the army, proved to be quite controversial. To begin with, it brought surgeons of volunteers (who had been selected locally) under the direct authority of the Medical Department. At a time when few respectable individuals would consider becoming a hospital patient and few physicians had more than a nodding acquaintance with the institution, the bill provided for the new military medicine to be administered largely through a hospital system organized on a national level. In another departure, leadership was to be chosen on professional grounds rather than by promotion through the ranks. The bill also opened the door for the imposition of a uniform set of standards on medical practitioners in the service, when most American practitioners were well accustomed to medical laissez-faire. . . .

[Senator James W.] Nesmith [Oregon Democrat] added that "people desire to introduce all sorts of conflicting theories and systems of medical practice into the Army, and I think, if the tastes and notions and prejudices of every soldier were to be consulted . . . it would be about as sensible to introduce clairvoyancers, spiritual rappers, homeopathists, and practicers of all other systems of medicine." But this intended *reductio ad absurdum* had little force. Already "large numbers of petitioners, some of them men of great eminence," were pressing for the employment of homeopathic physicians. To complicate matters, many congressmen were not sure what the difference was between the two major medical systems: was it the size of the dose, or the nature of the remedies employed? The actual status of homeopathy within army medicine was also an open question. Apparently no law or regulation existed which would prevent the appointment of homeopaths. However, as one senator put it, "the old school of practitioners have the control of the medical board, and they are jealous of the admission of any medical men of the new school." The surgeon general's office confirmed this: homeopaths "are not considered by this Department eligible or fit to be entrusted with the great responsibility of the health and lives of our brave soldiers," wrote Joseph R. Smith to Governor Richard Gates of Illinois. "This Department, while straining every nerve to make every proper provision for the care of the sick and wounded, is clear in its conviction that rather than employ an incompetent officer, it is preferable to employ none." But it seemed that some "homeopathists have been examined and passed on the supposition that they were allopathists." Because the qualifying examination was not standardized, it was quite possible that the questions which would distinguish between the schools might not be asked unless the candidate were suspected of homeopathic leanings. And there seemed to be nothing to prevent a physician from practicing on the homeopathic system, once in the service.

What all this meant was that physicians in the United State in 1862 simply did not form a unified community based on a shared training experience or body of medical knowledge. The general public was also divided. Even with "regular" medicine, a deep gulf separated the medical elite, with its reverence for laboratory science and its skepticism toward current therapeutic practice, from the medical rank-and-file, who tended to reverse these attitudes. . . .

The problem of hospital construction and administration lay at the heart of reorganization. Although few Americans in the mid-nineteenth century looked to the hospital for treatment, the institution was an important source of training, experience, and contacts for the leaders of the profession. Many factors would converge, by the end of the century, to transform the hospital into the center of American medical practice and research. Some of these factors were anticipated during the Civil War in the military context, when vast numbers of sick and wounded, far from their homes and without family to care for them, had to be collected, identified, treated, and (it was hoped) returned to their regiments or at least to their kin. It is thus significant, although perhaps not surprising from a twentieth-century standpoint, that the proposed reform of the Medical Department was designed (in Wilson's words) "to make a thorough organization of all our hospitals at stations and in the field, to bring all that science and experience could have brought to superintend, direct and control all the hospitals of this country in the camp and field and everywhere" and "to secure that efficiency in the administration of the hospitals of the country that shall save health and save money too." . . .

Probably no aspect of the reorganization of the Medical Department generated more confusion and hostility than the effort to establish and enforce uniform professional standards on doctors in the service. Yet here, too, "science" was able to exert a degree of authority rather surprising in view of the very limited assistance medical science was yet able to afford the practitioner. Few disputed the desirability of "weeding out" incompetent surgeons from the service; indeed, complaints about alleged incompetents recur frequently in the surgeon general's correspondence. But the staffing of medical examining boards by such professional leaders as Valentine Mott and T. M. Markoe of New York and Samuel D. Gross of Philadelphia had other significant implications. The scientific knowledge which they valued so highly provided the justification for excluding from practice many for whom neither minimal medical school graduation requirements nor unenforced state licensure laws had ever been an obstacle. Again, this was not without controversy, especially in view of the serious and well-recognized shortage of surgeons in the field. For example, Dr. A. P. Meylert, president of the examining board in Louisville, Kentucky, wrote to ask what he should do about regimental physicians who were "well informed in the practical portion of Surgery and Medical Practice—who are men of sound mind—good judgment and who have become perfectly familiar with the routine of duty . . . and have always given satisfaction . . . but are not well informed in Chemistry, Minute Anatomy, Physiology and Pathology, and perhaps not fully informed in Materia Medica." Indeed, irregularities in the administration of the examinations quickly became sufficiently widespread to damage the credibility of the entire system.

The idea of a standardized examination was so new that it had to be explained even to those who were to administer it. . . . "It is desirable, as far as possible, for the different examining Boards assembled for the same purposes, to adopt a uniform plan of examination and standard of proficiency," wrote Joseph R. Smith from the surgeon general's office to Dr. T. R. Azpell of St. Louis, president of the examining board there. He urged the use of a plan of examination he enclosed, and requested

monthly reports on the outcome. This plan (a far cry from the "standardized" medical examinations of the twentieth century!) had six components: a short written
medical autobiography; a written examination on anatomy, surgery, and practice of
medicine, consisting of four "well-selected" questions on each; an oral examination
on the above, and on general pathology; an oral examination on chemistry, physiology, hygiene, toxicology, and materia medica; a clinical examination (covering
medicine and surgery) conducted at a hospital; and where practicable, an examination using a cadaver to demonstrate surgical operations. . . .

Dozens, perhaps hundreds, of letters addressed to the surgeon general on the
subject of these examinations attest to the magnitude of the attempt by ordinary
doctors to comprehend and come to terms with the new standards. For example, a
Dr. Griffith of Louisville, Kentucky explained that "a constant field duty for eighteen
months" had left him without "sufficient opportunity for preparing . . . for so critical
an examination" as was required. He withdrew from the examination half-way
through, asking that the papers he had already written on anatomy be referred to
the surgeon general, apparently in the hope that he would be approved by the
higher authority. Charles R. Reber of Reading, Pennsylvania wrote to complain
that "the time allowed me, from Monday Ap. 20 to Saturday Ap 25th [1863], with
nearly the entire day of the 24th in the dissecting room was too short to do justice
to the questions submitted." He could have used three more days, but the examinations were cut off on Saturday so that the results might be taken to Washington; he
asked for another chance.

The precise nature of medical science was of less concern to congressmen promoting reorganization than the fact of medicine's existence as a "science," even
though most of these legislators knew little about what made modern medicine
"scientific." Wilson himself showed little interest in the philosophical or practical
differences between homeopathy and "regular" medicine, remarking merely that
"the difficulty would be in having these diverse systems of practice in the Army"
and that he thought it "better to have it all the one or all the other." Yet in rebutting
the democratic argument that every soldier had the right to choose his own doctor,
the Oregon Democrat James Nesmith declared that "the soldier must submit to discipline, and the Government must make provision for his care. . . . The system of
medicine, as practiced in our Army now, is deducted from scientific experiments,
from all the light and intelligence of the age, and from all that has been shed upon
it by former ages. It is supposed to be the very best." Nesmith's claims for the medicine of his time were surely exaggerated, but he may well have believed them
himself. Again we see "best-science elitism" as a broadly acceptable justification
for a new and authoritarian medical hierarchy. . . .

Recent Civil War historiography has emphasized the concept of "modernization," increasingly as a consequence rather than as a cause of the war. Eric Foner, for
example, has concurred with Raimondo Luraghi's judgment that the war "became
part of the process of 'building a modern centralized nation-state based on a national
market, totally and unopposedly controlled by an industrial capitalistic class.'" A
reevaluation of Civil War medicine in this context contributes to our understanding
of this process of "modernization" as well as to our grasp of this period in American
medicine. . . . More precisely, medical practice in the Union army illustrates well [as
historian George Fredrickson claims] "the industrialization of production . . . the

centralization and consolidation of . . . activity, the recruitment of leadership on the basis of merit or efficiency . . . and the mobilization of the general population to serve collective ends as defined by a dominant elite."

FURTHER READING

George Adams, *Doctors in Blue* (1952).

Bonnie Blustein, *Preserve Your Love for Science* (1991).

Gert Brieger, "Sanitary Reform in New York City: Stephen Smith and the Passage of the Metropolitan Health Bill," *Bulletin of the History of Medicine* 40 (1966): 407–429.

James Cassedy, "The Flamboyant Colonel Waring," *Bulletin of the History of Medicine* 36 (1962): 163–172.

James Cassedy, "Numbering the North's Medical Events," *Bulletin of the History of Medicine* 66 (1992): 210–233.

Horace Cunningham, *Doctors in Gray* (1958).

Eric Dean Jr., *Shook over Hell: Post-Traumatic Stress, Vietnam, and the Civil War* (1997).

John Duffy, *A History of Public Health in New York City* (1974).

John Duffy, *The Sanitarians: A History of American Public Health* (1990).

Gaines M. Foster, "The Limitations of Federal Health Care for Freedmen, 1862–1868," *Journal of Southern History* 48 (1982): 349–372.

George Fredrickson, *The Inner Civil War: Northern Intellectuals and the Crisis of the Union* (1965).

Margaret Humphreys, *Yellow Fever and the South* (1992).

Howard Kramer, "Early Municipal and State Boards of Health," *Bulletin of the History of Medicine* 24 (1950): 503–529.

Martin Melosi, ed., *Pollution and Reform in American Cities, 1870–1930* (1980).

Susan Reverby, *Ordered to Care: The Dilemma of American Nursing, 1850–1945* (1985).

Charles E. Rosenberg, *The Cholera Years* (1962).

Charles E. Rosenberg, *The Care of Strangers: The Rise of America's Hospital System* (1989).

Barbara Rosenkrantz, *Public Health and the State* (1972).

Jane Schultz, "The Inhospitable Hospital: Gender and Professionalism in Civil War Medicine," *Signs* 17 (1992): 363–392.

Richard Shryock, "A Medical Perspective on the Civil War," *American Quarterly* 14 (1962): 161–173.

Ann Douglas Wood, "The War Within the War," *Civil War History* 18 (Sept. 1972): 197–212.

CHAPTER
7

Reconfiguring "Scientific Medicine," 1865–1900

Nineteenth-century American physicians never doubted that their medicine was scientific, but their notion of what constituted scientific medicine changed over time. At the start of the century, rationalistic systems of pathology and therapeutics, drawn particularly from Scottish medical teachings, represented the forefront of medical learning. Later, from the 1820s through the 1850s, Americans influenced by the Paris Clinical School championed, in opposition to rationalism, an ideal of empiricism, stressing direct observation of the body and correlation of symptoms seen at the bedside of the sick with lesions revealed at autopsy. By the 1860s, other American physicians began to celebrate experimental laboratory science as a foundation for medical knowledge and practice, seeing it as the springboard for a cognitive and social transformation of their profession. The most lucid programmatic statement of a plan for regrounding medicine in the laboratory sciences was French physiologist Claude Bernard's Introduction to the Study of Experimental Medicine (1865). Yet it was chiefly from Germany that Americans selectively took the conceptual and institutional models in which they sought to anchor a reconfigured notion of what counted as scientific medicine.

During the 1860s American physicians studying abroad—often those who later became leading figures in the medical profession at home—shifted their attention from the hospitals of Paris to the laboratories and clinics of such German-speaking centers as Vienna and Berlin. Between 1870 and 1914 some fifteen thousand American doctors studied there and then returned to proselytize for a vision of the medical future that featured experimental laboratory science and clinical specialism as its hallmarks. In 1871, for example, Henry Pickering Bowditch returned from Leipzig to the Harvard Medical School, where he set up the nation's first laboratory for experimental physiology and occupied the first full-time post as a physiological researcher and teacher. The most dramatic change in practice imported by Americans returning from Germany was the rise of specialization. American ophthalmologists formed their own society in 1864, otologists in 1869, and during the 1870s other specialty societies proliferated—testimony to the increasing receptivity of the American public to claims to authority based on special knowledge.

Yet physicians who had consecrated themselves abroad to German models returned to an American profession sharply divided over what should be the proper sources of medical authority and the best foundations for an authentic, socially relevant scientific medicine. The multiple meanings of scientific medicine were vigorously contested and debated. Some physicians confidently believed that a new program relying on experimental laboratory science and the cultivation of clinical specialism would improve medical knowledge and practice and elevate the standing of the profession in American society. And the wider American public to a striking extent came to share much of their faith in the new scientific medicine. At the same time, other elite medical thinkers remained suspicious of the new order and, seeing in it more danger than promise, turned to such established anchors of professional stability as faith in clinical empiricism and allegiance to the American Medical Associations's Code of Medical Ethics in their efforts to temper the movement for thoroughgoing change.

Why were some Americans so optimistic about this new version of scientific medicine, and why were many others hesitant and sometimes vehemently opposed to this program? What did some foresee as its products and promise, and what did others fear as its intellectual, social, and moral dangers? What were the consequences of the ideology and technical conduct of the new scientific medicine that emerged in the final third of the nineteenth century for the image, organization, and practice of the medical profession? Once told as a linear story of progress, the contested changes in American medicine during this period, as recent historical analyses have shown, involved complex tradeoffs with far-reaching consequences both for the medical profession and for the place of medicine in American culture.

 ## D O C U M E N T S

In Documents 1 and 2, two Bostonians, both recent Harvard medical graduates who are studying abroad in 1869, recount in letters home their conversion to German ideals of medical science and their growing sense that they have a special opportunity to transmit new visions of scientific medicine to America. However, whereas for one of these young men the new "science" of medicine is characterized chiefly by laboratory experimentation, for the other it is distinguished above all by clinical specialization. The extracts from the letters of Henry Pickering Bowditch (Document 1) begin when he is studying in Paris, in the laboratory of physiologist Claude Bernard. Writing to his uncle—the eminent Boston physician and disciple of the Paris Clinical School Henry Ingersoll Bowditch—the young physician reveals the shift in his interests from the practice of clinical medicine to the pursuit of experimental physiology. Dissatisfied with French facilities for laboratory teaching, he moves on to Bonn and later to Leipzig, where he finds in the institute of German physiologist Carl Ludwig the model of experimental laboratory science he wishes to take back to his own country. The letters of Clarence John Blake (Document 2) are written chiefly from Vienna, where he is engaged mainly in clinical studies. Blake tells his parents about his growing interest in diseases of the ear, convinced that the model of clinical specialism he has encountered in Vienna represents the future course that the American medical profession should follow, and he speculates about his prospects once he returns to Boston and tries to establish practice as a specialist. Bowditch would return to Boston to become, at the Harvard Medical School, the first full-time professor of physiology in the United States, pursuing experimental investigations in his own laboratory;

Blake would return to the same city to become a leading figure in the emerging specialty of otology.

In Document 3, Roberts Bartholow, professor of therapeutics at the Jefferson Medical School in Philadelphia, opens the 1879–1880 academic course by giving students and colleagues his appraisal of the ongoing "revolution" in therapeutics. Experimental physiology, he asserts in his lecture, is the true foundation for a scientific therapeutics, and the shift from empiricism to "the physiological method" is the wellspring of therapeutic progress. He concludes with a defense of animal experimentation, on which experimental laboratory physiology relied, and attacks the emerging antivivisection movement. Document 4, selections from Baltimore physician Daniel W. Cathell's widely read *The Physician Himself and What He Should Add to the Strictly Scientific* (1882), gives Gilded Age physicians practical tips on how to succeed in the business of medicine.

To early proselytizers for the promise of experimental medicine, the slow advent of dramatic therapeutic products was frustrating—which made the appearance of therapies they could point to as "cures" for rabies in 1885 and for diphtheria in 1894 momentous occasions. Reflecting and promoting optimism about the therapeutic power of the recently announced diphtheria antitoxin, an 1894 article in the *New York Herald* (Document 5) launches a popular campaign to raise funds for the production of this "miraculous" new product of experimental medicine. Making this new and still scarce remedy available to the children of New York City's poor, the article emphasizes, will help safeguard the children of all classes in the community.

1. Henry P. Bowditch, a Recent Harvard Medical Graduate Studying in Europe, Finds in Experimental Laboratory Physiology the Path to a New Scientific Medicine, 1869

Paris, Jan 26th/69.

Dear Uncle Henry

Since I wrote to you last I have been giving nearly my whole time to Physiology. Bernard lectures twice a week & always after the lecture & often before he spends some time in the laboratory doing experiments & talking physiology. This is very instructive. He is engaged at present in the discussion of anaesthetics. . . .

I seem to be drifting farther & farther away from practical medicine. I wish I could see my way clear to devoting myself entirely to the science of the profession. I read in a late number of the Boston Medical [and Surgical] Journal an article by Dr Cheever on the importance of having some young men devote themselves to medical science so as to give instruction. He seems to think that America is in danger of being left very far in the rear if this is not done. What do you think about it? A life devoted to studies of this sort affords a pleasanter prospect to me than any other I can think of. I dont see why Americans are not as capable of doing good work in a scientific way as any other people. . . .

Excerpts from Henry I. Bowditch to Henry P. Bowditch, Paris, January 26, 1869; Paris, March 21, 1869; Paris, April 12, 1869; Bonn, May 30, 1869; and Leipzig, December 5, 1869, Henry P. Bowditch Papers [H MSc 5.1], Harvard Medical Library in the Francis A. Countway Library of Medicine, Boston, Massachusetts.

I hope to see Dr Ellis here in March & I shall then ask him what he thinks about my devoting myself to physiology pure & simple. Dr Wyman & Dr Holmes both advised me to do so before I came abroad & now I feel that I am much better fitted for that sort of life than for that of a regular practising physician. I am afraid that you think the idea rather a wild one. It has occurred to me that it might be possible to establish a physiological laboratory in connection with the technological school. I believe there is a chair of physiology there, is there not? . . .

Paris March 21st/69

. . . Dr. Ellis has been in Paris for a fortnight & we have been to several hospitals together. It is very pleasant to have him here. He is sitting in my room now waiting for me to finish this note, so I must be brief.

I have no objection to your letting it be known that I intend to make physiology my profession but dont blow my trumpet too loudly for when I get home people may be disappointed. . . .

Dr. Ellis sends his best regards to all the family. He wants me to tell you that he finds Paris nowhere compared to Germany. . . .

Paris Apr 12th/69

. . . I have met Prof. Kühne here in Paris. He was Virchow's assistant for a long while you know. He is now teaching Physiology on his own account at Amsterdam. I asked his advice as to the best course for getting a thorough Physiological education. He advised me to go first to Bonn to study Histology with Max Schultze for a few months & then in November to begin with Ludwig at Leipzic. He thinks I ought to spend a full year there so as to get the whole course & then divide another year between Helmholtz & Virchow. This marks out rather an extensive course but I dont know that I can do better than to follow it. At any rate, I shall probably start for Germany early next month for I am quite impatient to get to work there. . . .

Bonn May 30th/69

. . . Before I left Paris I obtained from Bernard a number of his cards directed to most of the physiologists in Germany so that I commence my German life quite well provided with introductions. Brown Sequard also gave me letters to several of his friends.

I have settled down in Bonn for the Summer session and am following Max Schultze's lectures on histology which are really very admirable. I can understand a great deal of them & am every day improving. I devote a great deal of my time to the German language & shall have to do so for a long time before I acquire any proficiency in speaking it. This learning foreign languages is no joke, German least of all. There is no use in trying to make believe that it is not a terribly hard language. How much time students lose in learning foreign languages! If only we had a common language such as Latin used to be in the last century we should save a great deal of time. . . .

Leipzig Dec 5th/69

I wrote to you last from Geneva a little over two months ago giving you the sad news of the death of your friend Dr Mannoir. Since then I have settled myself here in Leipzig & am fairly launched in [a] course of physiological work under the most favorable circumstances possible. People at home or even in France have very little idea of the way in which Physiology is taught & studied in Germany. Ludwig's laboratory is a large building something in this shape [an upside down capital U]. The main portion of the building is devoted to the study of physiology proper, vivisections etc. The two wings are devoted to chemistry & microscopy respectively. The little central projection contains the lecture room with seats for about 100 students.

The rooms are furnished with every imaginable sort of apparatus & if anything new is needed there seems to be no lack of money to supply it.

It seems to me desirable that a description of this model institution should be published in some of our medical journals in order that the medical profession may understand how science is valued here in Europe & if you think it worth while I will write a description for the Boston Med & Surg Journal. An account of the building will be much more intelligible if a plan can be printed with it. Please let me know what you think about it. The results of the work in this laboratory are published every year in a pamphlet of 200 pages or so & are very valuable contributions to physiological science. To give you an idea of the sort of work done here I will mention the principal investigations which are now going on.

The effect of the nervous system on the secretion of urine.

The influence of muscular contractility of fluids containing loosely combined oxygen (as Permanganate of Potash).

The action of the lung tissue on the inspired gases.

The course of sensitive nerve fibres in the spinal cord.

When I first came here I began some experiments on the accelerating nerves of the heart as demonstrated by von Bezold but for a thorough investigation of the subject it seems desirable to study more accurately than has hitherto been done the effect of asphyxia on the heart's movements as this seems to a certain extent to antagonize the action of the accelerating nerves. I have therefore begun a series of experiments to determine the effect of oxygen & carbonic acid on the movements of the heart. Ludwig is a most excellent teacher. His patience in explaining physiological problems & his constant good nature under trying circumstances are very remarkable.

The students in the laboratory form quite an international assembly. There are at present in the physiological department two Russians, one Norwegian, one Swiss, one American & two Germans. There is of course a great variety of character as well as nationality but we all get along very nicely together & I am enjoying as well as learning a great deal. I hear almost no English spoken from one week's end to the other, so it seems as if I *must* learn German sooner or later. It comes very slowly however. One doesn't realize what a hard language it is till one has been pegging away at it for a few months.

Give a great deal of love to all at home & my kind regards to Dr Ellis.

Ever aff[ectionate]ly your nephew
Henry

2. Clarence Blake, a Young Boston Physician Studying in Europe, Finds in Clinical Specialism the Path to a New Scientific Medicine, 1869

Vienna, Monday Mar 8[th] 1869.

Dear blessed Mater,

. . . [N]ow while smoking an after dinner cigar is the first good opportunity to continue [my letter], and I must go to work again soon having lately received some few new observations on polyps and carbolic acid by Dr Hagen. There is so much to be studied in this speciality. If a general scientific knowledge is required for general practice how much more is it needed for a speciality where one is continually treading new ground. Mater, to be an otologist of any standing and not merely an "Ear doctor" it is necessary for me to have a knowledge of and have studied the following things. 1 General Medicine and Surgery as taught in our University at home, including Anat., Mat[eria] Med[ica] &c—2 The especial Anatomy & Pathology, general and microscopic of the Human ear, and the more of the ears of animals the better. 3 Music and the laws of sound, Harmony &c. 4 Mathematics. 5 Certainly German and French and if possible Italian. All of the above is necessary to a good otologist; do you think that such being the case our "older practitioners" are right in their view that a speciality, such as the Ear for instance is narrowing to the mind.

I am sure I cannot think so. The science of medicine and surgery is the first of all sciences since it demands tribute from all, the fact of its precedence is proved by this—that to be a physician one must devote their life *to* it and be willing to sacrifice their life *for* it, as many do. [I]f a man will be a *true* physician he must make up his mind to it when yet young. . . .

Such an one who is a true physician can be that—and nothing else. [I]t is a common and great mistake in America that a man can be anything and everything he may turn his hand to. I wish we had a little of the German common sense in that matter in the "Land of the Free." Here they educate a man or woman to fill a place in the world, and educate them thoroughly. Look at their doctors and scientific men here they strive against all sorts of obstacles, want of money, and want of practice and stick to the thing, as they should do, against all odds and come out with a much higher stand then the same clan of men with us. . . .

The general feeling among the men studying abroad is that a revolution in medical practice which has already commenced here is to be extended to America, viz. the splitting up of the profession into specialities.

As yet it would hardly be wise of a *young* man to go home and declare himself for only a certain class of cases. [H]e must be able to treat his patients generally if they require it and not be so exclusive as to have to send a patient who comes to them for an ear or throat trouble to another practitioner because they desire also to have a sprain or rheumatism prescribed for. In many respects the scientific men here, though

---

Excerpts from Clarence John Blake's letters to his mother (Vienna, March 8, 1869); parents (Vienna, April 11, 1869); parents (Vienna, May 4, 1869); father (Vienna, May 19, 1869); father (Munich, June 8, 1869); and father (Munich, June 13, 1869), Clarence John Blake Papers [H MSc 19.1, Fds. 12–15], Harvard Medical Library in the Francis A. Countway Library of Medicine, Boston, Massachusetts.

they do squabble shamefully among themselves sometimes, are broader in their views then the same clan with us and to carry out still further what David Lincoln says in one of his book reviews—that science has no nationality, science should have also no personal feeling, no prejudice and no greed

Vienna. Sunday April 11th 1869.

Dear Pater & Mater,

    . . . [A]fter a careful study of the ground and a calculation of probabilities it seems to me that the domain of Aural Surgery will grow into a speciality much as the eye has done. The men taking it up now must be the builders up of it and be not merely givers of other mens prescriptions but above that, be observers and experimenters. . . .

    I am very anxious, if the thing is possible, to be as a specialist an Aural Surgeon. This desire is supported by the advice of Dr Roosa of New York and the men here. The specialty can never probably be so exclusive an one as that of the Eye, but from the large percentage of persons afflicted with deafness and the daily increasing knowledge of the subject it should be made to rank with Ophthalmology. I should like to go home especially, if not exclusively an Otologist, the exclusiveness can follow later in the day. This one study of diseases of the Ear "embryonic" as it is, is still so large as to be quite enough for an active mind to grasp thoroughly, and if the choice is given I had rather try and be an originator in a small field than an imitator in a larger one. The thoroughness with which these Germans go into any one subject and stick to it is rather astonishing to the more grasping and superficial (in one sense) American mind, and a fellow gets almost discouraged at the idea of fitting himself thoroughly in all the branches of his general practice; it cannot be done by any one man, midwifery, eye, or ear are quite enough for him to take up if he intends to be at all thorough.

    There are Americans here and in Berlin who have been studying "Eye" for two years or more and do not yet feel themselves fitted to practice and as for getting a sufficient knowledge of the Ear in six months it's mere nonsense; if I had not studied it before I should be all afloat, but with the time spent upon it when abroad before and the *exceptional* advantages enjoyed at present I hope to come home pretty well grounded in that one subject. If a fellow has studied abroad he is expected at home to be most perfectly fitted in *everything,* rather a mistake because the very thoroughness of study here obliges him to give his whole attention to one thing in order to grasp it fully, and so the Vienna school breeds American specialists. . . .

Vienna, May 4th 1869.

Dear Pater & Mater,

    . . . You ask dear Pater what you can do, I am very anxious to get a place as Aurist in the Boston Eye and Ear Infirmary when I get home, such a position will give material for study and be the best possible opening to practice as an Aural Surgeon, and that is what I should like exclusively to be, the field is not now a wide one but it can be made so, and that very fact is the greatest inducement for entering it. I dropped a hint to Cousin Percy on the subject in a letter to him . . . .

Vienna, May 19th 1869.

Dear Pater,

. . . One subject mentioned in your letter, the question of general or special practice, has been a matter of serious thought to me ever since leaving home. At that time
I was still undecided and since then have been weighing inclinations, expediencies,
and possibilities, and have finally come to the conclusion that it is better to make a
decided stand for the speciality of Otology. At least I should desire to do so. The
rapid advance of Med. Science as a whole makes specialities a necessity in our
cities. Every branch is being now so thoroughly studied that it is as much as one
man can do to work *thoroughly* in any one. America is becoming rapidly more
thickly settled and must of necessity follow the lead of older countries. Specialists
are rapidly multiplying at home and the prejudice against them felt by the older
members of the profession is being overcome. I am very much attracted by this
speciality and can see for it an enlarged future, it will require patient waiting and
hard work, experiment and observation in an extending field of labor, but these are
always the prices of professional success.

That the study and practice of a speciality by any one who loves Science for
itself has a narrowing effect upon the mind I confidently deny. The close study and
observation required by any one branch of Medicine keeps up the interest and is a
guard against superficiality.

Considered also in the light of expediency I cannot but feel that there is more
promise of a speedy reward in this than in a general practice. The number of general
practitioners is very large, the number of specialists comparatively few and in Boston
there is chance for one man with determination and a love of his work to take the
field against New England, and the ignorance among general practitioners of Diseases of the Ear is astonishingly great.

. . . Another matter and an important one mentioned in your letter, is the location
for an office. What changes have taken place since I left of course I cannot know.
[A]s a general practitioner I should judge Columbus Av. to be an excellent location,
as an Otologist I should think the preference might justly be given to the City
proper, the West End, or rather about Park St. Boston with all its virtues has a petty
tendency to cliques. Most of the specialists are in the lower part of the city and
there is a certain circle residing in that vicinity wh. I should like, and think I could
get into. The S. End is mostly filled up with younger men while lower down there
are many who have offered a helping hand to me as a specialist.

But there are many considerations wh. may present themselves only at the last
moment. My opinion is that the med. circle down town is the most select, though it
would never do to make such a statement openly and if this letter should go into
other hands it might be as well to draw a pen through the bottom of the last and top
of this page. . . .

Munich, June 8th 1869.

Dear Pater,

. . . A radical change is needed in the American system of medical education
and practice, and it devolves upon the young men who have gained [a] broader
view by studying on the Continent and in England, to inaugurate the change. Our

course of medical study at home is an exceedingly superficial one, even in the colleges of highest standing two sessions and a certificate from a country M.D. are considered sufficient to entitle the student to an examination which devotes ten minutes to each branch or a little more than an hour to the whole science of medicine, and which empowers him to take into his power legally the life of any patient that he can lay hands on. Worse than this, in some states, as Penn. for instance there are *no* laws governing medical education and the consequence is an Eclectic University of Philadelphia which takes students in the Autumn and turns them out full fledged M.Ds in the Spring. One of the Professors at this University maintains as one of the tenets of the practice inculcated by him, the exclusive use of vegetable remedies,—and prescribes Potass Bromide.

I cannot but think that this evil is to be most readily done away with by introducing to American medical practice the European system of educated specialists. . . .

Between ourselves dear Pater and the first lamp post you meet on your first walk; out here in Europe one learns to be a good diagnostician and therapeutics seem to take a stand wh. would be accounted for by all medical men following Shakespeares advice to "throw physic to the dogs." Here more stress is laid upon the Theory than upon the Practice, while at home on the other hand our young men are but too apt to be taught and but too apt to imbibe principles of medication by rule of thumb, much as if one hemisphere of the brain of our M.D. contained— Diagnosis and the other—Corresponding treatment. Still the Med. schools here turn out thorough practitioners because each is taught his diagnosis on the one hand and his drugs and their action in health and disease on the other and he is left to bring the two together from his own good judgment and a five year *experience* in walking the hospitals. . . .

Munich, Sunday P.M. June 13ᵗʰ 1869.

Dear Pater,

. . . Much obliged for your speaking to David about the Eye and Ear Infirmary as he may be able to give me a boost in that direction and I am *very* anxious to become connected with some such institution where I can have control of a clinique and opportunity for study and experiment as well as something to keep me busy for I have now gotten into first rate working trim and don't want to drop out of it. . . .

The advantages for following up any train of reasoning or proving any theory by experiment on the living subject are very great in Germany and I almost regret returning to America . . . were it not for the hope of having eventually some material to work upon at home. The abundance of material, the opportunities offered for scientific investigation and the consequent ease with which a scientific "idea" can be fully tested, would make a residence in Germany very tempting. I hope however that in due course of time and through the efforts of the American specialists who have had the advantages of an European education and the broader thought resulting therefrom we may stand at home on a par with our Continental brethren in the devotedness to and thoroughness in, scientific research.

Prof Rüdinger keeps me busy from 8.30 A.M. to 8 P.M. (with an interval of two hours for dinner) and I am enjoying every minute; his instruction is very valuable and establishes a fund of anatomical & pathological knowledge on wh. I can draw largely I hope at some future time. I shall certainly follow your good advice dear Pater with regard to "blowing my own horn," and as you see intend to report the very cases suggested in your letter. The world is most apt to take a man at his own estimate and also is able to see through any assumption sooner or later, but fortunately I can come home with the feeling that I do begin to know something about Aural Surgery, wh. feeling is one that I never had (except as a fledgling) in regard to general practice.

"Nothing ventured, nothing won" is true to the bottom, and I cannot but feel that it will be the wiser course to confine myself to my speciality. Other gentlemen have tried the half and half and have not succeeded. Dr J. Orne Green, who has done just what I proposed to do in the first place and who has not studied his speciality so long a time is having a first rate practice and Dr. Clarke left his Aural practice in his hands when he came abroad.

Specialists are growing in America, and are pushing their way into favor among the general practitoners as they have already done here. Popular feeling will be even more easily led and I cannot but feel that to enter practice as a specialist now, in Boston will be taking advance on an inrolling wave.

3. Roberts Bartholow, a Philadelphia Medical Professor, Celebrates Experimental Medicine and the Ongoing Therapeutic Revolution, 1879

Scientific physicians have usually held therapeutics in small esteem, doubtless because it had small deservings. . . . In fact, it was not until the birth of modern physiology that scientific therapeutics became possible, and that epoch was at a period within the memory of men now living. It may seem almost incredible, but it is true, that any considerable body of scientific facts in therapeutics has been the product of the last twenty years—for scientific therapeutics must always follow the course of discovery in physiology. Even now, there must necessarily be two methods pursued in advancing the knowledge of therapeutics: the empirical or rational, and the physiological or scientific. The empirical method is based on the principle, as ancient as our art, that a remedy which has cured a case of disease must also cure analogous cases. The scientific method is the application of physiological research to ascertain the actions of medicines, and on this sure basis is predicated the use of remedies in the treatment of disease. . . .

. . . Within a few years past a therapeutical nihilism has been the position occupied by many of the most influential leaders in modern medical thought. This movement is a result, in part, of the overshadowing importance of physiological and pathological studies. The founding of great laboratories and the brilliancy of discovery in these departments have attracted universal attention to those studies which have become the fashion. We see on every side the efforts put forth to give this direction to medical study and teaching. The desire of the time seems to be to make students, histologists, pathologists, microscopists, rather than sound practitioners,

Roberts Bartholow, "The Present State of Therapeutics. An Address Delivered at the Opening of the Fifty-Sixth Course of Lectures in the Jefferson Medical School," *Medical Record* 16 (1879): 337, 340–342.

full of the humble but necessary knowledge of the practical departments of our art and science. I hold this to be a perversion of the duty of a medical school. Its first and highest duty is to instruct students, not to pursue minute researches, but to become thoroughly accomplished physicians and surgeons. No fact is more evident than that the highest order of physicians and surgeons are not men remarkable for their knowledge of microscopy, of experimental physiology, and the other branches of theoretical medical science, and, conversely, that the microscopists and pure physiologists are not remarkable as physicians, and, indeed, cannot be. The attempt to pervert the proper purpose of medical schools, and to give a merely science aspect to medical teaching is a fashion of the time, which, if it gain more adherents, is likely to do serious mischief to the cause of medical education. For young men, allured by the glitter of scientific work, will neglect the important and really more difficult attainments of true professional studies. . . .

Many who have started out on a medical career with a competent knowledge of therapeutics have been disheartened by a failure to obtain the expected results. Failures of this kind arise from two causes: first, from an incorrect appreciation of what nature and art respectively accomplish; and second, from an inability to make a correct therapeutical diagnosis. The rage in our time is to make an accurate diagnosis of disease, and it is an enthusiasm to be encouraged, but there ought to be a corresponding desire to make an accurate therapeutical diagnosis—that is, to ascertain the remedy adapted to the form and character of the disease and the condition of the patient. Into this problem many complex questions enter, and he only can solve it correctly who has an intimate acquaintance with the phenomena of disease, and with the whole range of rational and scientific therapeutics.

What art, what nature can accomplish, is a wide subject which I must merely mention. It is a singular fact that but few young physicians, comparatively, recognize the limits of remedial power. The result is that they may begin with a blind, unquestioning faith, but they end with an unreasoning scepticism. . . .

Where must the reformation begin? . . .

We must begin by stripping the materia medica of its useless knowledge. We must relegate to the botanist, to the chemist, to the pharmacist, the subject-matters belonging to them, and retain those things having connection with the study and work of the physician. . . .

. . . I hold that the actions and uses of remedies is the point on which the greatest stress should be laid, and no information, empirical or physiological, should be neglected. Let the student have the minutest information from all possible sources of the physiological powers and capabilities of a drug, its behavior as influenced by idiosyncracy and dose, its applications in the treatment of disease, the fallacies which affect a proper estimate of its powers, the special conditions in which it is useful, why it should be preferred to another remedy of the same class, and in fact any information in regard to it which may facilitate the physician's use of his armamentarium. . . .

. . . But how demonstrate your therapeutical facts? This brings me face to face with the great vivisection question. Though an advocate for rightly conducted vivisections, I protest against cruelty to animals, who are God's creatures. I protest against those barbaric sports in which more animals suffer yearly—hunted to death— than have in all time been under the knife of the vivisector. More than all, I protest against that inhumanity to man—the outcome of an unreflecting sentimentality—which prevents those scientific investigations having for their end incalculable benefits to man. Some of our most important remedies and physiological knowledge of the highest importance have been, and only could have been, obtained by experiments on animals. If animals are sacrificed for the support of men's bodies, why should they not contribute to the improvement of men's minds? Your sentimental philosopher does not reflect on the humanity of the butcher, except for the toughness of his matutinal steak. Not to occupy further time with well-known arguments in favor of vivisection, I hold that the actions of drugs should be illustrated as far as practicable by experiments on animals, but the experiments must be decorous, not revolting, not cruel, and made strictly to advance or to impart knowledge for the benefit of our fellow-man. In these experiments animals have small occasion to suffer, for the medicament or the anæsthetic so far obtund the sensibility of the centres of conscious impressions that pain is not felt. . . .

The crusade against vivisection in England, which has attained extraordinary volume and force within a few years past, is an outgrowth of dog-worship, which has now become a form of religion in the upper classes of society. With hair perfumed, powdered, and curled, his canine worship sits at table with his mistress, rides in the park in the afternoon, sleeps on downy pillows at night; he has his maid to anticipate his wants, besides the undivided attention of his mistress, and when ill he is waited upon by a celebrated physician. He makes no return to society for the protection and benefits he receives; he pays no taxes; he merely barks and growls in return for the love of his mistress, and is altogether an ungrateful dog; but he has driven physiological research out of England, and the gentlemen who were engaged in an important series of investigations on the biliary secretion were compelled by him to go over to France. An epidemic of hydrophobia [rabies] and the loss of several titled ladies will be necessary to prevent the apotheosis of the dog, and to put vivisection in its proper position—for a cure for hydrophobia can only be arrived at by experiments on this at present distinguished member of society.

4. Daniel W. Cathell, M.D., Counsels Physicians on How to Succeed in Business, 1882

It is proper and advisable to display your library, microscope and other aids to precision; also your diplomas, certificates of society membership, pictures of eminent professional friends and teachers, anatomical plates, or anything else that has associations in your mind; but it is better to show such only as have relation to you as a student or as a physician. Professional relics and keepsakes whose history is connected with your medical studies, such as the human skeleton, either entire or in parts, pathological or anatomical specimens, and mementos of your dissections, are both appropriate and useful. A cabinet of minerals is also in good taste. Let no sharks' heads, impaled butterflies, miniature ships, stuffed birds, or anything else

D. W. Cathell, *The Physician Himself and What He Should Add to the Strictly Scientific* (Baltimore: Cushings and Bailey, 1882), pp. 11, 13, 18–19, 21–22, 35, 39, 41, 47–49, 59, 61–64, 86, 94–95, 119, 122–123, 126–127, 131–132, 145, 160–161.

be seen, that will place you in any other light before patients than that of a physician. Endeavor to lead them to think of you as a physician only. . . .

Do not let your office be a lounging place or a smoking room for horse-jockeys, dog-fanciers, gamesters, swaggerers, politicians, coxcombs, and others whose time hangs heavily on their hands. The public looks upon physicians as being singled out and set apart, and worthy of an esteem not accorded to such people, or to persons engaged in the ordinary business of life; the conversation of such companions is not believed to be in harmony with a meritorious physician's mind, it destroys public faith or prevents its growth, and on no profession does faith have such influence as on ours. Every circumstance in your manner, appearance, conversation, habits, etc., will be closely observed and criticised, more especially in the early years of your career. . . .

If, at your office, and elsewhere, you make use of instruments of precision—the stethoscope, ophthalmoscope, laryngoscope, the clinical thermometer, magnifying glass, microscope, urinary analysis, etc., they will not only assist you in diagnosis, etc., but will also aid you greatly in curing people by heightening their confidence in you and enlisting their co-operation. . . .

Take care to be neat in your personal appearance; above all else, wear a clean shirt and a clean collar; for, if you dress well, people will employ you more readily, accord you more confidence—expect a larger bill, and will pay it more willingly. . . .

You should get a respectable-looking horse and carriage, as soon as circumstances will possibly justify. A team is not only a source of health and enjoyment, in the beginning of practice, but it shows your practice is growing, and any one can ride into a full practice much quicker than he can walk into one. Besides, the unknowing public infer that one who rides must have had extensive experience and a successful practice, else he could not afford it.

A riding doctor has several advantages over the one who walks; he gets a rest while riding from one patient to another, and can concentrate his mind more fully on his case while riding than if walking; when he reaches his patient he is in proper mental and physical condition to begin his duties, while the walking M.D. arrives tired and in need of rest. Another is, he can salute persons as his carriage meets them and ride on, whereas were he on foot he might be compelled to stop, parley and lose valuable time with convalescent patients, old friends, etc. . . .

You will find it comparatively easy to get practice among the moneyless poor, and relatively hard to get it among the wealthier classes. You will readily get practice among the moneyless, because you can devote more time, and fix your attention on their ailments more anxiously, than could be reasonably expected of those engaged in extensive practice, and any special interest shown them is observed and appreciated. Your reputation will probably begin in alleys and back streets, where it will extend much more rapidly than in comfortable quarters; but no difference whether in mansion, cottage or hovel, every patient you attend, white or black, rich or poor, will aid in shaping public opinion by giving you either a good or a bad name. . . .

It is your duty to familiarize yourself with the Code of Ethics at the very threshold of your professional career, and never to violate either its letter or its spirit, but always scrupulously observe both towards all regular graduates practising as regular physicians. But remember that you are neither required, nor allowed, to extend their favoring provisions to any one practising *contrary to* the cherished truths that guide the regular profession, no difference who, or what, he is.

I am not sure that the medical profession of any country but ours, has a code of written ethics. Here, the very nature of society requires that physicians shall have some system of written ethics, to define their duties and regulate their conduct towards each other and the public. . . .

In our land this code is the balance-wheel that regulates all professional action, and no one, neither the eminent ones of the profession bedecked with honors and titles, nor the beginner in the ranks, can openly ignore it without overthrowing that which is vital to his standing among medical men. If you desire to act unfairly towards your brethren, this code will compel you to do the evil biddings of your heart by stealth, and even then your unfairness will seldom go undetected or unpunished. . . .

Every principle of honor and duty forbids you even to think of lending yourself as a medical cat's-paw in unjust malpractice suits against other physicians. These so-called "medical experts" often excite disgust and indignation at the sophistical attitudes they assume when they join hands with bad people and attempt to mulct a physician, or to clear a criminal from legal responsibility on the plea of "insanity" or other wicked absurdity gotten up to make money, or defeat justice. . . .

When circumstances require you to prescribe for females with delayed menses, where pregnancy is probably or possibly the cause, it is better, instead of giving a Latinized prescription, to order some suitable simple thing, such as hop tea, tincture of valerian, or wine of iron, under its common English name.

You must give a cautious, a very cautious opinion, if any, in cases of unmarried females whose menses have ceased, and pregnancy is feared; especially in cases where the suspected girl strenuously denies having had carnal intercourse. Erroneously to pronounce her pregnant, might blast her whole future and call down maledictions on you; if on the contrary, you too quickly declare her "not pregnant," it might injure you greatly; but this mistake would be nothing in comparison with the other. Temporize, or suspend your opinion for weeks, or even months, if need be, till positively certain.

When you are importuned to produce abortion, on the plea of saving the poor girl's character, or to prevent the child's father from being disgraced, or to prevent her sister's heart from being broken, or her father from finding it out and committing murder, or to avert the shame that would fall on the family, or the church scandal, etc., etc.; or to limit the number of children for married people who already have as many as they want, or for ladies who assert that they are too sickly to have children, or that their sucking child is too young to be weaned, etc., you should meet them with a refusal as cold as ice, as pure as snow: and never even seem to entertain the proposition. If they are too importunate and refuse to take "no" for an answer, get indignant.

How could any one but a fool be induced to take the burden from another's shoulders to his own, by doing a crimson crime; to violate both his conscience and the law; to risk exposure, social and professional ruin and the penitentiary, by putting himself into any one's guilty power, whether as a favor, or for a paltry fee?

Unmarried negresses and low females who fear they are pregnant, will occasionally consult you, consume your time and get your opinion, and when you discover that they are really pregnant, and refuse to produce abortion, will try to escape payment of your office fee. In all such cases inform them at the beginning how much your fee is for your time, and opinion, and advice, and that it must be paid whether your advice agrees with their wishes or not. After settling the fee question, study their case and give them your opinion and advice. If you doubt the existence of pregnancy, and give any medicine to women who believe themselves pregnant, order it under its plain English name, instead of giving a regular prescription, and tell them verbally how to take it. By avoiding concealment regarding the nature of the remedies you give, you will escape the suspicion or charge of giving abortifacients. . . .

No one can succeed fully without the favorable opinion of the maids and matrons he meets in the sick room. The females of every family have a potent voice in selecting the family physician. I have often thought the secret why so many truly scientific aspirants fail to get practice, is that their manner and acquirements do not appeal to the female mind. . . .

Give the right hand of fellowship to every regular, honorable physician, no matter what his misfortunes or how great his deficiencies; on the other hand, refuse it to all irregulars, no matter how great their acquirements, their reputation, or their pomp. . . .

Always feel and show respect for your seniors in practice. You may excel the older M.D.'s, in the dogmatic, and in severely scientific and technical points, but they have an experience, and an intuitive forecast of the necessities and the results of cases, that far outweigh mere book knowledge, and make them better logicians, and much better practitioners. Because knowledge gotten from observation and experience is more like part of one's very nature, than that gotten from any other source, and is fixed indelibly on both his senses and his reason. Remember that although younger doctors indulge more in scientific extras than older ones, yet that the art of curing disease owes more to common sense bedside experience, than to anything else.

When you have been a doctor long enough to make your patients feel that you alone are acquainted with their moral and physical idiosyncrasies, it will give you great advantage, and will make attending them much easier. You will occasionally be employed in cases because you have long ago attended other members of the family in similar affections, and are supposed to know the family constitution. You will find that "knowing people's constitutions" is a powerful lever. . . .

Make post-mortem examinations, and scientific use of your opportunities whenever proper cases present themselves. Experiments that require vivisections, etc., would not, however, add much to your reputation, as such things are supposed to have been studied as far as needful before leaving college. On the contrary, making clinical analyses of the urine, and other fluids, will not only lead you to invaluable information regarding your patient's condition, but will be a great element in giving you popularity and respect. Working with the microscope, on proper occasions, will not only increase your knowledge, but will also invest you with the benefits of a scientific reputation in public esteem. . . .

Do not be biased too quickly or strongly in new theories based on physiological, microscopical or chemical experiments. If you abandon the practical branches of medicine for histology, post-mortem phenomena, and refined diagnostics, your usefulness as a physician will almost surely diminish. I do not refer to teachers and experimenters who have hospital and laboratory facilities, and who do not look to their practice for support. Your most useful studies, as a practitioner will be hygiene and the art of treating diseases with success. . . .

You should keep a reference book for recording particularly good remedies, prescriptions for stubborn diseases, etc., also a case book for recording the date, diagnosis, treatment, etc., of unusually important cases. Nothing impresses a patient who has a complicated, or long-standing disease with a fuller conviction that you are interested in him, and that you intend to try to do him good, than to know that you keep a regular record of his case. . . .

School yourself to avoid crude therapeutic and cultivate conservative remedies instead of radical ones. Throw gross physic to the dogs. Fame for not being heroic and not giving much strong medicine, is a splendid item in a physician's reputation, one that might almost be adopted as a corner-stone. Of course, when duty actually requires you to act promptly or to use powerful remedies heroically, take the responsibility and do whatever is proper, without shrinking. . . .

Never turn your cases over to "*specialists*" unless they have features which render it an actual duty to do so. If you refer every case of eye disease to the oculists, every uterine case to the gynecologists, ear cases to the aurists, surgical to surgeons, and so on throughout the list, you will lessen your own scope, and soon lose all familiarity with the affections that specialists treat, and will degenerate into a mere distributer of cases, a medical adviser instead of a medical attendant—studying everybody's interest except your own, and making reputation for them out of that which sinks your own individuality and destroys your own fame. A good rule is this: whenever a case proves wholly unmanageable by usual treatment, or is so grave in prognosis as undoubtedly to require broader shoulders than yours to bear the responsibility, either call in a specialist to aid in its management, or turn it entirely over to him. Timidity and infallibility are both bad traits in a doctor, but the former is the greater drawback. . . .

Neither refuse to consult with foreign physicians, with doctresses, nor with colored doctors, provided they are regular practitioners, nor even with undergraduates if they are advancing in the regular line towards their M.D. You have no moral right to turn your back on sick and suffering humanity, by refusing to add your knowledge and skill to that of *any* honorable person whose professional acquirements and tenets give him a right to work in the professional field. It is not only unmanly to throw obstacles in the path of the less favored, but such a spirit is wholly incompatible with the objects of our art, and at variance with the spirit of science, which is cosmopolitan and knows neither caste, pride nor prejudice, and has no bounds except those of truth and honor. But your love of these twin virtues, *truth* and *honor,* will prevent you from ever entertaining a thought of consulting with Eclectics, Homeopathists, Hydropathists, or other irregular practitioners, under the specious plea of duty to humanity. Let their retirement be the prime consideration under which you assume charge. . . .

We of to-day know that three in every ten of those who send for doctors need no positive medication; and nine of the ten would get well sooner or later by proper hygiene and intelligent nursing and dieting, if there were not a doctor in the world; and we are naturally prescribing less and less. In children's diseases especially, we now, in many cases, trust almost entirely to nature and placebos, and see them get well from what look to be alarming conditions almost as if by magic.

The real secret, the very foundation, of the success of various systems of practice that have arisen within the last century, has been *nature's disease-limiting power,* and *"Allopathic"* adjuvants, adroitly interwoven with hobbies that have but little value except as advertisements. Homeopathy, the *ism* that Hahnemann created in 1796, got an extra start because it arose just when humoral pathology had satiated the world with crude remedies administered irrespective of form, taste, etc., and all were anxious for some change. It has become the chief delusion of our day, and has captivated many of those who, through disgust at our crude therapeutics, have joined *the opposition* and gone to an extreme reactionary limit. It has lasted much longer than it would have done, had not the regular profession been so slow to give up crude forms, over medication, etc. Were any one to originate such a system to-day, it would be still-born.

You can neither endorse nor follow its nonsense and follies, but you also can follow the fashion and *can* give to every fastidious or squeamish patient the smallest and most pleasant dose that his safety will permit, and can avoid giving any one crude remedies to a disgusting degree. Aim earnestly to please every one's taste and ideas of medicine as far as compatible with his safety. . . .

You are bound, as if by an oath, to use your best judgment for every one who puts himself under your care, but neither the Code of Ethics nor the Code of Honor prevents you from sailing as near to every popular breeze as truth and justice will allow. . . .

You will occasionally be called again to families who strayed in disgust from regular medicine long ago, when bleeding, etc., were fashionable, who will be surprised to learn that you no longer bleed and salivate, as they imagined. If you are careful, most of these can be permanently reclaimed.

It is well to look into the principles of Mesmerism, Homeopathy, Hydropathy, Galvano-therapeutics, Spiritualism, etc., to enable you to speak of them from personal knowledge, and to checkmate their representatives, who make great capital out of *knowing all about the "old school-system,"* which they, of course, aver does not compare with the "new school." . . .

As a doctor, you will sustain two relations to your patients; first, that of a person striving to relieve or cure the sick and the suffering; secondly, that of a person who depends upon those for whom he labors, for his support.

Business is business. The practice of medicine is the business of your life; it is as legitimate as any other. You must live by it, just as other people live by theirs, but cannot do so unless you have a business system, for upon *system* depends both your professional and financial success. Neither untiring study, nor unselfish devotion as a humanitarian, can lift you above the demands of the tailor, the instrument maker, the bookseller, the grocer, the butcher and other creditors, not one of whom will take your reputation of working for *philanthropy,* or your smiles, thanks and blessings for his pay, nay, even the conductor will put you off the street-car that carries you to your patient if you do not pay your fare.

5. New York Newspaper Launches Fundraising Campaign for "Miraculous" New Diphtheria Cure, 1894

ANTI-TOXINE FOR THE POOR.

Popular Subscription Started by the Herald

to Provide Dr. Roux's Great Remedy

for Diphtheria for the Public.

. . . Because of the undoubted efficiency of Dr. Roux's diphtheria anti-toxine, and the general and unsatisfied demand for such a valuable disease preventive and cure in this country, the HERALD announces its willingness to receive popular subscriptions for the preparation of the new remedy.

The HERALD contributes to the fund $1,000.

The serum to be thus supplied is for distribution among the poor of the city. The ravages of diphtheria among the children of the poorer classes have given philanthropists and physicians much food for thought. Through the patient research of years Dr. Roux, of Paris, has discovered a remedy which is almost miraculous in its effects. Because of the skill and time required, and the character of the materials necessary for the preparation of the serum, its cost is great, quite beyond the reach of the classes among which the disease is most prevalent. . . .

The details of the HERALD'S plan will be announced in due season. All who desire to subscribe to the fund may be assured that the preparation and distribution of the anti-toxins will be conducted under the immediate supervision of a committee of medical men in the very highest ranks of the profession.

NEW YORK HERALD **$1,000**

Who will be the next? . . .

Experts pronounce diphtheria one of the most fatal of diseases. Prior to Dr. Roux's discovery fifty per cent of those attacked died. In this city the yearly deaths from diphtheria range from 2,000 to 4,000. The experiments that have been made with the new medicine show that its employment has reduced the percentage of deaths from fifty to three per cent. . . .

"I regard the HERALD'S scheme as an extremely good one, and it will undoubtedly prove extremely popular," said Dr. H. Holbrook Curtis, a throat specialist. "As an evidence of my appreciation of the HERALD'S idea, I shall be glad to contribute $100. There is an urgent necessity for the diphtheria anti-toxine, and no time should be lost in equipping a place for the manufacture of the serum. It is the universal verdict that the serum is entirely efficacious. . . .

"In a general way I should think that the pathologists and bacteriologists of the city should be invited to act as an advisory board to manage the establishment [for manufacturing the serum]. All schools should be included. General practitioners,

"Anti-Toxine for the Poor," *New York Herald,* December 10, 1894, p. 3.

in my judgment, should be permitted to be free from active connection with the establishment so there would be no room for jealousies of any kind. . . .

"The possibilities for good in the HERALD's enterprise are many, and when it is successfully carried through, as it will be, thousands of children's lives will be saved and the work will be an enduring monument to newspaper enterprise and public spirit.

"There are many eminent bacteriologists in the city, and I think you will find them as enthusiastic as I am in this matter. An advisory committee, to include a member of the Pasteur Institute, Dr. F. Mitchell Prudden, Dr. Hermann M. Biggs, Dr. John M. Thatcher, Dr. Park and others, could select the staff for the manufacture of the serum, and the staffs for the reception pavillions to follow. The entire work should undoubtedly be left to the experienced bacteriologists and pathologists. Such an arrangement would prevent friction in medical circles and win the confidence of the public and the medical profession." . . .

Dr. George F. Shrady became enthusiastic when I told him of the HERALD's plan of establishing a place for the production of anti-toxine. He said it was just like the HERALD to take up a work like that.

He then brought from a room that was securely locked a small vial almost full of a fluid of an amber color and handed it to me. After examining it I handed it back and he immediately locked it up again.

"That," said he, "is all I know of in this country. I don't know where I could get any more; so you see, sir, I am very careful of it. I am afraid to use it now because a greater necessity may arise for it later."

He spoke about his children and added:—"I fear sometimes that something might happen to one of my children. I am going to hold on to that one bottle until I am sure another is coming from some place. It is awful to think of the little lives that are being lost every day when they might be saved by one dose of anti-toxine." . . .

I found Dr. Paul Gibler, director of the New York Pasteur Institute, in his laboratory.

"The HERALD can make a success of this proposed popular subscription," said Dr. Gibler. "There is a general appreciation of the value of the serum, which has been quite as successful in its way as vaccine virus is in preventing smallpox.

"The anti-toxine has an advantage over the vaccine virus, for while the latter is powerless to cure disease the anti-toxine can be administered in advance[d] stages of diphtheria, and frequently, even in the most desperate cases, effects a cure. I am confident public interest will be aroused, as the cause is eminently worthy, and the HERALD has demonstrated that it can do anything it sets out to do. When the Figaro launched its popular subscription in Paris the response in money was like a cataract.

"Persons of wealth appreciating that because of the lack of this material their own children were likely to die of diphtheria, promptly responded by contributions and in six weeks $100,000 had been raised. This sum was given to the Paris Pasteur Institute, of which Dr. Roux is a member." . . .

Dr. D. B. St. John Roosa said:—

"Every decent physician will co-operate with the HERALD in this work, and I feel sure that we have no indecent men in the profession. It has my heartiest good will in this work, and as president of the Academy of Medicine I feel that I can say, had you made this known last Thursday night, the Academy would have passed resolutions indorsing the plan. What more can I say? Every one is talking; every one is interested, and each physician is anxious to obtain some of the fluid. At present few seem to be able to get it. It is absolutely impossible to get even enough for a dear friend. . . .

"This subject brings me back four years, when I sat up all night with the child of a very dear friend that was suffering from the dreadful disease. Of course everything was done that could be done. We then knew nothing of anti-toxine. Had we possessed this anti-toxine I feel sure that the child would have recovered." . . .

"Well," said Dr. Alfred S. Loomis, "I think that is worthy and a good work, and deserves success. No doubt it will succeed. It is a public enterprise, and will be taken hold of by the public. As yet, however, we are hardly past the experimental stage. In fact, we are right in the midst of it, but I think that the results shown so far warrant an outlay of money to determine the exact value of this wonderful discovery.

"I think it should be under a bureau of capable men. They should be representative men from the different sections of the profession, in order that the work may commend itself to the public."

"I am glad," said Dr. Jacobi, "that the HERALD has taken hold of this thing. I know it can carry the plan through, and I feel sure it will receive the support of every one. Not a minute should be lost. Every minute may mean a human life, and if the HERALD can save lives it will indeed be a great work.

"If the direction of the work is given to any one outside the Board of Health, I think a committee of the Academy of Medicine should be appointed. There are no factions there."

E S S A Y S

In the first essay, Yale University historian John Harley Warner looks at the interrelated controversies over experimental therapeutics and the AMA Code of Ethics during the 1870s and 1880s as a way of exploring the confident optimism the new version of scientific medicine inspired in some physicians and the deeply felt apprehension it incited in other physicians. Those who gave their allegiance to the new scientific medicine, Warner shows, claimed that their science placed them above creeds, warranting the dissolution of medical orthodoxy in favor of a "scientific democracy." Divisive through the early twentieth century, this conviction would inform the 1903 revision of the AMA Code of Ethics and lift the proscription against professional consultation with practitioners so long demonized as "sectarians." City University of New York historian Bert Hansen, in the second essay, focuses on the popular attention excited in America when, in 1885, French experimentalist Louis Pasteur announced that he had demonstrated a successful cure for rabies. Hansen traces the public fascination with the power and promise of the new scientific medicine, which, starting in the 1880s, was expressed in such media as newspapers, cartoons, and popular museums. Both essays explore the complex and changing nature of medical authority in late-nineteenth-century America. The first investigates an internal professional debate over the most reliable sources of medical authority, whereas the second examines some of the factors that influenced how that authority was expressed in the wider community.

Professional Optimism and Professional Dismay over the Coming of the New Scientific Medicine

JOHN HARLEY WARNER

Claims for the clinical relevance of the basic sciences were not new to the nineteenth century, but in the United States they began to be voiced with unprecedented energy in the late 1860s. These were not simply familiar claims invigorated by the growing aspirations of basic scientists, however; they differed in kind from what had come before, positing a fundamentally new relationship between science and practice. Further, clinical skepticism of basic science was by the nineteenth century a long-established theme in medical discussions about the proper sources of knowledge. Yet during the final third of the century such skepticism took on a decisively different force and meaning. Above all, in American medicine the early arbitration of claims about a new relationship between basic science and clinical practice by and large was a matter of debate not *between* basic scientists and clinicians, but rather *among* practicing physicians. An understanding of the genesis and meaning of the ideal of applied science in medicine therefore demands close attention to a dialogue among medical practitioners about a proposed relationship between science and practice that they uniformly regarded as new.

My focus here is this relationship between science and practice as American physicians debated it between the end of the 1860s and the start of the 1890s. The science I shall consider is experimental physiology; the practice, medical therapeutics. One might look instead at another basic science such as bacteriology, but I have selected physiology because it was the field around which a program to make therapeutics an applied science first coalesced. One might also look at other practices, such as the practice of diagnosis or the practice of teaching, or at surgery rather than internal medicine, but I have chosen medical therapy as the task physicians still saw as most central to their professional role.

What is immediately striking about the exchanges among physicians over the newly proposed relationship between science and practice is the stridency of the rhetoric on both sides. There can be no mistaking the extraordinarily confident optimism of those who proselytized for experimental therapeutics—what Americans tended to call "physiological therapeutics"—their program for basing practice on experimental science; just as evident is the energetic, sometimes self-righteous denunciation by those who argued against it. This suggests my two leading questions: Why were some clinicians so vocally optimistic about the promise of experimental science to transform medical therapeutics? And why were many others so vehemently opposed to this program?

The debate over physiological therapeutics had an epistemological problem at its core: What kinds of knowledge should guide medical practice, and where should that knowledge come from? But to understand the uneasy emergence of a new ideal of science and its place in medicine, we must take seriously the social and moral

John Harley Warner, "Ideals of Science and Their Discontents in Late-Nineteenth-Century American Medicine," *Isis* 82 (1991): 455–458, 460–472, 476–478. Copyright © 1991 by the University of Chicago Press. Reprinted with permission of the publisher.

meanings doctors vested in these epistemological issues. American physicians, I want to suggest, identified particular epistemological positions with divergent conceptions of professional identity and professional morality. This was among the chief reasons why discussion about physiological therapeutics was so freighted emotionally. But the epistemological dispute was not an intellectual front to cover up the real issues; for physicians, redefining the relationship between science and practice was a process that inseparably bound together questions of medical epistemology with those of integrity. Indeed, as I shall argue here, the program for physiological therapeutics was premised upon a new ideal of science, one that posited a new relationship not just between science and practice, but also between science and professional identity and between science and moral legitimacy.

It is important at the outset to qualify a notion that has become a historiographic commonplace: the idea that basic science offered little to medical practice before the end of the nineteenth century. On the contrary, throughout the century American physicians maintained that basic science offered medical practice something valuable. That was one reason didactic physiological instruction occupied a place in the curricula even of third-rate proprietary medical schools at a time when American society required no formal education of a person who practiced medicine. Physiology informed a theoretical system that helped bring order to experience; it was an aid to memory and one source of reassurance that gave the practitioner confidence at the bedside.

In therapeutic practice, in other words, physiology *explained*—but it did little more than that. . . . [P]hysicians insisted that it was impossible to construct universally applicable therapeutic rules, a view that contrasted sharply with their assumption that such rules were precisely what should be sought in a basic science such as physiology. Proper treatment was individualized, varying according to such factors as climate, topography, and population density and the patient's ethnicity, age, gender, and occupation. In asserting that empirical clinical observation was the only sound foundation for therapeutic practice, physicians denied that knowledge about a basic science such as physiology could direct therapeutic activity. Basic science might inform therapeutic theory, suggest therapeutic possibilities, and explain what was clinically observed, but it could not direct practice.

In contrast, what was most radically new about the program for physiological therapeutics was the proposition that basic science should direct practice, not just explain it. This method of applying science to practice—"the physiological method," as adherents called it in explicit contrast to "the empirical method"—can be stated simply. The clinician first needed to know how processes in a disease deviated from those in health. Next he or she needed to know the physiological effects various drugs produced. While some of this knowledge came from bedside experience, much of it came from the physiology laboratory, especially from experiments on living animals. Knowing how diseased functions needed to be altered in order to be made normal, and knowing what drugs produced such alterations, the physician could then match the appropriate drug to the deviant physiological process. . . .

. . . Energetic claims about the promise of experimental science appeared at a time when doctors were profoundly despondent about the state and prospects of therapeutics. At no period in American history was therapeutic pessimism more pervasive. During the first two thirds of the century, skeptical empiricism had driven a critical reevaluation and dramatic decline in the use of traditional therapies such as bloodletting. But while the program for clinical observation proved effective in discrediting older practices, it generated little to take their place. Starting in the 1860s, physicians very deliberately put forward new plans for the future of therapeutics. Some advocated selective revival of traditional treatments, while others urged concentration on hygienic improvements more than drug therapy, or an intensification of empirical observation, or even a shift in emphasis from the task of healing individuals to the implementation of state-sponsored preventive medicine. But the only plan that offered even the possibility of rapid progress in therapy was the scheme for rooting therapeutics in basic science. The pessimism of the period made its proponents' optimism seem ever bolder by contrast.

These clinicians made it absolutely clear that in seeking to ground therapeutics on experimental physiology, they were in revolt against clinical empiricism. Empiricism, the Philadelphia physician and exponent of experimental therapeutics Horatio Wood noted sardonically, had sanctioned the therapeutic use of camel dung and dried frogs. Wood and the other advocates of physiological therapeutics claimed a legitimate place for rationalism, for reasoning from the laboratory to the bedside. They further claimed that there were universal laws in therapeutics, just as there were universal laws in the basic science, physiology, on which they sought to base it. Treatment, in turn, would be guided principally by the dictates of physiology, not fundamentally varied according to such individuating factors as ethnicity, gender, and geographic region. Roberts Bartholow, another leading proselytizer for physiological therapeutics as a program for what he called "applied medical science," put it plainly: "The special advantage of the physiological method is its exactness." . . .

The optimistic faith that experimental science would rapidly transform clinical practice, so characteristic of those who proselytized for physiological therapeutics, was one target for ridicule by its detractors. Alfred Stillé, in an address delivered on retiring from his chair in medicine at the University of Pennsylvania in 1884, condescendingly characterized that faith as the search for a medical "Cloudland." Conventional wisdom held that young physicians had greater faith in the power of drugs than practitioners sobered by years of hard experience, and the optimistic belief that physiology would transform practice seemed to fit this pattern neatly. As one physician asserted, "It is only our younger, less-experienced and over-sanguine members who feel such zealous and unhesitant confidence in their own skill and in the definite and mathematically estimable potency of remedies." . . .

More hostile was the charge that the program for physiological therapeutics was epistemologically invalid. It was presumptuous and wrong to think that practice could be derived from the basic sciences. Critics did not deny the medical value of physiology; but unless it could be shown to guide action, not just explain how remedies worked after the fact, physiology must remain an accessory to medicine. "It behooves us to remember," Stillé insisted, "that medicine is, above all else, humane as well as human, that its beginning, middle, and end is to relieve suffering, and that whatever is outside of this may indeed be science of some sort, but certainly is not medicine." . . .

The other thrust of the epistemological objection was that in elevating the authority of experimentation in the laboratory, the physiological therapeutists denied empirical clinical observation its rightful supremacy. "A fact not to be lost sight of is that the only reliable basis of therapeutical knowledge is clinical experience," the prominent New York physician Austin Flint typically wrote. "Great as are the difficulties in the way of determining the precise therapeutical value of drugs, clinical experience is the only tribunal from which there is no appeal." . . .

The proposition that science would bring precise rules to the bedside, then, threatened many clinicians at least as much as it promised to aid them. Once its epistemological presuppositions had been dismissed, the plan seemed not only simplistic but dangerous. As Stillé claimed, "There is an art of medicine [that] completely eludes, or flatly contradicts science, by means of empirical facts, and gives the palm to sagacity and common sense over laws formulated by experiment." "Clinical experience," he noted elsewhere, "is the only true and safe test of the virtues of medicines." . . . By making therapeutic behavior mechanical, physiological therapeutics denied the physician the exercise of judgment on which his identity was partly based. Clinical judgment drew upon scientific knowledge, but it also exercised a cultivated art. The proposal that experimental science could make therapeutics certain and exact—make it merely an applied science—jeopardized the physician's professional identity.

Moreover, it seemed to redefine professional responsibility in terms so narrow as to be doubtfully ethical. . . . Traditional canons of medical responsibility seemed to be subverted by the notion that correct behavior would flow naturally from a sufficiently sound command of science. This worry that overattention to science could undermine the moral order of medicine would be far more pronounced in the case of bacteriology, whose critics warned that the scientific physicians who narrowed their microscopic focus to bacteria were at risk of losing sight of their patients. But in experimental physiology, too, there was serious concern that clinicians would begin to see their responsibility as normalizing a deviant physiological process more than caring for a sick human being.

The stridency of this therapeutic debate, then, stemmed not only from the intellectual issues at stake, but also from larger concerns about the physician's identity and integrity. The dangers many clinicians perceived in physiological therapeutics, as well as the commitments of its defenders, can be clarified by situating attitudes toward this program within the context of a broader debate waged during the 1870s and 1880s over professional responsibility and propriety. Midcentury physicians had believed that the success of the profession at the sickbed and in society was rooted in shared medical and social values that informed responsible conduct. The physician's proper interactions with patients and fellow practitioners, as much as his mastery of medical knowledge, were critical to the regular profession's effectiveness and authority. In 1847 rules for right professional conduct had been codified in the "Code of Ethics" of the newly created American Medical Association (AMA), and this code was widely taken up by local and state medical societies. "To a young physician going forth into a life full of moral conflicts the wearing of this aegis would be one of his surest defenses," one AMA president later asserted: "next to the holy scriptures, and the grace of God, it would serve most effectually to guard him from evil."

Central to the maintenance of standards was the exclusion of unorthodox or irregular practitioners from regular institutions and intercourse. The chief concern here was with homeopathists, adherents of the heterodox medical system Samuel Hahnemann had founded in Germany late in the eighteenth century. Imported to the United States in the 1820s, by the 1840s homeopathy boasted practitioners better educated than many regular physicians, had its own institutions, and had grown to be a formidable rival to the orthodox profession. In treatment, homeopathy (*homoios* = like, *pathos* = suffering) employed drugs that would produce in a healthy person symptoms similar to those of the disease. This central dogma of "like cures like" posed a fundamental intellectual challenge to the orthodox conviction that treatment should counterbalance the actions of disease. Moreover, homeopathists maintained that dilution actually increased the therapeutic potency of a drug, and their minute doses offered the public a distinct alternative to orthodox heroic drugging, an aspect of regular practice that had come under widespread popular attack. Above all, both the metaphysical system and the mild therapies of homeopathy appealed especially to affluent, educated urban patients, the very clientele that leaders of the economically distressed regular profession most wanted for themselves.

The section of the 1847 AMA Code of Ethics that was to become the focus of contention prohibited regular physicians from meeting with irregulars in consultation on the grounds that the latter were medically and morally unfit. "No one can be considered as a regular practitioner, or a fit associate in consultation, whose practice is based on an exclusive dogma [i.e., homeopathic beliefs], to the rejection of the accumulated experience of the profession, and of the aids actually furnished by anatomy, physiology, pathology, and organic chemistry [i.e., a regular medical education]." . . .

In the 1870s and 1880s this Code of Ethics came to be challenged from within the orthodox ranks. Targeting the consultation clause in particular, some physicians in their local and state medical societies began to insist that they should be free to decide whom they would consult and called for annulment of the code or at least of the consultation clause. What is intriguing, and telling, is that . . . [a]mong the most vocal opponents of the code were physicians who believed that the advancement of science had rendered it obsolete and who, moreover, looked to science as a new source of professional authority and of more reliable criteria for professional integrity.

One prominent argument against the consultation clause was that an allegiance to science subverted the very idea of orthodox and unorthodox medicine. As one practitioner put it in explaining his opposition to the code, "There can be in medicine no heresy, because there is no orthodoxy." Science was the ultimate arbiter of propriety and had rendered distinctions between competing medical belief systems made on any other grounds meaningless. . . . It was for this reason that Abraham Jacobi, as president of the New York Academy of Medicine, could reassure its members in 1886 that "the absence of ethical codes" from the organization was testimony to "its scientific spirit."

Those who defended the code agreed that medicine was scientific but were disturbed by claims that science could be relied upon as an arbiter of right professional conduct. In their view it was precisely because science could *not* provide exact and invariant rules for practice that the physician needed the kind of guide to behavior the Code of Ethics provided. Austin Flint, the eminent physician (soon to be elected AMA president) who led the defense of the code, made this point plainly in linking support for the code with dismissal of the therapeutic certainty promised by experimental science. "The practice of medicine, when contrasted with other pursuits, is peculiar," he asserted in a treatise called *Medical Ethics and Etiquette* (1883), written in defense of the code. "The medical practitioner does not deal with facts and laws having the exactness of those pertaining to physics. . . . The problems of disease embrace many and varying elements, which can not always be estimated with absolute certainty. They offer a wide scope for the exercise of judgment in the practical applications of medical knowledge." This inbuilt uncertainty of medical practice, Flint argued, was the reason further guides to behavior were required. In overturning the code, its opponents were doing "warfare against the honor and dignity of the profession," as another practitioner put it. Thus after listening to criticisms of the code at a county medical society meeting in Ohio, one member declared that "what he had heard here in this discussion reminded him of the absurd cry of certain self-styled moral and social reformers, who claimed that the advanced civilization of the nineteenth century had outgrown the Bible." Medical reformers, in the name of science, were undercutting the moral order of the past that assured the integrity of the regular profession. As Stillé concluded, "It is a sign of decadence in the American social and medical systems that such laws are treated as obsolete."

The Code of Ethics debate suggests a larger context in which the concurrent debate over physiological therapeutics should be understood. Both conflicts expressed American physicians' attempts to sort out proper relationships among science, practice, and professional responsibility during a period of social and intellectual upheaval. The intercalation of the two controversies becomes even more evident when we see that the proselytizers for physiological therapeutics allied themselves with the opponents of the Code of Ethics, while some of those who most harshly denounced the program for physiological therapeutics were among the most vocal defenders of the code.

This alignment can be illustrated by the positions taken by the authors of four of the most prominent American textbooks on therapeutics and the practice of medicine in the 1870s and 1880s. Horatio C. Wood and Roberts Bartholow, whose textbooks unsparingly belittled clinical empiricism in favor of what one of them called "the modern physiological school of therapeutics," both thought the Code of Ethics was outdated. What is more, both used the example of physiological therapeutics to sustain their argument that physicians who trusted in the natural laws revealed by experimental science no longer needed the artificial laws embodied in codes of professional ethics. "Homeopathy and allopathy [i.e., orthodox medicine] are dreams of a by-gone time," Bartholow asserted. "Modern science is indifferent to Hippocrates and Hahnemann. The therapeutics of to-day rejects dogmas, and the therapeutics of the future will accept nothing that can not be demonstrated by the tests of science." . . .

Alfred Stillé and Austin Flint, on the other hand, condemned the notion that therapeutics could be grounded on experimental physiology and unabashedly presented their textbooks as bastions of clinical empiricism. These men were also among the most strident defenders of the Code of Ethics and all it stood for. Flint, who denied that precise rules of the sort promised by experimental therapeutics could ever be attained in clinical medicine, made the inescapable uncertainty of therapeutic practice a fundamental premise in pleading the necessity of "rules of conduct adapted to the peculiarities of medicine [that] constitute medical ethics." And . . . Stillé accused the advocates of physiological therapeutics of seeking to impose their scientific laws "like a new delivery of the decalogue." . . . In language he might just as well have used in assailing supporters of physiological therapeutics,

Stillé went on to denounce those who would overturn the code for what he called their "egotistical materialism." Such a position, he said, "tends to rob man of trust in . . . the established order of things."

. . . [T]he contours of the major battle lines drawn in the code controversy are worth closer notice, for they can clarify the wider context in which some American physicians brought forward claims about scientific expertise as a new foundation for professional identity and integrity, the issue so pivotal in disputes over physiological therapeutics. Skirmishes over the code were fought in local and state medical societies across the United States, but nowhere did they become more aggressive or divisive than in New York State. In 1882 a group of physicians in the Medical Society of the County of New York drafted a New Code of Medical Ethics and pushed it through a vote at the annual meeting of the state medical society. Many of these physicians wanted to abolish the Code of Ethics altogether but compromised with less radical reformers, and the New Code their coalition enacted differed from the Old Code of the AMA chiefly in its deletion of the consultation clause. Members of the state society were henceforth free to consult any legally qualified medical practitioner (by this time New York State had made provisions for the legal recognition of homeopathists). This overturning of what was called the Old Code or the AMA Code drew national attention, and at its annual meeting in 1882 the AMA refused to seat delegates of the New York society. During the next two years Austin Flint and his son Austin Flint, Jr., among other conservatives, led a vigorous campaign to have the Old Code restored by their state society, a move repelled with equal energy by the liberal coalition. In 1883 the AMA aggravated tensions by requiring that all delegates to the annual meeting sign a pledge of allegiance to the Old Code and by making the elder Flint president-elect of that national organization. Frustrated in their attempts to replace the New Code with the Old Code in the established Medical Society of the State of New York, however, in 1884 the conservatives split off to form a second state medical society, the New York State Medical Association, which ceremoniously restored the Old Code and was duly recognized by the AMA. Into the early twentieth century, New York had two state medical societies, split by dissension over the consultation clause of the AMA Code of Ethics.

The language of those who defended the Old Code typically was imbued with the moral indignation of people who saw the issue as the "survival of right over wrong" and who regarded the New Code as "a fire-brand of Nihilism in the profession." But this broader protest was sustained by more specific charges against those who sought change, particularly the accusation that the assault on the code was the self-interested work of "a horde of New York specialists." Critics correctly pointed out that the move to overturn the code had been led by urban specialists, members of a group distinctly gaining in prominence and power in the American medical profession, yet still somewhat new and suspect. New York City specialists such as Cornelius R. Agnew (an ophthalmologist), Fordyce Barker (a gynecologist), Abraham Jacobi (a pediatrician), Henry Piffard (a dermatologist), and Daniel B. St. John Roosa (an ophthalmologist) were the most active opponents of the Old Code, and votes for its overturn came disproportionately from physicians of Manhattan, Albany, Brooklyn, and Rochester. These specialists stood to gain the most financially from abolition of the consultation clause, for not only did they practice in the urban centers where there were the greatest concentrations of homeopathists, but their claims to special expertise meant that they were the physicians most likely to be called in for consultation by a homeopathist confronted with a difficult case. The overturning of the Old Code, one critic put it, "looks like a desperate endeavor on the part of those New York specialists who are itching to consult with all sorts of irregulars in order to increase their income." . . .

The seeming presumption of urban specialists that their claims to expert knowledge placed them above the established professional order drew further assaults from Old Code defenders against such symbols of medical specialism as instruments, which—tellingly—were also taken to be the most visible emblems of experimental science in clinical medicine. In his 1884 presidential address to the first annual meetingof the New York State Medical Association, the group newly organized to reembrace the Old Code, a physician from Onondaga County and leading defender of the Old Code . . . particularly warned against "the innumerable instruments of precision, which promise to substitute mathematical accuracy for vague guesses and which are too often used, not to supplement but to supplant other and valuable methods of investigation." There was real danger, he went on, in "all the 'scopes,' all the 'graphs,' and all the 'meters'" for which clinical authority increasingly was being claimed, particularly by specialists. "These rightfully challenge recognition and study, while with unappeasable appetite they devour our substance if we attempt to add them all to our *armamentarium.*" It was perhaps fitting that the elder Flint's last address, published posthumously as *Medicine of the Future,* not only cautioned that "the only solid basis of therapeutics is clinical experience" but ended by warning against medical specialization as "a dangerous tendency."

For their part, those who had rejected the Old Code insisted that the consultation clause was an infringement on the physician's personal liberties. No doubt some were enticed by the prospect of open professional interaction with homeopathists and its economic rewards, but other deeply held commitments also informed their stance. . . . As a rebuttal to Flint's defense of the Old Code and call for its restoration, published in 1883 as *Medical Ethics and Etiquette,* . . . later in the same year [they] compiled a volume, *An Ethical Symposium,* to present their stand. At a meeting held at the house of Drs. Abraham Jacobi and Mary Putnam Jacobi in 1883, members prepared a report clearly stating that the objective of the association was "to preserve to each physician perfect liberty to decide with whom he shall act in order to secure the best interests of the sick and the honor of his profession." . . .

It is against this backdrop that the alignment of proponents of physiological therapeutics with those who most energetically sought to overturn the Code of Ethics, and of the opponents of physiological therapeutics with defenders of the code, takes on broader meaning. What starts to become clear is that interwoven with the program for physiological therapeutics in American medicine, and with resistance to it, were newly emerging conceptions of professional identity and professional morality. The plan for applying experimental physiology to clinical therapeutics plainly expressed a new ideal of science and its role in medicine. But it called for much more than simply a new relationship between science and practice; it also called for a new relationship between science and the physician's identity and between science and moral legitimacy. . . .

. . . [I]n advancing a new relationship between science and practice, the advocates of physiological therapeutics . . . had embraced a conception of science that was new not merely in its conformity to a model of experimentation more than natural history, but also in its presentation as a powerful instrument of intervention. . . . Physiological therapeutics, which exemplified the new ideal of science, was one vehicle for a transformation in medicine that went far beyond the technical changes it would bring to the bedside. The idea of making medicine to some significant extent an applied basic science—a notion many others found more threatening than promising—was to these physicians a hallmark of the medical ethos they envisaged.

Popular Optimism About the Promise of the New Scientific Medicine: The Case of Rabies Vaccine

BERT HANSEN

When Louis Pasteur announced the successful inoculation of a human with his experimental rabies vaccine in 1885, he was already well known to the French public. The chemist had been celebrated in France for both intellectual and practical achievements: preventing spoilage of wine and beer, saving the silk industry from a silkworm disease, establishing the importance of molecular asymmetry, and inventing a vaccine to save cows and sheep from anthrax. Across the Atlantic, however, his science and his name were familiar to only a small number of Americans, largely younger physicians who had recently completed medical training in Europe. The survival of the first rabies victim to be treated by Pasteur's method seemed likely to be quickly forgotten in America with no lasting effect on popular consciousness. News coverage of Pasteur's discovery was hardly remarkable. The *New York Herald,* for example, announced it as part of a cable dispatch from Paris on October 29 and reported reactions by New York doctors and the American Society for the Prevention of Cruelty to Animals (ASPCA) on October 30. Another cable dispatch on November 1 was followed by more about local physicians' responses on November 3. A cable to the *Herald* mentioned it on November 8. Reports in the *New York Times* and the other papers gave it no greater attention. Then nothing more appeared until a local event made it newsworthy again.

On December 2, a new element entered the picture when a dog ran through the early morning streets of Newark, New Jersey, biting seven other dogs—and six children. This event made the afternoon papers. The day after the children were bitten, a local physician wrote to a local newspaper urging that the children be sent immediately to Paris for the new treatment and asking the public to contribute to their expenses if the children's families could not afford it. Within hours, working-men had collected donations and brought them to the office of this doctor, William O'Gorman. By cable, Pasteur was asked if he would receive the children; the papers carried his fast and precise reply in the original French: "Si croyez danger envoyez enfants immediatement" (If you think there is danger, send children immediately).

Bert Hansen, "America's First Medical Breakthrough: How Popular Excitement About a French Rabies Cure in 1885 Raised New Expectations for Medical Progress," *American Historical Review* 103 (1998): 373–376, 380–381, 384–385, 389–391, 393–398, 401, 406–407, 409–410, 414, 418. Reprinted by permission of the author and American Historical Association.

Arrangements were made for passage a few days later on a French steamer; more donations were accepted, with contributors' names printed in the newspapers. As interest in the boys' story grew, the press expanded its attention to include their families, the donation of warm clothing for their winter voyage across the North Atlantic, Pasteur's other discoveries, supposed remedies for hydrophobia, the problem of stray dogs in American cities, methods of dog control (the impounding, shooting, poisoning, or drowning of "stray curs"), the variety of opinions among local physicians and medical professors on hydrophobia, the mechanism of the inoculation process, Pasteur's experiments, the germ theory in general, and the outfitting of a hospital room in the steamer. Indeed, the boys' trip to Paris would create a media sensation across the United States and Canada. By this small accident, initially of only local interest, a trickle of modest news reports about a scientific announcement was abruptly transformed into a national torrent of news articles, features, illustrations, editorials, jokes, letters to the editor, cartoons, and even political satire. The sensation would last several months and catapult Pasteur and medical research to celebrity across North America.

. . . [T]he adventure prompted so much sustained attention by the press and the public as to change popular expectations about medicine more generally. When American newspapers and magazines devoted extravagant attention to the first Americans treated with Pasteur's brand-new rabies "cure," they were not simply reporting an event with broad human-interest elements, they were also elaborating a story of medical discovery as something useful and exciting to ordinary people. In the process, they were cultivating a sensation about medicine's being newly powerful, about scientific knowledge that makes a difference in a public arena beyond the walls of the medical school and the laboratory. As a result, Pasteur's rabies treatment, while far from the greatest discovery of the age and not connected with the United States except by accident, stimulated a series of events and expectations that set a pattern through which later discoveries would be experienced. . . .

As we shall see, several months of incessant attention to laboratory science prompted by the rabies vaccine helped to create new iconography and new institutions. In the process, an entirely new idea became embedded in popular consciousness: that medical research could provide widespread benefits. . . . Even with important new understandings under way by the 1880s in anatomy, physiology, cell biology, and bacteriology, medicine had seen very few successful therapeutic advances and none that made a sensation in the press. Yet, while the medical breakthrough was a novelty in 1885, press coverage of medical subjects was not. In the second half of the nineteenth century, American newspapers commonly ran stories on local disease outbreaks, epidemics near and far, accidents and injuries (including dog bites, food poisoning, medical and pharmacy malpractice cases), medical and scientific meetings, discoveries about disease, and the plans, policies, scandals, and failures of sanitary reform. Still, until late 1885, one would search in vain for a generally acknowledged and widely reported triumph, for any dramatic advance in the power of doctors to change the outcome of a person's illness. Although mechanical inventions by Thomas Edison and others had generated grand enthusiasms at times, a medical development had never before captured the headlines with sustained popular attention in America. Clearly, an important feature of the rabies vaccine distinguishing it from other developments of germ theory was that it was used as a therapy, not a preventive. It was technically the latter, as the injections were given to healthy people after a dog bite but prior to the onset of any disease symptoms. Yet, because people feared bites from a suspicious dog as tantamount to getting hydrophobia, this procedure was universally, if not accurately, viewed as a cure. This common misconception is important because, in the emotional ranking of popular enthusiasms, knowledge about disease without immediate application is hardly worth noting, preventives are mildly interesting, therapies are far more appealing, and successful cures (whether real or apparent) hit the top.

An appreciation of the feelings and attitudes in this enthusiasm is what I am seeking in the headlines, stories, pictures, cartoons, and popular entertainments that were spawned by the rabies cure. . . . The focus here is on changes in what ordinary people saw, read, thought, felt, and came to expect about science and medicine as enterprises, about research and discovery, about a human triumph and the potential for more such successes. . . .

When enthusiasm for a new triumphant medicine did appear in the United States, it did not spring from Pasteur's pioneering 1882 achievement of a vaccine for anthrax, nor from Robert Koch's identification of the cholera bacillus that same year, nor from Koch's discovery of the tubercle bacillus in 1883—all major landmarks in scientific medicine. Nor did it draw momentum from such earlier discoveries as inhalation anesthesia, introduced by American doctors and dentists of the late 1840s, or the antiseptic surgery developed and taught by Joseph Lister in the 1860s and 1870s. However much these advances appear momentous from our vantage point, they simply did not receive substantial treatment as news. The transformation in expectations came, rather, from Pasteur's triumph over a minor disease. Rabies was a malady that annually killed people by mere dozens, in contrast to such major killers as tuberculosis, pneumonia, smallpox, diphtheria, and infant diarrhea, which slew hundreds of thousands each year. Hydrophobia in the United States as in Europe and elsewhere—though well known and widely feared—was an infrequent illness. It was, however, invariably fatal. And since there was no sure way to determine whether an animal that inflicted a bite was rabid or not, fear of a horrible death followed every dog bite for some weeks before one could assume the incubation time had safely passed. A small wound or its quick healing did not mean one was out of danger, as people learned from frequent stories in the press. . . .

. . . Yet clinical features of this always fatal disease are not the only things that shape people's reactions to hydrophobia. Fascination with this disease seems to derive as well from its being so frequently caused by the animal known as "man's best friend." A dog bite leading to madness suddenly reverses many aspects of the seemingly natural order of things, in ways that other illnesses do not. Rabies evokes treachery and betrayal; it is the sudden and total disruption of the dependable bond between people and domestic animals. Hydrophobia, unlike the epidemic killers such as plague, cholera, or yellow fever, was not seen as caused by someone foreign or something hostile and alien but by a member of the family and the neighborhood. Furthermore, rabies turns the world upside down in another way, for the dying patients not only lose their human reason but also exhibit physical strength that appears superhuman or, perhaps more accurately, subhuman. Moreover, the laboratory research on rabies, like the police actions against stray dogs, could tap into profound emotional ambivalence about people's loyalty to animals, since this research required the medical sacrifice of seemingly innocent creatures, even though, like the wholesale drowning of strays by pound officials, the actions were deemed necessary to achieve public health and safety.

With a deep appreciation for the complexity of such attitudes and the power of rabies' fear and fascination, Louis Pasteur proclaimed in October 1885 that such tragedies were henceforth preventable. For Pasteur, the rabies treatment was only one among his many remarkable successes in applied biology and chemistry, but it was the one that most fully captured public interest and support. Before the rabies vaccine, he was well known in France and among some groups of scientists elsewhere; afterward, his would be a household name and his rabies treatment efforts a focus for charitable efforts around the world. . . .

. . . On December 4, a cluster of several interlocking stories appeared in long articles in most New York City and Newark papers. The *New York Herald* ran this stack of headlines:

IN TERROR OF HYDROPHOBIA.
SIX CHILDREN IN NEWARK BITTEN BY A DOG SUPPOSED TO BE MAD.
PASTEUR LOOKED TO FOR AID.
AN ATTEMPT TO BE MADE TO SEND THE VICTIMS TO PARIS FOR TREATMENT.

Four of the six bitten children were judged by local physicians to be hurt seriously enough to need the trip: Eddie Ryan (age five), Patrick Joseph Reynolds (age seven), Austin Fitzgerald (age ten), and Willie Lane, a messenger boy (age thirteen). On December 8, the *New York Sun* ran the first pictures of the four new celebrities. On December 9, the *New York World* added a picture of Dr. O'Gorman, who had alerted the public to this new French cure and coordinated the collection of funds. The same day, the *New York Times* took the opportunity to acknowledge the news of a girl in Pasteur's care who had died after being inoculated, but it carefully reported Pasteur's explanation that "the period of incubation had expired and the treatment was therefore too late." The paper also quoted the chemist's firm assurance: "I am confident my treatment will be successful if commenced at any time before actual hydrophobia sets in, even if a year or more elapses between the bite and the commencement of treatment."

All the December 9 articles reported on the boys and their families taking a ferry from Newark to New York and boarding the steamer, which was to embark the next morning for Le Havre. The *World* on December 10 carried pictures of them going aboard and of the room fitted out as their "hospital," as well as a portrait of Pasteur and of a Dr. Frank Billings, who was to accompany them and introduce them to Pasteur's laboratory, where, it was said, he had studied. In charge of the traveling party was Eddie Ryan's mother (eight months pregnant), who brought along her youngest son Willie, not bitten but too young to be left home without her. For the week the boys were at sea, there could be no news of them, so the papers kept the theme alive with more stories about the dog pound and the control of stray dogs, about a new rabies victim (with articles showing pictures not only of a Charles Kaufmann, who had been bitten, but also of the dogs involved), about Pasteur's earlier work, and even about the history of applied science in France more generally.

In the week or so since the Newark boys had been bitten, readers in the New York area—and throughout America, since the stories were widely reprinted in the papers of large and small cities all across the country—had been treated to such extensive coverage (including editorials, letters to the editor, and comments by one paper about another's reporting or illustrations) that the enthusiasm became a target for satire. On December 16, *Puck* ran a cartoon entitled "The New Scheme," showing two hoboes in conversation. The first proclaims, "Congratulate me, old man—I'm going to Paris." The second inquires, "How'd yer work it?" The first explains, "Said I was bitten by a mad dog—pop'lar subscription gettin' up to send me to Pastoor."

December 19 was the cover date for at least three magazines that ran illustrated versions of the story: *Frank Leslie's Illustrated Newspapers, Harper's Weekly,* and *Scientific American.* The *Frank Leslie's* article opened with a prescient forecast, calling this "an international episode of peculiar interest . . . which will occupy public attention in both France and America for some weeks to come." (While the French did not sustain a continuous fervor about *les quatre petits Américains,* the Americans would do so with a vengeance.) The "news sketches" in these magazines were becoming routine, unlike the originality shown the same day by the *New York Daily Graphic,* which covered its whole front page with nine drawings and cartoons about dogs, rabies, and the fashion of seeking cures in Paris—all surrounding the powerful image of a revolver aimed at a cowering dog. One of the cartoons, showing a young girl in a drug store, predicted vaccines as a commonplace of the future; her request to the clerk behind the counter was "Fifteen Cents Worth of Hydrophobia Virus, Please, for Pa."

By December 21, the boys had arrived in France, and the transatlantic telegraph cable could convey dispatches back to New York in about six hours, with reports daily and sometimes even more frequently. The next day, the *New York Times* carried these headlines on the front page.

IN PASTEUR'S LABORATORY.
THE NEWARK CHILDREN INOCULATED LAST EVENING.
THEY REACH PARIS ALL RIGHT, UNDERGO THE OPERATION BRAVELY,
AND THEN GO TO BED AND TO SLEEP.
BY COMMERCIAL CABLE FROM OUR OWN CORRESPONDENT.

. . . With exaggerated precision and mock seriousness, a cable dispatch from the *New York Herald's* correspondent captured the historic moment:

> Dr. [Grancher], who performs all the inoculations for M. Pasteur, told Lane to unbutton his jacket. At exactly twelve minutes before seven the Doctor inserted the point of a silver needle beneath the skin of Lane's abdomen and injected the virus. Lane has thus the honor of being the first American ever inoculated for rabies. As the needle was withdrawn he gave a slight squirm and burst into a boisterous laugh, explaining, "Why, it's like the bite of a big mosquito. It doesn't hurt a bit." Fitzgerald's turn came next. He watched the silver needle intently, and when pricked said, "How it tickles." Patsey Reynolds was next taken in hand. His stomach was bared, and when pricked he cried out, "Golly! Is that all we've come so far for?" . . . The children then scampered off as cheerful as jay birds and not a bit homesick. The inoculations took place in the same room of the laboratory where a man on Saturday died of rabies.

. . . On [January 3] . . . , the press announced the children's departure from Paris and their fond farewell from Pasteur's care. Even before the boys had arrived back in New York harbor, American commercialism saw profits to be made from the new folk heroes. A very popular wax museum, the Eden Musée, defined the boys a week later as a new sensation, advertising "The Topic of the Day, M. Pasteur Operating on One of the Newark Children." This entertainment venue, which had opened in 1883 in an elaborate building on 23rd Street just west of Fifth, "drew a largely conservative middle-class audience," presenting musical performances as well as the wax-figured exhibits.

But even more elaborate ways to satisfy the public's curiosity about the new miracles of medicine were available. Dime museums, clustered along the Bowery, provided entertainment to lower-middle- and working-class visitors with as many as twenty shows a day. More sensationalist than P. T. Barnum's American Museum or the Eden Musée, these smaller establishments, often in storefronts, charged the low admission price conveyed by their name. The 1880s were their heyday, though many survived well into the twentieth century. . . . The idea of putting the little Newark boys themselves on exhibit appeared on the front page of the *Newark Daily Journal* on January 13, just before they were scheduled to return. In a report about the parents' anxious wait for the steamer's arrival came word of the possibility. "The proprietor of a Bowery dime museum has been working assiduously for several days to secure the children for two weeks to place on exhibition. He offered the parents $15 a week. It is not likely that the proposition will be accepted." The boys' working-class families eventually acceded to the proposition, although they acted with ambivalence and embarrassment, facing condemnation from some middle-class newspapers and an investigation threatened by the New York Society for the Prevention of Cruelty to Children. But this was, after all, a very attractive offer, given that $12 to $15 a week were the wages of a skilled workman (though very popular freaks could command fees as high as $200 a week).

A lengthy article in the *Newark Daily Advertiser* on January 19 [credited] . . . the following paragraphs to the *New York Sun*.

> Three of the dog-bitten Newark children, little "Patsy" Reynolds, Austin Fitzgerald, and Willie Lane, were yesterday placed on exhibition at the Globe Museum in the Bowery. They were perched upon a pedestal, with the champion fat woman on one side and a white silk-haired man on the other. Crowds came to see them all day, and at night the museum was packed so full that the spectators could hardly get out.
>
> Prof. Hickey gave the sightseers a complete history of the children from the time they were bitten by the dogs until they were brought to the city for exhibition. He also gave a scientific explanation of Pasteur's method of treatment, and said that hereafter the boys might be bitten by any number of dogs and that it would have no dangerous effects. . . .

When the *World* reported on this exhibit a week later on January 27, the point of its story was not the proceedings themselves but their magnitude. "Three of the Newark boys draw crowds to a Bowery show-house. . . . Three hundred thousand persons have paid 10 cents apiece to get a look at them, and their popularity is increasing daily." Twenty times a day, the trio stood on stage. The managers had plans to exhibit them "in all the large Eastern cities." Now, 300,000 persons would represent over 20 percent of New York City's inhabitants at the time. But it is possible, if perhaps not likely, that the figure is not excessively exaggerated, as one historian has reported that attendance at a dime museum could sometimes run as high as 10,000 people each day. Although for much of the New York run, only three boys were on exhibit due to the absence of five-year-old Eddie, the *Newark Daily Advertiser* reported on January 29 that Eddie was due in the New York show "next Monday," shortly before the group's expected move to Philadelphia. A flier heralds that visit: "Palace Museum . . . One Week Only . . . The Newark Children . . . Pasteur's Patients from Paris! Whom we have induced to exhibit, for one week only, at the Enormous Salary of One Thousand Dollars."

Whatever the attendance figures and however many the cities where they appeared, the above reports demonstrate that a large share of the American public experienced a direct and personal engagement with Pasteur's miracle cure. The boys who received their shots in Paris became folk heroes—at least for a moment— achieving a momentary celebrity rather like that accorded some recipients of more recent medical miracles. . . .

. . . [J]ust at the time when the excitement over the Newark boys themselves began to fade during March, a new element entered the story, one with far-reaching potential, for at this point Pasteur announced plans to found a large new institute to provide inoculations, and a subscription campaign was begun. Such campaigns were prominent in the 1880s; not only had newspapers solicited the contribution of funds to send the Newark boys to Paris but an American subscription campaign, sponsored by Pulitzer's *World,* to build the pedestal for Frédéric-Auguste Bartholdi's Statue of Liberty had reached its goal of $100,000 only a few months earlier in August 1885. A successful fund-raising campaign promoted by newspapers around the world would establish the Institut Pasteur, which opened in Paris in November 1888; and, over these two and a half years, American papers reported regularly on the patients of varied nationalities being treated in Paris and on the progress of this campaign. . . .

From the deluge of publicity about Pasteur and his Newark boys came a number of further developments, which then took on lives of their own and continued to change the social contexts and imagery of medicine in America. The latest techniques started to displace traditional images of medical care in popular writings and graphics, Pasteur Institutes were founded in several American cities, a concept of "medical researcher" entered public awareness, and additional medical breakthroughs came to be expected. . . .

Institutional developments further reinforced the effects of the media coverage. In the United States within a month of the Newark dog's rampage, two Pasteur Institutes were organized (or at least attempted). Groups in both St. Louis and New York City announced in late December their intention to create facilities producing the biological material needed to treat dog-bite victims on this side of the Atlantic. Since it was believed the remedy needed to be given as soon as possible after the bites, nearby treatment (or at least without ocean travel) would surely save lives. . . . [S]everal other American treatment centers bearing the name "Pasteur Institute" were established over the years, and they treated dog-bite victims, often in large numbers: in Chicago from 1890 to about 1944, in New York from 1890 to 1918, in Baltimore from 1897 to 1909 at least, in Ann Arbor, Michigan, from 1903 to 1926 at least, and perhaps in Philadelphia (existence and dates unconfirmed). . . .

The public, in fact, moved ahead of the profession in its enthusiasm for rabies treatment, for microbes in medicine, and for optimism about a stream of new advances. During the 1880s, the medical profession for the most part did not share the public's unquestioning support of the rabies treatment. American doctors as a group had uncertain and conflicted responses to bacteriological science in general

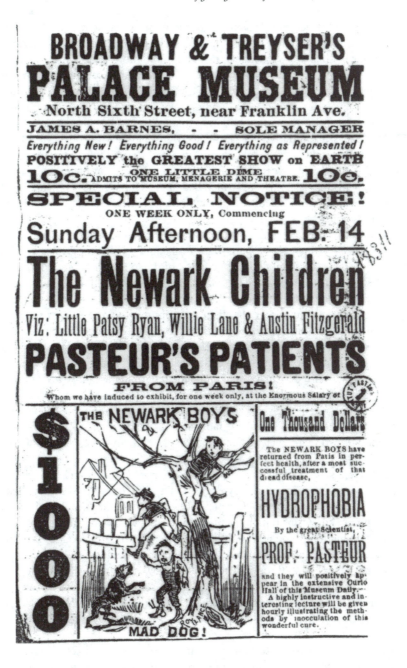

Handbill promoting the appearance of the Newark boys in a Philadelphia dime museum, *circa* 1886. Courtesy of the Institut Pasteur, Paris.

and were hesitant to accept its potential contributions to medicine. . . . But the profession did, in time, come to support the rabies vaccine and bacteriology in general in the decade or so after 1885. An exhaustive examination of the professional literature would be needed to determine just how the familiarity of laypeople with new discoveries and their enthusiasm for the first therapies that appeared from the lab might have played a direct role in doctors' reevaluation. But it clearly played at least an indirect role by shaping one major cause of change: the aggressive (and publicly successful) initiatives of Hermann Biggs and T. Mitchell Prudden at the New York City health department, starting in 1892, to use the new bacteriological laboratory as their major weapon against cholera, tuberculosis, and diphtheria in a very public way. Significantly, these men had observed the rabies enthusiasm firsthand and seem to have learned from it about the political leverage one could draw from public enthusiasms.

As the public became familiar with laboratory research, people also learned that such efforts needed financial support. Much of the initial willingness to make contributions to the cause was simply a continuation of the longstanding tradition of supporting needy patients through charity. Donations to send the boys to Paris were of this kind. Gifts to build the Pasteur Institute, solicited after March 1886, also tapped this old philanthropic impulse, rather than a commitment to research per se. But because of the Pasteur sensation, the excitement about the utility of discovery, and a growing hope for more, people came to see the value of investing in laboratory medicine. It seems to me more than coincidence that *public* funding for medical laboratories in America started up in the years immediately following this wave of popular enthusiasm about successful laboratory research, even though a direct connection would be hard to establish. Many other factors, of course, contributed to the trend, but it is striking that 1887 saw the establishment of the first federal public health laboratory and two municipal labs and that "by 1900 many states and all of America's forty largest cities boasted such facilities." One clear indication that some medical leaders saw a connection between popular enthusiasm and financial support for public laboratories is the way Biggs used the lessons of the Pasteur episode. He exhibited a profound appreciation for public relations and the cultivation of the public's support to ensure funding, especially in his work with the newspapers to promote introduction of the new diphtheria antitoxin, which he brought back from Europe after visiting research laboratories there in the summer of 1894. . . .

For subsequent breakthroughs, the public's new expectations of medical miracles engineered at laboratory benches came to shape the actions of scientists, physicians, and journalists. In the United States, the most important such episodes before the turn of the century were testicular extract (1889), tuberculin (1890), diphtheria antitoxin (1894), and the X-ray (1896). . . .

. . . [T]he 1885 Pasteur sensation continued to have an impact in shaping responses to advances. Yet the patterns of expectation, enthusiasm, and meaning that it pioneered would gradually change as successive new discoveries each came to take center stage. Attention-grabbing discoveries became ever more frequent and eventually routine. Losing its novelty, the medical breakthrough was transformed into an expected occurrence. By the twentieth century, a radically new medical therapy was no longer a surprise, nor always a sensation, and never again a once-in-a-lifetime event.

F U R T H E R   R E A D I N G

Michael Bliss, *William Osler* (1999).

Bonnie Ellen Blustein, *Preserve Your Love for Science: Life of William A. Hammond, American Neurologist* (1991).

Thomas Neville Bonner, *American Doctors and German Universities* (1963).

Donald Fleming, *William H. Welch and the Rise of Modern Medicine* (1954).

W. Bruce Fye, *The Development of American Physiology: Scientific Medicine in the Nineteenth Century* (1987).

Gerald L. Geison, "Divided We Stand: Physiologists and Clinicians in the American Context," in *The Therapeutic Revolution,* ed. Morris J. Vogel and Charles E. Rosenberg (1979), pp. 67–90.

Gerald L. Geison, ed., *Physiology in the American Context, 1850–1940* (1987).

Evelynn Maxine Hammonds, *Childhood's Deadly Scourge: The Campaign to Control Diphtheria in New York City, 1880–1930* (1999).

Bert Hansen, "New Images of a New Medicine: Visual Evidence for the Widespread Popularity of Therapeutic Discoveries in America after 1885," *Bulletin of the History of Medicine* 73 (1999): 629–678.

Susan E. Lederer, "The Controversy over Animal Experimentation in America, 1800–1914," in *Vivisection in Historical Perspective,* ed. Nicolas A. Rupke (1987), pp. 236–258.

Susan E. Lederer, *Subjected to Science: Human Experimentation in America Before the Second World War* (1995).

Russell Maulitz, "Physician Versus Bacteriologist: The Ideology of Science in Clinical Medicine," in *The Therapeutic Revolution,* ed. Morris J. Vogel and Charles E. Rosenberg (1979), pp. 91–107.

Regina Morantz-Sanchez, *Conduct Unbecoming a Woman: Medicine on Trial in Turn-of-the-Century Brooklyn* (1999).

Edward T. Morman, "Clinical Pathology in America, 1865–1910: Philadelphia as a Test Case," *Bulletin of the History of Medicine* 58 (1984): 198–214.

Naomi Rogers, "American Homeopathy Confronts Scientific Medicine," in *Culture, Knowledge, and Healing,* ed. Robert Jütte, Guenter B. Risse, and John Woodward (1998), pp. 31–64.

George Rosen, *The Structure of American Medical Practice, 1875–1946,* ed. Charles E. Rosenberg (1983).

Charles E. Rosenberg, *The Care of Strangers: The Rise of America's Hospital System* (1987).

Charles E. Rosenberg, "Making It in Urban Medicine: A Career in the Age of Scientific Medicine," *Bulletin of the History of Medicine* 64 (1990): 163–186.

Charles E. Rosenberg, *Trial of the Assassin Guiteau: Psychiatry and Law in the Gilded Age* (1968).

Barbara Gutmann Rosenkrantz, "Cart Before Horse: Theory, Practice, and Professional Image in American Public Health, 1870–1920," *Journal of the History of Medicine* 29 (1974): 55–73.

Barbara Gutmann Rosenkrantz, "The Search for Professional Order in 19th-Century American Medicine," in *Sickness and Health in America,* 2nd ed., ed. Judith Walzer Leavitt and Ronald L. Numbers (1985), pp. 219–232.

Andrew Scull, ed., *Madhouses, Mad-doctors, and Madmen: The Social History of Psychiatry in the Victorian Era* (1981).

Rosemary Stevens, *American Medicine and the Public Interest: A History of Specialization* (1971; 1998).

John Harley Warner, *Against the Spirit of System: The French Impulse in Nineteenth-Century American Medicine* (1998).

John Harley Warner, *The Therapeutic Perspective: Medical Practice, Knowledge, and Identity in America, 1820–1885* (1986; with new preface, 1997).

James Harvey Young, *Pure Food: Securing the Federal Food and Drugs Act of 1906* (1989).

CHAPTER
8

The Gospel of Germs: Microbes, Strangers, and Habits of the Home, 1880–1925

The germ theory of disease occupies a well-deserved place as a watershed in the history of American medicine and public health. Starting in the late 1870s, through the work of Louis Pasteur in France and Robert Koch in Germany, the new discipline of bacteriology amassed persuasive evidence identifying particular microbes as responsible for such deadly diseases as cholera, tuberculosis, gonorrhea, typhoid fever, scarlet fever, and diphtheria. Although some American physicians had reservations about "bacteriomania," as one prominent New York doctor in 1885 styled the zealous predictions of germ theory proselytizers, by the turn of the century Americans widely accepted the idea that microorganisms played a key role in causing disease. The germ theory transformed understandings of disease causation, prevention, and control, and exemplified the power and potential of laboratory science in medicine. It also disrupted long-standing assumptions about the relationships among dirt, moral culpability, and illness. The notion that particular, identifiable microbes were the culprits in causing specific diseases seemed to promise a profoundly new and objective framework for explaining and managing disease. And the realization that contagion could cross class and race lines as readily as cooks, laundresses, and other servants entered middle-class households proved a powerful impulse urging communal responsibility and social change.

Yet recent historical interpretations have drawn attention to the extent to which germ theory reconfigured rather than dissolved older expectations about the social and moral determinants of personal and public health and susceptibility to disease. Indeed, this episode in American medicine and public health offers a lucid example of how, amidst momentous changes, preexisting cultural values and social prejudices—especially assumptions about ethnicity, race, and class—were assimilated into a new explanatory framework. Racism, nativism, and class prejudice were in some ways bolstered as disease germs came to be associated in the thinking of many middle-class Americans with the poor, with immigrants, and with people of color. Within the United States, the new immigrants—Italians, eastern European Jews, and Chinese—represented a newly conceptualized threat of infection, reinforcing arguments for immigration restriction, just as apprehensions about contamination provided a new rationale for racial segregation. Abroad, the tendency to identify germs with the "other" also infused American imperialist ventures as authorities faced medical and public health problems in Cuba, Puerto Rico, Panama, and the Philippines.

With Koch's 1882 announcement of his discovery that the tubercle bacillus was the causative agent of tuberculosis, many physicians were exuberant about the therapeutic promise of bacteriology. But with only a few exceptions, hopes for effective antimicrobial therapies remained unrealized until the development of sulfa drugs and antibiotics in the 1930s and 1940s. In tuberculosis, for example, a leading cause of death, the only available therapy that killed the bacillus in the infected body without also killing living human tissue was education. Indeed, for the next half century, the germ theory of disease was chiefly a guide to prevention rather than to cure. Health departments continued to rely on sanitary cleanup and quarantine but increasingly focused on measures designed to prevent the spread of germs, warning the public about the dangers of what had been regarded as innocuous behaviors—sneezing, coughing, and spitting; failing to wash hands before eating; and sharing a common drinking cup.

Who is responsible for preserving health? Who is culpable for illness? How can disease be avoided? What constitutes risky, dangerous health behavior? Dangerous for whom? None of these questions were new, but the advent of the germ theory of disease compelled health professionals and the public alike to rethink the answers. What historian Nancy J. Tomes has called "the gospel of germs" was a campaign that not only provided answers in accord with the lessons of the germ theory but also specified how these lessons should govern the conduct of daily life. The antituberculosis movement pioneered the crusade against germs through a mass education program, enlisting such media as pamphlets, billboards, contests, pageants, parades, and films to promote the laws of healthy living. In the health education campaigns that became such a prominent feature of Progressive Era life, Americans were cajoled and frightened into reevaluating the disease-inducing potential of their domestic and civic environments, their neighbors, and their everyday behavior.

 D O C U M E N T S

Speaking at a "Symposium on Tuberculosis" at the 1900 meeting of the AMA, Elmer B. Borland, professor of hygiene at a Pittsburgh medical school, reports in Document 1 the results of his survey of municipal laws against spitting. Legislation and education, he argues, both have roles in changing a behavior newly valorized as dangerous and disease producing. In Document 2, Charles V. Chapin, head of the Providence, Rhode Island, health department and a leader of the New Public Health movement in America, addresses public health officials gathered for the 1902 annual meeting of the American Public Health Association (APHA). Broad-based programs for municipal cleanliness and "an indiscriminate attack on dirt," Chapin admonishes health officers in this well-known address, should give way to more focused attention on individuals to block the spread of infection by germs.

Documents 3 and 5 represent two strategies for preventing the spread of infection by the immigrant poor. In Document 3, Terence V. Powderly, commissioner-general of immigration, warns in a lay journal, the *North American Review,* about the growing disease menace of the new tide of immigration. Germ-carrying steerage immigrants from southern Europe and Asia, he argues, if not kept out, will undermine the nation's health. Warning middle-class Americans against the dangers to their own children, he advises them to see immigrants as a serious disease threat. Document 5, from a 1910 issue of the *Journal of the Outdoor Life,* published by the National Association for the Study and Prevention of Tuberculosis, offers antituberculosis activists a means of getting their message to people who "do not read books or pamphlets." The association, which vigorously employed the methods of modern advertising, offers a selection of seven 7' × 9' 8" billboards promoting healthy, tuberculosis-preventing behavior. In the tenement scene depicted here, dangerous habits spread a father's tuberculosis to his family.

Documents 4 and 6 exhibit the reform potential imbedded in the slogan "germs know no color line." In Document 4, John E. Hunter, an African American physician practicing in Lexington, Kentucky, addresses a 1905 meeting of the American Anti-Tuberculosis League in Atlanta. He assures his audience that the members of the National Association of Colored Physicians and Surgeons are ready to join with them in "the battle against the 'white plague'"—that is, tuberculosis. Using the by-this-time familiar argument that blacks were less afflicted by tuberculosis under slavery, he makes the case for environmental reform and education as the means of combating tuberculosis. Hunter subtly argues that preventing tuberculosis in the African American community directly serves the health interest of his European American listeners by preventing its spread to white families by black domestic servants. In Document 6, L. C. Allen, a Hoschton, Georgia, physician, addresses the general session of the 1914 meeting of the APHA. In remarks later published in the APHA's *American Journal of Public Health,* the nation's leading professional periodical in public health, Allen avows that black health is "one of the 'white man's burdens.'" His argument that tuberculosis in blacks threatens the European American population echos the reasoning of Hunter's 1905 address, though it is expressed in a distinctly different voice. More energetically than Hunter, Allen urges education as one means of reform, but like Hunter (though grudgingly), Allen too sees environmental reform as a necessary part of lasting improvement.

Document 7 comes from a pamphlet published in 1918 by the National Tuberculosis Association, which outlines the rules for its health game, the "Modern Health Crusade." Claiming an enlistment of over seven hundred thousand American children as "Modern Health Crusaders," this manual for teachers and parents displays the aims and educational methods of the children's crusade, including the child's progression to "knighthood" through the accumulation of points for performing health chores. Document 8 is a 1923 cartoon from the AMA's publication *Hygeia,* the most prestigious popular health magazine of its day. Jimmy Germ is depicted as a skinny, hook-nosed "villain" who strikingly resembles traditional caricatures of Jews and contemporary caricatures of southern European immigrants. This "trouble maker" is thwarted by a fair-haired child shown fresh from the tub but finds a prime "victim" in a dark-haired, dirty child shown sleeping with his windows shut and ignoring the laws of health.

1. A Professor of Hygiene Reports on the Success of Municipal Laws in Battling the American "Spitting Habit," 1900

Charles Dickens decided that, as a people, we lack the national instinct of cleanliness. He therefore designated Americans a nation of spitters. We no doubt deserve the designation, as the enlightened nations of Europe regard spitting on the floors and sidewalks as not only unsanitary, but an evidence of ill-breeding.

Five years ago the writer read a paper before the Allegheny County Medical Society recommending restriction and regulation of the spitting habit. Nine out of ten members who took part in the discussion agreed that restriction and regulation were needed. Six, however, of the nine thought any regulation impossible. "Women can, but men can not, change their filthy spitting habits."

The writer believed that most men had the natural instinct of cleanliness and could be educated in this respect up to the level with women; and further, that the ignorant, unteachable and vicious could be controlled by the absolute fiat.

The principal aim of this paper, however, is a brief review of what has been accomplished in this most important sanitary reform.

During the past year the writer has been in communication with the boards or bureaus of health of twenty-two principal cities of the United States. The following were the four principal questions asked:

1. Have you a special anti-spitting ordinance?
2. If you have not, do you attempt to restrict spitting under your general nuisance act?
3. Date of your special ordinance or order forbidding expectorating on public floors and sidewalks.
4. Result of enforcement.

An analysis of the replies gives the following information: Special laws have been enacted in one-half of these cities, and about one-forth are regulating partly or wholly under their general nuisance acts. These ordinances empower bureaus of health to abate or prohibit anything of an unsanitary character; indiscriminate spitting is included.

In the past five years, New York and Brooklyn, Newark, Columbus, Cleveland, San Francisco, Pittsburg, Washington, D.C., Rochester, New Orleans, Louisville and Baltimore have enacted special laws.

Denver, Atlantic City, and one or two others, have special laws under consideration.

The Boards of Health of Chicago and St. Louis have contented themselves with suggestions to the public, mainly through signs placed in street cars.

The Boards of Health of Philadelphia and Boston are doing good work under their general nuisance acts.

Elmer B. Borland, "Municipal Regulation of the Spitting Habit," *Journal of the American Medical Association* 35 (1900): 999–1001.

The Bureaus of Health of Detroit, Buffalo and St. Augustine are not in the working line. Hopes may be entertained for the two former, but, alas, St. Augustine! Poor St. Augustine! This ancient landmark answered the writer's inquiries thus: "Our native people would consider such an order an insult to their dignity. Can not stop a Florida cracker from spitting." May we interpret from this answer, that these people love darkness rather than light?

Many superintendents of bureaus of health do not seem to realize that they can regulate spitting under their general nuisance act. Others do not have backbone enough to promulgate and enforce an order. Special ordinances, however, attract the attention of the general public and are probably more easily enforced.

New York and Brooklyn are under one law, with a maximum fine of $500, or one year's imprisonment. . . .

Boston operates under her general nuisance ordinance, with a maximum fine of $100. The following is the text of this brief but concise order, issued by the Board of Health, in 1896, and revised in 1899.

> The board of health hereby adjudges that the deposit of sputum in public places is a nuisance, source of filth, and cause of sickness, and hereby orders: That spitting upon the floor, platform or steps of any railroad or railway station, car, public building, hall, church, theater, market, or any sidewalk immediately connected with such public places, be, and hereby is, prohibited.

In reply to the writer's special inquiry, the president reports: "The result of the enforcement is a most remarkable change from filth to cleanliness."

The courts of Newark and San Francisco have sustained their anti-spitting laws. The offenders were convicted and the penalties imposed. A millionaire was convicted by the superior court and the judgment sustained by the supreme court of California. He paid his fine of $25 and served one day in jail. Attorneys interested can secure data of the above cases by writing to the clerk of courts in either of the above-named cities.

The decision of the supreme court of California has established the fact that the passage of anti-spitting laws is a proper exercise of police power of the city. The entire Board of Health of San Francisco is composed of physicians, which probably accounts for the efficient work recently accomplished.

Men without scientific training or special fitness are frequently placed—by corrupt politicians—in charge of bureaus of health. The annual reports of these men often read like the minutes of a mutual admiration society, and their work is about as valuable. These reports and the inefficient work are sufficient evidence of the need of placing a medical executive board over all bureaus of health.

Public opinion is being rapidly educated, and if bureaus of health are inefficient, and anti-spitting laws are not well enforced in the near future, the question of first and second class electric and steam railway cars, to separate clean from indifferent people, will probably demand consideration, even in this democratic land. If rapid-transit street-car companies do not give this factor of car sanitation the attention it deserves, private motor carriages will crowd the streets, and this will delay and lessen street-car travel.

All communities have a few so-called scientific men, a few men in power, a few car conductors, a few "don't cares," who would rather wallow in public expectoration than set an example of cleanliness to the general public. There are also a few persons who consider it their sacred duty to clog the wheels of preventive medicine by opposing every useful reform and wailing over every offensive and dangerous institution as it falls.

Much has been done toward educating teachable people. The work is well begun. The pessimists of a few years ago are the astonished optimists of to-day. Thousands of earnest workers are now in the field where not a corporal's guard stood when the writer began agitating this factor of public health five years ago.

2. Charles V. Chapin, a Public Health Leader, Proclaims a New Relationship Among "Dirt, Disease, and the Health Officer," 1902

When our honored and lamented Reed went to Havana and discovered that yellow fever was transmitted by the bite of a mosquito, and Gorgas, by the most brilliant sanitary experiment ever made, put an end to this disease in its very stronghold, they drove the last nail in the coffin of the filth theory of disease. But it is to be feared that the devotees of this theory are loath to bury it, thus violating one of their cardinal principles. It seems to me that it is the duty of the health officers of this country to see that this ceremony is properly performed. The filth theory erroneously assumed that the infectious diseases were caused by emanations, gaseous or otherwise, from decaying matter. Everything decaying, and everything offensive to the sense of smell was dangerous. Everything dirty, everything nauseous, possibly, nay, probably would cause sickness. It was boldly taught that by removing all decaying matter the infectious diseases could be stamped out. For many years this idea dominated sanitary practice, the communicability of these diseases being almost entirely neglected. The English, who carried this notion of the danger of filth to the extreme, were assumed to be the leaders in public health work, and we blindly followed the leaders. Little stress was laid on *personal* uncleanliness. It was believed that the *municipality* was chiefly responsible for infectious diseases. Pure air, pure water, and a pure soil was the cry. Sanitary reform was engaged principally in protecting drinking water from organic contamination, in building sewers, in developing plumbing to a complicated and expensive art, in cleaning streets, in removing dead animals, in collecting garbage and removing household rubbish, in whitewashing and repairing tenements, in the regulation of offensive trades and the general suppression of all nuisances affecting the sense of smell. Of course there is some truth in the idea that dirt may be the cause of sickness. Some diseases are fecal borne and the danger from this source is sufficient to warrant our treating all fecal matter as suspicious. The protection of water supplies and the construction and utilization of sewers prevents disease and is worth all it costs. The secretions of nose and mouth are so often the carriers of infection that the personal cleanliness which avoids danger from this source is a potent factor in

Charles V. Chapin, "Dirt, Disease, and the Health Officer," *Public Health Papers and Reports Presented at the Thirtieth Annual Meeting of the American Public Health Association (1902)* 28 (1903): 296–299.

hygiene. But with minor exceptions, municipal cleanliness does little to prevent infection or decrease the death rate. Municipal cleanliness is no panacea. There is no more a royal road to health than to learning. It will make no demonstrable difference in a city's mortality whether its streets are clean or not, whether the garbage is removed promptly or allowed to accumulate, or whether it has a plumbing law.

There is no single procedure by which we can exterminate infection and prolong life. We have learned the true nature of infection and we have learned that the parasites which are its essence rarely propagate in filth and are seldom air-borne. We have, in the language of a distinguished American hygienist, been to a large extent, "barking up the wrong tree." Instead of an indiscriminate attack on dirt we must learn the nature and mode of transmission of each infection, and must discover its most vulnerable point of attack. We have learned that to fight typhoid fever and cholera we must keep human feces out of food and drink; in yellow fever and malaria we must destroy the *Stegomyia* and the *Anopheles;* in smallpox we must vaccinate, and in plague we must kill the rats. It is only along the line of patient investigation of each disease and practical deductions from ascertained facts that public health work can succeed.

There is nothing novel in all this and few will be found to dissent from the above. Rather, I fear, the criticism will be that I am threshing over old straw, and that the filth theory is buried as well as dead. I wish this were so, but I fear it is not, and I am sure that in my own city the outgrown traditions of the middle of the last century are still virile enough to decidedly interfere with real sanitary progress. Some of the most recent works on sanitation still reiterate the time-worn phrase about dirt and disease. The daily press and even the medical press speaks as if street cleaning, scavenging, modern plumbing and tenement house reform were the mainstay in fighting infection and reducing the death rate. The majority of even intelligent people today believe that Havana was made healthy by municipal engineering, while it was really accomplished by scientific effort specifically directed against certain infections. Our medical schools are also doubtless at fault, for many of even our younger physicians look for the source of malaria, typhoid and diphtheria in "unsanitary conditions," by which they usually mean defective plumbing, decaying vegetation, heaps of stable manure, or general yard rubbish. The great problem of sanitation today is how to deal with mild or unrecognized cases of contagious disease and with those persons, who, though well, are yet infected. This problem is not likely to be solved so long as physicians trace infection to the class of *things* mentioned, instead of to *persons*. There is also no question that we health officials, even against our better judgement, cling to discredited methods. An entirely disproportionate amount of time and money is devoted to plumbing regulation and the abatement of minor nuisances which have no direct relation to public health. We have far more sanitary inspectors than medical inspectors, and bacteriologists are not much in evidence except in the largest cities. Popular misconception as to the relation of dirt and disease is illustrated by the advertising cartoons of "Spotless Town," which is supposed to be so clean that the poor old doctor is dying of starvation. But we can rest assured that however spick and span may be the streets, and however the policeman's badge may be polished, that so long as there is found the bore so careless with his expectoration, and the doctor who cannot tell a case of sapolio from one of diphtheria, the latter disease as well as tuberculosis will continue to claim their victims.

Let me not be misunderstood. I am no lover of filth. I believe that personal cleanliness is the most important factor in the prevention of the infectious diseases. I as heartily believe in municipal cleanliness. It is one of the better phases of our modern urban life. The municipality ought to do much more than it ever has done to protect its citizens against nuisances of all kinds. Again, there is no question that municipal cleanliness does some good in the way of directly preventing disease, and also much in an indirect manner, by encouraging personal cleanliness. But there are very many other factors in modern life which tend to promote health far more than the one in question. But the health department, when it interferes with property rights as it does, and expends so much time and money in nuisance abatement, should have some stronger warrant than that it tends indirectly to promote good health.

I would plead with health officers for a more rational perspective in directing their efforts and to devote more attention to the isolation of infectious diseases, medical inspection, disinfection, vaccination and the control of milk supplies, and less to the abatement of nuisances; and in the latter, more attention to those nuisances which clearly and directly menace health, and less attention, or none at all to those which do not. Do not claim more for municipal house cleaning than the facts warrant. Teach, on all occasions, the true relation of dirt to disease. And lastly, pay a little less attention to finical defects in plumbing, to stable manure and garbage buckets, and more to the solution of those problems of infection which are so urgently pressing upon us. To attempt to solve these problems is not so easy as abating nuisances, but it will pay better in the end, and every health officer should do his part in the advancement of sanitary science.

3. Terence V. Powderly, Commissioner-General of Immigration, Warns of the Menace to the Nation's Health of the New Immigrants, 1902

Much has been said and much remains to be said of the evils likely to follow the admission of the alien criminal, pauper, anarchist and contract laborer who seek safety, an asylum or a workshop in the United States. The morals of the immigrant, the likelihood of his falling into distress and becoming a burden on our taxpayers, the possibilities of his carrying with him, or developing after landing, anarchistic tendencies, have all occupied the thought and attention of students of public questions; but the physical condition, the health, of the arriving applicant for the honor of American citizenship has not occupied the place in the discussion to which the gravity of that particular phase of the question entitles it. Many who study the immigration problem have in mind the immigrant as he presented himself at the port of landing in the early and middle decades of the last century,

T. V. Powderly, "Immigration's Menace to the National Health," *North American Review* 175 (1902): 53–60.

and they talk of him as he then was. They have before their mind's eye the sturdy Englishman, Irishman, Scotchman, Welshman, German and north countryman who came strong in limb and pure in blood. When opposition to immigration manifested itself in early days it was based on political or religious grounds; those who then wrote on the subject were actuated by a fear that the infusion of so much alien blood into our national system would pollute the stream of political life and weaken the strength of our institutions. They may have had cause for apprehension, they may have had reason to view the immigrants of their day with alarm, but it must not be forgotten that they were writing about an alien stream that had its source, or sources, in lands to which they looked with pride when tracing their own genealogy. The immigration of that day distributed itself over the entire country. With the massing of aliens in the centres of industry, grew a demand for the regulation of the system under which immigrants gained access to the United States. The popular idea is that immigration laws, passed during the last two decades, are intended to restrict, or lessen, the number of arrivals. No law has been enacted to prevent the strong, the willing, the honest, the moral or the healthy from landing, only certain classes are denied the right to come among us and take up a residence here. The proscription of these classes is intended to sift, rather than to restrict, immigration. . . .

The aliens . . . who give the immigration authorities the most trouble are those who come "suffering from a loathsome or a dangerous contagious disease"; and, of these, persons afflicted with Favus and Trachoma are most numerous. In other cases, excepting idiots, and these are so few as to give little trouble or concern to the government officials, admissions or confessions of the alien are required, but where Favus and Trachoma are present the alien presents the evidence to the Marine Hospital Surgeon who inspects all arrivals, it being external and difficult of concealment. The definition of Favus, as given in the Standard Dictionary, is: "A contagious disease of the skin, especially of the scalp, producing yellow flattened scabs and baldness, scaldhead, honeycomb, ringworm." The same authority defines Trachoma as: "A disease of the eye, characterized by hard pustules or granular excrescences on the inner surface of the eyelids, with inflammation of the membrane."

Until recently, the people of the United States were not familiar with either Favus or Trachoma; and until the tide of immigration swelled up, and began to flow in on us from the countries of southern Europe and the Orient, these diseases were not very prevalent. . . . When I assumed the duties of Commissioner-General of Immigration, I was ignorant of the nature of these afflictions. While the law expressly prohibited persons suffering from such diseases from landing, it was also held that, until an alien had been examined, pronounced entitled to admission and actually passed inward to this land of liberty, he was constructively on ship-board and, as a consequence, not landed. . . .

It was not to punish the steamship companies or the unfortunate aliens that the determination was reached by the Commissioner-General of Immigration to prevent, as far as possible, not only the landing of diseased aliens, but their embarkation at foreign seaports with the intention of landing in this country. The following, from the report of the Commissioner-General for the fiscal year ended June 30th, 1898, in which he refers to the bringing of persons "afflicted with a loathsome or a dangerous contagious disease" to the United States, will explain in part what was done to make the law effective:

> The last-named class represents virtually a new departure in the work of the Bureau, since the rejections on that ground rose from a single immigrant last year to 258 for the present fiscal year. This does not show, as may appear at first sight, laxity heretofore on the part of immigrant officials, but displays their increased efficiency in detecting and excluding cases of contagious diseases which are less obvious upon examination and of the nature of which less is known outside the medical profession than of the more generally recognized and easily detected forms of contagion.
>
> Most of the exclusions upon this ground represent aliens afflicted either with favus, a disease of the scalp, or trachoma, commonly known as granular eyelids. The former is confined almost exclusively to young persons, and, unless a careful inspection is made, the afflicted person may be admitted without detection. Protracted treatment is required in order to effect a cure, but experienced physicians contend that the disease is likely to become virulent, even after a course of hospital treatment.
>
> The difficulty in dealing with those afflicted with favus is that the separation of families is likely to follow the deportation of the afflicted immigrant, and this has occasioned immigration officials no little embarrassment and uneasiness. The question whether it would be better to deport such a person immediately on arrival and thus sunder family ties or, by delay of treatment, risk introducing this disease among the children of Americans, has been under discussion for some time, and it was decided to protect the children of the United States, even though hardship should follow the deportation of afflicted persons. . . .

The persons afflicted with Trachoma were comparatively few, and a doubt existed as to whether it should be classed as a contagious disease. To settle the disputed point the Supervising Surgeon-General of the Marine Hospital Service was appealed to for an opinion; the following is quoted from his answer:

> I have to refer you to an article on Contagious conjunctivitis, written by Dr. Miles Standish, of Boston, who is considered the very best authority. The article is as follows:
>
> "After these infections of the conjunctiva, the next most dangerous form of contagious conjunctivitis is the so-called granular lids, or trachoma. If this is of bacterial origin, the micro-organism has not as yet been recognized; nevertheless it will spread slowly through an orphan asylum, tenement house, or any other place where the poor are crowded together, unless special means are taken to prevent this result, leaving its victims handicapped for life and often nearly blind. Fortunately it is diminishing in this country, and is, compared with a few years ago, seldom seen except among recent immigrants from the eastern end of the Mediterranean, Polish and Russian Jews, Armenians, and others from that locality; and I may say in passing that the presence of acute trachoma in the conjunctiva of immigrants should be a good and sufficient reason for turning them back whence they came. A large proportion of these cases within a few months after their arrival become incapacitated and are public charges. And not only this, but were it not for the new cases thus introduced into the great tenement localities of our large cities, it is my opinion that the disease would soon become extremely rare in this part of the country."
>
> I have to add that I concur in the opinion of Dr. Standish as to the contagiousness of trachoma.

The agents of the steamship lines in Europe and Asia were notified that they should not sell tickets to persons suffering with either Favus or Trachoma, and in a large measure the traffic in diseased immigrants fell off. There were those, however, who paid little heed to the notice, and, trusting to the chance of passing their victims through without question, they continued to book them to points in the United States as before. . . .

. . . The one particular reason which determined the Commissioner-General of Immigration to prevent the landing, for any length of time or for any purpose whatever, of persons who had Favus or Trachoma was the importance of preventing the introduction of the germs, seeds or whatever else they may be called, of these diseases to the steerage of the immigrant ship. No other place under the sky is so well calculated to serve as a propagating bed for disease as the place where hundreds, and thousands, are crowded together for six or seven days, in an atmosphere that at best is unwholesome, while subsisting on food that contains no more nutrition than the law actually requires. Keep the disease out of the steerage, and it will not come out of the steerage to plague the children of America. Vice may come in the cabin or the steerage, in rags or fine raiment, and escape detection, but the diseases under discussion proclaim their presence and are their own detectors. That aliens who bring these diseases are for the greater part children does not lessen the gravity of the situation; on the contrary, it adds to it; for they go at once where large numbers of American children congregate, to the public schools and the crowded streets, to the tenement houses and attics of our large cities. That death does not follow contact with either disease is no reason why we should invite it to our shores. Statistics are not necessary to prove that disease is always dangerous; figures are not required to demonstrate that it should be avoided or warded off. No man would invite a person afflicted with a contagious disease beneath his roof, to mingle with the members of his own family. Rather would he shield his family from contact with disease; and as the nation is but a larger family every citizen should do his part, use his influence, to safeguard the homes of the poor of the United States against disease from abroad. If in future we should have occasion to trace the cause why our people are hairless and sightless through Favus and Trachoma, we should have ourselves to blame, for with proper precaution they may be warded off. One may complacently settle himself down in his comfortable chair, in his own home, and say: "It is no affair of mine if these children are afflicted, they do not associate with me, or mine." It is his affair and if he is conscious of the fact that disease is spreading in the community, it is a crime against society for him to remain silent and inactive. The men who, in the past, made the world better were obliged to disagree with others and with the world as they found it. It is not by tolerating evil, and submitting to those who advocate its continuance, that evil is checked. If we remain indifferent simply because these diseases do not prove fatal to life, we evade our duty; for the health of the nation is imperilled while one man is diseased. The old cry, "America is the asylum of the oppressed of the world," is too threadbare to withstand the assaults of disease. There is a danger that the oppressed may, through the burdens they fasten on others, become oppressors. At any rate, there exists no reason why the United States should become the hospital of the nations of earth, even though it does afford an asylum for those who come here to escape oppression.

4. John E. Hunter, an African American Physician, Admonishes Antituberculosis Activists to Recognize That Blacks and Whites Must Battle Germs as Their Common Enemy, 1905

Gentlemen of the American Anti-Tuberculosis League:

We bring to you the greetings of the National Association of Colored Physicians and Surgeons, and assure you that we are greatly interested in this work and gladly join in the battle against the "white plague." . . .

The history of the American negro before the war shows that he was comparatively free from tubercular infection, although no special statistics were very accurately kept along that line, as it concerned mostly his master. It is reasonable, however, to suppose that it was a very rare thing for him to fall a victim of that disease, or his commercial value would have been depreciated in those days.

The official statistics, as compiled, and that, doubtless, somewhat imperfectly, show that the death rate from tuberculosis is much greater at present in the negro than in the white race; and that increase has taken place since he became a free man. . . .

Digressing somewhat, since we have to admit the fact that the pendulum of mortality from tuberculosis has swung too far to our side, we can only content ourselves in this sad hour with the boasts of our fathers, that in the days of slavery they could eat with impunity and grow fat on the bacilli of yellow fever, while their beautiful young mistresses and athletic young masters would either have to take to the woods or suffer the ravages of the disease. We can say, however, that our birth rate is still at par, if not a little above. So, in view of the fact that we have kept out of the way of this monster since we have been free, by reason of the inexperience and vicissitudes that naturally follow a new birth of people, we come to you, gentlemen, whose race has never known the yoke of bondage, and whose civilization, education, and ruling power of the world are as old as the birth of Christ, that you may teach and help us improve our environments, so that we may lower this very undesirable mortality, and thereby help all mankind.

The study of the classes of the colored race reveals the same facts that such a study would reveal in any other race. Those who, by reason of industry, education, and morality, have lived above the environments that are conducive to tubercular tendencies, have a very low death rate from tuberculosis. The same is true, not only of classes of individuals of the same race, but also of nations. The death rate of the American Indian from tuberculosis exceeds that of any other race in the United States. This is due to his environments, lack of ability for self-government and of knowledge of hygiene and the laws of health. The same is true of the Chinese, whose death rate from tuberculosis exceeds that of any other civilized race of the world.

Tuberculosis in the negro is caused by the same tubercle bacilli that infect other races. The growth and development of these bacilli are influenced by the soil

---

John E. Hunter, "Tuberculosis in the Negro: Causes and Treatment," *Colorado Medical Journal* 7 (1905): 250–252, 254–257.

in which they find lodgment. Hence the cause and treatment of tuberculosis in the negro are the same as in other races.

Heredity does not balance the scale of environments. The consideration of tuberculosis would probably come under the heads of predisposing causes, preventive treatment, and the treatment of the disease itself.

While in bondage, the negro was not subjected to the crowded, unsanitary quarters of city life, for the reason that most large slaveholders lived in the rural districts, and had them engaged in outdoor work, reasonably well fed, and with such habits of life, together with fresh air, God's greatest blessing; hence he developed good chest expansion, robust and strong bodies. Along with the environments that confronted him when he became free, came the predisposing causes that brought about the increased mortality from pulmonary tuberculosis. Being turned loose from his former master in total ignorance of what was required in self-government, or of the laws of health, and likewise being a victim of many circumstances over which he had no control, he was made a subject of surroundings, habits, habitations and vices that were altogether different from his former life. . . .

The preventive treatment of pulmonary tuberculosis in the negro consists in eliminating all of those predisposing causes that render the body suitable ground for the reception, growth, and development of the tubercle bacilli. One great preventive treatment of this disease in the negro in lowly life would be the requirement and enforcement of property owners to make tenement houses more sanitary, both in construction and in location, prohibiting the building of so many houses in alleys that are cut off from sunshine and fresh air, and doing away with the one-room cabin in the country; demand the more frequent painting and whitewashing of tenement houses, and the disinfection of houses that have been occupied by people that have had any and all kinds of infectious diseases, compelling tenants to keep their homes clean, and also teaching them the knowledge and the proper use of some antiseptic, such as lime, carbolic acid, formaldehyde, etc. . . .

More attention should be given to the proper care of streets in colored settlements as a means of preventing disease; and instead of permitting the corners to be ornamented with cheap groceries and poison whisky in the rear parts of them, for a small license, it would pay better to have free city bath houses on said corners, for filth and bad whisky beget disease and crime, whereas cleanliness begets health and godliness. Such would bring better returns. Practical hygiene should be taught in the schools, teaching that tuberculosis is infectious, indirectly contagious, preventable and curable. Practical education along this line will prevent many of the diseases that tear down the system and open the doors to tuberculosis.

Every high official who advocates education for the negro as a means of bettering his condition is an anti-tuberculosis league in himself; and those who advise the withholding of it as a remedy for making him better are sowing the germs that may infect their own families.

If the master, the mule, and the cotton field saved the negro from tuberculosis before the war, protecting him by law in rural districts, giving him living wages, and education for his children, will keep him, to a great extent, a tiller of the soil in the fresh air of the country; and, therefore, he will not run to the miserable hovels of disease in the cities for protection, and thus create hotbeds for the germination of the various germs of the most loathsome of diseases.

The best anti-tuberculosis remedy for the negro discovered in recent years, although somewhat osseous and plastic just now, is the negro doctor. Right here I wish to say that, when the colored physician made his advent in this new field of work in the South, his greatest encouragement came from the professional friendship, helping hands and wise counsel extended him by the white brother doctors. This we cherish, and hope for its continuance.

We have not only entered the homes of our people as bedside advisers in cases of sickness, but have gone, and continue to go, and should go, into the homes of all classes with explanatory teaching of the laws of hygiene and health. We go into the meeting places, the schools, the churches of our people, and preach the gospel of pure air. We know the masses, their habits and needs as well. We have endeavored to decrease the death rate from this disease in our race, and, by the help of God, we expect to do more in the future. We have not only tried to check the spread of disease in the unsanitary places, where many are forced to live by reason of low wages, and others because of their bad habits and other circumstances over which they have not entire control; but we have been just as faithful in keeping its spread from the white families for whom these unfortunates work, as our fathers were faithful to their masters' families while they were in the battlefields fighting for the Confederate cause. We do our whole duty!

In view of these facts, do you not think that, where there are competent colored physicians, valuable help could come to a community by some of them being on the Boards of Health? They are on the Pension Boards, and are paid for it, and why should they not be on the boards that seek for the betterment of the health of all?

The treatment of this disease in the negro consists of fresh air and plenty of it, proper food and clothing and enough of them, and at the same time preventing the patient from infecting others and reinfecting himself. The question of travel for the negro of some means and intelligence, seeking health in sanatoria, is not worthy of consideration at this time; for a sick man traveling without civil rights, not knowing where he will be permitted to shelter his weakened body and quench his parching tongue, had better, yes, far better, remain at home with his family, and trust God for the rest. But with the brain and aid of such men in the front as constitute this organization, and that of municipalities, states, and federal government, together with our own greatest efforts, we may look up, with hope. . . .

When I moved into the home I now occupy [in Lexington, Kentucky], I was the only man and property owner of my race living in that square. As the city had not water pipes along that street, it became necessary for the property holders to build a private line. We came together, collected the money, and constructed the line. When completed, we all had water, and enjoyed all the benefits of its proper use. This was a common need of us all, and, as a business proposition, we united and got it. In the same home, I have had parties, and it has always been my choice to invite colored people, and all the people that have attended these parties have likewise been colored people. My white neighbors have also had their parties, and, as far as I know, all of their guests that were invited and attended were white people. I have never felt slighted, neither has my family, by not being invited to their social functions, and I do not believe they have felt slighted in the least by not being invited to ours, as they treat me and my family very neighborly still. This was a matter of choice, a social affair, one that always has and always will adjust itself if left alone. Socially, we are just as distinct and separate as the taps which lead the water into our different yards; but when it comes to the general good of the neighborhood, the best interests of the property holders, we are as the main pipe we all laid—united. Tuberculosis is a deadly scourge in the land, emitting its deadly germs seeking those they may devour, entering your home and my home, placing crape on our doors, causing tears and sorrow within. We must fight together and destroy this enemy, or else we ourselves will be destroyed, separately, by it.

5. Advertising Health, the National Association for the Prevention and Study of Tuberculosis Promotes Antituberculosis Billboards, 1910

The National Association for the Study and Prevention of Tuberculosis is trying to stimulate the campaign of education regarding tuberculosis in every part of the United States by means of posters, which will impress upon the public that tuberculosis can be prevented and cured. Many people do not read books or pamphlets, and are therefore most difficult to reach and yet most in need of instruction. They can only be attracted in some striking way, and the use of the bill-boards of the country for posting information regarding tuberculosis is a method of education which seems to meet these conditions.

The Associated Billposters of the United States have with great generosity offered all the vacant space on the bill-boards of the country to be used for displaying educational posters, and have offered, further, to put up free of charge the posters that are furnished. The Poster Printers Association, with similar generosity, have offered to print the posters gratis.

The designs shown in this circular have been selected from a large number of drawings offered by prominent artists and illustrators. As furnished they will be an eight-sheet poster 7 feet wide by 9 feet 4 inches high, and can be used on single eight sheet poster boards or in series on 24 sheet poster boards. These are printed in three colors and will attract attention at a distance. . . .

In addition to using the posters supplied by the Association, it is suggested that other posters containing reading matter be used. Suggestions for the text of these posters will be supplied by the National Association, and the printing can be done by any local poster printer.

For further information, or when ordering the posters, address the

National Association for the Study and Prevention of Tuberculosis,
105 E. 22d Street, New York City.

A Careless Consumptive is Dangerous to His Family

Don't spit on the floor
Don't make dust when sweeping

The National
Association
for the Study
and Prevention
of
Tuberculosis

POSTING
DONATED
By the
CITY
BILL POSTER.

The National Association for the Study and Prevention of Tuberculosis, "The Anti-Tuberculosis Bill Poster Campaign, Information Regarding the Procuring of Posters," *Journal of the Outdoor Life* 71 (1910): 390, 393.

6. A Georgia Physician Addressing "the Negro Health Problem" Warns That Germs Know No Color Line, 1914

The negro health problem is one of the "white man's burdens," and it is by no means the least of those burdens. It is at once the most serious and the most difficult health problem with which the people of the South are confronted.

The statement that "None of us liveth to himself, and no man dieth to himself" is as true today as it was when the Apostle penned it to the Romans nineteen centuries ago. And it applies with as much force to our "brother in black" as to any other man. Because of the fact that no negro liveth to himself nor dieth to himself the negro health problem is not alone a question of concern to the black man, but is one of equal moment to the white population in communities where the negroes are found in any considerable numbers. Disease germs are the most democratic creatures in the world; they know no distinction of "race, color, or previous condition of servitude." The white race and the black race will continue to live side by side in the South, and whatever injuriously affects the health of one race is deleterious to the other also. Disease among the negroes is a danger to the entire population.

Communicable diseases find their favorite propagating grounds in the dirty negro sections of our cities, and in unsanitary negro homes in the country. From dirty homes, in these disease-infested sections, negro people come into intimate contact with white people every day that passes. We meet them in our homes, offices, stores, in street cars, and almost everywhere we go. The fact is not pleasant to contemplate, but is nevertheless true, that there are colored persons afflicted with gonorrhea, syphilis, and tuberculosis employed as servants in many of the best homes in the South today. In every instance the employer is, of course, unaware of the risk being taken. Various diseases are often spread in this way.

It is undoubtedly true that the negro race has deteriorated physically and morally since slavery times. In some ways he is perhaps more intelligent, but freedom has not benefited his health, nor improved his morals. There is more sickness and inefficiency and crime among them now than before the war. All old physicians tell us that in slavery time consumption was practically unknown among the negro race. This fact, I believe, is thoroughly established. But how is it with them now? The figures speak for themselves. In the year 1911, as set forth in Census Bulletin number 112, the death-rate per one hundred thousand from tuberculosis of the lungs, in the registration area, was 162.2 for the whites, and 405.3 for the negroes. In other words, the death-rate of the colored people from this disease *is more than three times the death-rate of the white population*. In Jacksonville the rate for the whites 154.4; that for the negroes is 319.5. In Atlanta the white rate is 109.9, the black rate 297.4. In Savannah the white rate is 118, the black rate 328. Everywhere you look the proportion is about the same.

Because of the excessive death-rate among the negroes from tuberculosis the impression has gone forth, and has been widely accepted as true, that the negro race

L. C. Allen, "The Negro Health Problem," *American Journal of Public Health*, n.s. 5 (1915): 194–197, 199–202.

has a peculiar susceptibility to this disease. When all the facts are considered it seems to me that such a conclusion is not justified. Why was the negro free from tuberculosis during slavery time? The answer is obvious. Then he was disciplined; then he was made to bathe, and to keep clean; he was furnished a comfortable cabin in which to live, which he was required to keep scrupulously clean; he was given plain, but wholesome food, in generous quantities; he was made to stay at home at night, and rest, that he might be able to work; he was not allowed to roam the country, but was kept at work regularly, and was taught how to do his work in a skillful manner; he was not allowed liquor, nor indulgence in vicious pleasures; if he became ill the best physician obtainable was called to treat him. The health of the children was carefully looked after. It was to the slave owner's interest to do these things. The more efficient the slave the more valuable he was. A sickly negro was of very little value—a dead negro none. There was no more healthy race of people to be found anywhere in the world than the slaves of the South before the Civil War.

When freedom came, and all restraints removed, the negro began to indulge in all kinds of dissipation, and to practice all the vicious habits known to civilization. He now had to "shift for himself," and not having any experience in providing a living for himself and family (because the master had always done this) and thinking that freedom meant release from all work, he got along very badly. Like a child turned out in the world, homeless and penniless, he became the prey of any rascal who was disposed to take advantage of his situation. . . . The present generation of negroes have grown up amid very unfavorable surroundings, and without home training, or discipline. Many of them have not had a bath since infancy. They live very irregular lives. They often roam about at night, some of them indulging in licentious debaucheries of the most disgusting character. Their homes are filthy, and their home language unchaste. . . . It is the lack of physical and moral cleanliness that causes the death-rate to be so much more among the negroes than it is among the whites. . . .

I contend, then, that it is not a peculiar racial susceptibility to tuberculosis that is causing this disease to destroy so many people among the negro race, but his environment—his bad habits and his insanitary conditions of living. The same causes operate to produce a high death-rate from other filth diseases. . . . By an examination of the Census Bulletin referred to above, and other health reports, it may be seen that those diseases that are caused from filth, contagion, carelessness, insanitary living conditions, and exposure to cold have a high death-rate among the black population. The death-rate from pneumonia is 128.4 among the whites, while among the negroes it is 252.2. Other diseases that have a notably high death-rate among the negroes are: smallpox, typhoid fever, whooping-cough, rheumatism, influenza, and organic heart disease. . . .

Every one conversant with the facts admits that the negro health problem is an important problem, which imperatively demands attention. The question is: What are you going to do about it?

After all, the problem does not differ greatly from the same problem regarding certain portions of our white population. Ignorance and poverty are everywhere associated with disease and vice. Filth and contagion, coupled with ignorance and indifference, always bring about disease and death. The remedy of greatest importance is—*education*. But by the term "education" I hope I shall not be understood to mean the kind of learning the negro has been getting for the last fifty years. Millions of dollars have been spent, and thousands of teachers and others have devoted many years of earnest labor to the education of the negro, and as a result of it all we find the negro race as a whole in a worse condition than they were in slavery times. True a few negroes have accumulated property; a small number have become markedly intelligent; a few have become skillful laborers; but the great mass of common negroes are today densely ignorant and poverty-stricken. Most of them are unskilled laborers, working for small pay; not a few are vagrants; some are in our almshouses; a very large per cent. of them are diseased; and quite a large number of them are in our jails and chain gangs. These facts cannot be denied. I contend, therefore, that the kind of education we have been trying to give the negro has been a disappointment. . . .

The negro should be taught to work, and trained to keep regularly at it. He should be made to understand the value of time. He should be taught thrift. Proper ideas of cleanliness, sobriety, chastity, honor, and self-reliance should be instilled into his mind. These things are indispensable to his welfare. Some of the wisest negroes are beginning to see the wisdom of giving the negro an industrial education instead of teaching him Latin and Greek. . . .

A good friend of mine, a physician, says: "You might as well try to teach sanitation to mules as to try to teach it to the negroes." With this opinion I do not fully agree. I admit the task is a hard one. Progress will be necessarily slow. But the negro is not incapable of learning. It is our methods that are at fault. In some of the schools in our county, thanks to Frances Kinney, they have individual drinking cups, and nice lunch baskets made with their own hands. In this respect they are more advanced than some of our white schools. The trouble with the negro is not so much his inability to learn as it is his carelessness and indifference in doing that which he is taught to do. . . .

. . . Improvement clubs, formed somewhat after the manner of the boys' corn clubs, and the girls' canning clubs, organized at every schoolhouse in the land, would offer a sane and practicable method of solving the problem, or at least greatly improving the present conditions. On account of the negro's gregarious proclivities it should not be difficult to secure a large attendance at these club meetings. Capable teachers, physicians, and social workers should be induced to help in this work. These clubs should be a kind of school for all ages. In addition to improved methods of farming, stock raising, poultry raising, etc., hygiene and sanitation should be taught at these meetings. Prizes might be offered for various things, as for the woman who has the cleanest house and yard. By teaching these people a few simple facts an inestimable amount of good might be accomplished. The women should be instructed in cooking, and the care of infants. The manner in which tuberculosis spreads from the sick to the well, and the approved methods of preventing the same, should be explained. They should be made to know that typhoid fever is an infectious disease, and instructed in methods of disinfection and cleanliness, and informed of the benefits of typhoid vaccination. They should be told how the mosquito spreads malaria, and instructed in methods of prevention. They should be told of sanitary privies, and that houseflies are as dangerous as mad dogs. They should be especially instructed concerning the two twin enemies of the negro race—gonorrhea and syphilis. Many other things will naturally suggest themselves to you. Let them understand that disease, for the most part, is under man's control.

Divest their minds of the vague superstitions which most of them harbor concerning the causation of disease, and make them understand that disease is caused from uncleanliness, alcohol, germs, bad habits and bad morals. The negro should be inspired to think more of himself, and to place a higher value upon his life. Call their attention to the remarkable old age which many of their ancestors reached, but to which few of the present generation can hope to attain. They should be taught the great value of sleep, which they do not seem to appreciate.

In conclusion, the health of any people is the foundation upon which their happiness and prosperity and usefulness rests. If the individuals of any race yearly diminish in stature and physical strength, that race is doomed.

The negro race in America is deteriorating, and at a rapid rate. The death-rate among them from filth diseases is alarming. The race is headed toward destruction. Unless something is done to arrest the spread of disease among them the race will go as the American Indian went within a few generations.

7. The Modern Health Crusade Mobilizes Children for Health Reform, 1918

Ultimately measured, victory depends no more on the gains of the battlefield than on the quality of the men and women who carry on the work of the country after the war. The quality of these workers of to-morrow depends on the health of the children of to-day.

The Modern Health Crusade, an organized movement that has enlisted more than 700,000 American children, is adding strength to coming workers and protecting them from the increased disease and neglect which the war has brought to the children of Europe. It is a system of health education that grips the child's interest until health practices become habitual. Through children, it is educating parents and promoting community health.

The Modern Health Crusade supplies the child with a motive for patient work in acquiring health habits when the abstract advantages of health and the usual teaching of physiology do not call the child to action. "Material is educational just in so far as it creates an interest." With adults the *direct* motive for faithful observance of the laws of health is usually insufficient until sickness creates a desire for health through its absence. With children it is all the more essential to supply an *indirect* motive. The Crusade accomplished this by introducing the play element into the study and practice of hygiene. It transfers some of the romance of the medieval crusades to a vital quest of present-day children. It holds up to them the chivalry of health, the high ideals of strength, right living and the protection of the weak. It makes an instant appeal to the child through its titles and badges as well as by giving him something to do and honors to earn; but, throughout, it adheres to the laws of habit-formation. It applies the approved pedagogical principle of learning health habits by doing them.

The results of the Modern Health Crusade are physical improvement and prevention of disease among children and their families, moral discipline through

Modern Health Crusaders Manual (New York: National Tuberculosis Association, 1918), pp. 1–2, 7–8.

regular attendance to hygienic duties, and the awakening of community responsibility. Reports like the following are common:

> The father and mother and other children in the family (in a New York State city) also kept the crusaders' rules. The health of the entire family improved and the work continues.

> One teacher in a rural community (Indiana) states that the Crusade has affected the entire population, parents being every bit as enthusiastic as the children. It looks as if before the school year is over we will accomplish several important changes in public health conditions here.

> The teachers in charge (in Idaho) are all delighted with the work and do not hesitate to say that colds and usual epidemics are lacking where the health chores have been kept up.

The Modern Health Crusade is in essence a movement rather than an independent organization. While this manual indicates the method by which clubs of crusaders may be formed without reference to the schools or other established groups of children, the Crusade is carried on largely by schools and other organizations as a phase of their work. A prime objective of the Crusade, already carried out in many schools, is to establish its practical system of teaching hygiene in the elementary schools of the country and to render obsolete the question, "What shall it profit a child to gain the whole curriculum and lose his own health?" The Modern Health Crusade was founded by the National Tuberculosis Association, but the Crusade as well as the Association is not limited to tuberculosis. It relates broadly to the up-building of health.

Modern Health Crusaders are children between 6 and 16 years of age who qualify by doing the official health chores and by agreeing to the pledge printed on the certificate of enrolment and who receive this certificate from organizations or adult workers promoting the Crusade.

The certificate of enrolment covers membership for the balance of the year in which it is issued and through the ensuing year. It states that the boy or girl named "has agreed to *try* (1) to keep the Crusaders' health rules until the end of 1919; (2) to do nothing that may hurt the health of any other person; (3) to help keep home and town clean; has done at least 75% of the Crusaders' health chores for each of two weeks; and therefore is enrolled as a Modern Health Crusader through 1919." The 1918–1919 certificate carries, in reduced size, the illustrated "Daily Health Guide for Boys and Girls" of the National Tuberculosis Association, and is desirable for posting on the wall at home.

The health rules, printed on the back of the certificate, are:

1. Keep windows open or stay outdoors when you sleep, play, work or study. Breathe *fresh* air always and through your nose. Take ten *deep* breaths every day.

2. Eat wholesome food, including fruit and vegetables, and chew it thoroughly. Avoid greasy fried food, soggy breads, heavy pie and cake. Eat little candy; none that is impure. Drink plenty of pure water and use your own cup. Drink no tea nor coffee. Never take beer, wine or other alcoholic drinks or soft drinks containing injurious drugs. Do not smoke or use tobacco in any form.

3. Make sure that everything that you put in your mouth is clean. Wash your hands always before eating or handling food. Wash your ears and neck as well as your face and clean your finger-nails every day. Bathe your whole body twice a week at

least and shampoo often. Brush your teeth thoroughly twice every day, after breakfast and supper. Have all cavities in your teeth filled. Consult a dentist twice a year.

4. Play and exercise every day in the open air. Sit and stand up straight. Have a *regular* time every day for attending to toilet and each need of your body. Whenever you cough or sneeze, turn your head aside and cover your mouth with your handkerchief. If you must spit, spit only where it will be removed before person or fly can touch it. Have a complete medical examination each year.

5. Get a long night's sleep. Get up smiling. Keep your clothes neat. Brush your shoes before going to school. Keep your mind clean and cheerful. Be helpful to others.

. . . It is recommended that every Modern Health Crusade club hold a meeting every month following the list of subjects given herewith. Clubs in schools should have their meetings usually during school hours, but evening entertainments to which the public is invited are desirable occasionally. Ordinarily meetings should be held between the first and the tenth of the month.

SCHEDULE OF MEETINGS

January—Home and school gymnastics. Folk dances. Organized play in winter.

February—Fake cures and real medicine. Fresh air, wholesome food, exercise, rest. Methods of outdoor sleeping.

March—Nervous system. Influence of mind on health. Cheerfulness, anger, courage, purity.

April—Fly, mosquito and vermin campaigns. Clean-up work.

May—What and how to eat and drink. Regularity. Weight. Food protection. Clean hands. Typhoid fever.

June—Temperance. Alcohol, tobacco, injurious soft drinks.

July—Patriotism of health. Marching or military drills. Care of feet.

August—Outing or picnic. Field athletics and organized play.

September—First aid to the injured. Posture.

October—Care of teeth. Tooth-brush drill. Care of nose and throat.

November—Care of eyes, ears, skin and scalp. Baths.

December—Tuberculosis and respiratory diseases. How to prevent colds. Red Cross Christmas Seals. . . .

Every one of these twelve meetings can be made intensely interesting. A doctor, dentist, nurse, physical director, or scout master should be invited to give a talk and demonstration. . . .

Fifteen interesting health playlets designed primarily for children are published by the National Tuberculosis Association and sold for 1c. each. "The Play's the Thing," a circular summarizing their stories and telling how to use them, will be mailed free on request.

Where a motion-picture machine can be had, a club may make its meeting a popular success by showing one of the films to be rented from the National Association at 50c. a day. Particulars will be furnished on application.

8. Popular Health Magazine *Hygeia* Depicts the Germ as a Stereotyped Dangerous Alien Criminal, 1923

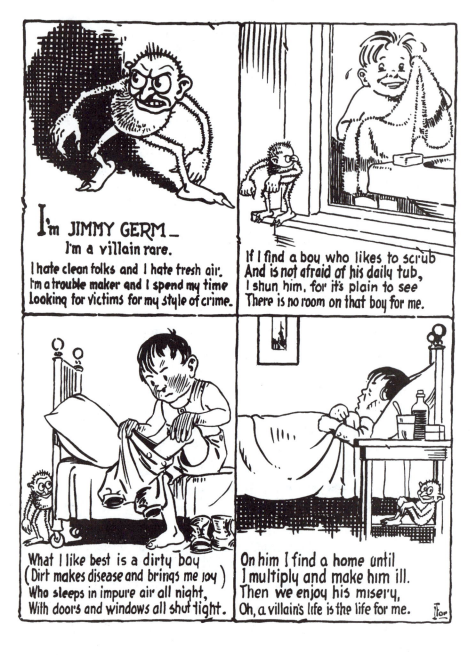

ESSAYS

In the first essay Nancy J. Tomes, a historian at the State University of New York at Stony Brook, explores the crusade against tuberculosis between the announcement in 1882 that the tubercle bacillus was the causative agent of tuberculosis and the 1910s, which saw a public health education campaign unprecedented in its scope and intensity. Tomes conveys a vivid sense of the texture of the mass health campaigns that became a prominent feature of American life and underscores how a wide range of personal habits were moralized in the public health campaigns that sought to change the every-day behavior of Americans. In the second essay, historian Alan M. Kraut of American University explores the Progressive Era apprehension that the new immigrants (Italians, eastern European Jews, and Chinese) threatened the health of the nation. Focusing on the medical inspection of immigrants at Ellis Island, he shows how the new science of bacteriology together with nativist ideology informed both national policies and the practice of Public Health Service physicians designed to safeguard American purity. In the final essay, medical historian Guenter B. Risse of the University of California at San Francisco uses the case study of the 1900 outbreak of bubonic plague in San Francisco, which initially occurred exclusively among the Chinese, as a way of exploring how germ theory did and did not alter patterns of expectation and regulation in which understandings of disease risk and danger were predicated on assumptions about race. He places the actions of public health officials and of the residents of San Francisco's Chinatown in a larger global context (the worldwide plague pandemic), inviting wider attention to medicine, public health, and turn-of-the-century American imperialism.

Germ Theory, Public Health Education, and the Moralization of Behavior in the Antituberculosis Crusade

NANCY TOMES

The germ theory of disease, which gained widespread acceptance after 1880, inspired mass health education crusades that intensified popular concerns about the contagious properties of the body and its by-products. Hygienic infractions once regarded as merely disgusting or ill-bred, such as indiscriminate spitting or coughing, now became defined as serious threats to the public health.

Nowhere was this intensification of concern about personal hygiene more evident than in the campaigns to prevent the spread of tuberculosis, the single most deadly disease of the period. The scientific revelation in 1882 that consumption, long thought to be a hereditary illness, was in fact caused by the tubercle bacillus prompted a great public health crusade to reshape the individual habits and social conditions thought accountable for its ravages. Until the discovery of effective drug treatments for the disease in the 1940s, prevention remained the central strategy of TB control.

In 1892 Lawrence Flick, who himself suffered from consumption, organized the first antituberculosis society in the United States: the Pennsylvania Society for the Prevention of Tuberculosis. By 1916 more than thirteen hundred local and state groups were conducting aggressive propaganda campaigns under the direction of the National Tuberculosis Association, founded in 1904. Municipal and state public health departments also made TB prevention a top priority of educational work. Together the private and public sectors of the antituberculosis movement mounted what constituted the first mass health education campaign in U.S. history. Through countless lectures, exhibits, posters, films, and pamphlets, millions of Americans from all walks of life were exposed to the same hygienic message: TB was a deadly communicable disease that had to be contained by hygienic measures such as spitting and coughing in a careful fashion, using individual drinking cups and dishes, and breathing fresh, clean air.

Because of its unprecedented scope and intensity, the turn-of-the-century crusade against TB had a profound impact on what might be termed public health morality, that is, the responsibilities that ordinary people assumed to guard themselves and others against infection. Extremes of dirt and disorder had long been associated with the risk of contagious disease, but the hygienic transgressions identified by this new crusade were far more commonplace and subtle: acts as seemingly inconsequential as coughing without covering the mouth, sharing a drinking cup, or dusting the house incorrectly could endanger otherwise clean-living individuals. Invoking laboratory evidence about how TB spread, public health authorities used categorical statements about "good" and "bad," responsible and irresponsible behavior to promote the observance of exacting hygienic rituals.

The antituberculosis movement offers a revealing case study of the impact that a changing scientific theory, in this instance the reconceptualization of consumption as a germ disease, can have on the moral significance of health-related conduct. TB is particularly instructive in this regard because unlike other highly visible diseases of the period, such as typhoid and cholera, its identity as an infectious disease was not well established prior to Robert Koch's discovery of the tubercle bacillus in 1882. Moreover, the bacteriological investigation of TB focused attention on commonplace behaviors, from spitting and sneezing to sharing drinking cups and tolerating flies, that had not previously been linked to the spread of deadly disease. In other words, the newly moralized behaviors associated with TB prevention reflected a significant dependance on experimentally derived hygienic truths. . . .

These historical reflections on the antituberculosis campaign and its conceptions of public health morality are particularly timely, given the new concerns raised by what the media have christened "superbugs." Not only has the AIDS epidemic shattered the complacency about infectious diseases that developed after the antibiotic revolution of the mid-twentieth century, but also after years of decline, tuberculosis rates have begun to rise again in recent years. Health officials and the public generally are concerned once again about the potential risks of infection posed by certain personal behaviors. As I hope to demonstrate, the history of the early-twentieth-century antituberculosis campaigns provides insight into both the contagion beliefs and the moral expectations Americans bring to the contemporary resurgence of anxiety about infectious disease. . . .

Early explications of the germ theory of disease built upon and reinforced the tendency, already apparent in sanitary thinking, to highlight the role of the human body as a polluter. Whether conceived of as an organic poison or as living germs, invisible particles of contagion had awesome power to multiply in the human body and its immediate environment, according to the late-nineteenth-century disease theory. Sanitarians and germ theory advocates alike stressed that under the right conditions, a single sick individual could start an epidemic. Thus, it was all the more essential that the public be educated about its responsibilities for disease prevention.

To this end, public health reformers promoted a new code of personal and domestic hygiene designed to control the disposal of dangerous human wastes, particularly fecal matter. In the 1870s and 1880s they conducted a vigorous campaign to get middle-class urbanites to open their homes to sunlight and fresh air, which were considered natural disinfectants; to install special plumbing to prevent dangerous "sewer gases" from polluting the household air; to isolate the sick and disinfect their bodily wastes, particularly fecal discharges; and to keep their homes and yards free of decaying organic matter.

Beginning in the late 1860s and 1870s, a small group of scientists, chief among them the French chemist Louis Pasteur, began to argue for a different explanation for why such hygienic measures worked to ward off contagion. Employing a new type of evidence, based on microscopic examination and laboratory experimentation, advocates of the so-called germ theory of disease posited that the real agents of infection were different species of living microorganisms, which entered the body through the nose, mouth, and skin. These living microorganisms spread from the sick to the well by means of the former's germ-laden discharges, either by direct personal contact or by diffusion into the air and water.

Throughout the 1870s and 1880s the medical profession in Europe and the United States debated the validity of this new explanation for contagion. Accustomed to thinking of disease as the product of complex environmental and individual factors, many physicians found the new emphasis on bacteria to be too simplistic. But gradually, improved laboratory methods, including pure cultures, staining methods, and rigorous animal experiments, overcame objections to the germ theory. Moreover, its advocates were quick to emphasize that it supported the preventive measures adopted by the previous generation of sanitarians. For all their differences over etiological explanations, both sides in the controversy agreed that individual and civic cleanliness were the best means to contain the threat of contagion. . . .

Addressing the Warren, Pennsylvania, Academy of Sciences in 1909 on the subject of "Preventive Measures Against Tuberculosis," Dr. M. V. Ball said [that] ". . . [t]he antituberculosis campaign has in it much of the fervor of a new religion." This fervor was explicitly grounded in the popular veneration of science so common among Progressive Era reformers. They believed that the scientific method, as they variously construed it, would produce an ever more accurate understanding of why diseases occurred; through popular education, the public would be shown the "light" and thereby be freed from disease and death. Pasteur, Koch, and [Edward] Trudeau [founder of the famous sanitarium in Saranac Lake, New York] were often invoked as modern-day saints whose courage and scientific skill had finally exposed the infective nature of the deadly white plague. Playing up the heroic dimension, a postcard designed to advertise the 1909 International Tuberculosis Exhibition in Philadelphia bore the legend "The two emancipators: Lincoln wiped out slavery. Science can wipe out consumption."

Although science was certainly their touchstone, TB workers invoked religious language and symbols in their hygienic exhortations as well. The recurrent use of terms such as *salvation, gospel,* and *crusade* along with the symbol of the double-barred cross imbued their work with a sense of spiritual mission. TB pamphlets were often referred to as "tracts" or "catechisms," and the rules of health they contained were called "commandments." . . . The National Tuberculosis Association's (NTA) Modern Health Crusade, an innovative child health education program begun in the 1910s, enlisted the young in a quasi-holy war against TB, reminiscent of the role nineteenth-century evangelicals accorded the "redemptive child." Observing the parallel with the medieval Christians' crusades against the infidels, one young crusader observed in her prize-winning essay, now "the germs are the Turks." . . .

Tuberculosis "religion" required rigorous adherence to a set of stringent rules designed to contain the dangers of contagion. This hygienic code envisioned the infective human body at the center of a series of concentric circles, moving outward from the individual body to the house to the public spaces of streets and buildings. Each circle of contagion posed its own special dangers and required its own special hygienic precautions. The TB workers' conception of these circles incorporated older sanitation mappings of the body's dangerous attributes. Prior to the 1890s, the main focus of hygienic precautions against infection had been the breath, feces, vomit, and skin particles of the sick, bodily by-products that had been implicated by long clinical and epidemiological experience with eruptive fevers such as smallpox and "filth diseases" such as cholera and typhoid. TB prevention reformulated older fears of the infectious breath into more specific concerns with the saliva, sputum, and droplets expelled by coughing and sneezing, which had not been so closely linked with lethal disease. In other words, the bacteriological investigation of tuberculosis intensified the dangers associated with discharges from the mouth and nose.

Spit was by far the most lethal new element added to late-nineteenth-century conceptions of bodily contagion. Etiquette and health authorities had long condemned spitting, especially of tobacco juice, as a breach of manners and general cleanliness. But prior to the 1880s, they had portrayed the negative moral and health consequences of spitting as limited to the transgressor himself; spitting was not condemned as a mode of spreading diseases to others. Only after microscopic investigation located the tubercle bacillus in the consumptive's sputum did the spitting habit become defined as a serious menace to the public health. . . .

These beliefs about the infective properties of the consumptives' bodily discharges, particularly their spit, led logically to an emphasis on the home as a source of disease. In frequently styling TB as a "house disease," Progressive reformers adopted and adapted older sanitarian preoccupations with home hygiene. The same zones of danger outlined in domestic manuals of the 1870s and 1880s, such as damp cellars, unaired bedrooms, and upholstered furniture, persisted in TB pamphlets for decades later. . . .

Although antituberculosis reformers saw the home as the primary site of infection, they also emphasized how contagion lurked in the outside world as well. Any public space or social interaction where human bodies and their by-products mingled represented a potential site for spreading the disease. Anxiety about preventing TB led to changes in the conduct of diverse institutions, including hotels, funeral parlors, commercial laundries, and public schools. For example, occupying a steamship cabin, a Pullman berth, or a hotel room involved the risk of inhabiting a space previously contaminated by a consumptive. Thus, the owners of such establishments had to take pains to assure clients that the room and its contents had been thoroughly cleaned and disinfected. To avoid the dangers of contaminated blankets, the *Pennsylvania Health Bulletin* advised in 1910, "The careful traveller will . . . insist that the blanket be covered by a fresh clean sheet the turn down of which shall cover it for a distance of two feet from the top," a custom that persists in many hotels to this day.

The fact that TB sufferers were often able to maintain a normal routine until their disease was far advanced made such vigilance especially important. Unlike cholera or smallpox victims, consumptives could move freely in society and spread the seeds of disease for many years. In an 1888 talk entitled "The Hygiene of Phthisis," Lawrence Flick conjured up a chilling vision of "consumptive tailors and dressmakers, consumptive cooks and waiters, consumptive candy-makers, consumptive bakers, consumptives indeed in every calling of life. These people do not suspect for a moment that they are spreading the disease, and take no precaution against doing so."

The dangers of contagion were all the more insidious because of the invisible, insensible nature of germs. Unlike the older, more straightforward concept of "filth," which usually announced itself by foul odor and squalid appearance, the menace of bacterial enemies was far harder to detect. Antituberculosis writings constantly repeated the warnings that things were not as they seemed, conjuring up images of the quaint wooden dipper laden with deadly germs or the seemingly healthy-looking dairy cows infected with bovine tuberculosis. . . .

The pedagogical techniques used by TB workers were morally heavy-handed, to say the least. They devised endless lists of "dos and don'ts," covering a multitude of behaviors: there were "right" and "wrong" ways to mop the floor, blow one's nose, prepare a baby's bottle, and set a table. Health exhibits specialized in "good" and "bad" rooms that laid out the proper floor coverings, drapes, and furniture styles to combat the scourge of the tubercle bacillus. The tone of admonitions was fierce, brooking no deviation: "It should be an absolute rule," intoned one author, "never to put a baby or a young child on the floor to play, as is so generally the custom." The extraordinary range of behaviors identified as potentially dangerous, from licking stamps to handling paper money, reinforced the message that even the tiniest infraction could lead to death. . . .

The moral framework for explaining why some people caught tuberculosis and others did not clearly emphasized individual responsibility: each person had an impelling duty to attend to public health directives and to practice protective rituals against consumption. But this emphasis on individual responsibility did not preclude more collective conceptualizations of health morality in the war against the white plague. The tuberculosis movement constantly acknowledged the interconnectedness of health behavior: imprudent behavior endangered not only the individual but those around him as well. Given the mobility and vitality of tuberculosis germs, there could be no simple dividing line between the potentially contagious self and the rest of society.

As in its conceptions of individual responsibility, the tuberculosis movement built upon older hygienic conventions of public health morality. Both in the older sanitarian tradition and the early formulations of the germ theory, nineteenth-century hygiene writers constantly emphasized how a better scientific understanding of contagion transformed and broadened one's civic responsibilities to prevent disease. As Harriette Plunkett wrote in her quaintly titled treatise *Women, Doctors, and Plumbers,* a neighbor was no longer just the man who lived next door, "but he also is the man whose premises the breeze may sweep, and bear its particles to our lungs and blood, at whatever distance, or at whichever point of the compas [*sic*] he abides." Germs were no respecters of persons, she concluded, and would fasten on a man "whether he be a millionaire or a shillingaire, with a perfectly leveling and democratic impartiality."

Progressive Era public health reformers repeated and elaborated on this interdependency theme endlessly. A particularly fine explication of the argument appeared in an article provocatively entitled "The Microbe as a Social Leveller," written by New York City Health Commissioner Cyrus Edson. "The microbe of disease is no respecter of persons," he wrote; "it cannot be guarded against by any bank account, however large." Wealth might protect the individual by allowing him to be "well nourished, warmly clad, and properly housed." But in this day and age, Edson warned, the "Socialistic side" of the microbe required that the wealthy be concerned for the poor. . . .

The recognition of collective responsibility for tuberculosis impelled many activists to endorse a broader agenda of social reform. . . . The elimination of TB became a powerful justification for strengthening municipal boards of public health, regulating tenement housing, inspecting sanitary conditions in factories, and providing school health services.

While encouraging concern about "how the other half lived," the TB crusade also expressed the infinite variety of ethnic and racial prejudices that abounded at the turn of the century. From the 1880s on, statistics collected by public health boards made increasingly evident that poor, immigrant, and nonwhite Americans were more likely to contract the disease than their affluent, native-born, white peers. As did Progressive reformers in general, TB workers disagreed over whether individual behavior, hereditary defect, or environmental conditions were most to blame for these group differences in the incidence of TB. Their conception of collective moral responsibility for infectious disease reflected a fundamental tension between portraying the diseased "other" simultaneously as victim and menace. . . .

Discussions of the "Negro problem" in the South exemplify the varied causal hypotheses and moral judgments that TB workers could derive from the often repeated observation that "germs knew no color line." In explaining why African Americans suffered higher rates of tuberculosis, conservative whites emphasized their intellectual and moral inferiority, and pushed for special measures to segregate the "colored consumptive." In contrast, African-American reformers and their liberal white allies pointed to the same disease statistics as evidence of the race's heavy economic and social disadvantages. In cities such as Atlanta, black antituberculosis societies used white fears about the disease to press their case for improved educational and municipal services for minority neighborhoods. . . .

Although the TB crusade certainly appealed to common stereotypes of the "other" as dirty and dangerous, and the woman citizen as social housekeeper, its public rhetoric tended to emphasize the integrative, as opposed to factionalizing, mission of health education. Certainly, compared to contemporary efforts to prevent disease by immigration restriction and eugenics legislation, the antituberculosis movement chose a more inclusive strategy. Its stated goal was not to ostracize groups at high risk for the disease but, rather, to bring them within a protective circle of hygienic knowledge. In a society split by ethnic, class, and racial differences, the crusade portrayed the common fight against an invisible enemy—the tubercle bacillus—as a positive means of redefining what it meant to be an American.

No aspect of the movement better symbolized the reintegrative role assigned the new codes of public health morality than the many antituberculosis parades and pageants staged in the early twentieth century. These community rituals recast nineteenth-century parade forms, which had displayed the serried ranks of society by class and occupation, into an army of citizens marching against disease. Conducted with circus-style promotional flourishes, antituberculosis parades were often led by children, befitting their special role as "evangelists" of health reform, and included delegations and floats from local businesses, labor unions, women's clubs, and the YM and YWCAs, in other words, the whole panoply of Progressive Era reform groups. In these symbolic public health demonstrations, disease prevention furnished a seemingly uncontested good whose pursuit cut across painful lines of difference.

In the ideology of the TB movement, the "socialism of the microbe" undergirded a new democratic society in which good health, particularly freedom from TB, could be identified as the birthright of every citizen, regardless of gender, ethnicity, class, or race. In the context of the Progressive Era, the TB menace had a unifying as well as a fragmenting effect on a diverse society: the yardstick of health morality could be used to compare different groups and chart the path of their reclamation, both in personal and social terms.

At the same time, the recognition that TB was a germ disease undoubtedly contributed to a harsher condemnation of those who contracted the disease. Social problems such as poor housing or low wages proved far harder to correct than individual deficiencies in hygienic knowledge and control. . . .

The TB crusade reserved its harshest moral language for the so-called careless consumptives, that is, individuals who knew they had the disease and refused to abide by the necessary precautions concerning their germ-laden discharges. For all TB workers' criticism of irresponsible landlords and factory owners, when it came time to personify the causes of tuberculosis, they almost always chose the homes and the habits of the consumptives themselves. In the NTA's stock lantern-slide lecture for the public, the only human faces shown to whom blame could be readily attached were "ignorant" consumptive parents exposing their innocent children to the disease. . . .

Not surprisingly, the "careless" or "unteachable" consumptive was usually poor, uneducated, and foreign-born or nonwhite. As the public health nurse Ellen La Motte wrote, "The day laborer, the shop girl, the drunken negro belong to a class which, *by reason of the very conditions which constitute it a class,* is unable to make use of what it learns" (emphasis in original). . . .

That the public health movement eventually adopted a more restricted vision of its social mission in the 1920s did not reflect a moral narrowness inherent in the germ theory of TB. Rather, declining rates of infectious diseases, changing conceptions of disease control, and a more conservative political climate combined to dim the reformist zeal of the antituberculosis movement. Deaths from tuberculosis began to decrease in the late 1800s, for reasons that historians and demographers still hotly debate. Improved nutrition and housing, as well as greater efforts to isolate the ill, probably all played a role in its decline. By the late 1920s, cancer and heart disease had displaced TB as the leading causes of death. The anituberculosis societies broadened their scope to include prevention and research concerning lung diseases in general, including lung cancer. The National Tuberculosis Association renamed itself the American Lung Association in 1954.

Regardless of how much public health education actually contributed to the decline of tuberculosis, the turn-of-the-century crusades clearly transformed personal and household habits of disease avoidance. By the 1920s the antituberculosis movement had done a remarkable job of making Americans of all backgrounds feel responsible for preventing the spread of infection by attending to the minutiae of personal behavior. These contagion rules continued to be passed on from parent to child, teacher to student, long after TB ceased to be the leading cause of death; with surprisingly little modification, they inform what adults teach children about avoiding germs and staying well to this day. Most people still think in terms of using their own cups, avoiding others' sneezes, and keeping up their resistance as the best means to avoid contagion.

Physicians and the New Immigration During the Progressive Era

ALAN M. KRAUT

In a 1902 *North American Review* article, United States Commissioner General of Immigration Terence Powderly called for stricter health controls on arriving aliens. Powderly cautioned that unless "proper precautions" were taken to detect two contagious diseases—trachoma, an eye infection, and favus, a dermatological disease of the scalp—the future American might be "hairless and sightless." He called upon Americans to refuse to allow their country to become "the hospital of the nations of the earth."

Powderly's dramatic image of what uncontrolled immigration might do to the American population was published during a peak period of American immigration. Between 1880 and 1924, 23.5 million immigrants arrived in the United States, largely from countries in southern and eastern Europe, but also in smaller numbers from China, Japan, Mexico, and Canada. Powderly's somewhat alarmist call for public support of stricter admissions standards struck a sympathetic chord with the many Americans who already feared that along with the millions of arrivals from nonnorthern European countries, speaking a cacophony of tongues, there might come other, even less welcome newcomers. These unwelcome others were silent travelers, germs that could spread infectious disease among Americans and genes that could undermine the country's rugged, Anglo-Saxon and Teutonic, pioneering breed with inferior genetic traits.

Alan M. Kraut, "Silent Travelers: Germs, Genes and American Efficiency, 1890–1924," *Social Science History* 12: 4 (Winter 1988): 377–385, 387–389. Copyright © 1998, Social Science History Association. All rights reserved. Reprinted by permission of Duke University Press.

Powderly's apprehensions were familiar to nativists who advocated tighter immigration restrictions to exclude those whose religion, race, or political persuasion they abhorred. Progressive reformers, who saw immigration as part of modernization's challenge, often shared the nativists' enthusiasm for restriction as a solution. Sociologist E. A. Ross of the University of Wisconsin was among the most prolific writers calling for exclusion because "the blood now being injected into the veins of our people is 'subcommon.'" Still, a great many reformers thought continued immigration advantageous, provided that it could be rationally regulated by experts and efficiently administered by a well-trained, forthright government bureaucracy. To the progressive mind expertise and efficiency seemed closely aligned. According to historian Samuel Haber, who described progressives as the preachers of a "gospel of efficiency," the term meant "social harmony and leadership by the 'competent.'"

Unclear in the matter of immigration were the "proper precautions" to which Terence Powderly alluded, and who were the "competent" individuals responsible for taking those precautions. Powderly's concern about the spread of trachoma and favus implicitly raised some larger issues. To what extent was the potential public health threat posed by immigration a matter for federal authorities? And what should be the proper role of the federal physician, the government's health "expert," in deciding the fate of those "huddled masses" being inspected at American immigration depots even as Terence Powderly published his dire prediction?

Immigration depots, especially New York's Ellis Island, opened in 1892, became laboratories where Progressive reformers tested, and, at times, even developed the clinical and administrative weaponry with which they hoped to bar harmful genes and germs from the United States. In 1907, the peak year for immigration in the twentieth century, 1,285,000 immigrants entered the country, [of whom] 866,660 (67.4%) came through Ellis. Not without good reason, then, the island became the flagship of federal immigration policy. At Ellis Island, the Progressives' twin deities, science and bureaucratic efficiency, became the bulwark of the nation's defense of its physical health and social vitality. . . .

. . . The germ theory of infectious disease developed by Robert Koch in Germany and Louis Pasteur in France had been embraced by federal authorities, as it was by a slowly increasing number of Americans in the health professions, by the 1880s. As early as 1887, the federal government ordered the beginning of cholera studies in a single room on the ground floor of the marine hospital at Stapleton, Staten Island. Dr. Joseph Kinyoun was in charge. The fear that immigrants carried Asiatic cholera had led the federal government to initiate research on bacteria, a program of research that evolved into the National Institutes of Health.

As historian Daniel Fox and others have suggested, there was a growing tendency in the late nineteenth and early twentieth centuries for Americans to separate health policy from social policy. Earlier, general social policy included health. Promoting health and preventing illness seemed to require no more than alleviating poverty and economic deprivation. But before the turn of the century, medical science was demonstrating that bacteria caused infection and that germs did not always recognize class boundaries. Though vestiges of the older view sometimes surfaced, increasingly, American officials trusted to physicians and their expertise to assess the health of individual newcomers, rather than relying on blanket, antiquated generalizations which suggested that poor and degraded classes were the vessels of disease.

Health certification of new arrivals was by the physicians of the United States Marine Hospital Service, which was renamed the United States Public Health and Marine Hospital Service after 1902, and finally, the United States Public Health Service in 1912, hereinafter referred to as the PHS. Ships entering New York Harbor were first boarded by New York State health officers, who conducted cursory inspections for what had become known as the "germ diseases": typhus, cholera, plague, smallpox, and yellow fever. Next the PHS boarding division inspected passengers fortunate enough to afford first or second class passage in their cabins. Immigrants in third class and steerage were ferried to Ellis Island to be checked by PHS physicians and then questioned by Immigration Bureau officials.

Upon arrival on Ellis, the immigrants, clutching their hand luggage, climbed the stairs to Ellis' main hall, quite unaware that their examination had begun. A physician stationed at the top of the stairs scrutinized the newcomer under the condition of physical stress produced by carrying often heavy hand luggage up the flight of stairs. Hands, eyes, and throats were closely examined. The newcomer's heart could be judged strong or weak after the climb, and the exertion would reveal deformities and defective posture, possibly the result of an illness or genetic malformity. This observation by a physician was the first step of the line inspection, an orderly procedure developed by the PHS to efficiently inspect large numbers of immigrants with limited numbers of doctors. . . .

Still, PHS physicians on Ellis prided themselves on their bureaucratic efficiency and impartiality. Dr. Alfred C. Reed wrote that "in all the manifold and endless details that make up the immigration plant, there is system, silent, watchful, swift, efficient." At the start of the line inspection, PHS physicians, working in teams of two, gave each immigrant a stamped identification card to hold in his or her hand. The physicians then observed the newcomers as the immigrants examined the card, checking each one for defective eyesight. In 1898, the examination for trachoma was given only to those who exhibited symptoms. However, beginning in 1905, physicians on Ellis and at other depots everted all immigrants' eyelids. Because no specialized instrument yet existed, physicians used conveniently shaped button hooks more commonly used to assist ladies in fastening their long, fashionable gloves. The doctors sterilized their instrument with a quick dip of the hook into a solution between examinations or a wipe on a Lysol-impregnated towel. Another doctor probed immigrants' scalps for lice and favus. He then requested the immigrant to turn his head so that his facial expression could be examined. Certain expressions were believed by physicians to be indicative of mental and physical disorders.

All who failed to pass the medical exam were detained for a more thorough inspection. Sometimes a few days of rest and some nourishing food was sufficient to prepare an immigrant for reexamination. On other occasions, a short stay in the Ellis Island Hospital, opened in 1902, might be sufficient to allow recovery from a minor illness or injury.

The PHS's triage could provide little more than a "snap-shot" diagnosis at best. However, in an era when sophisticated diagnostic technology was still limited and personal observation was a highly regarded method of diagnosis, the PHS physicians on Ellis took great pride in their ability to spot illness or disability. . . .

PHS physicians did not stop to consider that their professional demeanor could be forbidding. Euterpe Dukakis from Greece recalls that when her family arrived in

1913, her father called Ellis Island the "Palace of Tears, or sighs." She and her sister especially did not like it when "the doctor stuck his finger in her [the sister's] eyelid and turned it up for a very bad disease [trachoma] that was very communicable and infectious, contagious." Fannie Kligerman was certain that her eyes were examined by a "soldier"; an understandable mistake since, on Ellis Island, PHS officers wore uniforms. Reaction was similar from the Asian immigrants who arrived in San Francisco Bay and carved their apprehensions into the stone walls of the Angel Island processing center:

> I cannot bear to describe the harsh treatment by the doctors.
> Being stabbed for blodd [sic] samples and examined for
>   hookworms was even more pitiful.
> After taking the medicine, I also drank liquid,
> Like a dumb person eating the *huanglian*.

. . . PHS physicians did not comprehend that the garb designed to elicit the respect from their Coast Guard patients could be so misconstrued by the newcomers. . . .

Perennially, the chief ground for rejection was physical unfitness, trachoma being the most frequent of the loathsome contagious diseases that were grounds for exclusion. In fiscal 1911, a fairly typical year during the peak period of immigration, 749,642 aliens were examined upon arrival, of whom 16,910 were certified for physical or mental defects. Of these, 1,363 had loathsome or dangerous contagious diseases and 1,167 (85.6%) had trachoma. Yet, throughout the period and especially in the peak period from 1890 to 1924, those inspected and returned to their ports of origin because of poor health never exceeded 3% of new arrivals in any given year, and the average for the entire period was well below 1%. Clearly, the medical inspection at American immigration ports, including Ellis Island, did not markedly reduce immigration to the United States. What did change was the percentage of those debarred for medical reasons. From less than 2% in 1898, the percentage increased to 57% in 1913 and 69% by 1916.

. . . Recognizing the opportunity to shift the responsibility and onus for exclusion from policymakers to physicians, who could cite "objective" medical criteria as justification for immigration restriction, Congress passed a law in 1907 that gave physicians the option of stating on a medical certificate whether a particular illness or deformity might make a newcomer "likely to become a public charge." William Williams [Commissioner of Immigration of the Port of New York] was especially enthusiastic about this new opportunity. He saw in the new law a fresh mechanism for easing the administrative burden on the Boards of Special Inquiry that heard appeals from immigrants facing debarment.

What Williams had not counted on was the reluctance of PHS officials both on Ellis Island and in foreign ports to exceed their function as physicians making medical diagnoses and to involve themselves in the decision to debar particular immigrants. While Williams lamented that more medical certificates were not being issued by PHS physicians, laymen and physicians protested that these certificates called for a judgment that one critic characterized as "well beyond a professional medical opinion." Public Health Service doctors refused to be agents of exclusion.

. . . During World War I, the slower rate of immigration allowed PHS physicians in the laboratory of the Ellis Island hospital to conduct some medical research, using the newcomers as subjects. There was special interest in venereal disease. In June 1915 the Surgeon General reported that in addition to testing those actually suspected of having syphilis, Ellis Island physicians had done "about 1,000 Wasser-mann reactions" on persons in the line inspection. He further reported that studies of trachoma were made with "culture and smears" and that there had been "inocula-tions into animals." The report concluded with a request for another PHS officer in the laboratory because "there is not another place in the service where there is more opportunity for good research work from the laboratory side; and the expenditures involved would be very modest." Long before the vocabulary of patient rights en-tered the medical lexicon, immigrants processed on Ellis Island served haplessly as the subject[s] for psychological and physiological research. . . .

. . . On Ellis Island, each diagnosis constituted a negotiation between the bio-logical and the social. Ironically, even as PHS officers consciously refused to allow the agenda of immigration restrictionists to influence their medical assessments, the physicians were unconsciously swayed by their own ethnocentrism. Two such doctors, writing on trachoma, concluded that a perceived increase in the disease on Ellis was a direct result of the "change in the source of arriving immigrants and resulting differences in the character of the people."

But scrutinizing immigrants closely for specific diseases and debarring them accordingly was no mere matter of ethnocentricity. In a very real sense, PHS physi-cians navigated between their medical oath to minister unto the individual and their statutory responsibility to guard the health of the public at large. In steering between those two, often conflicting, charges, PHS officers made of Ellis Island an incubator for public health policy and a laboratory for scientific experimentation, a Progressive barricade against the germs and genes that Terence Powderly feared would leave Americans the blind, bald victims of immigration's silent travelers.

Bubonic Plague, Bacteriology, and Anti-Asian Racism in San Francisco, 1900

GUENTER B. RISSE

Early in the year 1900, an editorial in the *Journal of the American Medical Associa-tion* described the dangers posed by the relentless advance of bubonic plague towards the United States. In spite of high morbidity and mortality rates from the disease in China and India, the author sought once again to assure his readers that because of the "infinitely superior sanitary improvements of progressive civilization" in the West, a recrudescence of the pestilence would never again assume such dramatic characteristics as displayed during the Middle Ages. "There need be no fear of an introduction of the disease into the United States," the article concluded, "San Francisco, California, is already provided with the means to intercept infection."

This recurrent theme, already popular during the 1890s, was based in part on what the Surgeon General of the US Marine Hospital Service, Walter Wyman, and

---

Guenter B. Risse, "The Politics of Fear: Bubonic Plague in San Francisco, California, 1900," in *New Countries and Old Medicine,* ed. Linda Bryder and Derek A. Dow (Auckland, New Zealand: Pyramid Press, 1995), pp. 2–3, 5–9, 11–17. Copyright © 1995. Reprinted with permission.

others optimistically perceived as "the scientific advance of modern medicine." For Wyman, cause, method of propagation, and means to prevent the spread of plague were now "matters of scientific certainty." The small number of casualties among Westerners living in the notorious plague spots of Asia was mainly attributed to "European blood and stamina." The perceived superiority was not only considered genetic but equally environmental, a tribute to proper hygiene and nutrition. . . .

In the aftermath of the Spanish-American War [of 1898], the price for our new imperialism was heightened threats from a number of diseases, including cholera, yellow fever and plague. On 23 November 1899, given the imminent danger of plague transmission to American ports—two cases (introduced from Brazil) were discovered in New York—the President of the United States assigned twelve additional officers from the Marine Hospital Service to serve on US consulates abroad, gathering local epidemiological intelligence while also screening persons travelling to this country. Wyman, described in California papers as "the commander in chief of this new army who will save his country from the dreaded foe" of plague, had already forged what was described as "an impregnable chain of defenses": eleven national quarantine stations strategically located at some of the most important American ports.

However, such confidence-building rhetoric masked the reality of a divided and conflicted system of American public health much in evidence during the yellow fever epidemics afflicting the Gulf states during the previous two decades. Historically, the federal government had left public health functions to the states, and by further delegation to local authorities. A reluctant Congress enacted federal laws that continued to stress close co-operation with state and local governments and compliance with their regulations only when foreign and interstate trade seemed jeopardised. . . .

In spite of greater budget allocations by Congress to the Marine Hospital Service during the 1890s, the national quarantine station at Angel Island in San Francisco Bay remained a somewhat run-down complex of buildings. A new chief officer arrived on a cold foggy day in early June 1899: Joseph H. Kinyoun, considered one of the most prominent members of the service. Locals reassuringly interpreted the assignment as evidence of the President's and Surgeon-General Wyman's concern for their city in the face of an expected invasion by the plague. After all, Kinyoun was one of the new Pasteurians, having trained in Europe with the famous bacteriologists Koch and Roux. More recently, he had been the director of the service's prestigious hygienic laboratory in Washington, while also holding a professorship in bacteriology at Georgetown University. Little did San Franciscans know that Kinyoun's transfer had actually been the result of political intrigues in the nation's capital, engineered by no other than Wyman himself, who wanted to get rid of an independent-minded academic in favour of more pliable acolytes. . . .

[In] early January 1900, . . . [i]n spite of systematic screening and disinfection by federal quarantine authorities, bubonic plague came to the Hawaiian Islands; its victims were all Chinese. For some, the findings only confirmed the scientifically sanctioned view that the plague showed, as one San Francisco newspaper declared, "predilection for yellow meat." Just as in the slums of Hong Kong and Canton, filth and overcrowding seemed to create ideal conditions for the transmission of this disease. Following procedures previously employed by the Marine Hospital

Service for cholera, the Hawaiian Board of Health created a sanitary cordon around Honolulu's dilapidated Chinatown section, divided it into separate sections, and with the help of volunteers carried out a house-to-house inspection. Plague suspects and relatives of victims were forcibly removed to makeshift detention barracks erected outside the city. A few weeks later, during cleansing procedures that included burning down an infected building, Honolulu's Chinatown was accidentally set on fire and virtually destroyed, rendering 4,000 people homeless.

For more than a generation, San Francisco's own Chinatown had grown into the largest Asian settlement in North America, housing more than 25,000 people in a twelve square block area located in the heart of the city. For locals and tourists alike, it was an exotic window to the Orient on the North American continent, with its dark alleys, rooftop gardens, and colourful shops. Others, including local officials, considered it a filthy alien slum, populated with murderous gangs, where gambling, opium smoking, and prostitution flourished in spite of frequent efforts by local police officers who were rendered helpless in this maze of subterranean tunnels and rooftop hideaways. For decades, Chinatown was perceived as a menace to the public health of San Francisco, with health board members routinely calling, without success, for cleaning and vaccination campaigns in that district. Perceived as the eyesore of San Francisco, calls for razing Chinatown were periodically issued, and ignored, since most of the run-down properties belonged to wealthy, non-Asian San Franciscans living outside the district. In truth, Chinatown's commerce, tourist value, and easy money from drugs and prostitutes were important to the local economy.

Following the establishment of the early March quarantine, fearful Chinatown inhabitants immediately fled from the district, finding shelter in suburban laundries and vegetable gardens belonging to their relatives and friends. From the very outset, San Francisco's newspapers, commercial interests, and Chinese organisations vigorously opposed the notion that Chick Gin [a Chinese laborer found dead in a Chinatown cellar on 6 March] had died of bubonic plague. They also strongly condemned the inconveniences for local business brought on by the quarantine and the absence of Asian menial labour in the rest of the city. San Francisco's citizens, meanwhile, were reassured by their Democrat mayor, Mr Phelan, vowing that "scientific methods will be employed to protect the public health" during what would probably be just another temporary scare. . . .

. . . [I]n spite of concealments, three additional bodies of Chinese dwellers were discovered in Chinatown and bacteriologically diagnosed as having suffered from bubonic plague. Amid further local press claims that another "bubonic scare" was being manufactured, Hearst's *New York Journal* of 18 March—under the headline "Black Plague Creeps into America"—informed the entire nation that there was indeed plague in San Francisco. The sensationalised report used historical descriptions and iconography from the 1665 London plague to paint a dramatic picture of fear and panic. . . .

At this time there were deep divisions of opinion within the medical profession concerning the presence of bubonic plague in the city. The new bacteriology with its microscopic slides, germ cultures, and selective inoculations of experimental animals remained an alien world for most practitioners trained in an earlier age. They insisted that these procedures were at best ancillary to clinical information, and difficult to obtain given the fact that most plague victims in Chinatown were found dead. While clinicians had difficulties making a diagnosis of bubonic plague since the symptoms suggested many infectious diseases including venereal ones, bacteriologists argued amongst themselves about the morphological characteristics of the causative bacillus. To compound matters, the accepted epidemiology of plague still emphasised the primacy of human transmission through inhalation or ingestion of particles, thus linking the disease with notions of filth and dust, and thereby justifying public health approaches informed by miasmatic theory.

... [T]he state squared off against both the federal Marine Hospital Service and the local San Francisco Board of Health. The latter, encouraged by Wyman's offer of 20,000 doses of Haffkine vaccine, officially declared the existence of bubonic plague in the city to justify such an inoculation scheme without placing a new sanitary cordon around Chinatown, a decision that only produced a further exodus from the district. To monitor this new movement of people and to avoid a possible spread of plague across state lines, Kinyoun dispatched a number of his federal officers to California's borders with Nevada and Arizona, stationing them at railroad stations ready to inspect outbound travellers.

Almost immediately, the San Francisco health authorities encountered stiff resistance to the vaccination scheme from the inhabitants of Chinatown. Many were scared by rumours—supposedly spread by Caucasian physicians working in the district—that the Haffkine vaccine was experimental and highly toxic; others simply received death threats from highbinder gangs if they submitted to the procedure. Among the few who were initially vaccinated, severe reactions of pain, fever, and prostration only heightened the fear and opposition to the programme. In a telegram to the Chinese ambassador in Washington, the consul general strongly objected to the local vaccination scheme, indicating that Chinatown residents would rather return to their homeland before submitting to injections with the Haffkine serum. Aware of earlier resistances in India and China, Wyman suggested that Kinyoun "use tact and discretion" in promoting the voluntary vaccinations, as well as making sure that the vaccine was not exclusively administered to Asians.

Faced with the failure of the proposed vaccination campaign and convinced that he still had an obligation to stop plague suspects from leaving Chinatown and possibly bringing their infection to other parts of the country, Wyman now acted decisively. If local measures failed or were not available and the spread of infectious disease was imminent, the Quarantine Act of 1890 allowed for presidential orders and their implementation by the Marine Hospital Service. Thus, the Surgeon General sought and obtained authorisation from President McKinley to "forbid the sale or donation of transportation by common carriers to Asiatics or other races liable to the plague." Kinyoun was immediately notified that all Orientals without proper health certificates from the Marine Hospital Service could not purchase train or ship tickets, and that all means of transportation out of the state of California were to be henceforth monitored by federal agents placed at points of embarkation. ...

Within days, such blatant discrimination against Asians prompted a lawsuit in the US Circuit Court, filed on behalf of a Chinese merchant by the Six Companies. The defendants were Kinyoun and members of the San Francisco Board of Health. After a hearing, the presiding judge ruled in favour of the plaintiffs, indicating that the inoculation campaign was a clear violation of the equal protection clause of the

14th amendment of the US Constitution. In addition, Judge Morrow determined that "all public health measures, while lawful, are not totally immune to judicial scrutiny, and inasmuch as they impair personal liberties, totally arbitrary measures cannot be permitted to stand." . . .

At the federal level, Wyman's reaction to the ruling was simply to insist once more that the presidential order be applied to all persons, not just Asians, a critical shift in position. . . .

If San Francisco and California were destined to remain under a cloud of suspicion regarding the presence of bubonic plague, thereby hampering state business and inviting federal intervention, a smaller target had to be identified. Prodded by powerful railroad officials, San Francisco's commercial interests now shifted positions and pressured the local board of health and the Board of Supervisors to place a sanitary cordon around Chinatown. Not surprisingly, this time around the measure was also supported by the State Board of Health and state businesses increasingly concerned about embargoes against California goods. Without again expressly acknowledging the presence of bubonic plague, this move was designed to signal to the outside world that both the city and state were capable of containing within the perimeter of Chinatown whatever health problems existed in that despised slum.

For their part, the various San Francisco business associations promptly created a Citizens Relief Committee and pledged to raise by subscription $50,000 to carry out a comprehensive inspection and sanitation campaign within Chinatown. As part of this effort, the health board considered establishing detention centres outside the city for suspected plague victims and asked the federal government for space to house up to 7,000 persons. Amid complaints from the Chinese to the State Department that the quarantine was "without cause," and widespread fears of an evacuation of Chinatown as a preliminary step before razing the entire district, elements of the local press echoed the Honolulu experience in their continued attack on the designated culprit:

> In no city in the civilized world is there a slum more foul or more menacing than that which now threatens us with the Asiatic plague. The only way to get rid of that menace is to eradicate Chinatown from the city . . . clear the foul spot from San Francisco and give the debris to the flames.

From the start, Kinyoun and the Marine Hospital Service supported the municipal evacuation plan. To the federal government, this scheme, which had been implemented in other parts around the world, made perfect sense from a public health point of view. In fact, Kinyoun requested and was asked to assume control of the future detention camps at Angel Island and Mission Rock, and entrusted with the screening, cleansing and feeding of its inmates. The procedure would involve the transfer of "about five thousand coolies from the tenements by June 5"— Chinatown's "floating population." Once more, panic and fear gripped the inhabitants of that neighbourhood, now cast in their role as sacrificial lambs in the struggle between the various interested parties. Not surprisingly the Chinese immediately threatened to resist eviction from their homes by legal action and, if necessary, the force of arms. Indeed, on the appointed day, another legal suit, requesting an injunction against all quarantine measures, including the expected removal, was filed in the US District Court by the Chinese Six Companies which had hastily assembled a $40,000 fund for legal expenses. Again the shadow of events in Honolulu earlier that year cast a pall over the beleaguered population of Chinatown. Rumours of bribery offers to health officials, and threats of physical violence to anyone willing to be deported from Chinatown, circulated widely.

The legal proceedings once more exposed the differences of opinion among physicians concerning the presence of the plague in San Francisco, with affidavits from prominent medical men who emphatically rejected the diagnosis. Before a final verdict was reached, Governor Gage, in a turn-around, also testified on behalf of the plaintiffs. Seeking to further slant official opinion in favour of a plague-free San Francisco, he sent a telegram to the Secretary of State. To support his contention, Gage cited his own medical experts (including the presidents of three San Francisco medical colleges), as well as prominent local bankers and merchants. Shortly thereafter, the federal court handed down its decision in favour of the Chinese, declaring that the quarantine imposed by the local board of health was arbitrary and racially discriminatory. . . .

. . . The politics of fear had indeed done their deed. For the time being, the merchants' fears of a commercial embargo against California and San Francisco had been eased, and the Chinese fears of an eviction from their ethnic neighbourhood similarly relieved. . . .

Because the plague outbreak initially occurred exclusively among Chinese, it reinforced the long-standing and blatant sinophobia prevailing in California, including San Francisco. By establishing quarantines, carrying out inspections, and threatening resettlement, local officials tried to settle old scores with a stigmatised minority variously portrayed as alien and hostile to American values and laws. Under the circumstances, the fearful Chinese repeatedly tried to defend themselves, seeking protection through their commercial associations and in the federal courts. Not surprisingly, Chinatown inhabitants remained unfamiliar with modern Western disease constructions based on bacteriological criteria. Frightened by the prospects of harmful fumigations and vaccinations, they craftily concealed their sick and dead, smuggling them out to surrounding fishing villages around the San Francisco Bay and in the San Joaquin River delta. The postmortem dismemberments and cremations acceptable to Westerners, prevented the traditional custom of returning human remains to China for burial. It is very possible that the small number of official plague cases in 1900 were just the visible tip of a sizable underground epidemic claiming hundreds of victims as in Sydney, Rio de Janeiro, and Oporto. The ultimate goal, already expressed more than a decade previously, was to employ all sanitary regulations to disperse the Chinese population: "[T]he more rigidly this enforcement is insisted upon and carried out, the less endurable will existence be to the Chinese here, the less attractive will life be to them in California."

 F U R T H E R   R E A D I N G

Warwick Anderson, "Immunities of Empire: Race, Disease, and the New Tropical Medicine, 1900–1920," *Bulletin of the History of Medicine* 70 (1996): 94–118.

Barbara Bates, *Bargaining for Life: A Social History of Tuberculosis, 1876–1938* (1992).

Allan M. Brandt, *No Magic Bullet: A Social History of Venereal Disease in the United States Since 1880* (1985).

JoAnne Brown, "Crime, Commerce, and Contagionism: The Political Languages of Public Health and the Popularization of Germ Theory in the United States," in *Scientific Authority in Twentieth-Century America*, ed. Ronald G. Walters (1997), pp. 53–81.

James H. Cassedy, *Charles V. Chapin and the Public Health Movement* (1962).

Alfred W. Crosby, *America's Forgotten Pandemic: The Influenza of 1918* (1989).

Elizabeth W. Etheridge, *The Butterfly Caste: A Social History of Pellagra in the South* (1972).

John Ettling, *The Germ of Laziness: Rockefeller Philanthropy and Public Health in the New South* (1981).

Georgina D. Feldberg, *Disease and Class: Tuberculosis and the Shaping of Modern North American Society* (1995).

Victoria A. Harden, *Rocky Mountain Spotted Fever: History of a Twentieth-Century Disease* (1990).

Suellen Hoy, *Chasing Dirt: The American Pursuit of Cleanliness* (1995).

Alan M. Kraut, *Silent Travelers: Germs, Genes, and the "Immigrant Menace"* (1994).

Judith Walzer Leavitt, *The Healthiest City: Milwaukee and the Politics of Health Reform* (1982; 1996).

Judith Walzer Leavitt, *Typhoid Mary: Captive to the Public's Health* (1996).

Howard Markel, *Quarantine! East European Jewish Immigrants and the New York City Epidemics of 1892* (1997).

Martin V. Melosi, *Garbage in the Cities: Refuse, Reform, and the Environment, 1880–1980* (1981).

Katherine Ott, *Fevered Lives: Tuberculosis in American Culture Since 1870* (1996).

Martin S. Pernick, "The Ethics of Preventive Medicine: Thomas Edison's Tuberculosis Films: Mass Media and Health Propaganda," *Hastings Center Report* 8 (1978): 21–27.

Naomi Rogers, *Dirt and Disease: Polio Before FDR* (1992).

Naomi Rogers, "Germs with Legs: Flies, Disease, and the New Public Health," *Bulletin of the History of Medicine* 63 (1989): 599–617.

David Rosner, ed., *Hives of Sickness: Public Health and Epidemics in New York City* (1995).

Nancy J. Tomes, *The Gospel of Germs: Men, Women, and the Microbe in American Life* (1998).

Nancy J. Tomes, "American Attitudes Toward the Germ Theory of Disease: Phyllis Allen Richmond Revisited," *Journal of the History of Medicine* 52 (1997): 17–50.

Joan B. Trauner, "The Chinese as Medical Scapegoats in San Francisco, 1870–1905," *California History* 57 (1978): 70–87.

Strategies for Improving Medical Care: Institutions, Science, and Standardization, 1870–1940

At the end of the nineteenth century and the beginning of the twentieth, reformers brought together two powerful sets of issues—the shortcomings of the American medical education system and the need for new means of assuring a uniformly better quality of health care. This movement transformed the institutional structure of American medicine as scores of new programs and organizations were created and older ones were forced to adapt or disappear. To many reformers, the potential for rapid health care advances seemed unlimited in light of such recent laboratory breakthroughs as the identification of the tubercle bacillus (1882) and the development of salvarsan treatment for syphilis (1907). If products of the laboratory such as these could be incorporated into medical education and everyday practice, reasoned reformers such as Abraham Flexner, then the miracles of modern medical science would ensure a higher quality of health care. Hospitals, medical schools, and nursing schools were the institutions most immediately affected by this reform, but all facets of health care, even "alternative" practitioners and institutions in the most remote parts of the country, felt its impact. Changes essential to the reform movement—such as more stringent licensing laws, revised training guidelines, new qualifying exams, and accreditation requirements—ensured a broad effect.

Yet historical examinations of this movement make it clear that there was not a single cohesive reform group, but several groups that included a wide array of health professionals and laypersons. Among the doctors, nurses, educational reformers, and concerned citizens who were part of these groups, there was a shared core of values and reorganization techniques. The so-called Flexner report of 1910, which focused on medical education but was emulated by a variety of other reformers, epitomized these shared understandings. The report invoked the scientific method, the ideal of *efficient management, the standardization techniques of business, and at least the rhetoric of greater accountability to the public. Even with a set of shared beliefs, advocates of change often disagreed among themselves as they attempted to decide precisely what a healer needed to know in this age of "scientific medicine" and how best to implement these decisions. In addition, reformers met with some determined opponents and had varying degrees of success in their struggles. At its core this reform effort and the controversies it stimulated was a conflict over the control of resources—technologies, hospitals, and, ultimately, patients. Who won this conflict? Who lost? What were the consequences for future generations?*

The promised benefits of the new institutions and programs did not come without a cost. Recognizing that not all costs can be measured monetarily, does this sort of measurement require another kind of calculus more sensitive to such qualitative factors as denied opportunity and inequality of access? Did reformers succeed in creating a system of education and accreditation that served all potential students equally? If not, how did biases of race, class, and gender become integral parts of the new, scientifically oriented, research-based medical order? And was the medical system created out of this educational and professional reform movement able to provide America with the highest-quality health care?

 D O C U M E N T S

Document 1 is an excerpt from the controversial Flexner report, issued in 1910 by the Carnegie Foundation for the Advancement of Education. This classic piece of muck-raking investigation is written not by a physician but by a layman, educational expert Abraham Flexner. Using a yardstick derived from discussions with medical education reformers in the American Medical Association (AMA) and the American Association of Medical Colleges (AAMC) and embodied in the Johns Hopkins Medical School, Flexner wrote a scathing critique of the American system of training doctors. What makes his critique and model for the future of medical education so powerful? Document 2, written in 1917 by "college bred colored woman physician" Isabella Vandervall, makes it evident that the Flexnerian model disadvantaged some Americans.

Document 3, a 1918 report on the need for a clearly articulated set of national efficiency standards, prepared for the American College of Surgeons by its director, John G. Bowman, confirms the importance of the hospital in modern America. Motivated by a growing public concern with the variable quality of hospital care, and informed by the wider ideals of efficiency embodied in Taylorism (a popular business model that helped transform American industry), the American College campaigned for more effective self-policing by the medical profession. If the medical profession would use tools like the College of Surgeons' standards to police the practices of its members, reformers such as Bowman reasoned, "the proper care of patients" would be ensured. Using the same strategy of establishing a minimal set of standards that Flexner and Bowman employed, Josephine Goldmark examines the state of nursing and nursing education in Document 4. Her 1923 survey seconds the importance of the hospital in modern health care but, when juxtaposed with Bowman's and Flexner's reports, raises some troubling questions about the new order.

Document 5, a report commissioned by the Rockefeller Foundation's General Education Board in 1924 to survey the distribution of physicians in the United States, asks even more troubling questions about the consequences of reform. Prepared by social scientists Lewis Mayers and Leonard Harrison, the document provided the first comprehensive statistical data on where doctors practice medicine in America. Their study confirmed the widely held perception that rural communities were facing short-ages of physicians, in contrast to urban areas, which were experiencing an increase. These data, as Mayers and Harrison clearly recognize, sharpen the focus on a key question of the post-Flexnerian years: Was medical education reform lowering the quality of medical care by decreasing the supply of physicians?

1. Educational Reformer Abraham Flexner Writes a Muckraking Report on Medical Schools, 1910

The striking and significant facts which are here brought out are of enormous consequence not only to the medical practitioner, but to every citizen of the United States and Canada; for it is a singular fact that the organization of medical education in this country has hitherto been such as not only to commercialize the process of education itself, but also to obscure in the minds of the public any discrimination between the well trained physician and the physician who has had no adequate training whatsoever. As a rule, Americans, when they avail themselves of the services of a physician, make only the slightest inquiry as to what his previous training and preparation have been. One of the problems of the future is to educate the public itself to appreciate the fact that very seldom, under existing conditions, does a patient receive the best aid which it is possible to give him in the present state of medicine, and that this is due mainly to the fact that a vast army of men is admitted to the practice of medicine who are untrained in sciences fundamental to the profession and quite without a sufficient experience with disease. A right education of public opinion is one of the problems of future medical education.

  The significant facts revealed by this study are these:

  1. For twenty-five years past there has been an enormous over-production of un-educated and ill trained medical practitioners. This has been in absolute disregard of the public welfare and without any serious thought of the interests of the public. Taking the United States as a whole, physicians are four or five times as numerous in proportion to population as in older countries like Germany.

  2. Over-production of ill trained men is due in the main to the existence of a very large number of commercial schools, sustained in many cases by advertising methods through which a mass of unprepared youth is drawn out of industrial occupations into the study of medicine.

  3. Until recently the conduct of a medical school was a profitable business, for the methods of instruction were mainly didactic. As the need for laboratories has become more keenly felt, the expenses of an efficient medical school have been greatly increased. The inadequacy of many of these schools may be judged from the fact that nearly half of all our medical schools have incomes below $10,000, and these incomes determine the quality of instruction that they can and do offer.

  Colleges and universities have in large measure failed in the past twenty-five years to appreciate the great advance in medical education and the increased cost

Abraham Flexner, *Medical Education in the United States and Canada: A Report to the Carnegie Foundation for the Advancement of Teaching*, Bulletin #4 (New York: Carnegie Foundation, 1910), pp. x–xi, 20–22, 25–27, 159–161, 178–179, 180–181.

of teaching it along modern lines. Many universities desirous of apparent educational completeness have annexed medical schools without making themselves responsible either for the standards of the professional schools or for their support.

4. The existence of many of these unnecessary and inadequate medical schools has been defended by the argument that a poor medical school is justified in the interest of the poor boy. It is clear that the poor boy has no right to go into any profession for which he is not willing to obtain adequate preparation; but the facts set forth in this report make it evident that this argument is insincere, and that the excuse which has hitherto been put forward in the name of the poor boy is in reality an argument in behalf of the poor medical school.

5. A hospital under complete educational control is as necessary to a medical school as is a laboratory of chemistry or pathology. High grade teaching within a hospital introduces a most wholesome and beneficial influence into its routine. Trustees of hospitals, public and private, should therefore go to the limit of their authority in opening hospital wards to teaching, provided only that the universities secure sufficient funds on their side to employ as teachers men who are devoted to clinical science.

In view of these facts, progress for the future would seem to require a very much smaller number of medical schools, better equipped and better conducted than our schools now as a rule are; and the needs of the public would equally require that we have fewer physicians graduated each year, but that these should be better educated and better trained. . . .

. . . Society reaps at this moment but a small fraction of the advantage which current knowledge has the power to confer. That sick man is relatively rare for whom actually all is done that is at this day humanly feasible,—as feasible in the small hamlet as in the large city, in the public hospital as in the private sanatorium. We have indeed in America medical practitioners not inferior to the best elsewhere; but there is probably no other country in the world in which there is so great a distance and so fatal a difference between the best, the average, and the worst.

. . . The mastery of the resources of the profession in the modern sense is conditioned upon certain definite assumptions, touching the medical student's education and intelligence. Under the apprentice system, it was not necessary to establish any such general or uniform basis. The single student was in personal contact with his preceptor. If he were young or immature, the preceptor could wait upon his development, initiating him in simple matters as they arose, postponing more difficult ones to a more propitious season; meanwhile, there were always the horses to be curried and the saddle-bags to be replenished. In the end, if the boy proved incorrigibly dull, the perceptor might ignore him till a convenient excuse discontinued the relation. During the ascendancy of the didactic school, it was indeed essential to good results that lecturers and quizmasters should be able to gauge the general level of their huge classes; but this level might well be low, and in the common absence of conscientiousness usually fell far below the allowable minimum. In any event, the student's part was, parrot-like, to absorb. His medical education consisted largely in getting by heart a prearranged system of correspondences,—an array of symptoms so set off against a parallel array of doses that, if he noticed the one, he had only to write down the other: a coated tongue—a course of calomel; a shivery back—a round of quinine.

What the student did not readily apprehend could be drilled into him—towards examination time—by those who had themselves recently passed through the ordeal which he was now approaching; and an efficient apparatus that spared his senses and his intellect as entirely as the drillmaster spared his industry was readily accessible at temptingly low prices in the shape of "essentials" and "quiz-compends." Thus he got, and in places still gets, his materia medica, anatomy, obstetrics, and surgery. The medical schools accepted the situation with so little reluctance that these compends were—and occasionally still are—written by the professors and sold on the premises. Under such a régime anybody could, as [Harvard's] President Eliot remarked, "walk into a medical school from the street," and small wonder that of those who did walk in, many "could barely read and write." But with the advent of the laboratory, in which every student possesses a locker where his individual microscope, reagents, and other paraphernalia are stored for his personal use; with the advent of the small group bedside clinic, in which every student is responsible for a patient's history and for a trial diagnosis, suggested, confirmed, or modified by his own microscopical and chemical examination of blood, urine, sputum, and other tissues, the privileges of the medical school can no longer be open to casual strollers from the highway. It is necessary to install a doorkeeper who will, by critical scrutiny, ascertain the fitness of the applicant: a necessity suggested in the first place by consideration for the candidate, whose time and talents will serve him better in some other vocation, if he be unfit for this; and in the second, by consideration for a public entitled to protection from those whom the very boldness of modern medical strategy equips with instruments that, tremendously effective for good when rightly used, are all the more terrible for harm if ignorantly or incompetently employed.

A distinct issue is here presented. A medical school may, the law permitting, eschew clinics and laboratories, cling to the didactic type of instruction, and arrange its dates so as not to conflict with seedtime and harvest; or it may equip laboratories, develop a dispensary, and annex a hospital, pitching its entrance requirements on a basis in keeping with its opportunities and pretensions. But it cannot consistently open the latter type of school to the former type of student. It cannot provide laboratory and bedside instruction on the one hand, and admit crude, untrained boys on the other. The combination is at once illogical and futile. The funds of the school may indeed procure facilities; but the intelligence of the students can alone ensure their proper use. Nor can the dilemma be evaded by alleging that a small amount of laboratory instruction administered to an unprepared medical student makes a "practitioner," while the more thorough training of a competent man makes a "scientist." At the level at which under the most favorable circumstances the medical student gets his education, it is absurd to speak of an inherent conflict between science and practice. . . .

. . . Modern medicine cannot be formulated in quiz-compends; those who would employ it must trouble to understand it. Moreover, medicine is developing with beneficent rapidity along these same biological and chemical lines. Is our fresh young graduate of five and twenty to keep abreast of its progress? If so, he must, once more, understand; not otherwise can he adopt the new agents and new methods issuing at intervals from each of a dozen fertile laboratories; for rote has no future: it stops where it is. "There can be no doubt," said Huxley, "that the future of pathology and of therapeutics, and *therefore of practical medicine,* depends upon the extent to which those who occupy themselves with these subjects are trained in the methods and impregnated with the fundamental truths of biology." Now the medical sciences proper—anatomy, physiology, pathology, pharmacology—already crowd the two years of the curriculum that can be assigned to them; and in so doing, take for granted the more fundamental sciences—biology, physics, and chemistry—for which there is thus no adequate opportunity within the medical school proper. Only at the sacrifice of some essential part of the medical curriculum—and for every such sacrifice the future patients pay—can this curriculum be made to include the preliminary subjects upon which it presumes. . . .

. . . The preliminary requirement for entrance upon medical education must therefore be formulated in terms that establish a distinct relation, pedagogical and chronological, between the medical school and other educational agencies. . . .

So far we have spoken explicitly of the fundamental sciences only. They furnish, indeed, the essential instrumental basis of medical education. But the instrumental minimum can hardly serve as the permanent professional minimum. It is even instrumentally inadequate. The practitioner deals with facts of two categories. Chemistry, physics, biology enable him to apprehend one set; he needs a different apperceptive and appreciative apparatus to deal with other, more subtle elements. Specific preparation is in this direction much more difficult; one must rely for the requisite insight and sympathy on a varied and enlarging cultural experience. Such enlargement of the physician's horizon is otherwise important, for scientific progress has greatly modified his ethical responsibility. His relation was formerly to his patient—at most to his patient's family; and it was almost altogether remedial. The patient had something the matter with him; the doctor was called in to cure it. Payment of a fee ended the transaction. But the physician's function is fast becoming social and preventive, rather than individual and curative. Upon him society relies to ascertain, and through measures essentially educational to enforce, the conditions that prevent disease and make positively for physical and moral well-being. It goes without saying that this type of doctor is first of all an educated man.

How nearly our present resources—educational and economic—permit us to approach the standards above defined is at bottom a question of fact to be investigated presently. We have concluded that a two-year college training, in which the sciences are "featured," is the minimum basis upon which modern medicine can be successfully taught. If the requisite number of physicians cannot at one point or another be procured at that level, a temporary readjustment may be required; but such an expedient is to be regarded as a makeshift that asks of the sick a sacrifice that must not be required of them a moment longer than is necessary. Before accepting such a measure, however, it is exceedingly important not to confuse the basis on which society can actually get the number of doctors that it needs with basis on which our present number of medical schools can keep going. Much depends upon which end we start from.

The Medical Sects

In the reconstruction just sketched, no allusion has been made to medical sectarianism. We have considered the making of doctors and the increase of knowledge; allopathy, homeopathy, osteopathy, have cut no figure in the discussion. Is it essential that we should now conclude a treaty of peace, by which the reduced number of medical schools shall be so pro-rated as to recognize dissenters on an equitable basis?

The proposition raises at once the question as to whether in this era of scientific medicine, sectarian medicine is logically defensible; as to whether, while it exists, separate standards, fixed by the conditions under which it can survive, are justifiable. Prior to the placing of medicine on a scientific basis, sectarianism was, of course, inevitable. Every one started with some sort of preconceived notion; and from a logical point of view, one preconception is as good as another. Allopathy was just as sectarian as homeopathy. Indeed, homeopathy was the inevitable retort to allopathy. . . . But now that allopathy has surrendered to modern medicine, is not homeopathy borne on the same current into the same harbor? . . .

Modern medicine has . . . as little sympathy for allopathy as for homeopathy. It simply denies outright the relevancy or value of either doctrine. It wants not dogma, but facts. It countenances no presupposition that is not common to it with all the natural sciences, with all logical thinking. . . .

The ebbing vitality of homeopathic schools is a striking demonstration of the incompatibility of science and dogma. One may begin with science and work through the entire medical curriculum consistently, exposing everything to the same sort of test; or one may begin with a dogmatic assertion and resolutely refuse to entertain anything at variance with it. But one cannot do both. One cannot simultaneously assert science and dogma; one cannot travel half the road under the former banner, in the hope of taking up the latter, too, at the middle of the march. Science, once embraced, will conquer the whole. . . .

The Medical Education of Women

Medical education is now, in the United States and Canada, open to women upon practically the same terms as men. If all institutions do not receive women, so many do, that no woman desiring an education in medicine is under any disability in finding a school to which she may gain admittance. Her choice is free and varied. She will find schools of every grade accessible: the Johns Hopkins, if she has an academic degree; Cornell, if she has three-fourths of one; Rush and the state universities, if she prefers the combined six years' course; Toronto on the basis of a high school education; Meridian, Mississippi, if she has had no definable education at all.

Woman has so apparent a function in certain medical specialties and seemingly so assured a place in general medicine under some obvious limitations that the struggle for wider educational opportunities for the sex was predestined to an early success in medicine. It is singular to observe the use to which the victory has been put. . . .

Now that women are freely admitted to the medical profession, it is clear that they show a decreasing inclination to enter it. More schools in all sections are open to them; fewer attend and fewer graduate. True enough, medical schools generally have shrunk; but as the opportunities of women have increased, not decreased, and within a period during which entrance requirements have, so far as they are concerned, not materially altered, their enrolment should have augmented, if there is any strong demand for women physicians or any strong ungratified desire on the part of women to enter the profession. One or the other of these conditions is lacking,—perhaps both.

Whether it is either wise or necessary to endow separate medical schools for women is a problem on which the figures used throw light. In the first place, eighty per cent of women who have in the last six years studied medicine have attended coeducational institutions. None of the three women's medical colleges now existing can be sufficiently strengthened without an enormous outlay. The motives which elsewhere recommend separation of the sexes would appear to be without force, all possible allowance being made for the special and somewhat trying conditions involved. In the general need of more liberal support for medical schools, it would appear that large sums, as far as specially available for the medical education of women, would accomplish most if used to develop coeducational institutions, in which their benefits would be shared by men without loss to women students; but, it must be added, if separate medical schools and hospitals are not to be developed for women, interne privileges must be granted to women graduates on the same terms as to men.

The Medical Education of the Negro

The medical care of the negro race will never be wholly left to negro physicians. Nevertheless, if the negro can be brought to feel a sharp responsibility for the physical integrity of his people, the outlook for their mental and moral improvement will be distinctly brightened. The practice of the negro doctor will be limited to his own race, which in its turn will be cared for better by good negro physicians than by poor white ones. But the physical well-being of the negro is not only of moment to the negro himself. Ten million of them live in close contact with sixty million whites. Not only does the negro himself suffer from hookworm and tuberculosis; he communicates them to his white neighbors, precisely as the ignorant and unfortunate white contaminates him. Self-protection not less than humanity offers weighty counsel in this matter; self-interest seconds philanthropy. The negro must be educated not only for his sake, but for ours. He is, as far as human eye can see, a permanent factor in the nation. He has his rights and due and value as an individual; but he has, besides, the tremendous importance that belongs to a potential source of infection and contagion. . . .

. . . The negro needs good schools . . . to which the more promising of the race can be sent to receive a substantial education in which hygiene rather than surgery, for example, is strongly accentuated. If at the same time these men can be imbued with the missionary spirit so that they will look upon the diploma as a commission to serve their people humbly and devotedly, they may play an important part in the sanitation and civilization of the whole nation. Their duty calls them away from large cities to the village and the plantation, upon which light has hardly as yet begun to break.

Of the seven medical schools for negroes in the United States, five are at this moment in no position to make any contribution of value to the solution of the problem above pointed out. . . .

Meharry at Nashville and Howard at Washington are worth developing, and until considerably increased benefactions are available, effort will wisely concentrate upon them. . . .

The upbuilding of Howard and Meharry will profit the nation much more than the inadequate maintenance of a larger number of schools. They are, of course, unequal to the need and the opportunity; but nothing will be gained by way of satisfying the need or of rising to the opportunity through the survival of feeble, ill equipped institutions, quite regardless of the spirit which animates the promoters. The subventions of religious and philanthropic societies and of individuals can be made effective only if concentrated. They must become immensely greater before they can be safely dispersed.

2. Black Woman Physician Isabella Vandervall Laments the Racial and Gender Discrimination in the Program for Reforming Medical Education, 1917

For many years the colored woman physician has practiced and prospered; but now, in this twentieth century, this era when women in general are forging ahead, and the woman physician in particular is coming into great prominence, a huge stumbling block, one which seems almost unsurmountable, has suddenly been placed in the path of the colored woman physician. This stumbling block is a new law, the law of compulsory interneship, which requires the physician to have at least one year's service in a recognized hospital before being allowed to take the State licensing examinations.

One Monday afternoon the college from which I was graduated held a reception in honor of the opening of the new laboratories which have lately been acquired. As a member of the Alumnae Association an invitation was sent to me. With pleasure I planed [*sic*] the time to go. As I stepped off the "L" at the same old station my thought went back to the time when, not two years ago, I used to alight from the train at the same station every morning. I walked down the stairs and down the street, my spirit rising at every step as my mind flew back to my happy college days. At last I reached an old familiar corner which marked my near approach to the college buildings. Unconsciously my steps quickened, just as for four long under-graduate years they had quickened every morning in order that I might reach the college more quickly. I turned the corner and saw, across the street, a bevy of girls in cap and gown arranged in a long line in front of the college. At the foot of the line there were three girls holding a large American flag—three democratic American girls, students in a democratic American college, holding the banner of democratic America, the land of the free.

I went up the steps of the newly-acquired building, opened the door and went inside. At the foot of the stairway, which faced the entrance, stood a group of girl students, evidently the reception committee. One of them came hurriedly up to me as soon as I entered and said, "What do YOU want?" Imagine my feelings! My high spirits were suddenly dashed to the ground, my enthusiasm left me, my happiness and gladness in the prosperity of my Alma Mater left me. All that girl student could

Isabella Vandervall, M.D., "Some Problems of the Colored Woman Physician," *Woman's Medical Journal* 27 (1917): 156–158.

see was my dark face. She could not imagine that in the heart that lay beneath my dark skin was an interest in and a feeling for the college as great as hers; greater, perhaps, for I was a graduate and she was but an undergraduate; she could not know the deep feeling that comes over an alumna when she enters once again the doors of her Alma Mater. All that she saw in me was a dark speck, a foreign body in that gala assemblage, and her one thought was to oust me as soon as possible. So she gruffly asked me, "What do you want?" "What do you want?" in a tone which seemed to say "Get out!" And that is the greeting which meets the colored woman physician whenever and wherever she applies for what is freely granted to all white women physicians.

When white women first demanded hospital experience they met opposition, but opposition on account of sex. Soon that barrier was broken down, however, and the problem is now solved for the white woman physician. Last year, and also the year before, in 1915, when I graduated, I am told there were more hospital positions open to women than there were girls to fill them. They might have added one more person to their "list of women filling hospital positions"—women internes—but they would not add that one because she was colored.

Early in my senior year the news began to spread around that various States were gradually adding a year of service as internes as compulsory before license to practice would be granted. So the girls all busied themselves putting in their applications to various hospitals. In order not to be late with my application, I went, long before the Christmas holidays, to one of the members of our faculty, to whom the applications had to be made, and told her that I wished to put in my application as interne in our hospital—that is to say, the hospital attached to our college. Immediately, without thinking, this doctor said: "Oh, I wouldn't do that, Miss Vandervall," as much as to say, "What do you want in our hospital?"

"Why not?" I asked her.

"Not that I have any objection to you personally, Miss Vandervall," she said. And then she went on to say how, often in class when she told stories about an old colored man or an old colored woman or a negro or negroes, she had never thought of me as colored; she simply thought of me as one of the girls—in fact, she never thought about me as being colored—but now that I was applying for a position as interne the situation was different. The conference ended by her advising me not to apply, simply because I was colored. She could not doubt my ability; she could not doubt my fitness, for I was one of her own pupils. She knew I could stand the examinations, for I was then holding first place in my class, and had held it the year before, and also in my freshman year. But my skin was colored, a darker hue than that of the other girls, so she could not allow me to put in my application. Later on, in the same week, this doctor sent for me to come to her office. I went. She told me she had been thinking my case over, and that, after all, she thought it might be possible for her to do something for me. Anyway she had a plan by which she thought she could try me out. The plan was that I was to go into the hospital for the Christmas holidays as a substitute for one of the internes who was going to take a vacation at that time. She said that I would be observed very carefully during that week, and if there was any complaint from either nurses or patients, then the matter was to stand as it was—that I should not put in my application. But if, on the other hand, there were no complaints, she might consider my application. I spent the week in the hospital, then visited the doctor to ask her ultimate decision. She said she had received no complaints of any kind, but that every one considered it as a joke, and therefore it would be best for me not to put in my application. That ended my hope of getting an internship in my own hospital, so I turned my attention elsewhere.

Next I decided to try the Lincoln Hospital in New York City. I had been told that the Lincoln was a hospital which had been founded for colored people, so I thought certainly there could be no objection to me in that hospital. I knew the nurses were colored. This time I WROTE applying for the posotion [*sic*] as interne to the Lincoln Hospital, simply giving my name and stating the college from which I was about to graduate. A most favorable and gracious reply came back, saying that Lincoln Hospital had never had a woman interne, but that they would be glad to have one. The writer went on to ask me to call at his office at his convenience, as he could better explain then the work in the hospital and the scope of the hospital examination. When the doctor saw me and found that I was colored, he was astounded, and told me that he simply could not accept my application. I told him that I thought the Lincoln was a colored hospital, and therefore I did not see why he would not have a colored interne. He then told me that the Lincoln had very few colored patients— the majority were white—and that, although the nurses were colored, the physicians on the staff and the internes were white.

He proceeded to say the examination was in two parts—one written and the other practical—in which each applicant had to examine a patient under the supervision of a doctor of the staff. No one would know which was my paper, so there could be no discrimination as far as the written examination was concerned; but that when I went up to the practical examination, at which the doctors would see me, no matter how well I did, they would undoubtedly mark me so low in that part of the examination that the other part would count for naught, and in that way they would eliminate me. With that he dismissed me, and my second application was cast aside.

I next applied to the Laura Franklin Hospital, but there my former experiences were simply repeated. I had almost given up hope of securing an internship, when, one day, I saw a notice on the college bulletin board saying that the "Hospital for Women and Children in Syracuse, New York, wanted an interne." Here I thought was another chance. So I wrote, sent in my application, and was accepted without parley. A copy of the rules for internes was sent to me in a pleasant letter from the secretary, which told me when to present myself for duty. So to Syracuse I went with bag and baggage enough to last me for a year. I found the hospital; I found the superintendent. She asked me what I wantd. I told her I was Dr. Vandervall, the new interne. She simply stared and said not a word. Finally, when she came to her senses, she said to me: "You can't come here; we can't have you here! You are colored! You will have to go back." Go back! after making a trip of three hundred miles to accept a position which I had tried so hard to get! Give up so easily a position which had taken me so many months to find and secure? No, indeed, not I! So for three days I stayed in Syracuse, trotting hither and thither, seeing this authority and the other official. Everywhere I met the same answer: "No, we cannot have you. We do not doubt your ability, but you are colored, therefore we will not have you." They could not doubt my ability, they could not doubt my fitness, for they knew the college from which I came; they knew its reputation, and they knew the reputation of its graduates. That was why they sent there for internes, but when they got one they would not keep her because she was colored. So they sent me back home without any interneship. Luckily for me New York has not yet passed the law of compulsory interneship, and the law did not go into effect in New Jersey until 1916, so I can practice in New York and New Jersey.

The colored women who graduated last year (1916) and those who will graduate this year (1917) and in future years will not be so fortunate, for the law has gradually been adopted by many other States.

This makes the problem before the negroes a very serious one, for not only will those years—those valuable five to eight years—spent in the study of medicine be entirely wasted to the negro woman, but the negro people will be deprived of much needed medical attention. There are many communities in which the white physicians do not wish to attend colored patients; many hospitals object to the colored people; many negro women do not wish to be attended by male physicians, and do not wish to take their children, especially their girls, to one. Yet what are they going to do if they are to be denied women physicians of their own race? They must be treated, yet to whom can they turn?

So, my friends, you can see that this new law of compulsory interneship is far reaching in its effects. It affects not only those colored patients who feel that they have a right to have a woman doctor if they want one, and those ambitious colored women who aspire to join the ranks of the medical profession, but also it casts a serious reflection upon those white people—democratic and philanthropic Americans—who lavishly endow colleges and hospitals and allow colored girls to enter and finish their college course, and yet, when one steps forward to keep pace with her white sisters and to qualify before the State in order that she might do the same service for her colored sisters that the white woman does for hers, those patriotic Americans figuratively wave the stars and stripes in her face and literally say to her: "What do you want, you woman of the dark skin? Halt! You cannot advance any further! Retreat! You are colored! Retreat!" I ask, is this fair?

3. The American College of Surgeons Urges Standards for Hospital Efficiency and Physician Accountability, 1918

. . . As a people we are accustomed to hospital service; we look upon that service no longer as a luxury which we may buy, but rather as an inherent right. The humblest patient is entitled to the best of medical service. In the last twenty years especially this idea has taken hold of us. We regard the right to health today much as we regard the right to life.

It follows now that in so far as the right to health is a right of society, all hospitals in a broad sense are public service institutions. On the one hand, hospitals in which sound honest care is given patients may reasonably ask the confidence, good will, and support of their communities; on the other, all hospitals are accountable to the public for their degree of success. By general consent the time has come for an accounting on both sides of the equation. Such an accounting is inevitable. If the

John G. Bowman, "Standard of Efficiency of the First Hospital Survey of the College," *Bulletin of the American College of Surgeons* 3 (1918): 1–7.

initiative is not taken by the medical profession, it will be taken by the lay public; and this entire accounting is what we mean by hospital standardization. It is an analysis of the obligation of the public to support hospitals; and it is a practical accounting to the public of the business and scientific efficiency of hospitals. . . .

To come now to definite criteria upon which hospitals may be justly classified: The policy of the College in its first survey . . . is to define the few factors which are imperative in any hospital for the proper care of patients. . . .

1. Case Records

That the hospital keep in a systematic manner case records of its patients together with a convenient summary of each case; and that it utilize these records in analyses of its medical and surgical efficiency. . . .

. . . Case records, when properly kept, provide straightforward and truthful answers to these questions: What was the matter with the patient? What did the doctor do for him? What was the result? . . .

The usual purposes assigned for the keeping of case records are: first, their value in medical science; second, their value in the practical care of patients; and, third, their medico-legal value. And in addition to these purposes, the case records serve as an efficiency test in the care of patients which is most important in hospital standardization.

But, in detail, how do case records serve as an efficiency test? Obviously each hospital should undertake to care only for such cases as it is qualified by equipment and personnel to treat, unless the circumstances of its geographic situation or other reasons make it necessary that the hospital accept all cases which seek its aid. The integrity of the profession requires that each hospital should determine whether or not its cases are successfully treated and if not, why not; it requires that the staff by periodic review of its end-results determine the types of cases which, by equipment and training, it is qualified to treat and that, except under unusual circumstances, it limit its service to such cases. Case records provide the information for these reviews. They are not, therefore, merely a clerical procedure; they are the very index of the success of all clinical work in the hospital. . . .

. . . [Adequate case records] are in effect a pledge to the public for the integrity of all work done in the hospital. By earnest and constant attention to case records it often happens that an isolated and poorly equipped hospital makes up for its material deficiencies, first, because its staff is inspired always to its highest attainments; second, because by honest selection of its cases it will not undertake the treatment of cases for which it is not equipped. It follows, therefore, that such a hospital may be rated higher than a large hospital with modern equipment and scientific reputation.

2. Clinical Laboratories

That, as implied in the foregoing requirement concerning case records, the hospital provide either directly or indirectly the laboratory facilities which in the science of medicine are essential in the diagnoses and treatment of patients admitted for care under normal conditions.

While for economic reasons and expediency it is usually advisable that the clinical laboratories be owned and operated by the hospital, neither ownership nor control of the laboratories is essential. In many instances state, county, municipal, or private laboratories supplement to advantage the laboratory facilities of the hospital.

Because of the wide discrepancy in the range of diseases and illness treated by hospitals it is not feasible to stipulate minimum laboratory facilities. Efficient laboratory service is here emphasized rather than details of equipment. The laboratory requirement is, therefore, that the hospital have the constant use of clinical laboratory facilities adequate in the scientific diagnoses and treatment of its patients. . . .

3. Division of Fees

That the hospital trustees or governing authority in co-operation with the staff take action definitely to prohibit from all services of the hospital the practice of division of fees.

The evil of the division of fees is so widely recognized that emphasis of it here is not needed. The practice is prohibited by law in Kansas, Nebraska, Iowa, Minnesota, Wisconsin, Ohio, Alabama, West Virginia, Tennessee, and Colorado. Where it exists under any guise whatever, it is in reality the buying and selling of people who are ill. The consequences of the division of fees are, first, incompetent medical and surgical service; second, unnecessary surgical operations; and, third, the deadening of scientific incentive in the profession and the lowering of the whole profession of medicine into dishonesty. The fact is unchallenged that no intelligent community would tolerate this practice in its midst if the community were aware of the practice and of its significance. . . .

Neither the hospitals nor the College would ultimately be content with standardization which takes into account only the foregoing minimum standard. Having made a beginning of standardization and agreed upon a common meeting-ground, as stated in the foregoing pages, other important factors of hospital work call for attention. . . .

The Training of Internes.   The training of internes affects directly a comparatively small percentage of the hospitals. In a larger sense, however, it affects all hospitals and in fact all of the people of the continent, for it has to do, more than is generally realized, with the making of competent physicians and surgeons. Dr. Edward Martin, for instance, estimates that a doctor on graduation from medical school is only twenty per cent efficient as a practitioner of medicine, and that service as an interne under right conditions may provide nearly eighty per cent of the training of a doctor. . . .

The staff of each hospital where internes are engaged may well consider the following questions: Do internes receive training in the writing of case records? Do chiefs of departments give instruction to internes at the bedside of patients and throughout the procedure of each case as to the salient points of record keeping? Are internes under competent guidance trained in the clinical laboratory? Do they follow clinical cases to the laboratory? Do they receive systematic training in the making of postmortem examinations and in the preparation of sections of tissue from postmortems for microscopical examinations? Are they permitted to do independent major surgery or to take full charge of obstetrical cases in the first year of apprenticeship? Do the influences of the hospital make for high ideals of practice? Do they create the right start for a busy, happy, and useful professional career?

The Training of Nurses.   The training of nurses came into existence in hundreds of hospitals as a matter of expediency, and it is only in recent years that this subject has been given due consideration. The trained nurse is an indispensable aid in the care of patients. She is also a power in preventive medicine. In fairness now to the nurses themselves, and to the patients whom they are to serve, comes the question as to whether the three years required in the training school are really three years of educational training? Is a sound curriculum provided for the instruction of nurses? Is the teaching under competent supervision? Are pupil nurses sent out into families? If so, in what year? Are pupil nurses placed on special cases in the hospital? If so, in what year? Are fees received by the hospital for special duty of pupil nurses? Is the practice medically and educationally justified? The training of the nurse should be given the same thoughtful attention as that given to the interne.

Postmortem Examinations.   The keeping of case records implies that postmortem examinations are made whenever consent for such examinations can be obtained. The value of these examinations is here specially emphasized. The postmortem is a merciless criticism of the work of physicians and of surgeons. It is the sort of criticism, however, which physicians and surgeons who are guided by a scientific spirit welcome. There is probably no phase of hospital work which will so definitely put an end to incompetent and unnecessary surgery, and to careless and indifferent diagnoses in medical cases as will a consistent policy of postmortem examinations with staff review of the findings. Further, these examinations, if their results are regularly and fearlessly reviewed by the staff, will serve as a stimulus to scientific work and to valuable investigations. . . .

Obstetrics.   . . . In the next ten years it is reasonably certain that great advancement will be made in obstetrical services. . . .

If a hospital today does not provide for an obstetrical service, for what reasons is this service neglected? If an obstetrical department is provided, does it include a special delivery room? Does it include a nursery? Is prenatal work conducted in the department; in the out-patient department? Do nurses in the obstetrical department come into contact with patients of other departments? . . .

Cross Infections.   Does the hospital take all reasonable precautions against cross infection? Are examinations of patients on admission, especially of children, adequate in this respect? Are clean and septic operations conducted in the same operating room? Is the sterilization employed in and about the operating room effective? Is infection possible through the laundry or kitchen? Is constant check kept upon these matters? Are sufficient precautions taken with regard to the passing of nurses from one department into another who may carry infection?

4. Reform Committee Led by Josephine Goldmark Probes Nursing Education, 1923

On January 1, 1921, there were in the United States approximately 1,800 schools of nursing, having a total of 55,000 students and graduating each year approximately 15,000 nurses. According to the Biennial Survey of Education in the United States for 1919–1920, made by the Federal Bureau of Education, the rapid rate of increase during the last 20 years is shown by the following figures:

YEARS	NUMBER OF SCHOOLS
1899–1900	432
1904–1905	862
1909–1910	1,129
1914–1915	1,509
1919–1920	1,755

During the same span of time the increase in the number of students was from 11,164 to 54,953. . . .

On entering upon a study of nurse training today we are confronted by this dual character of the training school. It is indeed, as we shall see, the crux of our problem, the heart of our difficulty. For the school of nursing has sought to perform two functions: to educate nurses and to supply the nursing service for the hospital. But in these two functions there lies an ever present possibility of conflict. The needs of training and of hospital services may not coincide, and when the two are in conflict, the needs of the sick must predominate; the needs of education must yield. Whether or not, for instance, a student nurse has completed the services required for her training, whether or not she has had any experience with children or has had sufficient instruction in medical disease, if surgical patients are in need of care, to the surgical ward she is sent, though she may already have exceeded the time set for this service. . . .

. . . [A]t this point in our discussion we must first illustrate concretely how the training of nurses is sacrificed and prolonged in deference to the needs of the hospital. Today this cardinal point is unheeded, unrecognized. Were it once clearly established and its wide implications made plain, the fundamental error in the present relationship of hospitals and training schools would be abundantly evident. In such a showing lies the only hope of improvement. For the bar to progress at present lies precisely in ignorance of the facts. No action will follow until these facts sharply challenge the interest of those in authority; that is, first, the responsible hospital trustees and, behind them, the general public on whose financial support either directly through gifts or indirectly through taxation, the hospitals are dependent. . . .

. . . To many persons, including doctors as well as trustees, it is a new thought that the interests of hospital and training school are not one. That any legitimate conflict exists between the two is almost unthinkable. To them the school of nursing

Josephine Goldmark, *Nursing and Nursing Education in the United States: Report of the Committee for the Study of Nursing Education* (New York: Macmillan, 1923), pp. 187–188, 194–196, 209–210, 250–253, 483.

represents merely the department of the hospital, whose function it is to furnish the nursing service. They have tacitly assumed that the student nurses, in the course of three years, learn to care for the sick in the various divisions of the hospital and emerge at the end of that period as trained nurses. Thus the welfare of hospital and training school coincides. The work of the hospital is done and the students are simultaneously and automatically taught. And since a nurse should be equipped primarily for service, the difficulties and hardships of the work, such as they are, form an inherent and perhaps the most valuable part of the training, disciplining the nurse for any emergency as effectively as a more formal method would do. . . .

. . . It is evident that the dilemma of the training school is at bottom a financial one. Its failure—the worst failure of which an educational institution can be guilty— is the failure to teach. Now the cause of this failure is primarily the lack of money, without which the school cannot provide teachers, nor teaching equipment, nor even a place to teach; without which it is impossible to supply the supplementary nursing service to staff the wards while the students are given the classroom instruction that is to accompany, interpret, and illuminate their practical ward training. In a word, without sufficient funds, the wisest educational program must be frustrated.

Under the present system the school as a department of the hospital is given an allowance limited to the barest necessities, as viewed not from the standpoint of education, but of the hospital needs. A single striking instance illustrates this point. In its recent efforts to raise an endowment fund, a leading school of nursing points out that during its 31 years of existence it has grown from 17 to 250 students, and has graduated almost 1,000 nurses. During that period, says the appeal, the school of nursing "has provided through her student body the entire nursing care of the larger number of the 132,589 patients who have been admitted to the hospital." In addition to this it "has provided nursing supervision for the 2,000,000 patients who have come to the dispensary . . . and has extended this supervision beneficially into the homes of many of these patients."

Additional dormitories, the appeal continues, have been provided to meet the steady increase in the number of students. And "almost every year since the hospital was opened has seen either the expansion of existing services or the creation of entirely new ones," such as the psychiatric and the children's departments. "But no additions to any building have been made, no single new class or lecture room or laboratory has been provided, to supply the increased teaching facilities needed. The school outgrew its teaching equipment long ago." It has never been able to afford a librarian or clerical staff, and has urgent need of more teachers and supervisors. . . .

. . . [W]e face here a problem not only of education but of nursing service, and consequently of the public safety or danger. The hospital which uses students for its sole nursing staff, without adequate teaching, supervision, and suitable conditions of living, in effect jeopardizes the lives committed to its charge. . . .

Our next point for discussion is the legitimacy, sometimes challenged, of including these sciences in the nurses' training. "Why basic?" it is sometimes asked: "How related to the nurses' training, and why necessary at all in their curriculum? What need of the laboratory branches to teach nurses to be clean and deft?" . . .

. . . [A] knowledge, sound though comparatively elementary, of certain specific sciences and laws of science is indispensable for the nurses' training. In making this contention let us state bluntly at the outset that it is not to make nurses into doctors, but for the intelligent discharge of strictly nursing duties that this grounding in science is held indispensable. At best, only a relatively short time can be available for these courses. At best, they will be only elementary as compared with the intensive training of the physician or research worker. But we are concerned now not with the extent of courses but with the establishment of a principle, the need of adequate science teaching for nurses, often denied, often grudgingly provided for, rarely given its due weight in hospital training. . . .

The superior educational opportunities afforded by the university or the college as compared with those offered by the ordinary hospital school are abundantly evident. On the side of physical facilities, in the first place, the college and university have as a rule the standard plant and equipment for laboratory work in the sciences which the individual training school finds it so difficult if not impossible to command; supplies and material of all sorts are abundant, liberally provided and easy of access; there are extensive libraries and convenient reading rooms. All these facilities are frequently placed at the nursing school's service; where this is not the case they do perhaps as great a service in setting a standard for the new department. On the side of instruction, the training school, unendowed as it is, can rarely afford the best teaching; the college or university connection guarantees teaching by men and women who are not only specialists in their subjects but trained teachers as well.

Thus the standardizing influence of the university, in replacing as it does the inadequate equipment of the training school and the often unacademic grade of its teaching, can scarcely be overemphasized.

5. Rockefeller Foundation Reacts to a Growing Concern That Medical Education Reform Has Worsened Doctor Shortages in Rural America, 1924

Large and populous rural areas, ready, willing and able to support a physician, but unable to induce a physician to locate in them and compelled to rely for medical attention on the uncertain services of practitioners perhaps twenty miles distant: this is the picture which has been drawn with increasing frequency in the past few years wherever physicians or public health workers gather; and almost always the condition described, it is said, has come about only within recent years, and threatens to become more acute in the near future.

The causes assigned for this condition have been various; but certain factors related to the changes in medical education which have come about in the last ten or fifteen years have been charged with a large measure of responsibility—in some discussions, indeed, with sole responsibility. It has been alleged, first, that one reason why there are too few doctors in the rural areas is that there are too few in the country as a whole, in consequence of the fact that too few are being produced by the medical schools under the current régime of high entrance requirements and prolonged course of study; and second, that, even were their numbers adequate, the

Lewis Mayers and Leonard Harrison, *The Distribution of Physicians in the United States* (New York: Rockefeller Foundation General Education Board, 1924), pp. vii–ix, 3–5, 131–132, 144–145, 148–149, 152, 162 (table).

present-day medical graduates would refuse to locate in or near the rural areas. This reluctance is also ascribed to one or another of the characteristics of present-day medical education—its costliness in time and money, the location of schools in the larger cities, and the alleged emphasis on the importance of elaborate equipment and facilities in the diagnosis and treatment of disease. The conclusion is drawn that physicians can be obtained for the rural areas only by reducing the requirements for entrance upon and completion of the medical course; and so persuasive has been the line of argument by which this conclusion has been reached that in several states legislative action looking to a reduction of medical licensure requirements below the standards set by the better medical schools has already been proposed, and in one case taken.

It need hardly be said that the argument outlined, even where it has resulted in action, has been based upon no thorough-going examination of the facts. The causes behind the rural shortage have not been systematically studied; neither has a comprehensive attempt been made to ascertain its extent and character.

Because of the vital bearing of this problem on the development of American medical education, a systematic examination of the question has now been made, in order to develop as accurately as might be a picture of the distribution of the country's physicians to-day, and to compare the present condition with that formerly prevailing; to ascertain the causes which have determined the shifting of practitioners from one location to another, and the selection of initial locations by new graduates; to discover as far as possible any differences which there may be between the older and younger graduates, with respect to the size of towns selected for location and the type of practice favored, and finally, to obtain a comprehensive view of all factors, social, economic and psychological, which enter into the problem of obtaining adequate medical service for rural areas.

The problem being essentially one of detail, it was concluded that a more accurate picture could be obtained by studying carefully a number of representative areas than by attempting to examine all portions of the country with a less degree of care. The selection of the areas to be studied in detail was influenced by the changes in medical education in recent years. For this reason, especial attention was given to the South, east of the Mississippi, because in no other section have the developments of the last two decades produced so marked a decline in the number of medical schools, students and graduates, and correspondingly, in the number of new graduates locating in the section. In addition, two states of the South furnished particular reasons for study—North Carolina, because it has (with South Carolina) a lower ratio of physicians to population than any other state, showing a marked contrast indeed with its neighbors on the north and south; and Kentucky, because in no other state has complaint of extreme dearth of physicians in the rural areas been so insistent. Similarly, Maine, New York, and western Massachusetts were selected because in them, too, the rural medical situation has received much public discussion. Other states were chosen because they represented what seemed to be typical conditions in the sections in which they are respectively located. . . .

In the complex of economic, scientific and psychological factors which bear upon the distribution of physicians between town and country, one fact of overshadowing importance stands clearly disclosed. Always, and everywhere, the people of the towns have among them a substantially greater number of physicians than has an equal rural population. Such has been the situation in this country for fifty years back, beyond which our figures do not go; such is the situation to-day in all foreign countries for which figures are readily available, and, presumably, to an equal extent in countries for which they are not available.

Manifestly this cardinal feature of the distribution of physicians bears no relation to the need for medical service; for, on the basis of need, a given rural population, thinly scattered over an area served only by difficult roads, would require a substantially greater number of physicians than an equal population in a compact urban settlement. . . . What determines the distribution of physicians between town and country under the régime of individualism in medical practice is not the relative need for medical service but the relative attractions of the several towns, villages, and rural locations as possible fields for the practice of medicine.

It is not open to doubt that, from the standpoint of professional satisfaction, personal comfort and social environment, the city and the town have always offered to the average trained physician greater attractions than the isolated village; given equal income and prestige there are and ever have been but few physicians who would not choose practice in a fair-sized town, if not a large city, in preference to a remote rural location. It is the difficulty of obtaining a foothold in the towns and cities that has sent the young graduate to the lone village, or has kept there the established practitioner who fain would leave. So long as there exists a degree of free competition in the medical profession, accompanied by an ample supply, the superior personal, professional and social attractions of the town will unfailingly produce there a saturation, or, in the larger cities, a supersaturation of the demand; while the rural areas will attract physicians only to the extent that they offer a sufficiently superior financial prospect, and will retain what physicians they have only so long as the financial return is sufficiently great to outweigh the attractions of the town. . . .

The notion so widely current, in medical circles as well as out, that the standards of medical education alone determine the number of medical graduates, is usually found on inquiry to be based on the apparent experience of the past two decades—the sharp falling off in the attendance of medical schools concurrently with the elevation of their requirements. So direct does the connection seem to be that it is usually accepted as self-evident. On closer inspection, however, it develops that there are good reasons for doubting whether the connection is as direct as it looks.

The decline in attendance at medical schools began in 1905. The preceding twenty years, had, however, been a period of abnormal growth in attendance, which had increased far more rapidly that did the population. The number of medical graduates in the United States during the five-year period, 1886 to 1890, was 19,284. In the next five-year period (1891–1895) the number rose to 24,363, in the next (1896–1900) to 26, 238 and again (1901–1905) to 27,398. This growth was promptly reflected in the heavy increase in the number of physicians recorded in the 1900 census—an increase particularly heavy in the northern states, resulting in an overcrowding of the profession admittedly extreme. It is consequently more than likely that had there been no change whatever in the requirements for entrance to medical schools and for graduation there would still have developed, not long after 1904, a substantial reduction, relative if not absolute, in the number of medical students.

It has already been pointed out that, close on the heels of this decade of inflation, so to speak, in the number of physicians, there came the automobile, with its enlargement of the working capacity of the physician and the resultant intensification of the already severe pressure consequent on overcrowding. It is fair to assume that these conditions were effectual in discouraging, in the early years of the last decade, a not inconsiderable number of prospective or potential medical students who might otherwise have entered on the course.

Moreover, during the years in question not only have entrance standards risen, but the number of schools has sharply decreased. There were 150 medical schools in the United States in 1910; there were about 90 ten years later; and the schools that disappeared were schools that employed flagrant advertising methods. The drop in attendance is partially explicable by this fact. . . .

. . . [T]he facts [do not] lend much apparent support to the assertion, frequently encountered, that modern medical education spoils the country boy for rural practice in a way that the medical course of a generation ago did not, by accustoming him to the conveniences and diversions of urban existence. Implicit in this allegation is often found the belief that the older medical schools, which have passed away, were located in small towns, so close to the great open spaces that the student from the farm would hardly forget that God made the country but the devil made the town; while the school of today, to which the country boy must repair, is located in the great city. The fact is that far the greater number of the "diploma mills" of the last generation, and particularly those which attained the greatest size, were located in the large centers—often in the largest, as in New York, Chicago, Baltimore and St. Louis. . . .

Nor would it seem that the fact that the medical course now necessitates the country boy's absence from home in the large city for six years instead of four would be likely to be a decisive factor in increasing his distaste for rural life. Four years of city life surely was enough to give the medical student from the country (who had often enough, of course, despite the lax admission requirements, previously passed through a high school course in a fair-sized town) a sufficiently accurate notion of the relative attractions of city and country to neutralize any purely sentimental attachment to bucolic ideals. . . .

Quite aside from the increase in the length of the medical course, it is at times urged that the content and method of instruction are responsible for the apparent aversion of the recent graduate to rural practice. The medical course as at present conducted—so it is alleged—emphasizes the importance of the more recently developed instruments of precision and laboratory technique, and of highly specialized skill, till the student feels lost when out of reach of the facilities of the school. Hence the graduate tends to avoid the rural location, which demands from him the very type of service and skill which his medical course had done least to develop.

The authors of this report are not in position to express an opinion on the validity of these contentions; but it is clear that if they prove to any degree valid, the remedy would lie in a change in medical teaching, and not in a reduction of the length of the medical course. Indeed, the opinion has been expressed to us by some members of the rural profession themselves, that the greater responsibilities necessarily assumed by the rural physician, due to the inaccessibility of hospitals and specialists, render even the present extended medical course inadequate for the proper training of a rural practitioner. . . .

Finally, in charging the tendency to specialization with so large a share of the responsibility for the avoidance of the rural location by the recent graduate, there is usually implicit a misconception of the facts. Some of the assertions made in this connection would indeed appear to assume that the graduates of today no longer take any interest in general medicine, but that they usually enter on the practice of specialties immediately on graduation. How wide of the mark is such a notion may be seen in the figures of distribution of the graduates of 1916–20, no less than 18 per cent. of whom are found today in towns of less than 2,500 inhabitants, in which the practice of specialties is a rarity. Moreover, among specialists as a whole, in all the states selected for detailed study, the graduates of 1916–20 are found today in substantially fewer numbers, relatively, than are the older physicians, and in very much smaller numbers than are the graduates of 1911–15 and even those of 1906–10, which last may be regarded, with relatively few exceptions, as the product of the older order of medical education.

It is true that the graduates of those institutions which usually come to mind as the exemplars of the new order in medical education—Harvard, Johns Hopkins and Columbia, for example—are not found in the rural areas in equal proportions with those of schools less prominent, but the explanation for this is manifestly to be found in part in the character of the territory in which these schools are located— for despite their national fame their constituency is largely local—and in part in the fact that by virtue of their pre-eminence they attract a disproportionately large number of students who (often amply equipped with funds) have long aforetime fixed their eyes upon a career in research or in a specialty. Moreover, it must always be remembered that whether by express requirements—as in the case of Harvard, Cornell, Hopkins, Rush and others—or by means of selection from a great excess of applicants, or by both, these leading institutions in effect impose a standard of entrance requirement substantially higher than the standard fixed by the Council on Education of the American Medical Association or by the state licensing boards; and the required standard of performance in the course itself is substantially higher than in most schools. For all these reasons the distribution of the graduates of these schools furnishes no valid basis for appraising the compatability of current standards of medical education with the willingness to do rural practice.

In summary, to one taking a broad view of all factors, it seems reasonably clear that neither changes in the medical school constituency, nor changes in the mental attitude of the graduate induced by the current methods of instruction, have been more than a secondary influence in leading recent graduates to avoid rural locations, and that the primary factors have been substantially the same as in the case of the practitioners of longer standing—the increasingly superior financial, social and professional advantages of the larger places: factors which have appealed with equal force to all types of practitioners, including those who received their medical education under a régime far removed from that of today. . . .

If the conclusions reached in the present chapter are sound, no reduction of medical school requirements, either for entrance or graduation, that is at all within the realm of possibility, would be likely to have a significant effect upon the future supply of physicians to the rural areas; and the creation of a sub-standard class of physicians for those areas is quite impracticable. Whatever may be thought, therefore, of the necessity for taking measures to meet the problem of rural medical service, it seems clear that the situation does not call for any present action in the field of medical education in the direction of a reduction in requirements or a lowering of standards.

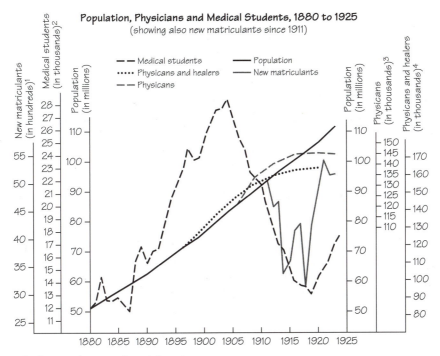

Population, Physicians and Medical Students, 1880 to 1925
(showing also new matriculants since 1911)

1. Academic year *beginning* with year indicated on curve.
2. Academic year *ending* with year indicated on curve.
3. Based on American Medical Directory.
4. Based on the U.S. Census.

 E S S A Y S

University of Wisconsin historian Ronald L. Numbers's account of the Flexnerian revolution in medical education underscores the importance of factors such as the passage of new, more stringent medical licensing laws by the states and the response of healers other than physicians to the effort to elevate professional standards. Tracing the unmistakable rise in the standing of the so-called "regular" or "allopathic" physician in the early twentieth century, Numbers deftly argues that organized medicine was not able to eliminate all competition—including competition from practitioners of alternative medicine—and exert complete control over the medical marketplace. In the second essay, Kenneth M. Ludmerer, a physician-historian at Washington University Medical School, St. Louis, who has written extensively about medical education, looks at another facet of this educational and professional reform process: the development of a new kind of patient care facility—namely, the teaching hospital. Many historians have seen the revolution in clinical teaching as a success, and Ludmerer does not disagree, but there were some unforseen consequences of this "success" that require attention. University of Pennsylvania historian Janet A. Tighe takes up this theme of unplanned outcomes in her case study of the struggle of one medical school—Temple in Philadelphia—to adapt to the new circumstances. Her essay gives us a glimpse into the complex world of local socioeconomic and political factors that affected the national movement to rebuild medical education and clinical practice. Together, these essays examine not merely the benefits but also the costs of this era of educational, institutional, and professional transformation.

Physicians, Community, and the Qualified Ascent of the American Medical Profession

RONALD L. NUMBERS

Medical education did . . . improve significantly during the latter half of the [nineteenth] century. Although the proliferation of substandard schools continued unabated, the best institutions lengthened their curricula to three years, offered a new set of courses each year, required some evidence of preliminary education, and, led by the Harvard Medical College, abandoned proprietary status to become an integral part of a university. The dramatic growth of laboratory-based medical science in the latter half of the century encouraged such reforms, as did the German training of approximately 15,000 American physicians between 1870 and 1914.

No event symbolized the reformation of American medical education more than the opening in 1893 of the Johns Hopkins School of Medicine under the leadership of the German-trained pathologist William H. Welch. At a time when, according to Welch, no American medical school required a preliminary education equal to "that necessary for entrance into the freshman class of a respectable college," the Hopkins faculty, at the insistence of its patron, demanded a bachelor's degree. Modestly following the Hopkins example, more than twenty schools by 1910 raised their entrance requirements to two years of college. This reform, Robert E. Kohler has argued, had far-reaching effects: it "stretched the financial resources of the proprietary school beyond the breaking point. . . . Higher entrance requirements disrupted the established market relation with high schools, diminished the pool of qualified applicants, and resulted in a drastic plunge in enrollments. Medical schools could not survive on fees."

A further prod to education reform came not from within the profession itself, but from the states, every one of which passed some kind of medical licensing act between the mid-1870s and 1900. Although physicians generally led the crusade to restrict the practice of medicine, they were not without external support. As society came to rely on physicians to certify births and deaths, to control infectious diseases, and to commit the insane, it became increasingly apparent that licensing served a public as well as a professional function. In 1888 the Supreme Court in a landmark decision, *Dent v. West Virginia,* upheld the authority of the state medical examining board to deprive a poorly trained eclectic physician of the right to practice. In the opinion of Justice Stephen J. Field, no one had "the right to practice medicine without having the necessary qualifications of learning and skill," and no group had greater competency to judge these qualifications than well-trained physicians. Thus society granted the medical profession one of its most cherished goals: the authority to exclude practitioners deemed unworthy. The fact that other professions won protective legislation at the same time suggests that the physicians' achievement resulted more from a change in social policy than

---

Ronald L. Numbers, "The Fall and Rise of the American Medical Profession," in *The Professions in American History,* ed. Nathan O. Hatch (Notre Dame, Ind.: University of Notre Dame Press, 1985), pp. 57–67.

from a recognition of the improved state of medical science, impressive though it may have been.

The state licensing boards influenced medical education in two ways. First, most of them required candidates to hold a diploma from a reputable medical school, that is, one requiring evidence of preliminary education and, perhaps, offering a three-year course of study, a six-month term, and clinical and laboratory instruction. This forced any school hoping to compete for students to upgrade its curriculum, at least superficially. Second, many states, especially during the late 1880s and 1890s, revised their laws to require all candidates, even those holding medical degrees, to pass an examination. Although some of the weaker schools quickly learned how to coach students to pass these tests, graduates from strong institutions had a much better chance of passing. A shallow medical education no longer paid. The success of the licensing laws convinced professional leaders of the great advantage of legal sanctions over moral suasion in reforming medical education. . . .

Medical practice acts not only set standards for licensing physicians but defined the very practice of medicine. The Nebraska act, for example, stipulated that anyone "who shall operate on, profess to heal, or prescribe for, or otherwise treat any physical or mental ailment of another" was practicing medicine and thus subject to the provisions of the law. For various political reasons, the states often granted exceptions. Many laws specifically exempted dentists, midwives, medical students, and persons who gave emergency aid; and a few states, especially in New England, provided immunity for Christian Scientists and others who engaged in mental healing. . . .

Since the appearance of rival sects in the first half of the century, regulars had sought to isolate and discredit them. Nevertheless, well-trained sectarians, especially homeopaths and eclectics, had prospered. During the latter part of the century it became increasingly difficult to distinguish between orthodox and heterodox practice, or to argue that one system was more efficacious than another. In the 1880s, for example, one life insurance company concluded that homeopathy was just as effective as allopathy in saving lives, while a comparative study at Cook County Hospital in Chicago showed the latter to have only a slight edge in mortality rates. Given the training, therapeutic success, and numerical strength of the sectarians, regulars found it impossible to legislate them out of existence; in fact, in at least twenty states they sat on the same licensing boards with homeopaths or eclectics—at a time when the AMA still banned professional intercourse. In only three or four instances did they obtain what they most desired: a single licensing board composed exclusively of regulars.

Although orthodox physicians liked to describe their efforts to suppress sectarians in humanitarian terms, evidence suggests that opposition stemmed as much from fear of competition as from a desire to safeguard the public. After all, as one homeopath perceptively noted, regulars made few attempts to police therapy among themselves:

> If you inform the people that you treat those who come to you according to Similia, so far as drugging goes, you are anathema with the "regular," but if you get inside his fold, you can use any old treatment you please—be it an "electro-therapeutist," a man of "suggestion," or of "serums," calomel, bleeding, anything, and be a "regular physician." Curious, isn't it? Looks as though the real thing at issue was the "recognition of the union" rather than the "welfare of the public."

In addition to battling sectarians, the regular medical profession zealously fought to subordinate and control allied health personnel. As the number of trained nurses increased after the Civil War, physicians expressed concern that these women would attempt to expand their role and presume to act as physicians. Thus doctors attempted to limit the amount of theoretical training nurses received and insisted that nurses strictly obey their orders. As the *Boston Medical and Surgical Journal* explained, the physician's relationship to the nursing staff was to be "like that of the captain to his ship." To win acceptance and approval from the medical profession, nurses themselves went out of their way to reassure the doctors. For example, in her influential *Nursing Ethics* (1900) Isabel Hampton emphasized discipline as the key to success: "The head nurse and her staff should stand to receive the visiting physician, and from the moment of his entrance until his departure, the attending nurses should show themselves alert, attentive, courteous, like soldiers on duty." Such an attitude posed no threat either to pocketbooks or egos.

Physicians experienced much greater difficulty trying to subdue male pharmacists, who not only sold medicines prescribed by doctors but frequently diagnosed minor ailments and suggested remedies. Pharmacists, warned one physician in the early 1880s, had "so industriously and energetically wedged themselves between the 'dear public' and the professional province of the physician" that they threatened to take over the practice of medicine. Incensed doctors denounced this intrusion as dangerous and illegal and sought to revise medical practice acts to ban practices such as over-the-counter prescribing. Their efforts, however, generally failed, and in at least one state (North Dakota) the pharmacists retaliated by securing passage of a law barring physicians from dispensing medicines. "If physicians wish to prevent encroachment on their domain," warned one pharmacist, "they should avoid invading others' property." . . .

In spite of substantial improvements in medical education and the passage of licensing laws, the medical profession at the end of the century still contained, according to one knowledgeable physician, "a vast number of incompetents, large numbers of moral degenerates, and crowds of pure tradesmen." By 1900 there were 151 medical schools, and even the worst institutions sometimes managed to prepare their graduates to pass ineffectual licensing examinations. In one notorious case, the weakest of Chicago's fourteen schools—"a school with no entrance requirement, no laboratory teaching, no hospital connections"—outperformed its thirteen rivals on the state boards. The medical practice acts, complained one contemporary, allowed all but "the most flagrant quacks and charlatans from carrying on their business unmolested." Thus after a half-century of reform much remained on the medical profession's agenda for elevating its status: the elimination of inferior medical schools, the enactment of stricter licensing laws, and the creation of a powerful national body to represent the interests of physicians.

The Reformation Completed

The professional leaders of American medicine faced the twentieth century determined to complete the reformation they had begun, that is, to reduce the quantity and increase the quality of medical practitioners. Although the ratio of physicians to patients had scarcely changed during the previous fifty years—in fact, it had actually decreased from 1:568 in 1850 to 1:576 in 1900—American doctors continued to view the overcrowding of their profession by poorly trained physicians as their greatest problem. Such individuals, argued the reformers, not only provided inadequate and sometimes dangerous care, but also depressed physician income. Well into the twentieth century, most American physicians earned less than $2,000 a year. In 1914, for example, less than 60 percent of Wisconsin's approximately 2,800 practitioners earned enough even to pay income taxes; and of those who paid, the average income was only $1,488—well below that of bankers, manufacturers, and lawyers, though more than twice what professors earned.

The profession's first order of business was to create a united front. Since its founding in 1847, the AMA had remained virtually impotent; it had, noted its president sadly in 1901, "exerted relatively little influence on legislation, either state or national." Only about 7 percent of the country's physicians had joined the association, and independent state and county societies often operated at cross purposes to the will of the national body. In response to this situation, an AMA committee in 1901 recommended a complete reorganization: the welding of local, state, and national units into one representative society that would "foster scientific medicine and . . . make the medical profession a power in the social and political life of the republic." Henceforth, membership in a local (generally county) society would automatically carry membership in the state and national organizations. This plan, approved at the 1901 annual session, produced immediate results. Most state societies fell quickly into line, and membership in the AMA multiplied over sevenfold within five years. For the first time American physicians possessed an organization large enough and strong enough effectively to further its interests.

Like its nineteenth-century parent, the reorganized AMA fought to control access to the profession by tightening the requirements for medical education and licensure. In 1904 it created a Council on Medical Education, which soon began inspecting and grading medical schools. A few years later the council cooperated with the Carnegie Foundation in producing Abraham Flexner's famous report on *Medical Education in the United States and Canada* (1910). This muckraking exposé described conditions—often abysmal—at each of the country's 155 medical schools. The adverse publicity generated by the AMA's inspections and the Flexner report, together with continuing pressure from licensing bodies and the growing expense of providing laboratory and clinical instruction, forced many institutions to shut down—and finally brought a halt to the overproduction of unqualified physicians. Between 1910 and 1920 the number of medical schools declined from 155 to 85, and it continued falling for the next two decades. In the same period the total number of physicians in the United States was dropping for perhaps the first time in history. The schools that survived this winnowing were, by 1930, generally requiring a bachelor's degree for admission and offering rigorous scientific and clinical training. Unlike the improvements of the nineteenth-century, which had little to do with the AMA, these changes often resulted from the AMA's cozy relationship with the state licensing boards, which delegated to the AMA (sometimes jointly with the American Association of Medical Colleges) the privilege of deciding which schools merited approval for the licensing of their graduates. By this means, and by accrediting hospitals for the training of interns, organized medicine gained considerable control over the education and supply of physicians.

The medical profession enjoyed much less success in its efforts to monopolize the practice of medicine by outlawing rivals and controlling allies. As we have seen, during the last quarter of the nineteenth century regular physicians often united reluctantly with their old nemeses, the eclectics and homeopaths, to win passage of state licensing laws. In 1903 the AMA took additional steps toward unity by deleting its ethical ban against consulting with irregulars and by welcoming as members eclectics and homeopaths willing to forsake sectarian dogma for scientific truth. This latter act proved to be the kiss of death for eclectic and homeopathic organizations, which, though still numerically strong, were now struggling to survive. Weakened by internal discord, defecting members, and the lack of state-supported medical schools, they soon ceased to be a factor in American medicine.

The demise of eclectics and homeopaths did not, however, eliminate sectarian competition. During the late nineteenth century, Christian Science, osteopathy, and chiropractic made their appearance, and by the early twentieth century these new "cults," as the medical establishment insisted on calling them, began threatening the therapeutic consensus based on scientific medicine as well as the economic goals of physicians. Despite an intensive and protracted campaign by the medical profession to have these sects declared illegal, all three won the legal right to practice their form of healing. The nature of their victory varied from state to state, but their experience in Wisconsin illustrates the various means they used to thwart the medical profession's monopolistic designs.

Like their spiritual leader, Mary Baker Eddy, Christian Science practitioners denied the existence of disease and the need for physicians. Instead of prescribing drugs, they relied on prayer and verbal persuasion to cure individuals who imagined themselves to be ill. Christian Scientists began practicing in Wisconsin in the 1880s, but physicians could do little to stop them before the state passed a medical practice act in 1897. Following enactment of this bill, authorities in Milwaukee arrested two Christian Science practitioners for violating the new law. At their trial the defendants argued that they were not guilty of practicing medicine "because they never administered drugs, never performed surgery, never manipulated the body or even touched their patients." Nevertheless, the court convicted them—only to be overruled by a higher court, which agreed that Christian Science had little in common with medicine. Therefore, Christian Scientists in Wisconsin faced only the insults of physicians, not the threat of arrest. In some other states, as we have noted, legislators specifically exempted them in defining medical practice.

Osteopathy was founded by a Missouri physician, Andrew Taylor Still, who turned against regular medicine after drug therapy failed to save the lives of his children. Convinced that the human brain functioned as "God's drug store," he attributed all disease to obstructions inhibiting the flow of blood and nervous fluid, which he sought to cure using manual manipulation, particularly of the spine. The first osteopaths arrived in Wisconsin in the 1890s, and by 1900 nineteen had located in the state. Charged in that year with illegal practice under the 1897 statute, the osteopaths lost their first court case. Seeking relief, they petitioned the legislature to create a separate licensing board for osteopathy. Regular physicians lobbied instead for the addition of an osteopath to the existing licensing board, believing that the "requirements are so high it is safe to say that but few, if any, osteopaths will ever be able to meet them." The regulars got their wish, but discovered to their chagrin that the underrated osteopaths routinely qualified for licenses to practice. Elsewhere, in over half the states, regulars suffered even greater humiliation, as legislators ignored their pleas and set up separate boards composed only of D.O.'s.

Chiropractic, the brainchild of an Iowa grocer, Daniel David Palmer, explained disease in terms of dislocations of the spine, which allegedly impeded the circulation of nervous fluid. Like osteopaths, with whom they were frequently confused, chiropractors relied therapeutically on adjustments of the spinal column. When the first of them moved to Wisconsin in the early 1900s, they landed in jail for practicing *osteopathy* without a license. Undeterred, they continued to practice illegally until 1915, when the legislature granted them immunity to work as unlicensed practitioners. Ten years later it disregarded the will of the medical profession and, like legislatures in many other states, voted to create a separate chiropractic board of examiners.

In the early 1930s one study of medical care in America reported that "the efforts of the medical profession to prevent legal recognition of the chiropractors have met with almost universal defeat." In fact, by this time nearly a quarter of American healers were Christian Scientists, osteopaths, chiropractors, or irregulars of some stripe. It was clear, concluded the same study, that "in the United States the legislative regulation of the healing art is not accomplishing its acknowledged purpose," that is, creating a monopoly for regular physicians.

Medical doctors encountered equal difficulty keeping assorted other health-care professionals from intruding on what they regarded as their rightful domain. Although they actually assisted podiatrists in achieving their independent status—on the grounds that corn-cutting like tooth-pulling was too trivial to control—they fought continually to limit the activities of such interlopers as optometrists, psychologists, and midwives, who competed directly with physicians specializing in ophthalmology, psychiatry, and obstetrics. The medical profession hoped to restrict the practice of such individuals by defining medicine comprehensively; however, unsympathetic judges and legislators time and again sided with its opponents. . . .

The Profession and the Public

A century after the founding of the AMA the American medical profession could look with pride on its various accomplishments. Although its efforts to monopolize the practice of medicine had fallen far short of its goals, it had, through its alliance with the law, eliminated overcrowding in the field, greatly reduced the number of incompetents practicing medicine, and acquired so much prestige and power that medicine became the envy of other professions. By the mid-twentieth century physicians had become the most admired professionals in the land, and, benefiting especially from the growth of health insurance, had passed bankers and lawyers to become the nation's highest paid workers. Despite mounting criticism of the medical profession during the past couple of decades, physicians have, by and large, retained their elevated position in American society. And despite the increasing intrusion of insurance companies, government agencies, and various allied health professionals into the medical domain, the gains physicians made during the first half of the twentieth century have, to a great extent, remained intact.

Balancing Educational and Patient Needs in the Creation of the Modern Teaching Hospital

KENNETH M. LUDMERER

[In the early twentieth century,] patients began to consult doctors more frequently in offices or hospitals rather than insisting that physicians make home visits as before. The common denominator to all these developments was that as the public increasingly relied upon physicians, it had a growing stake in how its doctors were trained. Now that the public sensed that proper training was indispensable for the practice of good medicine, the claims of medical educators as to what constituted proper clinical training carried much greater weight than ever before.

The growing sentiment in favor of the teaching hospital blossomed in full force in 1910. That year there were three seminal unions between medical schools and hospitals: the College of Physicians and Surgeons (Columbia) with Presbyterian Hospital in New York; Harvard Medical School with the Peter Bent Brigham Hospital in Boston; and Washington University Medical School with Barnes Hospital and St. Louis Children's Hospital in St. Louis. . . . In each case, Johns Hopkins served as the model for the arrangement. The universities were granted the right to appoint the medical staff of their affiliated hospitals, and the hospital trustees consented to permit the unfettered use of their hospital for medical instruction and research. These alliances marked the first major breakthroughs in the efforts to upgrade clinical teaching since the opening of Johns Hopkins.

The consummation of two of these alliances the same year as the Flexner report was a coincidence, although the Flexner report certainly gave great impetus to the teaching hospital movement nationwide. In Boston and New York the negotiations were already quite advanced at the time of the publication of the report, and these unions would have occurred even if the Flexner report had not appeared. In St. Louis, however, the Flexner report did help facilitate the arrangement between Barnes and Children's Hospitals and Washington University, largely through the influence of Flexner on Robert Brookings, the university president. Inspired by Flexner, Brookings became the prime mover in forging a relationship between the university and the two hospitals, as well as in building a nationally important medical school at Washington University. . . .

Planning for the three mergers proceeded in conjunction with one another. This was not surprising since the drive to establish teaching hospitals as well as the efforts to improve medical education were both national movements. Medical educators and hospital officials from all parts of the country met with each other regularly at regional and national meetings and remained in communication through professional publications and personal visits and correspondence. . . .

. . . [T]he aggressiveness with which the medical school representatives took their cases to the hospital trustees only partly accounted for the three affiliations that occurred. After all, medical school officials across the country had been doing so for

Kenneth Ludmerer, "The Rise of the Teaching Hospital in America," *Journal of the History of Medicine and Allied Sciences* 38 (1983): 389–414. Reprinted by permission of the author.

a generation without much prior success. The trustees, sympathetic though they were to the needs of medical education, were tough businessmen, loyal to the interests of the institutions they served. The novel affiliations with medical schools were not steps they undertook lightly. In Boston as late as 1908, after more than six years of discussions between Harvard Medical School and Peter Bent Brigham Hospital, it was not altogether clear that the Brigham would consent to the type of relation with Harvard that the medical school desired. Before it agreed to the affiliation with Washington University, Barnes Hospital had turned down similar overtures from three other St. Louis medical schools. Presbyterian Hospital, eager for an affiliation with a strong medical school for several years, still insisted that any alliance with Columbia University must allow "the maintenance of the independent corporate existence and individuality of The Presbyterian Hospital." The trustees, in short, agreed to the unions because they now believed that their hospitals stood to gain from an affiliation with a strong medical school. . . .

One advantage that representatives of the four hospitals saw in a medical school alliance was the provision of better patient care. In a teaching hospital "it is obvious that the routine care of patients will reach its highest efficiency," declared one speaker at the dedication exercises of Children's Hospital. An old argument, it was given a new urgency and timeliness in the early twentieth century as the modern hospital, laden with sophisticated technology and assuming more and more of a medical role, was developing. Whether a teaching hospital would provide what Presbyterian officials called the "best care for the sick and injured" was never proved, only assumed, but it was an assumption that hospital and medical school officials made with ease.

Part of their trust in the capability of the teaching hospital to deliver the finest patient care arose from the constant scrutiny that a teaching hospital, with its organized teams of attending physicians, house officers, and students, could provide. With such a large staff, doctors were always present. Acutely ill or unstable patients could be observed continuously, and someone was always present to handle an emergency. With students watching and asking questions, teachers were more assiduous in their work. With so many observers, patients were studied carefully and thoroughly, and the most accurate information about their condition could be obtained. . . .

In addition, the hospital officers thought that teaching hospitals could render better patient care by virtue of having the finest medical staffs. Because of the increasingly scientific nature of medical knowledge and practice, university and hospital officials regarded the medical scientists as the preeminent practitioners. The most skillful and knowledgeable clinicians in their eyes were now the academic physicians who devoted their entire time to the study of disease, not the local practitioners who formerly constituted the clinical faculties of medical schools. . . .

Hospital officials' respect for the academic doctor arose from the scientific advances of the late nineteenth and early twentieth centuries. As discoveries in chemistry, physiology, immunology, and bacteriology made their impact upon medicine, a greater knowledge of the basic sciences became essential even to the full-time practitioner. The practice as well as the theory of medicine was also changing, as standard clinical care increasingly made use of chemical and bacteriological tests of blood, urine, feces, and other body tissues as well as numerous histologic, radiologic, electrocardiographic, and serologic techniques. To ensure the most up-to-date care, hospital officials wished to employ the doctors who were responsible for the discoveries that affected clinical practice so dramatically. Said one speaker [in 1915] at the dedication of the new buildings of the Washington University Medical School: "Modern experience teaches that the fostering of a spirit of investigation is an effective means of keeping physicians in touch with advances in method. The scientific reports issued by a hospital may well serve as an index of how far its patients benefit from the developments of technical knowledge."

Accentuating respect for the academic physician was the growing recognition that the thought processes of clinical practice, when conducted properly, were similar to those of scientific investigation. Both utilized the same methods of verification: theory and hypothesis were subject to confirmation or refutation by empirical facts. The patient constituted the clinician's laboratory, and the history, symptoms, and physical findings provided his data. As a scientist would develop a hypothesis, a physician would construct a working diagnosis. Both hypothesis and preliminary diagnosis would stand in need of empirical confirmation. The test of the physician's diagnosis would be the response of the patient to the further investigations or treatments that might be suggested by the diagnosis. "The progress of science and the scientific or intelligent practice of medicine employ, therefore, exactly the same technique," observed Abraham Flexner. . . . [T]here was a growing conviction that "investigation and practice are . . . one in spirit, method, and object." The goal of medical education, a prominent physician told an entering class of Johns Hopkins medical students, was not that "every physician shall be a man of science," but that every doctor "shall have the scientific habit of mind." Such an outlook supported the assumption of hospital trustees that academic doctors, who presumably had mastered the scientific method, were also the best practitioners.

Officials of the four hospitals found a second attraction to the idea of merging with medical schools: such affiliations would enable the hospitals more effectively to pursue medical research. The trustees of each of these institutions were inspired by the emergence in the late nineteenth century of clinical investigation, which required a hospital for its execution. They had grown to accept the viewpoint that the function of hospitals was no longer just to provide care but to foster research as well. . . .

. . . In each of the affiliations under consideration, the medical schools agreed to maintain the hospitals' laboratories as well as to lend their own research staff, basic science facilities, and equipment to the hospitals in their joint effort to expand medical knowledge. Hospitals and medical schools would no longer be isolated from each other; the scientific talent and resources of the medical schools would be brought together with the vast clinical facilities of these major hospitals. The Barnes trustees boasted, "This contract [with Washington University] enables the Hospital to secure the services of the eminent men composing the medical staff of the University, and also insures to the Hospital, without any expense, the use of the magnificent laboratories and equipment of the new medical department of the University."

Hospital officials saw a third reason to affiliate with a medical school: such unions were economically mandatory if the hospitals and the universities were to do the work they desired. Complete laboratories and modern equipment, necessary for the best medical care, were very expensive. So were sophisticated laboratories for clinical research. . . . Barnes Hospital accumulated a deficit of $36,000 during its first year of operation alone. Even the Peter Bent Brigham Hospital, with over $6,600,000 in assets, complained loudly about expense. In its first report the president of the board of trustees warned that "the Corporation, while seemingly well endowed, finds its work always expanding, and the outlook for the future calls for ever-increasing expenditure." . . . Then, as now, no matter how wealthy a hospital might appear on the financial ledger, no matter how imposing its plant and facilities might seem to the outside observer, it would invariably complain of inadequate resources, protesting that its funds were insufficient to permit it to do the work it desired. No major hospital ever felt that it had enough money.

Formation of the alliances with medical schools allowed a division of labor that was to everyone's economic advantage, alleviating if not resolving the financial burdens of providing modern scientific medical care. In each case the hospitals made available to the universities superb teaching facilities that the universities could not have afforded on their own. In return the universities provided the hospitals with distinguished scientific staffs and equipped and maintained all the hospitals' laboratories. In St. Louis the financial benefits to the hospitals were the greatest of all, since the two hospitals and a new medical school plant were built next to each other. Washington University provided Children's and Barnes Hospitals with dispensary buildings, erected a pathological laboratory that served both hospitals, paid the salaries of all the physicians working in the hospitals (including the house officers), and constructed and operated a power plant that served the entire complex. With Children's and Barnes Hospitals adjoining each other, they could be served by centralized laundry, kitchen, and ambulance services. The businessmen who comprised the trustees of the four hospitals saw that the concept of consolidating resources into larger, more efficient units—the prototypical approach to solving the problems of commerce and government in progressive era America—could be applied in the medical arena as well. . . .

The unions in Boston, New York, and St. Louis represented the start of a broad movement. They served as catalysts, helping galvanize sentiment that had been accruing nationwide. Across the country medical schools succeeded in acquiring teaching hospitals under their direct control. They did so either by persuading trustees of established hospitals to consent to new arrangements or by influencing state and local governments to appropriate funds for new hospitals that would be run as teaching institutions. In 1914 the dean of the College of Medicine of the University of Nebraska, listing reasons why he felt the Nebraska legislature should appropriate funds for a university hospital in Omaha, could tell the president of the university that already "every Medical College of any standing in the country is associated either with a University Hospital, . . . or controls a large number of beds in a municipal institution. By 1921 every surviving medical school in the country had established an affiliation with a hospital that it often either owned or controlled. Hospitals, once intransigently opposed to the idea of involving themselves with medical teaching, now found that they liked the idea, and the public approved as well. In 1916, when the new Municipal Hospital of the University of Cincinnati opened after fourteen years of public skepticism, a local newspaper headline proclaimed: "Now The People Can't Understand Why It Was Not Built Sooner." Medical educators stood incredulous at the rapid acceptance of an idea that had encountered so much resistance only a few years before.

Many similarities existed between the subsequent mergers—as well as the successful lobbying before state legislatures to erect university hospitals—and the initial mergers that started the process. In virtually every case teaching hospitals were procured by aggressive medical staffs that initiated the negotiations. Physicians approached hospitals and governmental bodies with the same entrepreneurial flare and sense of mission that they manifested in approaching the American public at this time in their successful appeal to make medical schools the object of large-scale philanthropy. To this group of first-generation medical institution builders, the procurement of teaching hospitals and the establishment of a medical endowment were equally important tasks. Both were necessary for implementing their long-established goals of providing proper medical training and of making academic medicine a viable career. As early as 1899 Hunter H. Powell, dean of the Western Reserve Medical College, wrote that hospitals "must be convinced" by physicians "that one of the most important functions of a hospital is found in the advancement of medical education." Politically influential physicians such as Frank Billings and William Welch carried this appeal not just to their own institutions but to hospitals nationwide. The hospitals that listened to them were of the same kind: large, ambitious, technologically sophisticated institutions that had hopes of achieving international reputations. In case after case the rationale for becoming a teaching hospital was monotonously the same: the argument that teaching hospitals provided the best patient care, and the desire to serve a wide clientele and achieve broad recognition through medical education and research. The rise of the teaching hospital represented one more dimension of the widespread invasion of science into American life during progressive era America. . . .

The teaching hospital in many ways represented a success—but for whom, and at what cost? In one sense the hospitals achieved what they desired. Affiliation with medical schools assured their continued national and international importance. But the price they paid was the irreversible surrender of control over their own destinies. Hospital trustees, who in the nineteenth century had been responsible for all aspects of hospital policy formation and day-to-day decision making, now found themselves increasingly relegated to the role of fund raisers. In their place the medical boards were becoming the dominant policy setters and decision makers in the hospital, to whose recommendations the trustees would usually acquiesce. This change was occurring in all American hospitals at this time, but nowhere was it more pronounced than at the teaching hospitals.

Medical faculties, too, had achieved their objectives with the acceptance of the teaching hospital. Once done, however, it was seen that there were unanticipated consequences for professors as well. A readjustment of the balance of power within medical schools began to occur. Professors in the basic science departments, who had dominated the medical schools for the previous generation, were increasingly challenged by professors of the clinical subjects as these persons also became full-time. Not only did the basic scientists face a power struggle within the political structure of the schools, but they also encountered increased competition when applying for extramural funds. Even with the increasing amount of medical philanthropy, the amount of money available for medical research was finite and could be divided in just so many ways. Diffusion of the university spirit to the clinical faculty heightened the intensity of the competition for research support, particularly as the clinical investigators became as versed in the fundamental scientific disciplines as the basic scientists themselves. The Harvard pathologist William Councilman was but one of many laboratory investigators who had supported the development of stronger clinical teaching but who expressed disquietude afterward when clinical departments at his school began to receive priority in development over his own.

Medical students also emerged victorious, but their victory, too, was not entirely untainted. After the initial euphoria over having the opportunity to "learn by doing" wore off, it quickly became apparent that not all aspects of the clerkship were of equal educational value for the student. The line between learning by doing and being economically exploited as a source of cheap labor was a fine one that was frequently trespassed. A student did not have to draw many blood specimens for that act to cease to be of educational value. With the rush of the hospital routine, and so much of the ordinary work done by students, medical students during their clerkships often found themselves dehumanized more than at any other time in their lives. And if this problem was acute for medical students, for interns and residents it was critical.

Finally, what of the patient? Although many medical educators sanctimoniously rationalized the value of the clerkship to good patient care, in actuality the widespread implementation of the clerkship placed into sharp relief the tension between the needs of patients and the educational requirements of students that had been becoming increasingly apparent since the mid-nineteenth century. One need only examine the correspondence between the superintendent and the physician-in-chief of the Peter Bent Brigham Hospital to appreciate the impositions to patients that could arise by employing students as clinical clerks. Medical educators, of course, were not insensitive to the needs of patients and took many important steps to ensure that patient rights and privacy would not be infringed. However, even such a firm patient advocate as Harvard's Richard Cabot, one of the founders of hospital social work and an ardent champion of compassionate medical care, believed that patient "objection to [being used for] teaching is vastly less common than resentment for being passed by." The medical faculty of Fordham stated the matter more bluntly: "Patients must clearly understand from the beginning that they are admitted for teaching purposes and that they are to be willing to submit to this when pronounced physically fit." A new balance had clearly been struck. The tension between educational and patient needs had finally been resolved—in favor of education.

A Lesson in the Political Economics of Medical Education

JANET A. TIGHE

Philadelphia was one of the early stops in education reformer Abraham Flexner's 1908–1909 journey, undertaken for the Carnegie Foundation for the Advancement of Teaching, to examine the medical schools of the United States and Canada. The city, which had been the leading center of American medicine for much of the nineteenth century, offered Flexner an intriguing array of medical education styles and institutional structures. Five of the city's medical schools—Hahnemann, Jefferson, Medico-Chiurgical, the University of Pennsylvania, and Women's Medical

---

Janet A. Tighe, "A Lesson in the Political Economics of Medical Education," from *A "Key of Gold": Science, Money, and the Public Good in an American Medical School* (forthcoming).

College—had established reputations and identities. In stark contrast, the youngest Philadelphia medical school, the Medical Department of Temple College, scarcely had a past, having been founded in 1901. Even this brief history was, from the point of view of many medical educators, a problematic burden since most of Temple's first eight years of existence were as a night school for students with daytime employment. Evaluating the "midnight medical school," as most of Philadelphia's medical elite derisively called Temple, did not take too much of Flexner's time. In his now famous 1910 survey, Flexner declared that Temple had "absolutely no future." Lacking some of the most basic fundamentals necessary to teaching scientific medicine and with an unstable, market-oriented financial foundation, Temple was for Flexner a prime example of the kind of medical school that should be exterminated.

Temple's survival, despite its sometimes hostile, occasionally bewildered, and often distant relationship with the medical education elite, makes its history instructive. This history provides an opportunity to see the workings of a powerful group of cultural, political, and economic forces that have played as important a role as science in determining the nature of medical education in twentieth-century America. Temple's story makes it evident that embracing the reform vision set forth in the Flexner report was a much more conflicted and wrenching undertaking than most of its advocates were willing to admit. According to Flexner and his fellow reformers, there was only one method for getting science into the medical school: take the institution out of the market system; establish a strictly hierarchical, centralized financing and management structure; and employ a highly individualized, labor intensive teaching technique that required expensive equipment, laboratories, hospitals, and a large group of dependent sick people. Creation of the national system of university based, research oriented, elite institutions that medical education reformers dreamed about required not merely a massive investment of capital, but a reorientation of some basic American values and institutional structures. . . .

The ideals of scientific excellence that inspired American medical educators and the realities of survival in a capitalist democracy were often at odds. For most medical schools this struggle took place on a local rather than a national stage. Looking closely at the history of the Temple University School of Medicine discloses the force of local socioeconomic and political factors in the creation of America's medical education system. In the details of Temple's struggle we get a particularly compelling view of the power of state politics, local markets, and strongly held public beliefs about such ideals as the nature of opportunity in America.

Any understanding of the combination of forces that shaped Temple must begin with the career of one man, Baptist minister Russell Conwell, who founded both the Temple medical school and hospital. At the time that Conwell convinced his congregation at the Grace Baptist Church to take on the burdens of supporting a hospital and a medical school, his church in north Philadelphia was said to be one of the largest Protestant congregations in America. Celebrated for his dramatic oratorical style that combined Biblical exegesis with "true" stories of "real people" who had overcome life's adversities and achieved success, Conwell commanded sizable speaking fees and had been a major figure on the Chatauqua lecture circuit since the 1870s. These fees, particularly for his most famous speech, "Acres of Diamonds," provided a significant part of the funding for the ministries he and his Grace Baptist congregation came to embrace.

Recognizing that the core of Conwell's power was in a curiously mixed religious and commercial activity dedicated to spreading the gospel of success through education and hard work provides an important key to understanding his medical school plans. This insight also helps explain the tremendous gulf between Conwell and medical reformers such as Flexner. Unlike the medical education elite, Conwell had no qualms about mixing commercial activities with more sacred, or, in the case of his medical school, more scientific endeavors. Conwell also gave public service a much greater prominence in his institutional plans than the one assigned by Flexner and most other champions of scientific medicine. In 1901 Conwell declared his intention to create on the Temple College campus a new "workingman's medical college." Conwell's medical college was to be a night school, open to all, regardless of race, color, creed, or gender, charging a modest tuition and with a schedule flexible enough to accommodate students with daytime employment. Like all of Temple's educational programs, the medical department was to give "all classes the opportunity to rise from the middle, or even the most ignorant ranks of society, to the highest intellectual plane; and fit them to meet financial, moral and social responsibility, as real benefactors of mankind."

To achieve this dream Temple was forced to pursue a variety of creative social and financial arrangements, which drew it into a complex web of relationships with state and municipal governments, local community groups and charitable organizations, neighborhood businesses, and large corporations interested in medical products. These relationships powerfully affected the way Temple responded to the mandates of national medical education authorities. National scientific and organizational mandates had to be balanced against a variety of more locally oriented socioeconomic concerns and the demands of a democratic society for educational opportunity and public service. Although specifics differed, this pattern of entanglement and demand is evident in the great mass of medical education institutions unable to secure substantial funding from the larger medical philanthropies. In the land grant universities of the western United States, in the struggling institutions of the financially crippled South, and in the less prestigious schools of eastern urban centers a similar web of local demands exerted its force. . . .

At Temple, the web of local entanglements took a form most American physicians of the time would have recognized. Conwell and the medical faculty he assembled opened what was essentially a proprietary medical school. This institutional form was, for the average American physician trained in such schools, more familiar and better understood than the reform experiments initiated at Johns Hopkins and Harvard and lauded by Flexner. Temple was not a classic nineteenth-century proprietary school. It was not, for example, owned by a private group of physicians; it never made a profit; and it was associated with a nascent university. Nonetheless, during much of Temple's early years the school relied on the classic proprietary funding mechanism—student fees. Temple's medical faculty learned quickly—as did most early-twentieth-century medical schools—how inadequate the income from student fees was to their educational enterprise. Like most other medical schools, they sought financial help from private philanthropies as well as state governments. Temple, however, had only modest success in securing philanthropic and government support and explored a wide variety of entrepreneurial possibilities. By selling soap and coal, raising sheep, and providing medical services on a contract basis to manufacturing establishments in the area, Temple became an integral part of a local economy. This situation fostered an acceptance of commercialism very much akin to that of the early proprietary schools. Using business principles to achieve self-sufficiency (rather than profit) was always a clearly articulated goal at Temple. . . .

Some proprietary schools were the rapacious, intellectually bankrupt "diploma-mills" that reformers, particularly Flexner, so enjoyed denouncing. But a few, as even Flexner admitted, were moderately well organized facilities that did not let the pursuit of profit overwhelm their efforts to teach the "practical art" of medicine. Flexner believed that these practical schools, which he defined as anti-scientific, commercial, and hostile to research, did not produce physicians able to deal with the demands of modern medicine. He also believed that the United States required only thirty-one schools (not the 155 he inspected) to produce enough physicians for the nation. Flexner was not alone in these beliefs as a 1903 speech by AMA President John Shaw Billings confirms. Billings made a special point of denouncing night schools such as Temple. His objections included doubts as to whether the students who frequented these "sundown institutions"—"the clerk, the streetcar conductor, the janitor and others employed during the day"—were suitable material for the medical profession. The direct frontal assault on their democratic philosophy was quite clear to Conwell and his supporters. To them the "scientific" reform activities of such groups as the AMA were thinly disguised attempts to create a medical aristocracy. Many individuals who played a role in the creation of the American medical education system, particularly private practitioners, state legislators, and the general public, were as concerned about this elitist design as Conwell. This was particularly true at the time that Temple was founded, almost ten years before Flexner undertook his famous study. During these years and later, a spirited debate raged over the value of the so-called practical, community-oriented training. Temple and a number of other schools were able to take advantage of this difference of opinion and carve out their own niche.

. . . Although Conwell's faction was quite adept at defending their populist ideals, pressure on them was mounting. First, Temple's night schedule cost the school membership in the Association of American Medical Colleges (AAMC), which felt such programs were inherently inadequate and refused to admit any night schools to membership. By 1905 the Pennsylvania Medical Council, various other state licensing boards, and the AMA had joined the chorus of critics who openly encouraged Temple to give up evening operation. Yet, only after several state licensing boards, including Pennsylvania's, categorically refused to let Temple graduates take their examinations did the champions of the night school agree to its demise. With Conwell expressing profound misgivings and the resignation of at least one department chairman, Albert Robin, Temple ended its night school and gradually discontinued all of its evening classes between 1907 and 1911.

. . . While the elite medical reformers succeeded in eliminating the night school operations, stewardship and uplift did not disappear at Temple, but were translated into a more secular ideology of public service, equality of opportunity, and concern for the equitable distribution of the fruits of knowledge. By the 1920s, democratic politics—the politics of state appropriations—acted as a kind of countervailing pressure against the forces of medical science and medical education reform. The state of Pennsylvania and organizations such as Philadelphia's Welfare Federation accomplished this by introducing the messy, *quid pro quo* decision-making dynamic of the American political process into Temple's regular institutional life. In a sporadic, but often definitive fashion, the various legislators, Board of Public Charities members, governors, and other municipal and state bureaucrats who formed Temple's web of support made their nonscientific agendas felt. In these overtly political agendas the populist yearnings, the concern for "practical healing" and community medicine, and even the commercial spirit of Conwell's original creation found expression.

Initially, Temple met with little success in its efforts to attract state funding. Part of the trouble was simply bad timing. Temple applied for state money at a moment of considerable turmoil and criticism for the existing appropriation system. Historian Rosemary Stevens has noted in her account of Pennsylvania's "unusually strong" system of state subsidy for medical facilities that by the early twentieth century "the days of easy money were over." The number of institutions competing for tax revenues had increased dramatically. Compounding the effects of increased competition was the fact that tax revenues in Pennsylvania had peaked. Many institutions, including Temple competitors such as the University of Pennsylvania, Jefferson Medical College, and Hahnemann Medical College, were well-established members of the medical lobby in Harrisburg. These factors put Temple at a distinct disadvantage. But the disadvantage was not insurmountable. . . .

After a slow start in the 1910s, Temple began to learn the language of persuasive political lobbying by playing, for example, on Conwell's reputation as a champion of the hard-working common man and his penchant for the rhetoric of industrial growth and progress. The lobbyists representing Temple also developed an acute sensitivity to the many manufacturing concerns and working class neighborhoods of the institution's locale. In a state controlled by a pro-business Republican machine, such a location was a crucial bargaining tool. Temple could and did argue that it directly served the interests of the manufacturing powers by providing medical care, education, and hope for a better life to the myriad of industrial employees who lived and worked in North Philadelphia. By the end of the 1920s, moreover, having caught on to the legislature's emphasis on institutions that served state needs rather than merely local ones, Temple lobbyists expanded their service rhetoric to include the whole region. At appropriation time, Temple's representatives would take great care to enumerate the distribution of its graduates throughout the state and how its doctors and hospitals attracted patients from all over the region. To live up to this rhetoric it was necessary for Temple to retain at least part of the populist, practical service personality favored by founder Conwell, who died in 1925.

. . . The power of the state to affect life at Temple became evident in a dramatic fashion in 1919 and 1920. At the end of 1919, the AMA Council on Medical Education informed Temple's dean that the school had been downgraded from the "B" list of acceptable medical schools to the lowest rank of "C" schools. This "C" rating meant that most states would not allow Temple graduates to take the medical licensing examinations required to practice. It also meant that the AMA publicly declared Temple to be a school "in need of complete reorganization." The blow was devastating to the Temple faculty, particularly the dean, Frank Hammond, who wrote bitterly of being tricked by the false encouragement of a "B" ranking that lured the school into years of futile effort. After several months of tense negotiations with AMA officials, in April of 1920 University trustees, the medical faculty, and the school's worried students faced the grim prospect of closing the school.

Caught between the AMA's adamant demand for extensive reforms and the University's inability to finance them, Temple medical school appeared poised to finally succumb to the "killing process" of Flexnerian reform. In a last desperate attempt to survive, Hammond and University officer Charles Beury traveled to Harrisburg to make a special plea to the governor. Beury and Hammond focused on Temple's record of service to the population of one of Pennsylvania's largest manufacturing districts in their appeal for financial aid and assistance in convincing the AMA that Temple was worth saving. Prompted by the governor and much to the delight of Hammond and Beury, the legislature agreed and voted to add $100,000 to Temple University's biennial appropriation for the medical school. Governor Sproul also directed the head of the State Division of Public Health to arrange a conference for the AMA, state officials, and Temple medical faculty to discuss the school's future plans. By June of 1921 the AMA had returned Temple to the acceptable "B" rank. With renewed vigor and the encouragement of the state, Temple faculty embarked on an ambitious campaign to raise funds needed to complete AMA mandated reforms. Connections with the local community were strengthened, as alumni and local businesses and charities expanded their investment in the school. Precipitated by the growing strength of the policing forces of scientific medicine's elite, Temple's crisis of 1919–1920 bears ample testimony to the power of political forces to shape medical education.

From the 1920s onward Temple's fluency in the political language of public service and vote-trading increased. The subsidy from the state to Temple's various institutional components amounted to more than $500,000 by the end of the decade. But even so, Temple had serious financial problems as it struggled to cover the costs of the Flexnerian reform mandate and continued to explore other sources of support, including commercial opportunities. Certain state policies, particularly those encouraging medical school hospitals to expand their population of paying patients, provided a strong impetus to such revenue-seeking behavior. . . .

Temple responded by expanding dramatically the amount of private (for-pay) care it provided. During the 1920s and 1930s the school continued to experiment with a number of other entrepreneurial opportunities, but in an increasingly problematic setting. The scientific reform efforts that were rapidly changing medicine's institutional landscape were also redefining the rules of the medical marketplace. Proprietary medical schools are a glaring example of an earlier for-profit activity that had become illegitimate in the post-reform era. The status of many other commercial activities—including the production of pharmaceuticals, the running of laboratory tests, as well as biomedical product development and testing—were not so clearly defined during the second quarter of the twentieth century, as elites in both medical education and scientific research consolidated their power. The pressure brought by individuals such as Flexner, who wanted scientific research and education removed almost entirely from the commercial sphere, was having an effect, but in this era it was far from definitive. For example, when did medical school faculty collaboration with a pharmaceutical company in the production of a new therapeutic agent amount to science-invalidating collusion? Even physicians hailed as modern medical heroes, such as George Minot, developer of a successful treatment for pernicious anemia, and insulin discoverer Frederick Banting, had difficulty answering this question. In this murky environment, Temple's survival depended on finding a way to stay in the market while not running afoul of those in the emerging scientific and medical education elites who opposed commercialization. This search was done with the approval of the state of Pennsylvania, the city of Philadelphia, and most of its other commercial and charitable supporters. . . .

Temple did have to reach an accommodation with medical education authorities. By the 1930s, the alternative was institutional death. Yet, unwilling to abandon their effort to provide medical education for working people and unable fiscally and philosophically to meet all of the demands of the AMA and the other policing bodies, Temple continued to negotiate its own way. Temple's stubborn refusal to conform completely to the new standards was in many ways a shrewd assessment of both its economic and political position in Philadelphia and Pennsylvania. In the early twentieth century Philadelphia had four other medical schools: all received state funds and most were in better financial shape than Temple. In such a competitive situation, which would only worsen by the Depression, the crafting of a special identity—workingman's medical school—that accentuated an institution's service to a worthy, under-served community showed great political astuteness. Politics and the market place, whether Flexner and the reformers liked it or not, played and would continue to play a powerful role in the development of the American medical education system. . . .

Schools such as Temple, which came to define their purpose in terms of the community's need for practical physicians and educational opportunity for the common people, played a crucial role in enabling the American medical education system to support schools such as Yale, Harvard, and the University of Pennsylvania, which defined themselves primarily in scientific terms. Producing physician scientists was the goal articulated by Hopkins, Yale, and others in Flexner's top tier of schools. These schools were by definition elite and exclusionary, and did not produce adequate numbers of doctors to fulfill the needs of American communities, particularly in rural areas. Temple and schools with similar practical identities softened the effect of the nation's growing physician distribution problem by producing a large number of physicians who returned to their home communities to practice. Furthermore, the existence of schools like Temple, dedicated to serving America's vast middle class, also softened the elitism inherent in the modern medical education system. . . . Temple's history illuminates the network of relationships that bound American medical schools into a distinctive system that, for a time, balanced the demands of scientific elitism against those of democracy and the free market.

FURTHER READING

Thomas N. Bonner, *To the Ends of the Earth: Women's Search for Education in Medicine* (1992).

Thomas N. Bonner, *Becoming a Physician: Medical Education in Britain, France, Germany, and the United States, 1750–1945* (1995).

Charlotte G. Borst, *Catching Babies: The Professionalization of Childbirth, 1870–1920* (1995).

E. Richard Brown, *Rockefeller Medicine Men: Medicine and Capitalism in America* (1980).

Vanessa N. Gamble, *Making a Place for Ourselves: The Black Hospital Movement, 1920–1945* (1995).

Norman Gevitz, *The D.O.'s: Osteopathic Medicine in America* (1982).

Darlene Clark Hine, *Black Women in White: Racial Conflict and Cooperation in the Nursing Profession, 1880–1950* (1989).

Timothy C. Jacobson, *Making Medical Doctors: Science and Medicine at Vanderbilt Since Flexner* (1987).

Robert E. Kohler, *From Medical Chemistry to Biochemistry: The Making of a Biomedical Discipline* (1982).

Kenneth M. Ludmerer, *Learning to Heal: The Development of American Medical Education* (1985).

Kenneth M. Ludmerer, *Time to Heal: American Medical Education from the Turn of the Century to the Era of Managed Care* (1999).

Gerald Markowitz and David Rosner, "Doctors in Crisis: A Study of the Use of Medical Education to Establish Modern Professional Elitism in Medicine," *American Quarterly* 25 (1973): 83–107.

Steven C. Martin, "'The Only Truly Scientific Method of Healing': Chiropractic and American Science, 1895–1990," *Isis* 85 (1994): 207–227.

Barbara Melosh, *"The Physician's Hand": Work Culture and Conflict in American Nursing* (1982).

Ronald L. Numbers, *Almost Persuaded: American Physicians and Compulsory Health Insurance, 1912–1920* (1978).

Ronald L. Numbers, ed., *Education of American Physicians: Historical Essays* (1980).

Steven J. Peitzman, *A New and Untried Course: Woman's Medical College and Medical College of Pennsylvania, 1850–1998* (2000).

Susan M. Reverby, *Ordered to Care: The Dilemma of American Nursing, 1850–1945* (1987).

Naomi Rogers, *An Alternative Path: The Making and Remaking of Hahnemann Medical College and Hospital of Philadelphia* (1998).

George Rosen, *The Structure of American Medical Practice, 1875–1981* (1983).

Charles E. Rosenberg, *The Care of Strangers: The Rise of America's Hospital System* (1987).

David Rosner, *A Once Charitable Enterprise: Hospitals and Health Care in Brooklyn and New York, 1885–1915* (1982).

William G. Rothstein, *American Medical Schools and the Practice of Medicine: A History* (1987).

Paul Starr, *The Social Transformation of American Medicine* (1982).

Richard H. Shryock, *Medical Licensing in America, 1650–1965* (1967).

Rosemary Stevens, *American Medicine and the Public Interest* (1998).

Rosemary Stevens, *In Sickness and in Wealth: American Hospitals in the Twentieth Century* (1989).

Janet A. Tighe, "Never Knowing One's Place: Temple University School of Medicine and the American Medical Education Hierarchy," *Transactions and Studies of the College of Physicians of Philadelphia* 12 (1990): 311–334.

Morris J. Vogel, *The Invention of the Modern Hospital: Boston, 1870–1930* (1980).

Steven C. Wheatley, *The Politics of Philanthropy: Abraham Flexner and Medical Education* (1988).

Expert Advice, Social Authority, and the Medicalization of Everyday Life, 1890–1930

American society changed profoundly in the first third of the twentieth century. Some of the most basic patterns of daily life were transformed as the effects of America's continuing industrialization, open immigration policy, and urban expansion were felt by the mass of its citizens. New job opportunities, new places to live, new means of transportation and communication, and new forms of entertainment were just a few of the dislocations. Even when such circumstances were welcome, adapting was difficult and more than a little unsettling, for communities as well as individuals. Many men and women, as well as government agencies, sought help in dealing with the problems and opportunities unfolding around them, and the health professions and medical science became important sources of this help. The medical profession, in particular, took on a variety of new identities and a greatly expanded social authority.

Certain scientific and medical specialties, especially psychiatry and psychology, played a particularly visible role as advisors to the general public. Using new tools of diagnosis and treatment such as the intelligence test and the psychopathic hospital, the experts of the human mind embraced a greatly expanded realm of human behavior. Other health specialists—visiting nurses, pediatricians, and public health physicians—did very much the same thing, so that by the 1930s a wide expanse of "normal" everyday life had become the object of some form of expert medical attention. Raising children, feeding a family, deciding whether to consume alcohol, choosing a marital partner, even dealing with one's own sexuality became subjects on which the medical profession, many in the media, and even the federal government recommended consulting a health expert.

Historians often refer to this process as the medicalization of American life and cast health professionals in a very aggressive and self-aggrandizing role. Is such an image an accurate depiction of medicine's power in this era? Other institutions and professions such as the law and the government affect medicine's authority, as do lay expectations and demands. Popular movements that used medical ideas—for

*example, the temperance, eugenics, court reform, and maternal and infant welfare
movements—were made up largely of laypersons. Were the lay participants always
in agreement with medical ones, particularly when the health professional's
influence manifested itself as advice that had taken on the more preemptory tone of
a command? How did patients express their disagreement with medical judgments?
Did these disagreements have an effect on the doctor-patient relationship? Did such
factors as class, race, and gender play a role in how one reacted to these new forms
of medical advice and judgment?*

 D O C U M E N T S

Document 1, an exchange of letters that appeared in the popular magazine *The Outlook*
in 1911, highlights the confusion in the public mind about how to understand and deal
with individuals who drink alcohol to excess. Is such behavior, the reader asks the editor,
Dr. Abbott, a sin, a crime, or a disease? In Document 2, published in 1920, another
medical expert is consulted as Elizabeth MacDonald, a regular contributor to the
women's magazine *Modern Priscilla,* gives her readers the benefit of a recent "chat"
with an experienced physician. Although respectful of the doctor's advice and obviously
in favor of medical involvement in all aspects of child rearing, MacDonald suggests that
there are aspects of motherhood that "even doctors do not all sufficiently realize."

Augusta Scott, a psychiatrist working for the New York Probation and Protection
Association, presents an even more expansive argument for the extension of medicine's
authority in Document 3, an article in the reformist journal *Mental Hygiene.* Should
the courts become the "scientific, social laboratories" that Scott idealizes, or is
medicine intruding too far into the legal realm? The issue of the transforming impact
that medicine could have on traditional institutions and patterns of behavior comes
up again in Document 4, one of the specially developed psychological tests used by
the United States Army in its examination of recruits for World War I. What exactly
is being tested? Will Americans from all races and classes and both genders score
equally well on this test? What does it mean for the military to rely on such an instrument of evaluation?

There was a high rate of failure among the young men taking mental fitness tests
like this one, and many of the physicians and psychologists involved with the testing saw
these results as evidence of the inadequacy of the American health care system. A few
even drew eugenic conclusions. Supreme Court Justice Oliver Wendell Holmes came
to such conclusions in his classic 1924 decision, *Buck* v. *Bell,* which is Document 5.
Arguing that "three generations of imbeciles are enough," and ruling that forced sterilization was constitutional, Holmes gave voice to a widespread concern about the danger
of the United States being overrun by the "unfit." Who were these undesirables that
so concerned Holmes, Scott, and the creators of the army fitness tests? What role did
medical ideas and personnel play in their identification and control? In these discussions,
what was happening to the relationship between medicine and the government?

The issue of the appropriate role for government in the health lives of American
citizens comes up again in Document 6, letters seeking health advice from the federal
Children's Bureau between 1915 and 1932. In 1921 the U.S. Congress passed the
Sheppard-Towner Act, which established a federal program for providing improved
child and maternal health care to all states willing to participate. Administered by the
Children's Bureau and staffed primarily by nurses, this relatively short-lived (1921–1929)
program was popular with many Americans, particularly women living in medically
underserved rural areas. What do these pleas for advice and information say about the

health conditions in which many American families lived? Are they an argument, as many reformers at the time believed, for the reconstruction of the health care delivery system?

1. Questions Answered in a Leading Popular Journal About the Medical Status of Inebriety, 1911

INEBRIETY, A DISEASE? OR A SIN?

My Dear Dr. Abbott:

In an Outlook of recent date you print a letter of your own sent to Mayor Gaynor, June 16, 1911. In that letter you say: "I think all medical authorities, and practically all penological, are agreed that inebriety is a disease rather than a crime or a vice, though a disease that has been produced by vice and leads to crime." I have before me a copy of The Outlook of November 4, 1899. In that number is an article, "Ethics of Temperance Reform." In that article four points are made, and the first is as follows: "Drunkenness is always a sin. The drunkard is not a poor victim, but a sinner. He is no more a victim of his appetite than the murderer is of his passion, or the gambler of his greed." I assume that you were the writer of that article or editorial. It also seems to me that your letter to Mayor Gaynor is practically a flat contradiction of your former statement. If so, may I ask most courteously how you reconcile the two statements? or may I ask if your theory has changed? Indeed, may I be insistent enough to ask that some time you will give us in The Outlook a plain statement of your own theory of drunkenness, its cause and its cure?

A.G.

Minneapolis, Minnesota.

[Dr. Abbott's reply]

The inconsistency is more apparent than actual, more verbal than real. The explanation of the inconsistency is found in the statement in the first sentence, that inebriety, though a disease, has been produced by vice and leads to crime.

The appetites and passions should be under the control of the will, and so guided and directed by the reason as to promote physical, mental, and moral health. When they are not thus under the control of the will and are not thus guided by the reason, the result is intemperance. . . .

But while intemperance in all its forms is a sin, the disease which it produces is not a sin. Gluttony may produce dyspepsia; dyspepsia is not a sin, though it may be a result of sin. Excessive drinking of tea may, and often does, produce serious nervous disease; nervous disease is not a sin, though it may be a result of sin. Excessive drinking of alcohol produces a disease known as inebriety; that disease is not a sin, though it is always a result of sin. One of the effects of this disease is a loss of self-control. He who is afflicted with this in its most serious form is as unable to control his appetites as a man afflicted with locomotor ataxia is to control his muscles. To put a man afflicted with this disease in jail until he has recovered from the immediate intoxication, and then send him out again into temptations which he is powerless to

Letter to the editor, Dr. Abbott, from A. G. in Minneapolis, Minn., and Dr. Abbott's reply, *The Outlook* 98 (August 12, 1911): 816–817.

resist, is inexcusable folly. If a man has brought insanity upon himself by vice, we do not punish the insanity. We set ourselves to cure it. Inebriety is, in this respect, analogous to insanity. It is not to be punished; it is to be cured. This is none the less true because inebriety is almost always, as insanity is frequently, the result of vice. Society should distinguish between these three—vice, disease, crime—which it often confounds. The remedy for the vice of intemperance is largely moral and intellectual, or, in the broad sense of the term, character-building. The remedy for the disease which that vice produces is partly moral and partly physical. For the crimes into which the vice often leads the intemperate person society must, in self-protection, provide some form of punishment.

But, in our judgment, punishment, whether for the vice which produces the disease or for the crime which follows, should always be reformatory, not vindictive, in its character. The distinction between sin and disease is not easy to draw. . . . It has been well said that, if drunkenness produces poverty, it is equally true that poverty produces drunkenness. How far the boy who has grown up in a family where there is no control of the appetites, who has inherited from the father and mother a diseased appetite, who lives in an atmosphere which intensifies the craving for stimulants, whose inadequate or improper food further intensifies that craving— how far he is a guilty person to be punished, how far a diseased person to be cured, is a question to which no definite and final answer can be given.

What is true of drunkenness is true of other sins. They are partly the result of deliberate, intentional violation of law. They are partly the result of ignorance, ill-breeding, bad inheritance, and almost irresistible social forces. Society has tried for many years the experiment of curing sin by punishing it. It is high time that society tried the experiment of curing crime by removing the causes which produce it and by treating the criminal as a diseased or insane person, to be sent to a hospital for remedial measures. So much of vice and crime is due to disease, and so much of disease is due to vice and crime, that society might well treat all vice and crime as diseases to be remedied and all punishments to be administered for the purpose of remedy, and might well go further and recognize the fact that vice and crime are largely the result of abnormal and evil social organization, to be remedied, not only by individual treatment, but by fundamental social reforms.

2. A Doctor Advises Mothers in a Mass-Circulation Women's Journal, 1920

The Wee Editor had just had his monthly looking over, and the doctor sat in the big wing chair while we talked of mothers' problems, especially those of the young mother and her first baby.

"Suppose I were one," I said, "and suppose I knew nothing at all and that I was rather frightened, but solemnly determined to do my very best, what cautions would you give me, and what would you feel was most important for me to know?"

The doctor leaned his head against the high chair-back, and looked off through the long vista of maple leaves on the Avenue trees, dancing in the morning sun.

"Our Babies: A Talk with the Doctor," *Modern Priscilla* 34 (August 1920): 40.

"That question," he said, "I would have to answer by remembering the questions mothers most often ask me."

Here are the things the doctor said, just as they occurred to him, and as I put them down.

The safest way to keep a child well is to keep germ-carriers away. If anybody has a cold, we cannot tell whether that cold is the beginning of the measles, or scarlet fever, or diphtheria. . . .

Do not let anybody who has a cold come into the same room with the baby if it can be avoided. At any rate do not let such a person touch it.

If a mother is nursing a baby and is unfortunate enough to get a cold, she will protect her child by tying a handkerchief around her mouth and nose when she has to be near it to feed or change it.

There is another aspect of the contagion matter too, and this is the protection of other children in case your own child has something the matter with it. I have just had a case of the whooping cough where the mother was a clever and intelligent woman. The child was not very sick; the weather was fine and the mother knew that the child ought to be out-of-doors. She made a good-sized sign, "I have got the Whooping Cough," and pinned it on the front of the child's dress, and she explained to the child that she put it there so that the other children would not have to be bothered with the trouble that he was having, and sent him out to play. If more mothers adopted the same attitude there would be less little tragedies every year.

When you know your child has been exposed to the whooping cough, it is a good plan to have him vaccinated for it. This sort of vaccination is now accepted as entirely helpful, and it may prevent serious consequences which all too often follow in the wake of whooping cough. Another form of vaccination is that for smallpox. The child should have it preferably before he begins to walk about. Nobody knows when these infections are going to bob up, and protection against them is a form of simple insurance that is a sensible safeguard.

Unfortunately we cannot say that any milk is absolutely safe, especially in cities. It goes through so many hands that it is not humanly possible to guard against the danger of infection.

A special laboratory furnishing milk from its own herd of cows is as safe as anything can be, but even here, especially through the summer months, danger is possible. Pasteurizing milk or sterilizing it by bringing it up to the point where the thinnest scum forms over the top makes it safe, and kills any "bugs" which may have tumbled into it. . . .

While we are on the subject of milk we must not forget that even doctors do not all sufficiently realize the importance of breast milk to a baby.

There is no formula which can match it. It has a mysterious power for health-making that we have not been able to discover in any other kind of food.

Babies are taken off breast feeding many, many times for too slight a reason. The cases where breast feeding cannot be accomplished are very rare. In justice to your child, *stick to it* unless there is some most unusual reason why it should be discontinued. Nineteen times out of twenty it is not only better for the baby but better for you.

Work with your doctor. *Stick to him.* Never mind if the neighbor tells you that she knows of a baby in just the condition yours is and somebody gave it something, and it gained a pound a week. Never mind if a neighbor tells you that she is sure the doctor is not doing the right thing, and never mind, even if you see something in a magazine.

If you have picked your doctor intelligently and have faith in his skill, do exactly what he says, no matter what contrary advice you may have.

Sometimes when there are feeding troubles it may take the doctor a long time to solve the difficulty, but be patient and obey his orders absolutely, because his experience and his knowledge is superior to that of an untrained observer, or else he does not deserve his license to practise.

3. Psychiatrist Augusta Scott Proselytizes for Greater Legal Reliance on Medical Assessments of Mental Health, 1922

In the fall of 1920, the New York Probation and Protective Association, an organization that is intensely interested in the welfare of the girls and young women of New York, offered the part-time services of a psychiatrist to the Women's Day Court. It was not the purpose of the organization to undertake a survey or to carry out a statistical investigation. The idea was simply to gain an impression of the psychiatric material that presented itself in the court cases, to see whether a psychiatrist could be of service in helping the court and in aiding the probation officers in the handling of special problem cases. It was also the hope of the organization that the examiner would be able to help the individual girls to arrive at a better understanding of themselves and their difficulties. . . .

When a woman was found to be seriously defective, with vicious social tendencies or mentally sick, an effort was made to have her sent to the Psychopathic Ward of Bellevue Hospital to be observed and from there committed to one of the state institutions. . . .

The insistent question as to how many of the girls were normal came to be an annoyance, but one could easily counter with the reply, "Give me your standard of normality." The psychiatrist accepts the fact that there are varying standards of normality and is soon lost in the study of the individual and his assets and modes of reaction and self-expression, not as compared with any theoretical standard, but with reference to the question wherein this person, with his particular equipment, is making a failure. From the standpoint of conventional behavior, one could say off-hand that all of these women are abnormal, since they have deviated from social standards and have broken the laws that regulate social conduct. Probably most people mean by the question, how many have the capacity to make a successful social readjustment. Various case records from the thirty individuals of the normal type will be given to show the wide range of personalities within the group.

> *Case 4.* Anna is a sixteen-year-old girl who lived with her married sister in a very good home. Her mother is insane and was committed to a hospital six years ago. Anna was then ten years old, and she lived in a Catholic institution until one year ago. She had had no serious illness and no neuropathic traits. She finished the eighth grade in the parochial school, became a telephone operator, and has worked steadily, earning a good

Augusta Scott, "300 Psychiatric Examinations Made at the Women's Day Court, New York City," *Mental Hygiene* 6 (1922): 343, 347, 356–358, 360–361, 364, 367.

wage. Four weeks before being brought to court on a charge of incorrigibility, she had a quarrel with her sister about her hours and her recreation. She felt that she could not be in by eleven o'clock at night; therefore she ran away and took a furnished room. She was "crazy" about dancing and went out every night. She was going about with a man whom she met at a dance hall and was planning to go to Atlantic City with him, where he had promised to get her a better job. But the night before her departure she was arrested by a policewoman who had been searching for her. The girl was talkative, light-hearted, pleasure-loving, with no realization of the danger she had been in. Her mental age was 14.3 years, I. Q. 89, and she had no special difficulties except an undisciplined temper and a craze for dancing. Examination showed that she was a virgin and she was remarkably free from curiosity and ruminations about sexual matters. . . .

Case 10. Ruth, aged seventeen, an incorrigible girl, was brought to the examiner because she had broken her probation. During the last year she had run away from home five times. This time she was accused by the detectives who found her of consorting with negroes and practicing perversions. She was a rather pretty girl who coöperated well in the examination, giving in detail her version of the difficulties. Her intelligence was average—mental age 15.6, I. Q. 96. Her parents were strict orthodox Jews, and her earlier runaways were due to their uncompromising attitude and her craving for excitement. She was ambitious socially and felt that their home was not nice enough for her friends. She had had about two years in high school and then stayed at home while her mother attended to the shop. She had never been employed, and said she would not care to have an ordinary job, but might like to work in a first-class store and sell lovely things to nice customers. She confessed that she had had immoral relations with a friend two weeks before she left home the first time. She was partly threatened and partly persuaded into the act, but thereafter she was easily aroused and had repeated experiences. She denied the charges which the detective made, but admitted that she had been in colored cabarets. She did not deny that she prostituted when in need of money. This, however, was not without some conflict, for she said, "I know in my heart and soul I am not a prostitute, yet what else am I doing?" It seemed useless to send this girl home, yet there is no institution for Jewish girls. Probation officers and relatives were at a loss to know what to do. At that time it was reported that girls could be observed in the Bellevue Psychopathic ward and be admitted to Bedford Reformatory from there. After being at Bellevue for one month, she was returned to the court with the recommendation that she be committed to Bedford. Since the charge against her was incorrigibility, the judge again permitted her to go home. The hospital record stated that she undermined the morale of the ward, spoke disparagingly of other patients, had outbursts of temper, and became quite threatening in her attitude. It was also stated that she openly boasted of her immoral acts. After she went home, arrangements were made for her to reënter high school, but her teachers had to speak to her about her manner of dress and excessive use of rouge. They also said that she talked to other girls about her sex experiences. She deceived her parents and teachers and within a few weeks she again disappeared. . . .

Case 13. Hannah, aged twenty-six, convicted of prostitution, was an intelligent woman, dressed in good taste, refined in manner. Her mental age was 16.2, I. Q. 101, and she said that she was a college graduate. (A report from the college that she mentioned showed that she had not been enrolled there, but letters received from her mother confirmed her statements regarding her home life.) Her general health had been excellent, and she was in no way nervous or unstable. Her family live in the West and are in good circumstances. She came East to go to school. On account of her ambition to go on the stage, she also attended classes in a "school of oratory." While in the East, she had a love affair and entered into sexual relations, became pregnant, and had a miscarriage.

After she finished school, she taught in a high school for one year, but her stage ambitions were pressing, and she satisfied these cravings by becoming a Red Cross entertainer on a voluntary basis. Her parents have always supplied her with some money, but not enough for the pleasures she desires. For a number of months she was a man's mistress in a city in the Middle West. Over a year ago she came to New York hoping to get on the stage, but she made no real effort to attain her ambition. She went home this summer, but returned in a few weeks, taking a room with the girl with whom she was arrested. She denied that she prostituted for money, but said that she must have gayety and entertainment and was willing to pay the price. Intercourse meant nothing to her, and since she had "lost her virtue," what did it matter? She had not thought much about the way she was drifting in life and never worried over moral issues. The desire to go on the stage, she thought, arose from vanity. It was found that she had syphilis, and she was sent to Kingston Avenue Hospital. . . .

. . . With the spreading of the interest of the physician from the severe to the milder disorders, there has grown up a science of medical psychology, but for this, as for other sciences, there is a big field to be explored. Individuals vary so greatly in so many kinds of traits, abilities, defects, and modes of reaction, that it is futile to search for the "normal." What one can best do in the present state of our knowledge is to use descriptive terms and search for types. . . .

. . . As a result of this study of the 300 women, the opinion has grown more firm and definite that the problem of delinquency, antisocial conduct, and abnormal behavior is a very complex one that can be satisfactorily met only when judges, probation officers, criminologists, officers of correctional institutions, psychiatrists, and social workers pool their knowledge and experience. In fact, the problem is a community problem. The court is a clearing house for all sorts and conditions of people who are obviously making a failure in life. It should be a scientific, social laboratory of first importance.

4. The United States Army Tests the Mental Fitness of Recruits, 1921

In each of the sentences below you have four choices for the last word. Only one of them is correct. In each sentence draw a line under the one of these four words which makes the truest sentence. If you cannot be sure, guess. The two samples are already marked as they should be.

SAMPLES:

People hear with the   eyes   <u>ears</u>   nose   mouth

France is in   <u>Europe</u>   Asia   Africa   Australia

1. America was discovered by . . . Drake   Hudson   Columbus   Cabot
2. Pinochle is played with . . . rackets   cards   pins   dice
3. The most prominent industry of Detroit is . . . automobiles   brewing   flour   packing
4. The Wyandotte is a kind of . . . horse   fowl   cattle   granite

"Army Alpha Test #8 for Recruits to the U.S. Military," in *Psychological Examining in the United States Army,* ed. Robert Yerkes, vol. 15 of *Memoirs of the National Academy of Sciences* (Washington, D.C., 1921), pp. 227, 228.

5. The U.S. School for Army Officers is at . . . Annapolis   West Point   New Haven   Ithaca

6. Food products are made by . . . Smith & Wesson   Swift & Co.   W.L. Douglas   B.T. Babbitt

7. Bud Fisher is famous as . . . an actor   an author   a baseball player   a comic artist

8. The Guernsey is a kind of . . . horse   goat   sheep   cow

9. Marguerite Clark is known as a . . . suffragist   singer   movie actress   writer

10. "Hasn't scratched yet" is used in advertising a . . . duster   flour   brush   cleanser

11. Salsify is a kind of . . . snake   fish   lizard   vegetable

12. Coral is obtained from . . . mines   elephants   oysters   reefs

13. Rosa Bonheur is famous as a . . . poet   painter   composer   sculptor

14. The tuna is a kind of . . . fish   bird   reptile   insect

15. Emeralds are usually . . . red   blue   green   yellow

16. Maize is a kind of . . . corn   hay   oats   rice

17. Nabisco is a . . . patent medicine   disinfectant   food product   toothpaste

18. Velvet Joe appears in advertisements of . . . tooth powder   dry goods   tobacco   soap

19. Cypress is a kind of . . . machine   food   tree   fabric

20. Bombay is a city in . . . China   Egypt   India   Japan

21. The dictaphone is a kind of . . . typewriter   multigraph   phonograph   adding machine

22. The pancreas is in the . . . abdomen   head   shoulder   neck

23. Cheviot is the name of a . . . fabric   drink   dance   food

24. Larceny is a term used in . . . medicine   theology   law   pedagogy

25. The Battle of Gettysburg was fought in . . . 1863   1813   1778   1812

26. The bassoon is used in . . . music   stenography   book-binding   lithography

27. Turpentine comes from . . . petroleum   ore   hides   trees

28. The number of a Zulu's legs is . . . two   four   six   eight

29. The scimitar is a kind of . . . musket   cannon   pistol   sword

30. The Knight engine is used in the . . . Packard   Lozier   Stearns   Pierce Arrow

31. The author of "The Raven" is . . . Stevenson   Kipling   Hawthorne   Poe

32. Spare is a term used in . . . bowling   football   tennis   hockey

33. A six-sided figure is called a . . . scholium   parallelogram   hexagon   trapezium

34. Isaac Pitman was most famous in . . . physics   shorthand   railroading   electricity

35. The ampere is used in measuring . . . wind power   electricity   water power   rainfall

36. The Overland car is made in . . . Buffalo   Detroit   Flint   Toledo

37. Mauve is the name of a . . . drink   color   fabric   food

38. The stanchion is used in . . . fishing   hunting   farming   motoring

39. Mica is a . . . vegetable   mineral   gas   liquid

40. Scrooge appears in . . . Vanity Fair   The Christmas Carol   Romola   Henry IV

Answers

1. America was discovered by   Drake   Hudson   <u>Columbus</u>   Cabot
2. Pinochle is played with   rackets   <u>cards</u>   pins   dice
3. The most prominent industry of Detroit is   <u>automobiles</u>   brewing   flour   packing
4. The Wyandotte is a kind of   horse   <u>fowl</u>   cattle   granite
5. The U.S. School for Army Officers is at   Annapolis   <u>West Point</u>   New Haven   Ithaca
6. Food products are made by   Smith & Wesson   <u>Swift & Co.</u>   W.L. Douglas   B.T. Babbitt
7. Bud Fisher is famous as an   actor   author   baseball player   <u>comic artist</u>
8. The Guernsey is a kind of   horse   goat   sheep   <u>cow</u>
9. Marguerite Clark is known as a   suffragist   singer   <u>movie actress</u>   writer
10. "Hasn't scratched yet" is used in advertising a   duster   flour   brush   <u>cleanser</u>
11. Salsify is a kind of   snake   fish   lizard   <u>vegetable</u>
12. Coral is obtained from   mines   elephants   oysters   <u>reefs</u>
13. Rosa Bonheur is famous as a   poet   <u>painter</u>   composer   sculptor
14. The tuna is a kind of   <u>fish</u>   bird   reptile   insect
15. Emeralds are usually   red   blue   <u>green</u>   yellow
16. Maize is a kind of   <u>corn</u>   hay   oats   rice
17. Nabisco is a   patent medicine   disinfectant   <u>food product</u>   toothpaste
18. Velvet Joe appears in advertisements of   tooth powder   dry goods   <u>tobacco</u>   soap
19. Cypress is a kind of   machine   food   <u>tree</u>   fabric
20. Bombay is a city in   China   Egypt   <u>India</u>   Japan
21. The dictaphone is a kind of   typewriter   multigraph   <u>phonograph</u>   adding machine
22. The pancreas is in the   <u>abdomen</u>   head   shoulder   neck
23. Cheviot is the name of a   <u>fabric</u>   drink   dance   food
24. Larceny is a term used in   medicine   theology   <u>law</u>   pedagogy
25. The Battle of Gettysburg was fought in   <u>1863</u>   1813   1778   1812
26. The bassoon is used in   <u>music</u>   stenography   book-binding   lithography
27. Turpentine comes from   petroleum   ore   hides   <u>trees</u>
28. The number of a Zulu's legs is   <u>two</u>   four   six   eight
29. The scimitar is a kind of   musket   cannon   pistol   <u>sword</u>
30. The Knight engine is used in the   Packard   Lozier   <u>Stearns</u>   Pierce Arrow
31. The author of "The Raven" is   Stevenson   Kipling   Hawthorne   <u>Poe</u>
32. Spare is a term used in   <u>bowling</u>   football   tennis   hockey
33. A six-sided figure is called a   scholium   parallelogram   <u>hexagon</u>   trapezium
34. Isaac Pitman was most famous in   physics   <u>shorthand</u>   railroading   electricity
35. The ampere is used in measuring   wind power   <u>electricity</u>   water power   rainfall
36. The Overland car is made in   Buffalo   Detroit   Flint   <u>Toledo</u>
37. Mauve is the name of a   drink   <u>color</u>   fabric   food

38. The stanchion is used in   fishing   hunting   <u>farming</u>   motoring
39. Mica is a   vegetable   <u>mineral</u>   gas   liquid
40. Scrooge appears in   Vanity Fair   <u>The Christmas Carol</u>   Romola   Henry IV

5. Supreme Court Justice Oliver Wendell Holmes Upholds State Sterilization Practices, 1924

BUCK

v.

BELL, Superintendent of the State Colony for Epileptics and Feeble Minded
Argued April 22, 1927
Decided May 2, 1927

Mr. JUSTICE HOLMES delivered the opinion of the Court.

This is a writ of error to review a judgment of the Supreme Court of Appeals of the State of Virginia, affirming a judgment of the Circuit Court of Amherst County, by which the defendant in error, the superintendent of the State Colony for Epileptics and Feeble Minded, was ordered to perform the operation of salpingectomy upon Carrie Buck, the plaintiff in error, for the purpose of making her sterile. . . . The case comes here upon the contention that the statute authorizing the judgment is void under the Fourteenth Amendment as denying the plaintiff in error due process of law and the equal protection of the laws.

Carrie Buck is a feeble-minded white woman who was committed to the State Colony above mentioned in due form. She is the daughter of a feeble-minded mother in the same institution, and the mother of an illegitimate feeble-minded child. She was eighteen years old at the time of the trial of her case in the Circuit Court in the latter part of 1924. An Act of Virginia approved March 20, 1924 recites that the health of the patient and the welfare of society may be promoted in certain cases by the sterilization of mental defectives, under careful safeguard, etc.; that the sterilization may be effected in males by vasectomy and in females by salpingectomy, without serious pain or substantial danger to life; that the Commonwealth is supporting in various institutions many defective persons who if now discharged would become a menace but if incapable of procreating might be discharged with safety and become self-supporting with benefit to themselves and society; and that experience has shown that heredity plays an important part in the transmission of insanity, imbecility, etc. The statute then enacts that whenever the superintendent of certain institutions including the abovenamed State Colony shall be of the opinion that it is for the best interest of the patients and of society that an inmate under his care should be sexually sterilized, he may have the operation performed upon any patient afflicted with hereditary forms of insanity, imbecility,

Buck v. *Bell,* Superintendent of the State Colony for Epileptics and Feeble Minded (April 22–May 2, 1924), 247 U.S. 200, pp. 205–208.

etc., on complying with the very careful provisions by which the act protects the patients from possible abuse.

The superintendent first presents a petition to the special board of directors of his hospital or colony, stating the facts and the grounds of his opinion, verified by affidavit. Notice of the petition and of the time and place of the hearing in the institution is to be served upon the inmate, and also upon his guardian, and if there is no guardian the superintendent is to apply to the Circuit Court of the County to appoint one. If the inmate is a minor notice also is given to his parents, if any, with a copy of the petition. The board is to see to it that the inmate may attend the hearings if desired by him or his guardian. The evidence is all to be reduced to writing, and after the board has made its order for or against the operation, the superintendent, or the inmate, or his guardian, may appeal to the Circuit Court of the County. The Circuit Court may consider the record of the board and the evidence before it and such other admissible evidence as may be offered, and may affirm, revise, or reverse the order of the board and enter such order as it deems just. Finally any party may apply to the Supreme Court of Appeals, which, if it grants the appeal, is to hear the case upon the record of the trial in the Circuit Court and may enter such order as it thinks the Circuit Court should have entered. There can be no doubt that so far as procedure is concerned the rights of the patient are most carefully considered, and as every step in this case was taken in scrupulous compliance with the statute and after months of observation, there is no doubt that in that respect the plaintiff in error has had due process at law.

The attack is not upon the procedure but upon the substantive law. It seems to be contended that in no circumstances could such an order be justified. It certainly is contended that the order cannot be justified upon the existing grounds. The judgment finds the facts that have been recited and that Carrie Buck "is the probable potential parent of socially inadequate offspring, likewise afflicted, that she may be sexually sterilized without detriment to her general health and that her welfare and that of society will be promoted by her sterilization," and thereupon makes the order. In view of the general declarations of the Legislature and the specific findings of the Court obviously we cannot say as matter of law that the grounds do not exist, and if they exist they justify the result. We have seen more than once that the public welfare may call upon the best citizens for their lives. It would be strange if it could not call upon those who already sap the strength of the state for these lesser sacrifices, often not felt to be such by those concerned, in order to prevent our being swamped with incompetence. It is better for all the world, if instead of waiting to execute degenerate offspring for crime, or to let them starve for their imbecility, society can prevent those who are manifestly unfit from continuing their kind. The principle that sustains compulsory vaccination is broad enough to cover cutting the Fallopian tubes. . . . Three generations of imbeciles are enough.

But, it is said, however it might be if this reasoning were applied generally, it fails when it is confined to the small number who are in the institutions named and is not applied to the multitudes outside. It is the usual last resort of constitutional arguments to point out our shortcomings of this sort. But the answer is that the law does all that is needed when it does all that it can, indicates a policy, applies it to all within the lines, and seeks to bring within the lines all similarly situated so far and so fast as its means allow. Of course so far as the operations enable those who otherwise must be kept confined to be returned to the world, and thus open the asylum to others, the equality aimed at will be more nearly reached.

6. Families Seek Expert Advice from the Children's Bureau When Health Questions Arise, 1916–1926

Received August 1, 1925

More than a yr. ago, I wrote for information on raising my boy, who is now 3 yr. 8 mo. old. For more than a yr. he has been troubled with Colds. First in his ears, now I believe he has catarrah of the nose. And next, I expect, is suggestions to have the tonsils removed. Most of this is caused by improper housing at times & food. I had no work part [of] the time and couldn't hire the right place for him. . . . Altho the parties [who run child care] might have had the right food, they catered to his whims or his first demand, & would even hand him weinies just before breakfast, toasties & lots of sugar in winter, maybe 3 or 4 sausages, sauerkraut, or pork & beans for supper [with] syrup on top of it.

He then developed a terrible cold all thru his system. Even his eyes begin to look bad & I treated them with Argarol. Now I want to know if you will suggest some diet to build him up, as I can count his ribs, and at times he looks blue about his eyes & nose, and pale faced. For a yr. his teeth have been decaying. [He] has several to fill.

We live near the city hospital and the court lady who visits us suggest I get the children in [foster] homes or institutions. [She] says she could arrange to have our teeth fil[l]ed at the hospital, and I took the boy over and find out they do not do work of that kind there. If I try at other public places they could gather up a few diseases waiting in the crowds [for] our turn. [We waited] 3 hrs. the other day.

I had the baby looked at by a common physician. We were advised to move out of [our] place on the childrens behalf. Well, we moved into a room heated by a leaking gas heater. [We had to go] outside into a cold rooming house for eats a few awful blustery cold days before we could arrange to find any other place, & then we didn't get where the gas was piped correctly. It was hard on my eyes. My baby of 2 months had red streaks . . . in the White [of her eyes] for several days, then began holding her head to one side, and [was] troubled with flem in throat & gag[g]ed. . . . [Her] right ear had a bad odor. At [the] Hospital they advised 1/8 tablet aspirin 3 times a day, swab[b]ed the ears with a tooth pick wrapped in cotton & put in ear medicine containing alcahol. I had *been* putting warm boric acid water in [them]. . . . She coughs now. We pay $25.00 month for our two rooms. I don't believe children should be raised in rooms heated by gas. *And* I believe there should be laws against heating

---

These documents can be found in the Children's Bureau Records, Labor Department Record Group 102, Central Files, 1914–1940, National Archives, Files 4-3-0-3; 4-2-1-5; 4-5-8-1; 4-4-3-4. They can also be found in Molly Ladd-Taylor, *Raising Baby the Government Way: Mothers' Letters to the Children's Bureau, 1915–1932* (New Brunswick, N.J.: Rutgers University Press, 1986), pp. 49, 51–52, 112–114, 123.

rooms with gas not correctly piped for the general health of the people. It might lessen the no. of tonsil removals in school children. . . .

Will you send me some advise on the subjects of raising my children? The boy was born July 18, 1921. The girl Nov. 12th, 1924. Would you advise us to go to a dental college, where they fill teeth by students cheap? I hear that at the City hospital every thing is run by politicians and we do more waiting than anything else.

Will cod liver tablets be good for the children? And tomato juice for 4 months old baby? I have been trying to learn what different foods do for the body. . . . We live near a library. Can you suggest a certain book that would be somewhat complete on that subject?

I have a father at the State Hospital who has been *helping* for years to provide food stuffs & helping 6 hrs. [a] day for himself & inmates. We have payed also a few yrs $20 month. They wanted us to pay for every article of clothing, even to the shoe leather he trod out working. If we were well enough to do, [we] could furnish him with things to work with [that] he likes, a radio too, a Victrola, a car to take him in rides, etc. We would gladly care for him in my home and I believe he would be all right and happy.

Mrs. W. F., Kansas City, Missouri

August 12, 1926

Am writing to you to see if it is not possible to put out another Bulletin of information (or have added to your book on "Prenatal Care" more information for ignorant & expected mothers) that is [on] the danger of an instrument birth to a child—what to do with a child when seriously injured by instruments—that is, to take it to a hospital & and have it's little head operated on at once, while its little head is just cartilage, & its little brain not yet commencing to develop. Also explain the new method of operating on the mother & taking the child, thus avoiding such injuries & placing if possible these bulletins in [the] hands of nurses and Drs. to be given to their maternity patients.

I am begging the Department of Labor to try & get Drs. & nurses to take more interest in maternity work, as the life of one neglected child is such a costly experience for a[n] ignorant mother & father. I do not want any father & mother to suffer what we have thro ignorance. [That] is why I am writing you. We never knew of the danger of an instrument birth. We never knew the child could be taken by an operation. We never knew what to do with our child after it was hurt, until too late & the Drs. [we] had did not seem to know either. Until it was too late.

Our darling suffered 20 whole long months, to be operated on too late, & it cost her her life. Our only child leaving us, [our] hearts breaking from the suffering only a mother and father who worship[p]ed their child can know. So please try & help others through your department all you can & keep them from making the horrible mistake we made, & [from] the loss of the one whose place can never be filled. & what makes it so much worse is the fact it was so unnecessary, the seeming murder from pure ignorance. So please try & add this most necessary information for the ignorant to your helpful Bulletins. Cant you possibly do this? Am so anxious to know! & it is so badly needed. I speak from a heart full of aching practical experience, a loved one lost through ignorance. "The *one*" whose place *can never be filled.*

Do please try to help others? Surely such Bulletins should be in the homes of every married family, especially the young married couples who must get so much from experience. We never knew until too late & the experience is entirely too costly. Is all.

Sincerely.

Mrs. S. L., Louisiana

P.S. Please send me a copy of these or this bulletin soon as you put it out for public service & benefit, *wont you please?* Our babys head was badly hurt, the instruments crushed its little head in front—the forehead above the eyes—& it left pressure causing 20 months of suffering to be operated on too late. Please furnish the necessary information for such ignorance to expectant mothers you can reach thro your Bulletins.

June 18, 1918

Dear Sir

I saw in St Louis Weekly Globe Democrat Free book on Maternity. I am a wife of a soilder & will become a mother in about 8 months. My friend come out to See [me] with a baby Defarm[ed]; it[s] head like a snake. Can you tell wheather that would make my baby defarm[ed] by looking at It? I look at [it] about 10 Minutes. May was my first Month I didn't have my monthly so my time has come for June. Monday June 10 I was taken sick in my stomach, try to thro[w] up But could [not]. My head hurt Me & my side. I was sick Monday Eve then all day Wednesday & not since. So Please write; tell if that will defarm a baby & is there any thing I can take that will help it. I saw the baby Sat 15.

Can you let your Husband have it after you are in that kind of shape & how long. When would [we] hofto stop doing It? Will I Ingure the baby in any way? Please write & tell & send me your book. Can you send me some pretty names for boys & girls that would be nice to name a baby?

I always have my monthly on 29 or 30 of each month. When could you com[m]ence doing [it] after the child is born. How long do you hofto wait? Please give full information about such thing. I often hear they people [are] not having baby. What do they do not to have them? But I am crazy for Some Children & so is my Husband. I remain.

Mrs. E. G., Indiana

October 19, 1916

Dear Miss Lathrop:

I should very much like all the Publications on the Care of my self, who am now pregnant, also the care of a baby, both No. 1 and No. 2 [of the] series.

I live sixty five miles from a Dr. and my other babies (two) were very large at birth, one 12-lbs the other 10 ½ lbs. I have been *very* badly torn each time, through the rectum the last time. My youngest child is 7 ½ (and when I am delivered this last time it will be past 8 ½ yrs). I am 37 years old and I am so worried and filled with perfect horror at the prospects ahead. So many of my neighbors die at giving birth to their children. I have a baby 11 months old in my keeping now whose mother died—when I reached their cabin last Nov It was 22 below zero and I had to ride 7 miles horse back. She was nearly dead when I got there and died after giving birth to a 14 lb. boy. It seems awfull to me to think of giving up all my work and leaving my little ones, 2 of which are adopted—a girl 10 and this baby. Will you please send me all the information of the care of my self before and after and at the time of delivery. I am far from a Dr. and we have no means, only what we get on this rented ranch. I also want all the information on baby care especially right young new born ones. If there is *a[n]ything* what I can do to escape being torn again wont you let me know. I am just 4 months along now but haven't quickened yet. I am very Resp.

Mrs. A. P., Wyoming

 E S S A Y S

The first essay, by University of Wisconsin historian Rima D. Apple, shows the complex relationship that existed between physicians and the American public in the early years of the twentieth century. Drawing on advice manuals, medical textbooks, a host of popular journals, advertising copy, and her own broad understanding of women's history, Apple presents a compelling portrait of the social dynamics that went into the creation of "scientific motherhood." The lay population did not unequivocally accept doctors and other health advisors, Apple astutely points out. In reality there were alternating moments of acceptance and resistance and ebbs and flows in medicine's influence. These shifts in power had a profound effect on everyday health behavior and on medicine's status in society. The power dynamic at the heart of the second essay, written by Princeton University historian Elizabeth Lunbeck, looks quite different from the power dynamic in Apple's essay. Lunbeck's group of early-twentieth-century psychiatrists and social workers appear much more in control of the new diagnostic and therapeutic situations they were creating with the category of "hypersexual female." But were they? As Lunbeck explains, the revolution in sexual mores, particularly its manifestation among working-class youth, presented society, not just psychiatry, with a formidable challenge. Did the highly malleable medical theory that Lunbeck's psychiatrist created meet this challenge? More importantly, are assuaging middle-class concerns about a loss of social control and the creation of new categories of deviance a legitimate medical function?

Physicians and Mothers Construct "Scientific Motherhood"

RIMA D. APPLE

Scientific motherhood is the insistence that women require expert scientific and medical advice to raise their children healthfully. As the ideology emerged in nineteenth-century United States, a myriad of interested parties, including educators, social commentators, physicians, health reformers and mothers themselves, promoted the idea that mothers needed to learn about science and medicine. Women were advised

Rima D. Apple, "Constructing Mothers: Scientific Motherhood in the Nineteenth and Twentieth Centuries," *Social History of Medicine* 8 (1995): 161–178. Reprinted by permission of Oxford University Press and the author.

to seek out the most up-to-date and "scientific" information they could find. Doctors were popular sources, but so too were child-care manuals (produced by physicians, scientists, nurses, manufacturers and lay-writers), advice columns and letters-to-the editor in women's magazines and general interest journals, and the new field of domestic science or home economics with classes offered at all levels of a girl's education.

As scientific advice for successful child-rearing gained in prominence, the source of this expertise slowly changed. In its early manifestations, scientific motherhood encouraged mothers to find and evaluate information for themselves, to be actively involved in decision-making about the health of their families. By the twentieth century, the scientific motherhood ideology had been refined. Increasingly women were told not just that they needed to learn from scientific and medical expertise but rather that they needed to follow the directions of experts. This aspect of the ideology presented women with a tension-laden contradiction: it made them responsible for the health and welfare of their families, but it denied them control over child-rearing. In other words, women were both responsible for their families and incapable of that responsibility. Two advertisements clearly illustrate this transition.

A 1885 Mellin's Food advertisement from the child-care journal *Babyhood* is headed "Advice to Mothers" and the body of the copy cautions readers:

> The swelling tide of infantile disease and mortality, resulting from injudicious feeding, the ignorant attempts to supply a substitute for human milk, can only be checked by enlightened parental care.

The advertisement goes on to say most reassuringly:

> Men of the highest scientific attainments of modern times, both physiologists and chemists, have devoted themselves to careful investigation and experiment in devising a suitable substitute for human milk.

The result, of course, was Mellin's Food, a food "worthy the confidence of mothers."

In contrast another advertisement published in *Parents' Magazine* more than 50 years later has a young father objecting: "But your mother says he's much too young for vegetables!" And the modern mother replies, "Well dear, you'd better argue that with Doctor Evans. He says babies do better if they have vegetables early in life."

These two advertisements share several characteristics. Both are selling food products for infants; both seek to convince mothers to buy the product; both imply that use of the product will ensure good health for the baby; both suggest that science provides the best guide for raising children. Yet, despite these similarities, the two advertisements are quite dissimilar in form and tone. While both, to some extent, play on the emotions of the reader, the emotional content of the 1885 advertisement is more muted. It attempts to sell with gentle persuasion, informing the consumer of a problem, "the swelling tide of infantile disease and mortality," and explaining in rather technical terms that

> A compound suitable for the infant's diet must be alkaline in reaction; must be rich in heat-producers, with a proper admixture of albuminoids of a readily digestible nature, together with the necessary salts and moisture.

It then claims that Mellin's Food is the solution to that problem. It is a wordy advertisement, fairly typical of the day.

The 1938 advertisement attracts the reader with an eye-catching visual of a smiling baby and smiling parents. It graphically demonstrates the results of using Libby's Homogenized Baby Food. The copy . . . is informative, "special homogenization—which breaks food cells into tiny particles," but the information imparted in the text is less important than the emotional appeal. Of greater significance is the dialogue in the visual which cites a physician and urges readers to "Ask your doctor." Healthful child-rearing would not result from mother's, or grandmother's, experience, this advertisement suggests; nor would women study science for themselves. Rather, mothers interested in the health of their families would proudly follow the directions of their doctors. . . .

. . . Though new options took some women outside the domestic sphere into the worlds of paid labour and the women's club movement, the overwhelming majority of women became wives and mothers and popular imagery persisted in equating praiseworthy womanhood and the maternal role. "Women's labors and success in the various fields and affairs of life, are calling daily for more and more attention," noted one woman physician in her 1901 manual for women. But, she cautioned, "while we admire her in her new role, with her efforts toward success in society, literature, science, politics and the arts, we must not lose sight of her most divine and sublime mission in life—womanhood and motherhood."

Yet, even with the persistence of this image, over the decades the average American family size shrank and women spent fewer years in child-rearing. In 1880, the total fertility rate for white women was 4.24 children. The number decreased over the decades: by 1900 it was 3.56 and by 1930 the rate was 2.45, dropping to 2.19 in 1940.

In addition to declining family size, technological innovations and other social and cultural factors altered women's lives. Devices such as carpet sweepers, vacuum cleaners, refrigerators, and washing machines slowly became available to growing numbers of households. Cookery books became more "scientific," more exacting, speaking of a tablespoon of an ingredient, not a walnut-sized piece. The emerging commercial food industry further modified American women's cooking tasks, as the variety of canned foods first available in the mid-nineteenth century expanded greatly by the second decade of this century. Furthermore, modern and expanding networks of communication and transportation, including such developments as rural free delivery, mail-order merchandising, mass-circulation magazines, the telephone and railroads, facilitated the movement of goods and services and transformed the domestic experiences of women. . . .

. . . Scientific motherhood exalted science and devalued instinct and traditional knowledge. A 1915 anonymous poem from *Forecast: A Magazine of Home Efficiency* playfully captures this message:

A Modern Lullaby

Rock-a-bye, baby, up on the bough
You get your milk from a certified cow.
Before your eugenic young parents were wed
They had decided how you should be fed.
Hush-a-bye, baby, on the tree-top,
If grandmother trots you, you tell her to stop;
Shun the trot-horses that your grandmother rides—
It will work harm to your little sides.

> Mamma's scientific—she knows all the laws—
> She kisses her darling through carbolized gauze.
> Rock-a-bye, baby, don't wriggle and squirm:
> Nothing is near you that looks like a germ.

Though lighter in tone than other calls for educated motherhood, this poem is representative of the period.

Into the twentieth century, scientific motherhood more and more accentuated the positive necessity of mothercraft education. Giving birth made a woman a mother in the physical, biological sense only; a good mother had to learn about mothering from authoritative sources. The growing belief that science should inform mothering practices could and did lead to the claim that women should receive professional training for motherhood. Declared one mother of six writing in 1919, "It now seems to me that it is about as rational for a woman to learn by experience with her own children to be a good mother, as it would be for a doctor to get his education merely by practicing on his patients. Motherhood offers no less opportunities for success than do the professions of law or medicine." . . .

Not surprisingly, child-care journals and general women's magazines were among the leading proponents of scientific motherhood from the late nineteenth century onwards. As the magazine *Babyhood* stated in 1893, "there is a science in bringing up children and this magazine is the voice of that science." Other journals articulated the ideology of scientific motherhood through articles and advice columns such as "Mother's Corner," edited by a trained nurse for the *Ladies' Home Journal,* and the "Health and Happiness Club," edited by a physician for *Good Housekeeping,* another popular women's magazine. In 1910 in a more targeted move, Dr Emelyn Coolidge established the "Young Mother's Register" in the *Ladies' Home Journal.* Within one year over 500 mothers registered; they sent monthly reports to Coolidge and questions which the doctor promised to answer personally. By 1912, Coolidge proudly announced that "The young mother is fast becoming educated, being no longer satisfied to follow the advice of well-meaning but inexperienced neighbors, but preferring to turn to a higher authority for help in solving nursery problems." In this case, and increasingly, that higher authority was the scientific or medical expert.

In the twentieth century, another source for "scientific motherhood" was government pamphlets, most especially the federal government's pamphlet *Infant Care.* This most popular of all government publications was produced by the Children's Bureau. As a result of reformers' extensive efforts, the federal government had established the Bureau in 1912. Originally designed as a fact-finding agency to report on the welfare of children, the reformers who staffed the agency sought to maximize their influence through educational initiatives, and among the most important were their publications. *Infant Care* was first published in 1914. By 1940 over 12 million copies had been distributed and by the 1970s over 59 million. People could and did write in for the pamphlet, but it was also frequently sent unsolicited by Congressional representatives to their constituents with newborns. . . .

Books, mainly child-care manuals and home-medical manuals, also advocated the ideology of scientific motherhood. Dr L. Emmett Holt's book, though certainly not the first, was one of the most popular. First issued in 1894, Holt's *Care and Feeding of Children* went through 75 printings, 12 revisions and several translations by the 1920s. It was taken up by his son and, at least as late as 1957 was in print under the auspices of *Good Housekeeping*. Many other physicians published baby care books with varying success. And the tradition continues today with *Dr Spock's Baby and Child Care* in its fifth edition. And, physician-authored manuals face stiff competition from child-care books produced by psychologists and lay-writers.

In addition to publications, women learned about scientific motherhood and received training in other, more immediate settings. Beginning slowly in the early years of the twentieth century and growing rapidly in the 1920s and 1930s, school systems all over the country instituted home economics or domestic science classes. Often these courses were mandatory for girls. Educators rationalized that "It is expected that every woman will have at some time in her life the care of babies and young children. It is not reasonable to expect that she should know how to care for them wisely without definite instruction and training in the skill and art of mother craft." Domestic science instruction was preparation for a girl's life-work.

Middle-class home economists promoted their subject as beneficial for the future of individual girls and for society in general. They viewed with alarm what they and many other contemporaries saw as the break-down of American family life. All around they saw a society disrupted by increased urbanization, industrial-ization, and immigration. They believed they identified the remedy. Ellen Richards, founder of the Lake Placid Conferences, the first professional organization of home economists in the United States, confidently promoted home economics as "nothing less than an effort to save our social fabric from what seems inevitable disintegration." . . .

. . . [M]othercraft education was promoted through Little Mothers' classes, usually offered by city public health departments. These courses were first estab-lished in 1910 by Dr S. Josephine Baker in New York City. Her interest in educat-ing girls in mothercraft was spurred by the realization that many young children in the slums of New York were left for long periods of time in the care of only slightly older sisters. Baker had two goals in developing Little Mothers' Clubs. First she wanted the girls to receive practical instruction in child care, which she believed would improve the health of their younger charges. Secondly she intended that these young girls would, in turn, instruct their mothers and neighbours in scientific motherhood, making the girls, in Baker's words, "our most efficient missionaries." By 1912, some 20,000 girls attended weekly meetings of the City's Little Mothers' Leagues. Other states followed suit. For example, Wisconsin offered a series of ten 1-hour lessons on infant hygiene for school-age girls starting in the 1920s. If the student successfully completed the course, passed an oral or written examination, and demonstrated her expertise in bathing an infant and mixing a bottle formula, she received a diploma naming her a "Wisconsin's Little Mother." . . .

Evidently women came to accept the essence of the ideology: that successful and healthful child-rearing should be informed by scientific expertise. It is also evi-dent that women actively sought out expert advice. Women acted on the basic tenets of scientific motherhood, namely that while women maintained primary responsibil-ity for infant and child care, they were dependent on experts, scientific and medical, to tell them and to teach them how best to raise their children. Ultimately, they be-lieved that the most successful child-rearing was done under scientifically-informed medical supervision. This is not to say that all women everywhere and at all times slavishly followed the dictates of scientific and medical experts in raising their children. They could and did temper their faith in scientific expertise with greater or lesser doses of common sense and self-confidence in their own abilities. Indications that women accepted scientific motherhood and the balancing act are, on the whole, indirect and impressionistic.

Popular culture presents some hints of this balancing act. In the 1939 comedy film *Bachelor Mother,* Ginger Rogers is self-confident in her care of an infant; yet, as David Niven helpfully reads to her from a child-care manual written by a doctor with "twenty years' experience," she begins to doubt her ability. When Niven reads that Rogers should rub some warm food into the child's navel, she is torn between her methods, which have satisfied the child, and this "expert advice." She starts to lay the child down and undress him as if to follow the doctor's instructions. Then re-thinking the situation, she takes the book from Niven and discovers that in his reading several pages had stuck together and the instructions he read had concerned a treatment for colic. This scene captures very clearly the confusion that many women felt; they appreciated scientific-based advice but were perplexed when the "expert" opinion contradicted their own proven abilities and common-sense. Though an example from Hollywood, this film is one indication of the widespread recognition of the basic tenets of scientific motherhood in the United States.

The multitude of child-care books based on the ideology is another sign of its acceptance. These publications were extremely popular, running through many editions each. For example, Spock's book first appeared in May 1946. Within three years paperback sales reached one million copies annually. Despite stiff competition from a multitude of other child-care manuals, by 1985 Spock's had sold over 30 million copies in 38 languages. While historians may debate to what extent Spock's publication signified a major shift in the philosophy of child-care advice, in one very significant aspect at least Spock represents continuity with his predecessors. In the opening of his book, he counsels readers "You know more than you think you do. . . . Bringing up your child won't be a complicated job, if you take it easy, trust your own instincts, and follow the directions that your doctor gives you." . . .

The many letters received over the years by the Children's Bureau in praise of its pamphlet *Infant Care* . . . came from rural and urban mothers and cut across class and, to some extent, racial and ethnic groups. Women's acclaim for the Bureau's publications reached beyond the internal Bureau files. One mother, writing in *Cosmopolitan* in 1940, declared "My constant companion was that Bible of the 1940 young mother, the *Infant Care* pamphlet printed by the United States Government. The title was just too prosaic for the singing hearts of the mothers, so someone rechristened it The Good Book, and by that name it is generally known." Other letters and articles in women's magazines and child-care journals talk about raising their children "by the book" and counselled other readers to use child-care manuals. . . .

While letter-writers and authors of articles in women's magazines were primarily middle-class, the students in public-school home-economics classes spanned a wider range. Since home-economics educators as well as public health officials who established Little Mothers' Clubs were very pointed about the role of their courses in the uplifting and "Americanizing" of working-class and immigrant girls, the role of these educational efforts in the spread and popularity of scientific motherhood requires a complex, nuanced study of the education of girls in the period.

In the first four decades of this century, there were a few surveys that attempted to ascertain actual child-rearing practices among various class and ethnic groups. These investigations report that women read advice printed in sources such as Holt, and *Infant Care* and that they followed what they read. The Lynds' classic study of American culture, *Middletown,* disclosed the importance of published sources, classes and health practitioners to mothers raising children in Muncie, Indiana, though the specific forms popular with mothers varied among classes. My own interviews with women document their growing appreciation and reliance on scientific and medical expertise. Mothers who attended child-care classes at the university saved their books and notes and years later read them again while raising their children. One of my informants fondly remembered a University of Wisconsin course popularly called "The Bride's Course," which included instruction in prenatal and postnatal care. Years later she continued to refer to her class notes in raising her children. . . .

A most critical and as yet not fully examined component in the growing acceptance of scientific motherhood is gender. True, the experts were most frequently depicted as male, usually physicians; science, medicine and professionalism in general were described in male terms. Yet, scientific motherhood is more than an expression of male physicians intervening in the lives of female patients. Whether viewed as passive or active recipients of medical knowledge, mothers were actively involved in caring for their children in their homes, negotiating between the instructions of medical practitioners and the exigencies and beliefs of their own lives. Moreover, though medicine and medical science were gendered male, the insistence on the importance of medical expertise and experts came from a multitude of sources, including, very significantly, the emerging field of home economics. It is important to remember here that home economics was the only science gendered female; that is, a niche within which women could pursue science. . . .

Under the tenets of scientific motherhood, a woman's place remained in the home where mothers were accorded full responsibility for all things domestic, including, most significantly, the care and raising of children. At the same time, and with increasing intensity, scientific motherhood denigrated women's skills and knowledge by insisting that mothers needed the assistance of medical and scientific authorities in order to carry out their maternal duties successfully. The development of scientific motherhood did not represent a sharp break with past practices, but rather a gradual realignment of power relationships within the domestic setting. The nineteenth century promoted the image of woman as "queen of the nursery," responsible for and in control of her domain. Through the late nineteenth and early twentieth centuries, increasing numbers of advisors insisted on the importance of scientific expertise to the successful accomplishment of her tasks. By the second third of this century, the form of the expertise had shifted from counsel to direction. The image of the scientific mother changed from the queen of the nursery to the servant of science. By the twentieth century scientific motherhood endowed the image of women with positive and negative attributes: responsibility implies independence of action and strength— that mothers are important in child care; yet the need for assistance suggests dependence and weakness—that women lack intelligence.

Scientific motherhood was not and is not a disembodied, reified theoretical construct. It was and is defined by science, culture and society. It reinforced and reinforces, it reproduced and reproduces patriarchal sex roles: women in the domestic sphere, men outside; women instructed by scientific and medical authorities, males. Scientific motherhood was and is disseminated through cultural forms. The study of the development and spread of scientific motherhood can help us to understand the interrelationship between science, medicine, and social roles.

Psychiatrists, the "Hypersexual Female," and a New Medical Management of Morality in the Progressive Era

ELIZABETH LUNBECK

In the early years of the twentieth century, a number of prominent American psychiatrists identified the hypersexual female, the willfully passionate woman who could not control her desires for sexual pleasure, as an issue of pressing medical concern. Psychiatrists diagnosed women whose sexuality they deemed abnormally aggressive as "psychopaths"; these women, they explained, suffered from an inborn condition for which there was no remedy save institutionalization. Borrowing the term "psychopathic" from the nosologies of their German counterparts, who began using it in the late nineteenth century to classify male deviants (including vagabonds, criminals, anarchists, revolutionaries, and reformers), American psychiatrists employed it to account for what many agreed was the problem of women's sexual excess. Psychiatrists early identified prostitutes and female juvenile delinquents, most of whom had been charged with immoral behavior, as psychopaths; soon, a variety of other young women whose sexuality violated medical and social conceptions of proper female deportment swelled their ranks. . . .

In constructing the category of the female hypersexual, psychiatrists proclaimed themselves arbiters of rapidly changing sexual mores. They drew on their capital as medical experts in arguing for the indisputable fitness of an older Victorian morality that held women chaste and reticent. In so doing, they attempted to medicalize the discussion of the working girl's sexuality, to replace the prostitute, who in the nineteenth century had embodied all that was base in women's nature, with the hypersexual. In diagnosing women as hypersexual, psychiatrists in part were responding to the many demands that others placed on them—the families, police, and social workers who brought young women to their attention—to address the issue of female immorality and to find explanations and remedies beyond the outworn moral categories that saw the promiscuous woman as bad, and the sociological theory that cast her as a victim. Yet the particular solution psychiatrists chose—to diagnose these women as incurable psychopaths—was problematic. For these women manifested none of the usual symptoms of mental disorder, and psychiatrists readily conceded that psychopathic personality might be thought of as a conduct disorder rather than a disease. The significance of psychiatrists' intervention lies not in their success in

Elizabeth Lunbeck, "'A New Generation of Women': Progressive Psychiatrists and the Hypersexual Female," *Feminist Studies* 13 (1987): 513–526, 530–531, 535. Reprinted by permission of the author.

controlling, or even defining, female sexuality, but in identifying and attempting to comprehend a social change of singular importance: the emergence of the independent, sexually assertive woman in American society at the turn of the century.

This essay examines a moment in the largely unwritten history of female sexuality when psychiatrists first attempted to control the discourse concerning women's erotic nature. Drawing on case records from the Boston Psychopathic Hospital, one of the most highly regarded of American mental hospitals in the early years of the century, I will examine how psychiatrists constructed the category of the hypersexual psychopath and explore the worlds of the young women they considered oversexed. Psychiatrists saw these women as sick; middle-class social workers, bonded by gender but distanced by class, saw them as victims and sought both to protect and to discipline them. The women themselves fashioned their own interpretations of their predicaments from elements of both perspectives; they sometimes admitted, when pressed, to fears that they were not normal, that they were sick or bad, that they needed help and supervision. But they could also reject psychiatrists' and social workers' concerns altogether and argue for an end to the double standard of sexual morality that marked them as diseased. From this welter of confused perspectives a female voice emerged to challenge the strictures governing sexual conduct. This working-class voice was often halting and unsure. At times, however, it spoke with a strength and clarity rare in the annals of the historically invisible.

Psychiatrists argued that the sexual natures and needs of young women and men differed fundamentally . . . [holding] that social convention, which tolerated and even encouraged the fulfillment of male desire, only mirrored the immutable dictates of human nature. If it was for a girl once soiled, forever spoiled, while a boy could "sow an unusually large crop of wild oats," straighten up, and become a good citizen thereafter, this was the natural order of things. Men, unlike women, could weather a phase of intense sexual activity without breaking down under it; among men, psychiatrists agreed, "a separate standard of moral and sexual life" could and did prevail.

In its recognition of female desire the double standard that psychiatrists championed differed from that of the Victorian era. Middle-class Victorian sexual ideology had set the passionlessness of women against the lustfulness of men, elevating the former and excusing the latter, with tacit tolerance of prostitution as a necessary social evil. Although they paid a high price in their renunciation of passion, Victorian women managed to turn this ideology to their advantage; trapped in a society that offered them little outside marriage, they fell back on their supposed passionlessness to gain a measure of control over sexual relations with their husbands and thus over the timing and number of their pregnancies. Progressive psychiatrists, as they ceded some ground to women by recognizing their capacity for passion, stripped away from them all the protections Victorian ideology had offered. They not only overturned sexual Victorianism, but they reversed its equation of desire as well, casting women as sexual predators, men as sexual victims. If women wanted passion, they would give it to them with a vengeance.

Psychiatrists' recasting of the Victorian sexual drama is most starkly evident in their elaboration of the category of the hypersexual. Hypersexuality, like its elusive counterpoint, normal sexuality, first became apparent at adolescence. It was then that overdeveloped girls, girls who prematurely developed the womanly contours that so enfeebled male resolve, first began to constitute a real social menace. Upstanding men were absolutely unable to resist these young women. As psychiatrists related it, particularly attractive young women seduced many a hapless man over telephone lines, in automobiles, on public conveyances, and even in church; young temptresses led countless sailors astray. Invigorated by overwhelming desire, a young woman could haul a man through the windows of her residence or accost an innocent on the street and force him to submit, against his will, to intercourse on the spot! The city's abundant public places teemed with hypersexuals, ready to lure unsuspecting men into questionable establishments, to hire rooms for immoral purposes, to plague men with the demands of their insatiable immorality.

Psychiatrists elaborated this theory of female desire as they confronted the sexual mores of a generation of working-class new women. These women, born between 1890 and 1905, were among the first to achieve for themselves some limited freedom from family obligations, some limited freedom to earn and spend, and some limited freedom to associate with whom they pleased. . . . As parents and juvenile authorities conceived it, the years of a girl's life that corresponded to those of the boy's adolescence were filled with danger, not possibility. They were years in which she was to submerge, rather than to free, her yearnings for independence, years in which she was to reconcile herself to her dependence on men and the inevitability of marriage. They were years best avoided altogether; ideally, a girl would progress from childhood directly to the exalted state of motherhood.

These young women of the early twentieth century were the first to live in large numbers on their own in cities. . . . Living alone or in boardinghouses with others like themselves, working for meager wages, skimping on food to buy the fine clothing that conferred status and an air of sophistication, these young women, many country-bred, chose to participate fully in the life of the city. With little cash, without family obligations, and with few concerns for the future, they worked by day and pursued pleasure by night through the exciting commercial amusements—movies, dance halls, and theaters—that were just appearing on the urban scene. In these public, anonymous establishments, young women and their men, as they carried on the courtships formerly overseen by watchful parental and neighborly eyes, rewrote the code that governed their mutual relations. This code had long sanctioned sexual play—passionate kissing, petting, even intercourse—between young women and men who intended to marry. After the turn of the century, some young women sought, with varying degrees of self-consciousness, to engage in the same sorts of intimacies with men they did not intend to marry.

Participating in the sexual sphere was no easy task. With no construction of respectability available to her, the working girl struggling to define a morality that would enable her to do more than sit alone in her room at night was frustrated at every turn by the seeming timeless equation of the working girl and the prostitute. Codified in countless late-nineteenth and early-twentieth-century investigations that found her virtue wanting, this equation was assuming new and damning resonances as reformers campaigning to eradicate the necessary evil once and for all transformed the prostitute from a pitiable yet redeemable fallen woman into a hardened predator, a spreader of vicious disease. It was as well an equation to whose strictures she might be subject in her day-to-day dealings with men. Too often the working girl was taken for an easy mark, complained one woman who, because she had worn silk stockings to work one day, had suffered the taunts of her male workmates. Surely only a kept woman could afford such luxuries, they teased: "No one has anything on me," she shot back.

The working girl seeking a good time and respectability was frustrated, too, by the restrictions of poverty. Many girls worked long hours to earn between six and eight dollars a week, barely enough to cover room, board, and carfare. To gain entrance to the movies, shows, and dances that were the stuff of working-class leisure, some of them who claimed respectable status—who did not, that is, consider themselves prostitutes—chose to bargain with sexual favors, ranging from flirtation to intercourse, exchanged for men's "treats" to entertainments. Others thought such exchanges unworthy of a self-respecting young woman. Yet the urban working-class view of sex as a commodity shaped the heterosexual relations of even those working girls who thought "treating" beneath them. The woman who did not want to give herself to a man knew she must refuse any favors or money he might proffer; as one woman, pregnant, out of work, and desperate, explained, "I never approved of taking money from men. It places you in their obligations." . . . [M]en knew women had little in the way of capital besides sex and taunted them with this knowledge. As one young woman, desperate for money, told social workers, "Time and time again I have had chances to go astray, large sums of money and flattering remarks." She offered as an example of such the fellow who wanted to give her fifteen dollars "to go to a room with him, but I told him money could not buy me, he had the wrong girl." She continued, "Then he asked me, 'would I go as a gift,' and I said no and not for charity either."

If sex, or its promise, was the working girl's capital, to middle-class eyes it was capital she too readily squandered. It is hardly surprising that middle-class observers of the working-class sexual economy saw girls' behavior as promiscuous. Nor is it surprising that they focused on the dangers to which the young working woman was daily exposed: on her own in the anonymous metropolis, bereft of male protection, underpaid and overworked, the working girl was all too easy prey for male seducers, schemers, and white slavers. There was much that was true in this construction. Women in the case records I examined were often subject to exploitation at the hands of dishonest men; at least one woman was raped, by a man claiming to be an employment agent, as she looked for work in the city, and women regularly complained of having to rebuff unwanted advances.

Why, then, did psychiatrists and social workers absolve men of all blame? Why did women become the dangerous characters? And why did the sexual prowess of the young woman on her own assume such mythic proportions? . . . The sexual behavior of working-class men was of little concern to social workers, who saw that women bore all the untoward consequences of their new sexual freedom. Ignorant of any means of birth control other than abortion (to which they often resorted), women faced the prospect of pregnancy with each encounter. . . .

Still, this concern for young women's vulnerability does not fully account for the fact that psychiatrists and social workers blamed girls, not boys; women, not men. Nor does it explain why they cast the problem in terms of the "uncontrolled sex impulses" of one sex and not the other. Psychiatrists could understand the girl from a bad home who got into trouble. Her upbringing poor and her material pleasures few, this girl—the classic delinquent—traded favors for money. Material need, not passion, motivated her; most likely she felt no passion at all, like the sexually active young woman whom psychiatrists judged merely delinquent, not psychopathic, because, as she told them, she was "entirely without sexual feeling." The woman who did *not* receive money in exchange for her favors, who was "attracted to such acts by sexual passion alone," psychiatrists were at a loss to explain. Men were expected to seek sexual pleasure; indeed, a man's *failure* to do so might earn for him the designation psychopathic. It was, on the other hand, unseemly but increasingly all too common for a woman forthrightly to pursue sexual fulfillment. Women, according to conventional wisdom, properly relied on intrigue and feminine wile to attain their ends; men, on a "direct and open procedure," as one commentator put it. Women should be sly and devious, should seduce and tease. A woman who openly avowed passion, who could observe of her sexual exploits, like one putative psychopath, that "life is too short to worry. If you don't enjoy this life you might as well be dead," was, in psychiatrists' eyes, altogether without moral sensibility, altogether inexplicable, altogether pathological.

The psychopath's forthright sexuality was the most visible and disturbing manifestation of her social autonomy; the right to actively seek sexual fulfillment was but the most salient of male prerogatives she assumed. She wanted the freedom to earn and spend, like a man, free of supervision; she wanted to enjoy the pleasures of the city without having her character impugned; she wanted to make her own choices and live independently. Her independence of what many held were the proper and fitting constraints of family and home was nearly as troubling as her hypersexuality. Many hypersexuals had nothing to do with their families. Employed in factories or as domestic servants they enjoyed a freedom from adult supervision that many social commentators agreed was the source of their troubles. Others, in their twenties or thirties, eschewed marriage and chose instead to work and to live singly or with other women. To be sure, some of the young women psychiatrists diagnosed psychopathic looked forward to becoming respectable wives and mothers. One unmarried mother, for example, told psychiatrists she was "not worried about the morality of her act as many other young women have gotten into the same trouble and they have turned out alright and later established good homes." But others rejected the conventional female lifeprint that saw a woman passing from her father to her husband.

The concern over female autonomy that was implicit in the category of hypersexuality helps explain why psychiatrists considered failure to engage in heterosexual courtship—whether simple lack of interest or overtly lesbian behavior—just as psychopathic as a woman's too vigorous exercise of her seductive powers. The "spark of womanliness," for example, glowed but feebly in one psychopathic woman who lacked "ordinary feminine charm and appeal." Wrote one of the hospital's psychiatrists: "It would be difficult to imagine . . . even the most accomplished Lothario successfully drawing her into a flirtation or being able to keep a sustained interest in the pursuit." A more explicit rejection of heterosexuality, like that of a woman who lived with a female companion and questioned the institution of marriage, might mark a woman psychopathic as well. . . .

The sexual activities of these women who refused to seduce men were of little interest to psychiatrists, who focused instead on their gender-inappropriate independence. Before the mid-twenties, psychiatrists focused on the lesbian's supposed masculinity, not her sexual object choice; the lesbian's refusal to court men, not her preference for women, marked her as a sexual deviant.

It was in this context of growing concern over female independence and sexual deviance that psychiatrists settled on psychopathic personality as an explanation for female immorality. . . .

The women whom psychiatrists diagnosed as psychopaths at the Boston Psychopathic Hospital were overwhelmingly young (75 percent were younger than twenty-one), single, native-born whites. One-half were Protestant, one-third were Catholic, and the rest were Jewish. Although a few worked at middle-class occupations, such as teaching or office work, most, if employed at all, worked in factories or as domestic servants. Families, police, or courts committed one-half of them to the Boston Psychopathic Hospital for a variety of reasons; state social workers, or visitors, committed the rest.

Twenty-two-year-old Lillian Thomas's background, sexual behavior, and path to the hospital are typical. Thomas lived on her own in a home for young working girls. Her ties to her family had been severed long before; at age ten she had come under the care of the city as a neglected child. Court workers placed her with a woman who "looked after her very carefully and would not allow young men to call on her regularly." In her eighteenth year Thomas began living on her own, working as a waitress and "discouraging advances from young men for fear they might lead her into temptations." Within the year, however, she fell in love with a man she judged honorable and agreed to "illicit relations" with him. Finding herself pregnant, she considered his proposal of marriage. But she discovered he drank and, she told psychiatrists, she "preferred the alternative of living single and fighting out her own battle rather than being the wife of a drunkard." Thomas entered a home for expectant single women; one month after her boy's birth the matron of the home had her committed to the hospital to determine whether she was capable of caring for him. Social workers noted that Thomas's reputation was less than exemplary. At her previous lodgings she had been accused of entertaining men in her room at night; she "went often to dances and came home very late"; one man told them that she "could make up to men quicker than any girl he knew"; and, the case record notes portentously, "it is said she was discharged from one restaurant for underchecking accounts to men."

Thomas was a single working woman who adhered to a standard of sexual morality that many working-class women and men lived by, a standard that sanctioned sexual relations between those who intended to marry. Her only mistake, and the chief evidence of her hypersexuality, lay in withdrawing from the impending compact. Many of the other women committed to the hospital by their families, police, or courts, had, like Thomas, long been on their own. Some had run away from intolerable family situations, others had been orphaned, and still others, in their late twenties and early thirties, had chosen not to marry. Many lived in boardinghouses; in some cases the matrons of these homes, observing behavior they judged either bizarre or promiscuous, petitioned to have them committed to the hospital. The failed suicide attempts of lonely and despondent young women brought a few others under psychiatrists' purview; family members, deeming the behavior of a daughter or sister inappropriate, committed still other women.

The other group of women diagnosed as psychopathic were "state charges" brought to the Boston Psychopathic Hospital for observation as to their sanity.

Courts had already found these girls delinquent, primarily on the basis of their sexual behavior, and had committed them to the care of the State Industrial School at Lancaster, Massachusetts. Many of their parents, underemployed and alcoholic, burdened with large families (many of these girls had six or seven siblings) they could barely support, had originally petitioned for their commitment because they could not control them. Their daughters, they complained, went with undesirable companions, were on the streets at all hours, had immoral relations with boys, and, in general, ran wild. Some of this behavior, like taking to the streets, was a form of protest against overly strict parental control. Many widowed fathers, for example, expected their young daughters to keep house for them, prepare their meals, and wait on them as their wives had; many mothers expected daughters to perform heavy household labor—laundry, scrubbing, cleaning—as well as to care for younger siblings. Some of it, too, was textbook delinquent behavior; more than a few girls had consented to intercourse in exchange for various sums of cash, ranging from twenty-five cents for sex among the barrels at a beach resort to fifteen dollars—a substantial sum—for six episodes in a cheap hotel. But the relatively innocuous driving in automobiles with immoral persons; the frequenting of pool halls, dance halls, and saloons; the carousing with evil-minded girls and boys; and the casual sexual play that figured so prominently in parental and professional accounts of girls gone wrong point to the larger battle being waged between parents and daughters, between middle-class professionals and working-class girls, over the nature of working-class adolescent girlhood. Could a girl make her own life the same as a boy? To parents who expected their adolescent daughters to refrain from any sort of sexual activity, to hand over their wages without protest, and to assume the household duties of a wife, the girl who strayed undermined not only her own reputation but the fragile family economy, which depended on her services, as well. Her transgressions, then, provided sufficient cause for commitment to reform school. . . .

Psychiatrists' and social workers' conceptions of respectable, moral behavior rigidly divided good from bad women. The specter of the prostitute informed their prescriptions about girls' proper dress and deportment. To social workers, working girls who spent their meager incomes on frivolous ribbons and silk stockings and who purchased clothing on installment plans were no better than the "dolled-up" psychopathic prostitutes who found satisfaction in lavish personal adornment, plucking and penciling their eyebrows, and flaunting their wares as they strutted about in striking, cheap-rich styles of dress. But flashy dress, so tellingly tawdry to middle-class eyes, was the norm among working girls. Fine clothing compensated for the daily drudgery of work; it could bolster self-esteem flagging under the double burden of overwork and underpay; it could also enhance a young woman's desirability in the marketplace of pleasures. . . .

It was the readiness of psychiatrists and social workers to forever consign them, on the slightest of evidence, to the ranks of the promiscuous that young women found so irksome. Psychiatrists measured them against a middle-class moral code, a code that ensured that the middle-class woman would not squander her virtue, her most marketable of assets. But the strict morality they advocated held little appeal for working girls for whom a willingness to play fast was of equal value to the middle-class girl's chastity. A number of putative psychopaths struggled to define standards of sexual morality appropriate to the circumstances of their lives. Psychiatrists were puzzled that they could entertain any real self-respect—testified to in some cases by girls' refusal to accept money for their irregularities—while engaging in relations the psychiatrists judged promiscuous. Yet this distinction was central to these women who were trying to forge another standard of sexual morality. They objected to the double standard that marked them defective. . . .

If white immorality was a symptom of disease, black immorality, on the other hand, was entirely normal. "On the whole I have been very chary in making the diagnosis of psychopathic personality in these colored girls," one psychiatrist explained. "The level of the negro regarding conduct, using that term in the broad sense, is decidedly different [from] the conduct of the white." Psychiatrists contended that the fooling with boys that was a definite symptom of psychopathy in white girls was in blacks only the expression of the natural immorality of the race. A "normal negress" was unintelligent but high spirited, and her immorality could be shrugged off with the assurance that there was "nothing abnormal about her delinquencies. Some of us get caught, some do not." Adding a psychiatric twist to a very old set of beliefs concerning the sexual nature of black women, psychiatrists diagnosed as normal those with histories every bit as flamboyant as the supposedly psychopathic whites. Only black women whose immorality was of such proportions that it offended even the low standards of their race were psychopathic. . . .

It was a strange disease indeed that so respected social convention. Yet psychiatrists were firm in their conviction that psychopathic personality was an inborn and incurable condition. Unlike "simple" delinquents, who were "perfectly able to do otherwise if they wish" and who could learn from experience, the inborn defects of the psychopath rendered her unable to refrain from misdeeds. Some psychopaths thought differently, acknowledging their delinquent behavior but attributing it to poor upbringing, not inborn taint. Their mothers had been unable to care for them properly, several girls told psychiatrists; no one had taught them right living. Others, like Alice Lawson, insisted there was nothing at all wrong with them. As Lawson emphasized: "There is not a thing the matter with me. I eat and sleep well. I am perfectly normal. I have no hallucinations, illusions or delusions." She implored doctors to release her. "I am sure shutting a girl up—shutting her away from civilization does not help the girl any." . . .

In the twenties, as the sexual revolution reached the ranks of the middle class, and as behavior that psychiatrists labeled hypersexual became more prevalent and less easily ascribed to a deviant working-class minority, psychiatrists' interest in hypersexuality flagged. The sexual psychopath of the late twenties and beyond was male and most often homosexual; rapists, child molesters, and other sex offenders displaced working-class women as objects of psychiatric attention. As psychiatrists adjusted their theories to new sexual mores, they championed a sanitized heterosexuality that could be safely contained within marriage. Indeed, psychiatrists transformed the passion that had been such a mark of deviance into the very criterion of normality. Frigidity, not its obverse, marked the deviant woman; the lesbian, the all-too-independent woman who rejected men and patriarchy altogether, inherited the mantle of sexual deviance from the hypersexual who, however worthy of contempt, at least had played the game. As the hypersexual faded, the lesbian became the exemplar of female sexuality gone awry. . . .

But there was more to the hypersexual than this. Proclaiming women wholly sexual creatures, psychiatrists fixed on their sexuality in attempting to comprehend a larger process of social change that saw women moving out of the home and more visibly into the world of work. The psychopathic hypersexual was in part a product of psychiatric imagination; the confident hedonist who seduced men left and right was the working-class new woman, the woman with a little cash and a lot of savvy, seen through middle-class, mostly male, eyes. But the sexually assertive woman, the woman endowed with passion equal to that of a man, was real, and psychiatrists, however exaggerated their notions of her sexual prowess, were alone in recognizing her passion as dicey. For the moment, psychiatrists stood back, a bit awed perhaps, and attempted to comprehend this new phenomenon, the passionate woman. Reflexively, they turned to the familiar categories of the pure woman and the prostitute. At the same time they recognized this old dichotomy would not do. The uneasiness of the construct of the female hypersexual embodied their confusion and ambivalence toward women and their sexuality. With it they enjoined women to be at once chaste and seductive, to tease but not to conquer. The psychopathic hypersexual was at times a pathological deviant in psychiatrists' discourse. More often, however, she was Everywoman. If, as one authority proposed, "a clean and protected moron was not far from corresponding to the ideal woman of the Victorian age," the psychopathic hypersexual was her redoubtable twentieth-century counterpart.

 F U R T H E R   R E A D I N G

Elaine S. Abelson, "The Invention of Kleptomania," *Signs* 15 (1989): 122–143.

Rima D. Apple, *Mothers and Medicine: A Social History of Infant Feeding, 1890–1950* (1987).

Rima D. Apple, *Vitamania: Vitamins in American Culture* (1996).

Ronald Bayer, *Homosexuality and American Psychiatry: The Politics of Diagnosis* (1981).

JoAnne Brown, *The Definition of a Profession: The Authority of Metaphor in the History of Intelligence Testing, 1890–1930* (1992).

Joan Jacobs Brumberg, *Fasting Girls: The History of Anorexia Nervosa* (1989).

Karen Buhler-Wilkerson, *False Dawn: The Rise and Decline of Public Health Nursing, 1900–1930* (1989).

John C. Burnham, *Bad Habits: Drinking, Smoking, Taking Drugs, Gambling, Sexual Misbehavior, and Swearing in American History* (1993).

John C. Burnham, *How Superstition Won and Science Lost: Popularizing Science and Health in the United States* (1987).

David T. Courtwright, *Dark Paradise: Opium Addiction in America Before 1940* (1982).

Ian R. Dowbiggin, *Keeping America Sane: Psychiatry and Eugenics in the United States and Canada, 1880–1940* (1997).

Janet L. Golden, *A Social History of Wet Nursing in America: From Breast to Bottle* (1996).

Linda Gordon, *Woman's Body, Woman's Right: Birth Control in America* (1990).

Julia Grant, *Raising Baby by the Book: The Education of American Mothers* (1998).

Gerald N. Grob, *From Asylum to Community: Mental Health Policy in Modern America* (1991).

Nathan G. Hale, *The Rise and Crisis of Psychoanalysis in the United States: Freud and the Americans, 1917–1985* (1995).

Kathleen W. Jones, *Taming the Troublesome Child: American Families, Child Guidance, and the Limits of Psychiatric Authority* (1999).

Daniel J. Kevles, *In the Name of Eugenics: Genetics and the Uses of Human Heredity* (1985).

Molly Ladd-Taylor, *Mother-Work: Women, Child Welfare, and the State, 1890–1930* (1994).

Judith Walzer Leavitt, *Brought to Bed: Childbearing in America, 1750 to 1950* (1986).

Elizabeth Lunbeck, *The Psychiatric Persuasion: Knowledge, Gender, and Power in Modern America* (1994).

Richard A. Meckel, *Save the Babies: American Public Health Reform and the Prevention of Infant Mortality* (1990).

Martin S. Pernick, *The Black Stork: Eugenics and the Death of "Defective" Babies in American Medicine and Motion Pictures Since 1915* (1996).

Heather Munro Prescott, *A Doctor of Their Own: The History of Adolescent Medicine* (1998).

Philip R. Reilly, *Surgical Solution: A History of Involuntary Sterilization in the United States* (1991).

Barbara Sicherman, *The Quest for Mental Health in America, 1880–1917* (1967).

James W. Trent Jr., *Inventing the Feeble Mind: A History of Mental Retardation in the United States* (1994).

Leila Zenderland, *Measuring Minds: Henry Herbert Goddard and the Origins of American Intelligence Testing* (1998).

C H A P T E R
11

The Technological Imperative?
Hospitals, Professions,
and Patient Expectations,
1890–1950

From the beginning of the twentieth century, one of the most prevalently cited images of medicine has been that of a gleaming glass and steel hospital building filled to overflowing with a sophisticated array of complex machinery and technicians. The power of this image stems from its resonance with both the fears and the fondest wishes of people who have experienced the American health care system. For many observers of medicine, including a few historians, technology has taken on a dominating role. According to this interpretation there is a kind of technological imperative at work in American medicine that guarantees the use and generation of ever more complicated and expensive technologies. This chapter explores the meaning and consequences of the imperative, while at the same time examining other forces that have worked to mediate its effects. How has technology influenced patterns of care, social relationships, institutional structures, and clinical decision making? Has the influence of technology been the most powerful force shaping modern America's culture of health, or has this influence been less definitive, restrained by other, more powerful traditions in science and medicine?

The answers to these questions depend to a substantial degree on how the word technology is defined. In this chapter a broad definition is used. Technology refers not only to machines and instruments but also to clinical facilities (intensive care units and surgical suites); laboratory tests; an ever-expanding array of drugs; research techniques such as the randomized clinical trial; and, in fact, any "knowledge-producing tool" used for a medical purpose. This expansive definition makes it easier to see the complex negotiations that have been central to the creation of modern America's technology-based health care system. These negotiations have included a vast array of medical practitioners, patients, technology creators and

349

*manufacturers, and various levels of the United States government. They have
tapped into some of the most important values and beliefs of the American people,
including what many historians of the twentieth century have identified as the
public's love affair with the machine and the technological "quick fix." How
these attitudes have been balanced against equally powerful suspicions about the
depersonalizing and destructive potential of technology is an important part of
the problem this chapter explores.*

   *Equally important are the political and economic discussions that have re-
volved around the accessibility, efficiency, and cost-effectiveness of each new technology. At issue in these discussions is the concept historian Charles E. Rosenberg
has called "technological entitlement." If a technology exists, according to this
interpretation, all Americans should have equal access to it. When did such an
idea develop? Is there a relationship between the notions of technological entitlement and technological imperative? Moreover, how is this notion of entitlement
related to the dominant question of the early twenty-first century: Who pays for
the use of biomedical technologies?*

 D O C U M E N T S

In Document 1, an 1897 *Journal of the American Medical Association* article, Philadelphia physician Charles L. Leonard proselytizes for the greater use of x-ray technology, especially as a tool to improve diagnostic precision for surgery. Not even ten
years old, x-rays fascinated many in the medical profession and dazzled the general
public, but their power and potential as a medical tool were still elusive. How did these
"tangible shadows" change the diagnostic process and institutional structure of health
care? Document 2, an editorial published in the *Boston Medical and Surgical Journal,*
also explores the issue of the power of x-ray to transform modern medicine, but takes
it a step further. By 1912, physicians are discussing the usefulness of "precautionary
x-ray examination" for a wide range of conditions and promoting community subsidy
for a broad screening of Boston's citizens. The physicians writing these two documents
are obviously enthusiastic supporters of technological innovation. Document 3, layman William Armstrong's 1915 report for the popular magazine *The Woman's Home
Companion,* makes it clear that such enthusiasm was not confined to the medical
profession. Responding to a deluge of letters from the magazine's readers, inquiring
why a new method of supposedly painless childbirth was not available in the United
States, Armstrong recounts his visit to the German clinic that pioneered in this process
known as "twilight sleep." What does this document say about the power of popular
demand in negotiations over when, and often if, a new medical technology should be
introduced? What are the issues at stake in this debate?

   Document 4, written by Chicago physician Joseph Baer in 1915, attempts to
answer this question by using the scientific techniques of statistical and comparative
analysis. His measurement of the risks and benefits of the new procedure makes a
revealing comparison with Armstrong's view. What is the relationship between popular
and professional approaches to the question of technology evaluation? Who wins
when popular and professional demands collide? Document 5, a 1919 advertisement
depicting a white-clad doctor and nurse attending to a reclining patient, with the Draeger
Oxygen Apparatus Company's "Pulmotor" Resuscitative Device prominently displayed,
offers another kind of evidence for exploring the question of demand. This ad appeared
in the *Modern Hospital Year Book,* a trade journal and buyer's reference aimed at
physicians and hospital administrators. After the opening heading asks the value of a

human life, the advertising copy asserts, "For a hospital not to have a Pulmotor will soon be regarded as reprehensible negligence approximating malpractice." Was it? Or, is this just a high-pressure advertising strategy? What does this kind of advertising tell us about the role of commerce in American medicine, and the role of medical technology in the American economy?

Document 6, written in 1922 by Harvard Medical School faculty member Francis Peabody, urges all medical schools and hospitals offering internships to provide thorough training in laboratory methods. In this *Boston Medical and Surgical Journal* article Peabody tempers his enthusiastic embrace of technological training by adding a caveat that such education should be focused on "practical service," not overly specialized or research-oriented techniques. What are the most valuable technological lessons for practicing physicians? What does Peabody's somewhat guarded enthusiasm about the laboratory suggest about medicine's embrace of technology? Does Document 7—Howard University anatomist Montagu Cobb's review of pathologist Julian H. Lewis's 1942 book *The Biology of the Negro*—display similar skepticism? This review by prominent African American scientist Cobb, which appeared in the mass-circulation magazine *Crisis,* raises a host of questions. Why is Cobb concerned about Lewis's conclusions relating sickle cell anemia and "Negro blood"? What does this scholarly exchange reveal about the role of nonmedical ideas in the deployment of biotechnology and the ability of science to reinforce or overturn strongly held social attitudes, no matter how erroneous?

1. Physician Charles L. Leonard Extolls the Diagnostic Virtues of the New X-ray Technology, 1897

The application of the Roentgen rays to medical science has already given to surgery a method of diagnosis the precision of which makes it of the greatest value; this value lies in the absolute pictures which we are able to secure by its means, and loses its preeminence as soon as we are compelled to substitute for the absolute picture in black and white, mental pictures which always involve the personal equation of the observer.

It is worse than useless to suppose that any new method of forming mental pictures, no matter how startling or radical, can equal in accuracy or approach in value those which the science of medical diagnosis has already taught us to form with well-nigh infallible precision. It would be superogation on the part of anyone to think that the mental pictures which he might form by the use of the Roentgen rays could replace or even add much to the pictures which modern physical diagnosis is capable of presenting.

The property which gives this new method of diagnosis its greatest value and helps it to add to the sum of our knowledge, is its power to form real images, to make tangible shadows where only mental pictures were before possible. These tangible shadows eliminate the personal equation of the observer from the resulting diagnosis, and thus remove a source of error common to all methods that depend on the senses of the individual for the accuracy of their results. To this advantage is added the fact that they produce permanent data which different individuals may study in various stages of the same case or compare with other cases.

Charles L. Leonard, "The Application of the Roentgen Rays to Medical Diagnosis," *Journal of the American Medical Association* 29 (1897): 1157–1158.

The true value of the Roentgen rays and the advance made in their adaptation to medical diagnosis must be judged by the advance in our ability to replace or confirm by skiagraphs the mental images obtained by other methods. In cases where the lesion is extensive, where the symptoms and physical signs are pronounced, the skiagraph may only confirm the diagnosis, adding perhaps a few facts as to the exact shape of an aneurysm or the extent of the diseased area. It is, however, in the early stages of disease, during its inception, that it aids, chiefly by establishing a diagnosis which our most careful means of physical examination fail to make certain. This it does by differentiating between different areas of dullness, which by other methods present identical physical signs.

The application of this method to medical diagnosis is far more difficult than its application to surgery, for here we must deal with the relative opacities of structures which vary from one another by only slight degrees. To make this possible, the varying qualities of the X-ray must be under the control of the operator, so that he may employ more or less penetration as he may desire, and use at will the X^1, X^2 or X^3 rays. The results already attained in medical diagnosis are perhaps not as practical as those in surgery, but the possibilities which they open up are so great that this first insight gives promise of a future development of even greater value than in surgery. . . .

Although deprecating the prominence which some would give to fluoroscopic diagnosis, the author realizes its possibilities and has confirmed by personal observation the results attained by others. He believes, however, that its greatest usefulness is in the detection and study of motion, either normal or pathologic, in organs whose motion is beyond the field of ordinary vision. In the study of aneurysms and their pathologic expansile motion as observed by the fluoroscope there is, therefore, a definite addition to our knowledge. . . .

In reference to X-ray "burns," the author does not believe that they are due to the X-ray *per se,* but that they are the results of induced electric currents in the tissues of the patient. The X-ray depends for its production on the physical phenomena of electric induction, and it is certain that any conductor of electricity, as the patient's tissues, if approached sufficiently near to the X-ray tube, *i.e.,* within the field of electric induction, will have a current of electricity induced in it which may be capable of destroying its vitality. A substantiation of this theory is seen in the fact recently made known, that a sheet of aluminum if grounded and placed between the tube and patient, will prevent the burn, while interfering in no way with the X-ray phenomena. The induced currents are formed in the aluminum and carried by the wire to earth without injury to the patient.

2. Editor of Leading Medical Journal Urges "Precautionary X-ray Examinations," 1912

In our climate diseases of the chest, such as pneumonia and tuberculosis, cause great loss to the community through illness or death, but if they are recognized early illness may be shortened and the chances for recovery greatly improved. Here, then, is an opportunity for x-ray examinations because they not only give us another

Editorial, "Precautionary X-ray Examinations," *Boston Medical and Surgical Journal* 167 (1912): 560–561.

method for determining the conditions obtaining in the chest, but frequently enable us to recognize an abnormal condition earlier than is possible by the older methods of examination. With these latter methods we depend upon the senses of touch and hearing, while by means of x-ray examinations we have the use of another sense, that of sight. With the fluorescent screen the practitioner can study certain organs in motion. He can observe the shadow of the pulsating heart and that of the diaphragm as it moves up and down in expiration and inspiration. Further, by means of x-ray photographs, taken with an exposure of about one second, he can see some details that are obtainable in no other way.

So much has been said in recent years regarding tuberculosis of the lungs that the prevalence of this disease and the great mortality it causes, especially among young adults, is widely appreciated, so that it is a good example of the service precautionary x-ray examinations can render, for it is well known that if this disease is recognized very early most people recover. In a word, early recognition is vital.

The term "precautionary x-ray examinations" is a new one and needs a word of explanation. If a case of tuberculosis appears in a family, another case or cases often develop. It sometimes happens that all or nearly all the members of one family die of this disease, but such serious results could have been prevented if as soon as one member was known to have tuberculosis the lungs of the other members had been examined by means of the x-rays, *as a precaution.* Were this done it is probable that in one or more of them early signs of tuberculosis would be found that would not be so clear or definite by the other methods of examination. With this early warning such individuals would have an excellent chance of recovery before the disease had progressed so far as to make them a serious burden to their family, friends or the community. To illustrate: two sisters come to the hospital, one of whom has tuberculosis, the extent of which is definitely shown by an x-ray examination. The accompanying sister thinks herself perfectly well but is induced to be examined by the x-rays as a precaution. This examination reveals an abnormal condition of one lung and warns her that she should take care of herself. Or again, if a case of tuberculosis appears among people working together in groups, as in an office, for example, more cases are likely to follow, but x-ray examinations of other members of this group, as a precaution, would show slight changes in the lungs, if present, and thus afford an opportunity for saving lives and preventing a long, expensive, and comparatively hopeless illness. . . .

These examinations will also assist the physician to reassure the patient that he is not suffering from some disease of the chest that he fears is present, and that his dread is unfounded.

X-ray examinations are painless and, when properly made, harmless. They have been carried on at the Boston City Hospital, particularly with reference to diseases of the chest, for more than sixteen years, and no patient has been in any way injured.

In order that the community may have the benefit of precautionary x-ray examinations, the Trustees of the Boston City Hospital, upon the recommendation of the Senior Staff, have arranged to place the excellent equipment of the X-ray Department and the experience of its staff at their disposal.

This opportunity differs from the usual hospital clinic in that patients are to be examined, but not treated, and those who come from other institutions will be referred to those institutions with a report.

The Trustees of the Boston City Hospital and the City Government have thought it wise to expend the money necessary for this clinic to promote the well-being of our citizens, and perhaps also because the investment is one capable of yielding a large return, for anything which will save lives, especially of young adults, or shorten illness yields a return, even on a money basis, of many times its cost.

3. Journalist William Armstrong Reports to Women About His Investigation of the New Birthing Technology, "Twilight Sleep," 1915

The aim of this paper is to present the facts now authoritatively and scientifically known and acknowledged, for and against the scopolamin, or "Twilight Sleep," treatment of childbirth. An effort to obtain such a point of view requires the strict adherence to a neutral path; on one side of which rises ominously the pernicious spirit of skepticism, and on the other side the perhaps more pernicious spirit of maudlin enthusiasm. There has been so much written about this new method as the panacea for the pains and accidents of childbirth in *ALL* cases, so much that is superficial, and alarming, and sentimental, that it is time to call a halt and to investigate the exact status of this treatment: . . .

The history of the Twilight Sleep is no new one. Von Steinbüchel, in 1902, first suggested that it would be of value in controlling the pains of childbirth. Many foreign observers, notably, Doctors Steffens, Hocheisen and Veit, opposed it. It was used for a time by many men in this country; condemned by some, and praised by others. The treatment was further elaborated by Doctor Gauss in the clinic of Doctor Krönig at Freiburg, and in 1906 he published records of his first six hundred cases. In 1907 and 1908 the literature contains several articles by Doctor Gauss, Doctor Krönig, and Doctor Mansfeld, describing the administration of the method. Notwithstanding the good results claimed, Doctor Steffens and Doctor Hocheisen wrote strongly opposing its use after trial in three hundred cases, and Doctor Leopold and Doctor Veit gave it up as dangerous. The bad results reported were frequent asphyxia and death of infants, hemorrhage, and prolongation of labor.

Doctor Krönig at the American Gynecological Society in Chicago last fall, reported success in three thousand cases of confinements in his clinic, and his methods and results were identical with those reported at a recent meeting of the American Association of Obstetricians and Gynecologists. . . .

The fact that stands out brilliantly from the mass of more or less authentic claims is that *the scopolaminnarcophen treatment is of use in certain, scientifically-selected, individual cases, and where it is of use it is of enormous value.* In other words, the Twilight Sleep is effective when properly applied in appropriate cases: not every case responds to the treatment, nor should the treatment be tried in every case. Each case is a law unto itself. It is impossible to place too much emphasis upon this fact, for if it is kept in mind and valued in its true proportion, incalculable

William Armstrong, "Is the Twilight Sleep Safe—For Me?" *Woman's Home Companion* 42 (January 1915): 10, 43.

harm and danger to thousands, and perhaps millions, of women may be avoided. The unscientific articles written on this new boon to women state, or imply, that Twilight Sleep is successful and effectual for all women. Twilight Sleep cannot be employed indiscriminately—even the most enthusiastic supporters and "advertisers" of the treatment grant this truth, and they must grant it publicly if an authentic and honest publication of their data and results is made. . . .

. . . In order to determine whether or not the Twilight Sleep will be of use in a particular case, a woman should always have the opinion of an expert. As a corollary to this preliminary judgment by an expert stands the fact that, when the treatment is administered, it should be given by a trained obstetrician. There will be charlatans who will take every possible advantage of this new path to fortune, and there will be the type of physician who, when the patient insists upon having the Twilight Sleep, will, rather than lose the patient, administer it with insufficient knowledge of the processes. It is against these dangers that the WOMAN'S HOME COMPANION wishes to issue a distinct and timely warning.

Obstetrical experts are right when they maintain that it takes a great deal of time and experience to learn how scientifically to administer the Twilight Sleep. It entails a precise knowledge of the nature and results of the drugs, scopolamin and narcophen, and a nice observation of the symptoms and effects manifested by the individual mother-to-be.

The twentieth century stands for careful specialization, and this effort toward specialization should, of course, be directed especially toward the lessening of the pains and perils of maternity, the fundamental fact of life. The obstetricians of the world have been working toward the fortification of the general practitioner's knowledge of the science of obstetrics, so that the rate of death or mishaps may be minimized. The conservative physicians see in Twilight Sleep, when scientifically administered to suitable cases, an inestimable contribution toward the alleviation of the suffering of women.

But, on the other hand, they realize that, if any "fancy" variations or modifications are attempted by the tyro, this treatment becomes in his hands a weapon that can do incalculable harm. In other words, the operator must be an obstetrician as well as skilled in the technique. There is, of course, no reason why a physician should not learn the method; but he should not practice it until he has made it an art. If the operator is not thoroughly conversant and familiar with his subject dead babies and dead mothers will too often be the result of his ignorance. . . .

[A report published in the *American Journal of Obstetrics* in October 1914 states:] "The patient is drowsy and sleeps lightly between her pains. When a pain occurs, she manifests her suffering to a greater or less degree, and again dozes. But consciousness is not entirely lost. She responds somewhat tardily to questions, and usually obeys commands. Krönig lays great stress upon maintaining a condition of semi-unconsciousness, wherein the pains, though apparently perceived, are nevertheless immediately forgotten. The patient *perceives* a pain but does not *apperceive* it; in other words, she does not appreciate it. At any rate, on awakening, she has no recollection of anything that has occurred. The patient may complain that the treatment is not working and roundly abuse those in charge, yet half an hour after the birth have absolutely no recollection of her pains or of the coming of her baby. Thirty minutes after the birth of the child the woman is asked whether she has been delivered, and in the majority of cases she has actually no remembrance of the birth process and hesitates to believe that the child is actually hers."

A careful analysis of the foregoing statements reveals the fact that Twilight Sleep is a method that requires not only accurate knowledge of the technique but also expert watchfulness and constant attendance on the part of the physician. These demands are practically impossible of fulfillment in the busy life of the general practitioner—again a poignant argument in favor of the obstetrical specialist.

American obstetricians are practically unanimous in their vehement condemnation of the procedure which allows the mother to get out of bed the day following the birth and to shorten her convalescence in proportion. This is one very essential point of the method on which our specialists differ from the German specialists. The Freiburg method seems to derive great pride from the fact that a departure is made from the accepted fortnight of "lying-in," and the patient is often allowed to curtail her convalescence to astonishing brevity. Although many patients declare that they do not feel any more exhausted the day after the birth than they did the day before, and although some are anxious to get out of bed the first day, there seems to be no adequate reason why, in most cases, the routine length of the convalescence should be shortened. On the other hand, there seems to be every logical and sensible reason why the mother should stay in bed until the organs have returned to normal, and their repair is completed. . . .

The WOMAN'S HOME COMPANION has had so many letters from prospective mothers, inquiring as to the advisability of having the Twilight Sleep at their own homes that this question was referred to the specialist who read this article. It is his opinion that the treatment should, wherever practicable, be carried out in hospitals, where pavilions are now being especially equipped and fitted for this work. Of course the treatment is sometimes given in private houses, but in order to do this the patient must provide every resource of a hospital delivery-room, and the complete working force of the delivery must be transferred to her room for the entire duration of labor. This of course entails great trouble and great expense. The service of the attending physician and of one or two assistants is required throughout the course of labor.

A study of the opinions of the majority of the physicians whose judgments of the Twilight Sleep are adverse, shows that many of these men have not given the treatment a suitable trial under the conditions laid down as essential by the method. There is also the consideration of the adverse effect of impure scopolamin and of too much morphin. Often too, these men declare that they have "observed" certain facts usually used as conclusions against the method, but these "observations" might be less negative if they actually conscientiously studied and applied the method.

The lack of success in the use of the treatment, reported by many physicians, is often due to the fact that they do not realize how important is the effect of light and noise. This was certainly true when the treatment was in its incipent stages, and it has later been admitted by many doctors that the problem of these sensory impressions was not sufficiently regarded by them. Under disquieting conditions the patient, instead of being made calm by scopolamin, is excited. Hence the patient should be isolated, the room should be darkened, and when light is necessary, shaded lighting only should be used; the nurses wear felt slippers; the ears of the patient are occluded by the use of cotton soaked in albolene. At the time of the birth, the woman's face is covered with a towel, or smoked glasses used, in order to render her all the more impervious to sound and light; the cries of the child are often muffled by the sound of running water. . . .

The Editors of the WOMAN'S HOME COMPANION want to emphasize a timely and significant warning to American women who are interested in this treatment: Do not be lured by the quacks or charlatans, who will inevitably spring up like mushrooms, seeing in this cleverly-advertised method the means to reap a quick fortune. Perhaps the most pernicious element in the offered attractions of the "hospitals" or *"Frauenkliniks,"* a host of which are even now being planned by unscrupulous physicians, is the possibility of trading on the romance suggested by the name of the method. What possibilities of alluring and fascinating advertisement to attract women who, because of their condition or temperaments, or lack of discrimination, grasp too eagerly for any means that offers relief in the coming ordeal!

Like a glory of light revealing itself to womankind come the words of the summary of the report, from which we have already quoted, words important and symbolic: "We feel assured that we have in this (Twilight Sleep) a valuable method of abolishing the woman's recollection of the ordeal of labor in from sixty to seventy per cent of cases, and we believe that, in conscientious and painstaking hands, by strictly adhering to the above described technique, the possible dangers may be foreseen and avoided."

4. Doctor Analyzes Clinical Data to Determine the Safety and Effectiveness of "Twilight Sleep," 1915

A series of cases under scopolamin-morphin treatment was begun January 1, this year, in the Michael Reese Maternity, on the obstetric service of Dr. Lester E. Frankenthal, and continued on the service of Dr. Frank Cary. The series terminated February 5. . . .

Of the four delivery rooms in the Michael Reese Maternity, each constructed with cork-lined, sound-proof walls and sound-proof doors, the largest was chosen for the "twilight sleep" cases. Two nurses, both graduates with extensive obstetric experience, were especially engaged for day and night duty during the entire period of the series, and they remained constantly in the delivery room. The patients were furthermore under the continual observation of either the senior or junior intern on obstetrics, and of the day and night head nurse in charge of the maternity. All results were tabulated and the observations were constantly checked by Drs. Frankenthal, Cary and myself.

Patients in labor were sent to the third floor admitting room where they received a tub bath (sponge bath if membranes had ruptured), shaving of the genitals, and an enema, if not too far advanced in labor; when, if suitable for the series, they were taken to the delivery room, where treatment was begun with the following indications;

Joseph Baer, "Scopolamine-Morphine [sic] Treatment in Labor: A Critical Analysis of 60 Cases," *Journal of the American Medical Association* 64 (1915): 1723–1724, 1726, 1728.

in multiparas, when the pains recurred every ten minutes, and in primiparas when the pains recurred every five minutes. . . .

The total dosages varied from one-eighth to one-quarter grain morphin and from two doses of 1/200 to nine doses of 1/150 and eleven doses of 1/200 grain scopolamin, hypodermically. Subdued light, smoked glasses and avoidance of unnecessary and loud talking were strictly enforced. Observations on all points brought out in the literature were taken and recorded at half-hour intervals, and oftener when necessary. . . .

Results of Treatment

No Success, Twenty-six Cases

CASE 10.—Patient's memory was clear at all times. Patient was somewhat indifferent to the pains, but said that the pains were severe.

CASE 13.—Slight vertigo—memory clear at all times.

CASE 29.—Patient's memory clear throughout, slight flush and marked thirst being the only noticeable symptoms.

CASE 32.—At no time during labor had patient the slightest cloudiness of memory, sleeping between pains.

CASE 53.—Patient was delirious for several hours, doing foolish stunts and was very restless.

CASE 55.—Patient was very delirious, throwing herself about in a wild manner and later required restraint.

CASE 56.—Very restless—the drug increased her restlessness.

CASE 58.—Very restless, and during the second stage patient was absolutely unmanageable—could not be aroused and had to have restraining sheet.

CASE 61.—Treatment stopped after 5/150 grain scopolamin and 2/8 grain morphin because labor pains ceased. Patient also vomited and became restless, fetal heart tones dropped to 96 and forceps were used.

CASE 63.—Not much effect of the drug could be seen.

CASE 66.—Patient had a mitral insufficiency and myocarditis, a supposedly ideal case for the use of the treatment. After three doses subcrepitant râles appeared in the upper left lung, the pulse became fast and irregular and the fetal head stood in deep transverse arrest. Forceps and immediate extraction were followed by a pulmonary edema, from which the patient finally recovered. The baby was born in asphyxia pallida and was resuscitated with difficulty.

CASE 68.—No effect of drug noticed. . . .

CASE 11.—Delivery rapid following a somewhat quiet period. Patient quite indifferent, apparently having little pain, but somewhat cyanotic.

CASE 12.—Patient in the beginning was quiet; after the third dose became somewhat noisy and hysterical; memory was clear throughout labor.

CASE 14.—Child revived with difficulty. Later condition good. Treatment did not give desired effect of drugs.

CASE 19.—With heart tones at 108 from 124 after two doses, deemed it inadvisable to continue the treatment. Patient's mind was clear at all times and no effects of the treatment were noticeable.

CASE 25.—Patient had no disturbance of memory.

CASE 33.—Patient stopped for about four hours; after the fourth injection of scopolamin no effects of the drug were obtained.

CASE 37.—Patient's memory was clear at all times.

CASE 59.—Patient's memory clear throughout labor. After delivery became restless, then delirious, got out of bed and ran to window, getting onto the sill, was dragged off by the nurse, overpowered her, ran to the rear stairway, where three nurses finally succeeded in subduing her and getting her into the quiet room, where she was shackled and kept so four days, when she finally became entirely rational again.

CASE 62.—Patient's memory clear throughout. Case terminated by rupture of uterus. Patient, nonipara, had three doses of scopolamin 1/200 grain, and 2/8 grain morphin. After the last dose at 1:45 a. m., pains became less frequent and stopped at 4:30 a. m. At this time the fetal heart tones could no longer be heard, and the patient gradually became semiconscious. At 6:30 she was pale, and sweat appeared on the brow. The dilated cervix was found collapsed and the presenting head had receded. Diagnosis, rupture of the uterus, seen by Drs. Frankenthal, Cary and myself, abdominal section done, fetus and placenta found free in the abdominal cavity, a jagged transverse rupture in the lower uterine segment of the uterus, running straight across the whole width anteriorly just at the level of the fundus of the bladder and a huge retroperitoneal hematoma up to the kidney. Hysterectomy was done—patient died on the second day.

CASE 65.—No effect of drug noticed.

CASE 67.—No effect of drug noticed.

CASE 70.—No effect of drug noticed. . . .

Fair Success, Five Cases

CASE 8.—Patient's memory was clear throughout, but she appeared indifferent to what was going on.

CASE 43.—Patient was under influence of the drug as concerns amnesia for about one hour. Treatment lasted five hours and twenty-five minutes.

CASE 44.—Patient's memory was cloudy—excitation in the last half hour very marked, throwing herself about wildly. In the ward she had to be tied in bed.

CASE 45.—Patient was wildly delirious at time of pain, sleeping between pains, but throwing herself about for two hours before delivery in a wild manner.

CASE 57.—Postpartum hemorrhage half hour after patient returned to bed. Patient did not know when the baby was born. Abdominal muscles not used after the fifth dose of scopolamin. . . .

Completely Successful, Six Cases

CASE 23.—Patient had absolute loss of memory, but was very delirious, throwing herself about in a wild manner. Repair work was almost impossible on account of her wild actions, and restraint was necessary in bed. Child started breathing with little stimulation; ten minutes later stopped and artificial respiration had to be resorted to.

CASE 60.—Patient did not know when baby was born. Conduct during labor excellent.

CASE 42.—Patient's memory was only slightly cloudy prior to delivery, but amnesia was more marked after the birth of the child. Delivery was rapid.

CASE 46.—Patient was very quiet and slept all the time from one hour before delivery until several hours thereafter. Pains during second stage were good, regular and strong, but abdominal muscles were not used.

CASE 50.—Patient's memory was cloudy. Gave no expression of pain at time of birth and slept most of the time.

CASE 52.—Patient's amnesia was complete. Slept almost all the time, arousing only slightly at the return of each pain. . . .

From the foregoing results it seems reasonable to conclude that there are such dangers connected with the administration of the drugs, and that there is such a striking uncertainty of action in any given case, that the routine adoption of the treatment is not to be considered; moreover, it has been found impossible to "select" cases on any intelligent basis.

The lay press and magazines in their anxiety to outdo one another have published articles filled with the most extravagant phrases, but it is a bit out of the ordinary to read of a medical enthusiast announcing that by this treatment *the horrors of the delivery room are avoided.* The women must be few and far between who look back on the room in which they gave birth as a "chamber of horrors."

Summary

The prolongation of labor, the increase in the number of fetal asphyxias, the excessive thirst and intense headaches that are so distressing, the difficult control of patients and avoidance of infection by soiling of the genitals, the more frequent postpartum hemorrhages, the blurred vision, the ghastly deliriums persisting far into the puerperium, the inability to recognize the onset of the second stage unless by risk of more frequent examinations, the masking of early symptoms such as antepartum hemorrhage, rupture of the uterus and even eclampsia, the violence and uncertainty of the whole treatment, the general bad impression given to our patients who are being taught to approach the "horrors of labor" in fear and trembling, constitute so severe an arraignment of this treatment of labor cases that we feel compelled to condemn it, leaving open the question of the merits of a single dose of morphin and scopolamin in those cases in which we have hitherto given morphin and atropin.

5. Advertisement Insists That for a Hospital to Refuse to Buy Its "Pulmotor" Is Tantamount to Malpractice, 1919

WHAT IS THE VALUE OF A HUMAN LIFE?

"For a hospital not to have a Pulmotor will soon be regarded as reprehensible negligence approximating malpractice."

This statement was made recently by a hospital authority. It is a strong statement, but it was made with full knowledge of the fact that

The Pulmotor is the Resuscitative Device that will actually save life

It is automatic — can be operated by any of your nurses.

It is a scientific instrument, and its reputation is based on service performed, having saved more than 500 lives. The sale of this instrument was not promoted until its value was thoroughly established. Hundreds of hospitals and prominent physicians will back up our statements.

Can you assume the hazard of not having this life-saving instrument in your hospital?

The loss of a patient on the operating table or the failure to resuscitate any other case which would probably respond to the action of the Pulmotor would discredit your institution.

Full particulars on request.

THE PULMOTOR

Made in two sizes. Regular adult Pulmotor, with three sizes of masks. Infant Pulmotor for the new born only. The infant Pulmotor is almost indispensable for hospitals having a large number of maternity cases.

THE DRAEGER OXYGEN APPARATUS COMPANY, 415 First Avenue, Pittsburgh

Advertisement headed "What Is the Value of a Human Life?" in *The Modern Hospital Year Book: A Buyer's Reference Book of Supplies and Equipment for Hospitals and Allied Institutions* (Chicago: The Modern Hospital Publishing Company, 1919), back cover.

6. Medical Educator Francis Peabody Cautions Against Blind Faith in the Clinical Authority of the Laboratory, 1922

The important part which the laboratory has come to play in medical science is generally accepted and appreciated, but the relation which it should bear to clinical practice remains to be satisfactorily defined. It is obvious to all clinicians of experience that the laboratory never can become, and never should become, the predominating factor in the practice of medicine, but it is equally evident that sound medicine cannot be carried on without the support of the laboratory, and that in the future the dependence of the clinic on the laboratory will probably increase rather than decrease. Among the men engaged in active medical practice, however, only a small minority can ever hope to undertake extensive laboratory work in connection with their patients, and the great majority of physicians are and will continue to be confronted by the difficult problem of their relation to this growing influence in medicine. To the teacher of medicine, whose foremost duty is to prepare his students for the practice of the future, the same problem presents itself, for the students must be thoroughly trained in the laboratory methods that will be of practical service, but not burdened with those that are highly specialized or of questionable value.

The leading exponents of clinical laboratory work are the large hospitals—especially the hospitals associated with teaching institutions—and these exert a profound effect on private medical practice, but the conditions existing in them are such as to demand a separate consideration. In such hospitals, laboratory investigations fall into one of three categories. The first includes those which belong to the field of pure research, their object being to advance the limits of our knowledge of disease. With this we have, at present, no concern. The second consists of those laboratory methods that are applied in order to obtain direct aid in the diagnosis or treatment of individual cases of disease. This often means the use of standard methods of proved and known value—methods which have received general professional acceptance—but in addition it means the use of many methods of possible value, the significance of which needs to be thoroughly tested under conditions favorable for critical control. The trying out of newly advocated measures for the diagnosis and treatment of disease must always be an important function of the larger and better equipped hospitals. Many—indeed the majority—of such methods are found to be unreliable or of little practical value, and after their status becomes established they are discarded. Very rarely a new method withstands the test of prolonged observation and proves to be of such practical significance that it can be properly advocated for general adoption. This type of hospital thus serves as the court before which all such new ideas must stand trial and it is astonishing, if not depressing, to compare the enormous

Francis Peabody, "The Physician and the Laboratory," *Boston Medical and Surgical Journal* 187 (August 31, 1922): 324–328. The article was also published in *From Doctor and Patient: Papers on the Relationship of the Physician to Men and Institutions* (New York: Macmillan, 1930): 58–71.

amount of time and labor that is spent in gathering evidence with the comparatively meager results that pass the tests. The burden added to the hospital laboratories by such work is very great, but the importance of the function cannot be overestimated, for it filters out what is useful and protects the profession from much that is worthless.

The third category under which hospital laboratory work is carried on depends on the fact that every hospital is, or should be, an educational institution, and one of its primary duties is the instruction of all the members of the staff in the nature of disease. Many of the laboratory data, therefore, that fill the pages of carefully compiled hospital records do not have a direct diagnostic or therapeutic bearing on the individual case, but they contribute information which throws light on the pathological physiology and clarifies the disease process. In so far as the accumulation of such accessory laboratory observations is instructive to those who are studying the patients, the work is more than justified, but if, as sometimes happens, particularly with the younger members of the staff, it leads to the idea that all these observations are necessary for the proper diagnosis and treatment of any given case, the result may be most unfortunate. Properly used, such laboratory observations are enlightening and broadening; improperly used, they are blinding and narrowing. The real reason for taking an electrocardiogram on every patient with a cardiac arrhythmia is so that after one has studied the records of a large series of cases, he may understand the clinical manifestations of cardiac irregularities so well that he is able to recognize the type of arrhythmia without the electrocardiogram. His increased knowledge should, on the one hand, emancipate him from the need of the complicated apparatus in most cases, and, on the other hand, help him to appreciate the occasional case in which careful instrumental study is desirable. From this point of view, therefore, much hospital laboratory work may be regarded as of indirect significance for the individual patient, but aimed at the training of better clinicians. When, as sometimes happens, it results in the production of poor clinicians, unable to interpret disease except through the eyes of the laboratory, its purpose has failed, and failed seriously.

The physician engaged in the actual practice of medicine is directly concerned, therefore, with only a small part of the laboratory work which is carried on in the larger hospitals, for his attention must necessarily be focussed entirely on those methods which contribute immediately to the better care of his patients. The methods of the teaching clinic cannot and should not be carried into extramural practice. In the hospital all manner of tests can readily be performed in obscure or doubtful cases, but in private practice the economic factor usually restricts one to the tests which most obviously offer practical assistance. Fortunately, however—and this is apparently contrary to much present-day opinion—good medicine does not consist in the indiscriminate application of laboratory examinations to a patient, but rather in having so clear a comprehension of the probabilities and possibilities of a case as to know what tests may be expected to give information of value. Even so-called thoroughness should be tempered by reason, and the reason that must dictate the part which laboratory tests shall play in any given case must be the result of a combination of clinical experience with an understanding of the physiological significance of the available tests.

For the physician in private practice laboratory tests fall into two main classes. The first consists of those which every educated doctor should be able to carry out, and the second consists of tests which are more difficult in technique and which should be attempted only by a limited number of men who have been able to devote the time necessary to acquire specialized training. Fortunately, the first class is by far the more important of the two.

The laboratory tests which should be at the command of every practitioner of medicine are those which deal with the more important and practically useful examinations of the blood, urine, feces, gastric contents, spinal fluids, pleural and ascitic fluids. These are the tests that are customarily taught in the medical schools in the course in clinical pathology, and the instruction is usually designed to take up the laboratory methods that are absolutely necessary for good practice and those only. An experience in teaching this subject during the last seven years has emphasized the striking fact that in spite of the great contributions which the laboratory has made to clinical medicine there has been surprisingly little change in the character or number of the technical methods which are essential for good practice. . . . The methods for the examination of the urine, for instance, are taught much as they were two decades and more ago. . . . In the examination of the spinal fluid the cell count, which is the most important point, is merely an adaptation of the method of counting blood leucocytes, and not a new technical process. With regard to the examination of the gastric contents, body fluids, and feces, the same argument holds true; none of them involves difficult or prolonged examinations or expensive apparatus, and all of them yield information of the highest value to the man trained in their use and interpretation. Here, however, is the crux of the situation. All of these so-called routine tests are easy and consume little time in the hands of a trained man, but they are difficult, time-consuming, and of little value in the hands of an untrained man. What is really needed in the application of laboratory methods to the practice of medicine is not a knowledge of more technical procedures, but a much more exact knowledge of a few. Experience has shown that a proper degree of technical skill can rarely be obtained during the medical school course, and it should be the duty of every hospital to see that no house officer receives his diploma unless he has demonstrated an ability to perform satisfactorily all the simpler laboratory examinations and has shown a knowledge of how to use the results in the study of his patient. If every physician was so much at home with the technique of the simpler tests that it was quicker for him to apply them than to wonder whether they were worth while applying, and if he understood how to interpret these tests and gain the maximum information from them, the problem of the relation of the physician to the laboratory would be largely settled.

The second group of laboratory methods having a direct bearing on the practice of medicine consists of those which involve highly specialized technique and complicated apparatus. Electrocardiography, basal metabolism determinations, the Wassermann reaction, clinical bacteriology, and the various types of chemical analysis of the blood fall into this category. The information to be elicited from these and other analogous methods is often extremely valuable, but their application is necessary only in a comparatively limited number of cases. As a whole, these methods do not have the broad general significance and importance that characterize the simpler tests just referred to. It is, of course, highly desirable that they should be available to practicing physicians, so that they may be used in the cases in which they are particularly indicated, but fortunately there is no necessity for the great majority of physicians to both themselves about the details of technique. This should be relegated to a small number of men who are devoting their attention to specialized fields. Simplified technical procedures, supposed to be adapted to the use of practicing physicians, are continually being advocated as substitutes for the recognized standard methods employed in performing some of these tests, but they are frequently unreliable, or reliable only in the hands of one who has a thorough knowledge of all the sources of error, so that it is far wiser to avoid them and to obtain the dependable observations of experts. The clinician may, therefore, neglect the technical side of these more elaborate tests with a clear conscience, but in so doing he should not feel that he may drop the matter entirely. If he is ever to make use of them—and this the welfare of his patients may demand—he must have an understanding of their significance and of the physiology underlying them. He must know when they are indicated and when they cannot be expected to give important evidence. . . . [T]he physician should be able to interpret the results of the test in the light of his individual patient. A basal metabolism which is reported as 15 per cent above normal may or may not be significant, and an electrocardiogram showing a prolonged conduction time may be due to one of several factors, but in either case the physician should not be forced to depend for the interpretation on the man who does the laboratory work and who presumably has a less intimate knowledge of the clinical condition of the patient. The clinician himself should be able to appraise the laboratory findings if the patient is to derive the greatest benefit.

It is frequently alleged that many of our medical schools and teaching hospitals are producing "laboratory men" instead of clinicians. If it is true that the graduates of these institutions enter the practice of medicine handicapped by their dependence on the laboratory, then the system of training is wrong or—what seems more probable—it is imperfectly carried out. When schools and hospitals do their full duty their graduates will have had an opportunity to study disease intensively, checking and controlling their bedside observations by a variety of exact laboratory investigations. Such an experience will enable them to correlate the clinical manifestations of diseases with the underlying physiological processes, so that they can subsequently understand and interpret disease without recourse to all the laboratory procedures which were necessary in their student days. They will enter practice trained so thoroughly in a limited number of simple technical methods that they will not hesitate to use them, and they will understand all of their significance. They will also know when more complicated tests are indicated and how to interpret the results. In spite of the extraordinary influence which the laboratory has had on the development of medical science there is as yet no cause for the physician to feel that he cannot keep up with the requirements of the best modern practice. All of the more important elements are easily within his grasp. The need in clinical medicine continues to be, not for men trained in many laboratory methods but for men well grounded in a few methods—not for better technicians, but for better clinicians.

7. Prominent African American Anatomy Professor Montagu Cobb Questions the Assumptions of a Leading Textbook About the Biology of Race, 1942

THE BIOLOGY OF THE NEGRO
by Julian Herman Lewis, Ph.D., M.D.

This timely book, through which Dr. Lewis renders science and his people an important service, scores first with its paper jacket. The basic black tint shading into yellow-brown subtly but effectively emphasizes at the outset, the racial mixture represented by the Negro in the several parts of the world. One quickly perceives that the volume contains more data on its subject than have hitherto been assembled under one cover and so will be welcomed as a significant contribution to the long recognized need for a scientific reference volume on constitutional studies of the Negro. The usefulness of the book well justifies the patient labor obvious on every page.

The author, as a pathologist, is primarily interested in disease. This is clear from his preface and the fact that six of the nine chapters are specifically devoted to disease manifestations, while pathology distinctly has its hand in the other three. The chapters deal respectively with: population and vital statistics; anatomy of the Negro; biochemical and physiologic characteristics; medical diseases; surgical diseases; obstetrics and gynecology; diseases of the skin; diseases of the eye, ear, nose and throat; and dental diseases.

The book has professional value not only for its content, but for its convenience as a guide to a large literature. The general reader will be grateful for the lucid presentation of available information on many subjects of popular discussion, either as curiosa, such as steatopygia, racial odors and the principles of hair straightening, or as public health problems like tuberculosis and syphilis. The author's constant effort has been to preserve an impartial attitude. He "has no thesis to develop or disprove." The volume modestly "pretends to be nothing other than an arranged assembly of the observed and reported facts concerning the biology, including pathology, of the Negro."

Seldom cited contributions of the Negro to the building of our nation are of interest. Lewis records that the apparent immunity of the tropical Negro to malaria, subsequent to his heavy infection in infancy, is high. "Striking evidence of this was seen during the construction of the Panama Canal, which was made possible by the imported labor from the West Indies. The contrast in the mortality from malaria between these West Indian laborers and American whites was remarkable."

While at pains to stress that the American Negro is a socially and not a racially delimited group, and that no generalizations may be applied uniformly to all Negroes, Lewis believes the evidence clearly indicates the reality of racial differences in reaction to disease. This emerges from analysis of the data on nearly 90 clinical disease entities. The differences may refer to great susceptibility related to shorter historical

Montagu Cobb, Review of *The Biology of the Negro,* by Julian H. Lewis, *Crisis* 49 (1942): 394. The authors wish to thank The Crisis Publishing Co., Inc., the publisher of the magazine of the National Association for the Advancement of Colored People, for the use of this work.

exposure, as with tuberculosis, or to immunity acquired through longer contact, as with yellow fever and hookworm disease. They may be associated with anatomical racial features, as with differential Negro-white ratios in incidence of skin diseases, or with peculiarities of body reaction, as shown by the greater tendency to formation of fibrous tissue as in wound scars or in fibroid tumors of the uterus.

One disease, sickle-cell anemia, would appear to occur only in the Negro, with no apparent causal relationship. The author's special experience with this condition enabled him to enrich the book with a full clinical description such as would appear in a text on the practice of medicine. In his zeal to prove that sicklemia is exclusively a Negro disease, however, he approaches dangerously, the *reductio ad absurdum* which the Negro himself denounces in respect to so-called "tests" of Negro blood, such as nail pigmentation, split nasal cartilage, and the like. Lewis' arguments might be said to imply that a bona fide diagnosis of sicklemia in a white man is tantamount to evidence of some Negro blood, acquired either through unknown recent ancestry or through prehistoric infusion of Negro blood into southern European ancestry, but in reality, no known fact precludes the possibility of occurrence of authentic sicklemia in the white.

Lewis shows how modern improvement in coverage and accuracy of data has altered common opinion in respect to diseases such as diabetes and Buerger's disease, which formerly were believed to be of slight or rare occurrence in the Negro, but are now recognized to have a frequency which eventually may show little racial difference. We are given the facts and cautions concerning conditions such as diseases of the heart and blood vessels and of the kidneys, on which statistics though voluminous, are often unsatisfactory and difficult of evaluation. Discrepancies in conflicting theories which result from such inadequate information are pointed out. The excellences of the Negro as a surgical risk, related chiefly to his resistance to infection, are described and noteworthy facts in relation to special conditions cited.

On most subjects the evidence appears to have led to no sharp departure from current leading thought on the conditions described. One envisions that the work will soon be a handbook for members of medical societies and reading clubs in the preparation of the periodic papers they must regularly present.

 # E S S A Y S

In the first essay, physician-historian Joel D. Howell of the University of Michigan explores the role which two key diagnostic technologies (x-rays and electrocardiography) played in reshaping the organization of the hospital and the patient record. He also shows how institutional patterns and organizational structures can influence the use of new technologies. By focusing on how the machines and their products were actually used, Howell demonstrates the dynamic interplay between technologies and institutions. In the second essay, historian Judith Walzer Leavitt of the University of Wisconsin at Madison explores similar ground, but from the perspective of the lay community. The focus of her essay is the 1914–1915 controversy over the wisdom of importing the new anesthetic technology of "twilight sleep" from Europe to America for use during childbirth. As she takes us from the female-dominated culture of the midwife and home birth to the physician-guided hospital experience, the role of technology in medicine—in this case the American childbirth experience—emerges in a compelling way. Leavitt's powerful argument about the interplay of professional and lay interests in technological developments puts contemporary debates about techno-logical "quick fixes" in a new light. In the final essay, University of North Carolina historian Keith Wailoo investigates the role that a blood test developed originally for diagnostic purposes came to play in a larger cultural debate over racial identity. His finely drawn analysis of the development of Chicago anatomist Victor Emmel's test for sickling cells and of the scientific debate that ensued over its use sets out sharply the key question of the time: Was the test a diagnostic tool or a racial identifier? The use of a laboratory technology for other than medical purposes that Wailoo explores has a disturbing resonance in contemporary discussions of a whole range of biomedical technologies, particularly those associated with the burgeoning field of genetic testing.

Making Machines Clinically Useful in the Modern Hospital

JOEL D. HOWELL

Roentgen's description of x-rays in 1895 shocked the western world. The ability to see within the human body had a profound impact on both lay and professional communities, and the x-ray machine quickly came to symbolize the most advanced, scientific approach to medicine. In 1897, the Pennsylvania Hospital, like many other hospitals, purchased its first x-ray machine. While x-ray films were widely described in medical books and journals as useful for diagnosing fractures, description in medical literature is not the same as application in medical practice. Although trauma accounted for four of the five most common surgical diagnoses at the Pennsylvania Hospital, there is no mention of roentgenogram use in 1897. Five years later, in 1902, the x-ray machine was rarely used, and then only out of curiosity, not for patient care. . . .

A . . . 1902 example of the x-ray machine's use for curiosity, not patient care, is provided by the case of a gentleman admitted to the hospital, complaining of "inability to walk after being run over by a horse." The roentgenogram revealed a broken leg. This was not, however, an early diagnosis of fracture by x-ray, at least not in any clinically significant sense. The plate was exposed after 2½ weeks of uncomplicated hospitalization, during which the patient had been treated for an established diagnosis of a broken leg. The x-ray film was taken out of interest, not for patient care. Even a decade later, in 1912, roentgenographic examination was still quite an unusual event for the hospitalized patient. Patients with fractures severe enough to require surgery usually did not have a roentgenogram taken before going to the operating room for repair.

The person responsible for taking the x-ray films changed during the first 15 years. From 1897 to 1909, the chief resident operated the x-ray machine, one of his many duties; these duties also included running the operating room, sterilizing room, and photography room, as well as being responsible for the maintenance and care of "all apparatus and instruments." Clearly, the board of managers did not

Joel D. Howell, "Early Use of X-ray Machines and Electrocardiographs at the Pennsylvania Hospital," *Journal of the American Medical Association* 255 (1986): 2320–2323. Reprinted by permission of the American Medical Association.

anticipate that medical instrumentation would occupy a large part of the chief resident's day. X-ray equipment eventually assumed more time, and in both 1910 and 1911, the former chief resident stayed on for a year to run the x-ray machine. The first promptly declared the old equipment obsolete and insisted on the purchase of $940 worth of new machinery. His successor negotiated, with some difficulty, a pay raise from $25 to $50 per month.

The year 1912 marked a turning point in the operation of the x-ray machine, for in that year responsibility for running the machine shifted from a yearly succession of chief residents to a single physician who devoted his career to roentgenology. An x-ray department was established and David Bowen, MD, was named radiographer in charge, a position he maintained into the 1930s. Bowen, an 1894 graduate of Jefferson Medical College, was a country general practitioner until 1906, when he came across some discarded x-ray equipment that he was able to repair. The following year, he studied roentgenology for two weeks in Cincinnati and attended the annual meeting of the new American Roentgen Ray Society. He received further training from 1911 through 1920 in the radiology department of Jefferson Hospital, Philadelphia, published several articles, and became an editor for the *American Journal of Roentgenology and Radium Therapy*. From 1907 on, Bowen attempted to limit his practice to the taking and interpreting of roentgenograms.

The terms of Bowen's employment differed significantly from those of his predecessors, in ways that marked a qualitative change in the relationship between the physician, the machine, and the hospital. As compensation for devoting 50% of his time to the x-ray department, Bowen received a salary of $1,500 per year. In addition, his income included 75% of all fees generated by taking x-ray films of paying patients; the hospital retained 25%, an agreement reflecting the growing number of patients who paid for some part of their hospital care. At the same time as Bowen's 1911 appointment, an anonymous donor contributed $6,500 for the purchase of new x-ray equipment, marking a sharp increase in the hospital's capital investment in diagnostic machinery.

. . . The decision to establish a separate x-ray unit, run by a specialized physician with specific technical skills, was one part of a general increase in the complexity of the hospital's structure. Along with complexity came higher costs. Because the x-ray machine symbolized the exact, scientific nature of medicine, it was one way to attract paying patients. Indeed, the number of patients examined rose steadily, and in 1916 a nurse was assigned part-time to the x-ray department.

By 1917, roentgenograms had become routine for patients with kidney stones or limb fractures. Those with suspected broken legs often had examinations performed on admission, not 2½ weeks later, as in 1902. Physicians made specific diagnoses of tuberculosis, renal stones, and fractures solely on the basis of radiological evidence. However, patients were not admitted to the hospital specifically for an x-ray examination.

The First World War encouraged use of x-ray machines in two ways. First, dozens of nurses and physicians from the Pennsylvania Hospital staffed Base Hospital 10 in France. While caring for an unprecedented flow of casualties, they witnessed daily the value of x-ray films for diagnosing fractures and foreign bodies. Second, World War I stimulated technical advances in x-ray technique. X-ray pictures were originally taken on glass plates imported from Belgium. After 1914, these plates became difficult to obtain, and manufacturers were forced to use film to record x-ray pictures. Additional incentive for developing another medium came from the battlefield use of less powerful portable units, units that required faster film to take high-quality pictures. Both portable machines and more sensitive film were rapidly incorporated into civilian use. After World War I, the Pennsylvania Hospital X-ray Department expanded rapidly. A second physician was employed as assistant radiologist in 1919, and Bowen went from half-time to full-time radiographer in 1920, a year in which 4,005 patients were examined by x-ray film, and a portable unit was purchased.

The second major diagnostic technology introduced into the Pennsylvania Hospital, the electrocardiograph, provides a useful contrast with the hospital's experience with the x-ray machine. Unlike the sudden discovery of x-rays, the development of the electrocardiograph followed many earlier attempts to record the electrical action of the human heart. After Einthoven described the electrocardiograph in 1902, hospitals did not rush to buy one as rapidly as they had purchased x-ray machines in 1897. When the hospital finally purchased an electrocardiograph in 1921, they modeled arrangements for its use on those for the x-ray machine. The board of managers quickly approved the same 75%–25% split of fees for the "electrocardiographer" as they had earlier for the radiographer. Electrocardiographic (ECG) reports appeared on patients' charts within the year, usually on patients with irregular heart beats. A separate room was set aside to house the electrocardiograph.

By 1927, although not used as widely as the x-ray machine, the electrocardiograph was well on its way to becoming a routine part of patient care. The machine was applied frequently enough to require that a part-time technician be employed by the electrocardiograph laboratory. Attention and money were directed to heart diseases; a special heart clinic attracted large numbers of patients, and a fellowship in cardiac diseases was established. The x-ray department was also rapidly expanding. It performed 6,621 examinations in a new, 12-room, $21,000 suite, which had been featured in the 1925 annual report. The department boasted a stereo unit to examine the lungs, reports within the same day for 95% of cases, and, with three transformers, the ability to handle even emergency cases. Examinations for possible fractures were done at the time of admission, even when there was low suspicion that a fracture was actually present, and in almost every case diagnosed as a fracture an x-ray film was taken.

But in 1927, there was an even more significant transformation than the increased number of patients receiving an x-ray or ECG examination. For the first time, patient records indicate that individuals entered the hospital specifically "for study." This new indication for admission marks a distinct qualitative shift in the use of the hospital. The 19th-century hospital had been a home for the long-term care of the chronically ill, which gradually became a turn-of-the-century institution for acute management of accident cases as the community became increasingly hard pressed to care for the sick at home. Only in 1927 did the Pennsylvania Hospital start to function as a repository for complex diagnostic machinery. Why did this function not emerge until 30 years after the hospital originally bought an x-ray machine?

It would be appealingly simple to assert that technical improvements in diagnostic tools led directly to greater clinical utility. It is true that by 1927 a combination of new tubes, improved power supplies, and a moving grid had greatly improved the quality of x-ray pictures and made the x-ray a more useful clinical tool. However, the ECG, unlike the x-ray, was of very little clinical value in the 1920s. Its rapid integration into patient care cannot be explained by assuming that technical improvement with resulting clinical utility dictates how a machine will be used.

In 1897, there had been no structure into which the x-ray examination could easily fit. There were no physicians running machines for fees, no forms for reporting test results. Eventually the hospital employed a physician to take x-ray films, and by 1921 the roentgenogram had become an accepted part of hospital care. When the board of managers purchased an electrocardiograph, the hospital's experience with the x-ray machine had created a structure into which the new machine could be easily inserted. The routines were already in place, as was the idea that it was desirable to take precise, quantitative measurements with machines.

... [M]ore than simply organizational routines, financial reimbursement schemes, or standard operating procedures encouraged the introduction of machines. The hospital context became particularly receptive to information produced by machines as the practice of medicine became more complex, more quantitative, and more scientific—a change reflected in the form taken by hospital records.

In 1897, patient charts contained no pictures, no separate forms, few numbers, and no graphs save the temperature chart. The intern wrote the entire document by hand. By 1912, urinalysis results appeared on a small, printed slip of paper laid into the chart. The form defined specific examinations to be made on each urine specimen. Also in 1912, interns started to illustrate their physical examinations by drawing pictures of the patient's body. Such illustrations were consonant with the roentgenogram's visual, anatomic display of information, and served to communicate sensory evidence to the growing number of people involved in patient care. By 1917, laboratory results, including urinalysis, results of blood examinations, and pathological findings, were summarized on a single, full-size pink sheet, rather than being scattered on the earlier patchwork of pieces of paper pasted into the record. Also, no longer handwritten by the intern, a formal, official x-ray film reading was reported on a separate, standard form, signed by the radiologist.

Standardization and quantification proceeded apace after 1917, the year that the American College of Surgeons began a national drive for standardization of hospital records. Electrocardiographic reports written in precise, numerical terms appeared on patients' charts by 1922, along with handdrawn diet charts recording diabetic patients' intake of fat, protein, and carbohydrate in grams. The radiology department introduced forms for reporting results of gastrointestinal x-ray examinations on which the interpreting physician needed only to circle the appropriate description for each anatomic portion, thus limiting the possible descriptions of each to a few phrases. Even the visual display of anatomic information became standardized, as an inked stamp of the thorax replaced the intern's handdrawn effort.

The hospital record became progressively more visual and more quantitative. By 1927, interns charted a graphic representation of cardiac murmurs in addition to describing them with words. Physicians noted the heart's size with precise, quantitative measurements drawn on the standardized stamp of the patient's body. Colored bar graphs visually and quantitatively depicted the fluid intake and output of a patient with kidney disease. The handdrawn diet chart used for diabetics in 1922 had become, by 1927, a formal, standardized, printed form.

The use of forms to report results of diagnostic tests standardized information provided to those directly caring for the patient. This was explicitly true for gastrointestinal roentgenograms; to produce his report, the radiologist needed only to select which phrase to use. The language also was limited implicitly, as physicians interpreting each test came to report findings in a particular way. In both instances, standardized forms constrained the number of possible results that a test could provide. However, systemization improved communication between diagnostic units and treating physicians. It also aided clinical research by making it easier to follow findings on a single patient over time, and by facilitating quantitative comparisons between patients.

The widespread use of standardized forms both reflected and encouraged the rise of medical specialization. Forms emphasized the increasingly specialized nature of the knowledge produced by machines and, when signed by the director of a particular unit, reinforced the need for specially trained experts to interpret the results. These forms also symbolized the exact, scientific nature of the knowledge produced by machines.

The placement of x-ray machines in hospitals has been used to explain, in part, the rapid early 20th-century growth of hospitals. This study suggests the importance of other factors. Although the Pennsylvania Hospital purchased its first x-ray machine in 1897, it took three decades for such technology to draw patients into the hospital. This delay was caused not by technical inadequacies in the x-ray machine, nor by lack of medical justification for its use. Rather, the organization of the hospital had to change. . . .

Historical analysis should give us pause as we attempt to predict, using unequivocally rational and logical criteria, how new machines will eventually be applied. The x-ray machine was first used in an exploratory, experimental fashion, and pictures were taken of patients with many different conditions. Changes in the intellectual, social, and institutional system in which it was applied changed the indications for its application. The lesson of this study for contemporary technology assessment is that changes in both organizational and conceptual systems are critically important in determining how diagnostic technology is used, albeit difficult to predict.

"Twilight Sleep": Technology and the Medicalization of Childbirth

JUDITH WALZER LEAVITT

"At midnight I was awakened by a very sharp pain," wrote Mrs. Cecil Stewart, describing the birth of her child in 1914. "The head nurse . . . gave me an injection of scopolamin-morphin. . . . I woke up the next morning about half-past seven . . . the door opened, and the head nurse brought in my baby. . . . I was so happy." Mrs. Stewart had delivered her baby under the influence of scopolamine, a narcotic

Judith Walzer Leavitt, "Birthing and Anesthesia: The Debate Over Twilight Sleep," *Signs* 6 (1980): 147–164. Copyright © 1980 University of Chicago Press. Reprinted by permission of the publisher.

and amnesiac that, together with morphine, produced a state popularly known as "twilight sleep." She did not remember anything of the experience when she woke up after giving birth. This 1914 ideal contrasts with today's feminist stress on being awake, aware, and in control during the birthing experience. In 1914 and 1915, thousands of American women testified to the marvels of having babies without the trauma of childbirth. As one of them gratefully put it, "The night of my confinement will always be a night dropped out of my life."

From the perspective of today's ideology of woman-controlled births, it may appear that women who want anesthesia sought to cede control of their births to their doctors. I will argue however, that the twilight sleep movement led by women in 1914 and 1915 was not a relinquishing of control. Rather, it was an attempt to gain control over the birthing process. Feminist women wanted the parturient, not the doctor or attendant, to choose the kind of delivery she would have. This essay examines the apparent contradiction in the women's demand to control their births by going to sleep.

The attendants, location, and drugs or instruments used in American women's birthing experiences varied in the early decades of the twentieth century. America's poorer and immigrant women delivered their babies predominantly at home, attended by midwives who seldom administered drugs and who called physicians only in difficult cases. A small number of poor women gave birth in charity or public hospitals where physicians attended them. Most upper- and middle-class women, who had more choice, elected to be attended by a physician, usually a general practitioner but increasingly a specially trained obstetrician, rather than a midwife. At the turn of the twentieth century, these births, too, typically took place in the woman's home; however, by the second decade of the century, specialists, aided partly by the twilight sleep movement, were moving childbirth from the home to the hospital.

Physicians used drugs and techniques of physical intervention in many cases, although the extent cannot be quantified accurately. In addition to forceps, physicians relied on opium, chloroform, chloral, cocaine, quinine, nitrous oxide, ergot, and ether to relieve pain, expedite labor, prevent injury in precipitous labors, control hemorrhage, and prevent sepsis. In one study of 972 consecutive births in Wisconsin, physicians used chloroform during the second stage of labor in half of their cases and forceps in 12 percent. The reports indicate that drugs and instruments may have made labors shorter but not necessarily more enjoyable. Because most drugs could not be used safely throughout the labor and delivery, either because they affected muscle function or because they were dangerous for the baby, women still experienced pain. The use of forceps frequently added to discomfort and caused perineal tears, complicating postdelivery recovery. Maternal mortality remained high in the early decades of the twentieth century, and childbirth, whether attended by physicians or midwives, continued to be risky.

Most women described their physician-attended childbirths as unpleasant at best. Observers of the declining birthrates among America's "better" classes worried that the "fear of childbirth has poisoned the happiness of many women" and caused them to want fewer children. One woman told her doctor that her childbirth had been "hell. . . . It bursts your brain, and tears out your heart, and crashes your nerves to bits. It's just like hell, and I won't stand it again. Never." In scopolamine deliveries, the women went to sleep, delivered their babies, and woke up feeling vigorous. The drug altered their consciousness so that they did not remember painful labors, and their bodies did not feel exhausted by their efforts. Both the women who demanded scopolamine and the doctors who agreed to use it perceived it as far superior to other anesthesia because it did not inhibit muscle function and could be administered throughout the birthing process. It was the newest and finest technique available—"the greatest boon the Twentieth Century could give to women," in the words of Dr. Bertha Van Hoosen, one of its foremost medial advocates.

However, women's bodies experienced their labors, even if their minds did not remember them. Thus observers witnessed women screaming in pain during contractions, thrashing about, and giving all the outward signs of "acute suffering." Residents of Riverside Drive in New York City testified that women in Dr. William H. W. Knipe's twilight sleep hospital sent forth "objectionable" noises in the middle of the night.

A successful twilight sleep delivery, as practiced by Dr. Van Hoosen at the Mary Thompson Hospital in Chicago, required elaborate facilities and careful supervision. Attending physicians and nurses gave the first injection of scopolamine as soon as a woman appeared to be in active labor and continued the injections at carefully determined intervals throughout her labor and delivery. They periodically administered two tests to determine the effectiveness of the anesthesia: the "calling test," which the parturient passed if the doctor could not arouse her even by addressing her in a loud voice, and the "incoordination test," which she passed if her movements were uncoordinated. Once the laboring woman was under the effects of scopolamine, the doctors put her into a specially designed crib-bed to contain her sometimes violent movements. Van Hoosen described the need for the bed screens: "As the pains increase in frequency and strength, the patient tosses or throws herself about, but without injury to herself, and may be left without fear that she will roll onto the floor or be found wandering aimlessly in the corridors. In rare cases, where the patient is very excitable and insists on getting out of bed . . . I prefer to fasten a canvas cover over the tops of the screens, thereby shutting out light, noise and possibility of leaving the bed." When delivery began, attendants took down the canvas crib and positioned the patient in stirrups, familiar in modern obstetrical services. Van Hoosen advised the use of a continuous sleeve to ensure that patients did not interfere with the sterile field. The canvas crib and the continuous sleeve were Van Hoosen's response to a common need in twilight sleep deliveries: a secure, darkened, quiet, contained environment.

Twilight sleep became a controversial issue in American obstetrics in June 1914, when *McClure's Magazine* published an article by two laywomen describing this newly popular German method of painless childbirth. In the article, Marguerite Tracy and Constance Leupp, both visitors at the Freiburg women's clinic, criticized high-forceps deliveries (which they called the common American technique) as dangerous and conducive to infection. They contrasted these imperfect births to the safety and comfort of twilight sleep. The new method was so wonderful that women, having once experienced it, would "walk all the way [to Germany] from California" to have their subsequent births under twilight sleep. The physicians at the Freiburg clinic thought the method was best suited for the upper-class "modern woman . . . [who] responds to the stimulus of severe pain . . . with nervous exhaustion and paralysis of the will to carry labor to conclusion." They were less certain about its usefulness for women who "earn their living by manual labor" and could tolerate more pain.

The women who took up the cause of twilight sleep concluded that it was not in general use in this country because doctors were consciously withholding this panacea. Physicians have "held back" on developing painless childbirth, accused Mary Boyd and Marguerite Tracy, two of the most active proponents, because it "takes too much time." "Women alone," they asserted, "can bring Freiburg methods into American obstetrical practice." Others echoed the call to arms: journalist Hanna Rion urged her readers to "take up the battle for painless childbirth. . . . Fight not only for yourselves, but fight for your . . . sex." Newspapers and popular magazines joined the chorus, advocating a widespread use of scopolamine in childbirth.

The lay public's anger at the medical profession's apparent refusal to adopt a technique beneficial to women erupted into a national movement. The National Twilight Sleep Association, formed by upper-middle-class clubwomen, was best epitomized by its leaders. They included women such as Mrs. Jesse F. Attwater, editor of *Femina* in Boston; Dr. Eliza Taylor Ransom, active women's rights advocate and physician in Boston; Mrs. Julian Heath of the National Housewife's League; author Rheta Childe Dorr of the Committee on the Industrial Conditions of Women and Children; Mary Ware Dennett of the National Suffrage Association (and later the National Birth Control League); and Dr. Bertha Van Hoosen, outspoken women's leader in medical circles in Chicago. Many of these leaders saw the horrors of childbirth as an experience that united all women: "Childbirth has for every woman through all time been potentially great emergency." Dr. Ransom thought that the use of twilight sleep would "create a more perfect motherhood" and urged others to work "for the betterment of womenkind." Because they saw it as an issue for their sex, not just their class, and because many of the twilight sleep leaders were active feminists, they spoke in the idiom of the woman movement.

The association sponsored rallies in major cities to acquaint women with the issue of painless childbirth and to pressure the medical profession into adopting the new method. In order to broaden their appeal, the association staged meetings "between the marked-down suits and the table linen" of department stores where "the ordinary woman" as well as the activist clubwoman could be found. At these rallies, women who had traveled to Freiburg testified to the wonders of twilight sleep. "I experienced absolutely no pain," claimed Mrs. Francis X. Carmody of Brooklyn, displaying her healthy baby at Gimbels. "An hour after my child was born I ate a hearty breakfast. . . . The third day I went for an automobile ride. . . . The Twilight Sleep is wonderful." Mrs. Carmody ended with the familiar rallying cry: "If you women want it you will have to fight for it, for the mass of doctors are opposed to it."

Department-store rallies and extensive press coverage brought the movement to the attention of a broad segment of American women. Movement leaders rejoiced over episodes such as the one in which a "tenement house mother . . . collected a crowd" on a street corner where she joyfully told of her twilight sleep experience. Many working-class women were attracted to twilight sleep not only because it made childbirth "pleasanter" but because they saw its use as "an important cause of decreased mortality and increased health and vitality among the mothers of children." Some feared, however, that twilight sleep would remain a "superadded luxury of the wealthy mother" because it involved so much physician time and hospital expense. . . .

Van Hoosen emerged as the most avid advocate of twilight sleep in the Midwest. She received her M.D. from the University of Michigan Medical School and worked at the New England Hospital for Women and Children in Boston before setting up practice in Chicago in 1892. Her enthusiasm for the method came from two sources: her strong commitment to the best in obstetrical care and her equally strong commitment to women's rights. Through her use of scopolamine in surgery and obstetrics, she became convinced that twilight sleep offered women a "return of more physiological births" at the same time that it increased the efficiency of physicians, giving them "complete control of everything." She guided many other physicians to the twilight sleep method. In terms of safety and comfort, she could not imagine a better method of birthing.

Increasingly, doctors began to deliver twilight sleep babies. Some traveled to Germany to learn the Freiburg technique and subsequently offered it to both private and charity patients. A few physicians even became enthusiastic about the possibilities of twilight sleep. "If the male had to endure this suffering," said Dr. James Harrar of New York, "I think he would resort very precipitously to something that might relieve the . . . pain." . . . Another physician listed its advantages: painless labor, reduction of subsequent "nerve exhaustion that comes after a prolonged hard labor," better milk secretion, fewer cervical and perineal lacerations, fewer forcep deliveries, less strain on the heart, and a "better race for future generations" since upper-class women would be more likely to have babies if they could have them painlessly. There was also, it was claimed, an "advantage to the child: To give it a better chance for life at the time of delivery; a better chance to have breast-feeding; a better chance to have a strong, normal mother."

Despite the energy and enthusiasm of the twilight sleep advocates, many American doctors resisted the technique. They lashed out against the "pseudo-scientific rubbish" and the "quackish hocus-pocus" published in *McClure's* and simply refused to be "stampeded by these misguided ladies." These physicians did not believe that nonmedical people should determine therapeutic methods; it was a "question of medical ethics." Other physicians refused to use scopolamine because they feared its dangers either to the mother or the child. The *Journal of the American Medical Association* concluded that "this method has been thoroughly investigated, tried, and found wanting, because of the danger connected with it."

Because the evidence about safety was mixed, many doctors were frustrated in their attempts to find out whether scopolamine was harmful or safe for use in obstetrics. . . . In one journal, they read that the procedure was "too dangerous to be pursued," while another journal assured them that scopolamine, when properly used during labor, "has no danger for either mother or child." Increasingly, by 1915, medical journals published studies that at least cautiously favored twilight sleep (the January 1915 issue of *American Medicine* published nine such articles), although they frequently ran editorials warning of the drug's potential dangers and stressing the need for caution. Practicing physicians faced a dilemma when pregnant women demanded painless childbirth with scopolamine.

While physicians debated the desirability of using scopolamine in 1914 and 1915, the public, surer of its position, demanded that twilight sleep be routinely available to women who wanted it. Hospitals in the major cities responded to these demands and to physicians' growing interest in the method by allowing deliveries of babies the Freiburg way. In order to gain additional clinical experience, and possibly in response to some women's requests, some doctors used twilight sleep in hospital charity wards. But the technique was most successful in the specialty wards where upper- and middle-class patients increasingly gave birth and hospital attendants and facilities were available. By May 1915, *McClure's Magazine's* national survey reported that the use of twilight sleep, although still battling for acceptance, "gains steadily" around the country.

Because of the need for expertise and extra care in administration of scopolamine, the twilight sleep movement easily fed into widespread efforts in the second decade of the twentieth century to upgrade obstetrical practice and eliminate midwives. Both the women who demanded the technique and the doctors who adopted it applauded the new specialty of obstetrics. Mary Boyd desired to put an end to home deliveries when she advocated twilight sleep for charity patients: "Just as the village barber no longer performs operations, the untrained midwife of the neighborhood will pass out of existence under the effective competition of free painless wards." Not only did scopolamine advocates try to displace midwives, but they also regarded general practitioners as unqualified to deliver twilight sleep babies. "The twentieth century woman will no more think of having an ordinary practitioner attend her in childbed at her own home," said two supporters, "she will go to a [twilight sleep] hospital as a matter of course." Specialists agreed that "the method is not adapted for the general practitioner, but should be practiced only by those who devote themselves to obstetrics." . . .

. . . Another factor that might have pushed obstetricians to support twilight sleep was that births under scopolamine could be managed more completely by the physician. As one succinctly put it, anesthesia gave "absolute control over your patient at all stages of the game. . . . You are 'boss.'" Physicians' time at the bedside could even be used for other pursuits. "I catch up on my reading and writing," testified one practitioner, "I am never harassed by relatives who want me to tell them things."

Several factors contributed to the open tensions about the use of twilight sleep. One was safety. Many physicians rejected scopolamine because they did not have access to facilities like those at the Mary Thompson Hospital or because they believed the drug too risky under any circumstances. Because of the variability among physicians' use of scopolamine and the contradictory evidence in the professional journals, we know that safety was a guiding motivation of many physicians. However, this is not enough to explain physician reluctance since so many doctors administered other drugs during labor despite questionable safety reports. Differing perceptions about pain during childbirth also contributed to the intensity of feeling about twilight sleep in 1914 and 1915. Although many physicians believed that women's "extremely delicate nervous sensibilities" needed relief, others were reluctant to interfere with the natural process of childbirth. One anti–twilight sleep physician argued, "when we reflect that we are dealing with a perfectly healthy individual, and an organ engaged in a purely physiological function . . . I fail to see the necessity of instituting such a measure in a normal labor and attempt[ing] to bridge the parturient woman over this physiological process in a semi-conscious condition." . . .

Both sides in the twilight sleep debate grappled with a third important question: whether the women or the attendants should determine and control the birthing process. The women who demanded that doctors put them to sleep were partially blind to the safety issue because of the issue of control (over pain, bodily function, decision making) was so important to them. Control became important when doctors refused to allow women "to receive the same benefits from this great discovery that their sisters abroad are getting." Twilight sleep advocates demanded their right to decide how they would have their children. Tracy and Boyd articulated this issue: "Women took their doctor's word before. They are now beginning to believe . . . that the use of painlessness should be at *their* discretion." Although women were out of control during twilight sleep births—unconscious and needing crib-beds or constant attention to restrain their wild movements—this loss of control was less important to them than their determination to control the decision about what kind of labor and delivery they would have. Hanna Rion, whose influential book and articles had garnered support for the method, wrote:

> In the old-fashioned days when women were merely the blindfolded guardians of the power of child-bearing, they had no choice but to trust themselves without question in the hands of the all-wise physician, but that day is past and will return no more. Women have torn away the bandages of false modesty; they are no longer ashamed of their bodies; they want to know all the wondrous workings of nature, and they demand that they be taught how best to safeguard themselves as wives and mothers. When it comes to the supreme function of childbearing every woman should certainly have the choice of saying *how* she will have her child.

. . . This feminist emphasis on control over decision making appears in the writings and lectures of the twilight sleep movement; its followers sought simple relief from pain. Many leaders were active suffragists whose commitment to twilight sleep was rooted in their belief in women's rights. Although these activists agreed with most physicians that birth should increasingly be the domain of the obstetricians and that women should not suffer unnecessarily, they disagreed vehemently about who should decide what the birthing woman's experience would be. They clearly and adamantly wanted women to have the right to decide their own method of birthing.

In the face of advancing obstetrical technology, many physicians wanted to retain their traditional professional right and duty to decide therapy on the basis of their judgment about the medical indications. They refused to be "dragooned" into "indiscriminate adoption" of a procedure that they themselves did not choose. Even the doctors who supported twilight sleep believed that in the final analysis, the method of childbirth was "a question for the attending man and not the patient to decide." It was principally this question of power over decision making that separated the movement's proponents from its opponents.

In the very successes of the twilight sleep movement lay the seeds for its demise. Pressured by the clubwomen's associations and their own pregnant patients, doctors who had not been trained in the Freiburg method delivered babies with scopolamine. There was an enormous variation in the use of the drug, its timing through labor, the conditions in which the woman labored, and the watchfulness of attendants. As its advocates had feared, problems emerged when scopolamine was not properly monitored in a hospital setting. Following reports of adverse effects on the newborn, the drug fell into ill repute, and some hospitals that had been among the first to use it stopped administering it routinely. . . .

. . . A second inhibitory factor appeared in August 1915 when Mrs. Francis X. Carmody, one of the country's leading exponents of twilight sleep, died during childbirth at Long Island College Hospital in New York. Although doctors and her husband insisted that her death was unrelated to scopolamine, it nonetheless harmed the movement. Mrs. Carmody's neighbor started a new movement to oppose twilight sleep, and women became more alert to the question of safety than they had been. Doctors and some former twilight sleep advocates, emphasizing the issues of safety and difficulty of administration, began exploring other methods of achieving painless childbirth.

The obstetric literature after 1915 indicates that twilight sleep did not die in that year. The women's movement may have failed to make scopolamine routinely available to all laboring women, but it succeeded in making the concept of painless childbirth more acceptable and in adding scopolamine to the obstetric pharmacopoeia. In fact, obstetricians continued to use scopolamine into the 1960s during the first stage of hospital births. The use of anesthesia (including scopolamine) in childbirth grew in the years after 1915, since women, aware of the possibility of painlessness, continued to want "shorter and less painful parturition" and since physicians felt they could disregard these desires "only at great risk to [their] own practice." . . .

. . . Ironically, by encouraging women to go to sleep during their deliveries, the twilight sleep movement helped to distance women from their bodies. Put to sleep with a variety of drugs, most parturient women from the 1920s to the 1960s did not experience one of their bodies' most powerful actions and thus lost touch with their own physical potential. The twilight sleep movement helped change the definition of birthing from a natural home event, as it was in the nineteenth century, to an illness requiring hospitalization and physician attendance. Parturient feminists today, seeking fully to experience childbirth, paradoxically must fight a tradition of drugged, hospital-controlled births, itself the partial result of a struggle to increase women's control over their bodies.

The Power of Genetic Testing in a Conflicted Society

KEITH WAILOO

After sickle cell anemia was first discovered in 1910, a small community of physicians emerged who shared an interest in this disease. They were a community not because they shared a specialty like hematology or pediatrics, but because they spoke to one another through national and regional medical journals. In the period . . . 1920–1950, this community of scholars constructed knowledge about sickle cell anemia and its relation to thalassemia. By examining the writing of some of these

Keith Wailoo, "Genetic Marker of Segregation: Sickle Cell Anemia, Thalassemia, and Racial Ideology in American Medical Writing, 1920–50," *History and Philosophy of the Life Sciences* 18 (1990): 305–320. Reprinted by permission of Taylor & Francis, Ltd., http://www.tandf.co.uk/journals.

medical scholars, this paper explores how they came to see this disease as synonymous with "Negro blood," how this association informed racial thought, and how some physicians (but certainly not all) interpreted these biological features explicitly in their defense of racial segregation.

. . . [M]any physicians of the period saw "Negro blood" as a scientific term with clear biological, social, and public health implications. ("Blood" possessed the same scientific and popular resonances in that era as the term "genes" do today; "blood" collapsed categorical terms like community, clan, kin, character, and biological identity into one convenient shorthand term.) Accordingly, some physicians came to believe that "Negro blood" caused sickle cell anemia. Indeed, they saw it as a Mendelian dominant disorder—and this genetic character had important social and public health implications. According to their interpretation of Mendelian genetics, a dominant trait could be spread by any individual "carrier" parent to his or her offspring, regardless of the genetic endowment of the other parent. It could therefore spread outward from an affected population. This view was rooted not in confusion, but in what seemed at that time to be clear diagnostic evidence, and a prevailing scientific understanding of genetics.

But more than genetic, logic was at work in building this conception of the disease. Physicians also held to prevailing social assumptions about racial segregation, and these assumptions were particularly important in defining sickle cell as a disease caused by "Negro blood." Beginning in 1925, numerous case reports of "sickle cell anemia in whites" appeared in the medical presses. Some of these cases were undoubtedly what we might call thalassemia. For most physicians, these cases only confirmed that the taint (that is, the capacity for developing sickled cells) could be spread through miscegenation—racial intermarriage. One uncharacteristically blunt statement by a physician in 1943 proclaimed that: "sickle cell anemia is a national health problem, especially in the United States." He argued that "intermarriages between Negroes and white persons directly endanger the white race by transmission of the sickling trait . . . such intermarriages, therefore, should be prohibited by federal law." In less strident language, a 1947 editorial in the *Journal of the American Medical Association* confirmed this racial definition of the disease:

> Its occurrence depends entirely on the presence of Negro blood, even in extremely small amounts it appears that the sine qua non for the occurrence of sickle cell anemia is the presence of a strain, even remote, of Negro blood. . . . The disease . . . is regularly found in countries where there is frank interbreeding with African people. . . . Race is thus a strong etiological factor.

Miscegenation was characterized as the key vehicle of transmission of the disease. Throughout this period, the appearance of sickled cells even in so-called "white people" was treated as a genetic marker of "Negro blood."

How did this discourse evolve from 1920 to the 1940s? It is not enough merely to attribute such beliefs to a static "biological racism" or to the purposeful use of biology to promote the segregation and oppression of African-Americans. Historians and other scholars have shown that "race" means different things in different times and contexts. They have begun to explore the processes by which the meaning of race has changed over time in American society. Certainly, throughout the nineteenth and particularly the twentieth centuries the discourse and practice of the medical sciences have played a significant role in shaping the meaning of race. (Frequently, even today, when students of medicine, biology, or social history are told that "race" is an evolving social construct, some will point to one disease—sickle cell anemia—as evidence of established inherent biological differences between races.) My interest here is to examine the ways in which physicians in the past constructed ideas about race in their very discussions about this disease and their changing society. How did physicians dis-aggregate the complex symptoms they saw into some kind of meaningful order? How did they use diagnostic technology? Where did they look for models of interpretation (that is, to which allied sciences and social sciences)? Where did these "white" patients with sickle cell disease fit into their model? How were their ideas legitimated, sustained, and instantiated in the disease sickle cell anemia? How did sickle cell anemia become a disease of "Negro blood" and what did this mean at the time? . . .

In the late nineteenth century, one could read in medical and social science journals that the high mortality rates in emancipated blacks was a sign of racial decline, a decline set in motion by the challenges of freedom. By the early twentieth century, these dire warnings about the inevitable extinction of emancipated blacks in America had begun to subside in the face of significant demographic growth and mobility. This mobility—often referred to as the "Great Migration" into Northern and Southern urban areas—stirred discussions among medical professionals in the South as well as in the North. Physicians regularly commented on the high incidence of tuberculosis and venereal disease among blacks—was it the Negro "constitution," the moral failings of the race, or environmental and economic circumstances that explained this disease incidence? "Disease" proved to be a powerful idiom for expressions of fear and concern, provoking a variety of medical responses to the so-called "Negro problem." Thus, in 1923, when Virgil Sydenstricker of the University of Georgia at Augusta presented one of the earliest talks on this new sickle cell disease to a Southern medical audience, one of his colleagues arose to comment that: "it is of industrial, as well as medical importance. . . . As we have a plentiful supply of Negroes with us in the South, it is important that we acquaint ourselves with this disease. I am quite convinced there is more [of it] in the South than is at present realized. It is therefore a Southern problem for us to work out." The regional theme continued to attract commentary. More important, physicians saw sickle cell anemia as a latent, hidden disorder, to be uncovered and rooted out of the Negro community.

To understand how sickle cell anemia became synonymous with a hidden "Negro blood," it is necessary to understand the technique that Sydenstricker and others used for its diagnosis and definition. In 1917, a Chicago anatomist Victor Emmel created a diagnostic technique which physicians used from the 1920s until the 1950s to shape their thinking about sickle cell anemia. Emmel's technique was undoubtedly an important diagnostic achievement in the history of this disease, but my focus here will be on the pattern of interpretation informing many physicians' use of the new tool. In the year that Emmel published his article on the diagnostic test, only three cases of peculiar, elongated and sickle-shaped red blood cells in Negroes and mulattos had been reported. Emmel set out to investigate James Herrick's 1910 observations of sickle cells and the two subsequent cases, in which a wide range of symptoms and complaints—joint pains, lethargy, abdominal pain, leg ulcers, death from infection—were associated with the rare disease. He described a patient who appeared in the Charity Hospital in St. Louis (where he then worked), showing many of the same symptoms that Herrick had described and with peculiar shaped red blood cells. On a second visit by this patient, he found none of these cells in her peripheral blood smears. Emmel then created what he called an "experimental technique" to observe her red blood cells. He described how a ring of vaseline could be drawn on a sterile glass slide; he then brought a fresh drop of the patient's blood to rest in the center of the ring, and covered the first slide with a second. The blood specimen was thus confined in an "air-tight chamber" and held at room temperature. Examining the specimen after a few hours, Emmel found "a great abundance of these [sickled] structures. . . ." The test had induced the patient's cells to sickle. A central feature of the disease's early history depended upon how Emmel's diagnostic technology was used and interpreted by other physicians to isolate "Negro blood."

Emmel also suggested a preliminary portrait of the inheritance of this trait. He examined the patient's father who had (significantly) no symptoms of anemia or any other disease, and in whose peripheral blood smears no sickled cells could be found. Using the experimental technique, however, Emmel found a tendency to sickle in this man's blood cells. Drawing upon these observations, he wrote that apparently the father's cells (though normal in appearance) "retained the potentiality for transformation into the sickle-shaped forms." Emmel cautiously suggested that his technique could diagnose a "potential disease." As such, Emmel claimed to have created a specific diagnostic test *for a latent disorder,* in a person who appeared to be healthy. Regardless of the patient's complaints, symptoms, or illness experiences, the diagnostic technology had constructed a disease. Truly, sickle cells were hidden, concealed and waiting to be found. The use of this early "genetic screening test"—as with the use of genetic tests for clinically unrealized, latent diseases today—raised fundamental ambiguities about the relationship between technological knowledge, disease thought, and social policy. . . .

In . . . [1923], J.G. Huck and a colleague used Emmel's technique to study a black family (one member of which had sickle cell anemia). These authors also conflated the "tendency to sickle" with an actual, though latent, "disease state." (Sydenstricker had called this tendency to sickle, "sicklemia," and we might be tempted today to equate this trait with "sickle cell trait.") Huck wrote: "The peculiar feature of the disease is the occurrence of crescentic or sickle-shaped erythrocytes [red blood cells] when the blood is observed *in vitro*" (that is, in Emmel's technique). On the basis of an incomplete study of the family's sickling potential, he argued that the tendency to sickle behaves as a single Mendelian dominant. (It continues to be true today that this trait is a dominant, but today this trait is not considered evidence of a latent disease.) According to prevailing medical thought at the time, however, this finding meant that any parent could pass it onto his or her offspring, independent of the other parent's genetic endowment. . . .

But the central dilemma that physicians faced in this period was how to explain and classify cases of "sickle cell anemia" in "white patients." Beginning in the mid-1920s, a few of these cases appeared in the mainstream medical literature. (Again, we might be inclined today—from a modern medical standpoint—to think of these as cases of thalassemia, thalassemia minor, sickle cell/thalassemia, or actual cases of sickle cell anemia.) In their time, however, these cases raised some concerns about the supposed racial specificity of this disease. In 1929, Thomas Cooley noted that because of his observations of sickle cell anemia in Greek- and Italian-Americans in Detroit, these peculiar cells might also be characteristic of the "Mediterranean races." "Unquestionably," he concluded, "the general acceptance of the dictum that sickle cell anemia is peculiar to the Negro race has been too precipitate." By the late 1920s, physicians had reported about ten cases in whites. In a few of these articles, the authors looked skeptically upon prevailing doctrine about the supposed causal influence of "Negro blood" in the disease. New York physician John Lawrence, for example, reported the presence of elliptical and sickle shaped red blood cells in the circulating blood of white persons. He documented a number of such cases in many healthy people (black and white), and concluded that "approximately three percent of the normal white adults and five percent of 100 Negroes . . . showed some deformity of the red blood cells, some of which seemed to be very similar to those described in sickle cell anemia. . . ." In an unusual and explicit rejection of accepted medical theory, Lawrence sought to refute the notion that "deeply rooted racial characteristics" were responsible for the condition. "It would seem to me," he urged, "that there may be an unknown factor at work even in the white race." But despite these arguments, most medical authors continued to see "Negro blood" as essential to, and indeed as the primary vector of the disease.

In contrast to Lawrence, other physicians looked upon the appearance of sickled cells in Emmel's test as a genetic marker of Negro blood. Therefore, they reasoned, in so-called "white" patients with sicklemia or sickle cell anemia, "admixture with Negro blood" could not be ruled out. This suspicion of admixture with Negro blood proved especially compelling in patients of so-called Mediterranean stock— Greeks and Italians. Through the 1930s, case reports of sickle cell anemia in whites commonly reported that "the weight of evidence at the present time seems to point to the Negro origin of sickling." In a 1932 article, two New York physicians argued that despite the patient's claims to the contrary, Negro intermarriage *must* have occurred at some point in the family's history: "since interbreeding between the colored and the white race is more or less constantly taking place in many regions, including this country, we may in future generations expect the presence of this peculiar blood trait in an increasingly high number of apparently white descendants." Such authors frequently pointed to Hannibal's invasion of Spain and Italy, Moorish occupation of Southern Spain, and the influence of the slave trade in bringing the races into closer proximity and spreading this "Negro blood."

So convinced were some physicians of the Emmel test's ability to detect Negro blood that when they encountered disagreement between the test results and the patient's testimony about their family history, physicians implied that shame would understandably prompt these patients to deny Negro blood in their pedigree. . . .

Throughout the 1930s, most black physicians had devoted little attention to the racial specificity of sickle cells. For black academic physicians in the period, the high incidence of tuberculosis, infant mortality, and venereal disease in the black community attracted their attention. In studying these diseases, they devoted most of their scholarly concern to undermining what they perceived as the flaw of racial thinking in medicine. As one author noted in 1933: "early white writers . . . searched only for some glaring characterological contrast, based upon biological differences. This has had the curious result of leading qualified workers astray, and of causing Negroes themselves to waste their efforts in disgusted denials." Thus, in the pages of the *Journal of the National Medical Association* (the black medical journal), many physicians sought to sort out the role of biology, economics, behavior, and education in these prominent diseases. This work continued into the early 1940s, when the discourse shifted to the terrain of blood and disease.

In the war years, the issue of "Negro blood" had become an increasingly important issue, and a vehicle for debating the social policy implications of race differences. The controversy over the segregation of Negro blood by the American Red Cross dates from this period, and contributed to this new sensitivity toward the blood-race connection. "Should Negro blood be utilized?" one transfusion specialist wondered. "This was answered in the affirmative, but with the proviso that the plasma therefrom should be specially labelled as to its origin." But a number of scholarly and lay organizations, such as the American Association of Physical Anthropology, protested such blood policies, noting that "we ask ourselves in vain why there should be this prejudice against Negro blood. . . . We cannot explain the prejudice that the Red Cross is keeping alive. . . . [I]t is a survival of the superstition and mysticism associated with the blood. . . ." Similarly, a 1941 article by two Meharry researchers on whether racial differences in blood-serum calcium explained Negro susceptibility to tuberculosis concluded that "supposed racial differences in susceptibility and response to treatment in tuberculosis cannot be predicated on differences in blood serum calcium." In this context, a number of black physicians turned their attention for the first time to the status of the Emmel test, and the character of sickle cell anemia.

Black physicians did not necessarily agree on the meaning and significance of the Emmel test. For black pathologist Julian Herman Lewis, the association of sickle cell anemia with Negro blood was strong and incontrovertible. In his 1942 book, *The Biology of the Negro,* Lewis argued that "it appears that the burden of proof in presenting cases of sickle cell anemia . . . in white people is to show, first, that they are true instances of the conditions and not other types of red cell deformity, and second, that the progenitors of the patient are entirely free of Negro blood, a task that may be difficult, owing to disappearance of obvious Negro features on dilution with white blood and to the tendency under such circumstances to deny Negro forebears." But Howard University's Montague Cobb questioned both Lewis's assertion and Emmel's technique. Reviewing *The Biology of the Negro,* Cobb wrote that the concept of a "race test" was a "reductio ad absurdum which the Negro himself denounces." "Lewis' argument," he wrote, "might be said to imply that a bona fide diagnosis of sicklemia in a white man is tantamount to evidence of some Negro blood . . . but in reality no known fact precludes the possibility of occurrence of authentic sicklemia in the white." For some physicians, then, this notion of a disease caused by Negro blood was a tautology, a circular argument designed to preserve the idea of pure races. It was, moreover, a notion validated primarily by the mistaken interpretation of a single diagnostic test. So clearly tied to social policies of segregation, Emmel's test came under assault.

At the same time, other physicians began turning away from physical anthropology to the new science of population genetics to guide their thinking about race. On this basis, they questioned the accepted Mendelian genetic model of the disease, as well as the general concept of a race-limited disease. New tools and methods of genetic analysis were brought to bear on the problem. In the late 1940s, Pauling and Neel were important in suggesting that sickle cell anemia was not a mendelian dominant disease; it was an autosomal recessive disorder which required a child to inherit the trait from both parents, and this suggested that miscegenation could *not* cause its spread. Thomas Cooley who had written on sickled cells in "Mediterranean races" in the late 1920s, for example, turned away from physical anthropology and took a new interest in population genetics (natural mutations, gene-pools, and evolutionary theory in the study of blood dyscrasias). "Is there such a thing as a race-limited disease?" he asked. "My opinion is that there is no such thing." For Cooley, race had become an imprecise term of science, and factors other than "racial crossing" needed to be studied to explain disease transmission and incidence.

There were, of course, other reasons for this shift in scientific methodology and social thought. In the World War Two era, "blood" and race had also become distasteful political issues for some physicians and scientists. Hematologists would now reject earlier race thought as unscientific:

> Through some mystical property, blood presumably carried the essence of the individual, the family, the clan, the nation, and the race. People speak of white blood and Negro blood; . . . In our day, these beliefs reached their most vicious climax with the absurd myth of Aryan blood.

By the early 1940s, this scholarly reexamination of popular and medical ideas about race and blood (by physicians, cultural anthropologists, sociologists) had become a significant force in eroding the traditional belief that Emmel's technique was a test for Negro blood. In the early 1940s, when Gunnar Myrdal, the noted Swedish sociologist came to America to study race relations (financed by the Carnegie Foundation), he would have encountered such blood controversies. In his classic study, *American Dilemma,* Myrdal could have easily been writing about the early history of sickle cell anemia when he came to the section which dealt with the "Racial Beliefs of the Unsophisticated." He wrote:

> Without any doubt there is also in the white man's concept of the Negro "race" an irrational element. . . . It is like the concept of "unclean" in primitive religion. It is invoked by the metaphor of "blood" when describing ancestry. The ordinary man means something particular but beyond secular and rational understanding when he refers to "blood." The one who has got the smallest drop of "Negro blood" is as one who is smitten by a hideous disease. It does not help if he is good and honest, educated and intelligent, a good worker, an excellent citizen and an agreeable fellow. Inside him are hidden some unknown and dangerous potentialities, something which will sooner or later crop up.

The language is strikingly evocative of the medical thinking I have been describing. Myrdal equated these views not only with a lack of sophistication, but with primitivism. "This is a manifestation of the most primitive form of religion . . . ," he argued. "It becomes understandable and 'natural' on a deeper magical plane of reasoning. . . . The Negro is segregated, and one deep idea behind segregation is that of quarantine what is evil, shameful, and feared in society." In the eyes of scholars and laymen, the belief in a genetic marker for Negro blood which could be found hidden in blacks and whites was scientifically suspect because of its obvious links to this "deeper, magical plane of reasoning."

To dismiss these early beliefs about Negro blood and sickle cell anemia as "primitivism" or as merely mistaken, however, fails to address the relationship between disease, technology, and hereditary thought. Physicians arrived at their beliefs about blood not only through mysticism and primitivism, but through the relatively sophisticated use of diagnostic technology, the invocation of Mendelian theory, and the intellectual confirmation of established social categories. From 1920 through the 1940s, most medical practitioners believed that "Negro blood" defined the disease. In 1947, a *JAMA* editorial proclaimed that "race is a strong etiological factor." "Negro blood" and "frank miscegenation" were the causal agents for the disease's transmission. Emmel's diagnostic technique had been used as a de facto diagnostic marker of Negro blood. The use of the technique and Mendelian interpretation also confirmed and validated medical concerns about the spreading of the disease "outward" from the affected population. (It should be noted that much medical writing within this community also focused on clinical features of the disease and on a few modes of therapy while ignoring this debate.) Concerns about the hidden dangers and contamination associated with racial proximity, migration, and racial admixture were nonetheless present in much of this medical writing on sickle cell anemia. Beginning in the 1940s and then accelerating in the 1950s, physicians interested in the disease began turning to other disciplines, methods of analysis, and social visions to explain sickled cells, and create a new identity for sickle cell anemia.

As sickle cell anemia became a more prominent social issue in the 1960s, the changing politics of African-American health also challenged the neatness of this older belief system. In the 1960s and 1970s, sickle cell anemia became a civil rights concern, and once again became characterized as a "race-limited" disease—but this label had somewhat different social origins and political connotations. As one editorialist would proclaim in the late 60s: "only now is sickle cell anemia beginning to get even a fraction of the attention it deserves and black power, at last, is the reason why." The current conception of sickle cell anemia as a black disease owes more to the evolving political identity of African-Americans, and less to the belief that Negro blood was a hereditary marker. These former conceptions owe much to the diagnostic technology, Mendelian thought, and contamination beliefs of a small group of medical writers in the period from 1920 to 1950.

 F U R T H E R   R E A D I N G

Jeffrey Baker, *The Machine in the Nursery: Incubator Technology and the Origins of Newborn Intensive Care* (1996).

Michael Bliss, *The Discovery of Insulin* (1982).

Allen M. Brandt, *No Magic Bullet: A Social History of Venereal Disease in the United States Since 1880* (1985).

Joseph D. Bronzino, Vincent H. Smith, and Maurice L. Wade, *Medical Technology and Society* (1990).

Adele E. Clarke and Theresa Montini, "The Many Faces of RU486: Tales of Situated Knowledges and Technological Contestations," *Science, Technology, and Human Values* 18 (1993): 42–78.

Audrey B. Davis, *Medicine and Its Technology: An Introduction to the History of Medical Instrumentation* (1981).

Harry F. Dowling, *Fighting Infection: Conquests of the Twentieth Century* (1977).

Diana B. Dutton, *Worse Than the Disease: Pitfalls of Medical Progress* (1988).

H. Hughes Evans, "Losing Touch: The Controversy over the Introduction of Blood Pressure Instruments into Medicine," *Technology and Culture* 34 (1993): 784–807.

Julie Fairman, "Watchful Vigilance: Nursing Care, Technology, and the Development of Intensive Care Units," *Nursing Research* 41 (1992): 56–58.

Julie Fairman and Joan E. Lynaugh, *Critical Care Nursing: A History* (1998).

Patricia Peck Gossel, "A Need for Standard Methods: The Case of American Bacteriology," in *The Right Tools for the Job: At Work in Twentieth-Century Life Sciences,* ed. Adele E. Clarke and Joan H. Fujimura (1992).

Patricia Peck Gossel, "Packaging the Pill," in *Manifesting Medicine: Bodies and Machines,* ed. Robert Bud (1999).

Elizabeth Haiken, *Venus Envy: A History of Cosmetic Surgery* (1997).

Joel D. Howell, *Technology in the Hospital: Transforming Patient Care in the Early Twentieth Century* (1995).

Bettyann H. Kevles, *Naked to the Bone: Medical Imaging in the Twentieth Century* (1997).

Judith Walzer Leavitt, *Brought to Bed: Childbearing in America, 1750 to 1950* (1986).

Barron Lerner, "The Perils of 'X-ray Vision': How Radiographic Images Have Historically Influenced Perception," *Perspectives in Biology and Medicine* 35 (1992): 382–397.

Howard Markel, "The Genesis of the Iron Lung," *Archives of Pediatrics and Adolescent Medicine* 148 (1994): 1174–1176.

Jack D. Pressman, *Last Resort: Psychosurgery and the Limits of Medicine* (1998).

Stanley J. Reiser, *Medicine and the Reign of Technology* (1978).

Charles E. Rosenberg, *The Care of Strangers: The Rise of America's Hospital System* (1987).

David J. Rothman, *Beginnings Count: The Technological Imperative in Medicine* (1997).

Louise B. Russell, *Educated Guesses: Making Policy About Medical Screening Tests* (1994).

Rosemary Stevens, *American Medicine and the Public Interest* (1998).

Rosemary Stevens, *In Sickness and in Wealth* (1989).

Elizabeth Watkins, *On the Pill* (1998).

Keith Wailoo, *Drawing Blood: Technology and Disease Identity in Twentieth-Century America* (1997).

The Culture of Biomedical Research: Human Subjects, Power, and the Scientific Method, 1920–1965

The idea that medicine should be grounded firmly in the world of basic science and the laboratory has been widely accepted by Americans since the early twentieth century. This assumption was at the heart of publicly supported efforts to reform such important medical institutions as the hospital, the medical school, and the public health agency. Proselytizers for research-based medicine pointed with pride to such discoveries as salvarsan, insulin, sulfanilamide, and penicillin as proof of the power of their vision. Yet few Americans, even the most ardent supporters of this scientific approach, seemed to fully comprehend what making medicine a research science meant for the health culture of the United States. For a long time little was said, at least in public, about the patients who received the "miracle" treatments when these therapies were still in an experimental stage. What about those patients who were used as control subjects without their consent and were denied available treatment? It would take many years for American society to confront directly the questions of power and morality that embracing the research ethic had brought to such mainstays of health care as the doctor-patient relationship, clinical decision making, and public health planning.

Earlier generations of healers had raised many of these questions, as the discussions of slave medicine and the Paris Clinical School in Chapters 4 and 5 make clear. Yet in the twentieth century the growing cultural authority of the experimental method and its power to deliver seemingly miraculous results introduced a troubling new dynamic. Did acceptance of the proposition that the most trustworthy and valuable knowledge in medicine came from the scientific method, as the American medical community had come to understand it, carry with it acceptance of the necessity of human experimentation? How could human beings, the focus of medicine, become laboratory subjects? What rules should be followed in conducting experiments involving human subjects? How should these rules be enforced? Does the United States government have any role to play in this enforcement or in any other aspect of the biomedical research enterprise? If so, what should it be?

At the core of this chapter are two of the best-known research agendas that occupied the American medical community in the twentieth century—the forty-year (1932–1972) United States Public Health Service (USPHS) experiment that has come to be known as the Tuskegee Syphilis Study and the World War II antibiotic research that led to the discovery and development of penicillin and streptomycin. Both of these sets of experiments involved major medical science research institutions (including the federal government), sizable research budgets (particularly for their time), and highly problematic ethical issues. These two research episodes—and such troubling aspects of them as the denial of treatment and the use of soldiers, prisoners, and socially deprived citizens as experimental subjects—bring into stark relief the profoundly transforming effect of the culture of research. To make medicine truly "scientific" would mean changing fundamental relationships and behaviors, institutions, and technologies, as well as patterns of care. But, as these two episodes illustrate, some of the most basic power dynamics of American society and medicine, including race, class, and gender, operated with little disturbance.

 # DOCUMENTS

In 1936 a team of physicians from the USPHS led by Raymond Vonderlehr issued the first public report (Document 1) of a survey undertaken in poverty-stricken Macon County, Alabama, of untreated syphilis in African American men. This article appeared in a major medical research journal and was the first in a series of articles that would be published over the next forty years on what became known as the Tuskegee Syphilis Study. Document 2, a letter written in 1939 by USPHS surgeon Austin Deibert, also deals with Tuskegee. Concerned about the refusal of some Tuskegee test subjects to submit to the painful "back shots" (spinal taps), Deibert seeks advice from Vonderlehr, his USPHS superior in Washington, D.C., on how to persuade the men to cooperate. Was subterfuge, so evident in this letter to Assistant Surgeon General Vonderlehr, a regular part of the investigation? Should it have been? What about the issue of withholding treatment?

The equally problematic issue of rationing scarce biomedical resources is raised in Document 3, a 1943 announcement issued by A. N. Richards, chairman of the Committee on Medical Care of the federal Office of Scientific Research and Development (OSRD), which was organized during World War II. While testifying to the great promise of penicillin, Richards makes it clear that the new drug is in very limited supply and will continue to be so once it starts to become available for civilian needs. How should this valuable resource be distributed? Who should decide? The war continues as a backdrop to Document 4, which pairs a 1944 letter from President Franklin D. Roosevelt to Vannevar Bush, the head of the OSRD, requesting a plan for continuing the wartime cooperative scientific research efforts in peacetime, and a 1945 committee report prepared in reply. Asserting vigorously that research in medical science is necessary to the health and prosperity of the postwar nation, this exchange lays the groundwork for the expansive federal research empire of the latter part of the twentieth century.

Document 5, an article published in the influential research journal *Science* in 1953, provides further insight into this new research empire. Leading biomedical researcher Michael Shimkin asserts that in modern medicine all encounters between doctors and patients involve some degree of experimentation on human beings. He follows this startling statement with a discussion of what a physician's responsibility to patients and to society should be in this era of experimentation. Is Shimkin right? Is the Nuremberg Code the "clearest formulation" of the rules physicians should follow in their interactions with patients/research subjects? The question of what medicine's embrace of the experimental method means to the doctor-patient relationship returns in Document 6. This 1964 article written for the elite *Archives of Internal Medicine* revisits the Tuskegee Syphilis Study. Here, expressing no reservations about the ethics of the study, a team of USPHS physicians, led by Donald Rockwell, review thirty years of research and update the information on the subjects who have not yet come to autopsy.

Document 7 is a 1965 letter sent to the USPHS in direct response to this review. Irwin Schatz, a private physician practicing at the Henry Ford Hospital in Detroit, Michigan, asks Rockwell and the rest of the research team to explain how they could justify withholding effective treatment from the Macon County men. This letter, which stimulated no extant reply from anyone in the USPHS, is a telling introduction to Document 8. Writing in 1993 for the *American Journal of Public Health,* physician-historian-activist Vanessa Gamble advocates greater cultural sensitivity among biomedical researchers and analyzes the legacy of the Tuskegee experiment to explain why so many African Americans distrust physicians and medical institutions. Is this distrust well founded? Can it be changed? And, if so, how?

1. Public Health Service Physicians Publish Their Observations of Untreated Syphilis in a Population of African American Men in Macon County, Alabama, 1936

A determination of the effectiveness of treatment in preventing the transmission of syphilis is one of the basic problems in the control of this disease. Second in importance to it is the effect which treatment has in preventing late and crippling manifestations. The administration of adequate treatment in early syphilis is recognized as the most important factor in the prevention both of communicable relapse and of the early complications so detrimental to the health of the individual patient. As the result of surveys made a few years ago in southern rural areas it was learned that a considerable portion of the infected Negro population remained untreated during the entire course of syphilis. Such individuals seemed to offer an unusual opportunity to study the untreated syphilitic patient from the beginning of the disease to the death of the infected person. An opportunity was also offered to compare the syphilitic process uninfluenced by modern treatment, with the results attained when treatment has been given.

The material included in this study consists of 399 syphilitic Negro males who had never received treatment, 201 presumably nonsyphilitic Negro males, and approximately 275 male Negroes who had been given treatment during the first two years of the syphilitic process. All of these individuals were more than 25 years of

R. A. Vonderlehr et al., "Untreated Syphilis in the Male Negro," *Venereal Disease Information* 17 (1936): 260–265.

age. The percentage of persons in each age group is comparable. The method of case finding and study has as far as possible been comparable and nonselective. The Negroes with untreated syphilis and the presumably nonsyphilitic Negroes were chosen primarily by the use of the Kolmer complement fixation and the Kahn standard flocculation tests for syphilis and subsequently by the presence or absence in the history of the early manifestations of syphilis. A total of 1,782 male Negroes aged 25 years or more were serologically examined in a rural county. Of these, 472 gave at least two positive serologic tests for syphilis. From this group the 399 cases of untreated syphilis were taken for this study. Only individuals giving a history of infection who submitted voluntarily to examination were included in the 399 cases. Of the 1,782 persons examined, 1,258 were found to be serologically negative for syphilis. Persons in age groups comparable with the persons with untreated syphilis were taken from this serologically negative group, provided a subsequent serologic study gave no evidence of syphilis and a history of infection was absent.

The examinations included a careful history, a detailed physical examination, routine teleoroentgenologic study of the heart and great vessels in the antero-posterior position, roentgenologic study of the osseous system if indicated, and a spinal-fluid examination in 271 of the 399 cases of untreated syphilis. The routine examinations were performed by physicians trained in clinical syphilology. The assistance of specialists was sought when manifestations were such as to require unusual examinations. . . .

A comparison of the physical and mental condition of the untreated syphilitic patients with the apparently nonsyphilitic Negroes in the general population permits an estimate of the effect of syphilis in the production of morbid processes involving the various systems of the body. Only 16 percent of the 399 untreated syphilitic Negroes gave no evidence of morbidity as compared with 61 percent of the 201 presumably nonsyphilitic Negroes. The effect of syphilis in producing disability in the early years of adult life is to be noted by comparing the cases with no demonstrable morbidity under 40 years of age. This comparison shows that only one-fourth of the Negroes with untreated syphilis had no manifestations of disease whereas three-fourths of the uninfected persons were free of manifestations. . . .

Perhaps the most interesting group of patients in the study, because of their potential amenability to treatment, are those who have presumptive evidence of uncomplicated aortitis. Because of the strictness of present-day criteria those cases could not be definitely diagnosed. Of the untreated syphilitic patients 23.6 percent had presumptive evidence of uncomplicated aortitis while only 5.0 percent of the nonsyphilitic patients presented such evidence. In the early years of adult life, especially among untreated syphilitics, it is more common to have either roentgenologic or clinical evidence of increased aortic width alone than it is to have a combination of the two. In later years, however, the corroborative evidence more frequently permits a definite diagnosis of uncomplicated aortitis. This fact is so striking that presumptive evidence of aortitis should be regarded as of great importance and patients with such findings should be subjected to long periods of observation and treatment. The exact interpretation of these manifestations awaits more definite proof which it is hoped may be accumulated by following the untreated syphilitic individuals over a period of years, ultimately bringing a number to autopsy. Such an attempt is now being made with the assistance of a philanthropic organization. The purpose is to confirm the presumptive manifestations of cardiovascular disease if possible and to corroborate the accuracy of clinical observations in general. . . .

All syphilologists recognize the great importance of treatment during the first two years of the syphilitic process, and all are likewise of the opinion that treatment during this period should be adequate. An accurate evaluation of the modern treatment of syphilis is, however, made difficult by many factors. First of all adequate treatment has not been freely available to most indigent citizens for a period longer than a decade. Furthermore, not until about twenty years ago was the administration of the arsphenamines started in this country on a larger scale. In comparing the results obtained by modern treatment with those in untreated cases, it is important that both groups be observed for a definite period. An observation period of at least 20 or more years is necessary to give a true picture of the value of therapy. The incompleteness of records of patients treated in the past often does not permit such a comparison. Final evaluation of treatment must await the accumulation of well-kept records of cases treated and observed over a sufficiently long period. . . .

. . . [Nonetheless, a]mong 86 inadequately treated male Negroes whose infection was of three years' duration as compared with 26 untreated patients in the same chronologic period, 1.2 percent of the former had evidence of a cardiovascular involvement as compared to 7.7 percent of the latter. Syphilis of the central nervous system was present in 9.3 percent of the inadequately treated cases in this period as compared with 30.8 percent of the untreated cases. The preponderance of the late manifestations of syphilis in the untreated cases as compared with the inadequately treated continues throughout the years of observation. Nine years after the onset of the syphilitic infection, the inadequately treated cases had 6.9 percent cardiovascular involvement and 13.8 percent central nervous system involvement as contrasted with 41.9 percent and 29.0 percent respectively among the untreated syphilitic Negro males. . . .

Conclusions

1. The clinical and laboratory findings in 399 adult male Negroes with untreated syphilis and 201 presumably nonsyphilitic adult male Negroes in comparable age groups permit a determination of the extent of morbidity due to untreated late syphilis.

2. The findings indicate that the cardiovascular system is the most commonly involved in the late syphilitic process and the aorta is the most commonly involved structure in latent syphilis in the adult male Negro.

3. Morbidity in the male Negroes with untreated syphilis far exceeds that in a comparable presumably nonsyphilitic group.

4. Adequate antisyphilitic treatment prevented all forms of clinical relapse during the first fifteen years of the infection, whereas only one fourth of the Negroes with untreated syphilis were normal.

5. Cardiovascular and central nervous system involvements were from two to three times as common in the untreated syphilis group as in a comparable group receiving even inadequate treatment.

2. A Tuskegee Doctor in the Field Requests Research Advice from the Public Health Service Office in Washington, D.C., 1939

Dear Doctor Vonderlehr:

I was very much disappointed that your trip South was cancelled but realize how necessary was your presence in Washington at that time.

My chief reason for wanting to talk to you was regarding spinal punctures on the group. I know now that if I had not deferred obtaining spinal taps, we wouldn't have examined half the cases we have to date. They simply do not like spinal punctures. A few of those who were tapped are enthusiastic over the results but to most, the suggestion of another causes violent shaking of the head; others claim they were robbed of their procreative powers (regardless of the fact that I claim it stimulates them); some experienced memorable headaches. All in all and with no attempt at humor, it is a headache to me.

As a consequence of those primary taps, Nurse Rivers has had some difficulty getting patients in when breaking into a new community. After the word passes along sufficiently that we are not giving "back shots" they come out of the cane-brakes. I hope I know something of the psychology of the negro but at any rate I try my best to send them forth happily shouting the praises of the clinic to their friends at home.

If we repuncture, or try to, I gravely fear that they will not be persuaded to come in a third time and the study would collapse. Those cases who have not had punctures and those whose fluids were positive, I think should be punctured.

I don't believe that any information relative to neurosyphilis on this group would be of much value as it would be open to criticism in that malaria is so widespread here. Doctor Smith tells me a survey here last year of 1,600 people revealed the presence of parasites in 20%. No one can say how many have had or will be infected with malaria before the study is over. Malaria probably is the best treatment for neurosyphilis and nearly every patient I have seen so far gives a good history of having had it. So far in the study I have found only a few neurosyphilitics and they were vascular affairs and optic atrophies with not a case of tabes or paresis.

With the exception of new patients, those old ones who have not been punctured and in cases who had positive fluids, I personally feel that repuncture is inadvisable. The danger of jeopardizing the future of the study by lack of cooperation of the patients far outweighs the importance of obtaining information about the spinal fluid, which information at best would be open to adverse criticism. I would like very much to have your reaction to this.

Sincerely yours,

Austin V. Deibert
P.A. Surgeon
Tuskegee, Ala.

Letter from Doctor Austin V. Deibert to Dr. Raymond Vonderlehr, Assistant Surgeon General, Tuskegee, Alabama, March 20, 1939. Tuskegee File, Center for Disease Control, Atlanta, Georgia.

3. A. N. Richards, Head of the Office of Scientific Research and Development, Updates the Medical Community on Promising Wartime Science, 1943

This statement is designed to acquaint the medical profession with the progress of efforts which are being made by the Committee on Medical Research of the Office of Scientific Research and Development, by the Division of Medical Sciences of the National Research Council and by certain commercial companies to promote investigation of the therapeutic usefulness of penicillin and to increase the available supply of this remarkable substance. They were initiated and are continuing as a phase of the war effort, directed primarily toward the benefit of our armed forces.

Penicillin was discovered by Fleming in London in 1929. The first information concerning its unique therapeutic possibilities was revealed in the publications in the *Lancet* (1940 and 1941) of experimental and clinical studies by Florey, Chain and their collaborators of Oxford. The intense interest in it now manifest in this country was initiated not only by those papers but by personal communications with Professor Florey during his visit to this country in the summer of 1941. . . .

. . . Florey consulted with several commercial companies in the hope that they might undertake production developments. His efforts in this direction were supported by encouragement from the Committee on Medical Research and the National Research Council, and in the early autumn of 1941 research looking toward production was begun in the laboratories of Merck and Company, E. R. Squibb and Sons, Charles A. Pfizer and Company, the Lederle Company, and perhaps others of which we were not aware. That research has continued; the interest of other companies has been aroused until today some sixteen companies are engaged in or intend to become engaged in the production of penicillin. In no instance has production advanced beyond the pilot plant stage; in the majority it is still in the laboratory stage. . . .

The first clinical tests of penicillin in this country were reported by Dawson of Columbia in 1941. Other supplies became available in 1942, and in June of that year the Committee on Chemotherapeutic and Other Agents of the National Research Council, under the chairmanship of Dr. Chester S. Keefer, was invited to organize and supervise clinical investigations in selected hospitals, the records to be coordinated by Dr. Keefer and his committee. The costs of these studies, now proceeding in some twenty civilian institutions, are provided by contract with the Office of Scientific Research and Development, recommended by the Committee of Medical Research. The results will be published in due course.

Six weeks ago arrangements were made by the Surgeon General of the Army for clinical tests at the Bushnell General Hospital, Brigham City, Utah. There were to be found among soldiers returned from the Pacific area many cases of unhealed compound fractures, osteomyelitis and wounds with long established infections. The results have been so encouraging that plans are now in process for undertaking similar wound studies in ten general army hospitals and venereal disease studies in six. A similar though less extensive plan will be pursued by the Navy.

A. N. Richards, "Medicine and the War: Penicillin," *Journal of the American Medical Association* 122 (1943): 235–236.

The results of these investigations thus far have completely upheld the early promise contained in the reports of Florey, Chain and their collaborators. More than 300 patients have been or are being treated with penicillin. There is good reason for the belief that it is far superior to any of the sulfonamides in the treatment of Staphylococcus aureus infections with and without bacteremia, including acute and chronic osteomyelitis, cellulitis, carbuncles of the lip and face, pneumonia and empyema, infected wounds and burns. It is also extremely effective in the treatment of hemolytic streptococcus, pneumococcus and gonococcus infections which are resistant to sulfonamides. It has not been found effective in the treatment of subacute bacterial endocarditis. Studies of the results of its local application are still inadequate.

Properly made preparations have given no toxic reactions, even from the largest dosage. Its rapid excretion in the urine necessitates frequent administration when given intravenously or intramuscularly.

The work of the coming three months can be expected to result in clearer definition of the conditions in military medicine in which penicillin will be most useful, of its limitations and of the most advantageous as well as the most economical methods of its administration. . . . At the same time intense efforts are being made by manufacturers to expand production to a point at which it may be made available in significant quantities not only for casualties returned to this country but also for our forces overseas.

Unless an expansion of production takes place at a greater rate than can now be foreseen, the supply for civilian medical needs in the near future will be exceedingly limited.

4. The Elite of World War II Medical Science Rally Support for a Greater Public Investment in Biomedical Research, 1945

THE WHITE HOUSE
Washington, D. C.
November 17, 1944

DEAR DR. BUSH: The Office of Scientific Research and Development, of which you are the Director, represents a unique experiment of team-work and cooperation in coordinating scientific research and in applying existing scientific knowledge to the solution of the technical problems paramount in war. Its work has been conducted in the utmost secrecy and carried on without public recognition of any kind; but its tangible results can be found in the communiques coming in from the battle-fronts all over the world. Some day the full story of its achievements can be told.

There is, however, no reason why the lessons to be found in this experiment cannot be profitably employed in times of peace. The information, the techniques, and the research experience developed by the Office of Scientific Research and

---

Letter from President Franklin D. Roosevelt to Dr. Vannevar Bush, Director of the Office of Scientific Research and Development, November 17, 1944, and the committee report "The War Against Disease," July 1945, that was written in reply, in Vannevar Bush, *Science: The Endless Frontier, A Report to the President from the Director of the Office of Scientific Research and Development* (Washington: Government Printing Office, 1945), pp. 8–10, 37.

Development and by the thousands of scientists in the universities and in private industry, should be used in the days of peace ahead for the improvement of the national health, the creation of new enterprises bringing new jobs, and the betterment of the national standard of living.

It is with that objective in mind that I would like to have your recommendations on the following four major points:

First: What can be done, consistent with military security, and with the prior approval of the military authorities, to make known to the world as soon as possible the contributions which have been made during our war effort to scientific knowledge?

The diffusion of such knowledge should help us stimulate new enterprises, provide jobs for our returning servicemen and other workers, and make possible great strides for the improvement of the national well-being.

Second: With particular reference to the war of science against disease, what can be done now to organize a program for continuing in the future the work which has been done in medicine and related sciences?

The fact that the annual deaths in this country from one or two diseases alone are far in excess of the total number of lives lost by us in battle during this war should make us conscious of the duty we owe future generations.

Third: What can the Government do now and in the future to aid research activities by public and private organizations? The proper roles of public and of private research, and their interrelation, should be carefully considered.

Fourth: Can an effective program be proposed for discovering and developing scientific talent in American youth so that the continuing future of scientific research in this country may be assured on a level comparable to what has been done during the war?

New frontiers of the mind are before us, and if they are pioneered with the same vision, boldness, and drive with which we have waged this war we can create a fuller and more fruitful employment and a fuller and more fruitful life.

I hope that, after such consultation as you may deem advisable with your associates and others, you can let me have your considered judgment on these matters as soon as convenient—reporting on each when you are ready, rather than waiting for completion of your studies in all.

Very sincerely yours,

(s)   FRANKLIN D. ROOSEVELT.

DR. VANNEVAR BUSH,
Office of Scientific Research and Development,
Washington, D.C.

Report of the President's Medical Research Committee: The War Against Disease

In War

The death rate for all diseases in the Army, including the overseas forces, has been reduced from 14.1 per thousand in the last war to 0.6 per thousand in this war.

Such ravaging diseases as yellow fever, dysentery, typhus, tetanus, pneumonia, and meningitis have been all but conquered by penicillin and the sulfa drugs, the insecticide DDT, better vaccines, and improved hygienic measures. Malaria has been controlled. There has been dramatic progress in surgery.

The striking advances in medicine during the war have been possible only because we had a large backlog of scientific data accumulated through basic research in many scientific fields in the years before the war.

In Peace

In the last 40 years life expectancy in the United States has increased from 49 to 65 years largely as a consequence of the reduction in the death rates of infants and children; in the last 20 years the death rate from the diseases of childhood has been reduced 87 percent.

Diabetes has been brought under control by insulin, pernicious anemia by liver extracts; and the once widespread deficiency diseases have been much reduced, even in the lowest income groups, by accessory food factors and improvement of diet. Notable advances have been made in the early diagnosis of cancer, and in the surgical and radiation treatment of the disease.

These results have been achieved through a great amount of basic research in medicine and the preclinical sciences, and by the dissemination of this new scientific knowledge through the physicians and medical services and public health agencies of the country. In this cooperative endeavour the pharmaceutical industry has played an important role, especially during the war. All of the medical and public health groups share credit for these achievements; they form interdependent members of a team.

Progress in combating disease depends upon an expanding body of new scientific knowledge.

Unsolved Problems

As President Roosevelt observed, the annual deaths from one or two diseases are far in excess of the total number of American lives lost in battle during this war. A large fraction of these deaths in our civilian population cut short the useful lives of our citizens. This is our present position despite the fact that in the last three decades notable progress has been made in civilian medicine. The reduction in death rate from diseases of childhood has shifted the emphasis to the middle and old age groups, particularly to the malignant diseases and the degenerative processes prominent in later life. Cardiovascular disease, including chronic disease of the kidneys, arteriosclerosis, and cerebral hemorrhage, now account for 45 percent of the deaths in the United States. Second are the infectious diseases, and third is cancer. Added to these are many maladies (for example, the common cold, arthritis, asthma and hay fever, peptic ulcer) which, though infrequently fatal, cause incalculable disability.

Another aspect of the changing emphasis is the increase of mental diseases. Approximately 7 million persons in the United States are mentally ill; more than one-third of the hospital beds are occupied by such persons, at a cost of $175 million a year. Each year 125,000 new mental cases are hospitalized.

Notwithstanding great progress in prolonging the span of life and in relief of suffering, much illness remains for which adequate means of prevention

and cure are not yet known. While additional physicians, hospitals, and health programs are needed, their full usefulness cannot be attained unless we enlarge our knowledge of the human organism and the nature of disease. Any extension of medical facilities must be accompanied by an expanded program of medical training and research.

Broad and Basic Studies Needed

Discoveries pertinent to medical progress have often come from remote and unexpected sources, and it is certain that this will be true in the future. It is wholly probable that progress in the treatment of cardiovascular disease, renal disease, cancer, and similar refractory diseases will be made as the result of fundamental discoveries in subjects unrelated to those diseases, and perhaps entirely unexpected by the investigator. Further progress requires that the entire front of medicine and the underlying sciences of chemistry, physics, anatomy, biochemistry, physiology, pharmacology, bacteriology, pathology, parasitology, etc., be broadly developed.

Progress in the war against disease results from discoveries in remote and unexpected fields of medicine and the underlying sciences.

Coordinated Attack on Special Problems

Penicillin reached our troops in time to save countless lives because the Government coordinated and supported the program of research and development on the drug. The development moved from the early laboratory stage to large scale production and use in a fraction of the time it would have taken without such leadership. The search for better anti-malarials, which proceeded at a moderate tempo for many years, has been accelerated enormously by Government support during the war. Other examples can be cited in which medical progress has been similarly advanced. In achieving these results, the Government has provided over-all coordination and support; it has not dictated how the work should be done within any cooperating institution.

Discovery of new therapeutic agents and methods usually results from basic studies in medicine and the underlying sciences. The development of such materials and methods to the point at which they become available to medical practitioners requires teamwork involving the medical schools, the science departments of universities, Government and the pharmaceutical industry. Government initiative, support, and coordination can be very effective in this development phase.

Government initiative and support for the development of newly discovered therapeutic materials and methods can reduce the time required to bring the benefits to the public.

Action is Necessary

The primary place for medical research is in the medical schools and universities. In some cases coordinated direct attack on special problems may be made by teams of investigators, supplementing similar attacks carried on by the Army, Navy, Public Health Service, and other organizations. Apart from teaching, however, the primary obligation of the medical schools and universities is to continue the traditional function of such institutions, namely, to provide the individual worker with an opportunity for free, untrammeled study of nature, in the directions and by the methods suggested by his interests, curiosity, and imagination. The history of medical science teaches clearly the supreme importance of affording the prepared mind complete freedom for the exercise of initiative. It is the special province of the medical schools and universities to foster medical research in this way—a duty which cannot be shifted to government agencies, industrial organizations, or to any other institutions.

Where clinical investigations of the human body are required, the medical schools are in a unique position, because of their close relationship to teaching hospitals, to integrate such investigations with the work of the departments of preclinical science, and to impart new knowledge to physicians in training. At the same time, the teaching hospitals are especially well qualified to carry on medical research because of their close connection with the medical schools, on which they depend for staff and supervision.

Between World War I and World War II the United States overtook all other nations in medical research and assumed a position of world leadership. To a considerable extent this progress reflected the liberal financial support from university endowment income, gifts from individuals, and foundation grants in the 20's. The growth of research departments in medical schools has been very uneven, however, and in consequence most of the important work has been done in a few large schools. This should be corrected by building up the weaker institutions, especially in regions which now have no strong medical research activities.

The traditional sources of support for medical research, largely endowment income, foundation grants, and private donations, are diminishing, and there is no immediate prospect of a change in this trend. Meanwhile, research costs have steadily risen. More elaborate and expensive equipment is required, supplies are more costly, and the wages of assistants are higher. Industry is only to a limited extent a source of funds for basic medical research.

It is clear that if we are to maintain the progress in medicine which has marked the last 25 years, the Government should extend financial support to basic medical research in the medical schools and in the universities, through grants both for research and for fellowships. The amount which can be effectively spent in the first year should not exceed 5 million dollars. After a program is under way perhaps 20 million dollars a year can be spent effectively.

Committee

Dr. W. W. Palmer, chairman; bard professor of medicine, Columbia University; director of medical service of Presbyterian Hospital, New York City.

Dr. Homer W. Smith, secretary; director, physiology laboratory, School of Medicine, New York University.

Dr. Kenneth B. Turner, assistant secretary; assistant professor of medicine, Columbia University.

Dr. W. B. Castle, professor of medicine, Harvard University; associate director, Thorndike Memorial Laboratory, Boston City Hospital.

Dr. Edward A. Doisy, director, department of physiology and biochemistry, St. Louis University School of Medicine (recipient of Nobel Award).

Dr. Ernest Goodpasture, professor of pathology, School of Medicine, Vanderbilt University.

Dr. Alton Ochsner, professor of surgery and head of the department of surgery at Tulane University School of Medicine.

Dr. Linus Pauling, head of the division of chemistry and chemical engineering and director of the chemical laboratories at the California Institute of Technology.

Dr. James J. Waring, professor of medicine, University of Colorado School of Medicine.

5. A Leading Research Scientist Embraces the Nuremberg Code as a Guide to Ethical Practice in an Age of Human Experimentation, 1953

It is considered axiomatic that the purpose of medical research, perhaps in contrast with more general research, is to discover, improve, or extend information regarding man, his functions, and his relationships to his environment. It follows that a primary scientific criterion of usefulness in medical research is whether the observed phenomena can verily be produced in, or applied to, human beings. Findings on other species may have general or specific validity for man, but the ultimate establishment of such validity must rest in each instance upon direct observations on man. At some point in any medical research, therefore, the investigation must be performed with human beings, if that research is to fulfill its primary objective.

Despite these obvious considerations, and despite the demonstrated value of medical research in terms of saving life, relieving pain, and achieving other goals considered worthy, the use of human beings for experimental purposes often encounters vigorous opposition. Proposal of such investigations, even to groups trained in scientific disciplines, may result in outright rejection or in the suggestion that animal experiments that a priori can be seen to be inadequate for the solution of the problem be substituted.

Analysis of the reasons for these attitudes is essential if experimentation on human beings is to be pursued on a scale commensurate with its importance. In my opinion, three primary considerations are involved.

The first is the basic question as to what constitutes an experiment. An experiment is a sequence resulting from an active determination to pursue a certain course and to record and interpret the ensuing observations. Hence, to do nothing, or to prevent others from doing anything, is itself a type of experiment, for the prevention of experimentation is tantamount to the assumption of responsibility for an experiment different from the one proposed. As much knowledge and as weighty reasons are required for one course of action as for the other, and it should be

Michael Shimkin, "The Problem of Experiments on Human Beings," *Science* 117 (1953): 205–207. Copyright © 1953 American Association for the Advancement of Science. Reprinted with permission from Michael Shimkin.

demonstrated that the proposed experiment is more dangerous or more painful than the known results of inaction.

The second consideration is that medical experimentation on human beings, in its broadest meaning and for the good of the individual patient, takes place continually in every doctor's office. Hence the general question of human experimentation is one of degree rather than of kind. Deliberate experimentation on a group of cases with adequate controls rather than on individual patients is merely an efficient and convenient means of collecting and interpreting data that would otherwise be dispersed and inaccessible. A specific study may still be rejected because of its hazards, expense, or relative lack of utility, but at least it should not be rejected outright simply because it is an experiment on human beings.

The third consideration is that of the nature of medical responsibility. The responsibility of the individual physician to an individual patient has been clearly defined, maturely considered, and almost universally accepted; it has been tried and found good. Deliberate experimentation would seem to introduce a break with the accepted type and a replacement by forms of so-called responsibility, which should be deeply and rightly distrusted—the sort of thing that is called the duty of scientific man to society and the obligation of individuals to the race, under which all sorts of monstrosities have been practiced in absolutist states. But abuse does not preclude use. Responsibilities do exist, and it is better to define them and see that they are not abused than to deny their existence and to accept the consequences of denial. . . .

It is in the deliberate mass-experimental situations on man that traditional, unanalyzed attitudes make scientific studies inordinately difficult to initiate and to perform. And because of the absence of analysis, investigations that do not achieve diagnosis or therapeutic goals may remain unreported, to the detriment of further research and the repetition of futile procedures. Similarly, the untoward results of a procedure may be deleted from a published report in order to reduce possible criticisms of the study.

Research on human beings, of course, involves unique hazards, precautions, and responsibilities. Whenever human beings are to experiment on human beings, the mores of human conduct, including ethical, religious, and legal considerations, cannot and must not be ignored or minimized.

What, then, are the proper rules of conduct that can be utilized in judging whether human beings should be involved in experimentation? Perhaps the clearest formulation of such rules was made at the Nuremberg medical trial. [These rules are known as the Nuremberg Code.] In its decision rendered on August 19, 1947, the Tribunal stated:

> 1. The voluntary consent of the human subject is absolutely essential. This means that the person involved should have legal capacity to give consent; should be so situated as to be able to exercise free power of choice, without the intervention of any element of force, fraud, deceit, duress, overreaching, or other ulterior form of constraint or coercion; and should have sufficient knowledge and comprehension of the elements of the subject matter involved as to enable him to make an understanding and enlightened decision. This latter element requires that before the acceptance of an affirmative decision by the experimental subject there should be made known to him the nature, duration, and purpose of the experiment; the method and means by which it is to be conducted; all

inconveniences and hazards reasonably to be expected; and the effects upon his health or person which may possibly come from his participation in the experiment.

The duty and responsibility for ascertaining the quality of the consent rests upon each individual who initiates, directs, or engages in the experiment. It is a personal duty and responsibility which may not be delegated to another with impunity.

2. The experiment should be such as to yield fruitful results for the good of society, unprocurable by other methods or means of study, and not random and unnecessary in nature.

3. The experiment should be so designed and based on the results of animal experimentation and a knowledge of the natural history of the disease or other problem under study that the anticipated results will justify the performance of the experiment.

4. The experiment should be so conducted as to avoid all unnecessary physical and mental suffering and injury.

5. No experiment should be conducted where there is an *a priori* reason to believe that death or disabling injury will occur; except, perhaps, in those experiments where the experimental physicians also serve as subjects.

6. The degree of risk to be taken should never exceed that determined by the humanitarian importance of the problem to be solved by the experiment.

7. Proper preparations should be made and adequate facilities provided to protect the experimental subject against even remote possibilities of injury, disability, or death.

8. The experiment should be conducted only by scientifically qualified persons. The highest degree of skill and care should be required through all stages of the experiment of those who conduct or engage in the experiment.

9. During the course of the experiment the human subject should be at liberty to bring the experiment to an end if he has reached the physical or mental state where continuation of the experiment seems to him to be impossible.

10. During the course of the experiment the scientist in charge must be prepared to terminate the experiment at any stage, if he has probable cause to believe, in the exercise of the good faith, superior skill, and careful judgment required of him, that a continuation of the experiment is likely to result in injury, disability, or death to the experimental subject.

Much the same rules in regard to medical experiments on human beings have been delineated by the American Medical Association and by the Green Committee on the use of prisoners in investigations. Analysis of the rules shows that they can be reduced to two primary principles: First, the investigators must be thoroughly trained in the scientific disciplines of the problem, must understand and appreciate the ethics involved, and must thus be competent to undertake and to carry out the experiment. Second, the human experimental subject must understand and voluntarily consent to the procedure, and must not be selected upon any basis such as race, religion, level of education, or economic status. In other words, *the investigators and the subjects are human beings with entirely equal, inalienable rights* that supersede any considerations of science or general public welfare. Finally, research on human beings is too hazardous and implies too many responsibilities to be undertaken by lone investigators. It should be a group effort supported by a proper consultative body. Experimentation even on oneself without such collaboration and consultation seems as indefensible as similar experimentation on another individual. . . .

The complex problem of the use of human subjects in medical research involves many suprascientific considerations. The guiding principles that have been developed would have general acceptance within the framework of our culture. The application of these principles to specific experimental situations, however, is still open to individual interpretations and differences. It is appropriate to indicate in this connection that science per se is neither moral nor immoral; it become moral or immoral only as moral or immoral human beings use its powerful techniques.

6. Public Health Service Physicians Praise Thirty Years of Government-Sponsored Human Subject Research in the Tuskegee Syphilis Study, 1964

The year 1963 marks the 30th year of the long-term evaluation of the effect of untreated syphilis in the male Negro conducted by the Venereal Disease Branch, Communicable Disease Center, United States Public Health Service. This paper summarizes the information obtained in this study—well known as the "Tuskegee Study"—from earlier publications, reviews the status of the original study group, and reports the clinical and laboratory findings on those remaining participants who were examined in the 1963 evaluation.

In the late 1920's and early 1930's, surveys in rural areas of the South revealed a high incidence of syphilis among the Negro population, and it was determined that many of those infected remained untreated. Because of the lack of knowledge of the pathogenesis of syphilis, a long-term study of untreated syphilis was desirable in establishing a more knowledgeable syphilis control program.

A prospective study was begun late in 1932 in Macon County, Alabama, a rural area with a static population and a high rate of untreated syphilis. An untreated population such as this offered an unusual opportunity to follow and study the disease over a long period of time. In 1932, a total of 26% of the male population tested, who were 25 years of age or older, were serologically reactive for syphilis by at least two tests, usually on two occasions. The original study group was composed of 412 of these men who had received no therapy and who gave historical and laboratory evidence of syphilis which had progressed beyond the infectious stages. A total of 204 men comparable in age and environment and judged by serology, history, and physical examination to be free of syphilis were selected to be the control group.

The first published findings in 1936 by Vonderlehr et al showed that after infection of 15 years' duration only one fourth of the untreated syphilitics were normal and that most of the abnormal findings were in the cardiovascular system. Morbidity was noted to be approximately fourfold greater in the cardiovascular, central nervous, and bone and joint systems of untreated syphilitics under age 40 than in the controls of the same age.

In the first complete reevaluation of these patients in 1938–1939, it was found that many had received some therapy, usually only several injections of arsenic or mercury; however, a few, especially in the younger age group, had received more. Fourteen young, untreated syphilitics were added to the study to compensate for this. At this time it was also discovered that 12 of the controls either had had

Donald Rockwell et al., "The Tuskegee Study of Untreated Syphilis: The 30th [*sic*] Year of Observation," *Archives of Internal Medicine* 114 (1964): 792–797.

syphilis or had acquired it during the interim; these have been followed as syphilitics since that time.

Where possible, these patients have been followed with periodic history, physical and laboratory examinations, including serology, electrocardiogram, chest x-rays, and urinalysis—and autopsy.

Mortality records during the first 12 years of observation, as reported by Heller and Bruyere, revealed that 25% of the syphilitics and 14% of the controls of comparable ages had died. They calculated that at age 25 untreated male syphilitics would have a reduction in life expectancy of approximately 20%.

By 1952, after 20 years of follow-up, 40% of the syphilitics and 27% of the controls had died; at this time the life expectancy of individuals from ages 25 to 50 with syphilis was determined to be reduced by 17%. Fourteen per cent of the 159 syphilitics examined in 1952 showed evidence of late syphilis, approximately half being of the cardiovascular system. From autopsy information available through 1952, it was calculated by Peters and associates that a Negro male with untreated syphilis of more than ten years' duration and a sustained reactive serology would have approximately a 50-50 chance of having demonstrable cardiovascular involvement. Also, the primary cause of death in 30% of the infected group was attributed to syphilitic involvement of the cardiovascular or central nervous system. . . .

For the 30-year evaluation, a concerted effort to trace and examine as many as possible of the Tuskegee Study survivors was undertaken. As of Dec 1, 1963, of the original 412 syphilitics, 242 were known to be dead, 85 were known to be alive, and 85 could not be located and were considered lost to follow-up. Of the 14 young syphilitics added to the study in 1938, seven were alive, four were dead, and three could not be traced. Five of the control group who became infected have died, five were alive, and two were unaccounted for. One hundred ninety-two names of men listed as controls remain on the books. Three have not been seen since the original examination, and 36 others could not be located. Eighty-seven of the controls were dead, and 66 were alive. Therefore, of the original 412 syphilitics, 59% were dead, 21% alive, and 20% lost to follow-up, while 45% of the controls were dead, 34% alive, and 20% not traceable. . .

Eighty of the original syphilitics and ten of the syphilitics later added to the study group were examined during the summer of 1963, along with 65 of the controls. The syphilitic individuals continued to demonstrate more abnormalities, but these were not marked—a finding expected, since syphilis would be expected to have taken its toll earlier. After the age of 55 the processes of aging emerge and seem to become the significant factors in both groups. . . .

The treatment status of the surviving syphilitics is interesting, since 86 of the 90 examined this time have now received some therapy: 45 of these having received an average of five to ten injections of arsenic and bismuth; 11 others only several injections of mercury; 20 have probably received adequate treatment; and 10 more *may* have had adequate therapy. At the time of the second examination in 1939, it was found that approximately 42% of those examined had received some therapy. In 1963, a total of 69, or 77%, of those examined had received some therapy by 1939. The fact that a greater proportion of those who had received some, but inadequate, therapy were still living probably reflects only age differentials. . . .

The Tuskegee Study has been very useful in evaluating serologic tests through the years. Some analysis of the current results seems indicated since we now have 30 years of serologic tests for study. . . .

. . . [W]e have not attempted to analyze all the findings. Such a report awaits a reevaluation of findings and detailed analysis correlating duration of infection, ages, therapy, physical, laboratory, and autopsy findings; a complete review is now under way. We have attempted only to make a brief summary of the study and to report some of the findings of the 30th year of follow-up.

Summary

The syphilitic group continues to have higher mortality and morbidity than the uninfected controls, with the cardiovascular system most commonly involved.

As of Dec 1, 1963, approximately 59% of the syphilitic group and 45% of the control group were known to be dead, and the average age of the survivors in each group was 65 and 66, respectively.

Approximately 96% of those examined had received some therapy other than an incidental antibiotic injection, and perhaps as many as 33% have had curative therapy.

Twelve per cent of the syphilitics examined have clinical evidence of late syphilis, 64% being cardiovascular involvement; most of these have been known since 1948.

Sixty-six per cent of the syphilitics continued to have detectable reagin by the Venereal Disease Research Laboratory (VDRL) slide test, 91% had reactive *Treponema pallidum* immobilization (TPI) tests, and 97% were reactive by the fluorescent treponemal antibody absorption (FTA-ABS) test. The latter two tests were quite sensitive in detecting past syphilis infection which had passed the early stages, regardless of duration or therapy.

Factors in selection and therapy in this study, which must be evaluated more thoroughly, probably tend to minimize the effects of untreated syphilis.

7. A Private Physician Raises Questions That Go Unanswered About the Morality of the Tuskegee Experiment, 1965

Dear Dr. Rockwell:

I have recently read your paper on the Tuskegee Study of Untreated Syphillis appearing in the Archives of Internal Medicine in December, 1964.

I am utterly astounded by the fact that physicians allow patients with potentially fatal disease to remain untreated when effective therapy is available. I assume you feel that the information which is extracted from observation of this untreated group is worth their sacrifice. If this is the case, then I suggest that the United

---

Dr. Irwin Schatz to Dr. Donald Rockwell, Henry Ford Hospital, Detroit, Michigan, June 11, 1965, Tuskegee File, Center for Disease Control, Atlanta, Georgia.

States Public Health Service and those physicians associated with it in this study need to re-evaluate their moral judgements in this regard.

Yours sincerely,

IRWIN J. SCHATZ, M.D.
Head, Section of
Peripheral Vascular Disease

8. A Physician-Historian-Activist Explores the "Legacy of Distrust" Fostered by the Tuskegee Study, 1993

After the abuses of the Tuskegee Syphilis Study were revealed, the federal government strengthened regulations to protect the subjects of human experimentation. These increased safeguards, however, have not erased many African Americans' fear that they will be abused in the name of medical research. The tenacity of this conviction is understandable if one examines the broader history of race and American medicine. . . .

. . . As efforts begin to include more African Americans in clinical trials and to develop community-collaborative research programs, this legacy of distrust must be addressed, not dismissed as paranoia or hypersensitivity. The challenge is to understand and confront the historically based realities behind these sentiments. . . .

Law professor Patricia A. King warns that the Tuskegee Syphilis Study should serve as a caveat to medical researchers when they analyze racial differences between whites and blacks. She writes that "in a racist society that incorporates beliefs about the inherent inferiority of African Americans in contrast to the superior status of whites, any attention to the question of difference that may exist is likely to be pursued in a manner that burdens rather than benefits African Americans." The premise underlying King's comments is that medicine is not a value-free discipline. Rather, it has reflected and reinforced the beliefs, values, and power dynamics of the wider society. Accordingly, it has been influenced by issues of race and racism. . . .

The Tuskegee Syphilis Study continued until 1972. Throughout its 40-year history, accounts of the study appeared in prominent medical journals. Thus, the experiment was widely known in medical circles. As late as 1969, a committee from the Centers for Disease Control examined the study and decided to continue it. Three years later, a USPHS worker, who was not a physician, leaked details about it to the press. Media disclosure and the subsequent public outrage led to the termination of the study and ultimately to the National Research Act of 1974. This act, established to protect subjects in human experimentation, mandates institutional review board approval of all federally funded projects with human subjects.

Vanessa N. Gamble, "A Legacy of Distrust: African Americans and Medical Research," *American Journal of Preventive Medicine,* 9, Supplement 2 (1993): 35–38. Copyright © 1993 by American Journal of Preventive Medicine. Reprinted by permission of Elsevier Science.

After the study had been exposed, many black people charged that it represented "nothing less than an official, premeditated policy of genocide." This was neither the first nor the last time that the issue of genocide has been raised with regard to the relationship of African Americans and medical research. It has been associated with the development of birth control programs and with the sickle cell anemia screening programs of the 1970s.

Most recently, both genocide and Tuskegee have come up in connection with acquired immunodeficiency virus (AIDS). In September 1990, an article entitled "Is it Genocide?" appeared in *Essence,* a black woman's magazine. The author noted: "As an increasing number of African-Americans continue to sicken and die and as no cure for AIDS has been found some of us are beginning to think the unthinkable: Could AIDS be a virus that was manufactured to erase large numbers of us? Are they trying to kill us with this disease?" In other words, some members of the black community see AIDS as part of a deliberate plot to exterminate African Americans. The views of James Small, a black studies instructor at City College of New York exemplify this position. "Our whole *relationship* to [whites] has been of [their] practicing genocidal conspiratorial behavior on us, from the whole slave encounter up to the Tuskegee Study," Small contends. "People make it sound nice, by saying the Tuskegee 'study,' but do you know how many thousands and thousands of our people *died* because of that?"

It would be a mistake to dismiss such ideas as those of a paranoid extremist. In 1990 a survey conducted by the Southern Christian Leadership Conference found that 35% of the 1,056 black church members who responded believed that AIDS was a form of genocide. The legacy of Tuskegee has also influenced the wariness that many African Americans maintain toward needle exchange programs.

The Tuskegee Syphilis Study symbolizes for many African Americans the racism that pervades American institutions, including the medical profession. A lasting legacy of the study is African Americans' distrust of medical researchers. Dr. Stephen B. Thomas, director of the Minority Health Research Laboratory at the University of Maryland—College Park, laments, "Although everyone may not know the *specifics* of the Tuskegee experiment, they have enough residual knowledge of it so that they mistrust government-sponsored programs, and this results in a lack of participation in [AIDS] risk-reduction efforts." Alpha Thomas, a Dallas health educator, University Hospital, often confronts the legacy of Tuskegee. She notes that "so many African American people that I work with do not trust hospitals or any of the other community health care service providers because of that Tuskegee Experiment. It is like . . . if they did it then they will do it again."

The strengthening of safeguards and the reforms in research standards that followed the public disclosure of the abuses of the Tuskegee Syphilis Study have been insufficient to change African Americans' historically based fears of medical research. These apprehensions contribute to the low enrollment rate of African Americans in clinical trials. A 1989 study conducted by pharmacologist Craig K. Svensson demonstrated the underrepresentation of African Americans in clinical trials. He reviewed 50 clinical trials for new drugs that had been published in *Clinical Pharmacology and Therapeutics* for the three-year period 1984–1986. He discovered that the percentage of black subjects was less than their percentage in the cities in which the research was conducted and less than their percentage in the general population of the United States. More recent studies confirm this underrepresentation of African Americans in clinical trials for AIDS drugs.

Why this underrepresentation of black people? As one physician has put it, "We're battling centuries of mistrust based on historical actions of the very institutions involved." The attitudes and practices of medical researchers towards African Americans also cannot be discounted. Once at a job interview, I was told that black people are not included in clinical studies because "it is a well-known fact that they are noncompliant." Furthermore, in the past, most clinical researchers have used white men as the standard or norm from which to extrapolate data to the rest of the population. Young white men were presumed to be a homogenous population that had fewer confounding factors. Members of minority groups and women were frequently excluded from clinical studies. However, federal guidelines now call for the inclusion of these groups in studies unless a compelling reason exists for their exclusion.

Does it matter that African Americans have been excluded from therapeutic drug trials? In the case of the Tuskegee Syphilis Study, clearly the inclusion of the men in a nontherapeutic experiment was detrimental to their health; today, however, exclusion from a therapeutic one may be harmful. For example, recent studies suggest that there are racial and gender differences in the therapeutic efficacy of some drugs. In addition, it is crucial to have African Americans participate in clinical and public health studies that examine diseases and conditions that disproportionately affect them.

The researchers associated with the innovative research strategy to examine preterm delivery in African-American women recognize that a historically-based mistrust still influences African Americans' perceptions of biomedical research. They understand that these attitudes represent a significant research obstacle. These researchers have chosen not to cavalierly dismiss this legacy of distrust but to confront it. They have acknowledged that the voices and experiences of African-American women are crucial for the project's success. In a radical departure from traditional scientific studies, the investigators have actively solicited advice about the study from the African-American lay community. Their goal is to develop a collaborative research study that is conducted *with* African-American people, not *on* them. The efforts of these researchers are a significant step in eroding the legacy of distrust that has so profoundly shaped the relationship of African Americans to medicine.

 E S S A Y S

In the first essay, historian Harry Marks of the Johns Hopkins University examines the efforts of the United States government during World War II to develop a system for organized therapeutic investigation. As Marks shows, the wartime effort was a direct descendent of earlier efforts by the medical research community to engage in large-scale cooperative research endeavors. The crisis of war, however, created a special set of circumstances that transformed these earlier patterns of clinical investigation. Marks's detailed case history of the testing of the new antibiotics penicillin and streptomycin illuminates the interplay among politics, bureaucracy, public opinion, and science that has come to define modern medical research. The infamous Tuskegee Study of untreated syphilis in African American men is the subject of the second essay, by Yale University historian Susan Lederer. Lederer places Tuskegee in an often overlooked historical context, that of human dissection. Discussing several experiments besides Tuskegee, Lederer brings to life the kinds of negotiations in which research physicians and their subjects engaged as the pursuit of experimental truth became increasingly central to the production of medical knowledge. The conduct of the Tuskegee Study physicians, as Lederer frames it, appears less unique and more part of a broader pattern that stretches back into the nineteenth century.

The Politics and Protocols of World War II Venereal Disease and Penicillin Research Programs

HARRY M. MARKS

During World War II, the cause of organized therapeutic investigation received a substantial boost. The war provided an unprecedented opportunity for the nation's scientific elite to direct the conduct and organization of scientific research. In medicine, clinical investigators from the country's leading medical schools turned to cooperative studies to guide them in instructing the nation's physicians on how and when the newest wonder drugs—penicillin and streptomycin—should be used.

Like many in wartime Washington, medical scientists found themselves awash in an alphabetic sea of agencies, replete with overlapping jurisdictions and competing agendas. On June 24, 1941, President Roosevelt vested control over federal research money and policy in the hands of Vannevar Bush, head of the newly created Office of Scientific Research and Development (OSRD). In the case of medicine, Bush relied heavily on an existing network of committees at the National Research Council's Division of Medical Sciences. Created in World War I to provide scientific and technological advice to the military, the National Research Council (NRC) had developed an elaborate system of committees representing university scientists from multiple disciplines. Engaged during peacetime in advising corporations and foundations on questions of scientific research, the NRC returned to advising the military on medical affairs in mid-1940. By the time OSRD was created, the NRC's Division of Medical Sciences had eight major committees and thirty-three subcommittees reviewing problems of military medicine.

At OSRD, Vannevar Bush created a Committee for Medical Research (CMR) to oversee government planning and contracting for medical research. At its first meeting, the committee decided to rely heavily on the NRC: Lewis Weed, chairman of the NRC's Division of Medical Sciences, was appointed vice-chairman of the Committee on Medical Research, and the head of each of the NRC's major medical subject committees was appointed a consultant to the Committee on Medical Research. As a nongovernmental body, the NRC could not legally allocate

Harry M. Marks, *The Progress of Experiment: Science and Therapeutic Reform in the United States, 1900–1990* (New York: Cambridge University Press, 1997): 98–123, 126–127. Copyright © 1997. Reprinted by permission of Cambridge University Press. Excerpt from *Grand Rounds: One Hundred Years of Internal Medicine.* Edited by Russel C. Maulitz and Diana E. Long. Copyright © 1998 University of Pennsylvania Press. Reprinted by permission.

government funds, but its recommendations on investigators and projects usually governed CMR funding decisions.

The NRC's committees had never suffered from a lack of eminent and capable scientists. Having the resources to carry out their plans was another matter. Bush's decision to place the management of medical research in NRC's hands offered academic physicians the opportunity to put prewar ideals of clinical research into practice. For the first time in its history, medicine's intellectual elite had the opportunity not only to set an example for the rest of the profession but actually to direct the conduct of therapeutic research on a national scale. In each area of medicine, NRC's committees selected the topics to be studied and the best means of attack. Investigators willing to research the designated problems received ample funds. . . .

Among the many problems identified by the Committee on Medical Research, finding improved ways to treat or, ideally, to prevent venereal disease ranked high on the list. During World War I, syphilis and gonorrhea in the military services caused the loss of nearly seven million days of active duty. Giving up on efforts to "stifle the instincts of man" or "legislate his appetite," the army turned to chemistry and medicine for "adequate preventive measures."

Existing medical methods of prevention were imperfect, and dependent on soldiers' willingness to come forth for "chemical prophylaxis" after exposure. Newer methods, such as providing self-administered prophylactic doses of the newer sulfonamide drugs, carried less of a stigma, but the risks these treatments posed to military operations were unknown. Potential liabilities included adverse drug reactions; sensitization, which would affect subsequent use in more serious medical circumstances; and the possibility of producing undiagnosed gonorrhea carriers who might transmit the disease to other soldiers. . . .

Of the two diseases, syphilis and gonorrhea, the latter posed the greater scientific problem. In the case of syphilis, the immediate challenge was to adapt existing treatments to military circumstances. If new remedies arose, researchers had developed viable animal models for assessing the benefits and risks of treatment. Notwithstanding some difficulties in extrapolating animal studies to humans, systematic exploratory research could proceed. No such animal models existed for gonorrhea: developing a vehicle for experimental infections was CMR's first order of business. . . . Meanwhile, human studies provided the only means to evaluate treatment.

If studies in humans were necessary, the ideal approach from the researchers' point of view was to deliberately infect, then treat, human volunteers. Investigators could thereby control the timing and degree of the infection, and monitor their subjects carefully while under treatment. Army medical officials, however, doubted whether soldiers could be successfully isolated for the length of the study. Even if the logistic difficulties of confining soldiers could be overcome, army representatives were unwilling to subject draftees to "deliberate experimentation." The alternative was to study prophylaxis in "naturally occurring populations": individuals who had already been exposed to gonorrhea. Members of the NRC's committee on venereal disease, long familiar with the difficulties of interpreting such uncontrolled studies, were unwilling to rely on them. . . .

A prison study, proponents argued, would offer safeguards to the subjects, who could be closely monitored for the reactions characteristic of sulfa drugs. Most important, prisoners could be isolated from sexual activity for six months. Years of inconclusive research had convinced the specialists on the NRC committee that only sexual isolation would guarantee the experiment's scientific success. Without such measures, subjects might naturally acquire infections, hopelessly contaminating any evaluation of treatment outcomes. Neither civilian nor military volunteers, they reasoned, would subject themselves to the required degree of control. [Joseph Earle] Moore's committee did not believe that inmates of "institutions for the feeble-minded or insane" could offer meaningful consent to such a study. . . .

The engineers and physicists in charge of wartime research were less comfortable than their medical associates with the idea of deliberately inflicting gonorrhea. Science officials desired a more comprehensive assessment, one that took into account the proposal's political ramifications as well [as] its scientific merit. This review soon reached the highest levels of NRC and its parent organization, the National Academy of Sciences. . . .

According to [Frank] Jewett [President of the National Academy of Sciences], whether a human experiment was necessary was a "scientific" question; whether prisoners should be used in such a study was a matter of "public policy." . . . "My difficulty," Jewett explained, "resides in the fact that prison populations are not free populations and that so-called volunteers from such populations are not true volunteers in the ordinary sense. Their volunteering is or can be alleged to have been brought about by reasons which are entirely absent in a free population." . . .

Given the extensive deliberations preceding the study, its eventual outcome was anticlimactic. After several months of research on prisoners in the federal penitentiary at Terre Haute, John F. Mahoney reported that the procedure for inducing gonorrhea in humans was too unreliable to enable meaningful tests of prophylactic agents. Following his instructions to abandon the project if it proved "difficult or hazardous" to draw "sound conclusions" from the research, Mahoney stopped the study.

The merits of the gonorrhea research lay elsewhere than in its meager scientific yield, in the rationale for controlled experiments that emerged from negotiations between medical researchers and their lay associates. Research on humans worth doing was worth doing well. A less than adequate study from a methodological point of view was morally unacceptable.

While plans for investigating gonorrhea treatments were getting underway, CMR officials were beginning a much larger program of clinical investigation, to evaluate the therapeutic potential of penicillin. As early as 1940, British and American researchers had begun to demonstrate penicillin's remarkable abilities in uncontrolled staphylococcal and streptococcal infections. Under normal circumstances, these initial reports would be followed by a series of pharmacological and therapeutic studies conducted at various research centers around the country. . . .

Wartime circumstances provided academic physicians with the unusual opportunity to determine, more systematically and efficiently, when and how penicillin was best used. In the fall of 1941, Vannevar Bush and CMR chair A. N. Richards had initiated a crash program to develop industrial production of penicillin. In January 1942, Richards asked Perrin H. Long, the widely respected clinical expert on the sulfa drugs, to organize a research program under NRC auspices to evaluate the clinical uses of penicillin. By the summer of 1943 production capacity had expanded, but there was still far too little of the precious drug. In July, officials of the

War Production Board placed Chester Keefer, Long's successor at the NRC, in charge of all domestic supplies of the drug. The War Production Board action made Keefer virtual "penicillin czar" for the duration of the war.

Professor of Medicine at Boston University, Chester Keefer was a member in good standing with the academic elite of clinical investigators. A product of Hopkins and Harvard, Keefer turned naturally to organized cooperative investigations to study penicillin. He supplied the drug only to a handful of "experienced investigators" who agreed in return to work "under [CMR's] direction and supervision." As historian David Adams notes, rationing penicillin in the name of science enabled Keefer to defend the CMR's monopoly on civilian supplies of the drug against critics and queue jumpers. Government officials and drug manufacturers, fearful of the political fallout if money or privilege could buy access to the drug, similarly relied on Keefer's scientific authority to shield them from public criticism. . . .

Plans to evaluate the use of penicillin in syphilis did not begin until the summer of 1943 when Public Health Service researcher John F. Mahoney demonstrated that, contrary to earlier reports, the drug had a pronounced spirocheticidal effect in experimental infections. Security restrictions on all penicillin research did not prevent news of Mahoney's findings from circulating rapidly among experts on venereal disease. Mahoney's report that the initial syphilitic lesions in four sailors had promptly disappeared upon treatment with penicillin heightened military interest in the drug. . . .

By the fall of 1943, increased penicillin production made it possible to begin planning a civilian investigation of syphilis treatment, under the direction of Joseph Earle Moore, chairman of the NRC's Subcommittee on Venereal Disease. The NRC's studies had two aims: to determine the optimal ways of using penicillin to treat syphilis and to evaluate its efficacy under more carefully controlled circumstances. A cooperative study, operating according to a fixed plan, would meet both objectives. It would accumulate results more quickly, and more reliably, than a series of less focused individual inquiries. . . .

The clinics involved represented a handful of elite investigators, selected either for their expertise in syphilis or in the study of antiinfectious agents. Thanks to OSRD, they did not lack for funds or manpower in pursuing their researches. But these unusually favorable circumstances found researchers no less reluctant to surrender their intellectual autonomy, even in the pursuit of agreed-upon goals. . . .

Researchers' requests to use a portion of their penicillin allocations for autonomous investigations were repeatedly rejected by senior CMR officials. Not surprisingly, some individuals followed promising leads anyway, with the pursuit of scientific curiosity resulting in the neglect of patient follow-up in the cooperative study. Yet in a disease like syphilis, only data on long-term outcomes could address the question of cure. . . .

. . . Nearly half the cases accumulated during the war had to be discarded, because of incomplete information or the investigators' failure to follow the protocol. Loss of patients to follow-up hampered interpretation of the remaining data. Although researchers intended to compare standardized treatments across clinics, individual clinics rarely tested more than two or three of the numerous regimens being studied. Variations in race, gender, and stage of disease among the clinics further complicated investigators' efforts at interpretation, by confounding treatment with clinic effects. Before NCR researchers were ready to draw even tentative conclusions from the study, the war itself was drawing to a close.

Despite their obvious problems, cooperative studies had an appeal to therapeutic reformers, which the outbreak of peace did little to reduce. If studies conducted according to a standard protocol could guide military policy, Moore and his associates saw no reason why they could not also be used to shape the therapeutic practices of civilian physicians. As military pressures abated, their attention turned to evaluating treatment schedules and modes of administering penicillin that might prove useful in postwar civilian practice. . . .

In January 1946, the wartime Committee on Medical Research turned responsibilities for the penicillin study over to the Public Health Service. The transfer of authority did little to alter the membership of those directing the study, or their confidence in cooperative investigations. But with penicillin supplies increasing, senior investigators found it increasingly difficult to get participating researchers to stick to the study protocols. . . .

. . . It comes as no surprise that the specialists who guided the NRC's studies sought to maintain their influence on medical research after the war. During World War II specialists had consolidated their hold on *all* areas of medicine. But that the tradition of cooperative therapeutic studies should survive with them was by no means a foregone conclusion. Even under the most favorable circumstances—and for getting scientists to cooperate, national emergencies were the most favorable circumstances—obtaining the sustained cooperation of clinical investigators had been difficult to engineer.

At the end of the war, medical researchers faced the question of whether to continue working under a common yoke or be free to pursue their intellectual curiosity without restraint. In medicine, as elsewhere in the scientific community, opinions about the merits of organized, purposeful research were mixed. Therapeutic reformers would require more than their scientific ideals to continue the tradition of cooperative research after the war. They would need influential allies from outside medicine and a credible justification for withholding drugs from the rest of the medical community while they were studied. They would find both in the newest wonder drug: streptomycin.

The introduction of streptomycin toward the close of the war provided reformers a ready-made opportunity to continue the tradition of cooperative investigation. First isolated by microbiologist Selman Waksman in 1943, streptomycin initially received little attention from either the military or civilian authorities. Lacking federal encouragement, companies pursued only limited and exploratory research on the drug. But in September 1945, the announcement by two researchers at the Mayo Clinic (H. Corwin Hinshaw and William Feldman) that streptomycin showed promise in treating advanced cases of tuberculosis generated widespread civilian demand for the drug. With the army, private industry, and government planners soon "besieged by panic requests for the drug," all three turned to Chester Keefer and the NRC to "establish an integrated clinical research program" in which Keefer would once again take charge of allocating the drug to researchers who would be able to determine its most beneficial uses. . . .

As originally planned, the proposed streptomycin study was intended as a joint venture between the VA [Veterans Administration], the army, navy, and the

PHS. Lack of funding prevented the PHS from immediately joining a major research initiative. With 9,000 tuberculosis patients in its hospitals, and more on the way, the VA could not afford to wait: in June 1946, the first of its studies began.

The VA may have seemed like the ideal organization to conduct a controlled investigation of streptomycin treatment—a centralized bureaucracy, newly invigorated by an infusion of medical and scientific talent. The reality was somewhat different. Study organizers in Washington kept an eye on the veterans' lobbies, whose strength in many congressional districts gave local concerns substantial weight with the VA's central bureaucracy. The very idea that the VA was conducting experiments had to be approached gingerly: "We don't like to use the word 'experiments' in the Veterans Administration; 'investigation' or 'observations,' I believe is the approved term for such a study in the VA hospitals."

The VA's delicacy posed difficulties for what was initially planned as a controlled experiment. In principle, the arguments for including a control group were well understood. Clinical researchers had long been aware that spontaneous recoveries confounded the interpretation of treatment results. The experiences of the wartime penicillin investigators had only reinforced prewar concerns about studies that lacked a group of untreated control patients. Without "simultaneously run" controls, statisticians had found it difficult to distinguish between the effects of penicillin and the numerous other factors that might have affected treatment results: patient selection, adjunct therapies, and the complex natural history of syphilis itself.

The course of tuberculosis was similarly erratic: relapses and spontaneous recoveries were common enough events to confound treatment assessments. In the absence of an untreated control group, crediting improvements to streptomycin, or any novel treatment, was problematic. . . .

. . . [B]ut the VA investigators proved unwilling to abandon existing treatments purely in the name of science. Within a few months of starting the study, investigators fearful that the study hospitals held too few eligible patients dropped their plans for a control group. Sacrificing half their patients to a control group would impede the VA's ability to provide quick answers about the merits of streptomycin. What began as a pragmatic decision soon became a matter of policy. Fearful that withholding treatment would produce "undesirable repercussions" from "certain groups in this country," the researchers' commitment to untreated controls flagged. Despite the arguments of outside consultants that a control group was necessary, the study proceeded without such a safeguard.

The lack of an untreated control group forced the VA researchers to rely on ad hoc comparisons of study patients with the results of conventional therapy obtained in the recent past on comparable patients. The difficulties of interpreting such comparisons soon became evident. . . . But despite its methodological shortcomings, the VA study remained the largest, if not the only, program investigating streptomycin treatment: "Absolutely the whole profession is going to have to depend on the Veterans Administration to tell us what we are going to be able to learn about streptomycin. There is no other organization which is likely to be able to learn about streptomycin on such a wide scale." . . .

As with penicillin, publicity concerning streptomycin created a demand for the drug among both patients and physicians. Of the two groups, VA researchers considered patients and their families easier to manage: "What we tell the relatives is this—that this is an experimental drug, that its efficacy has not been proven and that we feel sure they would not want their own husband, father or brother being experimented upon because we have heard so many times, complaints about people being experimented upon." . . .

To nonmedical observers, the VA study looked like their idea of research: focused, purposeful investigation in a large bureaucracy. The watchword of the VA was organization, but the organizational means available to the VA study ultimately proved inadequate to the task. To the medical community, the VA's investigation of streptomycin demonstrated the limits of organization alone in producing convincing findings. Another avenue to producing reliable cooperative studies had to be found.

While the VA study was getting underway, the Public Health Service was planning its own researches into streptomycin. . . . To keep participating physicians in line, the planners called for a strictly defined protocol, with explicit rules about eligibility and treatment schedules. Physicians would be expected to continue treating patients on a given regimen, until authorized by a steering committee to discontinue treatment. . . .

. . . Advocates of a control group wanted backing from the medical authorities on the study's steering committee, in the form of a statement justifying the withholding of streptomycin. The limited amounts of streptomycin available, coupled with uncertainty about the drug's precise value, could serve as an initial justification. Skeptics doubted that any such statement would serve its purpose: to stiffen the backbone of investigators faced with a patient whose condition was deteriorating. The proposed compromise was "that physicians do not communicate to patients the fact that they are being considered for inclusion in this series. Hence patients who are in the control group are not to realize that they have been denied streptomycin."

The majority of investigators participating in the PHS study proved willing to go along with the idea of a control group. Unresolved was the question of handling control patients whose disease worsened substantially during the study. Should they receive the drug, and under what circumstances? Palmer and his PHS associate, Dr. Shirley Ferebee, proposed that investigators submit such cases to an appeals board, which would decide if an exemption was warranted. Provided the exemption criteria were sufficiently narrow, and specified in advance, only a few patients would be lost and the research design need not be compromised. . . .

The streptomycin studies conducted by the VA and PHS represent the principal attempt to carry on the tradition of cooperative studies immediately after the war. Once again, an innovative drug was in short supply and, once again, cooperative studies were proposed as a way of producing the most knowledge in the most efficient manner. The VA and PHS studies, without question, involved experienced investigators, knowledgeable about the vagaries of tuberculosis and the mechanisms of drug action and resistance. Yet what distinguished these studies from other research on streptomycin was not the involvement of specialists, but their apparent willingness in this instance to subordinate individual judgment to a common purpose.

If decisions about the future of the VA and PHS studies had been left solely up to the scientific community, it is an open question whether they would have been supported, or if they would have taken the precise form they did. But to those footing the bill, the streptomycin studies represented *organized,* purposeful research: a means of quickly finding answers to practical questions about the therapeutic use of streptomycin. What gave cooperative studies like these a competitive advantage, in the quasi-public debates over the direction and funding of postwar medical research, was not their association with better science but their reputation for efficiency. . . .

Long after the technical details of the procedures they employed were obsolete, the PHS's studies of streptomycin served as an example of scientific progress in therapeutics. Along with centrally controlled randomization, their use of objectively measured indicators of progress and blinded assessments of therapeutic outcomes constituted adherence to a program of methodological reform in the postwar era. The rationale contemporaries offered for such innovations was that they served to limit the exercise of subjective judgment: rather than pitting the clinical acumen of individual physicians against each other, evaluations conducted according to the new methodological canons would provide an objective measure of therapeutic progress. What went unmentioned was that these procedures also reduced the clinician's ability to deviate spontaneously from an agreed-upon plan of research, *whatever* the reason.

The Tuskegee Syphilis Experiment and the Conventions and Practice of Biomedical Research

SUSAN E. LEDERER

In 1997, President William Clinton apologized on behalf of the American people to the men and families of men who had participated in the notorious Tuskegee Syphilis Study, the longest nontherapeutic study in the history of medical research. Funded by the United States Public Health Service, the study began in 1932, when nearly 600 men, all African American and living in rural Alabama, were recruited without their knowledge or consent into a study of the effects of "untreated syphilis in the male negro." By the time the Department of Health, Education and Welfare (the forerunner of the Department of Health and Human Services) officially terminated the study in 1972, investigators had already determined that the death rate of the men infected with syphilis and aged 25 to 50 was 75 per cent greater than that of the control group (men in the study who did not have syphilis). At the formal White House ceremony held twenty-five years after the termination of a federally sponsored research program in which white doctors deceived their subjects and actively prevented their access to drugs which may have affected their disease course, Herman Shaw, one of the few remaining survivors, painfully recalled, "We were treated unfairly. To some extent like guinea pigs. We were not pigs. We were all hard-working men, not boys, and citizens of the United States."

The Tuskegee Syphilis Study (which some critics would prefer to see identified as the United States Public Health Service Study of Untreated Syphilis) understandably takes center stage in any discussion of racism and research in America.

Susan E. Lederer, "The Tuskegee Syphilis Study: Racism, Research, and Human Dissection," adapted by the author from "The Tuskegee Syphilis Study in the Context of American Medical Research," in Susan B. Reverby, ed., *Tuskegee's Truths: Rethinking the Tuskegee Syphilis Study* (University of North Carolina Press, 2000). Copyright © 2000 by the University of North Carolina Press. Used by permission of the publisher.

The shadow cast by the Tuskegee Syphilis Study on medical research continues to be experienced by researchers and other public health professionals especially in the area of AIDS and HIV treatment and prevention. Racism is hardly unique in the history of American medicine, nor is it rare in the history of sexually-transmitted diseases. Anthropologist Lawrence Hammar has described how researchers and physicians interested in another sexually transmitted disease, Donovanosis (*Granuloma inguinale*) also performed experiments on mostly African American subjects in the early twentieth century. Unlike the Public Health Service Study, which involved withholding treatment from already infected men, the Donovanosis experiments included deliberate efforts to transmit the causative agent of the disease. In 1926 University of Tennessee bacteriologist J. A. McIntosh described how he injected two hospital patients—a "colored man" hospitalized for liver cancer and a seventeen-year-old "colored girl" being treated with myelitis—with organisms taken from infected patients. Similar efforts to transmit the organism that causes Donovanosis continued on "volunteers" until the 1950s. So-called "voluntary" participation in these studies and the Public Health Service study of untreated syphilis cannot be taken at face value. Racism profoundly influenced the interactions of American medical researchers and black patients and subjects in this period.

The Tuskegee Syphilis Study is an infamous event in the history of American medical research. There are good reasons, however, to suggest that research may not be the most appropriate frame for understanding the Study. The conduct of the white government physicians may be better understood in the context of the history of human dissection, a history in which racism figured prominently. The Public Health Service investigators who staffed the Study over four decades regarded their African American subjects neither as patients, nor as experimental subjects, but as cadavers, who had been identified while still alive.

As historian James Jones has noted, the Tuskegee Syphilis Study did not originate as a fully developed research plan with clearly identified objectives or end points. The study began in 1932 when the Julius Rosenwald Fund, citing the adverse economic effects of the Great Depression, withdrew its funds for treating African Americans diagnosed with syphilis. At this point, Dr. Taliaferro Clark of the Public Health Service identified "a ready-made situation" in which to study the effects of untreated syphilis in Macon County. He proposed a short-term study, six months or one year, to follow a group of men infected with syphilis who were not receiving treatment for their disease. By 1933, however, Clark had been replaced by Raymond Vonderlehr in the Division of Venereal Diseases at the Public Health Service. At Vonderlehr's command, the study took a dramatic new course. Rather than bringing the study to a close as planned, Vonderlehr ordered the observation to be continued indefinitely. The men's participation in the study would now end with the post-mortem examinations following the deaths of the subjects.

The post-mortem examinations to confirm the effects of untreated syphilis became the most important focus for investigators. "The proper procedure," observed Vonderlehr in 1933, "is the continuance of the observation of the Negro men used in the study with the idea of eventually bringing them to autopsy." Like a twentieth-century version of Burke and Hare, the notorious nineteenth-century Edinburgh resurrectionists, Vonderlehr and his PHS colleagues identified bodies they wanted for dissection while the individuals were still alive. To further their goals, researchers took a number of steps to ensure the integrity of the bodies; in order to avoid contaminating their "study in nature," investigators actively prevented the men from gaining access to medical treatment for syphilis. In order to get the bodies of the dead black men to the autopsy table as quickly as possible (vital in Alabama in the days before air-conditioning), they worked closely with local physicians in Macon and surrounding counties to streamline the process. Unlike Burke and Hare, the PHS doctors did not kill their subjects. They allowed syphilis to take its painful, predictable course.

The Public Health Service investigators did not steal bodies or violate any laws. Instead they took considerable pains to observe the legal requirements for gaining permission from family members to conduct post-mortem examinations. To gain the cooperation of families, the researchers relied on Tuskegee nurse Eunice Rivers. A graduate of the Tuskegee Institute and well known and respected in the local community, Rivers approached the families for permission to perform the autopsy. Her task became much easier after 1935, when families who complied with the autopsy request received a $50 burial stipend. The $35 families received ($15 went to the pathologist) enabled them to bury their loved one. Made possible by funds from the Milbank Memorial Fund, the stipends were withheld if families refused to authorize an autopsy. Rivers proved enormously successful in getting familial compliance. In a 1954 *Public Health Reports* paper, Rivers recorded "only one refusal in 20 years and 145 autopsies obtained." The one refusal suggests how powerful an incentive the burial stipend represented in the impoverished Macon community. The PHS investigators did not have to resort to theft or deception when they had such funds to ensure compliance with the post-mortem examinations.

Why did these investigators who were willing to withhold treatment for syphilis, to deceive the men about the nature of their participation, to mislabel diagnostic tests as therapy go to such lengths to ensure that families gave consent for post-mortems? In part, investigators discovered that observing the laws furthered their own interests. Not only did burial insurance serve as incentive for gaining permission, but Rivers explained how community knowledge of the cash payments encouraged individuals to report deaths of participants: "They would let me know when somebody died because in those days $50 was a whole heap of money for a funeral."

Placing the Tuskegee Study in the context of human dissection may also explain the investigators' extraordinary compliance with rules regarding autopsy and the simultaneous breach of the operative rules regarding human experimentation. Even before the American Medical Association adopted its first formal principles regarding human experimentation in 1946, leading American medical researchers had identified by the early twentieth century several necessary conditions for ethical human experimentation. These included prior animal studies, consent of the patient/subject, and responsibility for harm to the subjects. The PHS investigators breached these conditions in the conduct of the Tuskegee Study, but they had apparently not violated any laws. Although federal and state legislatures had considered proposals for regulating human experimentation in the first two decades of the twentieth century, no federal regulations governing the conduct of human research were enacted until 1974 (on the heels of public disclosures about the Tuskegee Syphilis Study).

In the early twentieth century, American legislators had begun to regulate access to dead human bodies for dissection and autopsy. By 1932, when the Tuskegee

Study began, most state legislatures had enacted statutes involving the disposition and use of dead human bodies. Some of the laws explicitly noted the physician's responsibility to obtain consent from family members before a post-mortem examination. As attorney George Weinmann noted in 1929, "the general rule is that the unauthorized autopsy of a dead human body is a tort, giving rise to a cause of action for damages." An increasing number of Americans pursued lawsuits against hospitals and physicians for performing unauthorized autopsies on family members. Successful suits with monetary damages prompted pathologists and hospital administrators to urge more attention to the methods of obtaining written consent for autopsy as a protection against both individuals and institutions. There is some indication that African Americans and other ethnic groups were asked for permission. Explaining how Memorial Hospital improved a higher rate of cooperation with requests for autopsy, New York physician William Hoffman noted that doctors approached the family in business suits rather than white uniforms and avoided such words with "gruesome connotations" as autopsy, inquest, or necropsy. Using this new approach, Hoffman reported for the six months between July and December 1932 that of the seventy-one deaths in the hospital, the families of "all Germans, Danes, Irish, Negroes and all Italians but one consented to autopsy."

In the state of Alabama, an anatomical practice act permitted the distribution of unclaimed dead human bodies to medical schools for "the advancement of medical science." The law included provisions to allow surviving friends and family members to claim the body, so long as they could provide the money for burial. Although anatomical acts did not materially alter the social origins of the dead bodies available for dissection (in the 1920s, for example, interstate shipment of dead black bodies to northern medical schools continued), the law protected (at least, in theory) both whites and African Americans with money for burial from being turned over to medical schools. Intent on getting post-mortem evidence for the syphilis study, PHS investigators scrupulously complied with the legal requirements for family permission for the autopsy. For Vonderlehr and his colleagues at the Public Health Service, the dead took precedence over the living.

In the thirteen papers from the Tuskegee Syphilis Study published between 1936 and 1973, investigators identified the study participants as "syphilitics," "patients" or as "syphilitic Negro males." In no published paper did investigators characterize the men as research subjects, but in 1955 the men were, for the first time, described as "volunteers with social incentives." Once the study had ended amid a flurry of news reports and congressional hearings, some of the survivors of the study recalled being used as "guinea pigs" by government doctors. The equation of African Americans with laboratory animals has a history nearly as long as the term *human guinea pig* (introduced in 1906 by British writer George Bernard Shaw).

In the 1940s a University of Pennsylvania researcher elaborated a number of parallels between his Negro research subjects and laboratory animals. In an after-dinner speech intended to divert his colleagues, Abbott described some of his problems using "professional guinea pigs." In 1931 Abbott and his co-worker T. Grier Miller had developed a new technique for rapidly intubating the human intestine from mouth to rectum. Although advised to try the new device on animals, Miller and Abbott apparently never performed the animal studies. After numerous self-experiments, they attempted to locate subjects in the hospital wards, and finally turned to healthy men and women who would agree to the procedure. During the height of the Depression, Abbott and Miller approached a young relief administrator, hoping to gain cooperation in using unemployed men as subjects. Unlike her counterpart in Chicago who sent men on relief to laboratories to participate in research for payment, the Philadelphia administrator refused to send men to Abbott's laboratory, especially when she learned that they would be required to swallow a flexible twelve-foot tube to which a rubber balloon was attached and inflated once inside the intestine.

Frustrated by the employment bureau, Abbott asked the wives of his colleagues to distribute slips of paper instructing beggars to come to the hospital for a job paying $2 a day. He also used the bridge over the Schuylkill River as a "hunting ground" for potential participants, to no avail. Finally, his secretary suggested that the doctors call in their black janitor; they eventually promised Harry fifty cents for every healthy human subject who appeared at the laboratory door at 8:30 A.M. in a sober and fasting state.

Abbott's first subject, Flip Lawall, "tall, broad-shouldered, black as the ace of spades, and by profession a light-weight prize fighter," was joined by several other young black men. Employing this population as research subjects, Abbott insisted, was not without problems. Alluding in a stereotypical fashion to the men's penchant for thievery, Abbott complained that his "animals" also enjoyed a larger intake of corn liquor, pork chops, and chewing tobacco than the white rats in the medical school. He described how, on one occasion, he had attempted to insert a flexible rubber tube into one man's duodenum using fluoroscopic guidance, when he noticed a small piece of metal. Recognizing the tip of a .38 caliber revolver bullet, Abbott confronted his subject who admitted that the previous night his jealous "sweetheart" had shot him after seeing him with another woman earlier in the evening. Such events, Abbott explained, "led me to wish at times I could keep my animals in metabolism cages."

Abbott encountered more serious problems in the spring of 1935 when he scheduled an exhibit on intestinal intubation for the American Medical Association meeting in Atlantic City. Arranging for the men to be intubated at a local hospital before their appearance at the convention, Abbott was stunned when his "guinea pigs" threatened to walk out at the last minute unless they received double pay. Only an impassioned eleventh-hour appeal to the third-year medical school class and the offer of the same pay received by the "striking blackamoors" enabled Abbott to continue the demonstration using student volunteers. He fired all the black subjects and refused to have anything more to do with them.

After several months, Abbott reconsidered his position. "Those boys may have been short on morals but they were long in gut and in the end," he remarked, "I went to Harry once again to throw out a feeler." He discovered that his "boys" had "graduated from stealing inkwells to house furnishings"; all but two had been convicted of burglary, and his first subject, Flip Lawall, was serving a ten-year sentence in the state penitentiary for a rape conviction.

An advertisement in a local newspaper brought a fresh group of potential subjects to Abbott's laboratory. Some of the men and women who answered the ad winced at the description of swallowing the tubes, and many others apparently quailed at Abbott's insistence that they sign a statement prepared by the University attorney outlining every step of the experiment and stating that subjects recognized and accepted any risks associated with the procedure. (The document was more of an indemnification agreement than a consent form.) Abbott ended up with a roster of subjects, young and old, white and black, male and female, although he noted that his "clientele" generally dwindled down to hefty, older women, the human counterpart of the "big, lazy, overweight bitch [from the animal house] that could be counted upon to lie and wag her tail while being worked over."

Abbott's intubation experiments differed in a number of important ways from the Tuskegee Syphilis Study. His initial black subjects were all ostensibly healthy men, who knew that they were receiving payment for their participation in research. They were not patients. What the men actually understood about the risks associated with swallowing the tubes and the frequent x-rays is impossible to know. Abbott did refer to his own efforts to safeguard them from the effects of "overfrequent" radiation, but given his instrumental attitude toward the men, it seems unlikely that he explained the risks in any detail. Assumptions about race informed the investigators' attitudes toward the men, their reliability, and their level of comprehension.

Abbott jokingly equated his professional guinea pigs with laboratory animals, but reliance on Harry the janitor to arrange for the men to come to the laboratory bears remarkable similarity to the ways in which laboratories obtained both animals and human cadavers for study. Black technicians, janitors, and caretakers routinely located and supplied these materials—alive and dead. At Johns Hopkins, for example, the surgeon Willis Gatch recalled how each January William Halsted would call him into his office to inform him that he was ready to start his experimental work in the Hunterian Laboratory. Gatch would then hire a Negro boy to procure dogs and instruct him on how to etherize them. In a similar way, Nurse Rivers functioned as a conduit for the bodies of black men needed for post-mortem examinations.

The Tuskegee Syphilis Study, the Donovanosis experiments, and the intubation studies suggest a range of experimental encounters between African Americans and mostly white investigators. Although lack of financial resources, knowledge, and expertise often made African American patients vulnerable to experimenters, in one extraordinary case an African American woman looked to the courts for redress when a surgeon overstepped the bounds of appropriate experimentation. In the 1940s the mother of a young African American man sued a white physician in the District of Columbia whose surgical experiments caused severe injury to her son. Before the suit was eventually settled out of court, newspaper publicity about the case raised a number of questions about experiments on African Americans.

In 1940 John Bonner, a junior high school student, donated skin to a badly burned cousin for an experimental skin grafting procedure. Although Bonner was only fifteen at the time, surgeon Robert Moran did not obtain parental consent before undertaking the surgical experiment in the charity clinic of Episcopal Hospital. In an effort to treat the burned woman, Moran surgically removed a flap of skin and formed a "tube of flesh" from the boy's armpit to his waist, which he attached to the boy's cousin. The two remained surgically joined for four days, when Bonner began to experience shock and anemia. The boy lost so much blood that he required several transfusions, and spent nearly two months in the hospital recovering from his experience.

In 1941 Margaret Moore, the boy's mother, brought suit against the physician for assault and battery. Even though Bonner's mother had not given her consent, the trial court ruled in favor of the physician, noting that a minor's permission for the operation was sufficient in this case. Appealed to the District of Columbia Court of Appeals, the higher court ruled that although children could consent to medical therapy in exceptional cases, the Bonner case did not involve a therapeutic benefit for the boy.

> Here the operation was entirely for the benefit of another and involved sacrifice on the part of the infant [sic] of fully two months of schooling, in addition to serious pain and possible results affecting his future life. This immature colored boy was subjected several times to treatment involving anesthesia, blood letting, and the removal of skin from his body, with at least some permanent marks of disfigurement.

Although the appeals court instructed the lower court to retry the case, the parties reached an out-of-court settlement.

The case of *Bonner* v. *Moran* has been discussed in the bioethics literature in the context of legal precedents for allowing healthy children to donate kidneys. But the suit may be important for other reasons as well. The ruling of the appellate court suggests that there were in fact some legal (and financial) constraints on white physicians whose experiments on black subjects ended in injury or harm to the participants. Less tangibly, the "newspaper notoriety" surrounding the boy's heroism, which apparently resulted in public contributions of money for his future education, suggests a wider public appreciation for both the costs and benefits of human experimentation.

The Bonner case, Abbott's intestinal intubations, and the Tuskegee Syphilis Study illustrate different aspects of race and research in American medicine. Differences in study design, investigators, and subjects influenced the research experience, and race informed the conduct of these experiments as it did other aspects of American life. In the case of an "experiment in nature," as investigators termed the no-treatment syphilis study, investigators actively deceived their "patients" to retain them in their studies. In such explicitly non-therapeutic studies as the intestinal intubations, white investigators needed cooperation from their subjects; they reserved their contempt for their "guinea pigs" even as they furnished the money required to recruit them. Abbott's experience also illustrates how research subjects actively resisted the role of "human guinea pig," and attempted to negotiate more favorable terms for their participation as research subjects. John Bonner's mother repudiated the role of human guinea pig when she sued the surgeon for injuries to her son and won some monetary compensation.

In 1997, twenty-five years after the federal government brought the study to a close, five of the eight surviving participants of the Tuskegee Syphilis Study, elderly men some in wheelchairs, listened as the President apologized for the government's "shameful" silence on the no-treatment experiment. Ninety-five-year-old Herman Shaw explained that he was willing to put "the horrible nightmare" of the study behind him. Not everyone may be as forgiving. The legacy of the syphilis study and other experiments in which African Americans participated without their knowledge or consent seems likely to outlive Shaw and his fellow subjects.

F U R T H E R   R E A D I N G

David B. Adams, *The Greatest Good to the Greatest Number: Pencillin Rationing on the American Home Front, 1940–1945* (1991).

Saul Benison, A. Clifford Barger, and Elin L. Wolfe, *Walter B. Cannon: The Life and Times of a Young Scientist* (1987).

Michael Bliss, *The Discovery of Insulin* (1982).

George W. Corner, *A History of the Rockefeller Institute, 1901–1953: Origins and Growth* (1964).

W. Bruce Fye, *American Cardiology: The History of a Speciality and Its College* (1996).

Victoria A. Harden, *Inventing the NIH: Federal Biomedical Research Policy, 1887–1937* (1986).

McGhee A. Harvey, *Science at the Bedside: Clinical Research in American Medicine, 1905–1945* (1981).

Allen M. Hornblum, *Acres of Skin: Human Experiments at Holmesburg Prison* (1998).

James H. Jones, *Bad Blood: The Tuskegee Syphilis Experiment* (1981).

Susan E. Lederer, "Hideyo Noguchi's Leutin Experiment and the Antivivisectionists," *Isis* 76 (1985): 31–48.

Susan E. Lederer, "'The Right and Wrong of Making Experiments on Human Beings': Udo J. Wile and Syphilis," *Bulletin of the History of Medicine* 58 (1984): 380–397.

Susan E. Lederer, *Subjected to Science: Human Experimentation in America Before the Second World War* (1995).

Harry M. Marks, *The Progress of Experiment: Science and Therapeutic Reform in the United States, 1900–1990* (1997).

Jack D. Pressman, *Last Resort: Psychosurgery and the Limits of Medicine* (1998).

Robert N. Proctor, *Cancer Wars: How Politics Shapes What We Know and Don't Know About Cancer* (1995).

Thomas M. Rivers, *Tom Rivers: Reflections on a Life in Medicine and Science; an Oral History Memoir,* prepared by Saul Benison (1967).

George Rosen, "Patterns of Health Research in the United States, 1900–1960," *Bulletin of the History of Medicine* 39 (1965): 201–228.

Richard H. Shryock, *American Medical Research, Past and Present* (1947).

Stephan P. Strickland, *Politics, Science, and Dread Disease: A Short History of United States Medical Research Policy* (1972).

Donald C. Swain, "The Rise of a Research Empire: NIH, 1930–1950," *Science* 138 (1962): 1233–1237.

John P. Swann, *Academic Scientists and the Pharmaceutical Industry: Cooperative Research in Twentieth-Century America* (1988).

Public Health and the
State During an Age
of Biomedical Miracles,
1925–1960

In the middle third of the twentieth century establishing who was responsible for the health of the American people was a task fraught with problems. Was it the individual? Or was it the medical profession? Perhaps it was the government's job to ensure the safety and well-being of its citizens? In a capitalist democracy like the United States, such questions stimulated vigorous debate, especially after the preventive and therapeutic powers of medical science increasingly won public confidence during the second quarter of the twentieth century. For many of those involved in this debate the most controversial set of issues focused on the expansion of the federal government's role in regulating medical conduct and the health decision making of individual Americans. As the eighteenth-century inoculation controversy in Chapter 2 makes evident, government has played a significant part in the health lives of America's inhabitants since the colonial era. Until the twentieth century, as this chapter and others (particularly 6, 8, and 12) suggest, it was the state and local branches of government and the military that were the most active in this area, and even the actions of these agencies were subject to repeated inquiry. Americans asked themselves over and over again: If the government is to have a role in protecting health, exactly what should that role be? Should the government provide care, keep records, regulate health practices and products, provide funding, or simply leave these functions to private citizens and the market?

Although the answers to these questions changed dramatically over time, it is important to recognize that a pattern of compromise evolved in the mid-twentieth century between the forces of the private market and the powers of the state. Understanding this pattern requires the exploration of a complex network of interactions that involved the American public, a burgeoning mass media industry, and some of the latest communication technologies, as well as several of the nation's largest corporations and wealthiest philanthropies. This pattern of compromise also tested many of the nation's most sacred political institutions and economic beliefs. How was the nation to provide adequate information to a mass audience, to ensure equal access to valuable resources, and to protect the public safety while simultaneously guaranteeing the rights of individuals and private businesses to pursue their own interests? Were school boards mandating proof of vaccination or federal agencies regulating the safety of food, drugs, cosmetics, and other substances fulfilling these goals? Or were they overstepping the boundaries of democratic rule and a market economy? What about state-run public health programs, licensing authorities for health care providers, and patenting authorities for biomedical innovation? Most problematic of all is the perennial question of how to persuade individuals to abandon unhealthy habits and follow the behavioral dictates of medical authorities. What kind of persuasive techniques worked well in the mass society of the twentieth-century United States? And when, if ever, was coercion justified?

 D O C U M E N T S

Document 1, a flyer produced in the 1920s by the public education division of the Metropolitan Life Insurance Company, displays some of the complexities of government involvement in the health lives of American citizens. Here a private business is calling on residents to vote for tax support of a public tuberculosis hospital. Why would a business involve itself in such a campaign? What does this campaign say about American traditions of states' rights and local autonomy? The 1932 cartoon that is Document 2 is also designed to educate the public about the inadequacies of the United States health care system. Produced by the Committee on the Cost of Medical Care (CCMC), a privately funded voluntary health reform group, the cartoon's message that underemployed physicians ought to be matched with patients who need their services was not popular with all participants in the health care economy. Many of the CCMC's economic and statistical studies on the state of American health were equally controversial, particularly since many members of the committee favored such reforms as group practice and the expansion of government's role in health insurance.

Document 3, an excerpt from the *Congressional Record* of 1937, makes it clear that private businesses and voluntary organizations were not alone in pushing for medical and public health reform. Representative Maury Maverick of Texas makes an impassioned plea for a national cancer research center. Is such an expensive undertaking really in the nation's best interest? Should the federal government intrude so far into the world of research science? Document 4, an article from the popular women's magazine *Ladies' Home Journal,* published in the same year as Maverick's speech, provides further insight into the ways Americans answered these questions. The authors of this article are an intriguing pair: Paul de Kruif is the leading science reporter of his day and something of a gadfly to the medical community, while Thomas Parran is the Surgeon General and head of the United States Public Health Service (USPHS). Teaming up to write a deliberately provocative article, de Kruif and Parran decry the ignorance and mistaken modesty that they believe contribute to the spread of the "dread destroyer" syphilis. What are they asking American women to do? How are they pushing members of the medical profession to change their approach to patients? Why do they launch such a public health campaign through a magazine aimed at middle-class women?

Document 5, a 1947 address to Congress by President Harry Truman, casts the federal government in an expansive new role. Truman first began addressing Congress on the need to ensure that the "average American family has a decent chance for adequate medical care" in November 1945. With great regularity during his tenure in office he returned to this theme and his belief that "every American" should have the "right to adequate health care." Was he correct? What would guaranteeing this right mean to the development of both medicine and public health in the latter part of the twentieth century?

Bernard Devoto, a journalist, broadens the perspective on this debate over health rights in his 1947 article for *Harper's* magazine (Document 6). Offering a glimpse inside the annual American Medical Association (AMA) convention in Atlantic City, Devoto portrays the mixture of business, science, technology, and politics that characterizes the medical profession at work. How powerful was the AMA? Why did it oppose the Wagner-Murray-Dingell plan for compulsory national health insurance? Were there no curbs on the power of the AMA lobby? Document 7, a 1954 mass mailing to general practice physicians and pediatricians from the National Foundation for Infantile Paralysis (NFIP), is evidence of the power and trust midcentury Americans placed in the medical profession. Designed to help physicians answer the public's questions about the new poliomyelitis vaccine, the mailing was part of a campaign to ease the way for a massive clinical test of the Salk vaccine on American children. The vaccine field trials were a major undertaking, involving a sizable community of research scientists, state public health officials, the pharmaceutical industry, and thousands of children. What does it mean that the guiding force in this undertaking was the NFIP, better known as the March of Dimes, a private philanthropic organization with no official standing as either a regulatory or a scientific agency?

1. The Metropolitan Life Insurance Company Calls Out the Vote for a County Tuberculosis Hospital, ca. 1920s

Will You Vote YES or NO to Save Lives?

YOUR VOTE ON THE APPROPRIATION FOR A COUNTY TUBERCULOSIS HOSPITAL WILL ANSWER THIS QUESTION

Every voter will have a chance to vote on this Appropriation
on November Second

THINK WHAT YOUR VOTE MEANS

YES	NO
1. YES means that you save many persons in your home county from sickness and death from tuberculosis.	1. NO means that you are not doing what you can to prevent deaths from consumption.
2. YES means that you give consumptives the best possible chance to get well.	2. NO means that you are failing to provide the sick with the care which would give them the best chance of recovery.
3. YES means that you give the well, especially the children, protection against consumption by caring for the sick in a place where they will stay and where they will not spread disease.	3. NO means that you are willing to let tuberculosis spread unchecked—a constant menace to the health of all.
4. YES means that many lives will be saved—mothers saved to their children—workers saved to industry—wage-earners saved to families—young men and women saved to the county.	4. NO means that you do not understand the cost which consumption now puts upon the county by deaths, sickness, poverty and human suffering.
5. YES means that you make the best investment the county ever made—it means less orphans and less poverty.	5. NO means that you do not want your county to take the most important step in the battle against the white plague—a step which twenty-six other counties have successfully taken.
6. YES means that in many families among your neighbors you put happiness and health in the place of suffering, sorrow and neglect.	6. NO means that you vote for sickness, neglect and death, instead of health, scientific care and the welfare of the county.

VOTE *YES* ON THIS QUESTION NOVEMBER SECOND.

YOU WILL FIND THE QUESTION ON THE VOTING MACHINE, ON THE BALLOT WITH THE CONSTITUTIONAL AMENDMENTS OR ON A SEPARATE SMALL BALLOT.

VOTE *YES* ON THE TUBERCULOSIS HOSPITAL BEFORE YOU LEAVE THE BOOTH.

"Will You Vote YES or NO to Save Lives?" Flyer published and distributed by the Metropolitian Life Insurance Company, undated (ca. 1925). Metropolitian Life Insurance Co. Archive, New York, New York.

2. A Group of Private Citizens Organizes to Investigate and Reform the American Health Care System, 1932

THE DOCTOR and THE PATIENT

THE DOCTOR
WITHOUT A PRACTICE

THE NEEDY SICK
WITHOUT A DOCTOR

Chart No. 12

Adapted from a Cartoon by Rogers in the San Francisco News
Arranged by the National Forum

Published [in *A Picture-Book About the Costs of Medical Care,* 3rd edition] by the Julius Rosenwald Fund because of the demand for information in popular form concerning the economics of medical services. This pamphlet has not been copyrighted. Any of the charts, or the facts contained in this booklet, may be used or reproduced freely. Julius Rosenwald Fund, 4901 Ellis Avenue, Chicago, Illinois.

"The Doctor and the Patient," in *Picture-Book About the Costs of Medical Care,* third edition (Chicago: Julius Rosenwald Company, 1932), found in Sally Lucas Jeans Papers (#4290), the Southern Historical Collection, Wilson Library, The University of North Carolina, Chapel Hill, North Carolina.

Physicians today are given thorough and expensive training in medical schools. The tradition and the ethics of the medical profession place service to the sick above financial return. Physicians are generally ready and anxious to serve patients who need medical care.

Yet the average physician spends one-third of his time idle, waiting for patients.

On the other hand, many people go through serious illness without any professional care. Before the depression, studies covering over 24,000 persons of moderate or small incomes showed that 25 to 30 per cent of these people had gone through a disabling illness—not a minor one—without any care from a physician.

In California, the state which possesses most physicians in proportion to population, about one-third of the people studied in 1934, with family incomes under $1200, had no medical care whatever for disabling sickness.

3. Texas Congressman Maury Maverick Pleads for a National Cancer Center, 1937

Mr. MAVERICK.   Mr. Speaker, every year cancer kills 140,000 Americans. Between four and five hundred thousand are now crippled and helpless, suffering from this disease and awaiting a merciful death to release them. And so today I am going to talk to you about a bill which I have introduced concerning cancer. It provides for the establishment of a national cancer center. . . .

The first thing I will hear is economy. But there is no occasion to talk about economy in reference to this because the establishment of the cancer clinic will cost only three, or at the most, four million dollars to build and equip. Thereafter it will cost a million dollars a year to maintain. This is not a drop in the bucket by the side of other appropriations, normal or abnormal. This bill is good economy and virtually necessary whether times are good or bad. . . .

In the past, great epidemics like bubonic plague and Asiatic cholera ravaged humanity like great wars, but they have been conquered and almost forgotten. I can remember when smallpox was a menace down in Texas. When I was a youngster yellow fever was a menace, and until lately diptheria and typhoid.

Everyone in this Chamber can remember the campaign against tuberculosis, which still goes on. These diseases are known and understood and are under control. The hope that I have is that we may do the same for this terrible scourge of cancer. . . .

Now, let us talk about what is being done and what can be done.

At the present time, many kinds of experiments are being made all over America in cancer. Some work on irritations said to cause the disease. Some have shown it is hereditary in mice; others have made startling chemical experiments. The American Society for the Control of Cancer has done substantial work to educate the people and the profession as to the importance of early treatment. Advances are constantly being made. The American College of Surgeons has reported something like 25,000 permanent cures.

Maury Maverick, "Cancer Bill Is Good Economy," U.S. Congress, House, 75th Congress, First Session, May 25, 1937, *Congressional Record,* Appendix (81): 1318–1319.

But with all these various organizations and persons working, there should be some center for all activities. That is what this cancer bill provides, and it will make possible the accumulation of all this able work by institutions, groups, and individuals with definite coordination and cooperation. It will eliminate duplication of work that has meant great loss of effort, time, and money.

I understand from doctors it has gradually dawned on those most interested that cancer as a disease stands alone. It is not so simple of solution as our great infectious diseases. . . .

My colleagues, I have talked to numerous Members of this Chamber, and I find an exceptionally large number who have relatives who have died of cancer. All of us who were in Congress last year remember with deep affection our colleague, Mr. Jacobsen, of Iowa, whose son has succeeded him in Congress. Our deceased colleague did not even know he had cancer. He went to Mayo's for a checkup, and while there he died. Mr. JOHNSON, the gentleman from Minnesota, tells me that his father died of cancer. Several others tell me their mothers died of cancer. And listen again to this: One out of eight of us who are over 45 will die of it. I do not wish to horrify you, but it is of such grave importance that we certainly should personally consider and understand the subject, and then do something about it. . . .

I am told by doctors that there are only two methods of treating cancer—by surgery or treatment by X-ray and radium.

But the determination as to the correct treatment is a specialization of the highest order. It entails a knowledge of biochemistry, pathology, radiology, X-ray and other sciences. With this amount of knowledge at hand and knowing the situation, it seems to me that the time has come for the American Congress and the American people to stand behind our doctors and scientific laborers, who are working against terrific odds to solve our country's problems; to stand behind the great institutions and our public-spirited citizens who have borne the burden of the research.

And the time has come to stand behind them and to help the great medical profession, fighting this battle by placing at their disposal an institution to be used as a great clearing house for all cancer knowledge. . . .

Let me describe the bill.

It provides for the erection and maintenance of a national cancer center under the supervision of the United States Public Health Service, an institution which has done most distinguished service in America. This protection by the Public Health Service places it above all possible danger of interference by any and all local and self-seeking groups. As I have said, the cost will be very small.

Here are its real proposes:

First.   Its primary function shall be that of aiding in the collection of scientific information, research, and giving to the medical profession the benefit of this knowledge as it becomes available. It in no way interferes with the physician's close relation with the patient and in no way establishes anything like State medicine.

Second.   It brings together forces under one roof, making the availability of data to all parts of America quite prompt, which is otherwise impossible because of the scattered conditions of research laboratories and specialists.

Third.   The center would be a central training bureau for the scientists and technicians, who could then be sent out to man cancer clinics throughout the country.

These various classifications while receiving training could be in constant contact with specialists in varying fields. . . .

Mr. Speaker, this bill will be a great thing, and, as I said before, something that we as Congressmen can be proud of. It is much more noble to fight disease and to provide for human happiness than it is to fight enemies in battle and cause more misery and death. And the happy thing about this, is that although we do not know we can cure cancer, we do know we can do much to correct the situation and probably help control it. We may save the lives of millions of human beings at very small expense in money.

4. Science Writer Paul de Kruif and Surgeon General Thomas Parran Join Forces to Admonish Women About the Dangers of Venereal Disease, 1937

Of all death fights, the battle against syphilis is the most hopeful. The science is here, if we will use it, to make syphilis only an evil memory for our grandchildren. Moreover, the infection of wives and mothers—and transmission of the disease to their unborn babies—is the simplest and the easiest of all the forms of this disease to conquer. But before this battle can be begun, the situation must be bathed by what Dr. Herman Bundesen calls the cleansing light of universal knowledge.

There are facts, grim and hopeful, we must face. There are questions all of us—doctors, health men, husbands, wives, sons, daughters—must ask:

What is the peril of syphilis? What is its extent and prevalence among us? What can science *now* do to fight it? What is not being done today that could be? Why is it that the women of America are in a uniquely powerful position to lead this crusade?

Syphilis has been clamoring to be wiped out, to be really conquered, for a whole generation. Thirty-one years have passed by since the microbe, the pale spirochete of syphilis, was spied through his microscope by the supersharp eye of German searcher Fritz Schaudinn. Thirty years have gone by since the German wizard, Wassermann, devised his delicate blood test. It could spot the trouble in victims who showed no outward sign that they were infected. Twenty-seven years ago Paul Ehrlich cooked up a chemical, called "606," or salvarsan—a chemical that, injected into a syphilis victim, *quickly made him unable to give his sickness to healthy people.*

Then, since this spiral microbe can't generate itself spontaneously, since none can get it except from another human being who has already got it, you ask—why does syphilis exist at all today? With such powerful weapons in their hands, what have our doctors, what have our health men been doing all these years? What have we paid them for? Why is there no evidence that the prevalence of this so-long-ago-preventable plague has notably diminished—in our country—in the past thirty years?

Paul de Kruif and Thomas Parran, "We Can End This Sorrow," *Ladies' Home Journal* (August 1937), pp. 23, 88–90. Copyright © 1937, Meredith Corporation. All rights reserved. Used with permission of LADIES' HOME JOURNAL.

Any enemy, to be conquered, has got to be smoked out into the open. And the plain fact is that the hands of our death fighters have been tied. The plague itself has been hidden by an almost all-pervading hypocrisy—by a mass conspiracy of silence—a secrecy which has been, regrettably, the plague's most powerful friend. Our rank-and-file doctors were ready enough to report a case of smallpox. They were keen to notify authorities of the danger of a patient with open tuberculosis. But being human—feeling the community pressure—our doctors not only hesitated to put the stigma of the moral leprosy of syphilis upon their patients, they went farther—they even refused to suspect their sick ones of the disgrace of being tainted by it.

How, then, could the bulk of our physicians develop the skill to use those known tests to spot the terrible spirochete? Or learn generally to use the powerful chemicals that could stop a woman from passing her doom to a man—or a husband from infecting his wife—or a mother from endangering the babe developing within her? How, when doctors refused even to *suspect* that their patients might be suffering from this hidden disease?

Moreover, the syphilis germ is a treacherous one. It often vanishes underground, so to speak. After little treatment—even after no treatment!—its victim may *feel* fit as a fiddle, with no *evidence* of his illness. What more natural, then, than to neglect the long treatment needed to wipe out every last corkscrew microbe?

And what more dastardly than the way this microbe gangster then sneaks back out of his hiding? So that a husband, having long ago forgotten a past indiscretion, may then infect his wife. So that a mother, unaware the death has ever lurked within her, may pass it to the babe growing in her womb. In the case of many women, the disease does not make itself evident at the time of infection. *For syphilis fighters know that more than half of all women infected, when the blood test spots their sickness, are not aware they have ever harbored this microbe that is waiting to bring doom to their unborn babies.* Indeed, of the men, women and children in our country who suffer from syphilis, a large part of all these millions are absolutely innocent victims of this disease so long thought to be the reward of sin.

The syphilis microbe seems to want its victim to forget about it. Then ten, twenty, thirty years later, it springs to the attack, and the corkscrew germ strikes down humanity's most innocent. With no chance to know or to forfend it, mothers pass spirochetes through their blood to their unborn children, so that these babies are born dead before their time. Or a mother, happy to give the world what seems a healthy baby, may find that within a month it begins to sicken, only to die before it speaks its first baby talk. Or, worst of all—so patient is the syphilis spirochete—a boy or girl may grow to high-school age, husky, and brilliant in studies, with never a sign or an outward hint of syphilitic sickness. Then such a boy, pride of his mother, or such a girl, apple of her father's eye, may sicken, go insane with the terrible dementia called juvenile paresis. . . . Such are the perils of syphilis to the innocent.

You have the right to inquire whether these dangers, admitting that they exist for our children, are not exceptional. What, after all, is the prevalence, the true extent of the syphilitic peril to its innocent victims? Is it really widespread enough to demand that all interested in a stronger, more vigorous American people join in this crusade?

In this grave matter we must be careful to indulge in no wild estimates. We must commit no exaggerations. We must stir up no unfounded fears and suspicions in the hearts and brains of parents. And we must confess here the lamentable limitations of scientific knowledge. We must admit our ignorance of the true extent of the syphilitic danger to the innocent.

How could we be otherwise than ignorant? How could we know how much innocent syphilis exists, when doctors, health men, have never gone out systematically to find it?

Remembering, then, this gap in medical knowledge, this fact we know:

Of pregnant women who are known to be suffering from syphilis, and have not been treated, such women give birth to five babies dead, or syphilitic, for one that is alive and healthy.

But is there any hint at all about how many women of childbearing age harbor this microbe danger within them? There are conjectures, but, it must be admitted, no sure knowledge. Iowa City's syphilis fighter, Dr. P. C. Jeans, many years ago got together figures based upon the blood-testing of more than 5000 married pregnant women. Nearly ten out of every hundred of them showed a positive Wassermann reaction. Yet Jeans himself admitted that this figure could not be said to hold for America as a whole, for these women were "hospital" mothers, not representing a true cross section of our population.

One sure fact emerged from the careful toil of the many skilled obstetricians who now began to make Wassermann surveys of women who were going to have babies. To wit: that each searcher obtained figures that varied from all the others! Colored expectant mothers in some hospitals and isolated areas might, one out of three of them, show positive! And if there is any statistical agreement at all to be found from this maze of figures, it is that syphilis is two or three times as frequent in colored women of childbearing age as it is in their white sisters. . . .

If the danger to pregnant women is only spotted by a sufficiently early blood test, if women can be made to understand the awful chance of disaster to their unborn little ones so that they will begin the treatment early, *and stick to it* till just before their time, till they have been given a certain amount of the life-guarding drug—then *"syphilis in their offspring was not observed."* . . .

Since this science is so sure, then why hasn't syphilis of innocent babies and children begun to vanish from our land?

Why, if science has already known so well so long ago, then how explain the slow mending of this ghastly and now needless slaughter?

But has no progress at all been made? Yes. Where one gets at it, marked progress can be made. For example, at one large city hospital where routine tests have been made since 1915, there has been a reduction of syphilis among their obstetrical cases by 74 per cent. Certain other prenatal clinics, for which we have records since 1930, show a smaller but significant decline.

But how many other communities or states can report a like result? What is the record of the hospitals in your community?

And again, why do 25,000 unborn babies go on dying from syphilis every year, with no nationwide decrease perceptible?

The answer could not be simpler. It is to be found in the lack of general development of prenatal care of mothers. . . .

The women of America can band together to wipe out this infamy. It is their babies who have to do the dying. Theirs is the unforgettable sorrow for all these deaths. They have the care of our present thousands of syphilitic children with bad eyes, or blind, or deaf, or maimed, and, by reason of deformities and stigmas of their disease, in a state to which death would be preferable. Knowing, as they now can know, that this mass tragedy is almost entirely preventable, theirs, too, must be the self-accusation, the bitter "it-need-not-have-been."

They, the women of America, not only have the power to lead this fight; they have the tradition. Famed obstetrician Williams—he is the very one who made the practical prevention of this horror possible—admits that the great movement for prenatal care was not of medical origin mainly: For this lifesaving movement, Doctor Williams gives the credit to Mrs. William Putnam, plain laywoman, of Boston.

Now the wiping out of the syphilis of infancy and childhood is only one special form of good prenatal care. It is just that simple. And the general prenatal care of America's expectant mothers, by America's physicians, scientists and nurses, will be exactly as good as women demand. There are plenty of doctors who, if they are properly paid for it, will be able to perform this service.

In response to such a mass demand, there can be no alibis whatever. . . .

Women can see to it that the prenatal clinics and the dispensaries in all the hospitals of their communities make the blood-testing of all expectant mothers as much a matter of routine as the urinalysis and the taking of blood pressure is now. They can demand the same service of all private physicians; and if women are told that, at their social level, syphilis is rare, they can answer any detractors of their efforts with this basic truth:

The spirochete of syphilis is no respecter of race, creed, color or social station.

And, while they are fighting to make this mighty dragnet of the blood test a universal one, that will gather in every last poor woman who may be endangered, our women can see to it that all such endangered ones have that powerful treatment which has better than nine chances out of ten to bring them a healthy baby. They can bring it about that this treatment in every instance is given at the prenatal clinic itself. . . .

Our bands of crusading women will be asked this awful question:

"For the material for these blood tests: for the experts to make the tests; for the chemicals that we admit can guard your babies; for the skilled doctors to administer these treatments; for the all-important public-health nurses to find all pregnant women and, if they need it, to see that they stick through this wonderful treatment; for the follow-up of the babies to make sure they are not syphilitic, for these essentials, *where are you going to get the money?"*

To this our fighting bands of women can give, not a sentimental but an entirely practical, a hard-boiled, a business answer.

To the mayors and councils of their communities, to the governors and budget balancers of their states, to our national Congress and, yes, to the head of our nation, himself, our women can say:

"We are not demanding the weapons to wipe out this syphilis of the innocent because of our tears for babies born dead who might be alive and strong, or for babies born living but moaning with the pain of this death within them. Nor do we ask you even to sympathize with our sadness for thousands of children with impaired eyes, or blind, or deaf, or crippled, demented when they are preparing for useful citizenship. No. In the name of our anguished taxpayers, we only plead that you, our rulers, be economical.

"For, in unanswerable figures, we can prove that the cost of these babies dying, of maintaining these thousands of children sick, crippled, blinded, deaf, deformed or insane, is many times the cost of wiping out this syphilis of the innocent."

5. President Truman Confronts Congress About the Need for a National Health Program, 1947

To the Congress of the United States:

Healthy citizens constitute our greatest national resource. In time of peace, as in time of war, our ultimate strength stems from the vigor of our people. The welfare and security of our Nation demand that the opportunity for good health be made available to all, regardless of residence, race, or economic status.

At no time can we afford to lose the productive energies and capacities of millions of our citizens. Nor can we permit our children to grow up without a fair chance of survival and a fair chance for a healthy life. We must not permit our rural families to suffer for lack of physicians, dentists, nurses, and hospitals. We must not reserve a chance for good health and a long productive life to the well-to-do alone. A great and free nation should bring good health care within the reach of all its people.

In my message to the Congress on November 19, 1945, I said that every American should have the right to adequate medical care and to adequate protection from the economic threat of sickness. To provide this care and protection is a challenging task, requiring action on a wide front.

I have previously outlined the long-range health program which I consider necessary to the national welfare and security. I say again that such a program must include:

1. Adequate public-health services, including an expanded maternal- and child-health program.
2. Additional medical research and medical education.
3. More hospitals and more doctors—in all areas of the country where they are needed.
4. Insurance against the costs of medical care.
5. Protection against loss of earnings during illness.

I am pleased to observe that important advances were made by the last Congress toward realization of some of the goals which I set forth in my earlier message. But we must not rest until we have achieved all our objectives. I urge this Congress to enact additional legislation to authorize the program I have outlined, even though the fulfillment of some aspects of it may take time.

Our public-health services—Federal, State, and local—provide our greatest and most successful defense against preventable diseases. But in many States, cities, and counties in America, limited funds reduce the work of our public-health services to a dangerously inadequate level. Public services related to maternal and child health were expanded by the Seventy-ninth Congress, through amendments to

---

President Harry Truman, "National Health and Disability Insurance Programs—Message from the President of the U.S.," House, May 19, 1947, *Congressional Record* H261, pp. 5490–5491.

the Social Security Act. This action was gratifying, but the long-range need for additional health services for children and expectant mothers, and for care of crippled or otherwise physically handicapped children, should be carefully studied by the Congress.

The Nation's medical-research programs must in the future be expanded so that we can learn more about the prevention and cure of disease. The Congress has already recognized this by providing for research into the causes of cancer and mental diseases and abnormalities. Further dividends will accrue to our Nation— and to our people—if research can point the way toward combating and overcoming such major illnesses as arthritis and rheumatic fever, and diseases of the heart, kidneys, and arteries.

We still face a shortage of hospitals, physicians, dentists, and nurses. Those we have are unfairly distributed. The shortage of doctors, dentists, and nurses can be met only through expanded educational opportunities. The shortage of hospitals will be met in part through the action of the last Congress which provided Federal aid for the construction of hospitals.

In the last analysis the patient's ability to pay for the services of physicians or dentists, or for hospital care, determines the distribution of doctors and the location of hospitals. Few doctors can be expected to practice today in sparsely settled areas or where prospective patients are unable to pay for their services. Doctors tend to concentrate in communities where hospitals and other facilities are best and where their incomes are most secure. The unequal distribution of doctors and hospitals will plague this Nation until means are found to finance modern medical care for all of our people.

National health insurance is the most effective single way to meet the Nation's health needs. Because adequate treatment of many illnesses is expensive and its cost cannot be anticipated by the individual, many persons are forced to go without needed medical attention. Children do not receive adequate medical and dental care. Symptoms which should come early to the attention of a physician are often ignored until too late. The poor are not the only ones who cannot afford adequate medical care. The truth is that all except the rich may at some time be struck by illness which requires care and services they cannot afford. Countless families who are entirely self-supporting in every other respect cannot meet the expense of serious illness.

Although the individual or even small groups of individuals cannot successfully or economically plan to meet the cost of illness, large groups of people can do so. If the financial risk of illness is spread among all our people, no one person is overburdened. More important, if the cost is spread in this manner more persons can see their doctors, and will see them earlier. This goal can be reached only through a national medical-insurance program, under which all people who are covered by an insurance fund are entitled to necessary medical, hospital, and related services.

A national health insurance program is a logical extension of the present social-security system which is so firmly entrenched in our American democracy. Of the four basic risks to the security of working people and their families—unemployment, old age, death and sickness—we have provided some insurance protection against three. Protection against the fourth—sickness—is the major missing element in our national social insurance program.

An insurance plan is the American way of accomplishing our objective. It is consistent with our democratic principles. It is the only plan broad enough to meet the needs of all our people. It is—in the long run—far less costly and far more effective than public charity or a medical dole.

Under the program which I have proposed patients can and will be as free to select their own doctors as they are today. Doctors and hospitals can and will be free to participate or to reject participation. And a national health insurance plan can and should provide for administration through State and local agencies, subject only to reasonable national standards.

Finally, I should like to repeat to the Congress my earlier recommendation that the people of America be protected against loss of earnings, due to illness or disability not connected with their work. Protection against temporary disability is already provided by two States and is being considered in others. Comprehensive disability insurance should exist throughout the Nation. It can and should be a part of our social insurance system.

The total health program which I have proposed is crucial to our national welfare. The heart of that program is national health insurance. Until it is a part of our national fabric, we shall be wasting our most precious national resource and shall be perpetuating unnecessary misery and human suffering.

I urge the Congress to give immediate attention to the development and enactment of national health and disability insurance programs.

HARRY S. TRUMAN.

THE WHITE HOUSE, *May 19, 1947.*

6. Journalist Bernard Devoto Offers a Public Tour of the AMA's Annual Meeting and a Glimpse into the Mind of the Medical Profession, 1947

Back home—which might have been Iowa or West Virginia or Oklahoma—they probably called him Doc, and most likely Old Doc; for he would be close to seventy, his untidy Van Dyke [beard] was white, his shoulders were stooped and there was a slight tremor in his fingers. . . .

. . . One observer remembers him as clearly as anything else at the Centennial Celebration (and ninety-seventh annual meeting) of the American Medical Association, at Atlantic City in the second week of June.

Everybody else was there too, at least by type and category. There were the elite: bigshots, famous researchers, occupants of celebrated chairs, heads of great clinics and great hospitals, representatives of the various government medical services, Distinguished Foreign Guests. . . . There was every variety of physician and surgeon: young men recently out of the services and bewildered, older men looking for an opening, men of all ages apprehensive about their prospects or about what is happening to "medical economics" or about what is happening to the world.

But mostly they were your family physician, come from everywhere in the United States to Atlantic City, for the purpose of learning something about what has been going on, and for the further purpose of having a good time. . . .

Many acres of the exhibition floor were devoted to what the program called the Technical Exposition: in less scientific words, the advertising display. The program's estimate of "more than 282 firms" seemed conservative and the show was inexhaustibly interesting. It fascinated the profession; at any hour it was much more crowded than the other half of the floor, where the doctors themselves in the Scientific Exhibit displayed the results of their researches.

They had registered officially on arrival and they went on registering at the Technical Exposition, lining up in queues to make sure they got the house's literature. Their pockets gradually filled with comic devices like those you buy at a joke-shop and with samples of proprietaries small enough to be taken away. Samples of poison-ivy salves, vitamin tablets, liquids to be injected for bursitis, Old Doc's potassium iodide in a new and handier form—of the innumerable preparations that have just about relieved the modern physician from any need to study the United States Pharmacopoeia. Samples too of health breads, reducing wafers, dietary soups, a multitude of fruit and vegetable juices recommended for this or that condition, Pet and Carnation Milk, Heinz and Borden baby foods, Similac, Pablum. . . .

Everything that touched the doctor's life or practice was there. He could begin by hiring a receptionist from one of the employment agencies that listed girls who were trained in the techniques of meeting patients and keeping their records straight. He could furnish his waiting and consulting rooms in complete sets or piece by piece. Every conceivable appliance for sterilizing instruments, assisting diagnosis or treatment, or facilitating the routine of medicine was on display—X-ray and fluoroscopic equipment, a "cathode oscillograph," an "infatometer," ampoule openers, a "rhythmic constrictor for the treatment of peripheral vascular conditions," "Tidal Irrigators.". . .

Doctors like something for nothing as much as the rest of us and lined up by the hundred to receive a twenty-cent pack of cigarettes from the Philip Morris Company. While the queue inched forward they could read the placards and graphs that composed "A Tale of Two Cigarettes." This monograph dealt with the rigorously scientific test which had established that the use of diethylin glycol instead of glycerine as a hydroscopic agent makes Philip Morris by a wide margin the healthiest of all cigarettes. It was disconcerting, fifty yards away, to see other hundreds in queues scrutinizing another display which established by a similarly rigorous accumulation of scientific data that most physicians smoke a cigarette which obviously had not proved so healthy in that test. But the Camel Company was not only giving away a twenty-cent pack of its product; it was putting that pack in a ten-cent plastic case with Old Doc's name stamped on it while he waited. . . .

If the Technical Exposition made the medical profession look like the crowd at a county fair, the Scientific Exhibit put it in the light that we and the doctors themselves most like to see it in. Here several hundred exhibits reported on the current progress of medicine, and (since this was the centennial year) a number of others on the progress of a century, and (since this was the AMA) still others on the activities of the bureaucracy. Into these displays had gone a labor and ingenuity that reflected the labor and ingenuity of the researches they were summarizing. Most of them were by hospitals, clinics, research foundations, or medical schools, though a few were by individuals and a few others by societies or institutions not directly connected with organized medicine. Many of them lacked the detail and complexity and doubtless some lacked the authority of similar exhibits at meetings of the medical specialties. But they signalized one of the most heartening realities of life, the steady advance of medical science. . . .

Three theaters ran motion pictures, most of them in color and with sound, of surgical operations, new techniques in anesthesia, diagnostic procedures, and a miscellany of problems in public health, the treatment of convalescents, health education, and related subjects. Such movies have long been used in medical schools and shown at meetings of county medical societies; when it is feasible to make movies they have a quality that the static exhibits cannot achieve. One of them struck an ominous note; it was by the military and it was called "Operation Crossroads." A couple of goats that had survived Bikini were exhibited elsewhere.

For two days the convention met as a whole, morning and afternoon, to hear papers and panel discussions on stop-press news from the research centers by exceedingly distinguished medical men. Thus Sir Howard Florey, one of those who developed penicillin, reported that the evidence did not support a spreading suspicion that micro-organisms could quickly develop immunity to it. Specialists from the Mayo Clinic reported on two substances (one of them taken from fermenting hay) which have sharply reduced the mortality from certain thrombo-embolic conditions—they operate to prevent the formation of blood-clots and to break them up when formed. There were reports on the present status of streptomycin, of drugs used to treat various heart ailments, of experiments in the use of radioactive substances—and so on. . . .

. . . A past-president of the National Association of Manufacturers made a skillful speech. . . .

The past-president of manufacturers had a progressive mind, as he freely confessed, and so he realized that organized medicine must find some way of enabling people with small incomes to procure adequate medical care for themselves—to procure the kind of care for which the convention was repeatedly congratulating itself. He had applied hard thought to the problem, especially in relation to "politicians and reformers." And he had reached a conclusion: that we would be wise to adopt "the voluntary plans for hospital and health insurance" that the AMA recommends.

That was what he was brought to Atlantic City to say. And in the course of his inaugural address the new president of the American Medical Association found occasion to say it again. They were talking about a fearful bugaboo, a national health program, and they were voicing the party line of the present actual rulers of the AMA. In organized medicine there is a general realization that such a program is certain to come, a realization something like that of a town which learns by telephone that a dam up the valley has burst and a flood is on the way. The dam burst long ago and year by year the AMA has prepared to meet the flood by saying that it must not get here, that the flood waters are communistic, that we shall all be lost if they reach the city limits.

Systematically and tirelessly, with all the means available to one of the most powerful pressure groups and propaganda machines in the country, the AMA has opposed every measure in which it detected any connection whatever with what is surely coming. It has done so sometimes suavely, sometimes with amazing crudity, sometimes by individual pressure the most dishonorable, sometimes by flagrant mass appeals the most mendacious. . . .

It is only a few years since the Wagner-Murray-Dingell bill was, in the editorials of the *Journal of the American Medical Association,* pure communism instigated by conspirators in the national government who were acting on orders direct from Stalin. That bill contained six main provisions; since Stalin supposedly phoned his orders to the New Deal the AMA has, by official resolution, indorsed five of them. In 1938 it met with all the ruthless force at its command the challenge to its policies made by the Washington Group Health Association. That fight ended, disastrously for the AMA, in the Supreme Court of the United States, and in 1947 there is no possibility that such methods can be used against such institutions ever again. Many smaller defeats mark the slow abandonment of the impossible position which the rulers of organized medicine at first tried to maintain. All the outposts and subsidiary defences have been surrendered; the rulers are now defending what they regard as the citadel itself.

That ultimate and minimum is this: There must be no federally controlled health program; the program whose coming is seen to be inevitable must be based on states rights. There must be no national imposition of medical standards apart from those which organized medicine itself imposes. There must be no federal control over the practice of medicine and no government or public control of the bodies that will ulti-mately direct the program: all effective power must be reserved to organized medi-cine. There must be no form of *compulsory* health insurance—since this would make the previous provision impossible. There must be no "third party interven-tion," by any nonmedical board or panel or supervisor, between doctor and patient. (Medical third-party intervention is all right and nonmedical third-party intervention is accepted for the poor.) And nothing, at least nothing not a part of organized medi-cine, must interfere with "the free choice of the physician," a freedom which only a minute percentage of our population have now, which that percentage relinquish when they patronize any of the famous clinics, and which only a few of those who have it can exercise except ignorantly and as an act of faith. To sum up: organized medicine insists on complete, unsupervised control of any health program that may evolve; and it requires that plan to interfere with the fee-for-service system as little as possible, not at all wherever there is any way to maintain the system.

This stand, of course, is so unrealistic that is suggests the need of psychiatric scrutiny. Congress will not appropriate funds without providing for supervision of their disbursement, and if the AMA's propaganda were a thousand times as for-midable as it is it could not kid the public into accepting a plan which the public did not itself control. The greatest desideratum of any health program, the practice of preventive rather than remedial medicine, is impossible for most of the popula-tion without some kind of compulsory insurance. And finally without compulsory insurance there is no way of providing complete medical service, except by the group practice which organized medicine disapproves, or by setting the prices of "voluntary" schemes so high that they will be out of the reach of most people. . . .

Scarcity of objective thought, ignorance of economic and social developments, neophobia, docile acceptance of the fuehrer-principle, above all conditioned response in the automatic functioning of institutions which work as propaganda machines at the very moment when they are also working as guilds—these are the group characteristics one generalizes. They make the AMA, in regard to "medical economics" and the greatest single problem with which American medicine must deal, biased, obscurantist, and reactionary to an astonishing degree. But the AMA, like every other human institution, must yield to the pressure of events; and it is yielding now.

After all about thirty-five per cent of the doctors in the United States do not belong to the AMA; that is a sizable group and its attitudes and actions will necessarily influence the AMA's. Moreover, inside the AMA there are many groups whose attitudes toward the big problem are different from the official one, varying from passive dissent to active and sometimes violent opposition. The number and size of such groups are increasing; with whatever reluctance and however slowly, the AMA must maintain with them a working compromise that will constantly give ground, for it cannot afford rebellion and secession. In the county societies (in many ways far more important to the individual doctor than the AMA), the headlong social change of these times is constantly forcing more doctors to practice their profession in ways contrary to the official policies and therefore certain to alter those policies. A comparable influence is being exerted by medical schools and hospitals which have found that federal funds—so subversive and corrupt in the official view a few years ago—are increasingly desirable, and that the individual researcher who is supported by these funds is not a slave after all. From now on some of the ablest groups among the elite of the profession will have only formal reasons for supporting the party line. And there is the inescapable reality that the constant advance of medical knowledge constantly increases the cost of medical treatment and constantly reduces the number of people who can afford to pay for it under the present system. . . .

That seemed to be the moral of Atlantic City: the medical profession, so far as the AMA represents it, badly needs to bring a little of the laboratory method to the study of political behavior, and it needs some realistic instruction in the facts of modern life. Whether it will get them for itself or have them thrust upon it from outside made an interesting question to muse on as one watched the doctors strolling on the boardwalk in the fading afternoon. It seemed, as the former president of the NAM [National Association of Manufacturers] told them, later than they thought.

7. The National Foundation for Infantile Paralysis Instructs Parents and Physicians About Human Trials of a New Polio Vaccine, 1954

About The Trial Vaccine

A safe and promising polio vaccine is being studied now. Hundreds of thousands of children in the primary grades are taking part in tests to prove its effectiveness. After completion of the tests in early June, this vaccine will not be used again in 1954. *There will be none of it for anyone else this year.*

Polio Pointers for Parents, Public Relations Department of the National Foundation for Infantile Paralysis, 1954. Polio Ephemera Collection, Cushing-Whitney Library, Yale University School of Medicine, New Haven, Connecticut.

Only children in counties selected by State Public Health Officers and the National Foundation for Infantile Paralysis could be included in the tests. Not all of them received the vaccine, but the health records of all these children are important to the vaccine study.

After the 1954 polio season is over, a count will be made of polio cases which may occur in the test areas among children who received the vaccine and among those who did not. A comparison will show whether children who received the vaccine actually were protected when polio came to their neighborhood. The results will not be known until sometime in 1955. Until scientists declare this vaccine to be effective, it will not be produced for general use.

This vaccine study is financed by the March of Dimes at a cost of $7,500,000. . . .

50 Questions and Answers on the Polio Vaccine Trials

What Parents Want to Know

. . . 5. What is meant by "controls" in the vaccine trials?

Children of comparable age who will not receive the trial vaccine but whose health histories will be carefully kept for comparison with those who do receive it. Controls are needed to test scientifically how effective the vaccine is in preventing paralytic polio.

6. Who will give the trial vaccine?

Local physicians volunteering through their medical societies in cooperation with local health authorities.

7. Where will the trial vaccine be given?

In the schools.

8. How many doses will be given each child?

Three.

. . . 17. How can parents be certain it is safe?

Before delivery to local Health Officers each lot of the trial vaccine is tested for safety by three independent laboratories: the manufacturer's, Dr. Salk's and the Laboratory of Biologics Control of the National Institutes of Health in Washington.

18. Has the trial vaccine been used on human beings before?

Yes—on thousands in the Pittsburgh, Pa., area by Dr. Jonas E. Salk, who developed it under National Foundation grants to the University of Pittsburgh.

19. How much will it cost to have a child take part in the trials?

The trial vaccine will be given without charge. The trials are being financed with March of Dimes funds contributed by the public. Physicians and nurses as well as local health authorities are volunteering their services.

20. Will all participating children be volunteers?

Yes. Only school children in the designated grades whose parents request they be included will take part.

. . . 26. Why are only certain communities being selected for the vaccine trials?

Because only a limited amount of the vaccine can be made in time for the 1954 field trials and it must be used where chances for valid results seem best.

27. How were these communities selected?

> They were chosen by the National Foundation upon recommendation of State Health Officers. Factors considered were polio incidence during the past five or six years among children in the six-to-nine age group; size of population in each area; local health resources for the conduct of the trials and social, economic and geographical factors to achieve a cross-section of the whole country.

. . . 31. Who will make the evaluation of the tests?

> An evaluation of the effectiveness of the trial vaccine will be directed by Dr. Thomas Francis Jr., chairman of the Department of Epidemiology of the University of Michigan School of Public Health. Dr. Francis, a leading authority on epidemics, has organized a staff of researchers and scientists to conduct this independent evaluation.

. . . 43. Why is a "killed" virus used for the trial vaccine?

> Because a killed virus is safe and three doses of it seem to produce enough antibodies to protect against paralytic polio.

44. Is a "live" virus vaccine against polio contemplated for the future?

> Scientists are working to find one that will stimulate polio-protection quickly without danger of causing the disease. One may be found some day.

45. Will the trial vaccine, if successful, be the final answer to polio?

> No. Scientists will continue to work to improve the vaccine.

46. How does the scope of the polio vaccine trials compare with other such tests?

> It is the largest test of its kind in medical history.

 E S S A Y S

Historians Susan E. Lederer of Yale University and John Parascandola of the United States Public Health Service collaborate in the first essay to examine a revealing moment in public health education. Determined to try new ways to reach the public in the war against syphilis, the USPHS, under Thomas Parran, made the Warner Brothers movie *Dr. Ehrlich's Magic Bullet* part of a national information campaign. As Lederer and Parascandola demonstrate in their analysis of the exchange between Hollywood and Washington, new technologies—be they biomedical innovations such as Ehrlich's syphilis treatment salvarsan 606 or communications breakthroughs such as the motion picture—were changing fundamental relationships in American life, including the one between government and the individual citizen. In the second essay, Harvard University historian Allan Brandt analyzes the discovery, testing, and early distribution of the Salk polio vaccine in the 1950s. His account pays special attention to the role of the National Foundation for Infantile Paralysis (the March of Dimes), shedding light on the tension between the philanthropic and scientific functions of such organizations. Brandt also explores the role that public demand for the vaccine played in this drama. This analytic frame allows Brandt to underscore basic questions about the appropriate role for the federal government in producing and distributing the powerful tools of modern medicine.

Screening Syphilis: Hollywood, the Public Health Service, and the Fight Against Venereal Disease

SUSAN E. LEDERER AND JOHN PARASCANDOLA

In 1940 Warner Brothers Studios released a feature-length screen biography of Paul Ehrlich. The film, *Dr. Ehrlich's Magic Bullet,* starring Edward G. Robinson as the German scientist who introduced the drug Salvarsan for the treatment of syphilis, was both a critical and financial success for the studio. Against the backdrop of the Second World War, both the success of the film and the U.S. Public Health Service's on-going national campaign against syphilis prompted unusual cooperation between Warner Brothers Studios, which produced the film, and the federal agency. The Public Health Service abstracted a segment of the longer popular film to create a short film, *Magic Bullets,* which it included in its educational arsenal in the battle against syphilis. Both the making of *Dr. Ehrlich's Magic Bullet* and the subsequent use of the film biography of the Nobel Prize–winning Jewish medical researcher illustrate some of the tensions in public health education and the cultural meaning of sexually transmitted disease in the late 1930s and 1940s.

The decision to make a commercial film about the life of Paul Ehrlich reflected several trends in Hollywood film making and American life in the 1930s. Films featuring doctors, nurses, and hospital settings attracted large audiences. "The dramatization of medicine on the stage and screen was a response to popular tastes already apparent," noted historian Richard Harrison Shryock. The popularity of such films as *Men in White, Women in White,* and *The White Parade* made it seem "as though anything 'in white' was good for box-office returns." At Warner Brothers the box office appeal of such medical films and the studio's success with film biographies made a project on Ehrlich attractive. The Public Health Service's campaign against syphilis, launched by Surgeon General Thomas Parran in 1936, further stimulated the studio's interest in making a film in which that disease figured prominently.

In the 1930s a popular genre at Warner Brothers, like other major studios, was the feature film-length biography, or "bio-pic." In 1935 film makers at Warners had to overcome initial reluctance on the part of studio head Jack Warner in order to make the studio's first bio-pic about an eminent scientist. Although Warner, for example, had initially opposed making a film about "the story of a milkman," the decision to go ahead with *The Story of Louis Pasteur* proved enormously profitable for the studio. Not only did the film receive three Academy Awards, including Best Actor for Paul Muni in the title role, but the *New York Times* listed *Pasteur* as one of the best films of 1936. Even though the studio, convinced that the film would not attract an audience, had marketed the film to exhibitors for less than the usual percentage, *Pasteur* also proved to be one of the top moneymakers of 1936. More than that, however, a "prestige picture" like *Pasteur* enabled Warner Brothers to modify its image as purveyor of movies emphasizing gangster violence, crime, and sexual innuendo.

Susan E. Lederer and John Parascandola, "Screening Syphilis: Dr. Ehrlich's Magic Bullet Meets the Public Health Service," *Journal of the History of Medicine* 53 (1998): 343–370. Reprinted by permission of Oxford University Press and the author.

Following the success of the Pasteur film, production teams looked to other medical figures as potential screen projects. Film makers at Warners, for example, discussed and eventually discarded film biographies of Sigmund Freud, Joseph Lister, Joseph Goldberger, and Ignaz Semmelweis. The studio eventually released two additional medical screen biographies: the 1936 bio-pic of Florence Nightingale (*The White Angel*), a box-office failure; and, in 1940, *Dr. Ehrlich's Magic Bullet.*

The life of Ehrlich attracted studio interest in several ways. Like Pasteur, the German scientist was already well known to American popular audiences through his inclusion in medical writer Paul de Kruif's phenomenally successful *Microbe Hunters,* first published in 1926. Indeed, one can trace a de Kruifian connection to many of the screen treatments of medical science in the 1930s. . . . Paul de Kruif, who concluded *Microbe Hunters* with the chapter "Paul Ehrlich—The Magic Bullet," in fact attended a meeting in 1938 at which Surgeon General Parran discussed the possibility of a film about the discovery of a cure for syphilis with Will Hays, head of the Motion Picture Producers and Distributors of America.

As Parran's involvement implies, the syphilis theme also made the selection of Ehrlich as the leading character in a film attractive to the studio, enabling Warner Brothers to capitalize on the growing national preoccupation with venereal disease. Parran's campaign against syphilis was well known at Warner Brothers by 1938. Not only was "the shadow on the land," as Parran called the disease in his 1937 book of that title, the subject of articles in such popular magazines as *Ladies' Home Journal* and sermons in churches throughout America, but, as Warner's story editor Finlay McDermid recalled, "there was sufficient interest in Parran to have [Wolfgang] Reinhardt assign Heinz Herald to the task of looking up information on Parran's life to discover whether Parran himself might not be a suitable figure for a film biography."

Political developments in Germany in the 1930s also fueled the studio's decision to proceed with a film on the German-Jewish Ehrlich. American movie makers depended heavily on foreign markets for profits. When the Nazis came to power in 1933, they introduced a number of constraints on American studios, which maintained offices in Berlin. The Nazi government demanded, for example, that the studios terminate their employment of all "non-Aryans" in their German offices. Moreover, the government instituted a ban on films with Jewish actors and actresses and cut the number of American films that could be shown in Germany to twenty per year. Such changes angered studio head Jack Warner, who, like many Hollywood studio heads, was Jewish. As he worked on the screenplay, writer Norman Burnside developed an "anti-Nazi theme" in the Ehrlich material. "For Burnside's purposes," explained Warner story editor McDermid, "the reason for picking Ehrlich as a protagonist had very little to do with syphilis and its cure. Ehrlich happened to be a great humanitarian and a German Jew. For his part, producer Hal Wallis recalled his anger over Hitler's "widely quoted statement in 1938 that 'a scientific discovery by a Jew is worthless.'" The decision to pursue a film about Ehrlich's career assumed particular poignancy in August 1938, when the National Socialists removed the street sign for Paul Ehrlich Strasse in Frankfort.

Bringing the story of Ehrlich's efforts to develop an effective treatment for syphilis to the screen created considerable difficulty for Hal Wallis and his colleagues at Warner Brothers. No mainstream Hollywood film had ever succeeded in overcoming the strictures of the Motion Picture Code, which explicitly prohibited screen depictions involving sexually transmitted disease. To ensure that film makers followed the Motion Picture Code, Will Hays, President of the Motion Picture Producers and Distributors of America, had created in 1934 the Production Code Administration (PCA), commonly known as the Hays Office. No mainstream Hollywood film could be produced or shown without approval from the PCA and its director, Joseph I. Breen, who closely monitored scripts for depictions of violence and sex, including sexually transmitted diseases.

Despite the fact that an original book or play involved venereal disease, Breen and his staff routinely required studios to make substitutions. In 1934, for example, when RKO Studios sought script approval for the film version of Somerset Maugham's novel *Of Human Bondage,* Breen demanded that the prostitute with whom the disabled medical student falls in love suffer from tuberculosis instead of syphilis. . . . In 1936, when Criterion Pictures Corporation released *Marriage Forbidden,* a medical melodrama based on *Damaged Goods,* Upton Sinclair's 1913 novelization of the play by Eugene Brieux, the film's portrayal of syphilitic infection led the Hays Office to refuse a certificate to the film, a decision with major economic implications, as the film could not be shown in theaters associated with major film companies.

Even before submitting the Ehrlich idea to the censors, Wallis approached both Hays and Parran. When word of Wallis's proposal to make a film about the life of Paul Ehrlich was leaked to the press, the PCA notified the studio that the picture had not been approved. "Sex hygiene and venereal disease are not proper subjects for motion pictures," Breen informed the producers. Not content with the rejection, Wallis, who had already locked horns with the PCA over censorship issues, appealed directly to Hays. Persuaded by Wallis that the film was a biography of Ehrlich and not a treatment of venereal disease, Hays issued a special executive order allowing the studio to proceed with the film, but only after extracting a number of conditions from the producers, including changing the film's title from *Test 606* to *Dr. Ehrlich's Magic Bullet.* (Precisely why this particular change was deemed necessary is not clear.) For his part, Wallis agreed not to send out any advertising, exploitation, or publicity matter on the subject of syphilis, sex hygiene, or venereal disease. He also promised to reduce the number of references to venereal disease to a minimum, and to "rewrite the script and change, or eliminate, any clinical scenes involving syphilis patients or treatment of syphilis so that they will not be objectionable." . . .

Once the film had been approved, the research department at Warner Brothers began to compile extensive notebooks, known as "bibles," on Ehrlich, his laboratory, and other details required by the film makers. In addition to consulting *Reader's Guide to Periodical Literature* for references to syphilis in the years July 1937 to June 1939, the research department contacted members of the Ehrlich family. Warners paid the sum of $1,000 to Martha Marquardt, Ehrlich's longtime secretary, "for the right to represent and impersonate her in the photoplay and to use material contained in a published memoir on Ehrlich, which she had written." The studio also paid $42,500 to Ehrlich's widow (with the consent of her daughters and grandson) for the rights to represent Ehrlich's private life on screen. With the details accumulated from Ehrlich's family and staff, the film makers were able to re-create, in "the most painstakingly real and accurate settings ever built in Hollywood," laboratory sequences in Berlin and Frankfort.

As part of its investment in authenticity, studio make-up artists took considerable pains to enhance the physical similarities of Ehrlich and Edward G. Robinson, aided by recollections and insights from Hedwig Ehrlich, the scientist's widow. The research department continued to field a number of queries from the film makers during the production period. They answered questions about whether laboratory workers wore rubber gloves in 1910 and the exact date when gummed labels used for identifying the contents of laboratory glassware came into use. The department supplied information about the normal respiration, pulse, and body temperature (in both Fahrenheit and centigrade scales) of the experimental horses, guinea pigs, and snakes used in the production, as well as illustrations of Ehrlich's side-chain theory and a précis of ethical arguments both for and against animal experimentation. As further testimony to their desire for accuracy, film makers brought in several technical advisers. In addition to chemist Stanley Fox, two physicians, whose "professional ethics" forbade their receiving credit, offered expert advice on both scientific and medical subjects. According to the film's production notes, "the only color in the film was used to make the shots of bacteria absolutely authentic and life-like." The studio's self-conscious stake in historicity illustrates the extent to which authenticity became a marketing tool and why even such trivial matters as the weight of a guinea pig used in Ehrlich's laboratory received respectful attention from the research department.

The studio's scruples did not extend to accuracy in the historical events portrayed. As historian Fred Andersen has demonstrated recently, Warner Brothers (and other studios as well) was more concerned about authentic period sets and costumes in its bio-pics than with chronology or characters. . . . For Warners and other studios of the period, the creation of verisimilitude took precedence over the historical accuracy of events and actors.

For *Dr. Ehrlich's Magic Bullet,* film makers similarly invented several incidents to dramatize the scientist's commitment to discovering a cure for the scourge of syphilis. Early in the film, for example, Ehrlich is depicted as greatly distressed over his inability to treat the disease successfully when one of the syphilis patients he has just examined commits suicide out of despair. Yet no such incident is mentioned in standard biographies of Ehrlich; moreover, Ehrlich never worked in a dermatological clinic of a hospital as shown on screen. The scene in which Ehrlich's wife visits wealthy widow Franziska Speyer to seek financial support for her husband's chemical research was another filmic fabrication. According to biographical sources, the suggestion that Speyer fund Ehrlich's chemical research institute was made by Speyer's brother-in-law. Inaccuracies in chronology were also tolerated for the sake of simplification or dramatic effect. The Japanese scientist Sahashiro Hata appears in scenes in Ehrlich's laboratory at the time of the announcement of the discovery of the causative organism of syphilis (1905), although Hata did not actually arrive to work at Ehrlich's institute until 1909. Showing Hata in the earlier scenes, however, enabled film makers to make a point about the intolerance of the German bureaucrats, who criticized Ehrlich's "unGerman" attitude when he questioned the relevance of race in response to a query about why he had hired an "Oriental" to work in his laboratory.

Released in February 1940, the film received glowing reviews. Noting the film's careful treatment of syphilis, Frank Nugent, critic for the *New York Times,* praised Edward G. Robinson's performance as a "famous microbe hunter," and pronounced the film "richly human, lively, as exciting as any venture into the unknown can be—whether it is the unknown of the jungle or the unknown of pathology." *Variety,* too, endorsed the film's "intelligent handling" of syphilis: "Despite its straightforward presentation of the scourge of syphilis during Dr. Ehrlich's research for a cure, there is nothing offensive in either action or dialog. It's a straight clinical discussion and presentation, naturally confined in appeal to adult audiences, but a most effective preachment to youngsters in their late teens and of college age." . . .

Several groups quickly identified the film's potential as an educational tool. In the spring of 1940, the Good Housekeeping Club Service developed a bulletin and study program on the film, which encouraged women's clubs to use the film as an ally in the war on syphilis. Part of a larger series on Great Men of Medicine, the club bulletin emphasized the many "educational ramifications in the study of such a genius as Dr. Ehrlich." These included the film's explanations of elementary biology and chemistry "in terms that even the most unscientific can understand," the promotion of understanding about disease, and the "factual biography of a great man.". . .

In August 1941, Hedwig Ehrlich, who had left Nazi Germany for Switzerland in 1939, emigrated to the United States. Shortly after her arrival in this country, the American Medical Association hosted a reception in her honor, at which Surgeon General Parran gave the ceremonial address. In his remarks, Parran ranked Paul Ehrlich as a hero of the stature of Pasteur and Lister, and labeled the discovery of Salvarsan "the most brilliant in the series of great achievements of modern medicine.". . .

Parran's articles in magazines and his 1937 best-selling book, *Shadow on the Land,* were instrumental in breaking down the taboo in the popular press against the frank discussion of veneral disease. He sought to focus the battle against venereal disease on scientific and medical grounds, rather than emphasizing moral or ethical views concerning sex. However, Parran was by no means unconcerned with the moral aspects of venereal disease. Suzanne Poirier has recently pointed out that the Surgeon General saw "moral prophylaxis" as the ultimate goal for the eradication of syphilis and for the creation of a better world. Since this ideal, which would involve "the social regeneration of a whole people," was not immediately attainable, he emphasized the need to take other preventive measures against the disease. . . .

With the outbreak of war in Europe and the potential for U.S. involvement, Parran stepped up venereal disease control efforts, calling for "a major educational offensive to defend America's armed and industrial defense forces against the threats of syphilis and gonorrhea." As a part of its own efforts to combat venereal disease, the PHS prepared and supported the development of posters, brochures, radio programs, exhibits, and other public information tools. Among the weapons in the anti-venereal disease arsenal of the PHS were motion picture films. The perceived value of films in the campaign was great. "We feel very strongly," noted one PHS officer, "that motion picture films are a most important medium for health education. Well-written and produced films not only command large audiences, but as you know, actually instill more information into observers than does any other teaching aid."

Venereal disease films developed for the campaign included *Three Counties Against Syphilis,* produced for the PHS by the U.S. Department of Agriculture in 1939, and *Know for Sure,* produced for the PHS by the Research Council of the Academy of Motion Picture Arts and Sciences in 1941. *Three Counties Against Syphilis* depicted the work done by the PHS trailer clinic in the fight against syphilis among rural blacks in three Georgia counties and was designed for general lay audiences. *Know for Sure,* a sexual hygiene film aimed at working men, provided explicit information about how to recognize early symptoms of syphilis and stressed the importance of preventive measures against the disease.

At the same time that the PHS was supporting programs like the one in Georgia to diagnose and treat venereal disease in the African-American community and publicizing these programs through films and other media, it was also conducting the infamous Tuskegee syphilis experiment in Macon County, Alabama. In fact, Raymond Vonderlehr, who had been in charge of the field work when the Tuskegee study began in 1932 and later had administrative responsibility for it as Chief of the Venereal Disease Division, played an instrumental role in the development of PHS films concerning venereal disease.

Vonderlehr was also a key figure in bringing Warner Brothers and the PHS together on a project to adapt *Dr. Ehrlich's Magic Bullet* for use in the PHS venereal disease campaign. . . .

Part of Vonderlehr's interest in adapting film to public health education purposes reflected the rapid penetration of movies into many different aspects of American life. As Vonderlehr informed Donald Armstrong, a vice-president at the Metropolitan Life Insurance Company in New York City, the increase in the number of private and 16-millimeter sound units was "phenomenal." In the space of a year, the number of projectors with sound capabilities in the schools of West Virginia alone had grown from 6 to 175. Such an increase struck Vonderlehr as an unparalleled opportunity to bring the fight against syphilis to more and more Americans.

When Warner Brothers produced *Dr. Ehrlich's Magic Bullet,* the Venereal Disease Division of the PHS saw an opportunity to make use of the film in the battle against syphilis. Early in 1941, Vonderlehr visited Warner Brothers in Hollywood to inquire about the possibility that the studio release the picture to the PHS after it had lost most of its commercial value. Vonderlehr envisioned the PHS as producing and distributing a revised, shortened version of the film for educational purposes. . . .

One message in the film which fit in well with Parran's venereal disease campaign was the theme that syphilis is not necessarily "the wages of sin." Parran strongly believed that syphilis and gonorrhea would be conquered only when they could be spoken of openly in "polite society." He complained that the view that "nice" people do not have syphilis and do not speak about it was hampering the campaign against the disease. "He never tired of pointing out," historian Elizabeth Fee has noted, "that respectable physicians, innocent children, and heads of industry were among those infected."

Parran attempted to lessen the stigma of the disease by arguing that it might be transmitted in some cases by kissing and even through such casual contacts as sharing a drinking glass or a cigarette (although admitting that sexual contact was the chief means of spreading syphilis). . . . Emphasizing that syphilis could be "innocently" acquired furthered Parran's goals of convincing victims of the disease to come forward for diagnosis and treatment and encouraging the public to discuss the subject more freely.

Dr. Ehrlich's Magic Bullet includes a dramatic scene where the German scientist is intent on explaining his research to a potential patron at a dinner party. The guests are stunned when Ehrlich utters the word "syphilis." He informs his fellow guests, however, that syphilis is just like any other infectious disease, that it is caused by a microbe, "and people may get it in very innocent ways . . . even from public drinking cups . . . towels . . . public utensils." This scene, which echoes Parran's public pronouncements on the disease, was kept in the eventual PHS version of the film.

The evidence suggests that in private Parran and his PHS colleagues viewed nonsexual contacts as being much less important in the transmission of syphilis than in their public statements. For example, Vonderlehr, responding to the producer of a proposed motion picture at the "direction of the Surgeon General," criticized a synopsis of the film because it placed too much emphasis on "the rare occasions on which the disease is transmitted through the use of inanimate objects." On another occasion, a PHS officer, replying to a letter about a sexual hygiene film, stated that the PHS did not stress the avoidance of kissing as a means of preventing syphilis because the practice was "of relatively minor importance as a means of spreading infection."

Although in 1941 Vonderlehr did not succeed in convincing Warner Brothers to allow the PHS to use the film, he raised the issue again 2 years later, and this time the studio was more receptive to his request, perhaps because the film had by then exhausted most of its money-making potential. Wartime patriotic support for the campaign against venereal disease may have also encouraged the studio's participation. In the summer of 1943, the PHS contracted with Warner Brothers to produce a revised version of *Dr. Ehrlich's Magic Bullet* for PHS use. The adapted version of the film was 30 minutes in length and focused on the portion of the story that dealt with Ehrlich's discovery of Salvarsan and its use against syphilis. No new footage was shot for the PHS version, but where necessary, titles were inserted providing the connecting links between scenes. The PHS version of the film was given the title *Magic Bullets.*

Vonderlehr was convinced that the shortened version of the Ehrlich film would be "one of the most effective weapons in our educational armament." Because the United States was immersed in the Second World War when *Magic Bullet* was produced, the Office of War Information became a major distributor of the film. As in the First World War, venereal disease was viewed as a threat to America's fighting ability, and the film was described as "a definite aid in the war effort—fitting into the Public Health Service's national education and information program on VD (venereal disease)." . . .

For the PHS, the abbreviated version of the motion picture, *Magic Bullets,* was a valued addition to its arsenal of venereal disease educational films. The PHS understood that Hollywood-produced docudramas, with recognized stars, would be more likely to be shown by commercial theater owners, hence reaching a broad public, than poorly funded government documentaries.

Polio, Politics, Publicity, and Duplicity: The Salk Vaccine and the Protection of the Public

ALLAN M. BRANDT

The history of the Salk polio vaccine . . . marks an important episode not only in the growth of immunology, but, most significantly, in the history of public health. The demands made upon the government and the government's response to these demands provide critical insights into the recent course of public health in America. This paper will examine the history of the Salk vaccine in light of the ethical judgments involved.

The vaccine discovered by Salk in 1952 marked the culmination of the efforts of the National Foundation for Infantile Paralysis [NFIP] to secure an immunological agent against polio. The Foundation had grown out of efforts to raise funds for Franklin D. Roosevelt's Warm Springs retreat during the Depression. In consultation with public relations firms, Roosevelt's former law partner, Basil O'Connor, organized a series of "President's Birthday Balls" in 1934 with the slogan: "Dance so that others may walk." . . .

The creation of the Foundation signaled a major new direction in the history of American medical philanthropy. The appeal for funds now utilized sophisticated public relations techniques. Of significance was the dramatic extension of the traditional concept of philanthropy, as the National Foundation now sought funds from everyone, not just the affluent. Radio spots requested that dimes be sent directly to FDR in honor of his birthday on January 30, 1938. More than 2,600,000 dimes "marched" into the White House, inundating the mail room. Thus was coined the title "March of Dimes."

The Foundation pioneered in the techniques of modern fund raising with its mass appeals, use of media, public relations, and a corps of volunteers. The unprecedented doorbell campaign—the "Mothers' March on Polio"—began in earnest; the Foundation put its cadres into the streets. Their ability to raise funds, even during the most trying economic circumstances, must be rated remarkable. By the 1950s the National Foundation had developed the perfect form of philanthropy for the burgeoning consumer culture. The concept of philanthropy as consumerism— with donors promised personal benefits—was to a great degree the contribution of the March of Dimes.

Why did poliomyelitis become the rallying point for millions of Americans? One logical answer is, of course, Franklin Roosevelt's personal battle with the disease. Despite FDR's attempts to conceal his infirmity, a new media age made polio the most prominent of diseases. But Roosevelt merely symbolized a more general perception that polio was a peculiarly American malady. More dangerous in affluent nations, polio became America's target although other diseases and medical afflictions were really more common. An increasingly child-oriented society could not tolerate a disease which crippled its young. . . .

Allan Brandt, "Polio, Politics, Publicity, and Duplicity: Ethical Aspects in the Development of the Salk Vaccine," *International Journal of Health Services* 8, No. 2 (1978): 257–270. Baywood Publishing Company, Inc., Amityville, NY.

There can be little doubt that the Foundation put its funds into the right hands. Through the use of long-term, substantive grants awarded to eminent researchers and institutions, the NFIP insured the continuity of polio research. By 1948 a series of important epidemiological studies had been made under the Foundation's auspices. Most important was the discovery of Drs. John Enders, Thomas Weller, and Frederic Robbins, all of Harvard University, that poliovirus could be cultivated in nonnervous tissue. This Nobel Prize–winning discovery virtually assured that a polio vaccine could be produced. A race, with bitter political and personal overtones, ensued.

Dr. Jonas Salk began his research on polio immunization in 1951 under a grant from the National Foundation. Within a year he had successfully immunized monkeys in his laboratory at the University of Pittsburgh. Confident that he had found the key to immunization in a killed virus vaccine, Salk proceeded to test his discovery on human subjects. The first of these experiments was conducted on children from the D. T. Watson Home for Crippled Children. Risk was reduced by vaccinating these children, who had already had polio and were thus immune prior to injection. Salk inoculated 43 children with no adverse reactions. He later commented, "When you inoculate children with a polio vaccine, you don't sleep well for two or three months."

Salk continued his experiments at the Polk State School, where he again inoculated children with his test vaccine. Unlike the polio victims at the Watson Home, these children, who were mental defectives, had no history of polio and thus much lower antibody titer, significantly increasing the danger of the test. . . .

Fortunately, Salk's confidence in the vaccine was borne out by the results of these initial human tests. But Dr. John R. Paul, in his definitive history of poliomyelitis, pointed out what failure may have entailed:

> Had the experiments gone wrong at this point there might have been a tremendous outcry. Some would have called it unnecessarily hasty to use so many subjects all at once. . . . And others would have called it a crime to subject helpless children and adults to this sort of experimentation.

It would seem from this analysis that an experiment on human subjects is ethical if successful, unethical if a failure—a dubious formulation. No government guidelines or requirements for human testing existed at that time.

Salk's success buoyed his faith in the vaccine. In presenting his findings to the medical community, he was, however, more cautious:

> Although the results obtained in these studies can be regarded as encouraging, they should not be interpreted to indicate that a practical vaccine is now at hand. . . . It will now be necessary to establish precisely the limits within which the effects here described can be reproduced with certainty.

The task of establishing the effectiveness and consistency of the new vaccine would not be Salk's alone.

By the middle of 1953 the National Foundation had begun devising plans for a mass nationwide trial, the largest of its kind ever attempted. The Foundation established a Vaccine Advisory Committee (VAC) of eminent physicians and researchers headed by Tom Rivers to oversee the field trials. The NFIP's decision to conduct such a field trial meant that serious consideration of other forms of immunization, particularly the attenuated vaccine, no longer was possible. The Foundation's position, though clearly understandable in light of the embryonic nature of attenuated vaccine research, sparked controversy and aroused bitterness. From this time onward, criticism of the Salk vaccine would be an indeterminate mixture of scientific judgment and personal animosity.

The National Foundation conducted affairs on a grand scale; the field trials slated for early 1954 were to be no exception. The NFIP with its newly created Vaccine Advisory Committee proceeded to design the trials in a direct, almost autocratic manner. After his initial discovery, Salk found his influence diminishing over subsequent decisions concerning testing, as did a host of other scientific advisers to the Foundation. Basil O'Connor, anxious to move forward with all possible speed within the bounds of safety, pushed the VAC in the singular direction of conducting a definitive test.

Scientific advisers clashed over the design of the trials. Originally, the Foundation planned to vaccinate volunteers and compare the rate of paralytic polio among this group to a control group of nonvaccinated children. This format had the advantage of being easy to administer and evaluate, and in addition gave all volunteers the potential benefit of the vaccine. The Vaccine Advisory Committee insisted, however, that a "double-blind" test was necessary to eliminate the socioeconomic bias of the volunteer group and thus provide a scientifically unassailable evaluation. Under this test, half the volunteers would receive vaccine, half placebo. . . .

Though the National Foundation took full responsibility for the field trials, the VAC commissioned Dr. Thomas Francis of the University of Michigan to evaluate the trials. Francis, a pioneer in the fields of microbiology and immunology, commanded unquestioned respect in the scientific community. The Foundation assured the University of Michigan ample funds to assist in Francis' evaluation. He demanded complete control of the evaluation—with no outside pressure, timetable, or supervision—and O'Connor agreed to these stipulations. Francis also insisted on an injected control group in at least some states. The decision to have Francis assess the vaccine insured an irreproachable trial.

Before a trial could be attempted, however, the difficult transition from an experimental, laboratory-produced vaccine to a consistent, commercially manufactured vaccine had to be negotiated. Until commercial laboratories could produce vaccine, all talk of a field trial was really premature. Although the National Foundation contacted five major pharmaceutical companies to produce vaccine for the field trials, a complete draft of the requirements for production did not evolve until early 1954, only several months before the trials began. The Vaccine Advisory Committee supervised the shift to commercial production, making two critically important recommendations. First, the Committee required that Salk conduct an initial trial on at least 5000 children using commercially produced vaccine before undertaking nationwide trials. And secondly, *all* commercial vaccine for the field trials had to undergo safety tests in three laboratories—the producers', Salk's, and the U.S. Public Health Service's Division of Biological Control.

The decision to test commercial vaccine in the federally operated lab represents the difficulty of the government's position. The government had no legal role in the trial; no license was required for such an experiment. The Food and Drug Administration only required that the test drug be safe, not necessarily effective. A major medical advance was in the making, with the government's only capacity an essentially extralegal one. Moreover, when it came time for the licensing of the vaccine, the Public Health Service would be in the dark. "We wouldn't know enough about the vaccine and the ins and outs of its manufacture," remarked a Public Health Service official. "We would not be able to act on license applications for months. But the public would want action in hours."

With no official role in the testing of the vaccine but badly needing more information, the Public Health Service gladly accepted the functions allocated by the Vaccine Advisory Committee of the National Foundation. Indeed, the Division of Biological Control, under the direction of Dr. William Workman, scrutinized procedures to the point of threatening the trials. Workman and other government officials realized that, although they had no legal sanctions, they had the responsibility of insuring a safe, effective vaccine. Moreover, the National Foundation recognized the importance of having the blessing of the Public Health Service before conducting its trials.

Scientific opposition to Salk's vaccine remained formidable as the trials approached. Some scientists had difficulty duplicating Salk's inactivation process in their own labs, while others questioned the viability of a killed virus vaccine. . . . Dr. Albert Sabin, at work on an oral, attenuated vaccine, became Salk's chief antagonist. Only one month before the field trial was set to begin, Sabin called the test "premature." . . .

More troublesome than this criticism, however, were the continued difficulties of the commercial producers in their attempts to replicate Salk's vaccine *en masse.* Scientists at the Public Health Service's Division of Biological Control harbored serious doubts about the abilities of the manufacturers to produce consistently safe vaccine. This reflected, in part, inexperience in the histopathology of polio. But it also revealed a very real production problem. In March 1954, Dr. William Workman suggested that the field trials be postponed. . . . It should be emphasized, however, that the government had no legal means of postponing the trials. The National Institutes of Health and the National Foundation agreed that, rather than revising the safety tests themselves, companies must produce eleven *consecutive* lots of safe vaccine for any to be acceptable for use. With this agreement, plans proceeded for the field trials.

Despite the persistent opposition within the scientific community, the National Foundation and the press stimulated public optimism for the vaccine's success. The dual role of the National Foundation—philanthropic and scientific—created tensions. The profusion of positive press releases, essential to fill the Foundation's coffers, jeopardized scientific judgments. The National Foundation announced publicly the plans for a mass field trial months before a commercial laboratory had produced any vaccine. . . .

Although Salk and the National Foundation attempted to discourage such optimistic conjecture, [NFIP president] Basil O'Connor's euphoria could not be contained. He declared that the development of the vaccine had brought the fight against polio to the "verge of victory." The *New York Times Magazine* called the trials the "climax of a stirring medical drama."

The vaccine's notoriety undermined the control of the scientific community. The public now clamored for the vaccine, making it increasingly difficult for scientists with reservations to resist the demand for mass testing. Sabin's attacks on the vaccine became more personal in nature: "Let us not confuse justifiable optimism with achievement." And Salk's defense became less scientific: "I have the courage of my convictions. I couldn't do it unless I was more critical of myself than others are of me. It is courage based on confidence, not daring, and it's confidence based on experience." Salk continued to announce that he would take "personal responsibility" for the safety of the inoculation—a courageous, if ill-advised stand. . . .

The National Foundation must bear some of the responsibility for the public fervor which surrounded the field trials. Perhaps the most objectionable of all the Foundation's pronouncements was that the test was exclusively designed to test the efficiency of the vaccine. According to the Foundation, safety had already been conclusively demonstrated. In light of the production difficulties, this was a particularly bold assertion. The NFIP struck the word "experiment" from its literature; this was a "trial" vaccine, not an "experimental" vaccine. Although the test was conducted on a voluntary basis, the *quality* of informed consent is thus highly questionable.

On April 25, 1954 the Vaccine Advisory Committee set up final guidelines, giving its approval for the trials. . . . The next day the field trials began. With more than 1,800,000 children participating, the trials mark the largest clinical test using human subjects in the history of medical science. No medical experiment ever held such public attention. According to a Gallup Poll conducted in May 1954, 90 percent of the American people knew of the field trials, more than could identify the full name of the President of the United States.

The test, conducted in 45 states, used placebo controls in 84 areas and observed nonvaccinated controls in 127 areas. More than 400,000 children received three injections; about 200,000 of these actually received salt-water placebo injections rather than the test vaccine. Along with blood samples to test antibody titer, Dr. Thomas Francis now had the information needed for a conclusive evaluation of the vaccine. . . .

A critical problem faced the National Foundation during this interim period while awaiting Francis' report. Without a federal license (which could not be obtained until the vaccine was finally evaluated) and without advance orders, the pharmaceutical companies could not afford to continue to produce vaccine. It was not difficult to foresee a situation in which the vaccine would be found to be safe and effective, and yet there would be no vaccine available for the 1956 polio season. Basil O'Connor, with typical boldness, ordered $9 million worth of vaccine from six pharmaceutical companies—an expensive gamble on the vaccine's approval. Of course, if the Congress had been willing to allocate funds, this risk could have been avoided. But the government seemed content to let the National Foundation carry the ball.

On April 12, 1955, the tenth anniversary of Franklin Roosevelt's death, Francis released his evaluation, one of the most comprehensive epidemiological studies ever conducted. According to Francis, the safety of the vaccine was "powerfully affirmed." This is an interesting observation in view of the National Foundation's reluctance to consider the trials a test of safety. Francis found the vaccine 80 to 90 percent effective in placebo-controlled areas, slightly less in observed controlled districts. In short, the vaccine appeared to be a tremendous success. The nation celebrated; for many parents, it seemed, the anxious summers were over.

The successful development of the polio shot characterized the Eisenhower years as the moon shot did a later era. The image of the scientist-hero, unhampered by government intervention, held great appeal. The press proclaimed Salk a national demigod, while some colleagues, resentful of all the attention he received, suspected him a demagogue. The vaccine became a perfect cause for an age in which ideology was suspect. The scientific atmosphere of the 1950s was wrought with Cold War overtones. The vaccine, an affirmation of American scientific and technological progress, was viewed as a triumph of the American system. American science, pragmatic and purposeful, demonstrated the continued viability of the promise of American life.

In Washington, Mrs. Olveta Culp Hobby, Eisenhower's Secretary of the Department of Health, Education, and Welfare, signed licenses for six companies to produce vaccine. These companies had, of course, been producing vaccine all along; the licenses gave them authority to distribute it. The National Foundation's vaccination program for school children began immediately, with youngsters who had received placebo during the field trials given top priority. For all intents and purposes this should have been the dramatic conclusion to the conquest of polio. Unfortunately, it was not.

On April 26, 1955, two weeks after Francis' Ann Arbor proclamation of safety, five cases of paralytic polio were reported among children who had just received vaccine. All five victims, it was found, had received vaccine from the Cutter Laboratories in California. Surgeon General Leonard Scheele requested that Cutter recall all its vaccine pending an investigation. Remarkably, the government had no power to order the Cutter Labs to withdraw the vaccine, but Cutter readily complied. The infamous "Cutter Incident" would, however, eventually encompass 25 states and Hawaii, 260 cases of polio, and 11 deaths.

These cases of polio cast an ominous cloud over the Salk vaccine, the National Foundation, the pharmaceutical companies, and the National Institutes of Health. What had gone wrong with the most rigorously tested drug in medical history? The most obvious cause of the problems was that the careful triplicate testing of the field trials had not been continued for the licensed vaccine. Written protocols submitted by the manufacturers to the Division of Biological Control were the only legal requirement. The Division had the right to make spot checks, but did not exercise this option. Moreover, the consistency standards of repeated safe batches which had been devised for the field trials were not required of licensed vaccine. In brief, safety precautions for commercially produced, licensed vaccine fell far short of the guidelines used for the field trials.

During a series of meetings of top virologists and advisers called together by Surgeon General Scheele, it was decided to let the vaccination program continue. But this consensus began to erode quickly. . . . On May 7, Scheele *requested* that the national vaccination program be suspended pending further studies. . . .

On June 9, Scheele released a Public Health Service "Technical Report" on the Salk vaccine, an attempt to explain and correct the problems which produced the Cutter crisis. The "white paper," though not a complete whitewash, was carefully written to avoid directing blame. . . .

The irresponsibility of the Cutter Laboratories must not be overlooked in evaluating the crisis. Repeated difficulties in producing safe vaccine were experienced by the Cutter Labs; 9 out of 27 lots produced had contained live virus and were discarded. Yet Cutter failed to report this inconsistency to the Bureau of Biologics; the company only submitted protocols for batches which passed their safety test. Cutter officials never asked for assistance from NIH or Salk. Their ethical commitment to produce safe vaccine must thus be seriously questioned. But it also must be remembered that they acted entirely within the letter of the law. The NIH had no consistency requirement and did not require reports on discarded vaccine or production difficulties. . . .

. . . The Public Health Service revised the minimum requirements for production in light of the Cutter incident, making them mandatory standards. The Division of Biological Control was reorganized, becoming the Division of Biologics Standards with larger facilities and a fourfold increase in staff. . . .

The Cutter incident exposed the inherent weakness in the argument for governmental laissez-faire with regard to biologics control and pharmaceutical production. The limited role of the federal government clearly reflected the Eisenhower political philosophy. Olveta Culp Hobby eventually lost her job, largely because of the vociferous criticism of her handling of the vaccine program. In addition, the government's action was circumscribed by the minuscule legal powers of the Public Health Service, essentially unrevised since 1902, a time of relatively primitive pharmaceutical production. The government continued to assume that industrial interest in producing a safe product would ensure the public's safety.

In view of the federal government's minor role, the National Foundation assumed massive responsibilities in the development and distribution of the vaccine. Combining the functions of fund-raising, research, testing, and distribution, the National Foundation often found its multiple roles conflicting. Although well-intentioned, the publicity mill created an atmosphere in which demand threatened to outstrip sound scientific decision making. In such an environment, ethical questions can become obscured. The field trial, for example, though brilliantly engineered and promoted, and meticulously evaluated, lacked truly informed consent. . . .

The history of the Salk vaccine, from the initial research through testing and production, speaks clearly to the present. The institutional connections through which a new drug is channeled from laboratory to market remain uncertain, subject to frequent short-circuit. The time between discovery and production has steadily decreased, augmenting the difficulties implicit in regulation. Most importantly, the federal government has failed to keep pace with the rapid innovations in medical and pharmaceutical practice, at great cost to the public welfare.

 F U R T H E R   *R E A D I N G*

Allan M. Brandt, *No Magic Bullet: A Social History of Venereal Disease in the United States Since 1880* (1987).

James G. Burrow, *AMA: Voice of American Medicine* (1963).

Claudia Clark, *Radium Girls: Women and Industrial Health Reform, 1910–1935* (1997).

Alan Derickson, *Black Lung: Anatomy of a Public Health Disaster* (1998).

Elizabeth Fee, "Sin vs. Science: Venereal Disease in Baltimore in the Twentieth Century," *Journal of the History of Medicine and Allied Sciences* 43 (1988): 141–164.

Oliver Garceau, *The Political Life of the American Medical Association* (1961).

Micheal R. Grey, *New Deal Medicine: The Rural Health Programs of the Farm Security Administration* (1999).

James H. Jones, *Bad Blood: The Tuskegee Syphilis Experiment* (1981; 1993).

Steven Kunitz and S. Levy, "Dances with Doctors: Navajo Encounters with the Indian Health Service," in *Western Medicine as Contested Knowledge,* ed. Andrew Cunningham and Bridie Andrews (1997).

M. Susan Lindee, *Suffering Made Real: American Science and the Survivors at Hiroshima* (1994).

David McBride, *From TB to AIDS: Epidemics Among Urban Blacks Since 1900* (1991).

Fitzhugh Mullen, *Plagues and Politics: The Story of the United States Public Health Service* (1989).

David F. Musto, *The American Disease: Origins of Narcotic Control* (1987).

John R. Paul, *A History of Poliomyelitis* (1971).

Monte M. Poen, *Harry S. Truman Versus the Medical Lobby: The Genesis of Medicare* (1979).

Leslie J. Regan, *When Abortion Was a Crime: Women, Medicine, and Law in the United States* (1997).

David Rosner, ed., *Hives of Sickness: Public Health and Epidemics in New York City* (1995).

David Rosner and Gerald Markowitz, eds., *Deadly Dust: Silicosis and the Politics of Occupational Disease in Twentieth-Century America* (1991).

David Rosner and Gerald Markowitz, eds., *Dying for Work: Workers' Safety and Health in Twentieth-Century America* (1987).

Christopher C. Sellers, *Hazards of the Job: From Industrial Disease to Environmental Health Science* (1997).

Jane S. Smith, *Patenting the Sun: Polio and the Salk Vaccine* (1990).

Peter Temin, *Taking Your Medicine: Drug Regulation in the United States* (1980).

Robert A. Trennert, *White Man's Medicine: Government Doctors and the Navajo, 1863–1955* (1998).

Suzanne White, "Mom and Dad (1944): Venereal Disease 'Exploitation,'" *Bulletin of the History of Medicine* 62 (1988): 252–270.

James Harvey Young, *American Health Quackery: Collected Essays* (1992).

James Harvey Young, *The Medical Messiahs: A Social History of Health Quackery in Twentieth-Century America* (1967; 1992).

Rights, Access, and the Bottom Line: Health Politics and Health Policies, 1960–2000

Beginning in the 1960s, health issues became the focus of unprecedented political activity, including both organized party politics and more diffuse grassroots activism. No part of medicine or health remained untouched by this politicalization. Research, institutional structures, and access to care were the most visible targets of new kinds of power politics and policymaking. Yet at the same time the very nature of relationships between doctor and patient and among physicians was profoundly altered. One of the most important yet vexing consequences of this process was renewed attention to an issue that Americans struggled with for most of the twentieth century: Did the fundamental rights of citizenship extend to health? If so, what exactly did the right to health entail? Was it a right to health care, freedom to choose a caregiver, a guarantee of access to insurance coverage, or something more? Did the articulation of such a right disrupt the delicate balance between public and private interests that had been a hallmark of the American system?

Debates over three topics—Medicare, AIDS, and breast cancer—brought the challenge inherent in the notion of health rights sharply into focus. This chapter uses these debates in policy circles and among the general public to explore the changing dynamics and structure of health politics and policymaking in the late twentieth century. One of the most powerful forces shaping this transformation was a reorientation of American medical economics. Fed by post–World War II industrial expansion, the health care industry had, by the 1970s, become a major engine of economic growth and inflation. The federal government's health initiatives of the mid-1960s—most importantly, Medicare and Medicaid—had provided health care access for a large portion of those medically disenfranchised by America's third-party payer system. An ever-enlarging portion of the American labor force was

*absorbed into a vast array of new medical, scientific, and care-providing enterprises.
Profits rose for investors in the health sector, and incomes for many, particularly
specialists in newer high-technology areas, continued to increase.*

*Yet hidden among the rising incomes, expanding hospitals, burgeoning techno-
logical fields, and allied health professions was a profoundly troubling reality. By the
early 1970s costs had begun to escalate dramatically, and none of the schemas tried
by the government or by such private market players as health insurance companies
seemed capable of bringing this inflation under control. Furthermore, in this medical
marketplace many of the mechanisms that had helped to keep a buffer between medicine and commercial activity were altered, and the rules of behavior for most market
actors—particularly doctors and patients—became increasingly complex and tension
ridden. The stakes of health policymaking rose with each point of the Gross National
Product (GNP) that health care costs consumed (14 percent by 1999). At the same
time, the partisan political attention lavished on health topics increased significantly
as Democrats and Republicans vied for support from an electorate worried about
getting health care when they needed it. How is biomedical conflict handled in such
a highly charged political atmosphere? Are political problem-solving techniques
suitable for medical-scientific decision making? What is the role, if any, of the lay
public in resolving these issues?*

 D O C U M E N T S

Arnold Relman, editor of the prestigious *New England Journal of Medicine,* warns
Americans in Document 1 to pay close attention to the rise of what he calls the "new
medical-industrial complex." Playing on a phrase ("the military-industrial complex")
made famous in a 1961 speech by President Dwight D. Eisenhower, Relman raises
the specter of a dangerous combination of business and medicine. Why does the
for-profit health care empire Relman sees looming over the American economy in
1980 represent such a formidable challenge for both policymakers and the general
public? In Document 2, two AIDS posters produced in the 1980s—one for the Milwaukee AIDS Project and the other for the Aid for AIDS campaign of the California
Department of Health Project—present a very different set of questions about public
policy. These images, which combine familiar advertising techniques with health
education messages, are powerful reminders that persuading individuals to modify
their behavior received a crucial part of the government's public health attention.

Document 3, what many consider the most "masterful" speech of President
William J. Clinton's career, was broadcast on prime-time television on September 22,
1993. This speech was the opening salvo in Clinton's ill-fated campaign to craft and
win support for his Health Security Act, which would have created a national health
insurance program. Document 4 explores the issue of access to health care from the
perspective of a family struggling with the Medicare system. In this excerpt from
her 1993 book *Mama Might Be Better Off Dead,* journalist Laurie Abraham charts
the circuitous path that Mrs. Cora Jackson and her family must follow to acquire
health care.

In Document 5, a 1994 report by the Congressional Committee on Government
Operations concerning a revision of the National Cancer Institute's mammography
guidelines for American women, the focus shifts to the politics of scientific research.
This document pulls back the curtain on several important mechanisms of health
policymaking. Document 6, written by C. Everett Koop, arguably one of the most

famous U.S. Surgeon Generals (serving from 1981 to 1989), provides further insight into the policymaking process. In this memoir, Koop provides a compelling portrait of how, during the early 1980s, AIDS came to capture his and the nation's attention.

1. Medical Editor Warns About the "New Medical-Industrial Complex," 1980

In his farewell address as President on January 17, 1961, Eisenhower warned his countrymen of what he called "the military-industrial complex," a huge and permanent armaments industry that, together with an immense military establishment, had acquired great political and economic power. He was concerned about the possible conflict between public and private interests in the crucial area of national defense.

The past decade has seen the rise of another kind of private "industrial complex" with an equally great potential for influence on public policy—this time in health care. What I will call the "new medical-industrial complex" is a large and growing network of private corporations engaged in the business of supplying health-care services to patients for a profit—services heretofore provided by non-profit institutions or individual practitioners.

I am not referring to the companies that manufacture pharmaceuticals or medical equipment and supplies. Such businesses have sometimes been described as part of a "medical-industrial complex," but I see nothing particularly worrisome about them. They have been around for a long time, and no one has seriously challenged their social usefulness. Furthermore, in a capitalistic society there are no practical alternatives to the private manufacture of drugs and medical equipment.

The new medical-industrial complex, on the other hand, is an unprecedented phenomenon with broad and potentially troubling implications for the future of our medical-care system. It has attracted remarkably little attention so far (except on Wall Street), but in my opinion it is the most important recent development in American health care and it is in urgent need of study. . . .

. . . [In] 1968 there were only 769 proprietary hospitals, 11 per cent of the total. However, there has been a steady trend away from individual ownership and toward corporate control. During the past decade the total number of proprietary hospitals has been increasing again, mainly because of the rapid growth of the corporate-owned multi-institutional hospital chains.

There are now about 1000 proprietary hospitals in this country; most of them provide short-term general care, but some are psychiatric institutions. These hospitals constitute more than 15 per cent of nongovernmental acute general-care hospitals in the country and more than half the nongovernmental psychiatric hospitals. About half the proprietary hospitals are owned by large corporations that specialize in hospital ownership or management; the others are owned by groups of private investors or small companies. In addition to the 1000 proprietary hospitals, about 300 voluntary nonprofit hospitals are managed on a contractual basis by one or another of these profit-making hospital corporations. . . .

Arnold S. Relman, "The New Medical-Industrial Complex," *New England Journal of Medicine* 303 (1980): 963–970. An extract comprising two-thirds of the original article prepared by J. Tighe with Dr. Relman's approval. Copyright © 1980 Massachusetts Medical Society. All rights reserved.

Last year the proprietary-hospital business generated between $12 billion and $13 billion of gross income—an amount that is estimated to be growing about 15 to 20 per cent per year (corrected for inflation). A major area of growth is overseas—in industrialized Western countries as well as underdeveloped countries—where much of the new proprietary-hospital development is now taking place. Of the two or three dozen sizable United States corporations now in the hospital business the largest are Humana and Hospital Corporation of America, each of which had a gross revenue of over $1 billion last year. . . .

Proprietary nursing homes are even bigger business. In 1977 there were nearly 19,000 nursing-home facilities of all types, and about 77 per cent were proprietary. Some, like the proprietary hospitals, are owned by big corporations, but most (I could not find out exactly how many) are owned by small investors, many of them physicians. The Health Care Financing Administration estimates that about $19 billion was expended last year for nursing-home care in the United States. Assuming that average revenues of proprietary and nonprofit facilities are about equal, this means that about $15 billion was paid to proprietary institutions. This huge sum is growing rapidly, as private and public third-party coverage is progressively extended to pay for this kind of care.

Another large and rapidly expanding sector of the health-care industry, but one that is even less well defined than the nursing-home business, is home care. A wide variety of home services are now being provided by profit-making health-care businesses. These services include care by trained nurses and nurses' aides, homemaking assistance, occupational and physiotherapy, respiratory therapy, pacemaker monitoring, and other types of care required by chronically ill house-bound patients. The total expenditures for these services are unknown, but I have been told that the market last year was at least $3 billion. . . .

Last year, about $15 billion was spent on diagnostic laboratory services of all kinds. The number of laboratory tests performed each year in this country is huge and growing at a compound rate of about 15 per cent per year. About a third of the diagnostic laboratories are owned by profit-making companies. Most of these are relatively small local firms, but there are a dozen or more large corporations currently in the laboratory business, some with over $100 million in sales per year. . . .

A large variety of services are being sold by newly established companies in the medical-industrial complex. Included are mobile CAT scanning, cardiopulmonary testing, industrial health screening, rehabilitation counseling, dental care, weight-control clinics, alcohol and drug-abuse programs, comprehensive prepaid HMO programs, and physicians' house calls. Two markets that deserve special mention are hospital emergency-room services and long-term hemodialysis programs for end-stage renal disease.

With the decline in general practice and the virtual disappearance of physicians able and willing to make house calls, the local hospital emergency room has become an increasingly important source of walk-in medical and psychiatric services in urban and suburban areas. The use of emergency rooms has increased rapidly in the past two decades and has stimulated the development of emergency medicine as a specialty. Most third-party payers reimburse for services rendered in hospital emergency rooms at a higher rate than for the same services provided by physicians in their private offices. The result has been a vigorous new industry specializing in emergency services. Many large businesses have been established by entrepreneurial physicians to supply the necessary professional staffing for emergency rooms all over the country, and this has proved to be a highly profitable venture. In some cases, large corporations have taken over this function and now provide hospitals with a total emergency-care package. . . .

Long-term hemodialysis is a particularly interesting example of stimulation of private enterprise by public financing of health care. In 1972 the Social Security Act was amended to bring the treatment of end-stage renal disease under Medicare funding. When the new law was enacted, only about 40 patients per million population were receiving long-term hemodialysis treatment in this country, almost entirely under the auspices of nonprofit organizations. Forty per cent of these dialyses were home based, and renal transplantation was rapidly becoming an alternative form of treatment. The legislation provided for reimbursement for center-based or hospital-based dialysis without limit in numbers. The result was an immediate, rapid increase in the total number of patients on long-term dialysis treatment and a relative decline in home dialysis and transplantations. The number of patients on dialysis treatment in the United States is now over 200 per million population (the highest in the world), and only about 13 per cent are being dialyzed at home.

Proprietary dialysis facilities began to appear even before public funding of end-stage renal disease but the number increased rapidly thereafter. These facilities were usually located outside hospitals and had lower expenses than the hospital units. Many were purely local units, owned by nephrologists practicing in the area, but one corporation, National Medical Care, soon became preeminent in the field. This company was founded by nephrologists and employs many local nephrologists as physicians and medical directors in its numerous centers around the country. . . .

This, in barest outline, is the present shape and scope of the "new medical-industrial complex," a vast array of investor-owned businesses supplying health services for profit. No one knows precisely the full extent of its operations or its gross income, but I estimate that the latter was approximately $35 billion to $40 billion last year—about a quarter of the total amount expended on personal health care in 1979. Remember that this estimate does not include the "old" medical-industrial complex, i.e., the businesses concerned with the manufacture and sale of drugs, medical supplies, and equipment.

The new health-care industry is not only very large, but it is also expanding rapidly and is highly profitable. New businesses seem to be springing up all the time, and those already in the field are diversifying as quickly as new opportunities for profit can be identified. Given the expansive nature of the health-care market and the increasing role of new technology, such opportunities are not hard to find. . . .

In theory, the free market should operate to improve the efficiency and quality of health care. Given the spur of competition and the discipline exerted by consumer choice, private enterprise should be expected to respond to demand by offering better and more varied services and products, at lower unit costs, than could be provided by nonprofit voluntary or governmental institutions. Large corporations ought to be better managed than public or voluntary institutions; they have a greater incentive to control costs, and they are in a better position to benefit from economies of scale. We Americans believe in private enterprise and the profit motive.

How logical, then, to extend these concepts to the health-care sector at a time when costs seem to be getting out of control, voluntary institutions are faltering, and the only other alternative appears to be more government regulation.

That, at least, is the theory. Whether the new medical-industrial complex is in fact improving quality and lowering unit cost in comparison with the public or private voluntary sectors remains to be determined. . . .

Can we really leave health care to the marketplace? Even if we believe in the free market as an efficient and equitable mechanism for the distribution of most goods and services, there are many reasons to be worried about the industrialization of health care. In the first place, health care is different from most of the commodities bought and sold in the marketplace. Most people consider it, to some degree at least, a basic right of all citizens. It is a public rather than a private good, and in recognition of this fact, a large fraction of the cost of medical research and medical care in this country is being subsidized by public funds. Public funds pay for most of the research needed to develop new treatments and new medical-care technology. They also reimburse the charges for health-care services. Through Medicare and Medicaid and other types of public programs, more and more of our citizens are receiving tax-supported medical care. . . .

. . . [A] second unique feature of the medical-care market is that most consumers (i.e., patients) are not "consumers" in the Adam Smith sense at all. As Kingman Brewster recently observed, health insurance converts patients from consumers to claimants, who want medical care virtually without concern for price. . . . Hence, the classic laws of supply and demand do not operate because health-care consumers do not have the usual incentives to be prudent, discriminating purchasers.

There are other unique features of the medical marketplace, not the least of which is the heavy, often total, dependence of the consumer (patient) on the advice and judgment of the physician. . . . Probably more than 70 per cent of all expenditures for personal health care are the result of decisions of doctors.

All these special characteristics of the medical market conspire to produce an anomalous situation when private business enters the scene. A private corporation in the health-care business uses technology often developed at public expense, and it sells services that most Americans regard as their basic right—services that are heavily subsidized by public funds, largely allocated through the decisions of physicians rather than consumers, and almost entirely paid for through third-party insurance. The possibilities for abuse and for distortion or social purposes in such a market are obvious.

Health care has experienced an extraordinary inflation during the past few decades, not just in prices but in the use of services. A major challenge—in fact, *the* major challenge—facing the health-care establishment today is to moderate use of our medical resources and yet protect equity, access, and quality. The resources that can be allocated to medical care are limited. With health-care expenditures now approaching 10 per cent of the gross national product, it is clear that costs cannot continue to rise at anything near their present rate unless other important social goals are sacrificed. We need to use our health-care dollars more effectively, by curbing procedures that are unnecessary or inefficient and developing and identifying those that are the best. Overuse, where it exists, can be eliminated only by taking a more critical view of what we do and of how we use our health-care resources.

How will the private health-care industry affect our ability to achieve these objectives? In an ideal free competitive market, private enterprise may be good at controlling unit costs, and even at improving the quality of its products, but private businesses certainly do not allocate their own services or restrict the use of them. On the contrary, they "market" their services; they sell as many units as the market will bear. They may have to trim their prices to sell more, but the fact remains that they are in business to increase their total sales.

If private enterprise is going to take an increasing share of the health-care market, it will therefore have to be appropriately regulated. We will have to find some way of preserving the advantages of a private health-care industry without giving it free rein and inviting gross commercial exploitation. Otherwise, we can expect the use of health services to continue to increase until government is forced to intervene.

It seems to me that the key to the problem of overuse is in the hands of the medical profession. With the consent of their patients, physicians act in their behalf, deciding which services are needed and which are not, in effect serving as trustees. The best kind of regulation of the health-care marketplace should therefore come from the informed judgments of physicians working in the interests of their patients. In other words, physicians should supply the discipline that is provided in commercial markets by the informed choices of prudent consumers, who shop for the goods and services that they want, at the prices that they are willing to pay.

But if physicians are to represent their patients' interests in the new medical marketplace, they should have no economic conflict of interest and therefore no pecuniary association with the medical-industrial complex. . . .

What I am suggesting is that the medical profession would be in a stronger position, and its voice would carry more moral authority with the public and the government, if it adopted the principle that practicing physicians should derive no financial benefit from the health-care market except from their own professional services. I believe that some statement to this effect should become part of the ethical code of the AMA. As such, it would have no legal force but would be accepted as a standard for the behavior of practicing physicians all over the country. . . .

If the AMA took a strong stand against any financial interest of physicians in health-care businesses, it might risk an antitrust suit. Its action might also be misconstrued as hostile to free enterprise. Yet, I believe that the risk to the reputation and self-esteem of the profession will be much greater if organized medicine fails to act decisively in separating physicians from the commercial exploitation of health care. The professional standing of the physician rests no less on ethical commitment than on technical competence. A refusal to confront this issue undermines the moral position of the profession and weakens the authority with which it can claim to speak for the public interest. . . .

The increasing commercialization of health care generates still other serious problems that need to be mentioned. One is the so-called "cream-skimming" phenomenon. . . . [T]here are two types of "cream-skimming": elimination of low-frequency and unprofitable (though necessary) services, and exclusion of unprofitable patients (e.g., uninsured patients, welfare patients, and those with complex and chronic illnesses). The nonprofit hospitals could not employ such practices, even if they wished to do so, because they have community obligations and are often located in areas where there are many welfare patients. Another form of "skimming" by proprietary hospitals, whether intentional or not, is their virtual lack of residency and other educational programs. Teaching programs are expensive and often oblige hospitals to maintain services that are not economically viable, simply to provide an adequate range of training experience. . . .

Another danger arises from the tendency of the profit-making sector to emphasize procedures and technology to the exclusion of personal care. Personal care, whether provided by physicians, nurses, or other health-care practitioners, is expensive and less likely to produce large profits than the item-by-item application of technology. Reimbursement schedules are, of course, a primary consideration in determining what services will be emphasized by the health-care industry, but in general the heavily automated, highly technical procedures will be favored, particularly when they can be applied on a mass scale. Just as pharmaceutical firms have tended to ignore "orphan" drugs, i.e., drugs that are difficult or expensive to produce and have no prospect of a mass market, the private health-care industry can be expected to ignore relatively inefficient and unprofitable services, regardless of medical or social need. The result is likely to exacerbate present problems with excessive fragmentation of care, overspecialism, and overemphasis on expensive technology.

A final concern is the one first emphasized by President Eisenhower in his warning about the "military-industrial complex": "We must guard against the acquisition of unwarranted influence." A private health-care industry of huge proportions could be a powerful political force in the country and could exert considerable influence on national health policy. A broad national health-insurance program, with the inevitable federal regulation of costs, would be anathema to the medical-industrial complex, just as a national disarmament policy is to the military-industrial complex. I do not wish to imply that only vested interests oppose the expansion of federal health-insurance programs (or treaties to limit armaments), but I do suggest that the political involvement of the medical-industrial complex will probably hinder rather than facilitate rational debate on national health-care policy. Special-interest lobbies of all kinds are of course a familiar part of the American health-care scene. The appearance of still one more vested interest would not be a cause for concern if the newcomer were not potentially the largest, richest, and most influential of them all. . . .

If we are to live comfortably with the new medical-industrial complex we must put our priorities in order: the needs of patients and of society come first. . . . How best to ensure that the medical-industrial complex serves the interests of patients first and of its stockholders second will have to be the responsibility of the medical profession and an informed public.

2. Public Health Advocates Plead for AIDs Awareness, 1980s

None of these will give you AIDS.

There is no evidence that a person can get AIDS from handshakes, dishes, toilet seats, door knobs or from daily contact with a person who has AIDS.

For the facts about AIDS, call the Illinois State AIDS Hotline:

1-800-AID-AIDS
It's toll-free and confidential.

Reprinted by permission of AIDS Institute, N. Y. S. Health Department
Printed by Authority of State of Illinois
November 85-300M-50321

Reprinted with the permission of the New York State Department of Health. These documents were used by the Milwaukee AIDS Project and the California Dept. of Public Health's AIDS Project. Posters also reproduced in William Helfand, "Images of AIDS: The Poster Record," in *AIDS and the Historian: Proceedings of a Conference at the National Institutes of Health, March 20–21, 1998* (Bethesda: National Institutes of Health Publication No. 91-1584, March 1991), pp. 82, 90.

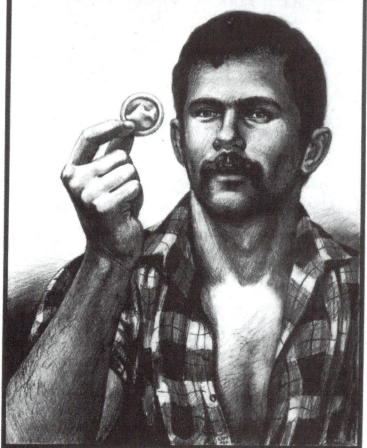

3. President Clinton Calls for a Health Security Act, 1993

The PRESIDENT. Mr. Speaker, thank you very much.

Mr. Speaker, Mr. President, Members of Congress, distinguished guests, my fellow Americans. . . .

. . . [T]onight we come together to write a new chapter in the American story. . . .

. . . [W]e are in a time of profound change and opportunity. The end of the cold war, the information age, the global economy have brought us both opportunity, and hope, and strife, and uncertainty. Our purpose in this dynamic age must be to make change our friend and not our enemy. To achieve that goal we must face all our challenges with confidence, with faith and with discipline, whether we are reducing the deficit, creating tomorrow's jobs and training our people to fill them, converting from a high-tech defense to a high-tech domestic economy, expanding trade, reinventing government, making our streets safer, or rewarding work over idleness. All these challenges require us to change.

If Americans are to have the courage to change in a difficult time, we must first be secure in our most basic needs. Tonight I want to talk to you about the most critical thing we can do to build that security.

This health care system of ours is badly broken, and it is time to fix it.

Despite the dedication of literally millions of talented health care professionals, our health care is too uncertain and too expensive, too bureaucratic and too wasteful. It has too much fraud and too much greed. At long last, after decades of false starts, we must make this our most urgent priority, giving every American health security, health care that can never be taken away, health care that is always there. That is what we must do.

. . . [T]onight I want to talk to you about the principles that I believe must embody our efforts to reform America's health care system: security, simplicity, savings, choice, quality, and responsibility.

When I launched our Nation on this journey to reform the health care system, I knew we needed a talented navigator, someone with a rigorous mind, a steady compass, a caring heart. Luckily for me and for our Nation, I did not have to look very far.

Over the last 8 months, Hillary and those working with her have talked to literally thousands of Americans to understand the strengths and the frailties of this system of ours. They met with over 1,100 health care organizations. They talked with doctors and nurses, pharmacists and drug company representatives, hospital administrators, insurance company executives and small and large businesses. They spoke with self-employed people. They talked with people who had insurance and people who did not.

They talked with union members, and older Americans, and advocates for our children.

President William Clinton, "Health Care Remarks—Address by the President of the United States," House, Wednesday, September 22, 1993, *Congressional Record* H6895. Also, a slightly edited version reprinted in *Solving America's Health Care Crisis,* ed. E. Eckholm (New York: Random House, 1993), pp. 301–314.

The First Lady also consulted, as all of you know, extensively with governmental leaders in both parties, in the States of our Nation, and especially here on Capitol Hill.

Hillary and the task force received and read over 700,000 letters from ordinary citizens. What they wrote and the bravery with which they told their stories is really what calls us all here tonight. . . .

And from them we have learned a powerful truth: We have to preserve and strengthen what is right with the health care system, but we have got to fix what is wrong with it.

We all know what is right. We are blessed with the best health care professionals on Earth, the finest health care institutions, the best medical research, the most sophisticated technology.

My mother is a nurse. I grew up around hospitals. Doctors and nurses were the first professional people I ever knew and learned to look up to. They are what is right with this health care system.

But we also know that we can no longer afford to continue to ignore what is wrong. Millions of Americans are just a pink slip away from losing their health insurance, and one serious illness away from losing all their savings. Millions more are locked into the jobs they have now just because they or someone in their family has once been sick and they have what is called a preexisting condition.

And on any given day over 37 million Americans, most of them working people and their little children, have no health insurance at all.

And in spite of all this, our medical bills are growing at over twice the rate of inflation, and the United States spends over a third more of its income on health care than any other nation on Earth, and the gap is growing, causing many of our companies in global competition severe disadvantage.

There is no excuse for this kind of system. We know other people have done better. We know people in our own country are doing better. We have no excuse. My fellow Americans, we must fix this system, and it has to begin with congressional action.

I believe as strongly as I can say that we can reform the costliest and most wasteful system on the face of the Earth without enacting new broad-based taxes. I believe—

I believe it because of the conversations I have had with thousands of health care professionals around the country, with people who are outside this city but are inside experts on the way this system works and wastes money.

The proposal that I describe tonight borrows many of the principles and ideas that have been embraced in plans introduced by both Republicans and Democrats in this Congress. For the first time in this century, leaders of both political parties have joined together around the principle of providing universal, comprehensive health care. It is a magic moment, and we must seize it. . . .

First and most important, security. . . .

Under our plan every American will receive a health care security card that will guarantee a comprehensive package of benefits over the course of an entire lifetime, roughly comparable to the benefit packages offered by most Fortune 500 companies. . . .

With this card, if you lose your job or you switch jobs, you are covered. If you leave your job to start a small business, you are covered. If you are an early retiree, you are covered. If someone in your family has unfortunately had an illness that qualifies as a preexisting condition, you are still covered. If you get sick or a member of your family gets sick, even if it is a life-threatening illness, you are covered. And if an insurance company tries to drop you for any reason, you will still be covered because that will be illegal.

This card will give comprehensive coverage. It will cover people for hospital care, doctor visits, emergency and lab services, diagnostic services like Pap smears and mammograms and cholesterol tests, substance abuse, and mental health treatment.

And equally important, for both health care and economic reasons, this program for the first time will provide a broad range of preventive services, including regular check-ups and well baby visits.

It is just common sense. We know, any family doctor will tell you that people will stay healthier and long-term costs to the health system will be lower if we have comprehensive preventive services. You know how all of our mothers told us that an ounce of prevention was worth a pound of cure? Our mothers were right.

And it is a lesson, like so many lessons from our mothers, that we have waited too long to live by. It is time to start doing it.

Health care security must also apply to older Americans. This is something I imagine all of us in this room feel very deeply about.

The first thing I want to say about that is that we must retain the Medicare Program. It works to provide that kind of security.

But this time, and for the first time, I believe Medicare should provide coverage for the cost of prescription drugs. . . .

I also believe that, over time, we should phase in long-term care for the disabled and the elderly on a comprehensive basis.

As we proceed with this health care reform, we cannot forget that the most rapidly growing percentage of Americans are those over 80. We cannot break faith with them. We have to do better by them.

The second principle is simplicity. Our health care system must be simpler for the patients and simpler for those who actually deliver health care: our doctors, our nurses, our other medical professionals.

Today we have more than 1,500 insurers with hundreds and hundreds of different forms. No other nation has a system like this. These forms are time-consuming for health care providers, they are expensive for health care consumers, they are exasperating for anyone who has ever tried to sit down around a table and wade through them and figure them out.

The medical industry is literally drowning in paper work. In recent years the number of administrators in our hospitals has grown by four times the rate that the number of doctors has grown. A hospital ought to be a house of healing, not a monument to paperwork and bureaucracy. . . .

I think we can save money in this system if we simplify it. And we can make the doctors and the nurses—and the people that have given their lives to help us all be healthier—a whole lot happier, too, on their jobs.

Under our proposal there would be one standard insurance form, not hundreds of them. We will simplify also, and we must, the Government's rules and regulations because they are a big part of this problem. . . .

And doctors, nurses, and consumers should not have to worry about the fine print. If we have this one simple form, there will not be any fine print. . . .

The third principle is savings. Reform must produce savings in this health care system; it has to. We are spending over 14 percent of our income on health care; Canada is at 10; nobody else is over 9. We are competing with all these people for the future. And the other major countries, they cover everybody, and they cover them with services as generous as the best company policies here in this country.

Rampant medical inflation is eating away at our wages, our savings, our investment capital, our ability to create new jobs in the private sector and this Public Treasury. . . .

. . . [H]ow will we achieve these savings? Rather than looking at price controls or looking away as the price spiral continues, rather than using the heavy hand of Government to try to control what is happening or continuing to ignore what is happening, we believe there is a third way to achieve these savings:

First, to give groups of consumers and small businesses the same market bargaining power that large corporations and large groups of public employees now have. We want to let market forces enable plans to compete. We want to force these plans to compete on the basis of price and quality, not simply to allow them to continue making money by turning people away who are sick or old or performing mountains of unnecessary procedures.

But we also believe we should back this system up with limits on how much plans can raise their premiums year in and year out, forcing people again to continue to pay more for the same health care without regard to inflation or the rising population needs. . . .

The fourth principle is choice. Americans believe they ought to be able to choose their own health care plans and keep their own doctors. And I think all of us agree.

Under any plan we pass, they ought to have the right. But today under our broken health care system, in spite of the rhetoric of choice, the fact is that that power is slipping away from more and more Americans. Of course it is usually the employer, not the employee, who makes the initial choice of what health care plan the employee will be in. And if your employer offers only one plan, as nearly three-quarters of small- and medium-size firms do today, you are stuck with that plan and the doctors that it covers. . . .

We also believe that doctors should have a choice as to what plans they practice in; otherwise citizens may have their own choices limited.

We want to end the discrimination that is now growing against doctors and to permit them to practice in several different plans. Choice is important for doctors, and it is absolutely critical for our consumers. We have got to have it in whatever plan we pass.

The fifth principle is quality. If we reform everything else in health care but fail to preserve and enhance the high quality of our medical care, we will have taken a step backward, not forward. . . .

Our proposal will create report cards on health plans, so that consumers can choose the highest quality health care providers and reward them with their business. At the same time, our plan will track quality indicators so that doctors can make better and smarter choices of the kind of care they provide. . . .

Our plan will guarantee that high quality information is available in even the most remote areas of this country, so that we can have high quality service, linking rural doctors, for example, with hospitals, with high-technology urban medical centers. And our plan will ensure the quality of continuing progress on a whole range of issues by speeding research on effective prevention and treatment measures for cancer, for AIDS, for Alzheimer's, for heart disease, and for other chronic diseases.

We have to safeguard the finest medical research establishment in the entire world, and we will do that with this plan. Indeed, we will even make it better.

The sixth and final principle is responsibility. We need to restore a sense that we are all in this together and that we all have a responsibility to be a part of the solution.

Responsibility has to start with those who profit from the current system. Responsibility means insurance companies should no longer be allowed to cast people aside when they get sick. It should apply to laboratories that submit fraudulent bills, to lawyers who abuse malpractice claims, to doctors who order unnecessary procedures. It means drug companies should no longer charge three times more for prescription drugs made in America here in the United States than they charge for the same drugs overseas. . . .

But let me say this, and I hope every American will listen, because this is not an easy thing to hear. Responsibility in our health care system is not just about them. It is about you. It is about me. It is about each of us. . . .

If we are going to produce a better health care system for every one of us, every one of us is going to have to do our part. There can not be any such thing as a free ride. We have to pay for it. We have to pay for it.

Tonight I want to say plainly how I think we should do that. Most of the money would come, under my way of thinking, as it does today, from premiums paid by employers and individuals. That is the way it happens today.

But under this health care security plan, every employer and every individual will be asked to contribute something to help here.

This concept was first conveyed to the Congress about 20 years ago by President Nixon, and today a lot of people agree with the concept of shared responsibility between employers and employees, and that the best thing to do is to ask every employer and every employee to share that. The Chamber of Commerce has said that, and they are not in the business of hurting small business. The American Medical Association has said that. . . .

To finance the rest of reform, we can achieve new savings, as I have outlined, in both the Federal Government and the private sector through better decision-making and increased competition. And we will impose new taxes on tobacco.

Over the coming months you will be bombarded with information from all kinds of sources. There will be some who will stoutly disagree with what I have proposed, and with all other plans in the Congress for that matter. And some of the arguments will be genuinely sincere and enlightening; others may simply be scare tactics by those who are motivated by the self-interests they have in the waste the system now generates, because that waste is providing jobs, incomes, and money for some people.

I ask you only to think of this when you hear all these arguments: Ask yourself whether the cost of staying on this same course is not greater than the cost of change. And ask yourself when you hear the arguments whether the arguments are in your interests or someone else's.

This is something we have got to try to do together. . . .

So I say to you, "Let us write that new chapter in the American story. Let us guarantee every American comprehensive health benefits that can never be taken away."

You know, in spite of all the work we have done together and all the progress we have made, there are still a lot of people who say it would be an outright miracle if we passed health care reform.

But, my fellow Americans, in a time of change you have to have miracles; and miracles do happen. . . .

Thank you very much and God bless you all.

4. Journalist Laurie Abraham Captures the Human Drama of Medicare, 1993

Since Rose (Jackie called nurses by their first names) was expected later that morning, Jackie decided to change her grandmothers's nightgown. She pulled the pink nylon one Mrs. Jackson was wearing over her head and replaced it with an identical blue-green gown. The whole time, Mrs. Jackson looked straight ahead, her eyes blank, her mouth set in a frown. The elderly woman had raised Jackie, and their recent shift in roles made Jackie uneasy. When Mrs. Jackson first became incontinent, she would stare silently at Jackie when she cleaned her up. "Close your eyes Mama," Jackie told her grandmother. "Don't look at me when I'm doing this." . . .

Rose rang the doorbell shortly after Mrs. Jackson was settled in her chair. The nurse was stopping by to check the stump of Mrs. Jackson's amputated leg, which had not yet healed completely, as well as to monitor her diabetes, high blood pressure, and heart disease. She also needed to check her darkening left toe and her bedsores, one on her buttocks and another one developing on her left heel.

Rose quickly went to work. She put a thermometer in Mrs. Jackson's mouth. While she waited for her temperature to register, she wrapped a blood pressure cuff around her arm. Mrs. Jackson kept her eyes lowered.

Next, Rose crouched down in front of the wheelchair to inspect Mrs. Jackson's foot. "I don't like the color of that toe," she said. But the toe was still warm to the touch and had a pulse, which meant gangrene had not set in.

"You're going to have everything cut off," Jackie said bluntly, perhaps trying to shock her grandmother into conversing with the nurse. Jackie wanted her grandmother to speak for herself; she worried that she might leave something out that could prove important. . . .

Jackie asked Rose whether Medicare or Medicaid would pay for the adult diapers her grandmother needed. Rose said she didn't think either would.

"I'll see you Monday. We'll look at your foot, your stump, and your behind," Rose said to Mrs. Jackson as she left.

Mrs. Jackson nodded.

Nurses, physical therapists, and other health professionals who visit sick people in their homes have become more important because of changes in federal health

Laurie Abraham, *Mama Might Be Better Off Dead: The Failure of Health Care in Urban America* (Chicago: University of Chicago Press, 1993), pp. 44–54. Copyright © 1993 University of Chicago Press. Reprinted by permission.

care financing for the elderly over the past decade. Congress liberalized coverage of home health care services under Medicare in 1980. The change eliminated a hundred-day annual limit on home health visits, as well as a requirement that patients be hospitalized for at least three days before qualifying for home care. A more well-known change that increased the use of home health services was Medicare's introduction of DRGs, or diagnosis-related groups, in 1983. In an attempt to control costs, Medicare began to pay hospitals predetermined rates for patients, depending on their diagnosis. Since hospitals receive a set amount for patients regardless of the cost of care, they have an incentive to discharge patients as soon as possible. The result is that patients who might have spent a few extra days in the hospital recuperating are now discharged "sicker and quicker" and need care from a home nurse. It also means that families are left with the responsibility of caring for more seriously ill relatives, a burden that falls heaviest on poor families like Jackie's, who have few resources to draw upon.

Despite the growth in Medicare reimbursement for home health services—a 24 percent annual rate of increase from 1974 to 1986—expenditures still are mostly for acute, hospital-based care. The $2.5 billion Medicare spent on home care in 1989 accounted for only 2.7 percent of the agency's total expenditures.

Mrs. Jackson and Jackie were expecting another visitor from Mount Sinai's home health agency that day, Sister Mary Ellen Meckley, a social worker who visits homebound patients to assess whether they are receiving the community services available to them. Sister Mary Ellen had not set a firm appointment but was expected sometime that afternoon, so Jackie decided to start on her grandmother's hair. She had just finished loosening her tiny braids, which had grown frizzy, when the buzzer rang again.

Sister Mary Ellen bustled into the living room. "How are you?" she asked Mrs. Jackson cheerfully. The lines around Sister Mary Ellen's eyes crinkled as she smiled; she looked genuinely pleased to see Mrs. Jackson again. The last time she had been out to the house Mrs. Jackson still had her leg; only her foot had been removed.

"All right," Mrs. Jackson said in a low voice that did not attempt to match Sister Mary Ellen's enthusiasm. . . .

Jackie told Sister Mary Ellen that Rose, the nurse, had informed her that neither Medicare nor Medicaid would pay for adult diapers, which cost $45 for a box of forty-eight. "No, no," Sister Mary Ellen corrected her, explaining that Rose was new on the job. "It's Medi*care* that doesn't cover diapers. Medi*caid* covers them. It's crazy."

"*Thank* you," Jackie said, putting a lilting emphasis on "thank" in the way that she does when another person confirms her beliefs.

Medicare pays for Mrs. Jackson's home health services and virtually all of her hospital costs, after she pays a $560 annual hospital deductible. For a $31.90 monthly premium, it also pays for 80 percent of her doctors' bills. The $7,428 annual income she receives from Social Security puts her about $1,400 over the federally defined poverty level, and so she does not qualify for a program Congress created in 1988 to exempt the poor elderly from Medicare's deductibles and copayments.

Ironically, even if Mrs. Jackson were poor enough, chances are she would still be paying those expenses out-of-pocket. A study conducted by a senior citizens' advocacy group concluded that about half of the four million poor elderly thought to be eligible for the extra benefit were not receiving it. That is because it is up to the elderly to apply for the program, and the agency that administers Medicare, the Health Care Financing Administration (HCFA), said it could not afford to identify and contact everyone who might be eligible. . . .

Deductibles and copayments aside, Medicare does not cover many things that Mrs. Jackson and other chronically ill people need, such as medications, transportation to doctors' appointments, and, as was the issue this day, adult diapers. According to HCFA rules, Medicare covers only services or supplies that are "medically necessary." And adult diapers are not, according to an official at HCFA's regional office in Chicago. "They are bought without a prescription; they are more of a convenience," she said. . . . Adult diapers, for instance, can prevent bedsores, as well as allow people to get out of their homes. Another example of shortsightedness, criticized in a report by the Institute of Medicine, a health policy group based in Washington, D.C., was Medicare's denial of coverage for grab bars in bathrooms. They are considered convenience items, although bathroom falls are a leading cause of hip fractures and other often devastating injuries among the elderly. . . .

Though Medicare covers both rich and poor, the poor, of course, are much more vulnerable to its shortcomings. Elderly people more affluent than Mrs. Jackson do not have to worry about coming up with $45 for a box of diapers. They also often retire with supplementary health insurance provided by their employers, or buy "Medigap" insurance, special policies that pay for some of the care Medicare doesn't cover. . . .

Since Medicaid covered the adult diapers, Sister Mary Ellen offered to call a medical supply company to order them. Jackie appreciated her help because the day before she had pored over the Yellow Pages trying to figure out which companies would bill one of the government insurers for the diapers rather than require cash up front.

Jackie's pleasure was fleeting. The suburban medical supply company, Peiser's Medical Supplies and Services, refused to fill the order for the diapers. The clerk said she had no proof Peiser's would be reimbursed by Medicaid. When she punched Mrs. Jackson's name into the computer, "spend-down not met" had popped onto the screen. Mrs. Jackson's $619 monthly income is too high for her to qualify outright for Medicaid. Her spend-down is akin to a deductible, a set amount of money she must spend every month on medical needs before Medicaid kicks in.

Jackie set down her jar of hairstyling grease and grabbed a piece of paper sitting on the hutch. It was a letter she had received from the Illinois Department of Public Aid, which administers Medicaid. It said her grandmother's spend-down had been met nine days earlier, starting the first of the month. . . .

Sister Mary Ellen guessed that Mrs. Jackson's spend-down problem stemmed from a delay at IDPA in entering her eligibility into the computer. But she could only guess because no one answered the phone.

"They're not supposed to go on break until 3:15," Sister Mary Ellen sighed. . . .

Sister Mary Ellen set down the receiver. "I guess the caseworker got an early break."

To get Medicaid without a spend-down in 1989, single elderly and disabled people could not bring in more than $292 a month—what is known as the medically needy level in Illinois. On paper, Mrs. Jackson received $686 from Social Security each month, but she actually got only $619 because Medicare's $31.90 monthly premium was taken from her check as was a deduction for an overpayment she erroneously received in years past. The Department of Public Aid based its calculations on what she was entitled to, however, not what she got, so Mrs. Jackson had to put at least $394 ($686 – $292) toward medical expenses each month in order to get a green card. . . .

It was Jackie's responsibility to gather medical bills or receipts month by month and take them to the local Public Aid office, a chore she understandably did not enjoy, especially since she felt like she was dumping the bills into a vacuum. The Public Aid caseworker told her she need not make an appointment to drop off her grandmother's receipts; she should simply leave them at the front desk. "It might be two days later until [the caseworker] comes to pick them up," Jackie complained. "How am I supposed to know?"

Two days can make a big difference. People become eligible for a green card on the day of the month that their medical bills and receipts show they have met their spend-down. If Mrs. Jackson meets her spend-down on the twentieth of the month, she qualifies that day for the rest of the month. So ten days after she becomes eligible, her coverage expires. As Jackie says, "By the time I get the card, it's time to do it again." . . .

If this all sounds incredibly confusing, that's because it is. Because the United States does not provide a basic level of health care to all its citizens, the country is left with a patchwork of state and federal programs among which inconsistencies are inevitable. People are divided into groups and subgroups, and then divided again. Administrative costs consume up to a quarter of America's health care spending (public and private), whereas they add up to no more than 11 percent in Canada. That country guarantees health care to all its citizens and does not fritter away dollars determining who should get care and, more to the point, who should not.

5. Federal Committee Criticizes Actions of the National Cancer Institute, 1994

From 1989 to December 1993, the National Cancer Institute [NCI] recommended that 40–49 year old women undergo biennial mammography screening, and annual mammography at 50. These recommendations formed the basis of a 1989 consensus guideline formulated by NCI and 12 medical and cancer organizations, including the American Cancer Society. Six years later, without the consensus of these 12 organizations, and against the recommendation of its own national advisory board, NCI eliminated its mammography guidelines for women in the 40–49 age group.

NCI's elimination of its mammography guidelines created a storm of controversy in the medical, scientific and women's health communities. After spending millions of dollars to educate women about the importance of mammography screening in the fight against breast cancer and after reaching national consensus on mammography screening, NCI stood virtually alone with its new proclamation.

Committee on Government Operations, *Misused Science: The National Cancer Institute's Elimination of Mammography Guidelines for Women in Their Forties* (Washington, D.C.: U.S. Government Printing Office, 1994), pp. 1–3, 6–17.

In light of the controversy created by NCI's action, the subcommittee investigated the internal processes at NCI that lead to the elimination of the mammography guidelines for women in the 40–49 age group.

Breast cancer is the leading cause of cancer death for women between the ages of 15 and 54. Based on the NCI SEER data base, the American Cancer Society calculated that in 1992, 40,000 breast cancers were diagnosed in women under 50 and of these cases, 28,900 cases were diagnosed in women between the ages of 40–49. Forty percent of the years of life lost to breast cancer occur in women diagnosed below age 50.

Mammography screening can add years to a woman's life. The American Cancer Society estimates that of the 46,000 breast cancer deaths in 1994, 13,800 women could have been saved with early detection. Women have a 93 percent 5-year survival rate if their breast cancer is diagnosed at the earliest stage. Diagnosis at the earliest stage of breast cancer is generally only feasible through mammography. If the breast cancer has spread regionally at the time of diagnosis, however, the 5-year survival rate falls to 72 percent, and for those with distant metastases at the time of diagnoses, the 5-year survival rate is 18 percent.

African American women are more likely to develop breast cancer between ages 30 and 40. Moreover, African American women have a 25 percent higher death rate from breast cancer as compared to caucasian women, due in part to the lack of access to early detection methods, like screening mammography.

The debate on mammography screening for women in their forties centers around the reliability of the scientific data from randomized clinical trials [RCTs] involving mammography screening. In such a trial, scientists randomly divide large numbers of women into demographically similar groups and then compare breast cancer deaths among screened women to the control group that is not screened. Most scientists agree that RCTs are the best scientific methods for demonstrating the value of mammography screening. However, to date, there have not been any *adequately designed and conducted* prospective randomized trials that can answer the question of whether mammography screening leads to reduced breast cancer deaths in women aged 40 to 49. . . .

In October 1993, the subcommittee began investigating the process by which NCI was revising its mammography guidelines. During a subcommittee hearing on women's health and health care reform, NCI testified that it was "considering whether or not those guidelines should be changed on the basis of the current scientific evidence."

On March 8, 1994, the subcommittee held another hearing to examine the process by which NCI changed its guidelines. Dr. Samuel Broder, the Director of NCI, testified on NCI's behalf. At that hearing, the subcommittee also took testimony from radiologists, medical doctors, the American Cancer Society, the former Director of the Early Detection Branch at NCI, breast cancer survivors under 50 years old, and the mother of a young woman who died of breast cancer at age 22.

On January 13, 1994, the subcommittee requested that NCI send it any and all documents and information relating to (1) NCI's decision to revise its mammography screening guidelines; and (2) NCI's decision not to follow the recommendation of the NCAB to retain NCI's then existing mammography guidelines. . . .

The subcommittee specifically requested all internal memoranda evidencing disagreement and varying analyses within NCI over the revision of the guidelines.

After two written requests for such documents, NCI failed to produce two highly relevant internal memoranda to the subcommittee: one by an NCI employee who found evidence that mammography benefits women between 40 and 49, and a response by his superior informing him to cease any further analysis on this issue so as not to prejudice NCI's work. The employee was later transferred out of the Division of Cancer Prevention and Control. . . .

. . . Publicly, NCI conducted its first review of the data in February 1993. On February 24 and 25, NCI held a 2-day International Workshop with experts on mammography screening. The purpose of this workshop was:

> to conduct a thorough and objective critical review of the world's most recent clinical trial data on breast cancer screening, consider the new evidence, assess the current state of knowledge, and identify issues needing further research.

The report of the International Workshop concluded that, "the randomized trials of women aged 40–49 are consistent in showing no statistically significant benefit in mortality after 10–12 years of follow-up." This report played a critical role in NCI's later actions and became the most important scientific basis for NCI's ultimate elimination of the mammography guidelines for women in the 40–49 age group.

In organizing the International Workshop, NCI used a model almost identical to the National Institutes of Health's [NIH] consensus conference. Generally, NIH consensus conferences are convened for the scientific and medical community to reach consensus on controversial biomedical issues. At these conferences, a broad-based panel listens to scientific data presented by experts, weighs the information, and then composes a consensus statement that addresses a set of questions previously posed to the panel. The conference is designed principally to develop useful guidelines for public health professionals and the public at large.

To ensure that balanced and objective attention is given to an issue, a 13-page set of guidelines governs the planning of the consensus conference. The foremost principle underlying these guidelines is non-partisanship. Accordingly, the consensus panel members who will actually write the recommendations must be carefully screened to exclude anyone with scientific conflicts of interest.

By contrast, the International Workshop lacked important safeguards to ensure the objectivity and the balance that are required of consensus conferences. The subcommittee's investigation revealed that NCI made no attempt to review a broad-based scheme of information at the International Workshop, nor were divergent views given an equal platform. Further, NCI appointed two known advocates of eliminating the guidelines as chair and senior member, respectively, of the International Workshop and as authors of its report. Further, though NCI's prior guidelines were issued with the consensus of the medical, scientific and public health communities, these very same groups were excluded from presenting information at the International Workshop. . . .

. . . Dr. Susan Fletcher, the chair of the International Workshop and author of the report, published an editorial, *while the workshop was being organized* analyzing the trials. In her editorial, "The Breast is Closer to the Heart," Dr. Fletcher concluded that the guidelines for women in their forties should be eliminated. . . .

Dr. Fletcher was chosen to head the International Workshop, less than a month after her editorial appeared. NCI was fully aware of her published article on mammography screening. In his testimony, Dr. Broder attempted to justify Dr. Fletcher's appointment. He said, "In some sense, it is better for Dr. Fletcher to have published her views and let everyone know where she stands, permitting her views to be shot at or objected to in advance under a scholarly format than for her to harbor private views which she doesn't disclose." This explanation is at odds with the principle of objectivity which NIH has established through its consensus conference guidelines.

In addition to Dr. Fletcher, the second senior author of the report, Dr. Sam Shapiro, had come out clearly against screening women 40 to 49 in previous lectures, as well as in his writing. In fact, 1 month after the International Workshop Dr. Shapiro drafted new mammography guidelines for NCI's physician data base that excluded recommendations for women in their forties. . . .

. . . [T]he International Workshop only considered data from the eight RCTs. The NCI organizers of the International Workshop excluded all other information on mammography screening from consideration, including data from NCI's SEER project and also NCI's own Breast Cancer Detection and Demonstration Project [BCDDP] which showed that 40–49 year old women benefited from mammography screening. The BCDDP was the largest study on breast cancer screening ever conducted by NCI. The exclusion of the BCDDP data is inconsistent with NCI's stated intention to gather all the "facts." . . .

. . . To date, the subcommittee has been unable to trace by whom, where and when the actual decision was made. NCI has also been unable to inform the subcommittee whether the decision was actually made at this meeting [NCAB meeting on November 23, 1993] or at another closed-door meeting. . . .

The absence of any documents recording the persons and discussion involved in making such a momentous policy move is troubling to the subcommittee. NCI has not stated what basis it used to overturn the NCAB. Further the fact that no record exists tracing this decision reflects a certain indifference to the import of NCI's new policy. It also suggests an unwillingness by NCI staff to take responsibility for overruling the Presidentially appointed NCAB and for creating NCI's new policy on mammography. Finally, the absence of documentation concerns the subcommittee because it has hindered the subcommittee's ability to conduct oversight and to investigate the internal processes that lead to this decision.

Conclusions

A. NCI's statement regarding the elimination of mammography guidelines have created confusion about the importance of mammography screening. . . .
B. NCI failed to examine objectively all the scientific evidence on mammography. . . .
C. In the process of revising its guidelines, NCI ignored the lack of data on American women, especially minority women. . . .

Recommendations

A. NCI should revise its mammography screening statement to provide a more balanced presentation of the evidence, pending a new conference on the issue which strictly adheres to the consensus conference guidelines. . . .
B. NCI's handling of controversial scientific issues, including screening and treatment guidelines, must be, and appear to be, objective and inclusive. . . .

C. NCI should maintain adequate records of the debates and decisionmaking process to support accountability both as an institution and by the individuals who comprise it. . . .

D. NCI should conduct further research to determine the efficacy of mammography screening on American women, and to pursue more effective early detection techniques.

6. Surgeon General C. Everett Koop Remembers the "Early Days of AIDS," 1995

Early in 1981, when I was designated as Surgeon General of the United States, I had never heard of AIDS. No one had ever heard of AIDS. As a matter of fact, there were only a handful of scientists who understood anything about immunodeficiency, and they did not have a name for it, much less know what it really was.

AIDS entered the consciousness of the Public Health Service (PHS) rather quietly, rather gradually, and with almost no fanfare at all. In June of 1981 the beginnings of what was to become the AIDS epidemic were reported at one of the senior staff meetings at the PHS, and it is now a familiar story. It was the story of those five homosexual males who developed *Pneumocystis carinii* pneumonia (PCP), a disease I had handled in my work with cancer patients at the Children's Hospital of Philadelphia. Five cases is not many, but for that disease (PCP), only a handful sounds like an epidemic, and so it turned out to be. Soon the reports began to trickle in about other cases elsewhere, and a month later, at an agency heads' meeting in the Humphrey Building in Washington, D.C., we had the second report from the Centers for Disease Control (CDC) concerning twenty-six young homosexual men recently diagnosed as having Kaposi's sarcoma. Twenty-six cases in one report, and in my lifetime I had seen but two. There was something very uncommon going on. . . .

By August of 1981, I and others were paying attention to the unusual news from the CDC, and learned that there were now just over 100 cases and that almost half of those affected had died. So I knew—everyone knew—that we were in for big trouble, but there was not much that I could do about it. I was not yet the Surgeon General of the United States. All through that awful summer of 1981, I was preoccupied by my long struggle for confirmation as Surgeon General by the Senate. But I realized that if ever there were a disease made for a Surgeon General, it was AIDS. But, for reasons of intradepartmental politics, which I still do not understand to this day, I was cut off from the inner discussions about AIDS and from making any statements about AIDS for the next three and a half years. I was told that I would have my hands full and that AIDS would become someone else's responsibility.

I was confirmed as Surgeon General in November 1981, but even in those early days of my tenure as Surgeon General, I had to learn about AIDS on my own. I learned about it from the newspapers, and from internal documents of the Public

C. Everett Koop, "The Early Days of AIDS as I Remember Them," in *AIDS and the Public Debate: Historical and Contemporary Perspectives,* ed. Caroline Hannaway, Victoria A. Harden, and John Parascandola (Washington, D.C.: IOS Press, 1995), pp. 9–18. Copyright © 1995 IOS Press. Reprinted with permission.

Health Service, to which, of course, I had access. I also read the *Morbidity and Mortality Weekly Report* and I did have discussions with colleagues.

There were two reasons, I think, why it took awhile for public health authorities to get a handle on AIDS in the beginning. First was the relatively small number of trained clinicians and researchers who were familiar with the rare diseases which were turning up as opportunistic infections, and which were occurring in places like San Francisco, Los Angeles, Chicago, and New York. The second reason was that the first patients with those conditions were homosexual men, most of whom had patronized physicians and clinics that were more understanding of their so-called "gay lifestyle." In making that choice for care, which was quite natural, these men effectively placed themselves outside of mainstream clinical medicine and therefore they were very difficult for us to know—to reach—and, of course, to help. As a result, our first public health priority, to stop the further transmission of the AIDS virus, became needlessly mired in the homosexual politics of the early 1980s. We lost a great deal of precious time because of this, and I suspect that we lost some lives as well.

By July of 1985, the CDC had reported just under 12,000 cases of AIDS and just under 6,000 of those people had died. Then only a week later, I recall that the numbers for both the cases and the deaths had jumped by 100. The AIDS epidemic was definitely progressing, and doing so at an accelerated rate.

. . . There were many charges of foot-dragging in those days, and they still continue in public television shows, but we learned as much about AIDS in the first six years as we had learned about polio in the previous forty. Although we acknowledged that there was much that we did not know, we had made extraordinary progress in understanding what we did know. We had identified the virus; we named it, then we renamed it. We understood the epidemiology relating to homosexual men and about the transmission of the disease through the sharing of the needles and equipment in intravenous drug abuse. We learned of homosexual practices that were hitherto barely mentioned, and we understood, perhaps for the first time, the extent of homosexual promiscuity.

. . . [W]e identified the antibodies to the virus and developed a screening test on the basis of that for the detection of these antibodies. This, in turn, made the blood supply relatively safe for transfusion. We learned how to kill the virus in the blood products and made clotting factors safe again for hemophiliacs.

. . . [A]bove all we were concerned about how the disease was transmitted. . . .

It was clear that, in spite of all kinds of unsubstantiated claims about mosquitoes, toilet seats, door knobs, and so on, AIDS could only be transmitted in four ways: through sexual contact; through blood contact associated with intravenous drug abuse; through pregnancy or delivery—contact between an AIDS-infected mother and her infant; and finally through transfused blood. But the most important information, and perhaps the worst, and the deadliest thing, that we learned, was the news that if a person had AIDS, his or her chances of surviving the next two or three years were not very good, and of surviving much beyond that time were essentially nil.

. . . Eventually my personal distance from AIDS information and policy came to an end when President Reagan asked me to write a report for the American people on AIDS. For the next two years, AIDS took over my life. . . .

I assumed that the report was meant to be simple and to be in language that could be understood by the average citizen; that it was meant to allay the panic of those who were afraid they might get AIDS but were never exposed to it; but it was also to warn those who were engaged in rather risky behavior what the inevitable outcome would be if they encountered the AIDS virus. But I also knew that the government clearance process could ruin any report that I might write and what I needed was the authority to write a report on my own without having it cleared by anybody. That was a very difficult thing to achieve in this government. What made it possible was the nice timing of the arrival of a new Secretary of Health and Human Services, Otis Bowen.

. . . I went to see Dr. Bowen several days after he arrived and told him that if his executive secretariat cleared my report on AIDS, it might come through that process looking like a Surgeon General's report on smoking. I made the brash request that I report only to him and that, when he approved of what I would write, we would jointly carry it to the president. He agreed.

My work in preparing the report amounted to walking a tightrope because I needed to be in touch with all of the national groups that were equally concerned, rightfully, about AIDS. I wanted to make sure that they knew what I was doing. I wanted to be sure that when we published the report they could not say that they had been kept in the dark or were blindsided in any way. But what was equally important was that I needed all the help I could get and I did value their input and advice. . . .

A few of the meetings that I had were especially helpful. The information provided by the National Hemophilia Foundation was absolutely critical. The Foundation's experience with hemophiliacs who had become infected with the virus allowed these tragic cases to be studied very carefully. . . .

. . . Six hundred families were very carefully studied. These family members, over a two-year period, touched each other, used the same utensils for cooking, kissed each other, and some shared razors, without passing the virus. Even in the 7 percent who shared toothbrushes—and that figure surprised me greatly—there was no transmission of the virus from infected patients to their toothbrush partners.

This was very important information. It meant, when joined with the information from other studies, that most Americans were not at risk for AIDS if they did not engage in high risk behavior with sex or drugs. It also meant that persons with AIDS should not suffer discrimination, and that the strident calls for quarantine or the denial of housing, insurance, employment, and public schooling had to be repressed. . . .

. . . [A]t long last, on October 22, I called a press conference and released the AIDS report. Of all the statements that I made, only two words seemed to be remembered: "Sex education." The next few days were spent fending off the press, and answering questions about my ideas on when sex education should begin. Many of the larger issues in that AIDS report were eclipsed temporarily by this distraction. . . .

By the spring of 1987, it had become obvious that one issue would shape official policy on AIDS in the United States, and that issue was testing for the antibodies to the virus. At first the suggestion was to test many people. With a killer disease on the loose, it seemed a good idea to test everybody and see who had it. But a little more thought on the issue fortunately revealed the shortcomings of that rather simplistic solution.

First, what was to be done with those who tested positive? Of course, I had already heard from those congressmen and others who wanted either to kill those infected or to put them in concentration camps. There was that little issue of the Constitution which did not allow the rounding up of people just because they were sick. AIDS became an issue, therefore, not only of health, but also of civil rights.

Widespread AIDS testing could result only in widespread discrimination against people who tested positive. Already the American people, at least those Americans who thought with justice and compassion, were horrified by stories such as that of Ryan White, the schoolboy who was driven by fear and hatred from his school and town in Indiana. Then there was the Ray family in Florida that had three young hemophiliac boys infected with HIV through no decision that they ever made. They suffered not only humiliating discrimination, but they saw their house burned down by arsonists, presumably fearful and hating neighbors.

Above all, mandatory AIDS testing would drive underground and away from counseling the very AIDS-infected people who needed help the most. Those, indeed, who needed help not only with their own health, but who needed help in reforming their behavior so that they would not infect others. Driven underground, these people would only continue to spread the disease. Health officials, unlike some laymen, were adamant about the importance of AIDS testing but knew it would serve its purpose only if the tests were voluntary and absolutely confidential. . . .

I have often noted, and will do so again, that the press did a remarkable and commendable job of communicating the issues of AIDS. The American people learned that, except for babies who got AIDS from their mothers, and except for innocent sexual partners of AIDS carriers who took no precautions, in order to get AIDS they had to engage in risky behavior. Fortunately, that kind of behavior many Americans thought was either illegal, or immoral, or both, in addition to being very risky. . . .

So we entered the third phase of AIDS in America, and that is the phase we are in now, when society, the health care system, and probably each American will have to come to grips with AIDS because of friends, and perhaps even relatives, who die from this horrible disease.

 *E S S A Y S*

The first essay, written by historical sociologist Rosemary Stevens of the University of Pennsylvania, focuses on the passage of the 1965 Medicare legislation and its dramatic impact on the American hospital system. The power of this legislation to reorient the entire medical economy becomes clear in Stevens's account, as does the rapid expansion of the government's influence into health care, which had been for the most part a private sector phenomenon. What does the redrawing of the line between public and private medical endeavors mean to the average citizen and to the nation as a whole? What kind of market has the post-Medicare politics of health created? University of Iowa historian Amy Sue Bix, in the second essay, takes a different tack in analyzing the shifting relationship between public and private aspects of health, comparing the campaigns to fight AIDS and breast cancer in the 1980s and 1990s. These campaigns were two of the most important health care initiatives of the late twentieth century, and, according to Bix, produced a distinctive, new pattern of political decision making. Why are grassroots organizations, like the Women's Health

Initiative and ACT-UP, so important? What does the rising power of these groups mean to the government agencies and medical professionals who formerly handled such questions alone? How do partisan politics figure into this dynamic? Should they?

Medicare and the Transformation of the Medical Economy

ROSEMARY STEVENS

Medicare Parts A and B, which became effective (under PL 89-97) in 1966, provided members of the population sixty-five years and over with substantial hospital and medical benefits; in 1972 the disabled and kidney dialysis and transplant patients were also included. Basic benefits initially included up to ninety days of inpatient hospital care per illness, outpatient care, posthospital care in a skilled nursing home of up to a hundred days per illness, home health services, and physician services, with various deductibles and coinsurance imposed upon patients. Hospitals were guaranteed payment by the program on the basis of "reasonable costs," and Medicaid was initially developed under the same system.

Nationally, the program was administered by the federal Social Security Administration. However, payment of hospitals on behalf of Medicare patients was organized through fiscal intermediaries. These third parties provided a buffer mechanism between the government and voluntary, for-profit, and local-government hospitals. In the negotiations surrounding the legislation the AHA [American Hospital Association] fought for the concept of intermediaries, arguing that the hospitals "needed protection" from the potential iron hand of government agencies. The ideal intermediary, from the hospital perspective, was Blue Cross, with its commitment to the strength and goodwill of the voluntary approach. Under Medicare, hospitals were allowed the privilege of picking their own intermediary; 90 percent chose Blue Cross. In another bow to the existing system, hospitals were guaranteed participation in the federal program by virtue of accreditation by the Joint Commission, as an alternative to government certification.

Thus with stroke of the pen the elderly acquired hospital benefits, the hospitals acquired cost reimbursement for these benefits, the Blue Cross Association was precipitated into prominence as a major national organization (since the national contract was to be with the association, with subcontracting to local plans), and the Joint Commission was given formal government recognition. Simultaneously, through the implementation of federally subsidized Medicaid programs in the various states, the poor, like the elderly, were brought into the "mainstream" of medicine. In theory, at least, most Americans might now be fully insured. . . .

With more than twice as many workers in 1965 as in 1950, hospitals attracted the attention of labor economists as a source of new jobs in an expanding economy, of union leaders looking for new fields to organize and of educational institutions as an outlet for expansion in training. More Americans were working in hospitals in 1960

Rosemary Stevens, *In Sickness and in Wealth: American Hospitals in the Twentieth Century* (New York: Basic Books, 1989), pp. 281–286, 349–350. Reprinted by permission of the author. Copyright © 1989. Reprinted, with an updated introduction, by Johns Hopkins University Press, 1999.

than for the interstate railroad, the automobile industry, or in basic steel. Yet at the same time, major social issues of the early 1960s played across the hospitals' facades: questions of access to care, of equity, of planning, and of public responsibility.

Medicare was a catalyst, testing the organizational resilience and the social altruism of the voluntary enterprise—testing, that is, its essential character. But some lines of development were already evident. Medicare and Medicaid together were to support the voluntary over the governmental hospital system. They affirmed the central importance of the hospital in American medicine, but left to individual hospitals the translation of this importance into networks and systems. There was little to push hospitals much beyond their exciting space-age image on TV. The altruistic aspects of voluntarism remained appealing, as did the continuing strategic connotations: freedom of action, political immunity, local initiative, and noninterference of government in caring for the sick. But maintaining voluntarism carried the paradox of voluntary controls, if strong government controls were to be avoided, as well as opportunities for voluntary initiative.

In Medicare, Congress recognized the central importance of hospitals over other types of health-service organizations. Yet voluntary hospitals borne along over the years by public approbation and increasing revenues, were marked by a series of unresolved tensions: the division between the hospital as an institution and its medical staff of attending physicians; the perplexing role of hospital governance by voluntary trustees, whose business acumen in their individual and several professional roles often vanished in the hospital board room; the maintenance of voluntary hospitals, legally, as tax-exempt, while their role was increasingly as a seller of services; the importance of buildings to demonstrate purpose; the lack of interest in patient-outcome measures; the fact that the hospital was not at risk for bad investment decisions because, increasingly, its costs were reimbursable; the tension between local community involvement and national standards and expectations; the division between acute care and long-term care; and, last but not least, the ambivalence between seeing the hospital as a cog in a major distribution system (with large units and regional networks) and seeing it as a local community institution.

Medicare responded to the prevailing questions, trends, and apparent needs of the early 1960s. Its great expansion made possible by the dollars available for reimbursement was to lead, first, to a rapid expansion in hospital services and expenditures, but along preexisting lines; and second, in sequence, to a focus on capital expansion, an overtly profit-making nexus, huge industrial growth, and federal regulation. The fruits of this process are the hospital system we have today: opportunistic and unsettled; ebullient and nervous; politically attuned and market-oriented. . . .

Medicare gave hospitals a license to spend. The more expenditures they incurred, the more income they received—until the system was changed in the early 1980s. Medicare tax funds flowed into hospitals in a golden stream, more than doubling between 1970 and 1975, and doubling again by 1980. Medicaid, though smaller, was equally expansive. In 1980 the two programs combined spent $35.5 billion on hospital care of all kinds. This was the equivalent of almost half the total expenditures of nonfederal short-term general hospitals. One major result of Medicare was to distinguish further the role of government as purchaser from that of hospitals as sellers of services in the marketplace. Another was a great increase in government power, through recognition of the power of the purse. Later, there was recognition of the similar power vested in major, nongovernmental purchasers, that is, employers.

The most obvious phenomenon of hospital history since 1965 is the over-whelming force of national government policy. This was expressed first in govern-mental pressures on hospitals from the 1970s to seek "private sector" (that is, business) solutions to perceived problems in hospital service. Under the basic (though untested) assumption that economic competition is more efficient than nonprofit enterprise, incentives pushed hospitals toward an industrial model of organization. From the late 1970s through the mid-1980s, the success of for-profit hospital chains on the national stock exchanges seemed to justify this policy of "privatization" and the "coming of the corporation."

The three major hospital sectors—voluntary, governmental, and profit-making—became, oddly, both more alike and more sharply delineated in the fifteen years following the Medicare legislation. All responded to the same signals from the federal government in the shape of Medicare reimbursement regulations, but each had a special challenge to its mission. Profit-making hospitals had to demonstrate that they were benevolent, voluntary hospitals that they were efficient, and local-government hospitals that they were necessary. Although profit-making hospitals, with less than 8 percent of all nonfederal short-term hospital beds in 1980, continued to be a rela-tively small part of the overall hospital system, they became the bellwether institu-tions of the 1970s, buoyed up and swept along by the political and economic conservatism that distinguished the Nixon, Ford, and Carter years.

Medicare and Medicaid—social programs which were designed to maintain the incomes of the elderly and poor—fed the market enthusiasms of the 1970s. It was now permissible (indeed admirable) for voluntary hospitals to post a surplus, indicating effective management. These hospitals were renamed, by the American Hospital Association, to suggest a subtle change in goals: formerly "nonprofit," they were now "not-for-profit." Proprietary, or profit-making, hospitals became "for-profit" or "investor-owned." Articles in major law journals in 1980 suggested that the major distinction between the not-for-profit and for-profit forms of organi-zation was their formal difference in tax status, rather than any necessary differ-ence in role or purpose. However, by stressing their parallelism with for-profit institutions, the voluntary hospitals opened themselves up to being judged by the free-market values of the profit-making system and to having their tax exemption seriously threatened. They were to face, too, the same kind of detailed federal and state regulation that distinguishes American business enterprise, but which voluntary institutions had long been able to avoid under the claim that they were autonomous, moral, "public" institutions.

What happened between the mid-1960s period with its mainstream egalitarian political rhetoric and 1980 with its strong market stance? How did the hospital complex shift so rapidly to market expectations? Three themes stand out. First, the Medicare legislation exposed the weaknesses of traditional vendor payment sys-tems as a vehicle for government entitlement programs. Second, decisions made about capital were key to the profit-oriented direction of all hospitals. And finally, Medicare supported voluntary hospitals as private institutions without giving them countervailing responsibilities—or the money—to operate as public agencies.

The act setting up Medicare specified that there should be "prohibition against any federal interference" with the practice of medicine or the way in which medical services are provided. But this statement was in part wishful thinking, in part legis-lative boilerplate, for a program as large as Medicare, even as initially envisaged, could not help but affect the health-care system. The experience of Blue Cross and commercial health insurance provided the precedent for the potential influence of governmental third parties on hospitals. From the beginning the inflationary potential of Medicare's payment policy was evident to officials in the Bureau of Health Insurance, set up within the federal Social Security Administration to run Medicare. Immediate federal concerns were to implement the program as quickly and efficiently as possible, and this meant insuring hospital cooperation, irrespective of cost. In retrospect, the hospitals, too, had little choice. It would have been foolish to repudiate the certainty of short-term gains for some nebulous expectation of long-term freedom from federal control, which might (or might not) be the consequence of presenting themselves as frugal, quasi-public agencies. Nevertheless, the hospitals put themselves into a box. Medicare, a federal program, would only survive without strong federal regulation as long as it remained relatively small (and thus of politically low visibility) and as long as it could be justified as effectively serving public needs. Neither of these conditions was to be met. . . .

Meanwhile, the overriding importance of financial incentives in hospital service has centralized and concentrated power over money in agencies extrinsic to both hospitals and patients. Economic power shifted in the 1980s from those who provide health services to the organizations that pay for them. But the interests of those served as patients are not necessarily identical with the financial interests of third-party payers. These include major employers, insurers, and specialists in "managed care," whose role is to identify potentially high-cost patients, such as a patient with AIDS, and organize a program designed for efficient utilization of resources. Individuals are being told, in effect, that doctors, as entrepreneurs, and hospitals, as businesses, are no longer to be trusted as agents and advocates for the consumer; but that the large payers *are* to be trusted, even though their goals are overtly the goals of management efficiency.

Hospital policy-making since 1965 has not been a steady, market-directed movement toward an industrial model for the hospital system. It has been a process of trial and error, spurred by federal incentives and restraints, both of which might easily change again in the future. In two respects hospitals have been enormously successful in the past ten years: in continuing to survive and prosper (for the most part) as major, expensive, visible social institutions, and in broadening the services they offer including, among others, incontinence control, rental of medical equipment for the home, menopause centers, centers for back pain, exercise centers, outreach clinics and primary care services, home care, and post-hospital nursing-home care. As a result, hospitals are now better attuned to broad patterns of health and disease—at least for those who can afford the services and choose them wisely—than in any other decade of this century. The hospital has become a multifunction health-care institution, in a constant search for a new market niche.

Nevertheless, accompanying these changes are troubling questions of social ideals and aspirations. Is American medicine now so routine that it has lost the glow of a higher purpose? Are hospitals primarily useful to U.S. culture as embodiments of the values of money, organizational success, and utilitarianism—and no longer important for suggesting cultural, religious, and altruistic aspirations? Do we need hospitals to articulate social class and to create community cohesion and a sense of common purpose? Are patients purely customers, hospitals machine shops, and doctors mechanics? The commercial model for hospitals, largely a product of the 1980s, has in many ways been a success. But it is no accident that the debates in major hospital groups—and elsewhere—are turning to questions of "quality" and "values" in the last few years of the twentieth century.

Breast Cancer and AIDS Activism Revolutionize Health Policies

AMY SUE BIX

Through the 1980s and early 1990s, the course of American health research was increasingly shaped by politically-aggressive activism for two particular diseases, breast cancer and AIDS (Acquired Immunodeficiency Syndrome). Even as national stakes rose, both in dollars spent and growing demands on the medical system, breast cancer and AIDS advocates made government policy-making for research ever more public and controversial. Through skillful cultivation of political strength, interest groups transformed individual health problems into collective demands, winning notable policy influence in federal agencies such as the National Institutes of Health (NIH) and Food and Drug Administration (FDA). Activists directly challenged fundamental principles of both government and medical systems, fighting to affect distribution of research funds and questioning well-established scientific methods and professional values. In the contest for decision-making power, those players achieved remarkable success in influencing and infiltrating (some critics said, undermining) both the politics and science of medical research. Between 1990 and 1995, federal appropriations for breast cancer study rose from $90 million to $465 million, while in that same period, NIH AIDS research rose from $743.53 million to $1.338 billion. . . .

. . . In previous decades, procedures for drug approval and research funding had not commonly elicited detailed public interest or sustained passion. Breast cancer and AIDS activism established FDA and NIH policy as regular topics for media analysis and high-profile public protest. Through activism, policy-making "insiders" (officials and researchers whose claims to expertise were secured by professional acknowledgement) were forced to cede some territory to "outsiders." Breast cancer and AIDS movements affected direction of funding and helped re-write official guidelines for research, testing, and drug approval, even as some scientists complained such changes endangered medical progress. Men and women without specialized education or research credentials found a decision-making place alongside scientists and agency executives. . . .

Challenging medical and agency authority was fundamental to AIDS and breast cancer activism, both as a philosophical commitment and as means for turning frustration over lack of medical advance into political mobilization. Activists operated on the assumption that research was primarily driven not by intellectual curiosity, but by the political climate, which could then be manipulated. They approached science and medicine not as disciplines of expertise to be judged on their own professional terms, but as potentially (if not actually) flawed social and political enterprises. Though scientific and medical workers themselves tended to value research as almost ideal objective analysis, activists accused researchers and federal officials of incompetence and unfairness, if not gender bias, racism, and homophobia. In sometimes conspiratorial-sounding language blaming "the system" for literally playing with lives, activists defined research as fair game for public confrontation. Surgeon/activist Susan Love likened the battle for breast cancer funds to past fights over "civil rights and war resistance and the early women's movement," while some AIDS activists adopted Malcolm X's slogan, "By any means necessary."

While observers in recent years have written volumes on breast cancer and AIDS separately, their policy-making significance for the 1980s and early 1990s can be best appreciated by examining them in tandem. . . . For both breast cancer and AIDS, activism coalesced around specific population and political subgroups: women and homosexuals respectively; though sexual orientation did not limit AIDS infection, gay groups took leadership in promoting action. In each case, mobilization, protest, and hard-fought campaigns brought public attention and political clout to disease-specific concern, winning activists recognition and policy concessions even as they questioned scientific and government authority.

1980s and early 1990s politicization of breast cancer was closely linked to general history of modern feminist concerns. Through the 1960s, as women organized around explicitly feminist motivations, they began scrutinizing gender dimensions of political, social and economic life, including health care. Under the maxim of "the personal as political," women's health was transformed from individual problems into a mutual concern and impetus for political action.

From its 1969 start, the Boston Women's Health Collective encouraged women to educate themselves about their physical well-being, to become informed health consumers who would refuse to tolerate condescending or inadequate treatment by the medical system. The group's 1974 reference *Our Bodies, Ourselves* described both medical details and women's own health experiences, from childbirth to contraception and more; within a decade, the text sold more than two million copies nationwide. In 1975, concerned parties established the National Women's Health Network to draw attention to female health issues and distribute information. . . .

Women's health mobilization also crystallized in response to two medical disasters: the Dalkon Shield, touted as a wonderful new 1970s IUD, turned out to cause miscarriage and pelvic inflammatory disease (some severe cases proving fatal), while the drug DES, once popularly administered to pregnant women in hope of avoiding miscarriage, was linked to cancer and reproductive problems extending even two generations down from users. Frustrated by seeming failure of doctors, lawyers, and politicians to provide information, health care, or compensation, concerned women formed grass-roots organizations such as DES Action to support affected women, raise public awareness, and maintain political, medical, and legal pressure.

By the late 1980s, feminist advocates argued that beyond disastrous products such as DES and the Shield, women's health had been systematically endangered by an entire medical establishment. Health was a gendered issue, critics contended;

despite evidence of important medical differences between men and women on such matters as cholesterol levels, researchers often investigated health questions or tested new drugs on male subjects alone. The multi-year Physician's Health Study especially troubled women's advocates; the report relied on an all-male sample of 22,000 doctors and so offered no evidence whether aspirin's cardiovascular benefits held true for females. The project head pointed to inherent constraints such as relative scarcity of older female doctors to complement the male study population, though critics asked why researchers could not draw on nurses or other predominantly female groups. The director maintained female subjects would also have confused results and increased expense of an already difficult project by introducing new scientific factors such as hormonal interactions, a fairly common attitude among researchers. He warned science would suffer if political pressure compelled researchers to alter studies, regardless of appropriateness, to fit a mandated gender balance; drug companies added their own cautions that potential harm to a fetus meant special risk in testing women of childbearing age.

Nevertheless, political forces had acquired momentum. In 1986, Public Health Service (PHS) officials spoke up for greater awareness of women's issues in medical studies, NIH then created policy encouraging all grant applicants to "consider the inclusion of women" and justify any research excluding female subjects. Four years later, however, a General Accounting Office (GAO) analysis confirmed women's suspicions that the new policy had been ineffective, that numerous research proposals still ignored gender considerations. The Congressional Caucus for Women's Issues subsequently introduced Women's Health Equity Act legislation which would, among other measures, create a special OB/GYN program at NIH and enforce rules for including female subjects in research. The Act drew growing attention, and soon House and Senate subcommittees adopted some of its provisions as part of NIH reauthorization. To try regaining credibility and demonstrate good faith on the question of women and research, NIH officials adopted strategy to separate and institutionalize responsibility for female health. In September, 1990, NIH established a new Office of Research on Women's Health, winning praise from Women's Caucus co-chair, Representative Patricia Schroeder, who had previously blamed male-dominated policy for leaving women's health "at risk."

The campaign for women's health united feminist advocates, sympathetic politicians such as Schroeder; individual doctors, scientists and medical researchers also supported the cause and organized groups such as the Society for the Advancement of Women's Health Research. By the 1990s, medical journals featured notable numbers of articles and editorials on the issue, as *JAMA* put it, whether there was "still too much extrapolation from data on middle-aged white men." . . .

In 1991, one week after confirmation as first female head of NIH, Bernadine Healy announced the agency was creating a $600 million, fifteen-year Women's Health Initiative to redress history of gendered research imbalance. Healy called this NIH's "awakening to a simple fact . . . that women have unique medical problems." Explaining that women at or past menopause had been doubly-neglected due to age as well as gender bias, the agency announced plans to concentrate on advancing medical knowledge of older women. As *Science* noted, that choice of focus also did credit to "Healy's political acumen," diverting attention from controversial reproductive topics "such as post-conception . . . birth control and fetal tissue transplant research."

Healy's announcement, making national news, won approval from women's groups, while NIH reported being flooded by letters and calls expressing "enormous" interest in the new program and praise. The head of NIH's Office of Research on Women's Health commented, "Women's health has risen to the public's consciousness in a way I would not have dreamed. . . ." The Initiative program confirmed the 1980s–1990s transformation of medicine into a gendered policy issue, granting seemingly unquestionable political victory for activists' case that women's health deserved special attention. Initiative research, planned to involve up to 160,000 women, would represent the biggest single clinical trial and research effort in NIH history. . . .

Within this context of activism for general women's health research, one particular disease, breast cancer, attracted increasing attention in the 1980s. New organizations were founded to focus public awareness and support concerned women; for example, the Susan G. Komen Breast Cancer Foundation, established in 1982, became known for organizing "Race for the Cure" runs in fifty-eight cities to raise money for research, education, and screening programs. Such groups gathered political strength, mobilizing to get government and public alike to recognize breast cancer as a unique concern and allocate special funds to fight the disease.

In this new political battle for breast cancer research, Susan Love, UCLA Associate Professor of Clinical Surgery and Director of the Revlon/UCLA Breast Center, established visibility and dual identity as both doctor and political player. Historically, other practitioners, from occupational medicine pioneer Alice Hamilton to pediatrician Benjamin Spock, had combined professionalism with social and political expression. However, Love increasingly defined her medical and activist breast cancer work as inseparable, even as many health professionals still felt uncomfortable positioning themselves to challenge the political and medical order. Love linked her political awakening to her promotion of her 1990 reference book for women concerned about breast cancer; after she tossed off a line proposing a "march topless on the White House" to "make President Bush wake up and do something about breast cancer," she found female listeners ready to take her seriously. Calling this group "fed up . . . that this virtual epidemic was being ignored," Love became increasingly vocal about breast cancer being as much a political as medical battle.

Following broader campaigns for women's health research, breast cancer concerns maintained that government and medical authorities had ignored the disease even as it approached epidemic proportion; news commentator Cokie Roberts observed that women's 44,500 breast cancer deaths in 1991 exceeded the total of American soldiers killed in Vietnam. Activists based their work on certain presumptions: without increased federal support, the country would make little progress on breast cancer, but given satisfactory resources, movement leaders promised, the disease could be conquered so modern women's daughters and granddaughters would not experience similar fear of breast cancer. To drive this agenda, Love helped establish the National Breast Cancer Coalition in 1991, linking separate advocacy groups to multiply their political effectiveness and muster parade rallies and other demonstrations of public support. Collecting thousands of signatures in petition drives to the President and Congress demanding more breast cancer research, the Coalition gained access to present its case to both Bill and Hillary Clinton.

Women's push for breast cancer money broke through partisan lines; Republicans such as Marilyn Quayle and Olympia Snowe joined Democrats Mary Rose

Oakar and Schroeder. Senators such as Edward Kennedy and Tom Harkin (who lost several relatives to the disease) proved useful allies in Congress. . . .

. . . Breast cancer could also be considered politically safe: while a campaign against women's lung cancer would have forced politicians to risk alienating Southern tobacco interests and defy the notoriously tough cigarette lobby, breast cancer did not seem to necessitate major confrontation. As Love acknowledged, advocates had demographics on their side; breast cancer had an image of affecting middle or upper-class Caucasian females, a crucial political constituency. For those reasons, supporting higher breast cancer funding became a way for politicians to exhibit awareness of women's issues. In 1991, government money for studying breast cancer rose $43 million, raising by half the previous level of $90 million; in 1992, funds soared to more than $400 million across various federal agencies. Within the National Cancer Institute (NCI) alone, breast cancer support jumped from $197 million to almost $263 million between 1993 and 1994; to place that in perspective, NCI devoted just over $90 million to lung cancer and under $50 million to prostate cancer in that same period.

Such developments reflected new reality: breast cancer had been established as *the* single most politically compelling part of women's medicine. In fact, politicians and advocates alike often equated feminist health concern with breast cancer issues, a powerful link. Corporate sponsors such as Revlon enlisted in fighting breast cancer, providing research funds and other resources while highlighting their support as showing the female market they took women's issues seriously. Public commitment to breast cancer research became a "safe" yet powerful symbol of sensitivity. . . .

Just as feminist organizations provided both philosophical and practical impetus for activists to demand increasing funding and attention for women's health in general and breast cancer in particular, so AIDS activism reflected mobilization of American's gay community. While the 1960s and 1970s had represented an alternately heady and frustrating period of personal concern and political organization for gays, the 1980s brought what seemed the greatest challenge yet, a devastating and mysterious new disease. By 1981, West Coast doctors treating the gay population started noticing clusters of immune deficiency problems. Physicians and researchers at the Centers for Disease Control (CDC) found unusually frequent reports of rare pneumonia and cancer forms. CDC medical detectives initially had to sort through a variety of possible causes, from chemical poisoning to recreational drug use, and perceived the threat as sufficiently urgent to warrant special studies of what some referred to as "Gay-Related Immune Deficiency" (GRID). . . . Gay aides on Capitol Hill tried pressing for increased federal research support. However, NIH representatives and Health and Human Services (HHS) Secretary Margaret Heckler officially assured skeptics that funding for AIDS work was "more than adequate." At various times, budget planners even proposed cuts of 10 percent or more. Meanwhile, between 1983 and 1985, United States AIDS cases jumped from three thousand to sixteen thousand, finally attracting significant national media coverage, especially after announcement of actor Rock Hudson's infection. Though Surgeon General C. Everett Koop began preparing to address the public on the nature and prevention of AIDs, concerned observers detected damning lack of leadership, if not outright sabotage, by the Reagan presidency and federal bureaucracy on research to fight the new fatal illness.

With increasing awareness of AIDS, 1980s gay community leaders mobilized resources for both medical and political efforts. Just as feminists had founded the Boston Women's Health Collective, National Women's Health Network, DES Action, and National Breast Cancer Coalition to call attention to women's health, so gay groups created new AIDS organizations. One West Coast group evolved into the San Francisco AIDS Foundation, while New York leaders established Gay Men's Health Crisis, along with the American Foundation for AIDS Research (Amfar).

The most brazen group, ACT-UP (AIDS Coalition to Unleash Power), had been organized in 1987, largely at New York writer/gay activist Larry Kramer's initiative. Members targeted public figures they believed had expressed insensitive attitudes or failed to show proper commitment to fighting AIDS, from Michael Dukakis and Ed Koch to George Bush and Jesse Helms. Hundreds of ACT-UP supporters took political confrontation to radical heights, designing strategies to draw media attention; most notably disrupting a December, 1989 mass at New York's St. Patrick's Cathedral to condemn church positions on AIDS, condoms, and sex education. Protesters also broke into government hearings, prime-time network newscasts, and political speeches across the country to vent opinions on the AIDS crisis.

Behind such public protest, AIDS activists organized special committees to help care for patients, prepare and distribute preventive public health information, and support research on the disease. As advocates educated themselves about medical details, that sense of knowledge helped some approach health experts on an informed footing, winning professional respect for their seriousness. But the late 1980s proved discouraging; while laboratories turned up apparently hopeful clues to disease mechanisms, converting such findings into practical treatments continued to be difficult and slower than even some experts had predicted. Linking this medical impasse to lack of adequate research funding, frustrated activists blamed government apathy for extending the crisis; Kramer called federal efforts to fight AIDS "murderously slow."

Advocates complained that once developed, medical treatments took longer than necessary to reach desperate patients, due to dragging government regulatory processes. In addition to familiarizing themselves with medical facts, AIDS groups also started learning how NIH and FDA operated, to challenge those authorities more effectively. Incensed with seemingly unconscionable bureaucratic delay in approving new drugs, ACT-UP staged sit-ins at NIH and "die-ins" in front of FDA facilities to dramatize demands. The call for action on a 1994 World AIDS Day poster ran, "Red ribbons are a nice gesture. It's red tape we won't stand for.". . .

Standard procedure before the 1980s allowed corporations, doctors, or other sponsors to register Investigational New Drug applications with the FDA after conducting basic safety studies on animals. The IND then provided go-ahead for three-stage human clinical testing (with continued animal tests): Phase I small-group clinical pharmacology tests designed to identify any negative side effects; Phase II controlled clinical investigations to evaluate effectiveness; and larger-scale Phase III double-blind work with placebo controls. Products passing all three levels were cleared to file a New Drug Application, with one last review of data to gain final market approval.

But by the late 1980s, AIDS groups such as Treatment Action Group (TAG) and Project Inform subjected established approval procedure to tough new scrutiny.

For victims of drastic terminal disease, advocates argued, conventional concerns about side effects and scientifically-measured efficacy were meaningless, while trials comparing new treatments with placebo controls or older drugs inhumanely denied subjects access to promising medicine. While activists fought the system, patients travelled to Mexico to acquire drugs not yet approved in the United States or patronized "black market" clinics which offered a wider range of treatment options than regular doctors. . . .

The 1991 appointment of pediatrician and law professor David Kessler as new FDA commissioner led the agency to acknowledge and deal more explicitly with AIDS groups' pressure, just as Healy's NIH work both reflected and affected the changing political context of breast cancer concern. Establishing new relationships with informed activists (among others), Kessler moved FDA toward a new image of responsiveness. . . . [and] agreed that "balanc[ing] the need to make drugs available quickly with the need to ensure that patients do not receive unsafe or ineffective products," FDA could afford to swing toward facilitating access for fatal diseases such as AIDS. For such desperate cases, the FDA soon instituted special accommodations for "accelerated approval"; while officials would still require basic safety tests, agency decisions could come before extensive trials proved effectiveness or without waiting for precise application terms to be refined.

Largely in response to such internal and external pressure, FDA's average time before deciding to approve or deny new drug applications dropped 42 percent between 1987 and 1992, from thirty-three months to eighteen, the GAO reported. In December, 1995, the FDA proudly pointed to record speed in approving the new protease-inhibiting AIDS drug saquinavir, just over three months from the manufacturer's first submission. In fact, officials announced, all six anti-AIDS drugs approved in the preceding seven years had come through government review in six months or less. . . .

. . . AIDS advocates had established their legitimacy, a sense of a right to be involved with policy-making at NIH and FDA, the administration and Congress. In December, 1995, activists gathered at the first White House conference on HIV and AIDS, along with researchers and medical officials, to encourage and pressure Clinton to maintain government's fight against the disease. Meanwhile, the CDC announced AIDS stood as the leading source of fatality for white men twenty-five to forty-four years old, and the third cause for women that age (behind cancer and injury), with 41,930 overall American AIDS deaths reported in 1994.

AIDS and breast cancer advocacy, of course, were not absolutely identical. For example, though women concerned with health issues were able to draw on increased female Congressional representation after 1992, gay groups could not count on having as many "natural" allies come forward in the political establishment. Overall, however, activist development for breast cancer and AIDS displayed significant parallels; in both cases, mobilized organizations transformed a group's specific medical problem into concerns defined as politically crucial. Both AIDS and breast cancer could leave victims feeling powerless, a sense reinforced by consciousness of women's and gays' status as "outsiders." Political activity offered a way to rechannel frustration, away from individual battles against an enemy inside (disease itself), into organized campaigns challenging stubborn outside forces ("the political establishment," "medical system," or both). Even if policy changes and renewed research funding came too late to bring a particular patient/activist any personal medical help, organizations drew the individual into a broader fight, promising their commitment would broadly benefit entire groups of others, even curing or preventing future disease. Both breast cancer and AIDS activists operated from conviction that previous medical funding and research policy had been systematically biased against investigation of "their" disease. Some almost-moralistic undertones insisted government and medical authorities confess previous "injustices," then to be atoned for by generous new spending.

Similarities between AIDS and breast cancer activism should not be surprising. From the late 1980s on, leaders in the two camps studied each other's work, modelling new efforts in light of what had succeeded for the other cause. Breast cancer advocates adopted tactics initiated by AIDS activists and vice versa, cooperating where they saw common need for action. For example, members of Women's Health Action and Mobilization (WHAM!), sharing ACT-UP's aggressive political inclination, joined the 1989 St. Patrick's protest against certain Catholic moral precepts. Each movement developed special fund-raising and public awareness events (from breast cancer-benefit fashion shows, to AIDS-benefit theater, music, and art events). Both causes even acquired shorthand symbols of support: red ribbons for AIDS and pink for breast cancer, fashionable accessories among regular Americans and Hollywood celebrities wishing to display political and philosophical solidarity with activists....

Fundamentally, AIDS and breast cancer activists were challenging and politicizing not only funding, but the structure and scientific values of research itself. Under ongoing criticism that NIH had not effectively mandated gender balance in research pools, 1994 agency changes set new guidelines requiring clinical trials to make "valid analysis" of whether the treatment in question affected women and minorities differently than white males. Some scientists resented the policy as imposition of political correctness which would cause delay and add to research cost; a Johns Hopkins biostatistician called it "very foolish and very harsh law that is not in the public's interest." Similarly, for AIDS, some researchers feared that FDA policy change granting more generous access to experimental drugs actually undermined scientific need to acquire knowledge about new medicines. A 1994 FDA review of accelerated approval showed that after treatments such as DDI and DDC became available, manufacturers never completed follow-up research proving effectiveness. While it was one thing for advocates to win political battles, it remained another matter to convince researchers that resulting policy change did not hurt medical progress.

Some AIDS and breast cancer activism explicitly challenged fundamental scientific method such as randomized research trials comparing new promising treatment against placebos or older drugs. AIDS groups objected that random tests might leave some patients stuck with ineffective medicine; a tombstone-shaped poster at one protest read, "I got the placebo." Some FDA officials and researchers feared such objections might end up undermining necessary studies of new AIDS medicine, if "compassionate" or accelerated approval policy offered patients alternate access to experimental drugs without risk of "getting the placebo." ... Though scientists relied on random clinical trials as a vital scientific method for eliminating bias and so yielding objective results, outside observers did not necessarily value the procedure similarly.

In other cases, breast cancer and AIDS patients actually rejected scientific testing procedures. According to a 1995 report, NCI tests of bone marrow transplants as breast cancer treatment had been undercut because women feared they might be randomly placed in control sections receiving less aggressive therapy. When possible, patients simply chose to avoid enrolling in NCI trials, instead just finding providers willing to give them transplants directly. Worrying that failure to recruit enough subjects might make it impossible to conduct valid tests, the NCI project head hoped physicians might "take a stand and not let this stampede to bone marrow transplant continue"; however, women themselves were expressing reluctance to "be a guinea pig." Similarly for AIDS, some observers suggested that patients had become so infuriated with complex eligibility requirements surrounding research projects that they engaged in "rampant 'lying and cheating' " to be accepted into promising studies. In other cases, subjects might drop out of testing if they suspected they had gotten placebos, or else might share medication with others, adjust dosages as they saw fit, or secretly continue alternate types of treatment. According to one analysis, such individuals could "justify non-compliance with protocols" by adopting a "coercion defense"; if society and science refused to recognize their need for medical support and free choice of treatments, patients bore no obligation to comply with the medical system's rules. . . .

Questioning of medical authority on breast cancer and AIDS came in a period which also showed broader American skepticism of conventional medicine. According to one 1990 report, over 33 percent of AIDS patients used unorthodox therapies such as acupuncture, imagery, megavitamin doses, and unapproved medicine. A more general 1993 study correspondingly shocked the medical profession, showing one-third of adults supplementing visits to regular physicians with chiropractic care, relaxation technique and other alternative treatments for physical pain (back and headaches) and other problems (anxiety, depression, and insomnia). Such therapy found a home within mainstream health institutions; by end of 1995, the relatively new NIH Office of Alternative Medicine had given out almost $8 million in research support, while Harvard, UCLA, and thirty other medical schools offered classes on unconventional treatments. . . . But for many scientists, the new NIH office and medical courses confirmed fear that non-scientific work was gaining a foothold in respectable institutions, violating the ultimate divide between objectivity and quackery. . . .

While breast cancer and AIDS groups were not the first American organizations to fight for specific medical causes and research money, the 1980s–1990s activism was unique in two respects. First, as those organizations gained political power, they reached for unprecedented influence on government agencies, demanding a voice in distributing research funds, changing policy, and setting research agendas. While in earlier decades the March of Dimes had raised significant sums to fight polio, the group followed mainstream medical opinion on the best direction for using such research funds; by contrast, a 1996 breast cancer petition asked the President and Congress to "mandate that . . . breast cancer activists help determine how the money gets spent." Second, breast cancer and AIDS activists went beyond other medical causes in posing broad and direct challenges to scientific authority; again, polio groups had not disputed the objective value of research or fought to reverse specific rulings. Breast cancer and AIDS groups did not deny the ultimate value of medicine itself; in fact, they expressed repeated confidence that with significant increases in funding and national commitment, researchers would find better treatments, cures, and preventive measures for such terrible diseases. Yet to achieve such gains, activists contended, the medical community needed to reform its entire approach, even re-considering the value of randomized testing and supposedly "objective" results to accommodate sensibilities of patients and politics.

FURTHER READING

Virginia Berridge and Philip Strong, eds., *AIDS and Contemporary History* (1993).

Peter E. Dans, *Doctors in the Movies: Boil the Water and Just Say Aah* (2000).

Harry F. Dowling, *City Hospitals: The Undercare of the Underprivileged* (1982).

Steven Epstein, *Impure Science: AIDS, Activism, and the Politics of Knowledge* (1996).

Elizabeth Fee and Daniel M. Fox, eds., *AIDS: The Burdens of History* (1988).

Elizabeth Fee and Daniel M. Fox, eds., *AIDS: The Making of a Chronic Disease* (1992).

Leon Fink and Brian Greenberg, *Upheaval in the Quiet Zone: A History of Hospital Workers' Union Local 1199* (1989).

Daniel M. Fox, *Health Policies, Health Politics: The British and American Experience, 1911–1965* (1986).

Daniel M. Fox, *Power and Illness: The Failure and Future of American Health Policy* (1993).

Daniel M. Fox and John K. Iglehart, eds., *Five States That Could Not Wait: Lessons for Health Reform from Florida, Hawaii, Minnesota, Oregon, and Vermont* (1994).

Eli Ginzburg, *The Medical Triangle: Physicians, Politicians, and the Public* (1990).

Caroline Hannaway, Victoria A. Harden, and John Parascandola, eds., *AIDS and the Public Debate: Historical and Contemporary Perspectives* (1995).

James Kinsella, *Covering the Plague: AIDS and the American Media* (1989).

Fitzhugh Mullan, *White Coat, Clenched Fist: The Political Education of an American Physician* (1976).

Dorothy Nelkin and Lawrence Tancredi, *Dangerous Diagnostics: The Social Power of Biological Information* (1994).

James T. Patterson, *Dread Disease: Cancer and Modern American Culture* (1987).

Robert Proctor, *Cancer Wars: How Politics Shapes What We Know and Don't Know About Cancer* (1995).

Richard Rettig, *Cancer Crusade: The Story of the National Cancer Act of 1971* (1977).

Charles E. Rosenberg, "Meanings, Policies, and Medicine: On the Bioethical Enterprise and History," *Daedalus* (1999): 27–46.

Louise B. Russell, *Educated Guesses: Making Policy About Medical Screening Tests* (1994).

Randy Shilts, *And the Band Played On: Politics, People, and the AIDS Epidemic* (1987).

Theda Skocpol, *Boomerang: Clinton's Health Security Effort and the Turn Against Government in U.S. Politics* (1996).

Robert Stevens and Rosemary Stevens, *Welfare Medicine in America: A Case Study of Medicaid* (1974).

Rosemary Stevens, *In Sickness and in Wealth: American Hospitals in the Twentieth Century* (1989).

Richard M. Titmuss, *The Gift Relationship: From Human Blood to Social Policy* (1971).

CHAPTER
15

The Persisting Search for Health and Healing at the End of the Twentieth Century

American medicine and public health underwent dramatic and, for many, profoundly disorienting changes during the final decades of the twentieth century. Never had medicine's technological prowess been greater or had its ability to explore the secrets of the human body more assured. Yet this was also a time of widespread discontent both within medicine and in the larger culture. New biopathological developments, most prominently AIDS, stimulated the rethinking of fundamental principles of medical science. Such basic premises of medicine and public health as what constitutes evidence of a disease were questioned. Relationships between doctors and patients, nurses and physicians, scientific researchers and human subjects, and government and health care professionals were radically reoriented. The very profile of the country's health was transformed, as the increasingly large role of chronic disease in comparison to infectious conditions finally received sustained attention. No aspect of health care—from therapeutic modalities to diagnostic capabilities, from public health policy to financing and organizational structure—was left untouched in this era of raucous debate. Americans began a new millennium with a medical and public health legacy of glistening possibilities and deeply troubling unresolved conflicts.

As the twentieth century ended, an ever-expanding chorus of critics itemized the failures and limitations of the medical profession, hospitals and laboratories, the pharmaceutical and health insurance industries, biomedical researchers, and the health policies of the United States government. Everyone, it seemed, had betrayed the trust of the American public. At the same time, such seemingly fundamental concepts as health and disease had lost their clarity for many both inside and outside the health professions. The struggle for meaning and for care was particularly poignant for groups of recent immigrants, particularly Hispanics and Southeast Asians, whose traditional beliefs and practices often clashed with those of Western biomedicine. In such an era, who could be trusted in the quest for reliable information—the family doctor, the members of a lay self-help group, the vitamin industry, the alternative practitioner, the representatives overseeing NIH, or perhaps the insurance companies and HMOs who underwrote payment for medical care? If these various advisors gave different answers, how was the conflict resolved? Who could be relied upon in a time of crisis?

As Americans struggled with these issues, their concern with the equally troubling question of responsibility for health also returned. In this era of high-cost, technologically intensive, commodified medicine, much emphasis was still placed on the individual's role in preserving his or her own health. This concern for individual responsibility, accountability, and culpability, while evident through-out American history, took on another dimension with the introduction of powerful new tools for identifying and eliminating health risks. For example, the discovery of genetic markers for diseases such as Tay-Sachs, Huntington's chorea, and even some forms of breast cancer raised unsettling questions about birth control, abortion, and prophylactic removal of healthy breasts. Did the existence of this kind of knowledge place some sort of obligation on the individual to avoid health-risking behavior? Or, were Americans at the end of the millennium free to live any kind of health life they chose? What did the newer genetic information, diagnostic technologies, and tests that revealed the mere possibility of future disease really mean to the individual and the society as a whole?

 D O C U M E N T S

The work of a women's collective, excerpts from the 1971 first edition of the self-help text *Our Bodies, Ourselves,* make up Document 1. This classic in feminist medical literature is a far more politically radical document than the edition now on the shelves at college bookstores. The excerpts convey some sense of the anger that motivated critics of the medical establishment during the early years of the feminist health movement.

Document 2 is another type of response to a changing world of patient care. Written by psychiatrist Jerold Kreisman, this 1975 article from the *American Journal of Psychiatry* presents two cases of "schizophrenic" (the author's diagnosis) Mexican-American patients who were successfully treated in a Denver hospital with an approach that integrated *curanderismo,* traditional Hispanic healing, with the conventional therapies of biomedicine.

In Document 3, a poignant excerpt from African American poet Audre Lorde's *Cancer Journals,* published in 1980, another kind of insight into the modern biomedical approach is captured. This reading shows how different some of the most promising high-technology solutions to a life-threatening health problem look from the perspective of a breast cancer patient who has just undergone a radical mastectomy. The glimpse that Lorde gives of the role of fellow sufferers and self-taught laypersons in late-twentieth-century health care is confirmed in Document 4, Chicana midwife Jesusita Aragon's account of her experiences practicing in Nevada. Having learned midwifery from her grandmother in Mexico, *la partera* (midwife) Aragon tells how she adapted her techniques to a new land and new challenges.

Document 5 continues the exploration of challenges facing healers as pediatrician Perri Klass takes a thoughtful look at the role of women in the late-twentieth-century medical profession. Trained at Harvard in the 1970s and practicing pediatrics in Boston, Klass has published regularly in popular journals and newspapers about her experiences as a medical student and a physician. This particular article illuminates a larger issue: the medical and cultural significance of the steady increase in the number of women becoming physicians. Document 6, journalist Anne Fadiman's powerful 1997 depiction of the clash between Hmong family customs and American biomedicine, underscores the fact that it is not just the population of caregivers that is changing but the patient population as well. Fadiman explicates both Hmong apprehensions of American doctors and American doctors' misunderstandings of Hmong convictions, giving a compelling portrait of the powerful tensions that lurk beneath the surface of the American health care system.

1. Feminists Reclaim Women's Health Care, 1971

Doctors' attitudes toward patients are terrible condescending, especially toward women. You aren't supposed to read the record of your own body, and you are scolded like a child if you do. Doctors withhold information that you are dying. They withhold information that you might have a difficult pregnancy or childbirth. In playing God, their attitude is that you must have complete confidence in them to make all of your decisions for you. Why should they make your decisions?

Doctors see women as patients more frequently, women average 25% more visits to the doctor per year than men, not counting the many times they accompany their children. A standard complaint of doctors is that they are tired of neurotic women with nothing wrong with them who come in because they are lonely or dissatisfied with life. Psychiatrists get more women patients. A study showed recently that conceptions of behavior of normal men and normal adults coincided, but behavior stereotypically feminine was not thought by psychoanalysts to be normal adult behavior. No wonder more women end up on the couch, where they are supposed to learn to adjust. It is also true that many women have a more difficult time adapting to "their roles" in society.

The system fails to provide basic preventive medicine for people. For example, cancer of the cervix or the uterus can be totally cured by early detection by the Pap smear and early treatment. The Pap smear was developed about thirty years ago, and yet today (1970) only 12% of American women regularly get Pap smears. It would be simple (but boring) to have a mass screening campaign. A great proportion of the 14,000 deaths per year from uterine cancer could have been prevented. A young internist recently remarked that he rarely did pelvic examinations of his women patients because it embarrassed him. How many women die because doctors have hang-ups about their genitals?

On the other hand, unnecessary and cruel surgery is often performed. In a study at Columbia, one-third of the hysterectomies reviewed were judged as having been done without medical justification. The study covered 6,248 operations. 30% of the patients aged 20–29 who had hysterectomies had no disease whatsoever. In individual hospitals, the percentage of unnecessary hysterectomies has been as high as 66%. In Appalachia, doctors have removed healthy reproductive organs from 11 and 12 year old girls to get the $250 fee. Unnecessary surgery is common in America. We have twice as much surgery, per capita, as England. The unnecessary operations are called "remunerectomies" (done for monetary remuneration). How many remunerative testectomies do you think are done? . . .

Boston Women's Health Course Collective, *Our Bodies, Ourselves*. Reprinted with the permission of Simon & Schuster. Copyright © 1971, 1973, 1976 by the Boston Women's Health Book Collective.

The AMA (American Medical Association) has been an extremely powerful force in insuring that medicine is practiced for the doctors, not the patients. Although it does not speak for every doctor as an individual, it does write the rules that all doctors must follow. Milford O. Rouse, M.D., last year's AMA president, has asserted that there is a threat to medicine in the concept of health care as a right rather than a privilege. The AMA has the richest lobby in Washington, spending $1.1 million in 1965. In 1968, AMPAC, the AMA's front for political contributions, gave $680,000 to candidates for national office who think our resources should be allocated to death: wars and guns and ABMs and MIRVs [antiballistic missiles and multiple independently targetable reentry vehicles] rather than to clinics and more doctors. It is estimated that five times this amount is spent at the local level. . . .

The AMA has opposed free inoculations against diphtheria and polio, free vaccinations against smallpox, the establishment of Red Cross blood-banks, federal grants for medical school construction and medical student loans, national health insurance and Medicare. . . . In 1955, after Salk developed his vaccine, the AMA House of Delegates passed a resolution demanding "immediate termination" of free distribution of the vaccine. The Federal Government's program to inoculate people was called "a violation of the principles of free enterprise." In New Jersey, the state medical society forbade physicians to participate in the free programs except when the patients were paupers. Half of the vaccine purchased by the Federal Government went unused in the first year of the program, due to doctors' unwillingness to participate in free programs. The doctors charged $5 a shot. They get most vaccines free.

The AMA has fought any form of practice of medicine that promotes preventive measures rather than curative treatment. The AMA's positions on pollution, smoking, car safety, and working conditions all show that they put the freedom of the corporations above the concern of keeping people healthy. 45% of the AMA's operating budget comes from the drug and medical supply industries, so the AMA is interested in laws which bolster the exorbitant profits of these industries. An example of such a law is the ability of the drug companies to obtain a patent on a new drug, thus inhibiting competitive pricing. Dr. Milton Rouse has stated the purpose of the AMA by saying that the AMA should "concentrate [its] attention on the single obligation to protect the American Way of Life. That way can be described in one word: capitalism." . . .

Instead of having health teams to give continuous care necessary for the protection of health, the system in this country is that patients are treated only after they become sick enough for admission to a hospital. (When was the last time a doctor came to your house?) Hospitals are centers for dealing with crisis medical problems. Yet only a few hospitals can do this well. The others do not have enough personnel, equipment, experience, or desire. . . . The source of the financing of the public and voluntary hospitals does not differ greatly (eventually, tax money), but they are benefitting different people. Most of the people who can't pay for their care and who don't have insurance are supposed to go to the publicly-financed public hospitals while private patients go to the publicly-financed "private" hospitals. But there are many more private and voluntary hospitals than public. . . .

A teaching hospital is any hospital which takes medical students for teaching purposes. The teaching hospitals are run mainly by the medical schools. All of the major hospitals in Boston have relationships with one or more of the three medical schools. Here is one place to look for medical empires. Although the trend is allegedly changing, the medical students practice mainly on "charity" patients, that is, poor people who come in without a private doctor. The hospital is dependent upon the medical school for personnel to do the routine scut work. Taking advantage of medical students and treating them roughly insures they will continue the tradition when they have the power to do so. The medical schools could not teach without patients to work with. . . .

The medical schools are becoming an increasingly dominant force in the way medicine is coming down to people. Doctors are doctor chauvinists as well as male chauvinists. Most women doctors are no exception to this, having taken a role of "honorary men." Although 70% of hospital employees are women, 7–10% of the doctors are women. Two percent of doctors are black. . . .

The purpose of clinics is to provide care for the patient who can't afford a private doctor. They are run with this in mind. Most of the poor people in Boston go to the clinics at Boston City Hospital, where facilities are so understaffed and undersupplied that a doctor was heard complaining about his inability to find a clean tongue depressor. This concentration of patients is changing a little with the other big hospitals expanding their clinic facilities. BCH serves over 1000 people a day in assembly line fashion. You may see as many as six doctors in the course of your pregnancy. In no case is any effort made that you see the same doctor for any longer than the duration of one particular illness. Disease is regarded as a purely technical matter, the malfunctioning of a machine (the heart is a pump . . .). Work is arranged so that the students, interns, and residents of the teaching hospital can see the maximum number of "cases" in a short period of time. They fail to take the whole person into account, to see that he/she follows as good a diet as possible, to recognize his/her fears and anxieties which may be exaggerating his/her sickness, to see that her/his life is making her/him sick.

In the out-patient department at Boston City, most patients wait two or more hours to see a doctor. Much of the human contact comes in the form of "Alright, numbers one through ten line up and get weighed." There are only two nurses and two aides for sixty patients each morning in the Ob-Gyn clinic. Some new liberal administrators at BCH are concerned that the service is inhuman. They think that the solution is an appointment system, which the Ob-Gyn clinic has had for a long time. Only about half the patients keep their appointment, which messes up the system. The liberal administrator interprets the unkept appointment as a lack of the middle class value of the importance of time, so they plan to give lectures to the waiting patients on the value of keeping their appointments. A few conversations with patients would reveal that when you wake up in the morning, two or three bus trips from the clinic, a household to care for, children to find a babysitter for or lug on the bus with you, not feeling well, and anticipating the bureaucracy and coldness of the clinic, you think twice about going. It takes a lot of will power to go. The appointment system doesn't necessarily decrease the amount of waiting anyway, because patients always come in without appointments. . . .

So far, the existing medical institutions have been unable to give proper medical care to all the people. Because of this inability, small groups in a few places have gotten together to form clinics of their own. In the spirit of the idea that health care is a human right, most of these clinics have been free. Our society and the medical world do not take kindly to these clinics, they are not the American Way. The Black Panther Party of Boston has set up a free clinic in Roxbury on the pattern of the Judson Mobile Health unit in New York in which the patients are encouraged to ask questions, and are invited to look through microscopes at their own blood samples, and participate in the decision making. Watch out for harassment. The Free Clinic in Berkeley was attacked by the Berkeley police with cannisters of CS gas during a fight over People's Park. One of the cannisters was shot through the window of the clinic during regular clinic hours. CS is a dangerous substance, especially when used against already sick people. Many medical and scientific personnel in this country spend all their time on research, development, and testing of chemical-bacteriological weapons, yet the Hippocratic Oath says, "I will use treatment to help the sick according to my ability and judgment, but never with a view to injury and wrongdoing." . . .

The medical institutions we have do just exactly what they are intended to do. The drug and supply companies make money, the AMA protects capitalism. The medical schools train a small number of people to fit into the system. The hospitals treat some sick people. The clinics see some people and offer study material to students. None of them is responsible for the health of the people. . . .

We believe that health care is a human right and that a society should provide free health care for itself. Health care cannot be adequate as long as it is conceived of as insurance, which is the business of taking in $100 from 100 people to guarantee them against loss by a contingent event and then paying out $40 to the people the event happened to and pocketing the rest. The profit system guarantees that certain people will benefit and the rest will be exploited. We will gain nothing by pumping more money into our present system. Health care for everyone is possible only outside of the profit system. Elitist attitudes and patients being regarded as "consumers" would not be supported if society and its institutions were run by and for all of the people.

2. A Psychiatrist Integrates Folk and Medical Healing Practices, 1975

Modern psychiatry must extend treatment to people of many different backgrounds. However, such assistance often fails to acknowledge and work within an individual's cultural frame of reference. The Hispanic population is Denver's largest minority group, and, despite acculturation, the Hispanic culture is pervasive in many areas, particularly the concept of illness. Unfortunately, there is little integration of these unique cultural considerations into a definitive treatment plan for Spanish-speaking patients.

This paper describes two cases involving Mexican-American schizophrenic patients in which conventional therapy was seriously stalled until treatment was adapted to the patients' culturally bound concept of their illness. The therapy was

Jerold J. Kreisman, "The *Curandero*'s Apprentice: A Therapeutic Integration of Folk and Medical Healing," *American Journal of Psychiatry* 132 (1975): 81–83. Copyright © 1975, the American Psychiatric Association. Reprinted by permission.

modified to conform appropriately to a model of *curanderismo,* the Hispanic concept of healing.

. . . [T]he Mexican-American family is typically a tightly knit unit; distrust of
agencies outside this unit prevails. Since illness may be perceived as a hereditary
defect, the family strives to determine that a member's illness is due to external,
extrafamilial factors, often seeking the services of a *curandero* (healer), who will
support such an etiology. The *curandero* is a very religious and highly respected
member of the community who retains many of the customs of Mexico, maintaining cultural bonds for even the acculturated Mexican-American.

Case Reports

Case 1.   J.S., a 31-year-old Mexican-American woman, was brought to the hospital by the police because of disorganized, bizarre speech and behavior. She had been
hospitalized twice previously with a diagnosis of paranoid schizophrenia. At the time of
admission, the patient was confused, suspicious, resistive, and actively hallucinating.

On the ward, she was given trifluoperazine and she partially reintegrated over a
two-week period. Although oriented and exhibiting more appropriate behavior, she remained withdrawn and secretive. She vaguely but inconsistently acknowledged auditory
hallucinations and continued her reticence in psychotherapy, exhibiting no insight.

After several weeks of stalled therapy, the suggestion was introduced that she
might be *embrujada* (bewitched). She responded with great affect and relief, confirm-
ing the suggestion and expressing surprise at the therapist's grasp of the problem. At
that point, the therapist described a course of *curanderismo,* relating that he had worked
with a *curandera* who had granted him use of her herbs in combination with a prescribed ritualistic regimen designed for victims of *embrujada.* The therapy included
prayer, isolation, and personal deprivation, in combination with the prescribed herbs—
actually doxepin hydrochloride (Sinequan).

She described immediate improvement when the course of *curanderismo* was
added to the regimen and has functioned well since discharge. There has been a marked
deemphasis of the etiological significance of the folk illness, although upon direct
questioning she confirms that she is no longer troubled by "spirits." More important,
immediately following discussion of her concept of her illness, the patient for the first
time began openly revealing and discussing pertinent parts of her history and important
intrapersonal conflicts. . . .

Case 2.   D.M., a 22-year-old unmarried Mexican-American woman, was admitted
for the first time to the hospital with psychotic behavior one week after the birth of her
first child. At the time of admission, she appeared grossly psychotic and suspicious, di-
vulging little information. She was given haloperidol and improved within several days,
although she retained a markedly flat affect.

She was discharged after two weeks in the hospital, but was readmitted one week
later with the recurrence of symptoms. At the time of her readmission she also exhibited
significant signs of depression. After antidepressants were added to the haloperidol regimen, she again partially recompensated, but the flat and inappropriate affect persisted.
Her family clamored loudly for her release, simultaneously expressing dissatisfaction
with the hospital's treatment and the conviction that the patient was well enough to return home. The patient continued to be very resistant and the therapy was stalled.

At this point, the patient told a Mexican-American staff member about the possibility that a hospitalized patient might actually be "hexed." At a subsequent interview, the
therapist remarked that he had observed a similar case in which a patient had felt she

was *embrujada*. The patient responded enthusiastically to this suggestion, acknowledging that her mother had been trying to find a *curandero* for her.

She eagerly responded to a proposal to utilize the *curandero*'s herbs in the hospital and rigorously prepared herself for the ordeal with prayer and isolation. She also devised specific criteria by which she could judge when she was no longer *embrujada*. Her improvement in the hospital continued but, although acknowledging she was regaining her health, she insisted that only after receiving the *curandero*'s magic would she be totally cured.

Prior to the initiation of the hospital *curanderismo,* the patient, while on a pass, was taken by her mother to a local *curandera* who administered "medicine." She returned to the hospital complaining of xerostomia, blurred vision, tremulousness, and the return of persecutory auditory hallucinations. She also exhibited nystagmus, mydriasis, and tachycardia. As her symptoms persisted over the next few days, the patient requested the hospital *curandero*'s herbs, which she felt could counteract the local healer's drug. Within one day after initiation of the regimen (doxepin hydrochloride), her symptoms disappeared and she had also fulfilled her own criteria that indicated she was free of *embrujada*.

Over the next several weeks the patient began to progress significantly in psychotherapy and a firm rapport was solidified with her as well as with her previously hostile family. However, she retained a markedly flat and often inappropriate affect, failing to regain her state of health before her encounter with the local *curandera*. A course of electroconvulsive treatment was eventually initiated, and the patient responded exceptionally well. She has regained her premorbid status, retaining her previous job and assuming mothering responsibility for her child.

. . . A major problem in dealing with folk illness is recognizing when this concept is a significant factor in the malady. It may not be necessary to explore this ground unless the patient's conflicting view of his illness interferes with therapy. However, . . . it is unusual for the Mexican-American patient to volunteer to the Anglo therapist the belief that he is *embrujada,* although he may well respond enthusiastically to such a suggestion from the psychiatric worker. Therefore, the therapist must be aware of subtle signs which indicate that a patient's concept of cultural illness is conflicting with a traditional therapeutic program.

As the case reports I have presented illustrate, patients in whom such a conflict exists may display mistrust and evasiveness, often as a reflection of their inability to translate culturally defined concepts of disease to a socioculturally distant therapist. . . .

Probably the most significant indicator in the recognition of folk illness as a significant factor in a patient's psychopathology is the reaction of the family. They may demand the patient's release, expressing a desire to take the patient to their private doctor and criticizing the hospital care. This usually reflects the family's anxiety over the patient's illness and their conviction that he will not regain his health until the *curandero* intervenes.

If the therapist feels that folk illness is a significant factor in a patient's illness, he is faced with the dilemma of how best to confront this issue. Several alternatives are available and may be referred to as approaches that ignore, compete, cooperate, or integrate.

The first approach, the most obvious as well as the most frequently used, is to totally ignore the patient's concept of his disease, dealing only with a medically oriented model. The prevalence of this attitude stems primarily from ignorance of an individual patient's frame of reference. Although this approach may be acceptable in some cases, it is probable that few patients are best treated by completely ignoring their cultural biases.

The second approach is to acknowledge and discuss the patient's concept of his illness but to compete against it. The traditional medical view of disease is offered as the one true, rational construct; the patient's own culturally biased understanding is denigrated. Although some patients may respond to an outsider's admonitions that the folk explanation of illness is nonrational, logical argument cannot pretend to negate an individual's lifetime training.

A third alternative is the cooperative approach, in which the therapist benignly accepts the patient's concept of his illness and avoids competition with this belief. Here, traditional psychiatric care and *curanderismo* maintain a kind of separate but equal status. The patient's realization that the Anglo doctor may truly appreciate the problem in its proper context may encourage him to open up further in therapy. . . .

In the approach that stresses integration, the therapist may not only accept the patient's cultural beliefs but may encourage their expression, actively seeking to integrate his therapeutic regimen within a framework consistent with the patient's understanding. The therapeusis is employed within the appropriate cultural bias, but unpredictable outside forces are not introduced. Folk and scientific treatments are equal but not separate in this approach; they are integrated under the total control of the therapist. Such a technique was utilized with success in the two cases I have cited.

3. Patient Audre Lorde Confronts Breast Cancer Treatment, 1980

In September 1978, I went into the hospital for a breast biopsy for the second time. It all happened much faster this time than the year before. There was none of the deep dread of the previous biopsy, but at the same time there was none of the excitement of a brand new experience. I said to my surgeon the night before—"I'm a lot more scared this time, but I'm handling it better." On the surface, at least, we all expected it to be a repeat. My earlier response upon feeling this lump had been— "I've been through this once before. What do we do for encore?"

Well, what we did for encore was the real thing.

I woke up in the recovery room after the biopsy colder than I can remember ever having been in my life. I was hurting and horrified. I knew it was malignant. How, I didn't know, but I suspect I had absorbed that fact from the operating room while I still was out. Being "out" really means only that you can't answer back or protect yourself from what you are absorbing through your ears and other senses. But when I raised my hand in the recovery room and touched both bandaged breasts, I knew there was a malignancy in one, and the other had been biopsied also. It was only for affirmation. I would have given anything to have been warmer right

Audre Lorde, *The Cancer Journals* (San Francisco: Aunt Lute Books, 1980), pp. 27–33, 36, 38, 41–44, 46–47. Reprinted by permission of the Charlotte Sheedy Agency. Copyright © 1980 Aunt Lute Books.

then. The gong in my brain of "malignant," "malignant," and the icy sensations of that frigid room, cut through the remnants of anesthesia like a fire hose trained on my brain. All I could focus upon was getting out of that room and getting warm. I yelled and screamed and complained about the cold and begged for extra blankets, but none came. The nurses were very put out by my ruckus and sent me back to the floor early. . . .

In the next two days, I came to realize as I agonized over my choices and what to do, that I had made my decision to have surgery if it were needed even before the biopsy had been done. Yet I had wanted a two-stage operation anyway, separating the biopsy from the mastectomy. I wanted time to re-examine my decision, to search really for some other alternative that would give me good reasons to change my mind. But there were none to satisfy me.

I wanted to make the decision again, and I did, knowing the other possibilities, and reading avidly and exhaustively through the books I ordered through Frances and Helen and my friends. These books now piled up everywhere in that wretched little room, making it at least a little bit like home. . . .

I considered the alternatives of the straight medical profession, surgery, radiation, and chemotherapy. I considered the holistic health approaches of diet, vitamin therapy, experimental immunotherapeutics, west german pancreatic enzymes, and others. The decision whether or not to have a mastectomy ultimately was going to have to be my own. I had always been firm on that point and had chosen a surgeon with that in mind. With the various kinds of information I had gathered together before I went into the hospital, and the additional information acquired in the hectic three days after biopsy, now more than ever before I had to examine carefully the pros and cons of every possibility, while being constantly and acutely aware that so much was still not known. . . .

On Wednesday afternoon I told Frances that I had decided to have surgery, and tears came to her eyes. Later she told me that she had been terrified that I might refuse surgery, opting instead for an alternative treatment, and she felt that she was prepared to go along with whatever I would decide, but she also felt surgery was the wisest choice.

A large factor in this decision was the undeniable fact that any surgical intervention in a cystic area can possibly activate cancer cells that might otherwise remain dormant. I had dealt with that knowledge a year ago when deciding whether or not to have a biopsy, and with the probabilities of a malignancy being as high as they were then, I felt then I had no choice but to decide as I did. Now, I had to consider again whether surgery might start another disease process. I deluged my surgeon with endless questions which he answered in good faith, those that he could. I weighed my options. There were malignant cells in my right breast encased in a fatty cyst, and if I did not do something about that I would die of cancer in fairly short order. Whatever I did might or might not reverse that process, and I would not know with any certainty for a very long time.

When it came right down to deciding, as I told Frances later, I felt inside myself for what I really felt and wanted, and that was to live and to love and to do my work, as hard as I could and for as long as I could. So I simply chose the course that I felt most likely to achieve my desire, knowing that I would have paid more than even my beloved breast out of my body to preserve that self that was not merely physically defined, and count it well spent.

Having made that decision, I felt comfortable with it and able to move on. I could not choose the option of radiation and chemotherapy because I felt strongly that everything I had read about them suggested that they were in and of themselves carcinogenic. The experimental therapies without surgery were interesting possibilities, but still unproven. Surgery, a modified radical mastectomy, while traumatic and painful would arrest any process by removal. It was not in and of itself harmful at this point, since whatever process might have been started by surgery had already been begun by the biopsy. I knew that there might come a time when it was clear that surgery had been unnecessary because of the efficacy of alternate therapies. I might be losing my breast in vain. But nothing else was as sure, and it was a price I was willing to pay for life, and I felt I had chosen the wisest course for me. I think now what was most important was not what I chose to do so much as that I was conscious of being able to choose, and having chosen, was empowered from having made a decision, done a strike for myself, moved. . . .

The year before, as I waited almost four weeks for my first biopsy, I had grown angry at my right breast because I felt as if it had in some unexpected way betrayed me, as if it had become already separate from me and had turned against me by creating this tumor which might be malignant. My beloved breast had suddenly departed from the rules we had agreed upon to function by all these years.

. . . Until 5:00 a.m. the next morning, waking was brief seas of localized and intense pain between shots and sleep. At 5:00 a nurse rubbed my back again, helped me get up and go to the bathroom because I couldn't use the bedpan, and then helped me into a chair. She made me a cup of tea and some fruit juice because I was parched. The pain had subsided a good deal.

I could not move my right arm nor my shoulder, both of which were numb, and wrapped around my chest was a wide Ace bandage under which on my left side the mound of my left breast arose, and from which on the right side protruded the ends of white surgical bandages. From under the Ace bandage on my right side, two plastic tubes emerged, running down into a small disc-shaped plastic bottle called a hemovac which drained the surgical area. I was alive, and it was a very beautiful morning. I drank my tea slowly, and then went back to bed. . . .

On the morning of the third day, the pain returned home bringing all of its kinfolk. Not that any single one of them was overwhelming, but just that all in concert, or even in small repertory groups, they were excruciating. There were constant ones and intermittent ones. There were short sharp and long dull and various combinations of the same ones. The muscles in my back and right shoulder began to screech as if they'd been pulled apart and now were coming back to life slowly and against their will. My chest wall was beginning to ache and burn and stab by turns. My breast which was no longer there would hurt as if it were being squeezed in a vise. That was perhaps the worst pain of all, because it would come with a full complement of horror that I was to be forever reminded of my loss by suffering in a part of me which was no longer there. I suddenly seemed to get weaker rather than stronger. The euphoria and numbing effects of the anesthesia were beginning to subside. . . .

On the second day in the hospital I had been crying when the head nurse came around, and she sent in another woman from down the hall who had had a mastectomy a week ago and was about to go home. The woman from down the hall was a smallbodied feisty redhead in a pink robe with a flower in her hair. (I have a permanent and inexplicable weakness for women with flowers in their hair.) She was about my own age, and had grown kids who, she said, wanted her to come home. I knew immediately they must be sons. She patted my hand and gestured at our bandages.

"Don't feel bad," she said, "they weren't that much good anyway." But then she threw open her robe and stuck out her almost bony chest dressed in a gay printed pajama top, saying, "Now which twin has the Toni?" And I had to laugh in spite of myself, because of her energy, and because she had come all the way down the hall just to help make me feel better.

The next day, when I was still not thinking too much, except about why was I hurting more and when could I reasonably expect to go home, a kindly woman from Reach for Recovery came in to see me, with a very upbeat message and a little prepared packet containing a soft sleep-bra and a wad of lambswool pressed into a pale pink breast-shaped pad. She was 56 years old, she told me proudly. She was also a woman of admirable energies who clearly would uphold and defend to the death those structures of a society that had allowed her a little niche to shine in. Her message was, you are just as good as you were before because you can look exactly the same. Lambswool now, then a good prosthesis as soon as possible, and nobody'll ever know the difference. But what she said was "*You'll* never know the difference," and she lost me right there, because I knew sure as hell *I'd* know the difference.

"Look at me," she said, opening her trim powder-blue man-tailored jacket and standing before me in a tight blue sweater, a gold embossed locket of no mean dimension provocatively nestling between her two considerable breasts. "Now can you tell which is which?"

I admitted that I could not. In her tight foundation garment and stiff, up-lifting bra, both breasts looked equally unreal to me. But then I've always been a connoisseur of women's breasts, and never overly fond of stiff uplifts. I looked away, thinking, "I wonder if there are any black lesbian feminists in Reach for Recovery?"

I ached to talk to women about the experience I had just been through, and about what might be to come, and how were they doing it and how had they done it. But I needed to talk with women who shared at least some of my major concerns and beliefs and visions, who shared at least some of my language. And this lady, admirable though she might be, did not.

"And it doesn't really interfere with your love life, either, dear. Are you married?"

"Not anymore," I said. I didn't have the moxie or the desire or the courage maybe to say, "I love women."

"Well, don't you worry. In the 6 years since my operation I married my second husband and buried him, god bless him, and now I have a wonderful friend. There's nothing I did before that I don't still do now. I just make sure I carry an extra form just in case, and I'm just like anybody else. The silicone ones are best, and I can give you the names of the better salons."

I was thinking, "What is it like to be making love to a woman and have only one breast brushing against her?"

I thought, "How will we fit so perfectly together ever again?"

I thought, "I wonder if our love-making had anything to do with it?"

I thought, "What will it be like making love to me? Will she still find my body delicious?"

And for the first time deeply and fleetingly a groundswell of sadness rolled up over me that filled my mouth and eyes almost to drowning. My right breast represented such an area of feeling and pleasure for me, how could I bear never to feel that again?

The lady from Reach for Recovery gave me a book of exercises which were very helpful to me, and she showed my how to do them. When she held my arm up to assist me, her grip was firm and friendly and her hair smelled a little like sun. . . .

After she left, assuring me that Reach for Recovery was always ready to help, I examined the packet she had left behind.

The bra was the kind I was wearing, a soft front-hooking sleep-bra. By this time, the Ace bandage was off, and I had a simple surgical bandage taped over the incision and the one remaining drain. My left breast was still a little sore from having been biopsied, which is why I was wearing a bra. The lambswool form was the strangest part of the collection. I examined it, in its blush-pink nylon envelope with a slighter, darker apex and shaped like a giant slipper-shell. I shuddered at its grotesque dryness. (What size are you, she'd said. 38D I said. Well I'll leave you a 40C she said.)

I came around my bed and stood in front of the mirror in my room, and stuffed the thing into the wrinkled folds of the right side of my bra where my right breast should have been. It perched on my chest askew, awkwardly inert and lifeless, and having nothing to do with any me I could possibly conceive of. Besides, it was the wrong color, and looked grotesquely pale through the cloth of my bra. Somewhere, up to that moment, I had thought, well perhaps they know something that I don't and maybe they're right, if I put it on maybe I'll feel entirely different. I didn't. I pulled the thing out of my bra, and my thin pajama top settled back against the flattened surface on the right side of the front of me.

I looked at the large gentle curve my left breast made under the pajama top, a curve that seemed even larger now that it stood by itself. I looked strange and uneven and peculiar to myself, but somehow, ever so much more myself, and therefore so much more acceptable, than I looked with that thing stuck inside my clothes. For not even the most skillful prosthesis in the world could undo that reality, or feel the way my breast had felt, and either I would love my body one-breasted now, or remain forever alien to myself.

Then I climbed back into bed and cried myself to sleep, even though it was 2:30 in the afternoon. . . .

I was very anxious to go home. But I found also, and couldn't admit at the time, that the very bland whiteness of the hospital which I railed against and hated so, was also a kind of protection, a welcome insulation within which I could continue to non-feel. It was an erotically blank environment within whose undifferentiated and undemanding and infantalizing walls I could continue to be emotionally vacant—psychic mush—without being required by myself or anyone to be anything else.

Going home to the very people and places that I loved most, at the same time as it was welcome and so desirable, also felt intolerable, like there was an unbearable demand about to be made upon me that I would have to meet. And it was to be made by people whom I loved, and to whom I would have to respond. Now I was going to have to begin feeling, dealing, not only with the results of the amputation, the physical effects of the surgery, but also with examining and making my own, the demands and changes inside of me and my life. They would alter, if not my timetable of work, at least the relative pieces available within that timetable for whatever I was involved in or wished to accomplish.

For instance, there were different questions about time that I would have to start asking myself. Not, for how long do I stand at the window and watch the dawn coming up over Brooklyn, but rather, how many more new people do I admit so openly into my life? I needed to examine and pursue the implications of that question. It meant plumbing the depths and possibilities of relating with the people already in my life, deepening and exploring them.

The need to look death in the face and not shrink from it, yet not ever to embrace it too easily, was a developmental and healing task for me that was constantly being sidelined by the more practical and immediate demands of hurting too much, and how do I live with myself one-breasted? What posture do I take, literally, with my physical self?

4. Mexican Immigrant Jesusita Aragon Recounts Her Work as a Midwife, 1980

When I'm sad my friends come, and I feel better. Friends help. And now I am the oldest, of neighbors and relatives and everything; now there's just me.

So many things change over the years. Many things change in how we deliver babies. When I first be a midwife, some mothers give birth the old way; the way that's gone now. They squat down when they have their baby. They tie a little round stick on the string, on a little rope. Then they put the rope over the *vigas,* the beams in the ceiling. They put it over so it's like a handle for her, and she squats down and holds onto the stick. Oh, it helps. I like that way, and sometimes somebody hold her from the back. They hold her back against their leg so she doesn't fall over.

I deliver two that way, and one of them was my sister-in-law. I don't know why, but with her first baby, she kneels down, and she says, "I feel better that way." So kneeling down is not too hard. And another lady, she does the same thing. It helps. I don't know why they stop doing that way, why they start laying on their backs. I think because to squat down is an old-fashioned way.

And we used to do different with the placenta. As soon as the placenta comes out you're supposed to take that placenta to some other room or to the bathroom, or take it out and bury it right away. Because they say the mothers feel bad when the placenta's in the room with them; they feel cramps or sometimes upset.

You know, when that lady is having her baby, I'm praying, but not loud. Praying for that lady to be OK, and for that baby, 'cause I learn to pray from my grandmother. My grandmother says, "Pray when you have a patient, pray for her and pray for that baby." So I learn everything. I pray in my mind, not loud. I pray in my heart by myself. I always pray for them, always.

Fran Leeper Buss, *La Partera: Story of a Midwife* (Ann Arbor: University of Michigan Press, 1980), pp. 63–65, 68–71, 74, 78–79. Copyright © 1980 by the University of Michigan Press. Reprinted with permission.

I have paintings of the saints in the room I use for the babies. My San Luis belonged to my great-grandmother and is very old. During the deliveries I pray to those saints:

> San Martín de Porres,
> ayúdame que salga con bien.
> San Antonio, cuídalas.
> San Luis Gonzaga, cuídame
> asi tambien que salga todo bien.

It means:

> San Martín de Porres,
> help me that it comes out fine.
> San Antonio, take care of them.
> San Luis Gonzaga, take care of me
> also so everything will be all right.

And I learn how to baptize from my grandmother, too. I baptize many. When the mothers think their baby is going to die, they tell me, "Baptize my baby." . . .

Now if there are tiny babies, premature babies, they take them to the hospital and into the incubator, but long ago I had two babies, two-pound babies, and they grow; they're alive. One is a nurse at the hospital in Pueblo; that's my nephew. He weighed two pounds when he was born. He was only six months along. He didn't have nails, nor hair, nor nothing. Nothing, just a tiny little baby. And when he opens his mouth you don't hear any sound because he's too little to have sound yet.

We say, "We should take him to Las Vegas, to the hospital."

But his mother says, "No, by the time you get there my baby will die." So we don't take him, but she is scared all the time and would say, "My baby's going to die; he's going to die." But they take care of him in a little box on the oven door, and they keep just a little piece of wood in the stove so to have low heat, for two months they do this. It is hard because at night one of them has to watch for several hours and the other one another hour, something like that. They feed him with a dropper, but he lives and is all grown now.

My grandmother teaches me how to take care of sick babies. She teaches me how to breathe in babies' mouths if they don't breathe themselves. I don't know if the other midwives know how to do that, but I know how. . . .

Today I still deliver babies. The ladies come to me when they think they're pregnant. They go to public health too, for the tests. When she first comes I check to see if the baby's in good position. I check with my hands, by the way they feel. When the baby's a breech baby the head is up at the top.

I tell the lady the supplies she needs. She needs blankets and binders for the baby, diapers, olive oil, and things for the lady. And I have the string, tape, nylon for the cord on my own. I used to get them here at the clinic, but they don't have them anymore for me. And I have to buy my own gauze for the cord, because I'm an old-fashioned midwife. I learned that things from my grandmother, to take care of the cord and put a binder around it, and to put a binder around the patient too. Yes, it's old fashioned.

You know, I can't use my rubber gloves. But I think doctors use them because they go from one infection to another, and they're scared they'll give that infection to a mother. But I wash my hands real good, with a brush, and I have short nails and everything. . . .

They say, "Oh, you have so nice hands, smooth." I don't have smooth hands; I have hard hands, but they feel my hands are smooth. I don't touch them hard nor nothing. I touch them just gentle and pet them. It helps. They feel so good, and they say, "Oh, Jesusita, I love you."

And I talk with them and sometimes I make them laugh. Yes, they feel better, and sometimes I tell them, "Get up and sit here in the kitchen and talk with me. I'm going to make supper." Or dinner, or breakfast. And that way they feel better talking. We get their things out, and I say, "Stay here; don't worry. I'm here; I'm ready." They feel better that way.

But if you are mad with them, they don't feel good. No. They say to the midwife, "I mustn't come here." 'Cause I hear them sometimes, talking about the other midwives, but I look like that I don't hear nothing.

Some of the midwives got mad, though. I know that there was a midwife that used to slap them when they cry or get nervous, but she didn't last too long. They disqualify her. They took her certificate away because the people say at the clinic what kind of midwife she is. Now I get a license, and every year they send it from Santa Fe to me.

Sometimes the ladies cry during labor, 'cause it hurts. Some of them get mad too, like they're blaming me, and they say, "Don't touch me. Get away from here." But I know that's normal, sometimes. When I went to school I learned those things.

Sometimes they try to pinch you or scratch you, but, little by little, they calm. I never get mad with them; I tell them, "Don't scratch me, don't be like that. Don't blame me on that, that's your own fault," I say.

Sometimes they laugh, or sometimes they say, "Oh, shut up."

When the mother's in labor I check her inside to see how far she's open and when she's coming. I can tell if there's a slow birth. If they have their contractions, and the womb won't open, but a little slow, it will be a long birth. . . .

When the babies come, I like the mothers to lay down, but some of the mothers are getting new ways. Well, I don't like those; I'm not used to them. There is a book when they're on their hands and knees, but I'm not used to it. And if they're sitting, they're on the baby's head that way, so that baby have to come out up, not down like he's supposed to go. I like the old ways.

And when the lady is opening for the baby's head, I pour a little olive oil on the lady, on her perineum, by her vagina, so that part gets soft and smooth and tender, and it won't cut. So it won't tear when the baby's head come out. I massage it; I rub it so it bends more, and it doesn't rip and tear. Then I pour a little more olive oil on it and rub it some more, and the mothers feel good.

My grandmother taught me how to do that. My grandmother was a good midwife; she was number one at Trujillo. When the other midwives couldn't do it, they go and bring my grandmother, and she do it in a little while.

When the baby's head is coming out I get a white rag, and I hold it on the bottom where the baby's head is coming. I hold the head so it comes slow until it is out, and then I put the rag down below on the bed and hold the baby's head and body so it won't pop out too fast. Then, as he comes all the way out, I hold his head and hips and lay the baby down.

I clean the baby's face and eyes so the baby breathes. He's usually crying and waving his little hands, and sometimes he's scared, sometimes. Then I have to get the cord in my hand until it stops to beat. I tie it a little long, and then four fingers longer, and I tie another string. Then cut on the middle.

I wrap the new one in a blanket and give the baby to the mother for a little while. She usually is, oh, so happy and talks to her new little one. Then I take the baby back and clean the baby with olive oil and cotton. I wipe the baby all over and put drops in the eyes. And I bind the baby round with gauze. That way, when he cries, where the cord was won't pop out. Finally, I weigh the baby, and then the next day I give him a bath.

Sometimes I have to give mouth-to-mouth breathing to help that baby, sometimes. Consuelo my granddaughter helped me do it some years ago. Because sometimes she likes to help me, and once she said, "Oh, Tita, this baby's not crying; he's going to die!"

I told her, "No, shut up. If you're going to help me, shut up, and come and give mouth-to-mouth." So she did. Oh, she was proud because she makes that baby cry.

I didn't want Consuelo to scare the mother. I don't say anything to scare them. If she have a breech baby I never let her know, because they get so scared. A breech is a little hard for the mother 'cause it's a little big. First his bottom comes out and then his legs and feets. Then you have to put your left hand under the baby's chin when his head starts to come. You raise the feets a little bit, not too much, so that head will slide down. Now I take the mother with a breech baby to the hospital, but I used to deliver her. . . .

Sometimes I have to get blood for special tests. The doctors bring me little bottles. So I can get that blood, and they're supposed to take it to the hospital. They have to check it from the cord and the afterbirth. I put the cord in the bottle, one big bottle and the other small. . . .

I know how people can hurt. That's part the reason I don't charge too much. They ask me the other day, on the clinic, "Why don't you charge one hundred dollars? Everything is going high; why don't you Jesusita?" Because I don't want to, and I work for my own. I'm my own boss; that's why they don't make me. I want to help the people; they need help. I know they have money, some of them, they can give one hundred dollars for their time, but I don't want to do that. I feel better to charge fifty.

Sometimes somebody comes in here, and they're crying and saying, "Jesusita, I need you, but I don't have any money. I'm going to have a baby, and I don't have any money."

So I tell them, "OK, just come in. You can have your baby here, and you don't have to pay me if you don't have any money." And when they go home, in a month or two, they come and bring my money.

It's hard to be good midwife sometimes. It's not easy, no. . . .

Sometimes I help a man. They maybe twist a foot, a wrist, or his neck, something. But I don't like to do that, no, but I do it, sometimes I do it. And I fix one man who had a wound in his stomach that wouldn't heal. I fix some herbs and put it on and before long, it's better.

And sometimes I help the children. I help them with the *empacho.* I don't know if there's English for it; I don't think so. The kids get it when they eat or chew or swallow something bad for them, and it's stuck in there. Maybe they eat too much cold lunch or too much potato chips with coke, so I have to rub the stomach and back to put it down, and I pull the skin up and clack it, so it's loose in there. I learn this from my grandma long ago.

I know what's good for a fever besides aspirin. Rubbing alcohol on the body and *azafrán,* if you make a tea. It's a flower, a red thing, and you make a tea and give it to them. We used to do that in Trujillo. We used to plant too many azafrán. I can't hardly find the seed now, it's a little white weed.

There are others. The *escoba de la víbora,* that's snake-weed; it's for ulcers. Make tea and drink it, and *mastranzo* just the same, for the same thing. And *romerillo* is for hemorrhages. There are so many that I can't remember. But I remember some of them. They used them when people were sick when I was little, and sometimes now.

This mastranzo is good for those little things that grow in the vagina, the yeast infection. Use mastranzo and *añil del muerto.* Just boil it, make tea, and put them in a douche bag and douche with it. And drink some. I have some; yes, everybody brings me herbs. . . .

My grandmother showed me how to use these things. When I was little. She learned them from her mother. Everybody knew them back then, and they teach each other. Yes, I know many things now. I'm partera, a midwife, and some people say I'm médica. I'm médica, the healer.

5. Perri Klass, a Physician and Writer, Ponders the Feminization of the Medical Profession, 1992

There was a conundrum which used to turn up now and then, when I was in high school, designed to test your level of consciousness: a father and son go fishing, and on the way home, they're in a car accident. The father is killed instantly, the boy is rushed to the hospital, where the surgeon takes one look at him and screams, "Oh, my God, it's my son!" What is the relationship between the surgeon and the child?

Well, obviously, the surgeon is the child's mother. Surely no one had to think twice about that? Well, fifteen years ago, lots of people would ponder that puzzle, making up complex stepfather/grandfather linkages, trying to explain how a child could have no father, but still have a parent who was a doctor.

In 1969, 9.2 percent of the first-year medical students in America were women; in 1987 it was 36.5 percent. In 1970, women accounted for 7.6 percent of all the physicians in America and 10.7 percent of the residents. In 1985, 14.6 percent of all physicians and 26.2 percent of all residents were female. Perhaps the most important and most interesting question that confronts female M.D.'s as they become more and more a fact of life in the medical profession is this: are women actually changing medicine, are they somehow different as doctors—or does the long and rigorous medical training produce doctors who are simply doctors, male or female?

I did not go to medical school during the pioneering age. When I started, in 1982, 53 of the 165 students in their first year at Harvard Medical School were women. Moreover, I chose to go into pediatrics, a field that has the highest percentage of female residents of any medical specialty—fifty percent nationwide. I have never had the experience of being the only woman in the lecture hall, the only female resident in the hospital. Occasionally, I have been the only woman on a particular medical team, but often I have been on all-female teams. During my own medical training, so far at least, I have not had reason to feel like a scholarship student from an alien tribe. . . .

When I interviewed women doctors, I came always to the point where I asked, are women doctors different? And with only a couple of exceptions, I got versions of the same response from the doctors I interviewed, young or old, avowedly feminist or not. First you get that disclaimer, the one I just offered; I've known some wonderful male doctors, I've known some awful female doctors, generalizations are impossible. And then, hesitantly, even apologetically, or else frankly and with a smile, comes the generalization. Yes, women are different as doctors: they're better. . . .

Nevada Mitchell, M.D., practices internal medicine. Her subspecialty is geriatrics. She was born in Kansas City, went to college at Vassar, then came back to KC, got married, started teaching—she had thought about medical school, but didn't feel she had what it would take to go. But reading in the Vassar alumnae magazine about classmates who had gone to medical school, she decided she wanted to try for it, and five years later she was in medical school. Dr. Mitchell has no doubt at all about the difference between male and female doctors. "There's a world of difference. The women I come into contact with are less aggressive, more likely to have one-on-one-type relationships with patients than men, less likely to go for high volume of patients—but also less likely to be out here in private practice." Dr. Mitchell returned several times to the issue of being "out here," explaining that many women take jobs with HMOs, which offer regular salaries and limited working hours. "You need a certain aggressiveness to choose private practice," she said, with some satisfaction.

Dr. Mitchell feels that older patients are often more receptive to women doctors, since they are looking for more than medical therapy. Her original decision to go into geriatrics was related to watching her younger colleagues in medical school trying to deal with the many elderly patients, and feeling those patients were often neglected or taken for granted. Her medical practice now includes many older patients, but she also does general internal medicine. With a smile, she ticked off the various groups on her fingers: older people are fine, younger and middle-aged women usually have no problem with a female doctor, younger men are initially hesitant, feel self-conscious about the complete physical examination.

Dr. Mitchell cannot think of a female doctor she wanted to be like. "I didn't have that many examples. I developed my own style and image." She did, however, tell me that I ought to talk to the doctor who had operated on her when she needed some gynecological surgery. She felt that when she had discussed the medical issues with a male doctor, he had placed less of a priority on maintaining the option of future pregnancy. Dr. Mitchell, who is thirty-nine and has a sixteen-year-old daughter, wanted to keep her options open, and felt that a female doctor, Marilyn Richardson, had been more willing to take this seriously.

Ironically, Dr. Richardson herself thinks that's nonsense. An obstetrician-gynecologist specializing in reproductive endocrinology, she was a pianist for years before she went to medical school. She is highly professional, authoritative, and decided in her opinions. Patients who come looking for a female gynecologist, she says, are "erroneous—it's a patient's misconception that has evolved with consumer awareness, an erroneous belief that women doctors are more compassionate, more understanding. Well, I don't have menstrual cramps, I didn't have severe pain in labor. Women who come asking for a female doctor are looking for a buddy, and they're not going to find that in me." . . .

. . . "It was a male mentor who taught me sensitivity toward the preservation of fertility." Her style, she says, is a composite of this mentor and of her father, also in Ob-Gyn, and of techniques of doctoring she has developed for herself.

I mention to Dr. Richardson that one of the places I always felt a very sharp difference between male and female doctors was in the operating room. I ask whether she believes this is also erroneous. No, she agrees, the way that women run an OR is different. "Women manage more efficiently if they can strike a balance of authoritativeness and humaneness. Men are often arbitrary, demanding, and disrespectful, and the level of efficiency suffers. Women don't usually command quite as fiercely, will *ask* for an instrument . . . you get camaraderie with the other staff members."

Dr. Susan Love agrees. One of the first two female surgical residents at a major Boston teaching hospital, Dr. Love finished her training in 1980. She went into private practice in general surgery, though she initially had trouble getting a position on the staff of the hospital where she had just been chief surgical resident. In her practice, she found she was seeing many patients with breast disease, who preferred to go to a woman doctor, and she eventually decided to specialize in this field. She now has a partner, another woman surgeon, and they have as many patients as they can handle. Dr. Love feels strongly that she had to suppress many of her basic values in order to get through her surgical residency: "Most women have problems—unless they can block out their previous socialization. Surgeons don't really like having women, don't make it comfortable for them. Things that women like, talking to patients, aren't important, it's how many operations you've done, how many hours you've been up, how many notches on your belt. If you get through your five or six years of training, you can regain your values, but it's a real if. Most men never get them back."

Dr. Love runs an operating room, she says, by "treating the nurses like intelligent people, talking to them, teaching them. I'm not the big ruler." . . . A concrete example of something she does differently, something no one taught her: before the patient is put to sleep, she makes it a practice to hold the patient's hand. "I'm usually the only person in the room they really know, and it's the scariest time. The boys scrub, come in when the patient's asleep. I got razzed for it, but they're used to it now."

Unlike Dr. Richardson, Dr. Love does think that women doctors behave differently with their patients. "I spend more time in empathy, talking, explaining, teaching, and it's a much more equal power relationship." And then there's not taking people for granted—she tells the story of a recent patient, an eighty-four-year-old woman with breast cancer who was asked by a male surgeon, "Are you vain?" Embarrassed, the woman said she wasn't. The surgeon advised her, in that case, to have a mastectomy, rather than a more limited procedure—"But then her niece pointed out, but you bought a new bra to come to the doctor, but you combed your hair over your hearing aid." The doctor had simply assumed that an elderly woman would have no particular desire to keep her breast, no vanity left to speak of. Dr. Love's anecdotes are often sharp—she describes a male surgeon who explained that a particular implant used in breast reconstruction felt just like a normal breast; he meant, of course, that to someone touching the breast, the texture was close to natural, not that the woman actually had normal feeling in the implant.

I heard over and over that women are better at talking to people, better at listening. Dr. Carol Lindsley, a rheumatologist at the University of Kansas, says the female medical students are "more sensitive to patient and family needs, more patient, pay more attention to detail." Dr. Marilyn Rymer, a Kansas City neurologist, says that many of her female patients come looking for a woman doctor, some because they feel they can talk to a woman more easily, others because "they find that women listen better, are more empathic, care about explaining things, dealing with the family." Dr. [Linda] Dorzab agrees: "My patients say women listen better, are better at acknowledging when something is bothering the patient." On the other hand, Dr. Debbie Stanford, a resident in internal medicine at the University of Alabama in Birmingham, feels that there is no difference at all between the male and female interns she supervises: "Capabilities, compassion, endurance—no difference." ...

It is generally agreed, among women doctors, that we have to be more polite and more careful with nurses than our male colleagues; a fairer way of putting this would probably be to say that nurses have had to take a lot of rudeness and bad behavior from doctors over the years, and that while they make some of the traditional female allowances for traditional male patterns, they are unwilling to accept these same behaviors from women. Or, to quote Dr. Richardson again, "When you make a big mess in the operating room, there's something different in your mind when you walk out and leave it for another woman to clean-up." I have found in my own training that nurses generally expect me to clean-up after myself (i.e., to gather up all the little alcohol pads and pieces of gauze left on the bed after I draw blood from a baby), to do a fair amount of my own secretarial work, and not to take too high-and-mighty a tone. What would be taken as normal behavior in a male (especially a male surgeon; they have the most traditional doctor-nurse power structure) is considered aggressive and obnoxious in a female. ....

Medical training and medical practice are stressful for everyone, male and female. Women often face additional pressures; the issue of combining family and career comes up constantly when you try to write about women in medicine. ....

These difficulties are not, of course, unique to the women. Males also have to cope with the hours, with not being there when their children need them, with promises made and broken. They are somewhat more likely to have spouses who delay their own careers. Still, I have heard complaints about male colleagues of mine who are too eager to leave the hospital and get home to their families; some men may even be much less self-conscious about this precisely because they bear no if-I-make-a-fuss-about-my-kid-they'll-think-women-shouldn't-be-doctors burden. No one, after all, is likely to say that fatherhood and medicine don't mix. The fact is, though, that certain intensities of career are essentially incompatible with any kind of parenthood. You don't have very much to do with your child if your ideal is to spend every waking moment in the hospital, whether you are the father or the mother. The influx of women into medicine, we can hope, will help us design medical careers for both men and women that will enable doctors to follow some of their own recommendations (reduce stress, eat a healthy diet, keep regular hours, spend time with your family—we pediatricians, for example, are always telling parents how important it is that they pay lots of attention to their children).

6. Journalist Anne Fadiman Chronicles the Collision of Healing Cultures, 1997

It was said in the refugee camps in Thailand that the Hmong in America could not find work, were forbidden to practice their religion, and were robbed and beaten by gangs. It was also said that Hmong women were forced into slavery, forced to have sex with American men, and forced to have sex with animals. Dinosaurs lived in America, as well as ghosts, ogres, and giants. With all this to worry about, why did the 15,000 Hmong who gathered on the Ban Vinai soccer field to voice their deepest fears about life in the United States choose to fixate on *doctors?*

A year after I first read the account of that gathering, as I was attempting to deal out a teetering pile of notes, clippings, and photocopied pages from books and dissertations into several drawerfuls of file folders, I had a glimmering of insight. There were hundreds of pages whose proper home I was at a loss to determine. Should they go in the Medicine folder? The Mental Health folder? The Animism folder? The Shamanism folder? The Social Structure folder? The Body/Mind/Soul Continuum folder? I hovered uncertainly, pages in hand, and realized that I was suspended in a large bowl of Fish Soup. Medicine *was* religion. Religion was society. Society was medicine. Even economics were mixed up in there somewhere (you had to have or borrow enough money to buy a pig, or even a cow, in case someone got sick and a sacrifice was required), and so was music (if you didn't have a *qeej* player at your funeral, your soul wouldn't be guided on its posthumous travels, and it couldn't be reborn, and it might make your relatives sick). In fact, the Hmong view of health care seemed to me to be precisely the opposite of the prevailing American one, in which the practice of medicine has fissioned into smaller and smaller subspecialties, with less and less truck between bailiwicks. The Hmong carried holism to its ultima Thule [expression meaning "farthest extreme"]. As my web of cross-references grew more and more thickly interlaced, I concluded that the Hmong preoccupation with medical issues was nothing less than a preoccupation with life. (And death. And life after death.)

Not realizing that when a man named Xiong or Lee or Moua walked into the Family Practice Center with a stomachache he was actually complaining that the entire universe was out of balance, the young doctors of Merced [town in central California] frequently failed to satisfy their Hmong patients. How could they succeed? They could hardly be expected, as Dwight Conquergood [International Rescue

Committee ethnographer] had done at Ban Vinai [refugee camp in Thailand], to launch a parade of tigers and *dabs* through the corridors of MCMC [Merced Community Medical Center]. They could hardly be expected to "respect" their patients' system of health beliefs (if indeed they ever had the time and the interpreters to find out what it was), since the medical schools they had attended had never informed them that diseases are caused by fugitive souls and cured by jugulated chickens. All of them had spent hundreds of hours dissecting cadavers, and could distinguish at a glance between the ligament of Hesselbach and the ligament of Treitz, but none of them had had a single hour of instruction in cross-cultural medicine. To most of them, the Hmong taboos against blood tests, spinal taps, surgery, anesthesia, and autopsies—the basic tools of modern medicine—seemed like self-defeating ignorance. They had no way of knowing that a Hmong might regard these taboos as the sacred guardians of his identity, indeed, quite literally, of his very soul. What the doctors viewed as clinical efficiency the Hmong viewed as frosty arrogance. And no matter what the doctors did, even if it never trespassed on taboo territory, the Hmong, freighted as they were with negative expectations accumulated before they came to America, inevitably interpreted it in the worst possible light.

Whenever I talked to Hmong people in Merced, I asked them what they thought of the medical care they and their friends had received.

"The doctor at MCMC are young and new. They do what they want to do. Doctor want to look inside the woman body. The woman very pain, very hurt, but the doctor just want to practice on her."

"One lady, she is cry, cry, cry. She do not want doctor to see her body. But this country there is the rule. If you want to stay here you must let doctor examine the body."

"Most old people prefer not to go to doctor. They feel, maybe doctor just want to study me, not help my problems. They scary this. If they go one time, if they not follow appointment and do like doctor want, doctor get mad. Doctor is like earth and sky. He think, you are refugee, you know nothing."

"It took us an hour to see the doctor. Other people who are rich, they treat them really well and they do not wait."

"This lady she had some blisters inside the mouth and the doctor he say, you need surgical treatment. She say, no, I just need medication for pain only. And he say, I know more than you do. He completely ignore what she ask."

"My half brother his body was swollen and itchy, and the doctors say, hey, you got a cancer and we need to operate. He agreed to sign the operation but then he didn't want to do it. But he say to me, I already sign everything and the doctor going to send me to jail if I change my mind."

"Hmong should never sign anything at MCMC. The student doctors just want to experiment on the poor people and they kill the poor people."

"The doctor is very busy. He takes people that are sick, he produces people that are healthy. If he do not produce, his economic will be deficit. But the Hmong, he will want the doctor to calmly explain and comfort him. That does not happen. I do not blame the doctor. It is the system in America."

All of the people quoted here speak English, and thus belong to the most educated and most Americanized segment of Hmong society in Merced—the segment most likely to understand and value Western medical care. Nonetheless, their version of reality fails to match that of their doctors pretty much across the board. From the doctors' point of view, the facts are as follows: MCMC is indeed a teaching hospital, but this works to its patients' advantage, since it has attracted skilled faculty members who must constantly update their knowledge and techniques. The young residents are all M.D.s, not students. The Hmong spend a long time in the waiting area, but so does everyone else. Patients who change their minds about surgery do not go to jail. The doctors do not experiment on their patients. Neither do they kill them, though their patients do sometimes die, and are more likely to do so if, like the Hmong, they view the hospital as a dreaded last resort to be hazarded only when all else fails.

Although the doctors at MCMC are not aware of most of the Hmong's specific criticisms—they would be unlikely to ask, and the Hmong would be unlikely to answer—they certainly know the Hmong do not like them, and that rankles. The residents may be exhausted (since their shifts are up to twenty-four hours long, and until recent years were up to thirty-three hours long); they may be rushed (since many clinic appointments are only fifteen minutes long); but they are not—and they *know* they are not—greedy or spiteful. Most of them have chosen the field of family practice, which is the lowest-paying of all medical specialties, for altruistic reasons. "Of course, some of the subspecialists would say we went into family medicine because we weren't smart enough to be urologists or ophthalmologists," Bill Selvidge, MCMC's former chief resident, told me. "If we *were* urologists, we'd be making a lot more money and we wouldn't have to get up so often in the middle of the night."

Bill is an old college friend of mine. It was he who first told me about the Hmong of Merced, whom he described as being such challenging patients that some of his fellow doctors suggested the preferred method of treatment for them was high-velocity transcortical lead therapy. (When I asked Bill what that meant, he explained, "The patient should be shot in the head.") Bill himself did not seem to find the Hmong quite as exasperating as some of his colleagues did, perhaps because of the lessons in cultural relativism he had learned during the two years he had spent with the Peace Corps in Micronesia, and perhaps because, as he pointed out to me, the Hmong acted no stranger than his next-door neighbors in Merced, a family of white fundamentalist Christians who had smashed their television set and then danced a jig around it. (The neighbor's children had then offered to smash Bill's set as well. He had politely declined.) Bill was the sort of person I'd always wanted to have as a doctor myself, and before I came to Merced, I found it hard to believe that his Hmong patients weren't prostrate with gratitude.

When refugees from Laos started settling in Merced County in the early 1980s, none of the doctors at MCMC had ever heard the word "Hmong," and they had no idea what to make of their new patients. They wore strange clothes—often children's clothes, which were approximately the right size—acquired at the local Goodwill. When they undressed for an examination, the women were sometimes wearing Jockey shorts and the men were sometimes wearing bikini underpants with little pink butterflies. They wore amulets around their necks and cotton strings around their wrists (the sicker the patient, the more numerous the strings). They smelled of camphor, mentholatum, Tiger Balm, and herbs. When they were admitted to the hospital, they brought their own food and medicines. The parents of one of

Neil Ernst's [pediatrician in Merced] patients, a small boy with a gastrointestinal disorder, once emptied his intravenous bottle and replaced its contents with what Neil described as green slime, an herbal home brew whose ingredients the doctors never determined. Hmong patients made a lot of noise. Sometimes they wanted to slaughter live animals in the hospital. Tom Sult, a former MCMC resident, recalled, "They'd bang the crap out of some kind of musical instrument, and the American patients would complain. Finally we had to talk to them. No gongs. And no dead chickens."

Neil Ernst and Peggy Philp [pediatrician in Merced] were shocked to discover quarter-sized round lesions, some reddish and some hypopigmented, on the abdomens and arms of some of their pediatric patients. They looked like burns. Some of the lesions had healed and others were still crusty, suggesting that the skin had been traumatized on more than one occasion. Neil and Peggy immediately called the Child Protective Services office to report that they had identified several cases of child abuse. Before the cases were prosecuted, they learned from a San Francisco doctor that the lesions were the result of dermal treatments—rubbing the skin with coins or igniting alcohol-soaked cotton under a tiny cup to create a vacuum— that were common among several Asian ethnic groups, and that they were a "traditional healing art," not a form of abuse. (I once attended a conference on Southeast Asian health care issues at which a prominent doctor showed some slides of coin-rubbing lesions and told the audience, "It doesn't hurt." The young Lao woman sitting next to me whispered, "Yes it does.") Dan Murphy remembers that when he was a resident, he heard a story about a Hmong father in Fresno who was sent to jail after black marks were discovered on his child's chest by an elementary school teacher. The father hanged himself in his cell. The story is probably apocryphal (though it is still in wide circulation), but Dan and the other doctors believed it, and they were shaken to realize how high the stakes could be if they made a tactical error in dealing with the Hmong.

And there were so many ways to err! When doctors conferred with a Hmong family, it was tempting to address the reassuringly Americanized teenaged girl who wore lipstick and spoke English rather than the old man who squatted silently in the corner. Yet failing to work within the traditional Hmong hierarchy, in which males ranked higher than females and old people higher than young ones, not only insulted the entire family but also yielded confused results, since the crucial questions had not been directed toward those who had the power to make the decisions. Doctors could also appear disrespectful if they tried to maintain friendly eye contact (which was considered invasive), touched the head of an adult without permission (grossly insulting), or beckoned with a crooked finger (appropriate only for animals). And doctors could lose the respect of their patients if they didn't act like authority figures. The young residents at MCMC did not enhance their status by their propensities for introducing themselves by their first names, wearing blue jeans under their white coats, carrying their medical charts in little backpacks, and drinking their coffee from Tommee Tippee cups. Doctors could get into trouble if they failed to take the Hmong's religious beliefs into account. For example, it was important never to compliment a baby's beauty out loud, lest a *dab* overhear and be unable to resist snatching its soul. Similarly, when a seventeen-year-old Hmong patient once asked if her failure to get pregnant might be attributable to the *dab* who frequently visited her in her dreams, sometimes sitting on the edge of her bed and sometimes having sexual intercourse with her, it was fortunate that the resident on duty in OB-GYN Clinic listened with calm attention instead of diagnosing an acute psychosis and dispatching her to a locked ward. On the other hand, bending over backwards to be culturally sensitive did not always work. Bill Selvidge once examined a depressed middle-aged Hmong woman with severe headaches. Surmising that some of her problems stemmed from cultural dislocation and that her spirits might be buoyed by traditional treatment, he recommended that she see a *txiv neeb*. However, as he reported in his clinic note, "She is reluctant to go to a shaman, partly because she is now Catholic and partly because it takes too many chickens and/or pig that have to be killed in her home for her to satisfy shamans and traditional healers. She may have tried this in the past because she indicates a previous landlord told her to leave home after police were called when some members of her family were just about to sacrifice a pig." Disappointed, Bill prescribed aspirin.

 E S S A Y S

In the first essay, Columbia University historian David Rothman exposes the structural and attitudinal barriers that have arisen in the doctor-patient relationship in the years since 1945. Changes in the hospital, in general medical practice, and in medical education, as well as increasing reliance on technology and specialization, have, according to Rothman, helped to make "the doctor a stranger." His analysis of this process makes understandable the sense of distance and distrust that pervades many Americans' encounters with modern medicine, a malaise animating an ideological orientation that encompasses such notions as a "patient's bill of rights" and bioethics. In the second essay, historian Allan Brandt of Harvard University examines the same era in American health history but chooses a very different vantage point. He begins his essay by sketching changes in major epidemiological patterns. He then uses these statistical patterns as the backdrop for an exploration of what really interests him—namely, how Americans gave meaning to these shifting disease patterns. Brandt captures a kaleidoscope of changing attitudes toward health risks and responsibilities as he investigates such key episodes in late-twentieth-century health history as the tobacco wars, the self-help and fitness movements, the AIDS epidemic, the emergence of the discipline of bioethics, and the enunciation of a patient's rights ideology.

The Doctor as Stranger: Medicine and Public Distrust

DAVID J. ROTHMAN

Practically every development in medicine in the post–World War II period distanced the physician and the hospital from the patient and the community, disrupting personal connections and severing bonds of trust. Whatever the index—whether ties of friendship, religion, ethnicity, or intellectual activity—the results highlight a sharp

David J. Rothman, "The Doctor as Stranger," from *Strangers at the Bedside: A History of How Law and Bioethics Transformed Medical Decision Making* (New York: Basic Books, 1991), pp. 127–147. Reprinted by permission of the author. Copyright © 1991.

division between the lay world and the medical world. . . . In a spate of recent medical self-help books writers have advised patients to prepare to enter a hospital as though they were going on a trek in Nepal—take food and organize family and friends to provide necessary help. It has even been suggested that patients hang up school diplomas and pictures of their children to make certain that the chieftains of this exotic place know that they are valued persons in the outside world.

To read some of the critiques, one would think the problem is mostly a matter of educating medical students by emphasizing communication skills (so doctors learn better how to interview and how to listen) and incorporating the humanities into the curriculum (on the theory that studying the classics will increase empathy). But however worthwhile these efforts, a reliance on the education of the future practitioner as the vehicle for change minimizes the structural barriers to recasting the doctor-patient relationship. The organization and delivery of medical care almost guarantees that at a time of crisis patients will be treated by strangers in a strange environment. This circumstance has transformed many patients' behavior, encouraging a style closer to that of a wary consumer than a grateful supplicant. Moreover, this distancing helps explain why a cadre of outsiders felt compelled to enter the medical arena and promote a commitment to a more formal and collective type of medical decision making, including administrative guidelines and review committee oversight.

The first and most obvious of the structural changes that distanced patients from doctors in the post-1945 decades was the disappearance of the house call. By the early 1960s, home visits represented less than one percent of doctor-patient contacts. Surprisingly, the demise of the house call is a relatively unexplored phenomenon, but it reflects a combination of professional and technological considerations. By bringing the patient to the office and hospital, physicians increased their own efficiency and incomes, enabling them to examine many more patients in much less time. The change also served to give patients quicker access to medical technologies (at first, X-ray and electrocardiogram machines; later, computerized scanners and magnetic imagers). But whatever the reason, the effect was to remove patients from familiar surroundings and deprive the doctor of a firsthand knowledge of the patients' environment. In both symbolic and real terms, doctors and patients moved apart.

This distance was further enlarged as medical specialization and subspecialization transformed the profession in the post–World War II years. The fears of the 1930s became the realities of the 1950s and 1960s; only 20 percent of physicians now identified themselves as general practitioners, and occasional efforts to increase the pool through training programs in community medicine or family medicine showed few results. Not only were doctors now trained so intensely in the functioning of a particular organ or system that they might well lose sight of the patient's presence, but specialization meant that patients and doctors were not likely to have met before the onset of the illness, let alone to have developed a relationship. . . . Even those with a primary physician could not be certain that the doctor would be able to follow them into the hospital; since admitting privileges to tertiary-care medical centers were often very restricted, the odds were that as the stakes in illness mounted and decisions became more critical, the patient was more likely to be in a strange setting surrounded by strangers. . . .

After the 1950s, even sectarian hospitals no longer relied on such criteria as religion or ethnicity to select most of the house staff and senior physicians. Put another way, choice by merit accelerated the process by which the ethnic hospital lost its special relationship to its patients. It became increasingly difficult to define what was Presbyterian about Presbyterian Hospital or Jewish about Mt. Sinai Hospital, and the answer could not be found in the characteristics of either the patients or the attending physicians. (Catholic hospitals have withstood this trend to a degree, but they barely resemble their predecessors of the 1930s, which were dominated by the nursing sisters.) The trustees of Montefiore Hospital in New York, for example, celebrated the hospital's 100th anniversary in 1985 by amending its charter and eliminating the provision that a majority of its board had to be Jewish. Although the revision paid homage to the scientific ideal of universalism, it also reflected the decline of the ethnic character of the hospital. . . .

In much the same way, the hospital as a neighborhood institution almost disappeared. In New York City, for example, between 1963 and 1978, thirty-five hospitals closed; and they were, typically, smaller facilities that served a special section of the population. As the authors of one report concluded: "The communities for which these institutions had been established—generally comprising either the educated and affluent or immigrants of a single particular ethnic group—had vanished in a massive turnover of population." The same process has affected smaller communities. Since the 1970s many rural and small-town hospitals have closed, reflecting mounting costs, inefficiencies of size, and patients' preference for hospitals staffed by specialists and equipped with advanced technologies. The trade-off, of course, is that seriously ill patients must travel to a distant regional hospital to be cared for by strangers.

Not only the anonymity of the doctor and the hospital but the new style of medical practice have made it nearly impossible to maintain a personal and intimate link between the patient and the health care providers. . . . Compared with the pre–World War II period, the patient population in major medical centers has become more seriously ill. This increased severity of disease reflects a shortened length of patient stay—usually achieved by curtailing the period of in-hospital recuperation and recovery—and a closer scrutiny over patient admissions to make certain that they really need a hospital bed. Whether the driving force is the need to cut costs or to spare the patient days in so alien an environment or to reduce the likelihood of iatrogenic complications, the result has been to transform the practice of hospital medicine.

On the wards, doctors typically scramble from crisis to crisis. No sooner do they stabilize a patient and get her on the road to recovery, than she is discharged and the next acutely ill patient takes the bed. House staff, who actually do most of the scrambling, often devise ingenious strategies to keep a recuperating patient in bed, not as a favor to the patient but as a way of reducing their workload. But ploys, like lining up an additional test, do not work for very long, for as clever as house staff might be, hospital administrators are not far behind. So physicians soon are again performing intake exams, diagnosing symptoms, devising a treatment plan, and responding to emergencies, knowing that the moment they rescue one patient, the cycle will inevitably begin again.

. . . [O]f course, the hospital had become the prime, almost exclusive, setting for treating serious illness, bringing with it isolation from family and friends which hospital policies only exacerbated. The most compelling critique of this change came from Dr. Elisabeth Kubler-Ross, one of the first physicians to make dying her specialty. "I remember as a child the death of a farmer," she wrote in her 1969 best-seller, *On Death and Dying*. "He asked simply to die at home, a wish that was granted without questioning." He called in his children, arranged his affairs and asked his friends to visit him once more, to bid good-bye to them." By contrast, we now "don't allow children to visit their dying parents in the hospitals," and the patient himself undergoes a kind of torture: "He may cry for rest, peace and dignity, but he will get infusions, transfusions, a heart machine, or tracheostomy." The loneliest, and cruelest, setting was the intensive care unit. Kubler-Ross recounts the frustration and agony of an elderly man allowed only a five minute visit every hour with his desperately ill wife in the ICU. "Was that the way he was to say good-bye to his wife of almost fifty years?" Kubler-Ross well understood that "there are administrative rules and laws" and "too many visitors in such a unit would be intolerable— if not for the patients, maybe for the sensitive equipment?" But surely, we have to find a way to reduce the distance between hospital, patient, and family.

However important these structural considerations, they are not the totality of the story. To understand the separation of the medical and nonmedical worlds, one must also reckon with changes in the patterns of recruitment to medicine and training in medicine in the post–World War II period. For here too lie elements that have promoted the insularity of physicians and their separation from the nonmedical world. In very dramatic fashion these changes undermined the patient's confidence in the exercise of physician discretion. It made sense in an earlier era to trust to the wisdom of the doctor, knowing that his decisions would be informed not only by his greater experience—he had been there many times before—but by the ethics of the community, which he, too, shared. But in the postwar decades this confidence eroded. The doctors' decisions, like the researchers', seemed likely to reflect their own or their subspeciality's idiosyncratic judgments.

The process that encapsulates physicians in their own universe begins surprisingly early in their lives. A study in the 1950s of six successive classes of medical students at the University of Pennsylvania revealed that just over half the students were already considering a medical career by the time they were thirteen; if their fathers were physicians, the percentage climbed to three-quarters. . . .

. . . The pre-med student, noted one graduate, "narrows his horizons, intensifies his efforts in physics, chemistry, and biology and limits the amount of his general cultural baggage during precisely the three or four years that offer the last chance of a liberal education."

Once in medical school, most medical students face time demands—to say nothing of the substance of the curriculum—that further separate them from their peers. By comparison to law, business, or graduate school in the arts and sciences, the daily class schedule and the academic terms are very long; and the medical campus is often distant from the other parts of the university, so even those inclined to mix with other graduate students are unable to do so. The isolation only increases during the years of residency and fellowship training. Time not spent on the wards is usually spent catching up on sleep. Thus, when physicians earn the requisite degrees and pass the national and specialty board exams, they have spent some fifteen years since high school on the training track, most of this time, segregated in a medical world.

The stuff of medicine is also isolating. To deal on a daily basis with injury, pain, disfigurement, and death is to be set apart from others. Modern society has constructed exceptionally sturdy boundaries around illness, confining it to the hospital and making it the nearly exclusive preserve of the medical profession. In effect, the hospital does for illness what the insane asylum intended to do for mental illness: enclose it in its own special territory. To be sure, this process is not new, but it has surely accelerated over the last several decades. The two great rites of passage, birth and death, have both moved into the hospital, the first by the 1920s, the second by the 1950s. The isolation of illness is certainly not complete, however. Epidemics, whether Legionnaires' disease or AIDS, rivet public attention; chronic disease is more likely to be treated in the community; and bookstore owners devote more space than ever before to self-help books explaining everything one wants to know about heart disease, diabetes, and cancer. Nevertheless, serious disease is not the substance of everyday discourse, and in more ways than might be at first recognized, this division of labor cuts doctors off from others. . . .

Whether the isolation of physicians is self-imposed or socially imposed, the results are apparent in a variety of contexts. Physicians are notable for their lack of political involvement, particularly given their high status and incomes. Because the American Medical Association has been so vocal a lobby, one tends to forget just how removed most doctors are from politics. Questionnaires distributed to the 1959 and 1963 Harvard Medical School classes, for example, revealed that only 4 to 6 percent of the students intended to be politically active. That they, and other physicians, meant what they said, is evident if one looks at the number of physicians in high office or active at the state and municipal levels—probably less than 100 if one excludes agencies dealing directly with matters of health or research policy.

In fact, medical practice seems to leave very little room for any other activity. Physicians report an average workweek of fifty-four hours, not including time spent reading professional journals or educational activities. Almost 30 percent spend over sixty hours a week at work, roughly 8:00 A.M. to 6:00 P.M., six days a week. Their hobbies are remarkably few, and their range of interests narrow. One sample of physicians reported spending less than three hours a week in cultural activities and less than four hours a week on family outings. . . .

Medicine has never lacked critics. As the historian John Burnham noted in a 1982 article aptly entitled "American Medicine's Golden Age: What Happened to It?" there is a venerable tradition of denigrating doctors that stretches from Aristophanes to Molière, and on to Ivan Illich. But as a sense of doctors as strangers and hospitals as strange places permeated American society, the thrust of the critique changed, and so did the implications for public policy.

From the 1930s through the 1950s, most of the attacks on medicine were inspired by shortcomings in the system of health care delivery, particularly because medical care was often beyond the reach of the poor and increasingly placed a heavy financial burden on the middle class, especially the elderly. To critics, like journalist Richard Carter, problems began with the fact that the AMA was a powerful trade lobby and the doctor, a rapacious businessman. The opening pages of his 1958 book, *The Doctor Business,* tell about an accident in which a young boy fell into a well; after volunteers worked unstintingly for twenty-four hours to dig him out, his parents took him to a local doctor, who proceeded to bill $1,500 for his services. A public outcry followed (one U.S. senator spoke of "the outrage in my soul"), and even the AMA disassociated itself ("Not one doctor in a thousand would have charged a fee"). Pointing to this story, Carter criticized the "fee-based relations" between doctor and patient, concluding that "without presuming to tell a single M.D. how to care for a single appendix, the public can upgrade medicine from the bazaar." . . .

A very different critique characterized the late 1960s and 1970s, inspired not by economics but by distance and distrust, not by considerations of cost but of sentiment. To be sure, even earlier there had been numerous complaints about the unfeeling specialist or busy doctor, but they had never before reached the pitch of these protests or served as the basis for new organizations. The distinctions between the two sources of discontent . . . appeared . . . vividly in the approach of the women's rights movement, a movement that at once fed on and reinforced a sense of separation—the doctor as stranger, indeed as male stranger.

. . . [T]he new feminism challenged social practices in the physician's office. They redefined doctor-patient relationships that had once seemed natural and appropriate (the good patient as compliant) as part of a larger male design to keep women powerless, and at the same time, as part of a professional design to keep all laypeople powerless. Feminist scholars and advocates denounced both the inherited politics of gender and the politics of the professions, so that the issue of men dominating women was inseparable from doctors dominating patients. Medicine, in fact, was a sitting target, first, because its ranks were almost exclusively male, and at least in obstetrics and gynecology, all the patients were female. Second, the medical establishment had been expansive in its reach, medicalizing phenomena that had once been outside the doctor's ken, capturing for its own professional territory the area of reproduction, childbirth, and sexuality. To the feminists and their supporters (like Illich), these matters ought to have remained in the lay world, particularly with the women in that world.

Feminist scholars explored the history of medicine not to celebrate great discoveries or to trace the scientific progress of the profession but to analyze the dynamics by which male doctors had excluded women and enlarged their own domain. The articles and books were passionate, even bitter, as they described physicians' opposition to women's education (on the grounds that their frail bodies could not tolerate the strain), the exclusion of women from medical schools (on the assumption that they were not sufficiently dedicated to or temperamentally suited for medicine), and the insistence that women's proper place was in the private sphere (in the belief that anatomy dictated destiny, that God had fashioned a uterus and then built the woman around it). Feminist researchers then went on to explore more generally the medicalization of American society. When doctors expelled midwives from the delivery room, or when doctors replaced women as the authors of popular child-rearing tracts, the change spoke to a reduced role not only for women but for all laypeople. When male doctors discriminated against women physicians, they were minimizing the role of sympathy against science in the profession, and thereby encouraging an impersonal and distant style of medical practice.

Feminists presented these same points to a wider public in such best-selling publications as *Our Bodies, Ourselves,* originally published in 1971. Their primary target was gynecologists, but the onslaught extended to all (male) doctors, and the prescriptions were not gender specific. . . . The concluding advice to women—really, to all patients—followed logically on the critique: "We want you to be more alert to your responsibility in the relationship, just as you would in any other adult relationship where you are purchasing services." The rules for patients had changed: docile obedience was to give way to wary consumerism. Thus, if kept waiting, a patient should take her business elsewhere; if denied information, she should find another source. The adage "never trust a stranger" now expanded to "never trust a doctor."

One final piece of evidence confirms just how widely shared this judgment was becoming in the post-1965 period, namely, the mounting sense of crisis around malpractice litigation. The apparent increase in litigation (record-keeping methods varied so greatly from state to state that firm conclusions on actual increases were difficult to reach) spurred a 1969 congressional study (chaired by Connecticut's Senator Abraham Ribicoff) of what role the federal government might play in resolving the problem. Then, two years later, President Richard Nixon appointed a HEW commission to study the causes and issue recommendations, and the AMA also organized a survey. Although these various committees noted that American society was becoming more litigious generally, they agreed that one critical element in the rise of malpractice suits was the breakdown of the doctor-patient relationship. The overwhelming majority of suits were filed against specialists, not general practitioners because here the distance between physician and patient was greatest. Thus, it was experts in malpractice law, not consumer activists, who counseled doctors: "When the physician-patient rapport remains at a high level of trust and confidence, most patients will ride out a bad result, but when that rapport is inadequate in the beginning or is permitted to deteriorate in route, a suit is likely to follow." Not only were patients distrustful of strangers, they were ready to sue them.

No one document better illustrates how new social attitudes and practices redefined both the concept of the good patient and the obligations of health care professionals and institutions than the Patient Bill of Rights, promulgated first by the Joint Commission on the Accreditation of Hospitals (JCAH) in 1970 and formally adopted by the American Hospital Association (AHA) in 1973. The initial inspiration for the document came, fittingly enough, from the National Welfare Rights Organization (NWRO). Dedicated to bringing a rights orientation into areas dominated by concepts of charity and worthiness, its leaders devoted most of their energy to making relief and welfare policies responsive to a concept of entitlement. But the NWRO also focused on other institutions that affected the lives of the poor, including public schools, and most important in our context, voluntary and public hospitals. Recognizing that the hospital system was essentially two-track, with the poor typically consigned to twelve-bed wards, treated by medical students and house staff, and, apparently, disproportionately experimented on by investigators, the NWRO attempted to impose a rights model on hospitals. In 1970, it presented a list of twenty-six proposals to the JCAH, and after negotiations, the JCAH incorporated a number of them into the preamble to that group's "Accreditation Manual." This preamble was the only document composed by health care professionals that *Our Bodies, Ourselves* reprinted and credited.

As befit its origins with the NWRO, the preamble first addressed issues that particularly affected the poor. First, "no person should be denied impartial access to treatment . . . on the basis of . . . race, color, creed, national origin, or the nature of the source of payment." In this same spirit, all patients had a right to privacy, including the right not to be interviewed without their consent by "representatives of agencies not connected with the hospital," that is, welfare agencies. A patient's right to privacy also meant a respect for "the privacy of his body," and so, regardless of source of payment, the patient should be examined "shield[ed] . . . from the views of others" and should be made a part of clinical training programs (for medical students) only voluntarily. These points made, the preamble framers then addressed concerns that affected all patients, whatever their social or economic status. The process of defining rights moved across tracks, from concerns more relevant to the poor to concerns relevant to everyone. Thus, the document continued: "The patient has the right to receive . . . adequate information concerning the nature and extent of his medical problem, the planned course of treatment, and prognosis." In brief, all patients had the right to be told the truth about their medical condition.

The preamble served as the basis for the 1972 Patient Bill of Rights, adopted by the AHA after a three-year discussion by a committee that included not only the trustees of the association but four outsiders representing consumer organizations. The first of the twelve points in this bill of rights was a general statement of the right to "considerate and respectful care," and then the document addressed the most central concern, patient consent. It enlarged on the JCAH standard for truth telling by insisting that explanations be given in ways that "the patient can reasonably be expected to understand," and spelled out, in language reminiscent of the FDA stipulations, the requirements for obtaining consent both in treatment and experimentation. Its remaining points emphasized the patient's right to privacy and to a "reasonable" degree of continuity of care.

To be sure, the document disappointed a number of patients' rights activists. They were quick to note that rights would not be achieved when they were handed down from on high by the medical establishment. Willard Gaylin, a psychiatrist who at that moment was helping to organize the Hastings Institute of Society, Ethics and the Life Sciences, charged that the process amounted to "the thief lecturing his victim on self-protection." Others observed that none of these documents (or the variants on them that particular hospitals adopted) included any procedures for enforcement or for levying penalties, and still others criticized them because the stipulations on truthtelling allowed a major exception: when doctors believed that bad news would be harmful to the patient, they were to convey it to the family. Indeed, the provisions on consent generally amounted to be self-serving restatements of legal precedents intended to reduce the frequency of patient dissatisfaction with physicians, and thereby, the frequency of malpractice suits.

But these objections notwithstanding, the preamble and bill of rights had both symbolic and real importance, affecting attitudes and practices of both doctors and patients. . . .

. . . Leading national professional organizations, responding to external pressures, were now adopting the language and concepts of rights to delineate medical obligations. Behind the transformation lay, first, the recognition that the social distancing of doctor from patient and hospital from community rendered obsolete inherited maxims and practices.

Risk, Behavior, and Disease: Who Is Responsible for Keeping Americans Healthy?

ALLAN M. BRANDT

Although biomedicine, and the germ theory in particular, led to a far more complete understanding of the causes and nature of many diseases, it did not lead to immediate or effective therapeutic modalities. Nevertheless, infectious diseases did decline, and in fact, as more demographic data were sifted, it eventually became clear that most important infectious diseases were declining even before the elucidation of the germ theory. The leading causes of death in 1900 were tuberculosis, pneumonia, and diarrhea. In 1990, heart disease, cancer, and stroke constituted the principal causes of death; cancer and heart disease alone accounted for almost 60 percent of all deaths. What accounts for this truly revolutionary change in the patterns of disease? Although many associated this epidemiological and demographic shift with the rise of the germ theory and "scientific" medicine, most data suggest that this transformation was well under way before medicine developed any decisive technologies to fundamentally alter patterns of disease and death. Changes in the material conditions of life—sanitation, nutrition, and birth rates—led to fundamental changes in patterns of infection and longevity.

For any understanding of the relationship of culture and science, the problem of causation is critically important because it reflects directly on the question of responsibility for disease. Despite the anomalies implicit in the germ theory and the reductionist qualities of the biomedical model, the bacteriological revolution had the effect of "depersonalizing" disease. Under the microscope, diseases could no longer possess the same moral valence they had possessed in the past. In the increasingly secularized and rational world of medicine and science, microorganisms came to be viewed, almost unilaterally, as the cause of disease. This offered at least the possibility of disconnecting disease from its historic associations with sin, moral turpitude, and idleness. There were, of course, a number of diseases that continued to have powerful moral meanings: mental illness, alcoholism, and the sexually transmitted infections, to name but a few. But many diseases came to be seen as the result of a random chain of events that brought together a microorganism (a vector) and human beings. Disease was no longer seen as necessarily reflecting the personal attributes of the sick individual. The biomedical model had the effect of depersonalizing and secularizing disease.

It was in this historically specific context that the attribution of disease had the effect of reducing individual responsibility. Disease, in this biomedical paradigm, became a secular and scientific phenomenon, freed from traditional moral linkages. This accounts for the eagerness with which the founders of Alcoholics Anonymous, for example, seized the notion that alcohol dependence was a disease. It was not so much a desire to medicalize the phenomenon of habitual alcohol consumption as it was to free those with the habit from moral stigma, to "remoralize" the behavior. A

Allan M. Brandt, "'Just Say No': Risk, Behavior, and Disease in Twentieth-Century America," in *Scientific Authority and Twentieth-Century America,* ed. Ronald G. Walters (Baltimore, Md.: Johns Hopkins University Press, 1997), pp. 82–98. Copyright © 1997 Johns Hopkins University Press.

similar phenomenon occurred in the early twentieth-century movement to transform homosexuality from a crime into a disease, an indication of psychopathology. The implication was that those who suffered from the "disease" should be relieved from the traditional culpability associated with their behaviors. Disease implied a lack of volition or, at least, a failure of individual agency. The concurrent move to expand the nature of the insanity defense during the first decades of the twentieth century is yet another example of this significant trend.

In the biomedical model, the occurrence of disease largely came to be seen as the result of discrete phenomena. Susceptibility was defined as a lack of antibodies to a particular organism; resistance could be acquired through natural exposure to the organism or through vaccination to stimulate antibody production. In keeping with this particular paradigm, biomedicine focused on destroying pathogens or inducing resistance to them. With the introduction of sulfa drugs in the 1930s and antibiotics in the 1940s, the germ theory had spawned effective technologies to combat infection. The promise of Paul Ehrlich's "magic bullets"—specific chemotherapies used to root out and destroy "invading organisms"—had at last been realized. Diseases that a mere decade earlier had posed a serious threat to life could now be quickly and definitively treated; antibiotics now routinely saved those previously damned. The golden age of American medicine had begun.

In spite of the critics and theoretical limitations of the biomedical model, it is not difficult to recognize its appeal. If disease was caused by a single microorganism, then destroying these microorganisms—either in the environment (through sanitation) or in the body (through therapy)—offered the promise of conquering disease through definitive technologies. The elegance of magic bullet medicine has remained one of the most compelling metaphors in modern medicine. The possibility of dramatic cures after centuries of stalemate inspired a new awe regarding scientific investigation and medical intervention. . . .

During the course of the twentieth century, the epidemiological shift to the predominance of noncommunicable, chronic diseases exposed the problems inherent in magic bullet medicine. For the persistent problems of cancer, heart disease, and stroke, diseases in which it was impossible to specify a single cause, it proved impossible to specify a single solution. And even for infectious disease, specific therapies proved to have limitations—organisms could become resistant to previously effective chemotherapies. Even when effective treatments were available, they could not always be delivered on a timely basis. Moreover, the notion of specific causality neglected the complex interactions between agent, host, and vector. Clearly, some human beings were more vulnerable than others. As a result of heredity, geography, or environment, some individuals were apparently more susceptible to a number of microorganisms.

Implicit in this shift from infectious to chronic, systemic disease was a transformation in the meaning of disease and the assumptions concerning its causes. Epidemic infectious disease was typically perceived to be the result of external forces. During the nineteenth century, physicians had debated whether disease resulted from environmental decay—miasmas, poverty, pollution—or from foreigners bringing contagion to new soil; disease was a "visitation." Disease was episodic, and it did not originate or reside in the body. The chronic diseases of the late twentieth century were preeminently diseases of the body. Diseases were no longer caught, they were acquired. The limits of the germ theory to address systemic chronic disease led to a new recognition of environmental and behavioral forces as determinants of disease in the postwar era.

This change in patterns of disease ultimately challenged the ascendancy of the germ theory. By the 1960s, the promise of the biomedical revolution had begun to fade. Despite the firepower of magic bullets, these drugs simply could not target the systemic chronic diseases, which now accounted for the preponderance of deaths in the United States and other developed countries. The war on cancer, a national commitment to finding a cure for cancer in the laboratory, had stalled as the promise of any definitive victory dissipated. The technological "fix" for the remaining problems of disease proved illusory, despite remarkable technological advances. Cure proved the exception in the battle against the chronic diseases of later life. . . .

The significant change in patterns of disease that occurred during the first half of the twentieth century . . . encouraged a "new" epidemiology. From tracking microbes, which were uniformly seen as the "cause" of disease, researchers began to identify *risks:* the social, environmental, and behavioral variables that were statistically associated with patterns of chronic disease. The nature of causal inference in the sciences became a contested domain in the context of this demographic transition. Although some researchers continued to explore theories of specific causes of chronic disease, especially hereditary predispositions, the recognition that many factors were likely to contribute to the development of diseases such as cancer and heart disease led to a revolution in epidemiological technique. The rise of modern biostatistics and the development of controlled prospective trials offered the opportunity to explore the relationship of a host of environmental and behavioral variables to patterns of health and disease.

A prime example of this complex historical process of legitimating new approaches to causal inference lies in the history of the cigarette. The recognition that cigarette smoking causes serious disease followed by the decline in smoking is characteristic of the postwar shift regarding risk, disease, and behavior. It was no simple task to "prove" that cigarettes cause disease. By the end of World War II, cigarette smoking had become an enormously popular social behavior in American life, an icon of the consumer culture. The cigarette, an unusual and somewhat stigmatized form of tobacco consumption at the turn of the twentieth century, had become—through creative marketing and industrial consolidation—a symbol of affluence, leisure, personal power, and attractiveness. But despite its categoric success, concerns persisted about its impact on health. Lung cancer, virtually unknown in 1900, had begun to rise alarmingly. By the 1940s, spurred by the findings of life insurance actuarial studies, major prospective studies of cigarettes, lung cancer, and mortality began in the United States and Great Britain. These studies concluded that cigarettes constituted an enormous risk to health, not only as a cause of lung cancer and other lung diseases but also as a contributing factor in heart disease.

The epidemiological studies of cigarette smoking culminated in the surgeon general's report of 1964. The report, written by a group of eminent scientists under the auspices of the surgeon general, reviewed the epidemiological evidence indicting cigarettes as a cause of disease and concluded that these studies, in fact, conclusively demonstrated the risks of smoking. Implicit in this research was an influential critique of the whole notion of specific causality. This type of quantitative epidemiology touched off an important debate within the scientific community about the nature of causality, proof, and risk. At stake were the very epistemological foundations of scientific knowledge: How do we know what we know? What is the reliability of causal inference from statistical data? At the basis of the epidemiological argument was the clear limitation of laboratory experimentation for making determinations about probability and risk. The debate about smoking and health revealed an intraprofessional battle between epidemiology and laboratory science (the science of germ theory)—their values, assumptions, and expectations.

. . . The surgeon general's report made a fundamental contribution to medical studies of causality. Members of the committee realized the complexity of the relationship—of the impossibility of saying simply that smoking causes cancer. Many individuals could smoke heavily throughout their lives and apparently never suffer adverse consequences; cause implied a process in which *A* would, by necessity, lead to *B*. Therefore, they acknowledged the complexity: "It should be said at once," the report explained, "that no member of this committee used the word 'cause' in an absolute sense in the area of this study. Although various disciplines and fields of scientific knowledge were represented among the membership, all members shared a common conception of the multiple etiology of biological processes. No member was so naive as to insist upon the mono-etiology in pathological processes or in vital phenomena." This statement, a clear criticism of the germ theory's emphasis on specific causality, lent new credibility to the entire field of modern epidemiology. The report underscored the nature of the social process of scientific proof. This authoritative study now constituted the "proof" that cigarettes "cause" cancer and signaled the beginning of a major battle between the tobacco industry and public health forces in the United States.

Congress responded to the surgeon general's report by legislatively mandating that cigarette packs be labeled. The Federal Cigarette Labeling and Advertising Act of 1965 required that all cigarette packages carry a warning: "Caution: Cigarette Smoking May be Hazardous to Your Health." Given that the surgeon general had found that smoking *causes* lung cancer, the warning was remarkably weak, indicating the effectiveness of the tobacco lobby on Capitol Hill. It further reflected the relative lack of experience most legislators had with scientific findings, especially if they were contested. At the hearings concerning this legislation, tobacco spokesmen challenged the findings of the surgeon general. By treating all perspectives as those of "interested" parties to be brokered in the political process, members of Congress sought compromise. Moreover, powerful economic interests, especially of tobacco-growing states, acted forcefully to moderate any regulatory initiatives. Nevertheless, as scientific studies collected in subsequent surgeon general's reports continued to indict the cigarette as a major cause of serious disease, Congress took additional action. In 1971, the label was changed to "Warning: The Surgeon General Has Determined that Cigarette Smoking Is Dangerous to Your Health." And, in 1985, four rotating labels were mandated. Although originally viewed as an educational and regulatory measure, cigarette labeling served the purpose of shifting responsibility for smoking and its risks from the industry to the individual smoker. Cigarette smoking—given the clear warnings printed on every pack—had become the preeminent example of a "voluntary" health risk. . . .

With this logic, and a growing body of supporting data, the meaning of disease in American culture underwent a radical shift. By the early 1970s an emerging critique of modern biomedicine and medical technology centered attention on the question of responsibility for disease and its prevention. Few could disagree that disease prevention and health promotion were laudable goals. According to critics such as John Knowles, president of the Rockefeller Foundation, American society had reached the point of diminishing returns from its heavy investment in medical high technology and tertiary care. The failure, claimed Knowles, was in prevention of disease. The goal of health and longevity rested firmly with individuals, who in the last decades had forfeited their health in an "orgy" of greed, avarice, and over-eating, the "diseases of affluence." . . . Knowles suggested that "the idea of a 'right' to health should be replaced by the idea of an individual moral obligation to pre-serve one's own health . . . a public duty if you will." According to this perspective, control of the persistent health problems of the United States—the chronic diseases of middle and later age such as cancer, stroke, and heart disease—depended directly on individual behavior and habits. . . .

The emphasis on individual responsibility for health, as well as the epide-miological studies that demonstrated the significance of specific behaviors such as cigarette smoking, diet, and exercise offered the possibility of control over one's health. No longer would disease be viewed as a random event; it would now be viewed as a failure to take appropriate precautions against publicly specified risks, a failure of individual control, a lack of self-discipline, an intrinsic moral failing. By the late 1970s, Knowles's views had entered the political mainstream. In 1978, Secretary of Health and Human Services Joseph Califano, eager to find a way to reduce growing health expenditures, explained: "We are killing ourselves by our own careless habits. . . . We are a long way from the kind of national com-mitment to good personal health habits that will be necessary to change drasti-cally the statistics about chronic disease in America. . . . Americans can do more for their own health than any doctors, any machine or hospital, by adopting healthy lifestyles." . . .

. . . The calls for individual responsibility and reform of personal behavior draw on deep cultural values and social psychologies concerning the nature of disease. At stake in the process by which health risks come to be elucidated and defined in twentieth-century America are several critically important political and economic conflicts. In this respect, cultural norms and values are fundamentally related to political conflicts. Is there a "right" to health care or a "duty" to be healthy? How do we distinguish between assumed risk and imposed risk as they related to patterns of behavior and disease? Indeed, these distinctions probably reflect specific (and changing) historical assumptions about the nature of human behavior rather than any empiric reality.

Again, the cigarette provides a telling example of the historical issue. Shall we consider smokers ignorant and stupid for maintaining an "unnecessary" behavior that has been defined as highly dangerous? Or shall we recognize the power of ad-vertising and cultural conventions as well as the power of the biological and psycho-logical factors in addiction, all of which constrain individual choice? . . . Simply identifying individual behavior as the primary vehicle for risk—even with substan-tial epidemiological data—negates the fact that behavior itself is, at times, beyond the scope of individual agency. Behavior is shaped by powerful currents—cultural, psychological, and biological—not all immediately within the control of the individual. Behaviors such as cigarette smoking are sociocultural phenomena and are not merely individual or, necessarily, rational.

The emphasis on personal responsibility for risk taking and disease has come at the very moment when cigarette smoking is increasingly stratified by education, social class, and race. In 1985, 35 percent of blacks smoked, compared to 29 percent of whites. For college graduates, the proportion of smokers fell from 28 percent in 1974 to 18 percent in 1985; for those without a college degree, the decrease during the same period was from 36 to 34 percent. Thus to stress individual accountability is to deny that some groups may be more susceptible to certain behavioral risks, that the behavior itself is not simply a matter of choice. Nevertheless, individuals who "take"—note the voluntaristic bias—such risks are considered ignorant, stupid, or self-destructive. Identifying disease as an essentially voluntary process demonstrates the cultural imperative for control. If disease can be avoided by carefully following a set of prescriptions regarding personal behavior, then individuals can take control over their bodies and, thereby, their lives. By this logic, the persistent (and growing) differentials in the burden of disease between blacks and whites, for example, become but an artifact of the vicissitudes of individual behaviors.

The very nature of these causal frameworks for understanding disease has been to make complex phenomena seem simple. In this process, important cultural values are expressed. Take, for example, the well-known "Just Say No" antidrug campaign of the 1980s. Implicit in this educational campaign, whose legitimate goal was to invigorate individual assertion over peer pressures, was the notion that simple self-denial can solve a complex social problem. The pathology of drug abuse is shifted; rather than the problem reflecting certain external social conditions, it now resides in the individual. Drug use becomes preeminently an aspect of individual agency: Just Say No.

To evaluate the power of this set of cultural assumptions one need take but a cursory look at the first decade of the AIDS epidemic. AIDS, of course, contradicted some of the most basic assumptions of postwar medicine: the era of infectious epidemics was supposed to be over; ours was a time of chronic diseases that struck late in life, debilitating the growing ranks of the elderly. AIDS strikes the young, is communicable, and is caused by a deadly pathogenic organism. But despite these characteristics, AIDS has been placed strongly within the paradigm of responsibility. If one "merely" avoids the risk behaviors associated with the transmission of the virus—unprotected sexual intercourse and the sharing of intravenous drug paraphernalia—one can avoid AIDS. Therefore, infection is a clear, and usually terminal, marker of individual risk taking, of engaging in behaviors held to be deviant or criminal. According to this view, those who are infected are responsible for their plight; AIDS is caused by a moral failure of the individual.

Labeling this perspective as "victim blaming" is to miss its full historical implications. Certainly, it does hold victims of disease socially accountable for their illness, disability, or even, death. But it also underscores implicit cultural values about the nature of behavior, responsibility for disease, and access to care and services. The triumph of a social ideology of individual control marks a powerful denial of our relative lack of control. Because external risks appear so difficult—if not impossible—to modify, the tendency in the last two decades has been to focus on those risks for which individuals do have some modicum of control. . . .

At particular historic moments, social forces have eroded the rigid allocation of responsibility for disease. Just as the Great Depression demonstrated that destitution could be the result of powerful forces beyond the control of the individual, so, too, did contemporaneous attitudes about disease reflect an ideology of randomness. The fact that the major voluntary health insurers have their origins in the Depression reveals a social and economic recognition of a shared vulnerability to sickness and its costs. When Blue Shield and Blue Cross were organized in the 1930s they were committed to the idea of community rating: anyone could join at the same cost. The essential philosophy behind this premise was that risks should be equally shared by everyone in the community. In an age of magic bullet treatments and heightened expectations of medicine's ability to cure, political sentiment for the "right" to health care intensified. Calls for universal insurance were one result of this political impulse and, eventually, the enactment of Medicare and Medicaid in 1965.

. . . By the mid-1970s, discussions of the right to health care had been transformed to the duty to be healthy. In this context, full access to medical care was viewed by some as possibly encouraging unhealthful behaviors. As physician-philosopher Leon Kass notes: "All the proposals for National Health Insurance embrace, without qualification, the no-fault principle. They therefore choose to ignore, or to treat as irrelevant, the importance of personal responsibility for the state of one's health. As a result, they pass up an opportunity to build both positive and negative inducements into the insurance plan, by measures such as refusing benefits for chronic respiratory disease care to persons who continue to smoke." By the 1980s, when new voices supported national health insurance, it was typically to limit rocketing health expenditures—more than 12 percent of the gross national product—than to provide everyone equal access to health care. Equality of access came to be seen as a potential windfall of asserting central control over medical costs.

This . . . [essay has focused] on the cultural implications of fundamental demographic and epidemiological change. The way any society comes to understand patterns of health and disease, and their causes, is revelatory of basic cultural norms and expectations. Whether these changes are the result of purposeful human insight and intervention—as they so rarely have been—or of basic changes in the material conditions of life, they do have a dramatic impact on assumptions about human behavior and notions of responsibility and morality. In the United States in the twentieth century, the good life came fundamentally to mean freedom from disease; health became the ultimate goal in a pluralistic, secular culture. And freedom from disease came fundamentally to mean assertion of control over the vagaries of one's body. The ephemeral nature of the effort has yet to discourage this intense capacity for personal reform.

 # F U R T H E R   R E A D I N G

Renée R. Anspach, *Deciding Who Lives: Fateful Choices in the Intensive-Care Nursery* (1992).
Robert Aronowitz, *Making Sense Out of Illness: Science, Society, and Disease* (1998).
Charles L. Bosk, *All God's Mistakes: Genetic Counseling in a Pediatric Hospital* (1992).
Charles L. Bosk, *Forgive and Remember: Managing Medical Failure* (1979).
Joan Jacobs Brumberg, *The Body Project: An Intimate History of American Girls* (1997).